# GREENBERG'S GUIDE TO

# LIONEL TRAINS:   1945-1969

# By Bruce C. Greenberg, Ph.D.

# Edited By Roland LaVoie

## Photographs from the Eddins Collection
## and by courtesy of Frank Hare, Iron Horse Publications
## and Tom McComas of TM Productions

Copyright 1984

**Greenberg Publishing Company**
7543 Main Street
Sykesville, MD 21784
301 795-7447

Manufactured in the United States of America

Greenberg Publishing Company offers the world's largest selection of Lionel, American Flyer and other toy train publications as well as a selection of books on model and prototype railroading. To receive our current catalogue, send a stamped, self-addressed envelope marked "catalogue."

Greenberg Publishing Company sponsors the world's largest public model railroad shows. The shows feature extravagant operating model railroads for N, H0, 0, Standard and 1 Gauges as well as a huge marketplace for buying and selling nearly all model railroad equipment. The shows feature, as well, a large selection of doll house miniatures.

Shows are currently offered in New York, Philadelphia, Pittsburgh, Baltimore, Washington, D.C., Williamsburg and Boston. To receive our current show listing, please send a self-addressed stamped envelope marked "Train Show Schedule."

## Library of Congress Cataloging in Publication Data

Greenberg, Bruce C.
    Greenberg's guide to Lionel trains, 1945-1969.

    Includes index.
      1. Railroads--Models.  2. Lionel Corporation.
I. LaVoie, Roland, 1943-      . II. Title.
TF197.G667  1985        625.1'9          85-763
ISBN 0-89778-021-3

# INTRODUCTION

**Greenberg's Price Guide for Lionel Trains, 1945-1969**, fifth edition, is our most comprehensive report on the toy train marketplace. This edition records a very uneven pattern of price changes. At the present time, however, in the fall of 1984, prices are stable.

## PURPOSE

The purpose of this book is to provide a comprehensive listing with current prices for Lionel locomotives, rolling stock and accessories, in 0 and 0-27 Gauges, produced from 1945 through 1969. We include those variations which have been authenticated. In a few cases we ask our readers for further information where information is missing or doubtful. Values are reported for each item where there have been reported sales.

## DETERMINING VALUES

Toy train values vary for a number of reasons. First, consider the **relative knowledge** of the buyer and seller. A seller may be unaware that he has a rare variation and sell it for the price of a common piece. Another source of price variation is **short-term fluctuation** which depends on what is being offered at a given train meet on a given day. If four 773s are for sale at a small meet, we would expect that supply would outpace demand and lead to a reduction in price. A related source of variation is the **season** of the year. The train market is slower in the summer and sellers may at this time be more inclined to reduce prices if they really want to move an item. Another important source of price variation is the relative strength of the seller's **desire to sell** and the buyer's **eagerness to buy.** Clearly a seller in economic distress will be more eager to strike a bargain. A final source of variation is **the personalities** of the seller and buyer. Some sellers like to quickly turn over items and, therefore, price their items to move; others seek a higher price and will bring an item to meet after meet until they find a willing buyer.

Train values in this book are based on OBTAINED prices, rather than asking prices, along the East Coast during the summer of 1984. We have chosen East Coast prices since the greatest dollar volume in transactions appears there. The prices reported here represent a "ready sale", or a price perceived as a good value by the buyer. They may sometimes appear lower than those seen on trains at meets for two reasons. First, items that sell often sell in the first hour of a train meet and, therefore, are no longer visible. (We have observed that a good portion of the action at most meets occurs in the first hour.) The items that do not sell in the first hour have a higher price tag and this price, although not representing the sales price, is the price observed. A related source of discrepancy is the willingness of some sellers to bargain over price.

Another factor which may affect prices is reconditioning done by the dealer. Some dealers take great pains to clean and service their pieces to that they look their best and operate properly. Others sell the items just as they have received them, dust and all. Naturally, the more effort the dealer expends in preparing his pieces for sale, the more he can expect to charge for them. This factor may account for significant price differences among dealers selling the same equipment.

From our studies of train prices, it appears that mail order prices for used trains are generally higher than those obtained at eastern train meets. This is appropriate considering the costs and efforts of producing and distributing a price list and packing and shipping items. Mail order items do sell at prices above those listed in this book. A final source of difference between observed prices and reported prices is region. Prices are clearly higher in the South and West where trains are less plentiful than along the East Coast.

## CONDITION

For each item, we provide four categories: **Good, Very Good, Excellent and Mint.** The Train Collectors Association (TCA) defines conditions as:

FAIR Well-scratched, chipped, dented, rusted or warped

GOOD Scratches, small dents, dirty

VERY GOOD Few scratches, exceptionally clean, no dents or rust.

EXCELLENT Minute scratches or nicks, no dents or rust

MINT Brand new, absolutely unmarred, all original and unused, in original box.

In the toy train field there is a great deal of concern with exterior appearance and less concern with operation. If operation is important to you, then ask the seller whether the train runs. If the seller indicates that he does not know whether the equipment operates, you should test it. Most train meets have test tracks provided for that purpose.

We have included MINT in this edition because of the small but important trade in pre-1970 mint items. However there is substantial confusion in the minds of both sellers and buyers as to what constitutes "mint" condition. How do we define mint? Among very experienced train enthusiasts, a mint piece means that it is brand new, in its original box, never run, and extremely bright and clean (and the box is, too). An item may have been removed from the box and replaced in it but it should show no evidence of handling. A piece is not mint if it shows any scratches, fingerprints or evidence of discoloration. It is the nature of a market for the seller to see his item in a very positive light and to seek to obtain a mint price for an excellent piece. In contrast, a buyer will see the same item in a less favorable light and will attempt to buy a mint piece for the price of one in excellent condition. It is our responsibility to point out this difference in perspective **and** the difference in value implicit in each perspective, and to then let the buyer and seller settle or negotiate their different perspectives.

We do not show values for Fair or Restored. **Fair** items are valued substantially below Good. We have not included **Restored** because such items are not a significant portion of the market for postwar trains. As a rough guide, however, we expect that Restored items will bring prices equivalent to Good or possibly Very Good. The term professional restoration refers to highly proficient technical work. There is disagreement among restorers as to what constitutes approproate technique and finished product. There are substantial differences in the price that consumers are willing to pay for restored items.

As we indicated, prices in this book were derived from large train meets or shows. If you have trains to sell and you sell them to a person planning to resell them, you will not obtain the prices reported in this book. Rather, you should expect to achieve about fifty percent of these prices. Basically, for your items to be of interest to a buyer who plans to resell them, he must purchase them for considerably less than the prices listed here.

We receive many inquiries as to whether or not a particular piece is a "good value." This book will help answer that question; but, there is NO substitute for experience in the marketplace. WE STRONGLY RECOMMEND THAT NOVICES DO NOT MAKE MAJOR PURCHASES WITHOUT THE ASSISTANCE OF FRIENDS WHO HAVE EXPERIENCE IN BUYING AND SELLING TRAINS. If you are buying a train and do not know whom to ask about its value, look for the people running the meet or show and discuss with them your need for assistance. Usually they can refer you to an experienced collector who will be willing to examine the piece and offer his opinion.

# ACKNOWLEDGEMENTS

Thanks to the generosity and scholarship of train enthusiasts, this new book, is the most detailed and complete book we have ever published concerning the 1945-1969 years of Lionel production.

We thought that the last edition of this book represented a large increase in postwar data, but it pales in comparison to the veritable hurricane of data which blew our way after the volume was published. In the space of one year, we have accumulated no fewer than five hundred additions, corrections and changes to the text, eight new scholarly articles and many new photographs. What a tribute this is to the thoroughness and enthusiasm of you, the Lionel collectors and operators!

We could not talk about the scholarly articles in this book without mentioning the revised version of **Richard Vagner's** article on postwar gondolas. Richard has not only contributed a fine article, but also set new standards of data collection for many varieties of trains. He has established himself as one of the foremost train scholars in the country. **Pat Scholes** has given us two excellent and well-researched articles on the Pennsylvania S-2 Steam Turbine varieties and the Electronic Train Set. These articles give highly desirable information on one of Lionel's most popular postwar items. **Ron Griesbeck** has given us a meticulously detailed research article on Lionel's Berkshire steam engines; the excellence of his prose and photography speak for themselves. **Norman Anderson**, a man who has much experience with the prototypes, has cleared up several problems in nomenclature with his article defining plug door boxcars and refrigerator cars and Lionel's attempts to imitate them. In a similar fashion, **William Meyer** has written a fine essay concerning Lionel's confusion between the SW-1 and NW-2 diesel switchers. **David Fleming** and **Jerry Schuchart** have detailed the history of the most popular of all Lionel's accessories, the Automatic Refrigerated Milk Car. **William Schilling** has written an article which sorts out the production variations of Lionel's postwar tank cars. Last, but definitely not least, is **Michael Ocilka's** masterful analysis of Lionel flatcar molds and dies. His is a work of painstakingly detailed research which breaks new ground in that category.

For this edition, **I. D. Smith** has revised his original listings of postwar catalogues, service station bulletins and billboards. These listings are now more complete than ever. He was assisted by written material provided by **Pat Corrigan, who was himself aided by Joe Snuggs, Don Simonini, William Mekalian, J. E. Felber, Jim Gates** and **George Shewmake.**

As always, there are major contributors to thank whose efforts for this edition have gone above and beyond the call for assistance. This editor owes a great deal to **Joe Bratspis** and **Joe Gordon**, the proprietors of the Toy Train Station in Feasterville, Pennsylvania, who have graciously allowed me to examine their awesome store stock in the pursuit of my own research. They also provide a venue for the camaraderie between hobbyists which is so important to the meaningful exchange of information - not to mention a "hangout" for the editor on Friday evenings! **Dr. F. Richard Ervin** proofread the entire steam locomotive manuscript and made many beneficial changes based upon his own experience and vast collection. As a result of his efforts, that chapter is more thorough than it has ever been. **Chris Rohlfing** went through the manuscript of the entire book and sent in over a hundred additions and corrections for postwar alone; I can only imagine the hours of labor this effort took. He also supplied some vital pricing information, as did **Richard Lord**, a dealer and collector of vast experience who gave us new pricing information on rare items in the postwar catalogue.

Not very long ago, **Glenn Halverson**, a college student and train enthusiast, sent us a note that he had some information for us. He subsequently sent us an astonishing variety of new additions, factory errors and everything else. Glenn's enthusiasm is a model for all of us, and at a young age he is rapidly becoming an expert train scholar. His diligence is truly admirable. When we wanted to begin a new chapter on uncatalogued sets, our major source of information was **Paul Ambrose**, whose specialty that area is. Paul also made helpful recommendations and further corrections and additions. Mike Ocilka did not limit his contribution to the article on flatcar molds by any means; several new variations are the result of his fine work. **Tom Budniak** wrote us several long letters detailing new variations and additions from his vast collection and long experience. He also straightened out a number of the editor's misconceptions concerning certain pieces of rolling stock. **Joe Algozzini** is a specialist on factory errors; the extensive additions to the new section on factory errors are largely the result of his work. He also expanded the known varieties of several important pieces of Lionel rolling stock. In addition to expanding and updating the catalogue and billboard sections, I. D. Smith proofread letters and manuscripts, sent in further additions to nearly every chapter and generally let us take shameless advantage of his talent. Finally, no book of ours would be complete without a significant contribution from one of the most observant train researchers in captivity, **Jim Sattler**. This time, Jim gave us a detailed description of the 3454 Merchandise Car which proves his talent for close observation. This editor learned more from him in half an hour than from everyone else in a year!

Many contributors sent information concerning one particular area of interest, and some of this information was extremely valuable. **William Davis** added to Jim Sattler's description of the 3454 by describing a version of this car previously unknown to us. **Tony Arpino** sent us a long and well-detailed list of variations from his collection. **John Diggle** photographed and described a significant construction difference in the Aerial Target Launching Car. **Ed Kraemer** sent us some very useful and timely information concerning Lionel's factory errors. **Doug Feldman** sent us a fine description of his Sears General set, and **Tom Hawley** was a big help with the nomenclature and descriptions of the wheelsets and trucks. **Paul R. Beavin** sent us photos and descriptions of a truly incredible Sears Allstate train set which may have been the finest set ever made by Lionel. **Bernard Stekoll** was of great assistance when we delineated the variations in the Lionel searchlight cars, and **Lawrence J. C. Backus** sent a detailed description of some significant construction variations in the 3351-55 log dump car. **Warren Blackmar** helped us correct some misconceptions we had about the 224 and 1666 prewar and postwar steam locomotives. We still may not have the differences completely right, but Warren is working on an extensive article which will banish our collective ignorance of these locomotives. **Frank J. Cordone** sent us a nice note about his X616 uncatalogued set which made a good addition to that chapter. **Ken Markley** is more frequently a contributor to our prewar volume, but he sends us intelligent and perceptive letters which keep us mindful of the philosophy behind these trains. **Jim Whittam's** comments to this editor perform the same function.

In addition to the people mentioned above, the following individuals made contributions of one kind or another during the past year. We are not unmindful of the many individuals who made contributions to previous editions, but space would not let us list them here, and the pages of this book are dotted with individual entries secured from them. If for any reason I have forgotten anyone, the error is mine and is certainly not deliberate. I hope that I will be apprised of any omissions so I can make amends.

We are grateful for the assistance of the following people: **Jerry Abraham, Jerry Alvatrain, Carl J. Anderson, Louis Bohn, Frank Bowers, John Breslin, Robert Maxwell Caplan, Dr. Philip Catalano, Richard Clothier, George Cole, Carl Cummings, Joe Cusumano, Clyde Darasko, David M. Dixon, Everett E. Dodd, Jr., David Dunn, Henry Edmunds** and **David Ely.**

Also: **Robert Frangillo, Ray Gallahan, Michael Goodwin, Joe Grossano, Eugene Heid, Kurt Hessler, William Hudzik, Jack Kirby, Terral Klaassen, Joseph Kotil, Ken LaFayette, Cliff Lang, Allan T. LaRue, Gary Magner, Ernest Mancinelli, Louis Manz, Roscoe McMillan, III, Brian J. Michel** and **Ed Minch.**

Also: **Ron Niedhammer, Norman L. Oswald, Sr., Al Otten, David Otth, Marc A. Powell, Harold Powell, C. Adair Roberts, Mark Rohlfing, Perry Rothenberg, John Roskoski, Bob Royer, Glenn Salamone, Edmund Schwartzel, Richard Shanfeld, John R. Shoemaker, Joseph Siachitano, David Stonecipher, Lewis E. Striebeck, Jr., Pastor Philip Smith, Donald Shaw, A. Gordon Thompson, Eugene Trentacoste, John P. Uptegraft, Al Weaver, Victor Weisskopf, Richard White, Gordon Wilson** and **Jeff Wilson.**

That's quite a list of people! We must also make mention of all the people who have proven to be faithful and accurate proofreaders and, generally, good people to corroborate our thinking. The Guide was ably edited by **Cindy Floyd** and **Linda Wyant** on our Computers. It was proofread by **Donna Price.**

This editor would also like to thank Bruce and Linda Greenberg for their kindness, tolerance, patience and votes of confidence. I am honored to have my name attached to this document, and to the Greenbergs I owe, most of all, the full realization of the fun this hobby can be.

If you have additions for our next edition, please send them either to Bruce Greenberg at his Sykesville business address or to me at 137 Pine Valley Road, Cherry Hill, NJ 08034. Your letters will be acknowledged by one or both of us, and your help is appreciated because that assistance has made this book the fine volume that it is. We hope that you get as much enjoyment out of perusing its pages as we have had in tracking the mysteries of Lionel down. Thanks to all of you for your help!

Roland E. LaVoie, Editor
Cherry Hill, New Jersey
December, 1984

\*　　　\*　　　\*　　　\*

As a publisher, I am most appreciative of Roland's total involvement with and dedication to describing and evaluating Lionel trains. His commitment to thorough research and his boundless enthusiasm for the job at hand make working with him a truly collaborative and envigorating activity.

Bruce C. Greenberg
President, Greenberg Publishing Company
December 26, 1984

# TABLE OF CONTENTS

# Chapter I
# STEAM LOCOMOTIVES

### STEAM LOCOMOTIVES
#### By Roland LaVoie

Most people now tentatively entering middle age have fond childhood memories of "those little white pills you could drop down the stack" for smoke, the mellow sound of a steam whistle and the sight of spinning wheels and rods. These were the prominent characteristics of the Lionel Corporation's steam engines throughout the whole postwar period. Lionel made an astonishing variety of miniature "iron horses" for its trains; there was a steamer for every inclination and pocketbook by the time Lionel reached its zenith in the early to middle fifties.

As a rule, Lionel's steamers can be grouped roughly into three highly variable categories. The large "premium" steamers included the Hudsons, Berkshires, S-2 Turbines and J Class locomotives, all of which had six or more drivers and at least one four-wheel trailing or leading truck. The medium steamers included all the remaining six-drivered engines such as the K-4 Pacifics and the 637/2037 class. The smaller engines, by far the most numerous, included the steam switchers, the Scout locomotives of the late forties and early fifties, and all the metal or plastic four-driver engines included with 027 inexpensive sets.

The large steamers represented the finest locomotives which Lionel could produce. The 773 Hudson was made to scale, and if it was not quite the awesome engine which the prewar 700E Scale Hudson was, it was still the tin plate state of the art. Even the cheapened 1964 version of this locomotive commands both respect and a healthy price among collectors. Not too far below this locomotive in overall esteem was the 1957-1958 746 Norfolk and Western streamlined "J" class 4-8-4 locomotive, a beautiful engine with deep red trim whose prototype is said to be the finest steam engine ever made in America.

The 773 and 746 may have been the best of the premium steamers, but they were certainly not the only ones. The stories of the Pennsylvania S-2 Turbine and the 2-8-4 Berkshire are related by Pat Scholes and Ron Griesbeck in their articles within this section. However, the Hudsons deserve a strong mention because they were the most numerous of the big steamers and are perhaps remembered best of all Lionel's postwar steamers. These strong, handsome 4-6-4 steamers came with two essential boiler types. The "Alco" boiler, larger of the two, was modeled after prototypes of the New York Central; and the "Baldwin" boiler, sometimes called the "Junior Hudson", was detailed after engines used by the Santa Fe. The easiest way to tell the two types apart is to look at the cab windows. The Alco-boilered Hudson has a square, three or four-paned window, while the Baldwin-boilered Hudson has a rectangular, two-piece cab window.

There are many variations of the Hudsons besides the two basic boiler types. Some confusion can arise because these locomotives had a dual numbering system, depending upon whether they were used for 0 or 027 sets. For example, the 646 and 2046 are identical, but the three-number version was meant for 0 Gauge sets and the four-number version for 027 sets.

Some Hudsons had feedwater heaters on their boiler fronts; others had square-backed tenders instead of the Pennsylvania-type streamlined tenders. The engine numbers changed with the dropping of magnetraction in 1952; then they changed back but with slightly different characteristics. All of the Hudsons are fairly common, but they are desirable because they are smooth runners and good-looking locomotives.

The medium-sized, six-driver locomotives included two carry-overs from the prewar period, the rather nice 224 and the inexpensive but good-quality 1666. Lionel produced other locomotives in this series almost immediately. The 221 was a small streamlined locomotive roughly resembling the Dreifuss-styled Hudson of the New York Central; it pulled a few medium-priced passenger sets in 1946-1947. In 1947, Lionel changed the 225 boiler to produce the 675/2025 Pennsylvania K-4 Pacific - even though Lionel never produced it with the correct 4-6-2 wheel arrangement. The 675/2025 originally came with Baldwin nickeled disc drivers in a 2-6-2 wheel arrangement. Later, it got magnetraction and a four-wheel trailing truck. The 1666 boiler was revamped into the 2-6-4 637/2037 pair of the middle fifties, a steamer produced in great quantities for the middle-priced sets of the time. One variety of the 2037 became the notorious 2037-500 Girls' Train locomotive painted in shocking pink! Many other numbers and variations were produced within this broad category of steamers.

The small steam locomotives (except for the switchers) are rather neglected by most collectors, who generally chase after the "glamour" steamers of Lionel's production. However, they are a fascinating study all to themselves, and a collector interested in them can build up a considerable collection of them at a modest cost. The majority of these steamers were made with a 2-4-2 wheel arrangement. Only a few of them had smoke units, but most were at least lighted. Their tenders could be square metal, square plastic or slope-back plastic. The Scout locomotives (and many later engines in this series) came with a notoriously unreliable sealed motor with movable brushes for reversing. It is an absolute beast to repair, and during production years the factory would replace it with a conventional motor if the customer was insistent. The majority of these engines with conventional motors had the less expensive two-position reversing unit, and the last years of production cheapened these locomotives still further; some had no reverse at all. Still, for families with modest toy budgets, these locomotives headed sets which gave children joy at Christmas Time at a very low cost. Lionel built these locomotives in great numbers to meet the challenge of the Marx train sets, which made a strong bid for the low end of the toy train market all throughout the postwar years.

No discussion of the steam locomotives would be complete without a discussion of several special types. In the early postwar years, Lionel built 0-4-0 steam switchers, the 1656 and 1665, almost comparable to the magnificent switchers of the late prewar period. These engines had terrific detail, working back-up lights and operating bells in the tenders. Later, less detailed versions of these locomotives were also made. In 1959,

Lionel made its "General" locomotives in three numbers, 1862, 1872 and 1882. This locomotive was a finely detailed replica of the locomotive used by the Andrews Raiders during the Civil War. All the right details were there - balloon stack, bright colors, big drivers and colorful tender with a fake woodpile. It is entirely possible that this locomotive was inspired by the Walt Disney movie, **The Great Locomotive Chase**, a thrilling account of the Andrews Raid starring Fess Parker of "Davy Crockett" fame. Authentic period coaches were made to be sold with this locomotive.

Any collector who would want to build a complete collection of Lionel's postwar steam engines had better reserve a great deal of shelf space! During the long postwar period, Lionel offered instant nostalgia through its wide variety of steamers. Great arguments have been advanced concerning which of these locomotives was the best looking, the best "runner" and so on. However, that is not the real significance of these locomotives. More than any other Lionel product, the steam engines take us all back to a time when life seemed much more innocent. Perhaps that is why these engines have never lost their appeal.

## LOOKING AT THE LIONEL BERKSHIRES
### By Ron Griesbeck
NOTE: This article first appeared in the June 1979 **The Lion Roars** (Lionel Collectors' Club of America). Used by permission of the author. Photographs were printed by Ray Nikolai.

If your enthusiasm for things Lionel is most evident in the pursuit of postwar steam locomotives, you know the frustration of pursuing the elusive and expensive 733 Hudsons. These magnificent locomotives seem to stay beyond the reach of most collectors. The 746 Norfolk and Western locomotives are rapidly approaching the same status. Owners of either or both of these pieces are truly to be envied. However, one of Lionel's most desirable and stately postwar steamers is still (relatively speaking) a bargain within the reach of many collectors. This is the Lionel 726-736 2-8-4 Berkshire steamer.

Sales of the Berkshire spanned the entire postwar to Fundimensions period, cresting with the golden years of the Lionel Corporation and foundering with its decline. In spite of the overshadowing 773 of 1950 and 1964-1966, and the brief but flashy 746 of 1957-1960, the Berkshire retained its dignity and its popularity. It reigned prestigiously not for just a few years, but for more than two decades over the metal-bodied realm of steam, that multitude of rod-spinners. Moreover, its 0 Gauge rank was never compromised by demotion to 027 status, unlike its "poorer" cousins, the Hudsons and the Turbines.

A big locomotive of 2-8-4 wheel arrangement, the Lionel Berkshire is handsome, powerful and of excellent quality in all of its variations. Since little has been revealed concerning the scarcity of some of these variants, most models sell at comparatively low prices. The 726 Korean War model of 1952, for example, is possibly just as scarce as the coveted Norfolk and Western 726 "J" class, but it sells for less than a third of its price!

The Berkshire family embodies most of Lionel's postwar to Fundimensions steam locomotive innovations, since its production ran continuously from 1946 to 1966. This long 21-year run put a considerable number into circulation, so they are not too difficult to acquire (that is, if any old "Berk" will do). However, assembling a collection in decent condition is somewhat challenging!

Such a collection can vary in number, depending upon how finely the collector wishes to split variation hairs. I will deal with nine examples which I feel are representative of all the types manufactured: 1946 (726); 1947 (726); 1948-1949 (726); 1950-1951 (736); 1952 (726); 1952 (726RR); 1953-1954 (736); 1955-1956 (736); and 1957-1966 (736). I have combined 1957-1960 with 1961-1966, as only a tender variation occurred during that period.

The following discussion and accompanying photos will show varieties which were apparently created deliberately by engineering or styling modifications. Much of the material has been covered by other books and articles. My goal is to add my findings to the known data and to condense the total picture to a reference catalogue which new collectors might find valuable.

In an effort to avoid repetition and overlap, I have arranged the photos and text categorically rather than chronologically. A completely charted variations chronology follows the article for convenient reference.

FIGURE 1: 1946-49, 52 left, 1950-51 right.

## CAB NUMBERS

Although the Berkshire began life as model 726 and evolved eventually into 736, the evolutionary process was complicated by shortages of magnetic magnetraction materials during the Korean Conflict. The silver "726" number rubber-stamped in the "fat and fancy" style appeared on the first-year models of 1946 and continued through 1949 (Figure 1, left). The year 1950 saw the introduction of magnetraction, and the number "736" heralded the innovation (Figure 1, right). The new number, however, carried only through 1951. Enter the "Korean Connection".

FIGURE 2: 1952 left, 1953-66 right.

Because of the Korean War, magnetic materials became scarce, and Lionel responded in 1952 by omitting the magnetraction feature and reverting to the "726" number in two variations: the old 1946-1949 type of numbers and a new style, thin and condensed "726" numbers with small capital letters, "RR", below (Figure 2, left), to indicate that the locomotive was a "rerun".

As peacetime returned, so did magnetraction, and the "736" numbering for 1953 came in a new heat-stamped white version (Figure 2, right). This final numbering, thinner and cleaner, would carry unchanged to the termination of production in 1966.

The photos in Figures 1 and 2 also exhibit an interesting and somewhat random quirk in cab window arrangement. A three-window type, with the rear horizontal frame omitted, turned up somewhat sporadically throughout the years of production. I doubt that the window strut was removed or broken by owners, as has been suggested, since all are symmetrically opposite and on the same year models. The "broken-window" theory sounds too much like a conspiracy to be credible!

The four-window type appears to have run irregularly during 1946-1949, 1952 and 1961-1966. The three-window variety filled the gaps: 1950-1951, 1952 RR. The irregularities suggest that combinations of features may be rather abundant.

FIGURE 3:  1945-52 on the left, 1953-66 on the right.

### BOILER DETAILS

Two front boiler assemblies are isolated (Figure 3) to compare the headlamp housing of 1946-1952 (left) with the 1953-1966 version (right). A small brace cast into the plate below the housing (arrow, right) gave more rigidity to the housing and may have been Lionel's response to complaints about bent or broken headlights.

FIGURE 4:  The 1946-49 assembly on the left and 1950-66 on the right.

A view from a different angle reveals further internal modifications to the boiler fronts (Figure 4). The assemblies are seen from bottomside with the smokebox door open. In 1946 through 1949, the assembly was attached by two lugs (left). In 1950, the lower lug (A) vanished along with a notch (C) and a small hole (B) in the headlamp plate. The new top lug (D) was beefed up in width (right). The bulb clip (E) appeared in 1947, when smoke lamps were phased out in favor of a new resistance-coil smoke unit. Both boiler fronts fit all Berkshire boilers, unlike the similar conversion of the Turbines, where the 1946 boiler front will not fit later models.

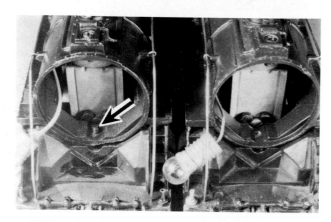

FIGURE 5:  1946-49 on the left and 1950-66 on the right.

Locomotives from which the boiler front examples were taken (Figure 5, left) show the frame-to-boiler screw (arrow) extending beyond its hole. It loosely retained the lower lug of 1946-1949 fronts, as the lug hole was oversized and untapped. As the lower lug was omitted, the screw furnished was shorter (right).

FIGURE 6:  1946-47 on the left and 1948-66 on the right.

The pair of pilots (Figure 6) compare the 1946-1947 model without coupler (left) to the more detailed redesign of 1948-1966 (right). (A similar detailed redesign occurred on the smaller 675 and 2025 locomotives.) A somewhat scale-sized drop coupler is sculpted with its attending lift gear. The brake hose is shackled by chain. Note the deeper depressions between thinner vertical bars of the pilot.

On the corners of two pilot beams (Figure 7) are the two types of flagstaffs. The hexagonal base of 1946-1954 (left) is contrasted to the round base of 1955-1956 (right). These flagstaffs are found in aluminum or painted black somewhat randomly. Some locomotives turn up with no evidence of ever having flagstaffs installed in their empty holes.

FIGURE 7: 1946-54 on the left and 1955-66 on the right.

On the top of the boiler castings (Figure 8), the 1946 sand dome (left) appears small and round. In 1947 (right), it was lengthened aft to nearly double its former dimensions, and a rectangular hatch finished its appearance. Above the newer sand dome is evidence of the new E-unit, with its lever protruding through a transverse slot.

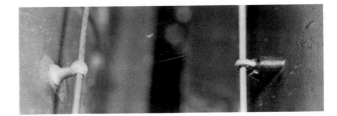

FIGURE 9: 1946 on the left and 1947-66 on the right.

FIGURE 8: 1946 on the left and 1947-66 on the right.

The prewar influence is apparent with a nicely turned stanchion guiding the handrail on the initial model of 1946 (Figure 9, left). Four of these stanchions were fastened with small brass nuts on each side of the boiler. For 1947 (right), inexpensive cotter pins were inserted through projections cast into the boiler, the method all further models would adopt.

The three inverted boiler castings reveal their simulated reverse gear details (Figure 10, boxed area). The easily broken 1946 open-type casting (left) was strengthened in 1947 (center) and ran through 1949. It was further simplified in 1950 (right) and ran unchanged for the balance of production.

FIGURE 10: 1946 on the left, 1947-49 in the center and, 1950-66 on the right.

FIGURE 11: 1946 on the left, 1947-56 in the center and 1957-66 on the right.

The 1950-1966 boiler received a flat projection (arrow) indicating adaptation of the Berkshire boiler shell to other Lionel locomotives. This projection had no purpose whatever on the Berkshire models. New steamers, such as the 2046 Hudson, used the same boiler. It was attached to their frames by the use of a long Phillips screw which attached to this projection.

## FRAME AND DRIVE

The pilot-cylinder casting was riveted to the frame on the first 1946 Berkshire. A unique frame assembly with drop-out wheels, axles and gears, it was a serviceman's delight. A long cast plate (Figure 11, left), with collector arms attached, retained the entire drive train and wheels in their channels.

The first and fourth axles were geared and driven by a long, longitudinal worm shaft. Despite the impressive construction, the 1946 Berkshire was slow, gear noise was horrendous and traction proved disappointing.

A new frame emerged in 1947. Simulated spring suspension and lower boiler contours were added to the frame casting, filling in the previously open area between boiler and frame (Figure 12). Axles now passed through holes across the new frame, and wheels were pressed on in conventional fashion.

Center-rail collector assemblies are of three types (Figure 11). In 1946, the cast four-screw plate described above held the

FIGURE 12: 1946 top, 1947-66 bottom.

collector arms. From 1947 through 1956, a smaller two-screw stamping was utilized (center). The same arms and wide rollers were attached. A total redesign appeared in 1957 (right). Smaller and with narrow rollers, the assembly was attached with a single large-head screw; this arrangement ran through 1966.

FIGURE 13: 1950-51, 53-66 on the left and 1952 - 726, 726RR on the right.

An extraordinary performance improvement in 1950 - magnetraction - employed a cylindrical magnet (Figure 13, left, A) mounted in a cavity between the third and fourth driver axles. Magnetic flux was conducted along iron side plates (B) which flanked the frame. In 1952, the war postponed the feature, resulting in the omission of magnet and plates (Figure 13, right). They returned in 1953 to run through 1966.

FIGURE 14: 1946 on the left, 1947-66 on the right.

Pilot truck guide plates (Figure 14) were attached by two screws in 1946 (left). In 1947, the plate was staked to the pilot underside (right) and provided with a hole for access to the frame-boiler screw. This became the standard practice through 1966. The other pair of holes added to the cylinder casting had no purpose on the Berkshire. Again, interchangeability with other steamers necessitated the alteration.

## DRIVERS AND RODS

Driving wheels of 1946 through 1949 models of the Berkshire were the attractive "Baldwin Disc" type, as lettered on the counterweights (Figure 15, left). These wheels were also used on other steamers of the period, such as the 224, 675 and 2025. Nickeled tires were pressed onto the cast wheels in prototype

FIGURE 15: 1946-49 on left, 1950-66 on right.

fashion. However, with magnetraction in 1950 came the traditional spoked wheel of sintered iron (right). In reality, locomotive wheels evolved from spoked-type to disc-type; Lionel's Berkshire demonstrated reverse chronology in this regard.

FIGURE 16: 1947-66 locomotive.

FIGURE 17: 1946 locomotive.

FIGURE 18: 1946 on left, 1947-66 on right.

Eccentric cranks were given a tiny notch in 1947 (Figure 16, arrow). This notch appeared on all models to follow. In addition, the connecting rods of 1946 were embossed with a small bump on the simulated coupling (Figure 17, arrow). In 1947 and thereafter, this surface was flat. The rods themselves were nickel-plated from 1946 through 1952. Brighter cadmium plating was employed thereafter.

## PILOT AND TRAILING TRUCKS

In 1946, the pilot truck wheels had a hollowed area surrounding their inner raised centers (Figure 18, left). Two square spokes radiated at 180 degrees across this hollow area. Conventional wheels followed in 1947 through 1966 (right). Original equipment pilot trucks on the Berkshire and many other Lionel steamers are good indicators of a locomotive's "mileage". Any derailment would result in a shower of sparks from beneath the pilot truck as it dragged across the power rail, causing a short circuit. A glance back at Figure 14 will show the progressive wear of the soft iron axle housing.

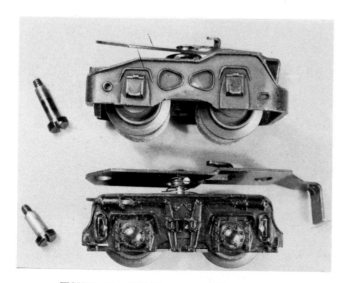

FIGURE 19: 1946-54 on top, 1955-66 on bottom.

The four-wheeled rear truck of 1946 was framed in one piece of cast metal (Figure 19, top). It wrapped completely around the wheels, sides, front and rear. The assembly was installed with a long-shanked screw and was used through 1954. A cheaper rear truck (Figure 19, bottom) with a stamped metal

bolster and black plastic side frames appeared in 1955. Well detailed but light in weight, it ran through 1966. A shorter screw was provided to fasten it to the frame.

FIGURE 20: 1946-49 left, 1950-54 center, 1955-56 right.

A top view of three rear truck assemblies (Figure 20) shows various combinations of truck and draft gear used. The 1946-1949 type drawbar (left) was short and coupled the tender prototypically close to the locomotive cab. Lengthening the drawbar by 1/4" in 1950 (center) allowed clearance for the new tender design of that year. In 1955, the new plastic-sided truck mentioned earlier was equipped with the same longer drawbar (right).

## ELECTRICAL SYSTEMS

In Figure 21, motor and reversing systems are shown in profile. A 1946 horizontally mounted 726M-1 motor (top) shows its tubular brush holders and jack plug, while the leverless E-unit lies prone and is equipped with a return spring. The slanted 671M-1 motor installation (identical to the one employed in the 671 PRR Turbine) debuted in 1947 with a smaller casing. This chassis also came with the new vertically mounted E-unit with lever and gravity return which would appear on all future models of the Berkshire. A ballast weight of lead alloy bolted between the E-unit and the motor was an attempt to enhance traction on 1947 through 1949 locomotives.

In 1949, the motor brushes were integrated with the back plate on the new 681-100 motors (bottom). The absence of tubular projections is apparent. The example also shows the ballast deleted. Since this particular locomotive chassis is of 1961-1966 vintage, magnetraction eliminated the need for added weight. Incidentally, ballast was not used on 1952 models in spite of omission of the magnetraction feature during that year. The same group of chassis is viewed from both rear and top (Figures 22 and 23) to show these three basic types of installations.

Being "deluxe" items, all Berkshire locomotives were equipped with smoke units. In 1946, the first models were produced with the marginally-performing 18 volt lamp type of

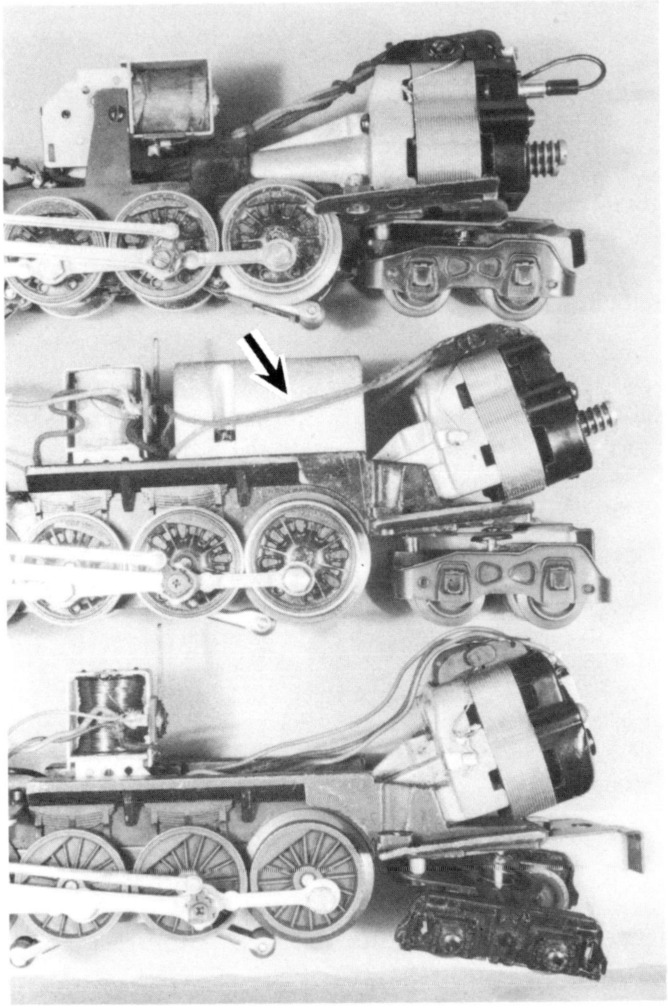

FIGURE 23:   1946 top, 1947-48 center, and 1949-66 bottom.

FIGURE 21:   1946 top, 1947-48 center and 1949-66 bottom.

FIGURE 22:   1946 "LIONEL ATOMIC PRECISION MOTOR" left, 1947-48 "LIONEL PRECISION MOTOR" center, and 1949-66 "LIONEL" right.

smoke unit. The same lamp also provided illumination for the headlight. The unit used a wire "flapper shaft" to pump smoke. All locomotives to follow received a new resistance coil smoke unit with a stamped metal smoke lever pump; this unit required the addition of a headlight socket to be attached to the smokebox door. A felt stack gasket sealed both old and new units. Occasionally, 1946 locomotives will be found with the newer smoke unit, since Lionel offered conversion kits to service stations for any owner wishing a conversion to the newer unit.

FIGURE 24: 1946 2426W top (A), 1950 671W second (B), 1952 2046W third (C), and 736W on bottom (D).

## TENDER VARIATIONS

Since the Berkshires were sold as premium 0 Gauge locomotives, it was appropriate that their tenders be first class (Figure 24). All had motor-driven two-tone whistles. The first Berkshire of 1946 was sold with the highly desirable 2426W tender (A). This tender was lavishly detailed. Turned metal stanchions guided wire railings around its deck. The all metal die-cast body shell also had separate cast steps on its front and stamped metal steps on its rear, as well as a plastic inlaid coal pile fastened by two screws. This tender, which weighed over two pounds, was rubber-stamped "LIONEL LINES" in white serif lettering on its detailed flanks. Silver lettering also appeared on a small quantity of 1946 tenders. It rolled on six-wheel passenger car trucks and had a coil coupler. The

same tender came with the celebrated 773 of 1950; after its discontinuance, its like would not be seen again until Fundimensions revived the tender type in 1981 with its Chicago & Alton Hudson passenger set.

A plastic "PENNSYLVANIA" type streamlined tender with a water scoop became the standard Berkshire tender in 1950 and thereafter (Figure 24, B, C and D). This tender had several variations. The 1950 Berkshires were trailed by a 2671WX tender with "LIONEL LINES" widely spaced in small letters decorating its sides (B). The same six-wheel trucks and couplers were retained. The drawbar had two 45-degree bends within its length, compared to the two 90-degree bends on that of the earlier tender. The plastic body shell was retained by a screw at each end.

This tender received a new lettering treatment (C) and a new number, 2046W, in 1952. The expanded and larger "LIONEL LINES" is easily differentiated by an examination of the "O" in "LIONEL". It appears round on 1950-1951 models and flattened or elliptical on 1952-1960 tenders. This tender received four-wheel cast metal freight trucks with a magnetically operated coupler. A manual tab was added to the coupler in 1955.

The streamlined tender was altered again in 1961 (D). This time, "PENNSYLVANIA" was heat-stamped on its side in white letters, and it was renumbered "736W". This tender ran until the end of Berkshire production in 1966. It was furnished with cheaper plastic-sided Timken four-wheel trucks and a plastic disc-operating coupler typical of Lionel's practice at this time with its freight cars. The cheapening of this tender was the sign of bad times to come; Lionel was declining rapidly towards the end of Berkshire production.

FIGURE 25: 1946-49 2426W on the left and 1950-66 2671WX, 2046W or 736W on the right.

The tops and the front ends of these tenders are compared to illustrate the basic body design differences between 1946-1949 and 1950-1966 tenders. Note the apparent massiveness of the earlier model. The 2426W tender looked expensive - and it was!

An interesting view of the three tenders shows back end variations (Figure 27). The 2671WX (center) had three small holes. These became backup lights when the tender was sold with a small number of 1948 671 Turbine locomotives. The idea was never popular and was too expensive, so the holes were filled in for the years 1952 and afterwards (right). Another very subtle difference on the 2671WX can be seen at the top vertical

FIGURE 26:  1946-49 2426W on top and 1950-66 2671W, 2046W or 736W on bottom.

FIGURE 28:  1946-49 2426 W on the left and 1950-66 2671W, 2046W or 736 W on the right.

bars of the ladder (arrows), which appear separated from the tender body shell. This separation was filled on all post-1951 models.

"Under the hood" of the tender, a pair of whistle mechanisms are compared (Figure 28). The mechanism of the 2426W (left), with its heavy die-cast metal housing, is mounted on its side. This mechanism produced a much clearer, more mellow sound than did its successor in 1950 and later (right), which was mounted in a "shaft-upright" position and was made of marbled plastic in its earlier years and black plastic later on. The later mechanism's air intake used the water scoop for its air duct.

During the declining years of Lionel, the continued production of the Berkshires became a poignant reminder of the Lionel Corporation during its heyday. Today, the 726 and the 736 stand as reminders of the excellence once achieved by the old Lionel Corporation.

It was inevitable, then, that Fundimensions would reintroduce the Berkshire, and indeed this occurred in 1980 with the production of Chessie Steam Special and Union Pacific models. Two years later, a magnificent Berkshire was produced in Nickel Plate Road markings, this time with its original premium metal 2426-style tender. It is only fitting that these Fundimensions products represented what the original Berkshire was - the very best in steam locomotives. Indeed, the Nickel Plate Road Berkshire, with its electronic whistle and Sound of Steam, might represent the ultimate in Berkshire production.

My personal need for a comprehensive but handy guide resulted in the chronology chart which follows this article. It is revised frequently as more data is discovered. Hopes are that the chart, coupled with the text and photos, will enhance significantly the much-deserved interest in the fine Berkshire locomotive series.

FIGURE 27:  1946-49 2426W on the left, 1950-51 2671WX in the center and
1952-66 2046W or 736W on the right.

# Lionel 726-736 Series Steam Locomotive
## 2-8-4 BERKSHIRE TYPE (226 BOILER DERIVATIVE)
## VARIATIONS CHRONOLOGY (1946-1966*)

| | MODEL YEAR | 1946 | 1947 | 1948 | 1949 | 1950-1 | 1952 | 1953-4 | 1955-6 | 1957-60 | 1961-6* |
|---|---|---|---|---|---|---|---|---|---|---|---|
| | **Cab Number** | '726' Rubber Stamped—Silver | | | | '736'RS—Silv. | '726' RS, Silv. / 726 RR' RS, Silv. | '736' Heat Stamped—White, Thinner Typeface | | | |
| **ELECTRICAL** | **Motor** | 726M-1 'Atomic' | 671M-1 | | 681-100 | | | | | | |
| | **Drive** | Horizontal, Dual Worm | 30° Slant, Single Worm | | | | | | | | |
| | **Brushes** | Tubular Receptacles | | Receptacles Integrated with Motor Backplate | | | | | | | |
| | **E-Unit** | Horizontal, Spring Return, Jack Plug | Vertical, Gravity Return, Lever Thru Top of Boiler | | | | | | | | |
| | **Collector Asm.** | 4-Screw Cast Mount | 2-Screw Stamped Mount | | | | | | | 1-Screw Smaller Stamped Mount | |
| | **Smoke Unit** | Lamp Type, 18V | Resistance Wire Heating Element | | | | | | | | |
| **WHEELS** | **Drivers** | Zinc, Lettered 'Baldwin Disc', Steel Tires | | | Sintered Iron, 1-Piece, Spoked | | | | | | |
| | **Axles** | Bottom Drop-Out | Thru-Frame | | | | | | | | |
| | **Traction Aid** | None | Ballast Weight | | | Magnetized Drivers | None | Magnetized Drivers | | | |
| | **F & R Trucks** | Cast Metal Frames – Front and Rear | | | | | | | Rear—New Style, Stamped Frame, Plastic Sideframes | | |
| | **Pilot Plate** | 2-Screw Mounted | Staked to Pilot/Steamchest Casting, Access Hole for Screw | | | | | | | | |
| **CASTINGS** | **Boiler** | Short Sand Dome, Open Valve Gear Hanger Detail | Long Sand Dome, Filled Valvegear Hanger Detail, Cast Stanchion Posts | | | | | | | | |
| | **Cab Windows**\*\* | 3 & 4 Window | 4-Window | | 3 & 4 Window | | | 3-Window | 3 & 4 Window | | |
| | **Frame** | Open Bottom | Closed Bottom, Simulated Lower Boiler and Suspension Added | | | Magnet Cavity, Iron Side Plates | Cavity, No Side Plates | Magnet Cavity, Iron Side Plates | | | |
| | **Pilot** | No Simulated Coupler | Cast, Simulated Coupler and Lift Pin Assembly | | | | | | | | |
| | **Boiler Front** | 2 Small Mounting Lugs—Top and Bottom, 2 Notches Horizontally Opposite | | | 1 Large Mounting Lug—Top Only, 1 Notch at Locking Snap | | | | | | |
| | **Smokebox Door** | No Bulb Clip | Bulb Clip Added | No Headlamp Brace, Hole in Headlamp Baseplate | | | Cast Headlamp Brace, Baseplate Hole Deleted | | | | |
| **HARDWARE** | **Side Rods** | Coupling Embossment | Nickel Plated | Notch in Eccentric Crank, Coupling Flat | | | | Cadmium Plated (Slightly Brighter) | | | |
| | **Hand Rails** | Turned Stanchions with Nuts | Cotter Pin Attached | | | | | | | | |
| | **Flagstaffs** | Hexagon Base | | | | ? | Round Base | | | | |
| | **Headlamp Lens** | Flat Plastic Disc | | | Solid Lucite | | | | | | |
| | **Draft Gear** | Short (Engine and Tender Close Coupled) | | | Lengthened ¼ Inch | | | | | | |
| **TENDER** | **Frame Number** | 2426W | | | 2671WX | 2046W | | | | 736W | |
| | **Body Style** | Die Cast Large Box-Type, Derived from 2226W Pre-War | | | One-Piece Plastic, Streamlined Pennsylvania Type, with Water Scoop | | | | | | |
| | **Misc. Details** | Plastic Coal Pile, Turned Stanchions, Wire Handrails | | | 3 Back-Up Lamp Holes | Back-Up Lamp Holes Filled | | | | | |
| | **Lettering** | Silver or White | White Only | "LIONEL LINES"—Rubber Stamped | | "LIONEL LINES" Small Letters | "LIONEL LINES"—New Typeface, Larger | | | | "PENNSYLVANIA" |
| | **Trucks** | 6-Wheel, Plastic Sideframes | | | 4-Wheel, Cast Metal Sideframes | | | | | | 4-Wheel, All Plastic |
| | **Coupler** | Electromagnetic | | | Spring-Loaded Plate | | | Manual Tab Added | | | Plastic, Metal Disc, No Tab |
| | **Whistle** | Cast Metal Housing, Motor Shaft Horizontal | Plastic Housing, Motor Shaft Vertical | | | | | | | | |
| **MISC.** | **Major Variants** | 1946 | 1947 | 1948-9 | | 1950-1 | 1952 2-Varieties | 1953-4 | 1955-66 | | |
| | **Catalog Price** | N/A | $37.50 | | $42.50 | | $43.50 | | $45 | $47 | $49 | $50 | $60 |
| | **MODEL YEAR** | 1946 | 1947 | 1948 | 1949 | 1950-1 | 1952 | 1953-4 | 1955-6 | 1957-60 | 1961-6* |

\*Not manufactured after 1966, sold until 1968

\*\*3 and 4-window variations are known to exist in many (possibly all) 226 derived boiler/cab castings, (i.e., 646, 726, 736, 2046, 2056).

NOTE: Changeover datelines are variable for certain common parts such as flagstaffs, rods, etc. Such parts were often used until supplies were exhausted, in spite of availability of replacements.

Compiled by **Ron Griesbeck**
Revised **March, 1982**

## LIONEL STEAM TURBINES: HOW DO THEY DIFFER?
### By Pat Scholes

NOTE: This article first appeared in the **Rocky Mountain Division Newsletter** of the TCA, Volume 6, Number 2, Summer 1980. Used by permission of the author. Photographs by Roger Bartelt.

Few postwar Lionel locomotives captured the imagination of the train-buying public more than did the Lionel model of the Pennsylvania Railroad's innovative S-2 steam turbine. From its introduction in 1946, the Lionel Turbine was a runaway success; it was the first locomotive to be produced with Lionel's smoke units and it included nearly every deluxe feature available. This popularity has continued with collectors. Now, as then, the turbines have been excellent sellers, and many hobbyists still run them regularly as the best "haulers" in their operating collections.

How many variations of this impressive locomotive did Lionel produce from 1946 until its last year of production, 1955? Such a long production period would suggest that there were quite a few variations, especially in view of the popularity of the engine. In fact, no fewer than 18 variants of this locomotive have been identified!

Variations may not be every collector's priority. However, tracing the turbine variations through the 10 years of Lionel production gives a fascinating account of the attempts to "catch the eye" of children and adults interested in toy trains. Equipped with a prototypical 6-8-6 wheel configuration, Lionel's turbine sported a total of 20 wheels! The sight of all this imagined power churning furiously down tin plate track has always been spellbinding and impressive indeed, especially when the turbine is coupled with the 1948 12-wheel tender.

The purpose of this article is to outline the progression and variations of the 20-wheel steam turbine from its introduction in 1946 until its discontinuance in 1955. Some of the variations are quite subtle, while others are pronounced. Most of my observations are from examples which appear to have a history of not being altered after they left the factory. This, of course, can be very difficult to verify, but sometimes the originality can be inferred if the locomotive is purchased from original owners (or dealers who have bought it from original owners). In any case, much effort has been expended in examining many sets to arrive at the following information. Readers are asked to write with any additional information they might have.

As with automobiles, the turbines were changed on a "model year" basis. In the first four years of production, 1946-1949, there were three "lines" of turbines with three different number designations: 2020, 671 and 671R. With each year, a change in one of these lines was accompanied by changes in the others. In other words, the design changes in the 1948 2020 were the same as the design changes in the 1948 versions of the 671 and 671R. Since there were design changes each year in the first four years, this accounts for 12 variations (four years x three lines per year).

In addition to the engine number, some other characteristics to observe are:
- Presence or absence of thick nickel rims on the drive wheels.
- Presence or absence of thin blackened rims on the drive wheels.
- Extruded wheel weights on the drive wheels, as opposed to inset or recessed versions.
- Presence or absence of the E-unit lever protruding from the top of the cab.
- Presence of "Electronic" decals.

671W       2671W       2046W-50

Three different tenders that came with Lionel turbines. 2466-type (numbered 671W in this example) and two different versions of the long, low 2046-type tender: 2671W (in center) with 12 wheels and backup light holes and 2046W-50 (on right) with eight wheels and filled-in holes. Bartelt photograph.

- Tender design. There were two basic types. One was the short, high 2466-type tender. It is different from those found on other locomotives of the period in that it has vertical handrails on all four corners. The second type was the long, low, water-scoop Pennsylvania tender, which was produced with six-wheel and four-wheel trucks.

There are two other distinguishing characteristics which are covered in the hobbyist literature in great detail. For completeness, however, both are included here:
- The position of the motor mounting (horizontal or slanted).
- The presence of additional valve gear linkage on the front drive wheels.

This is found on the 682, along with a white stripe on the edge of the catwalk down each side of the engine.

The short, high 2466-type tender was catalogued as 2020W, 671W or 4671W. Bartelt photograph.

### TENDERS

An examination of the tender varieties available with the turbine is an interesting part of a study of engine and tender variations. As mentioned earlier, the turbine was accompanied by two basic tender types. These were the high, short 2466-type and the long, low 2046-type. An example of each type can be seen in the photos. According to the 1946 catalogue, the 2020 occasionally came with the 2466 WX tender, which has no vertical handrails on the corners. I have not been able to confirm this combination. All 1946 engine and tender sets I have studied which appear to be original have had the tender with vertical handrails attached. In fact, the picture in the 1946 catalogue shows handrails on all the 2020 sets. All other sets in 1946 had the tenders with vertical handrails. These tenders were numbered 2020W, 671W or 4671W, depending upon the engine number. Another complication is that the numbers were not stamped on the undersides of the tender in 1946, as they were later.

At Lionel, the tender variations from the basic design were sometimes denoted by adding or changing a digit in front of the number. Thus, the electronic tender in 1946 was numbered 4671W. Since the digit was "4", this leads us to conclude that the long, low Pennsy 2671W tender was on the drawing boards as the 1946 catalogue was being printed, even though it didn't appear until 1948. The 4671W was produced unchanged until the Electronic Set was discontinued after the 1949 model year. It was basically a 671W tender with chassis modifications to accommodate the radio receiver.

The 2046-type tender later came with eight wheels. It was catalogued as 2046WX but usually rubber-stamped 2046W-50 on its underside. Bartelt photograph.

The long, low 12-wheel tender with water scoop catalogued as 2671W and later 2671WX. We call this the 2046-type tender. Bartelt photograph.

In 1947, none of the tenders were changed. In 1948, however, the 2671 Pennsylvania tender made its debut. Early production models had backup lights in the three portholes in the end of the tender, as did the prototype. There is some evidence that a few of these early models with backup lights were numbered 2671WX - the number which later denoted the same non-lighted tender with "LIONEL LINES" markings. The backup lights were soon discontinued, probably due to production cost compared to added value. The run was so short that the lighted tenders are, in my opinion, a prize all their own. (The feature is easy to install on non-lighted tenders, but original installations can be detected by the protrusion of three plastic knobs, part of the original plastic lens, out of the portholes. Post-factory additions would simply have a flat plastic lens glued inside the tender). The light holes in the plastic tender shell were to persist through 1953, when they were finally filled in.

Another change to the tender occurred in 1948. Lionel was converting its couplers from the original coil-operated version to the mechanical flap-type coupler. Rolling stock which underwent this change and had a four-digit number was customarily denoted by changing the first digit from "2" to "6". Thus, the 2020W tender would become a 6020W. Oddly, though, I can find no evidence that the coupler was changed from coil to mechanical on the 6020W tender, despite the number change. It appears to have remained equipped with the coil coupler until it was discontinued after 1949. In fact, it may not have been planned to change the coupler on this tender, since the tender was due to be phased out. Since the 2671W tender had six-wheel trucks, it retained coil couplers because the mechanical coupler had not yet been developed for the longer trucks. Of course, the 4671W tender (and the other electronic cars) were forced to continue with coil couplers because they had to be activated from track power through the radio receiver; this would have been impossible with a mechanical coupler.

The last year for the production of the 2020 turbine - and its 6020W tender - was 1949. Likewise, the 4671W would not

return in 1950; the Electronic Set was being discontinued. However, the 2671W was alive and well. In 1950, this tender continued to be pulled by a turbine, the new 681 model. (The engine number increased by ten when magnetraction became a feature of certain locomotives.) The 681 was a redesigned 671 equipped with magnetized wheels for pulling power and stability. This combination remained until early 1952, when the Korean War caused magnetic materials to be in short supply. Since the 1952 engine reverted to 671 to signify the omission of magnetraction, Lionel apparently took the opportunity to cut production costs on the 2671W tender. The company outfitted it with four-wheel trucks so that it was basically the same as the tender pulled by the 2046 Hudson, which was, of course, the 2046W. However, the Hudson's 2046W had "LIONEL LINES" on its sides instead of "PENNSYLVANIA". Therefore, the Pennsy eight-wheel tender was distinguished as a separate unit by numbering it 2046W-50, although it was referred to in the catalogue as 2046WX. This configuration remained through 1953.

In 1954, the turbine was modified and numbered 682. The tender remained 2046W-50, but it had a different plastic tender body shell. The backup light holes, unused since 1948, were filled in so that only an outline of the circles remained. The "PENNSYLVANIA" lettering on the tender was shorter, measuring 5-5/8" rather than the 6" length which existed from 1948 to 1953. There were no changes in 1955, the last year of production.

## ENGINES

As previously mentioned, the steam turbine series was introduced in 1946 as the 2020, 671 and 671R. They had no E-unit lever protruding from the top of the cab. The motor was horizontally mounted, and all eight drivers had thick and shiny nickel rims. The wheel weights were extruded, not inset (this characteristic would remain through 1949). A pair of receptacles on the brushplate was used to activate or disable the E-unit, depending upon which receptacle had the plug-in wire inserted into it. The tenders were not numbered, but they were the 2466-type with vertical handrails on all four corners.

In 1947, the cab casting and running gear were changed. The motor was mounted on an angle in the chassis to accommodate a single worm-drive, rather than a double one as used in 1946. This slanted motor mounting continued through the rest of production. The cab casting had a slot in its top for the E-unit lever. Close scrutiny of the two castings can reveal several detail changes. All eight drivers still had nickel rims. The smoke unit was changed from the bulb-activated unit to a resistance coil unit which was to continue through the rest of production. Due to the presence of the E-unit lever, the

A 1947 Chassis from a 671 with resistance coil smoke unit, vertical E-unit and nickel rim drivers. The motor is stamped "LIONEL PRECISION MOTOR". Bartelt photograph.

receptacles on the brushplate were no longer needed, so they were discontinued from production of the 671 and 2020. However, the 671R retained them for connection from the electronic reversing unit in the tender. The tenders now had the numbers stamped on the underside, usually in silver. The boiler showed extra piping detail just behind and below the smokebox, where the steam chest would be on a conventional steam locomotive. Since Lionel offered a conversion kit to install the new resistance-coil smoke unit, some 1946 castings will be found with a resistance smoke unit. Finally, a small number of early production locomotives had the numbers "671" or "6200" rubber-stamped in silver on the boiler front Keystone instead of the more common red and gold decal. The exact manufacturing sequence for this change is not clear. Similar stampings are found in the 1947 production models of the 675 and 2025 locomotives as well.

The 671 was coupled with the 2671W tender in some cases in 1948 (or possibly the 2671WX). The 2020 was equipped with the 6020W tender, which was unchanged from the 2020W tender except for its number. All three turbines had thin, blackened rims on the front and rear pairs of drivers only; the two middle pairs had no rims.

The year 1949 was one of little change. The main item of significance was that the rims on the drivers were discontinued completely.

In contrast to 1949, the year 1950 brought about many changes. The 2020 was discontinued, probably because Lionel wanted to concentrate sales of the turbine upon the 0 Gauge market (the 2020 had been marketed as an 027 locomotive). The 671R Electronic Set was also discontinued. (One prototype 4681 locomotive was produced.) The 671 itself was fitted with magnetraction and became a 681. In the process of designing and manufacturing the wheels to be responsive to the magnetic

bar in the chassis, the drive wheel weights were inset rather than extruded, as they had been. The 681 pulled the 2671W tender, as had the 671 in 1949. No changes were made to the engine or tender in 1951.

The shortage of magnetraction alloys in 1952 caused that feature to be eliminated shortly after production started. Although the 1952 catalogue was printed with the anticipation of materials shortages, some train sets were apparently produced with the 681/2671W combination. One of my own train sets, purchased new in 1952, has the cars exactly as catalogued in 1952, but they are pulled by a magnetraction 681! It was purchased as part of an unbroken set. In any event, Lionel soon had to cease 681 production and manufacture 671 locomotives, which were in reality 681 locomotives without magnetraction. The firm apparently still had 671 cabs left over from 1949, so these were put on the non-magnetraction 681 chassis. The 2671W was discontinued in favor of the less expensive eight-wheel tender, the 2046W-50. These 1952 671 engines can be distinguished from their 1949 671 counterparts, which also had no rims on the drivers, by the inset wheel weights and the hole through the frame between the first and second axles, where the magnet bar was omitted.

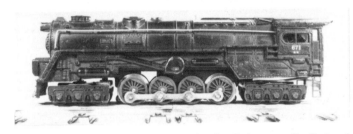

The 671 RR from 1952 had a space in the chassis between the first and second drivers where the magnets, if available, would have gone. Also note that the wheels do not have nickel rims.

This year of 1952 eventually led to a further merry mix-up of cab and number configurations. Lionel apparently exhausted its stock of leftover 671 cabs, so the company reissued them as 671 RR (re-run). This number was the only change to the locomotive. The tender remained the 2046W-50. Still later, another 1952 variation emerged. Apparently, the magnetic materials for magnetraction became available again before Lionel had used its complete stock of cabs marked 671 RR. So, being prudent business people, they finished their 1952 production by manufacturing some 671 RR locomotives with magnetraction! The example of this locomotive which I possess

A 1946 Lionel 2020 turbine with 2020W four-wheel tender. The tender has vertical handrails at the corner, the locomotive does not have a reverse unit lever protruding throught the boiler top, however, there are two receptacles on the brushplate for activating or disabling the E-unit; its drivers have thick shiny rims. Holden Collection, Bennett photograph.

The 1951 model of the 681 did not have nickel, the 2671W 12-wheel tender. Holden Collection, Bennett photograph.

seems to be authentic. Although the magnetraction 671 RR is interesting from a historical point of view, I do not consider it particularly valuable because it would be simple to fabricate one by interchanging cabs. Early 1952 saw the end of the impressive 2671W 12-wheel tender; it would not return.

671 from 1952. Note opening in chassis behing first driver. LaVoie Collection, Greenberg photograph.

The 682 is distinctive because of the whistle stripe on the running board and its lubricator linkage attached to the first driver. Bartelt photograph.

So, the year 1952 produced four variations:
• 681/2671W with magnetraction
• 671/2046W-50 without magnetraction
• 671 RR/2046W-50 without magnetraction
• 671 RR/2046W-50 with magnetraction

The year 1953 saw the reemergence of the 681, this time with the 2046W-50 tender. Except for the tender, it was identical to the 1951 model.

The 682 is distinctive because of the white stripe on the running board and its lubricator linkage attached to the first driver. Bartelt photograph.

In 1954, the 682 turbine arrived; this version has been the one most sought after by collectors. It is not as rare as other variations, but it is definitely in a class by itself because of the detail changes Lionel made to it. This locomotive had extra valve oiling gear on the front drivers and long white striping along each side. The paint wore off quickly with handling, and it is difficult to find with the white paint fully intact. If you possess a 682, let me caution you against running it too much. A little bit of wear on the extra linkage can cause it to jam the drivers. The inertia of the engine is usually enough to break off

the fragile linkage, and this seriously impairs the appeal and value of the engine. The 682 ran unchanged in 1955, which was the last year of production for the engine.

The chart at the end of this article summarizes the variation sequence, but if you have additions or corrections to it, please make them known.

The crowning irony of the Lionel S-2 Turbine is that Lionel sold many thousands of these locomotives as toys, but their prototype was a coal-devouring failure on the Pennsylvania Railroad, and only that one prototype was built.

But the story of the Lionel Turbine may not be over yet! After an absence of 30 years, Lionel's successor, Fundimensions, has announced its plans to reissue the turbine as part of its Famous American Railroads Series. The new turbine, to be marketed in the spring of 1985, will be the most spectacular version of this locomotive ever produced. Lionel's turbines were a uniform black, but this one will have Brunswick Green upper works and a silver smoke box. In addition, the new model will have a big 12-wheel tender with Sound of Steam and whistle, magnetraction, white striping and whitewall drivers, smoke, the extra oiling linkage of the old 682 (reinforced, one hopes!) and even backup lights in the tender! This locomotive promises to rekindle a long and interrupted love affair with a truly magnificent tin-plate masterpiece.

**1946** 3 variations - 2020/2020W, 671/671W, 671R/4424W: All tenders are short 2466-type. No tender numbers. No E-unit lever. Receptacles for E-unit wire on motor brushplate. Smoke bulb. Thick nickle rims on all drivers. Extruded wheel weights. Horizontal motor, no magnetraction.

**1947** 3 variations - 2020-2020W, 671/671W, 671/4671W: Tenders have numbers. E-unit lever in cab. No receptacles for E-unit wire on motor brush plate (except 671R). Smoke heater unit. Slanted motor.

**1948** 3 variations - 2020/6020W, 671/267W, 671R/4671W: Thin blackened rims on front and rear drivers. No rims on center drivers. Tender 267W is long, low, water scoop-type. It has long (6") "Pennsylvania" lettering, open light ports in back and 12 wheels.

**1949** 3 variations - 2020/6020W, 671/2671W, 671R/4671W: No rims on any of the drivers. 2671WX not produced with "Pennsylvania" lettering.

**1950** 1 variation - 681/267W: Has magnetraction and inset wheel weights.

**1951** 1 variation - 681/2671W: Same as 1950.

**1952** 3 variations - 681/267W: Same as 1950 & 1951.
671/2046W-50: No magnetraction. No magnet in frame. Inset wheel weights. 2046W-50 has 8 wheels; otherwise very similar to 2671W.
671RR/2046W-50: Number-board re-printed with "RR" under "671". Otherwise, same as 671 above.
671RR/2046W-50: Same as above, but WITH magnetraction.

**1953** 1 variation - 681/2046W-50: Same as 1950 681 except with 2046W-50 tender.

**1954** 1 variation - 682/2046W-50: Extra valve gear linkage. White stripe down side of engine. 2046W-50 tender has short (5-5/8") "Pensylvania" lettering and has filled-in light ports in back.

**1955** 682/2046W-50: Same as 1954 682.

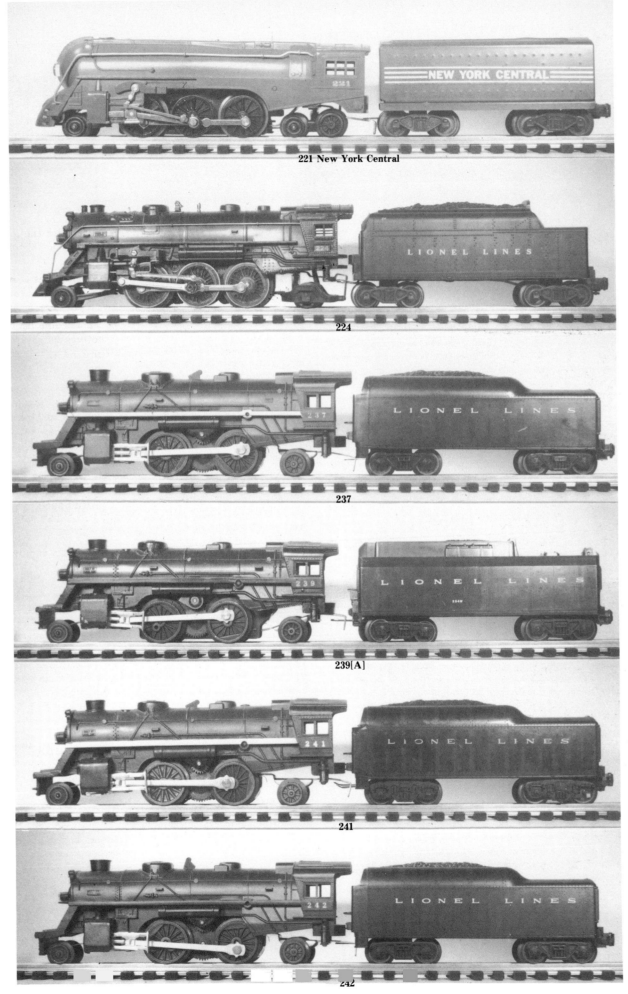

221 New York Central

224

237

239[A]

241

242

The 671R Electronic control turbine was numbered "671" beneath the window but had distinctive decals on both the locomotive and tender. Note the radio receiver under the tender. Holden Collection, Bennett photograph.

## STEAM LOCOMOTIVES

**With the assistance of Ronald Niedhammer**

Gd VG Exc Mt

**221** 1946-1947, 2-6-4 die-cast boiler, New York Central streamlined prototype, handrail from the pilot to the cab, very shallow stamped bell and whistles, large lens with refracting qualities, drive and connecting rods, valve gear, crosshead integral to body casting, motor with brushplate on left side and forward, casting opened up to provide room for brush holders; motor held in by screw behind smokestack and rod in front of cab, right side has large, medium and small gears, readily visible sliding shoes, blind center driver, "221" apparently rubber-stamped in silver or white/silver. 221T tender marked "New York Central" with decal in black and silver, metal trucks, staple-end, coil coupler, also came with 221W whistle tender. It is reported that the 1946 and 1947 castings are quite different. Ely observation. We would appreciate reader explanations of those differences.
(A) 1946, gray body, aluminum-finished drivers without tires.

30 50 65 90

(B) 1946, gray body, black-finished drivers, without tires.

20 30 45 65

(C) 1947, black body, black drivers with nickel tires. 20 30 45 65
(D) Black body, silver drivers without tires. Niedhammer observation.

20 30 45 65

(E) Black body, black drivers without tires. Niedhammer observation.

20 30 45 65

(F) Gray body, black drivers with nickel tires. Niedhammer observation.

20 30 45 65

**224** 1945-46, 2-6-2, black die-cast boiler; Baldwin nickel-rim disc drivers; 0 Gauge motor with gears on left and brushplate on right; drive, connecting and eccentric rods; die-cast front and rear trucks; cab detailed with two fireboxes; headlight; trim rods run from cab to pilot on both sides; nickel-plated bell on bracket; motor held by screw at top rear of boiler and horizontal rod across boiler just above steam chest; rear of cab floor rounded with short drawbar. The 2466W whistle tender (or 2466T non-whistle tender) has staple-end metal trucks and a coil coupler with sliding shoe. Two versions of the coil coupler are found: early version has open assembly and "whirly" wheels and later version has metal plate covering shoe support bracket and solid wheels. Both tenders feature metal trim, including wire guardrail which goes around the back deck. This engine was also made prewar as 224 or 224E in either black or gunmetal. It has a squared-off cab floor and a longer drawbar with ears; its tender has the older box couplers. Priced for postwar version. The later tender is the 2466WX. The prewar version of this engine was probably carried over into postwar production; if so, it was equipped with an early coupler assembly and whirly wheels, and it was produced only during late 1945. Ervin and LaVoie comments.

35 45 60 110

**233** 1961-62, 2-4-2 black plastic boiler, plastic side motor 233-100, two-position reverse, smoke, light, magnetraction, 233W tender with whistle.

12 15 25 35

**235** 1961, uncatalogued, 2-4-2, black plastic boiler, two-position reverse, smoke, light, magnetraction, plastic side motor 236-100.

14 18 28 50

**236** 1961-62, 2-4-2, black plastic boiler, white lettering, drive rod only, liquid smoke, light, plastic motor with ridged bottom, two gears visible on left side, brush holder on right side, rolled metal pickup, magnetraction, fine cab interior detail, slope-back tender with operating coupler.

10 15 25 35

**237** 1963-66, 2-4-2, black plastic boiler, drive rod only, liquid smoke unit, light, plastic motor 237-100 with ridged bottom, two gears visible on left side, brushplate holder on right side, middle rail pickups are rolled metal, rubber tire on right rear driver, fine detail inside cab, white stripe runs length of body, two-position reverse unit with fiber lever through boiler top; streamlined tender lettered "LIONEL LINES", Timken trucks, ground pickup fingers on front truck, rear truck with fixed coupler, tender not numbered, see 1101 for discussion of body types. 10 15 25 35

**238** 1963-64, 2-4-2, black plastic body, plastic side motor, Scout-type two-position reverse, smoke, light, rubber tires, 243W tender with whistle; see 1101 for discussion of body types.
(A) Tender lettered "LIONEL LINES". 10 20 35 50
(B) Tender lettered "CANADIAN NATIONAL". NRS

**239** 1965-66, 2-4-2, black die-cast body, step for bell, no bell.
(A) Plastic motor with ridged bottom, two gears showing, rubber tire on right rear wheel, liquid smoke unit, 16-spoke wheels, light, fiber lever on two-position reversing unit. 10 20 35 50
(B) Better grade 0-27 metal side motor with three-position reverse unit with control lever down, readily accessible brushes, locomotive retains slot in top for two-position reverse unit, 239 (B), has a lighter stamping and a different type-face than does 239(A). 10 20 35 50

**240** Circa 1964, 2-4-2, uncatalogued by Lionel. Came as part of Sears space set 9820 only. Black plastic boiler, plastic side motor, two-position reverse, smoke, light, rubber tires (see 1101 for full discussion of locomotive types). This locomotive is particularly interesting because of its set, which included a 3666 cannon car, a 6470 exploding boxcar, an unnumbered flatcar with a green tank, a 6814 (C) rescue caboose, what appears to be a Marx - made transformer and a number of other pieces. This set, illustrated in color in the flatcar section, is described in more detail under the 3666 boxcar listing. Set value:

300 400 600 750

These observations are the result of the contributions of Vergonet, Bohn and Jarman. Some sets, possibly made in 1968 and numbered 11600, also came with an olive-colored range launching unit (add $100 to set values). Locomotive and tender value: 15 35 85 150

**241** 1958, uncatalogued, 2-4-2, die-cast body, white stripe along locomotive sides, fiber lever for reverse unit between domes, 239-100 motor with ridged bottom, gears on left side, brushes on right side, liquid smoke unit, finely detailed cab interior, rubber tires. Tender with Scout side truck frames with magnetic coupler; tender cab is fastened to base with two tabs in rear and screw in front; see 1101 for discussion of boiler types and comparisons with 237 and 242. 10 13 18 30

**242** 1962-66, 2-4-2, black plastic body, motor with grooved bottom, light, main rod each side, two gears visible on left side, brushes on right side, highly detailed cab interior, fiber lever for reverse unit through boiler top, stack has large hole because red gasket for smoke unit is not present. Tender with Timken trucks, one disc coupler, cab held to frame by two tabs

243

244

245

246[B]

246[A]

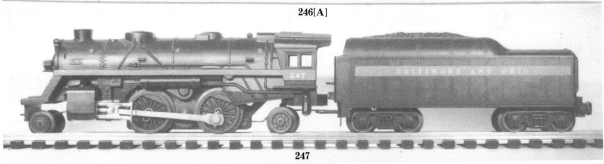

247

249

250

637[A]

646

665[A]

671RR

in rear and Phillips screw in front; motor held in by slide on front and pin through cab on rear; see 1101 for a discussion of boiler types and comparisons with 237 and 241.                                    **10   13   18   30**

**243** 1960, 2-4-2, black plastic body, two-position reverse unit with metal lever coming through boiler near cab, one drive rod on each side; 0-27 metal sided motor with two gears showing on left side and brushplate on right side; liquid smoke unit with bellows, highly detailed cab interior, motor held on by screw in front of reverse lever and plate in front of drivers, rubber tires, light. 243W tender, Timken trucks, disc coupler, one pickup roller for whistle and one wire for ground; see 1101 for a discussion of boiler types and comparison with 237, 241 and 242.            **10   13   18   30**

**244** 1960-61, 2-4-2, black plastic body, bell ledge between stack and first dome, no bell, reverse lever between second dome and cab; liquid smoke with bellows, light, 0-27 247-100 motor with metal sides, two gears on left side, brushes on right side, weight under cab. Tender lettered "LIONEL LINES", Timken truck in front, arch bar truck in rear with fixed coupler, tender cab mounted by two tabs in rear, screw in front, came with either 244T or 1130T tender.                              **10   13   18   30**

**245** 1959, 2-4-2, black plastic boiler, bell ledge between stack and first dome, no bell, small molded generator unit immediately in front of cab, motor mounted by pin through boiler and mounting plate in front, weight under cab, two gears visible on left, brush holder on right, smooth bottom plastic motor No. 245-100, two-position reverse unit with fiber lever, detailed cab interior. Tender with arch bar trucks, fixed coupler, see 1101 for discussion of body type.                         **10   13   18   30**

**246** 1959-61, 2-4-2, black plastic boiler, bell ledge between stack and first dome, no bell, reverse lever slot between first and second domes; single main rod on each side, light, no smoke unit, magnetraction. In late 1961, this locomotive came as part of set X-600, a special Quaker Oats promotion wherein the purchaser sent in two Quaker Oats box tops and $11.95 for the set, which included a 6406 flatcar with automobile, a 6042 gondola with canisters, a 6076 hopper car, a 6047 caboose, a 1016 transformer and track. Further details are requested concerning the cars in this set.
(A) No molded generator unit in front of cab, ridged bottom plastic motor 246-100, magnetraction, 244T or 1130T tender, tender not numbered.
                                                **10   15   20   30**
(B) Molded generator unit in front of cab, smooth bottom plastic motor 246-200, no weight under cab, slope-back tender, partially open in front pilot.                                             **10   15   20   30**

**247** 1959-61, 2-4-2, black plastic body, blue stripe with white lettering; tender lettered "BALTIMORE & OHIO", reversing unit, motor held by screw in rear and casting mounting in front; light, liquid smoke unit with bellows. 247T tender with Timken trucks, disc coupler; cab fastened to frame by tab fasteners in rear, screw in front; see 1101 for discussion of body types.                           **15   25   35   50**

**248** 1958, not catalogued, 2-4-2, black plastic boiler, 0-27 motor with metal sides, two-position reverse unit.          **12   18   25   40**

**249** 1958, 2-4-2, black plastic body, bell ledge, no bell, black generator detail between reverse lever and cab, orange-red stripe with white lettering on both locomotive and tender. Tender lettered "PENNSYLVANIA", drive rod on each side, No. 249 0-27 motor with metal sides, brushplate on right side, two-position reverse unit, metal weight underneath cab, no light in locomotive. 250T tender with Timken trucks, disc coupler, see 1101 for discussion of body types. Came with 1130T tender (written on tender box) as part of set No. 1609 Budniak observation.      **15   25   40   60**

**250** 1957, 2-4-2, black plastic body, bell ledge, no bell, generator detail in front of cab, no reverse lever slot, orange stripes on locomotive and tender with white "PENNSYLVANIA" lettering; 0-27 metal side motor, three-position reverse unit, lever down, weight under cab floor, light in front of locomotive, no lens, two gears on left side, brushplate on right side, motor held in by Phillips screw behind second dome and slot in front of motor, cab interior highly detailed. 250T tender with Timken trucks, disc coupler; see 1101 for discussion of body types.              **15   25   40   60**

**251** 1959 (date confirmation requested), 2-4-2, black die-cast boiler, light, two-position reverse with fiber reverse lever, brushes right side, white "251" on cab beneath window. Clark Collection.
(A) Slope-back tender with Timken trucks, fixed couplers.
                                                **12   17   22   35**
(B) 250T-type tender, Timken trucks, fixed couplers.   **12   17   22   35**

**637** 1959-63, 2-6-4, catalogued as Super 0 but shares 2037 metal boiler casting, black with white lettering, smoke, magnetraction.
(A) 2046W tender with whistle, lettered "LIONEL LINES", 1960.
                                                **40   60   85   150**
(B) 2046W tender lettered "PENNSYLVANIA", 1961-63.
                                                **40   60   85   150**

**646** 1954-58, 4-6-4, smoke, three-position reverse unit, shares boiler casting with 2046 and 2056, boiler casting evolved from 726 casting. 2046W tender with whistle, water scoop, bar-end metal (1954-56) or trucks with disc couplers (1957-58), two pickup rollers; with either heat-stamped or large or small rubber-stamped cab numbers. This boiler casting and all other New York Central "Alco" boiler castings (726, 736, 2046 and 2056) can be found with two types of cab windows. One type has a full cross-brace which divides the window into four equal-sized small windows. The other is missing one part of the cross-brace so that there are three windows instead of four. It is often mistakenly believed that the three-window casting has a broken window support brace. Griesbeck and Ervin observations.
(A) 1954, Die-cast trailing trucks, small rubber-stamped number. Foss Collection.                                   **75   125   175   250**
(B) 1954-58, trailing truck with plastic side frames, large rubber-stamped number. Foss Collection.                      **75   125   175   250**
(C) Same as (B), but heat-stamped number. Ervin Collection.
                                                **60   85   120   210**

**665** 1954-59, 4-6-4, pill-type smoke unit, three-position reverse, magnetraction, feedwater heater in front, plastic side frame on trailing trucks, shares Santa Fe Hudson boiler casting with 685, 2055 and 2065, with either rubber-stamped or heat-stamped cab numbers.
(A) 6026W tender with whistle, bar-end metal trucks, magnetic tab couplers.                               **60   110   125   225**
(B) 2046W tender.                            **60   90   125   225**
(C) 1966, 736W tender, "PENNSYLVANIA". Hutchinson Collection.   **NRS**

**670** 1952, 6-8-6, Pennsylvania Steam Turbine shown in advance catalogue but not made.                               **Not manufactured**

**671** 1946-49, 6-8-6 model of Pennsylvania S-2 Steam Turbine.
(A) 1946, double worm-drive, horizontal reverse unit, smoke lamp with bulb with depressed area that used Special #196 tablets, silver rubber-stamped number under cab window, no external E-unit lever, motor labeled "ATOMIC MOTOR", slotted brush holders, jack receptacles, red Keystone on boiler front with gold lettering, shiny nickel rims on drivers, 671W tender with grab-rails front and back, railing on rear deck, white "LIONEL LINES" lettering, Ervin observation.           **50   100   150   250**
(B) Same as (A), but black Keystone with white heat-stamped "6200". Ervin observation and Rothenberg Collection.   **50   100   150   250**
(C) Same as (A), but red Keystone rubber-stamped "6200" in silver. Griesbeck and Taylor Collections. Niedhammer observation. Additional observations requested.                                    **NRS**
(D) 1947, single worm-drive motor, vertical reverse unit with E-unit lever projecting through boiler, new smoke unit with resistance coil and bellows, white rubber-stamped number under cab window, motor stamped "LIONEL PRECISION MOTOR", non-slotted brush tubes, no jack receptacles, piping detail added to boiler immediately behind air pumps, bottom plate reads: "S-2 TURBO LOCOMOTIVE MADE IN THE ..." red Keystone on boiler front, 671W tender with grab-rails front and back, railing on rear deck, "LIONEL LINES" lettering.               **50   100   150   250**
(E) 1948, similar to (C), but thin blackened steel rims on flanged drives (1st and 4th axles), bottom plate on middle rail collector reads "MADE IN THE ...", metal ballast, new streamlined, twelve-wheel 2671W tender lettered "PENNSYLVANIA", tender has water scoop and plastic whistle case with whistle lying on side with opening through the water scoop, tender has back-up lights, light bracket is similar to those found on pre-war 0 Gauge cars, inside the tender is a piece of red-painted plastic for the red light and clear plastic for the two side lights, coil couplers.
                                                **100   175   250   400**
(F) 1948, same as (D), but tender does not have backup lights.
                                                **50   90   140   200**
(G) 1949, same as (F), but no rims on drivers. Ervin Colletion.
                                                **50   90   140   200**

(H) Same as (F), but has 2671W tender with wide-spaced "LIONEL LINES" and backup lights; same tender as 736 produced in 1950-51. Klaassen Collection.
**40    80    130    200**

NOTE: In 1972, the Train Collectors' Association produced a special boiler front designed to fit the 671, 681, 682 and 2020 S-2 turbines. This boiler front was made for the 1972 Pittsburgh convention and had special TCA stickers on the pumps and smoke box front. The casting differs from Lionel's original casting. Reader comments on the specific differences are requested. Although this is only a component, and not made by Lionel, it is closely associated with Lionel production and is located here for reader convenience.

**671R** 1946-49, 6-8-6, electronic control set, Lionel Precision motor with two jacks, decaled with black decal smaller than a dime and white-lettered "ELECTRONIC CONTROL" and "L" in center, boiler front has red Keystone with gold number "6200", smoke unit. Locomotive numbered "671" on cab. 4424W or 4671W tender with Type RU electronic control receiver affixed to frame underside, "LIONEL LINES" heat-stamped in silver, special electronic control decal, light gray with white-lettered "ELEC-TRONIC CONTROL", tender has handrails on rear deck and rear end and handrails on tender front, wire connects locomotive with tender, staple-end metal trucks, coil coupler operated by electronic control receiver; gray decal on tender matches gray button on control unit. The changes in this locomotive correspond to the changes in the regular 671 issue. In 1946-47, the Electronic Control Set included the 671R engine, a 4424W whistle tender, a 4452 gondola, a 4454 boxcar, a 5459 dump car and a 4457 caboose. It also included a special electronic control unit, ECU-1. In 1948, a 4357 SP-type caboose replaced the 4457. The set remained the same in 1949. Lord and Ervin Collections.
(A) Locomotive and tender only.
**70    100    150    225**
(B) Price for set.
**200    300    425    600**

**671RR** 1952, 6-8-6 Pennsylvania Turbine, see 671 for background. This locomotive is mechanically similar to 681 but does not have magnetraction due to a shortage of Alnico magnetic material for axles due to the Korean War. Locomotive may be marked either 671 or 671RR on cab beneath the window. Locomotive has one-piece wheels made from sintered iron. Although the illustration of this locomotive shows it with a 671W tender, the correct tender is a 2046W-50. This tender has 2046W-50 stamped on the frame in silver, though its box is labeled "2046W, PRR, WITH WHISTLE". It has four-wheel bar-end metal tracks, "PENNSYLVANIA" lettering in white, open holes at the tender rear and a marbled yellow plastic whistle housing. The locomotive number is rubber-stamped on the locomotive cab, and there is a hole in the chassis between the first and second pair of drive wheels where the magnets for magnetraction would have been placed. LaVoie Collection.
(A) "671" on cab.
**50    90    140    200**
(B) "671RR" on cab.
**50    100    175    250**

The Lionel 675 has a striking resemblance to the Pennsylvania Railroad's K-4 locomotive. Note that the headlight is located on the top of the boiler, the pumps are located just over and between the second and third drivers and the fire box flares outward in front of the cab. The K-4 illustrated had the number 5353 on its boiler keystone while some of Lionel's models were numbered 5690. The photograph was taken by Robert L. Long and records the last steam passenger engine to operate on the PRR Pemberton to Camden, New Jersey line on November 12, 1957.

**675** 1947, 2-6-2, die-cast boiler, Pennsylvania K-4 prototype, rubber-stamped cab numerals, drive, connecting and eccentric rods, smoke, light; label on cab roof underside reads "to remove the whitish smoke deposit

from locomotive body, apply a little Lionel lubricant or vaseline and polish with a soft clean cloth", Baldwin disc wheels with nickel rims. 2466W or 2466WX tender with rear deck handrail, staple-end metal trucks, coil couplers, lettered "LIONEL LINES", whistle.

A closeup of the rubber-stamped 675 numbering. Note the right window does not have a horizontal divider. Bartelt photograph.

(A) Early 1947, "675" heat-stamped in silver on boiler front Keystone, unpainted aluminum wide-rim stack.
**45    80    100    180**
(B) 1948, "5690" in gold on red decal on boiler front. Kauzlarich Collection.
**45    80    100    150**
(C) 1948, similar to (B), but with new pilot with simulated knuckle coupler and lift pin; smoke stack reduced in size.
**45    80    100    150**
(D) 1949, similar to (C), but with 6466WX tender with magnetic couplers
**45    80    100    150**
(E) Same as (C), but 2666T tender. Dorn comment. Additional observations requested.
**NRS**

675: 1952 version. Bennett photograph.

(F) 1952, 2-6-4, spoked drivers, Korean War issue without magnetraction. four-wheel stamped sheet metal trailing truck, hot stamped "675" on boiler front, 2046W tender with bar-end metal trucks, magnetic couplers, illustrated in Lionel Service Manual and 1952 catalogue. Hutchinson comment. Powell, Arpino and Ervin Collections.
**50    75    125    200**

(G) Same as (F), but has pilot like (C) and came with 6466W tender. Budniak Collection.
**50    75    125    200**

(H) Same as (B), but came with 6466WX tender, coil couplers and staple-end metal trucks. Tender may be misnumbered, since a 6000 number usually meant magnetic couplers. Further observations requested. Budniak Collection.
**NRS**

**681** 1950-51, 1953, 6-8-6, smoke, three-position reverse unit, worm-drive motor, magnetraction, 6200 on decal cab front. 2671W tender stamped "PENNSYLVANIA" in white or silver, six-wheel trucks with blind center wheels, water scoop, three holes in tender rear; 0 Gauge locomotive, rubber or heat-stamped cab numerals.
(A) 1950-51, "681" rubber-stamped on loco and "PENNSYLVANIA" rubber-stamped on 2671 or 2771 WX tender in silver or white letters. Griesbeck and Ervin Collections.
**55    45    170    250**
(B) Late 1951 and 1953, "681" and "PENNSYLVANIA" in heat-stamped white lettering, 2046W-50 tender with four-wheel trucks, Griesbeck and Ervin Collections.
**55    115    170    250**

NOTE: An original 2671W tender shell for the 681, 682, 726 and 736 locomotives can be faked by removing the number from the back nameplate of a Fundimensions tender shell. I.D. Smith observation.

675

681

682

685

726[B]

726RR

Top photo: The 1947 model of the 675 had an aluminum stack, and a slotted head screw attaching the rods on the center driver. Lower photo: The 1948 model of the 675 had its smoke stack cast as part of the boiler. A Phillips-head screw attached the rods to the center driver. Bartelt photographs.

**682** 1954-55, 6-8-6, Pennsylvania S-2 Turbine prototype, similar to 681, but with lubricator linkage and white stripe on running board, 6200 on boiler front Keystone, heat-stamped "682". 2046-W-50 tender with whistle, water scoop, bar-end metal trucks, magnetic couplers, three holes on tender rear filled in, tender lettered "PENNSYLVANIA", 0 Gauge locomotive.

**110   175   225   325**

Left: 685 heat-stamped in white. Right: 685 rubber-stamped in silver. Staebler photograph.

**685** 1953, 4-6-4, shares Santa Fe Hudson-type boiler with 665, 2055 and 2065; comments from those apply; 6026W tender has metal trucks with bar-ends, magnetic couplers, two pickup rollers and whistle, 0 Gauge locomotive.
(A) Early production: 2046W tender, bar-end metal trucks, magnetic couplers. Locomotive has embossed drive rod like 2046; later production lacks this embossing. Raised projections on crosshead guide plate where screws attach. Fleming Collection. **75   135   175   300**
(B) Rubber-stamped 685 in silver below cab windows, 6026W tender with bar-end metal trucks. J. Wilson Collection. **85   145   195   350**
(C) Same as (B), but 685 is heat-stamped in white below cab windows. Eddins Collection. **75   135   175   300**

**686** Uncatalogued, c. 1953-54, 4-6-4. Confirmation and additional information necessary. Hutchinson comment. **NRS**

**703** 1946, 4-6-4, scale Hudson, postwar version of 763, catalogued but not made, prototype exists in MPC archives. Bohn comment.

**Not Manufactured**

**725** 1952, 2-8-4. Berkshire shown in advance catalogue but not made.

**Not Manufactured**

**726(A)** 1946, 2-8-4, Berkshire, die-cast Baldwin disc drivers with pressed-on metal tires, Lionel atomic precision motor with double worm gear, boiler casting is modified prewar 226 boiler, turned handrail stanchions, two-plug receptacles on brushplate to disconnect E-unit or lock E-unit in place. One receptacle locks E-unit in forward, neutral or reverse and other plug activates E-unit so that it sequentially reverses, early smoke bulb unit, nickel-plated drive and connecting rods, valve gear, smoke box door swings open on hinges, flag holders, nickel-plated motor side not covered by cowling as on 726(B); plate that covered the bottom of the motor extends beyond ashpan and beyond beginning of last driver, in contrast to 726(B); the plate may be removed, allowing the drive wheel axle sets to be taken out. This is a revival of the prewar "BILD-A-LOCO" motor design. Ashpan integral part of motor base casting; motor on bottom says "726 O-Gauge Locomotive, Made in U.S. of America, the Lionel Corporation, New York", compare to lettering on 726(B). When bottom plate is removed worm driving and copper wheel busings are visible, metal tires on Baldwin disc wheels, center drivers are blind, pilot truck guide plate is screwed on 726(A), and riveted on 726(B), wheels on trailing truck on 726(A), have hollow area with bridge across 726(B), concentric. Same difference for pilot truck wheels. 2426W tender has metal top cab with six-wheel trucks, plastic side frames, coil coupler with sliding shoe, handrails and longrails on front, longrails and black deck railing with six stanchions; highly desirable tender, worth at least $100; same tender came with 773, 1950 version. Second version of 1946 has different frame and motor; early motor cannot be used on later frame because reinforcement was added to rear of chassis. Early locomotives which retain the original smoke bulb arrangement are considerably more scarce than the converted or later versions. Fleming comment. In addition, the casting of the early 1946 locomotive is open where the eccentric rod attaches to the boiler casing; in later production, this area is closed, Bratspis observation. **150   225   325   500**

**726(B)** 1947-49, generally similar to (A), but revised boiler casting with lengthened sand domes, cotter pin-type handrail stanchions, E-unit mounted vertically with lever penetrating top of boiler; plug receptacles on brushplate are eliminated; simulated coupler lift bar on front pilot, black flag holders, bottom plate reads "Made in U.S.A., the Lionel Corporation, New York, New York", riveted metal retaining plate for pilot truck, cowling added to side of motor to hide motor, simulated springs visible from side of locomotive, ash-pan part of bottom frame but ends at rear set of drivers, resistance coil smoke unit. Large cab metal tender, 2426W; 0 Gauge locomotive. **155   225   275   425**

**726(C)** 1947 only, plain pilot without simulated front coupler, otherwise like (B), has 2426W metal tender, but with cast metal whistle soundbox, locomotive has 671M-1 motor. Griesbeck comment. **150   180   225   300**

**726RR** 1952, 2-8-4, "RR" for Korean War issue without magnetraction, cadmium-plated drive and connecting rods, valve gear, smoke unit, three-position reverse unit. Tender has four-wheel staple-end metal trucks, two pickup rollers, holes in tender rear filled in, whistle; less desirable tender than 2426W; 0 Gauge locomotive.
(A) As above. **95   170   225   300**
(B) Similar to (A), but larger "726" and no "RR" on cab, nickel-plated rods, 2046W tender, holes in rear of shell, bar-end four-wheel trucks with magnetic couplers. Griesbeck and Fleming Collections.

**90   155   200   250**
(C) Same as (A), but six-wheel tender with "LIONEL LINES" in small white serif lettering widely spaced on the tender side. Klaassen Collection. **NRS**

**736(A)** 1950-51, Berkshire, spoked-style drivers without tires, die-cast trailing truck, nickel-plated drive and connecting rods, valve gear, worm-drive motor, three-position reverse unit, magnetraction, smoke, whistle, hinged smoke box door, rubber-stamped cab number; 2671W tender with six-wheel trucks, heat-stamped "PENNSYLVANIA" lettering, plastic truck sideframes, water scoop, coil-operated couplers, holes in rear deck; 0 Gauge locomotive. Griesbeck comment. Also came with 2671WX tender having six-wheel trucks and "LIONEL LINES" markings. Ambrose comment. **125   175   250   400**

**736(B)** 1953-54, similar to (A), but heat-stamped lettering on cab, small bracket wedge on headlight casting, collector assembly attached with two screws, die-cast trailing truck, cadmium-plated rods; 2046W tender with four-wheel trucks, 0 Gauge locomotive. Griesbeck and Ervin comments.

**95   175   225   350**

**736(C)** 1955-56 similar to (B), but collector assembly attached with two screws; sheet metal trailing truck with plastic side frames; 2046W tender

736[A]

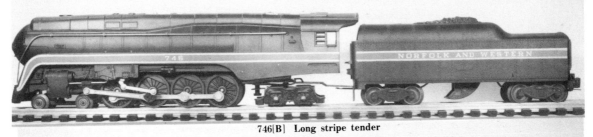

746[B]  Long stripe tender

746[A]  Short stripe tender

773[A] New York Central Hudson [1950]

773[C] New York Central Hudson [1965-66]

1001

with four-wheel trucks, 0 Gauge locomotive. Griesbeck and Ervin comments.                                                          **95  175  225  350**

**736**(D) 1957-60, same as (C), but collector assembly attached with one screw; 2046W tender. Griesbeck comment.          **95  175  225  350**

**736**(E) 1961-66, same as (D), but 736W tender. Griesbeck comment.
                                                                    **95  175  225  350**

**746** 1957-60, 4-8-4, model of Norfolk and Western J, three-position reverse unit, magnetraction, liquid smoke; 746W tender with whistle, bar-end metal trucks, magnetic coupler with tab, two roller pickups; engine and tender have red band outlined in yellow stripes, yellow lettering; "746" rubber-stamped on cab, tender lettered "NORFOLK AND WESTERN", 0 Gauge locomotive. Short stripe tender also lettered "746W".
(A) 1957 only, tender with long, full-length stripe and no 746W raised numbering, Rubin and Weiss observations.          **300  500  700  1000**
(B) 1958-60, tender with short stripe and 746W raised numbering. Friedman observation.                                 **250  400  600  750**

**773**(A) 1950, 4-6-4, scale model of New York Central J-3 Hudson. Postwar version of prewar 763 and its more detailed brother, the 700E. The 773, unlike the 763 and 700E, will run on regular 0 Gauge tubular curve track and offers smoke and magnetraction. Locomotive has plug jacks in cab for connecting three-position reverse unit. Label on underside of cab states: "To remove the whitish smoke...." Catalogued as 0 Gauge locomotive.
(A) Has lighter stamping of "773" on cab compared with (B). Comes with very desirable 2426W tender with six-wheel trucks. 1950 version has slide valve guides.                                                      **475  700  1000  1300**

1950 Steam cylinder with slide valve guide

1964 cylinder without slide valve guide

(B) 1964, similar to 773(A), but with heavier heat-stamped number on cab, slide valve guides omitted from steam chest casting, steam chest not interchangeable with 773(A). "PENNSYLVANIA" tender with Timken trucks, disc coupler, two pickup rollers; "773" is more heavily stamped than on 773(A).                                           **400  525  700  950**
(C) 1965-66, similar to (B), but with tender marked "NEW YORK CENTRAL".                                                   **400  550  750  1050**
(D) Similar to (B), but has 2426W tender with plastic whistle casing, 1964-style 773 stamp, no steam chest valve guides, white marker lights on boiler front and 1950-style roller pickups. Reportedly made for Macy's in 1956. Reader comments invited. Klaassen Collection.      **NRS**

**1001** 1948, 2-4-2, first Scout locomotive, specially designed motor, 1001M-1 with two-position reverse unit integral to motor, motor has plastic sides and smooth bottom, with two pieces of copper rolled to form pickup rollers, awnings over windows. 1001T sheet metal Scout tender, Scout trucks and coupler, galvanized base, 0-27 locomotive. C. Rohlfing comment. The Lionel 1948 catalogue (page four) shows what appears to be the same locomotive (note horn atop boiler front and window sunshades!). The 1001 appears to be the first plastic boiler ever used by Lionel. This was also the first offering of the notoriously unreliable plastic-side Scout motor, which used a highly unusual engineering design for its reverse unit involving movable brush holders. Although Lionel's obvious intent was to reduce costs, this motor proved so difficult to repair that if a customer complained loudly enough, the factory or the service station would replace this motor with the conventional metal-framed motor used in the 2034. The procedure is outlined in the Lionel service manual in section LOC-1110(1951), page 1, June 1953, and section LOC-2034, page 1, August 1953. Although the plastic boiler casting for this locomotive was highly detailed, it did not appear again until 1959, when in obvious financial distress, Lionel brought it back. There is a Marx plastic body which is almost identical to the 1001. Was the usual role of copier and copied reversed in this instance? Reader comments invited. Bartelt comment.                          **6  12  15  25**

**1050** 1959, uncatalogued 0-4-0, plastic side motor, forward only, light, side rod, 1050 slope-back tender; 0-27 locomotive.          **7  10  15  25**

**1060** 1960-61, 2-4-2, same boiler as 1050, no reverse, main rod only, light. This engine was not shown in the consumer catalogue, since it was intended "to meet the needs of the low priced toy train market.... for pricing and delivery information, see your wholesaler or Lionel representative". The engine came with two different tenders with at least three different sets and is illustrated in the 1961 Lionel Advance Catalogue. It has a plastic boiler with highly detailed cab interior and a curved metal piece for center rail pickup. It is classified as an 0-27 locomotive. One of the tenders is an 1130T with arch bar trucks. Rohlfing observation.
(A) 1130T tender, part of No. 1109 Huntsman Steamer set which has a 6404 flat with auto, a 3386 Bronx Zoo giraffe car and a 6047 caboose. All rolling stock has arch bar trucks and non-operating couplers. This set was offered as a Green Stamps premium set in 1960. Fleming comment. Locomotive and tender value:                                            **7  10  15  30**
(B) With 1050 slope-back tender, arch bar trucks and fixed coupler, part of No. 1123 Pacesetter set which included a 6406 flat with auto, a 6042 gondola with canisters and an unlettered, unnumbered caboose. Reader assistance is asked in determining the original wholesale price and the numbers printed on the boxes. Rina comment. Locomotive and tender value:
                                                                    **7  10  15  30**
(C) With 1130T tender, 3409 flat with helicopter, 6076 Lehigh Valley hopper and an unlettered, unnumbered caboose. Reader assistance is asked in determining the original wholesale price and the numbers printed on the boxes. Rina comment. Locomotive and tender value:  **7  10  15  30**

**1061** 1963-64, 0-4-0; also catalogued in 1969 as a 2-4-2, black highly detailed plastic boiler, similar to 1060 and 1062, plastic side motor, rolled metal pickups, drive rod without crosshead, no reverse, no light, slope-back tender with fixed coupler lettered "LIONEL LINES". This locomotive was part of set 11420, which sold for $11.95 in 1963-64 (the 1969 price was not included in the catalogue). This set possesses the dubious distinction of being Lionel's least expensive set since the thirties. On the other hand, the set could be viewed as Lionel's very creative response to a difficult marketing situation. Lionel was buffeted by Marx production on one hand and race cars and space related toys on the other. This set gave Lionel a chance to offer a competitive, inexpensive product. However, Lionel weakened its profit-making mechanism by such production - high quality toys at a premium price. Locomotive and tender value:          **7  10  15  25**

**1062** 1963-64, 0-4-0, highly detailed plastic body, plastic side motor, rolled metal pickups, drive rod without crosshead to reduce costs, two-position reverse with lever on boiler top, rubber tire on one driver, headlight, slope-back tender lettered "LIONEL LINES", 0-27 locomotive. This locomotive is included in the No. 11430 set listed in the 1964 catalogue. Priced at $14.95, the set came with a 6176 hopper, a 6142 gondola, a 6167-125 caboose, a 6149 remote control track, a 1026 25-watt transformer and track. Winton Collection. The locomotive was shown in the 1963 catalogue as an 0-4-0. Rohlfing Collection.

(A) Short headlight, drive rod without crosshead, slope-back tender, Timken trucks, fixed coupler, galvanized tender base, tender cab fastened by two tabs, contacts on tender front truck provides locomotive ground.
                                                                    **7  12  15  25**
(B) Long headlight, no drive rod or crosshead, large unnumbered tender, with Timken trucks, fixed coupler, contacts on tender front truck provide locomotive ground.                                                  **7  12  15  25**

**1101** 1948, 2-4-2, Scout locomotive, die-cast boiler, sliding shoe pickups, drive rod with solid crosshead, three-position reverse unit, interior cab detail, 12 rib wheels, stripped down version of 1655 powered with regular 1655-2 motor; tender with metal bottom, top; Scout trucks and coupler.
                                                                    **7  12  15  25**

The 1101 die-cast body has a small cast bell on a small step on the boiler's left side between the smokestack and its first dome. The 1101 body design was the basis for the later 230, 240 and 250 series locomotives. Some of the later locomotives retained the step even though the bell was no longer present, i.e., 241 and 243.

The 1101 has a straight slot for the E-unit lever since the lever moves in a straight line. When the 1101 design was adopted for the 243, the slot was changed to a curved design to accommodate the movement of the two-position reverse lever.

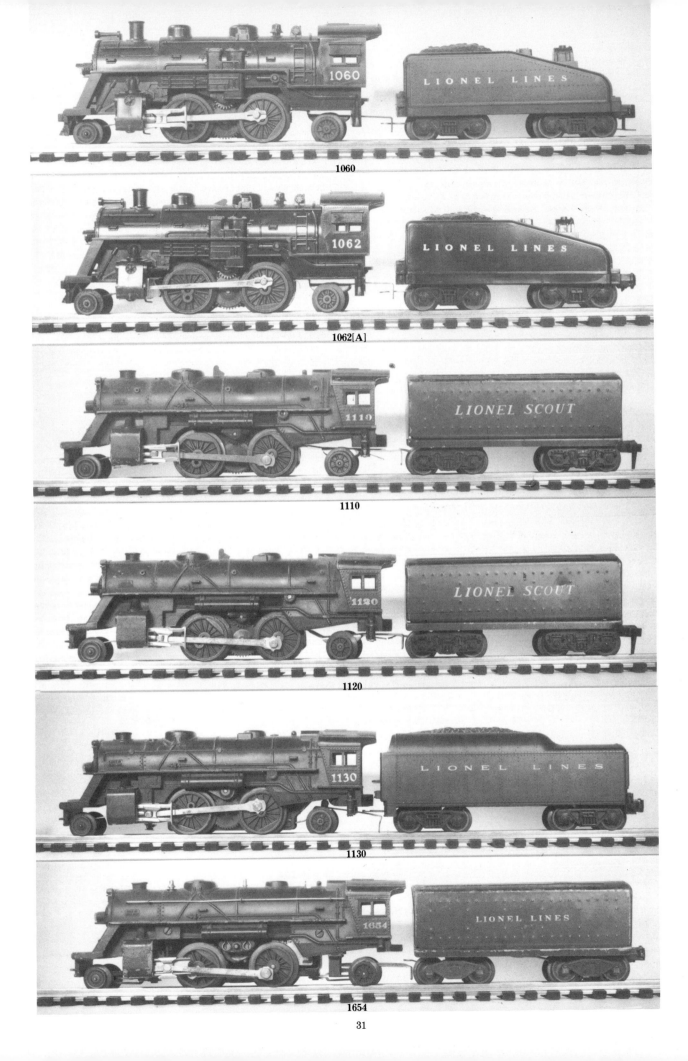

1060

1062[A]

1110

1120

1130

1654

Other factors distinguish the 230, 240 and 250 series locomotives. Some have holes in the cab floor for weights (the 241 and 243), others do not. Some have thick running boards, others have thin ones. On some the reverse slot is between the first and second dome, on others between the second dome and cab.

**1110** 1949-52, 2-4-2, Scout with "LIONEL SCOUT" tender, die-cast boiler and cab similar to the 1101 but not interchangeable with it; Scout motor with plain plastic bottom, rounded copper pieces for pickups; drive rod with crosshead, fiber reverse lever, two-position reverse; tender with metal frame and top, Scout trucks, one Scout coupler. Lord comment.

(A) 1949, no hole on boiler front for smoke draft.    **7   12   15   25**
(B) 1951-52, hole in boiler front for smoke draft but no smoke unit.

                                              **7   12   15   25**

**1120** 1950, 2-4-2, Scout with "LIONEL SCOUT" tender, die-cast boiler, headlight, no lens, fiber reverse lever, two-position reverse, plastic side motor with inaccessible brushes; rolled copper pieces for pickups; tender with metal frame and top, Scout trucks, one Scout coupler.

                                          **7   10   15   25**

**1130** 1953-54, 2-4-2, black plastic body similar to die-cast 2034; 2034-100 motor with three-position reverse unit, short lever points down, headlight lens, main rods with guides, roller pickups which slide in and are held by a clip, large gear seen between drivers on left, brushplate on right. 1130T tender, bar-end metal trucks, operating coupler; 0-27 locomotive. Lord comment. Engine produced in 1953 came with set No. 1500; had 6066T tender with Scout trucks and magnetic couplers. The 1954 version of this engine had an 1130T tender with Scout trucks and magnetic couplers. Rohlfing and Powell comments.

(A) As described above (either version).    **7   12   15   25**
(B) Die-cast body instead of plastic. Niedhammer and Szabat Collections.

                                                     **NRS**

**1615** 1955-57, 0-4-0 Switcher, black die-cast body, B6 on PRR oval builder's plate on boiler right side, red marker lights (sometimes omitted), 0-27 motor with brushplate showing on left side and two gears showing on right, operating disc coupler in front, "L" shaped locomotive drawbar has brass spring to insure good electrical ground with tender, detailed cab interior, small 027 contact rollers, 1615T hollow plastic slope-back tender (too light for good operation when pushing cars), no bell in tender, metal trucks; 0-27 locomotive, locomotive number either rubber or heat-stamped. Niedhammer and Philip Smith comments.

(A) 1955, number rubber-stamped in silver, blackened tender drawbar. Ervin Collection.    **55   100   160   225**

(B) 1955-57, number heat-stamped in white, non-blackened drawbar. Ervin Collection.    **55   100   160   225**

(C) Same as (B), but Timken trucks on tender. Ambrose Collection.    **40   75   125   200**

1625

**1625** 1958, 0-4-0, Switcher, black die-cast body, "B6" on PRR oval builder's plate on right side of smoke box, red marker lights (sometimes omitted), 027 motor with brushplate showing on left side and two gears showing on right, dummy coupler in front, "L" shaped locomotive drawbar has brass spring to insure good electrical ground with tender, detailed cab interior, small 027 contact rollers, cadmium-plated rods, 1625T hollow plastic

slope-back tender, no bell, 027 locomotive. The Lionel Service Manual specifies a dummy front coupler, but an operating coupler is easily installed. The 1958 catalogue drawing shows the spring for the operating coupler. Philip Smith comment.

(A) As described above.    **65   125   200   300**
(B) Same as (A), but tender has Timken plastic trucks. Ambrose Collection.    **65   125   200   300**

**1654** 1946-47, 2-4-2, black die-cast boiler, nickel trim pipe on each boiler side, nickel bell and whistle, three-position reverse unit, metal reverse lever through boiler; sliding shoe motor 1654M-1 with brushplate on left side, motor fastened to boiler in part by long pin that goes through back of boiler casting, large gear between drivers on right side, drive and connecting rods attached to solid crosshead; 0-27 locomotive, operates on 0-27 track but not switches or crossovers, 1654W tender with whistle (or 1654T without whistle), metal base and top staple-end metal trucks, coil coupler.

                                       **8   12   20   35**

**1655** 1948-49, 2-4-2, heavy black die-cast body with fine cab interior detail; light, drive and connecting rods, two sliding shoe pickups, improved 1655M-1 motor using double reduction gears (compare with 1654); brushplate left side, four visible gears, solid crosshead, 12-spoked wheels, nickel bell and whistle, three-position reverse, metal reverse lever through boiler near cab. 6654W metal box tender with whistle, metal trucks.

                                       **8   12   20   35**

1656

**1656** 1948-49, 0-4-0, Switcher, black die-cast body, B6 on right side, red marker lights; light, nickel bell on bracket; 1656M-1 motor identical to 1655-1 except equipped with contact rollers rather than sliding shoes; coil-operated front coupler; two plug/jack connections from locomotive to tender; left plug connects locomotive coupler to tender, rear truck pickup shoe; center plug provides extra ground for locomotive through tender wheels and body. 6403 slope-back tender, staple-end metal trucks, coil coupler. Tender has bell, wire handrails and working backup light. I.D. Smith observation.

(A) "LIONEL LINES" closely spaced on tender.    **125   175   250   350**
(B) "LIONEL LINES" spaced out on tender.    **125   175   250   350**

1665

**1665** 1946, 0-4-0, Switcher, black die-cast body, red marker lights, coil-operated front coupler and wire handrails, 1662M-2 motor shared with prewar 1662 with four gears showing on left side, brushplate on right, three-position reverse unit, two wires from tender plug into locomotive: left wire connects locomotive front coupler coil to tender sliding shoe, other wire provides better ground. 2403B slope-back tender with metal frame, body, bell and metal trucks; backup light on tender, "LIONEL LINES" heat-stamped on tender; staple-end metal trucks, coil coupler, wide-spaced lettering, separate Bakelite coal pile casting and wire handrail (although illustration does not show handrail). I.D. Smith comment.

                                     **125   200   275   400**

A comparison of two different Postwar 1666 locomotives. Note the bell and hanger on the left and the single piece bell on the right locomotive. Also note the hatches on the top of the forward dome of the left locomotive. Riley Collection, Bartelt photograph.

### THE POSTWAR 1666

#### By Warren Blackmar

The 1666E, a 2-6-2 Prairie-type steam locomotive, first appeared in the 1938 catalogure in gray with the 1689T-type sheet metal tender. In 1939, it was painted black and came with the 1689T tender again. In 1940, some versions were equipped with a new Bakelite tender with coal pile. This combination continued with minor casting changes until World War II interrupted production of Lionel trains.

The 1666 was one of four prewar locomotives, two of which carried their old numbers, that reappeared as train production resumed. It is reasonable to assume that some engines were assembled with available parts and sold after the war which are identical to the late prewar models with the exception of the tender trucks. The new die-cast trucks with knuckle couplers were used with the earliest units equipped with trucks having the "floating shoe" pickup.

Lionel did not catalogue the 1666 in 1945. It is possible that 1666's were manufactured and sold in 1945, but we have no data to support this supposition. However, Lionel did catalogue and sell the 1666 in 1946. The 1666 was not catalogued in 1947.

The first postwar 1666s differed from the prewar 1666s in several ways. The cab floor end was rounded rather than square as on the prewar version. The postwar 1666 came with a 2466WX tender with staple-end trucks with late coil couplers while the prewar models had tenders with box couplers. The early postwar 1666 was similar to the prewar model in a number of ways. It had number plates with "1666" in silver on a black background. The bell mechanism consisted of two parts: a cast bell with horizontal shaft mounted on stamped-steel bracket which in turn was fastened by a screw to the boiler. The pilot and steamchest were mounted by screws, which fitted in drilled and tapped holes in the boiler casting, the front truck was cast, the center drive wheel on each side had slots to receive the nibs of the cast eccentric crank, the eccentric crank was attached by a slot-headed screw, the rear truck mounting plate holes were drilled and tapped in the casting and the headlight socket had a screw base.

However, later 1666s also probably manufactured in 1946, had noticeable changes. The two-part bell was replaced by a

single-piece casting riveted to the boiler. The number "1666" was rubber-stamped in silver on the cab beneath the windows. The steamchest pilot casting was peened to studs in the boiler casting. The front truck was stamped-steel, the center drive wheel on each side had cast in studs on which to attach the steel eccentric crank, the eccentric crank was attached by a hex-head screw. The boiler casting had undrilled depressions at both front and back that had been drilled and tapped on earlier engines.

Both of these 1666's have the rounded cab floor, but top photo is rubber-stamped, and the bottom photo has metal number plates. Bartelt photographs.

**1666** 1946, 2-6-2, black die-cast locomotive, green marker lights, came with two different kinds of bells, three-position reverse unit mounted between the smokestack and the first dome, limited cab interior detail consists of two firebox doors, rounded rear cab floor, and either stamped-steel or die-cast pilot and trailing trucks. Came with several different tenders: 2466W, 2466T and 2466WX with staple-end metal trucks with early coil coupler. The 1666 was also manufactured prior to World War II and differs most noticeably from the postwar versions in that it has a square rear cab floor, a long shank hook and a tender with box couplers.

(A) Number plates with "1666" in silver on a black background. The bell mechanism consisted of two parts: a cast bell with horizontal shaft mounted on stamped-steel bracket which in turn was fastened by a screw to the boiler. The pilot and steamchest were mounted by screws, which fitted in drilled and tapped holes in the boiler casting, the front truck was cast, the center drive wheel on each side had slots to receive the nibs of the cast eccentric crank, the eccentric crank was attached by a slot headed screw, the rear truck mounting plate holes were drilled and tapped in the casting and the headlight socket had a screw base. The 2466WX tender had late coil couplers. Rohlfing Collection.      **25   40   60   75**

(B) The number "1666" was rubber-stamped in silver on the cab beneath the windows. The bell was a single-piece casting riveted to the boiler. The steamchest pilot casting was peened to studs in the boiler casting. The front truck was stamped-steel, the center drive wheel on each side had cast in studs on which to attach the steel eccentric crank, the eccentric crank was attached by a hex-head screw. The boiler casting had undrilled depressions at both

Closup of number plate on prewar 1666. Number plates are also found on postwar 1666 locomotive. The prewar locomotive cab floor did not extend beyond the cab side walls. Bartelt photograph.

front and back that had been drilled and tapped on earlier engines. Blackmar Collection.                    25    40    60    75

We also have reports of 1666s with an X about 3/8" high stamped on the left fire box door and models without the X. We do not have other details about these models and hope that our readers will assist us. We also have illlustrated a 1666 with 6654W metal box tender. We do not know if the combination was factory produced.

A comparison of the pilot trucks of an early postwar 1666 above and later 1666 below. The left truck is die-case while the right truck is stamped-steel. Bartelt photographs.

**1862** 1959-62, 4-4-0, modeled after Civil War "General", gray boiler, red cab, green 1862T tender, 0-27 Gauge, without magnetraction, two-position reverse, light; lacks some boiler banding and applied piping details found on 1872, does not have smoke or whistle, price for locomotive and tender only. The 1959 production of this locomotive had a red headlight. In 1959-60, the screw on the cab rear was small and protruded beyond the cab. In 1960, this became a larger screw which was recessed. Vagner comment.
(A) Gray stack.                    75   125   175   275
(B) Black stack.                   75   125   175   275

**1872** 1959-62, 4-4-0, modeled after Civil War "General", gray chassis and boiler, red cab and pilot, black, red and green 1872T tender with gold lettering; 0 Gauge, magnetraction, smoke unit, three-position reverse, came with coach 1875W with whistle in set. The 1960 production of this locomotive had a black headlight. Vagner comment. Price for locomotive and tender only.                    100   150   250   400

1882

**1882** 1959-62, 4-4-0, modeled after Civil War "General", uncatalogued by Lionel, sold by Sears, black boiler and smokestack, orange pilot and cab with gold lettering, does not have smoke unit or whistle. This engine was part of the Sears General set, which included the 1882, the 1866 mail car, a blue 1885 passenger car and the 1877 horse flatcar, circa 1960. The set also included an Allstate transformer which may have been made by Marx. Feldman Collection. Price for locomotive and tender only.
(A) Black stack. Weiss Collection.            150   225   425   650
(B) Gray stack. Hutchinson Collection. Further observation requested.
                                                         NRS

**2016** 1955-56, 2-6-4, light, does not have smoke or magnetraction, similar to 2037 with box on pilot, three-position reverse unit, "LIONEL 0-27" plate on bottom, cadmium-plated drive rod and connecting rod; 6026W tender, lettered "LIONEL LINES", bar-end metal trucks, magnetic coupler with tab, 0-27 locomotive.            20    35    60    90

**2018** 1956-59, 2-6-4, box on front pilot, cadmium-plated drive and connecting rods, smoke, three-position reverse unit. 6026W tender and whistle, bar-end metal trucks, magnetic coupler, "LIONEL LINES" on tender side; 0-27 locomotive. Came in sets with 1130T tender. Budniak observation.
(A) Black.                              25    40    65    100
(B) Blue, from Boy's Set, two known to exist.              NRS

**2020** 1946-47, 6-8-6, model of Pennsylvania S-2 Steam Turbine. See discussion under 671. Catalogued as 0-27 but identical to 671 which was catalogued as 0 Gauge.
(A) 1946, double worm-drive, horizontal reverse unit without external E-unit lever. Since lever does not penetrate boiler, locomotive cab interior includes two jacks on the brushplate holder. Plugs are inserted to disconnect the E-unit or lock the E-unit in one position. Motor labeled "ATOMIC MOTOR", slotted brush holders, shiny nickel drive rims. Locomotive has smoke bulb, part #671-62, with bulb marked GE797, 15 watts, 12 volts. The bulb has an indentation to hold "early" smoke tablets. The bulb did not produce sufficient smoke and bulb was replaced by the resistance coil (see B). However, Lionel furnished a kit to its service stations to convert the bulb unit to resistance unit coils. Consequently, 2020(A)s will be found with resistance coil units. 2020W tender lettered "LIONEL LINES", staple-end metal trucks, coil couplers. Tender has trim on rear deck and rails on both rear and front ends. Tender stamped 2020W on bottom, Shewmake Collection and Rohlfing comments.            50    80   120   175
(B) 1946, Same as (A), but 2406WX tender. Walsh Collection.
                                         50    80   120   175
(C) 1947, single worm-drive motor, vertical reverse unit with E-unit lever projecting through boiler, new resistance coil-type smoke unit with bellows, no plug jacks on motor brushplate, non-slotted brush tubes. 2020W tender with magnetic coupler, and plastic whistle box. Griesbeck Collection.
                                         50    80   120   180
(D) 1948, Same as (C), but flanged drivers have darkened rims, 6020W tender. Ervin Collection.        50    80   120   180
(E) 1949, Same as (D), but no rims on drivers. Ervin Collection.
                                         50    80   120   180
(F) Same as (A) early unit, but has red Bakelite motor brushplate. Possible saleman's sample. Se also 726 entries for Factory Errors and Prototypes. Bratispis Collection.                        NRS

**2025** 1947, 2-6-2, same as 675 (except number) but catalogued as 027, 5690 on boiler front of (C) and (D). 2466WX tender with whistle, metal trucks, coil-operated coupler, railing on tender rear deck.
(A) Early production: "2025" heat-stamped in silver on black Keystone, unpainted large aluminum smokestack. Numbers on Keystones had a tendency to wear off easily; however, number indentations remain. Solid black Keystones once had decal. Comments here also apply to production of 675, 671 and 2020 locomotives. LaVoie Collection.        30    50    80   110
(B) Same as (A), but cab number heat-stamped, number on Keystone rubber-stamped. Gallahan Collection.          30    50    80   110
(C) 1948-49, same as 2025(A), but pilot with simulated knuckle and lift pin. 6466WX tender with magnetic coupler, 5690 in gold on red and gold Keystone on boiler front.                    30    50    80   110
(D) 1952, 2-6-4, black steel frame, sintered-iron wheels, smoke, light, no magnetraction, 6466W tender with whistle.          30    50    80   110

2037-500[B] Girl's Set loco with square type tender

(E) 1948, same as (B), but 2466WX tender stamped "6466WX", wire-wound coupler, staple-end trucks. Hutchinson Collection.

| | 20 | 35 | 50 | 80 |

(F) Same as (A), but 2466WX tender and "2025" on Keystone decal instead of "5690." The same number change occurred with 675; these examples are extremely scarce. Ervin Collection.  **NRS**

**2026** 1948-49, 1951-53, 2-6-2, based on 1666, feedwater heater, box added to pilot, sand dome enlarged, smoke, light, sliding shoe pickups, drive rod, connecting rod, eccentric; die-cast trailing truck, steel-rimmed drivers. In 1948, the pickup wire was mounted erroneously on the front truck. In 1949, the error was corrected. Ervin observation.

(A) 1948-49, 6466WX tender with whistle.    **30  40  50  70**

(B) 1951-53, 6466W or 6466T tender, rimless drivers, 2-6-4, no eccentric rod, roller pickups, stamped sheet metal trailing truck. I.D. Smith observation.    **30  40  50  70**

(C) 1952, spoked sintered-metal wheels, no tires, no magnetraction because of Korean War Alnico magnetic metal shortage, 2-6-4 with four-wheel stamped sheet metal trailing truck, 2046-type tender, shown as a 2-6-2 in 1952 catalogue, also shown in the Lionel Service Manual, Hutchinson and Bartelt observations.    **30  40  50  70**

**2029** (A) 1964-69, 2-6-4, light, smoke, rubber tires, main rod, side rod, 243W tender with whistle, available in 1967 although no catalogue was issued, O-27 locomotive.    **13  25  40  60**

(B) 1968, 2-6-4, plate on bottom reads "THE LIONEL TOY CORPORA-TION, Hagerstown, Maryland 21740;" the trailing truck has "Japan" embossed on it; drive rod, connecting rods, brushplate on left side, blue insulating material covers E-unit and motor field coil; gears on right side, motor has both brass and dark colored gears; motor attached by bar through back of firebox area and held in by grooves on front end; bracket holding the front truck is shiny metal, smoke unit bottom is also shiny metal; three-position reverse unit, smoke. 234W Santa Fe-type tender with Timken trucks and center rail pickup on both trucks, fixed coupler, whistle, "LIONEL LINES" heat-stamped in white as is 234W; from the Hagerstown set which consisted of 25000 hopper, 6014 box, 6315 tank, 6560 crane and 6130 work caboose; price for locomotive and tender only.

| | 15 | 25 | 40 | 60 |

**2029W** Locomotive with 1130T uncatalogued tender, "Southern Pacific", Hutchinson comment, LCCA magazine, Volume 5, #2. More information necessary.    **NRS**

**2034** 1952, 2-4-2, die-cast body, 2034-100 motor with three-position reverse unit, light, very similar to 1130 which has plastic body and Scout plastic side motor, O-27 locomotive.    **10  15  20  30**

**2035** (A) 1950, 2-6-4, based on 2025 but with magnetraction, drive rod, connecting rod, eccentric rod with new crank using half-moon fitting into wheel recess, trailing truck stamped-steel, sintered-iron drivers. 6466W tender with whistle but without handrails, 0-27    **20  30  45  75**

(B) 1951, same as (A), but crank fastened by two projecting pins, motor has armature plates (not on 2035(A)), and has pickup rollers with fixed axles.    **20  30  45  75**

(C) 1950, 2-6-2, uncatalogued, illustrated in November, 1950 **Model Railroader**, apparently 675-212 trailing truck. Reported by Lower, Rapp and Jodon. We need additional confirmation of pieces that are known to be original with this truck arrangement.    **NRS**

**2036** 1950, 2-6-4, similar to 2026(A) but with magnetraction, rimless drive wheels, no smoke, sheet metal trailing truck, no handrails or eccentric rod. 6466W tender without handrails, 0-27 locomotive.    **18  35  45  75**

**2037** 1954-55, 1957-58, 2-6-4, derived from 2026 and 2036, light, smoke, magnetraction, "2037" heat-stamped in white.

(A) 1957, 6026W tender.    **25  35  50  100**

(B) 1954-55, 1958-60, 6026 tender.    **25  35  50  100**

**2037-500** 1957, 2-6-4, pink body for "Girl's Set" with blue 2037 numbers beneath the cab window (2037-500 does not appear on cab), smoke, headlight lens, green marker lights, battery box on front pilot, nickeled simulated bell, three-position reverse unit, magnetraction, drive rod and connecting rod only, brushplate on left side, gears on right side. Set includes hopper, gondola, two boxcars, caboose and 1130T tender. Reproduction locomotives have been made which are difficult to distinguish from originals, Bohn comment. Set:    **600  800  1200  1800**

(A) 2230T streamline tender.    **200  300  400  500**

(B) 6026 square-type tender, may be one of a kind. Degano Collection.    **NRS**

See also Factory Errors.

**2046** 1950-51, 1953, 4-6-4, die-cast New York Central-type boiler, gears on left side, brushes on right, drive rods, connecting rods, valve gear, three-position reverse unit, magnetraction, shares casting with 646 and 2056, evolved from 726; 2046W tender with whistle, bar-end metal trucks, two pickups, magnetic coupler, with or without "2046W" lettering; 0-27.

(A) 1950, metal trailing truck, number rubber-stamped in silver. Ervin and Ocilka Collections.    **65  100  140  225**

(B) 1951, same as (A), but number is heat-stamped in white. Ervin and Ocilka Collections.    **65  100  140  225**

(C) 1953, same as (B), but plastic trailing truck. Ervin and Ocilka Collections.    **50  70  90  150**

**2055** 1953-55, 4-6-4, die-cast Santa Fe-type boiler, magnetraction, drive rod, connecting rod, valve gear, smoke unit, light, boiler front pops out, shares boiler casting with 665, 685 and 2065, 0-27.

(A) 1953, number rubber-stamped, 6026W square tender, bar-end metal trucks, magnetic coupler, whistle, "LIONEL LINES". Ervin Collection.    **65  100  140  225**

(B) 1953-57, heat-stamped    **65  100  140  225**

**2056** 1952, 4-6-4, die-cast NYC-type boiler, smoke, three-position reverse, gears on left, brushplate on right, reversing lever slot directly in front of cab; 2046W tender has water scoop, whistle, metal trucks with bar-end, magnetic coupler, tender lettered "LIONEL LINES" in larger type than that found on tender that came with 2046, catalogued as 0-27, Korean War issue of 2046 minus magnetraction. Ervin Collection.    **90  150  200  300**

**2065** 1954-57, 4-6-4, die-cast Santa Fe-type boiler with feedwater heater above boiler front, smoke, magnetraction, drive rod, connecting rod, valve gear, boiler casting on left is relatively plain. Trailer truck casting with plastic sides same as both 2065 and 2055, casting detail also shared with 665 and 685; 665 has a feedwater heater while 685 does not.

(A) 1954, rubber-stamped number on boiler, 2046W tender with whistle. Ervin Collection.    **45  70  90  140**

(B) 1955-57, heat-stamped number on boiler, 6026W tender. Ervin Collection.    **60  100  140  200**

**2671** 1968, TCA Convention tender shell only, 2046-type shell with large "TCA" in white, TCA circular logo in white, "NATIONAL CONVENTION 1968 CLEVELAND, OHIO" in white, two lines over and underscored. Versions with gold and silver lettering also exist. Quantities produced: 1,146 white, 43 gold and 11 silver-lettered, Bratspis observation. Although this chapter is devoted to locomotives with tenders, we have listed this

1655

1666

2016

2018[A]

2020

2025[A]

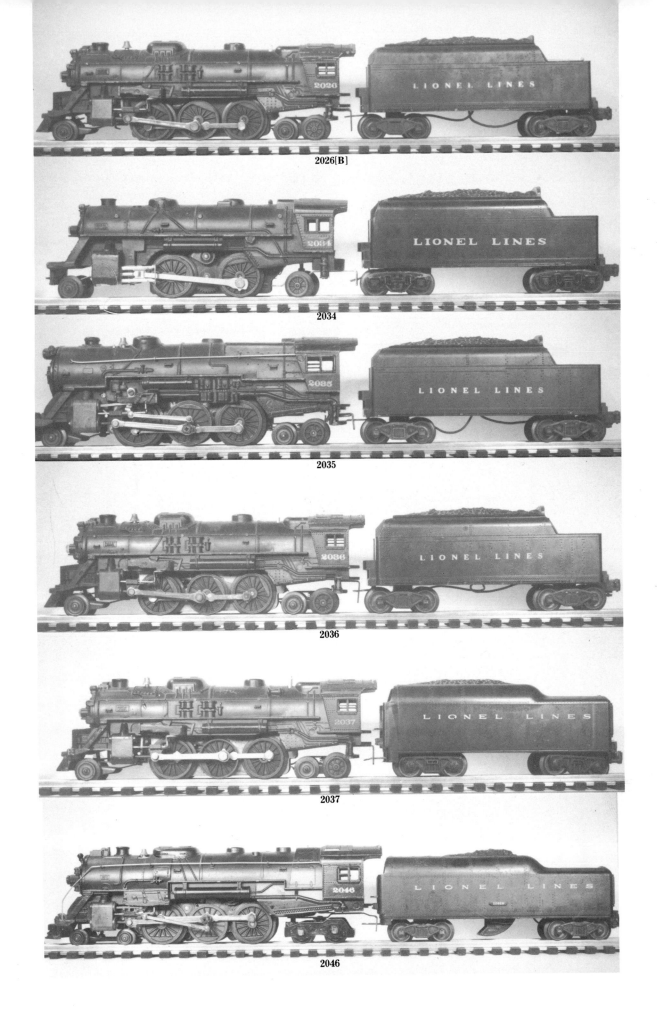

2026[B]

2034

2035

2036

2037

2046

2055[A]

2056

2065

4671   Electronic control loco

6110

Two versions of the 2037-500 Girl's locomotive. Left has plain heat stamped lettering; right has bold fancy rubber stamped lettering. Griesbeck Collection.

tender in this chapter since it is more easily located by our readers. Priced for white lettering. — — — **75**

**4681** 1950, 6-8-6 electronic control locomotive and tender with set. Although catalogued, this locomotive was apparently never made for production purposes. This conclusion is based upon the absence of comments by readers about the omission over the last six years. However, one prototype set is known to exist with this engine. Ervin and Lord observations. **Not Manufactured**

**6110** 1950-51, 2-4-2, black die-cast boiler, drive rod with crosshead, fiber reverse lever, two-position reverse, no light, magnetraction, 6001T tender, 0-27 locomotive. This Scout locomotive, similar to 1001, 1110 and 1120, does not use a conventional E-unit for reversing. Lionel created a very imaginative—and trouble-prone motor design which made the reversing mechanism part of the motor itself and reduced costs. This motor has a two-part field. One part is pivoted to permit it to move when attracted by the energized winding on the stationary section of the field. As the movable field pivots downward, it moves a pawl engaging the geared drums of the brush holders, causing them to rotate. The rotation changes the connections to the armature windings with respect to the field windings, and thus reverses the motor direction. The movable field and pawl stay in the low position, locking the brush holder drums as long as the field winding is energized. When the current is interrupted, the pawl spring returns the movable field and pawl to their up positions. The Scout motor includes a fiber lever which protrudes through the boiler and locks the locomotive in either forward or reverse, as no neutral position is possible with this design. This locomotive has a smoke generator, but not the usual piston and cylinder arrangement found on more expensive locomotives. Rather, smoke is driven up the stack by air which enters through a hole on the boiler front. Consequently, forward motion is necessary for smoke! Its magnetraction, like that of early magnetraction diesels, uses a permanent magnet fixed transversely between the rear wheels, rather than having magnetic axles carry the magnetic flux through the wheels. The magnetic circuit is completed through the sintered-iron rear drivers. The tender came in a box marked 6001T and has "LIONEL LINES" in white lettering. The tender has no lettering on its bottom and Scout trucks. Although the tender shell omits the hole to the lower right of "D" in the diagram has one 1/4" hole, one 1/8" hole and a large rectangular opening. This engine came in set 1461S, which contained a 6002 black gondola, a 6004 boxcar in a box marked 6004 and 6007 Die #3 caboose. The set sold for $19.95. These observations are compiled from the comments of Lord, Kotil and I.D. Smith.

    **7   12   15   25**

# MOLD IDENTIFICATION OF SQUARE PLASTIC TENDERS
### by Joseph F. Kotil
### Frame Identification for Postwar Tenders

There are four versions of the 1666T-4

All molds are identified by the number 1666T-4 on the inside top of the tender.

Unlettered holes are common to all tenders

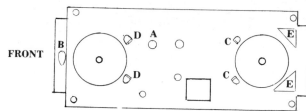

**FRONT**

---

**Type I** Four small holes at the front for handrails; the holes may or may not go through to the inside; all prewar and early postwar tenders are Type I. Whistle tenders have rounded corners, elongated holes punched in the front and a coal pile.

**Type II** Four small holes not present. The tender has a rectangular hole at the front and a hole molded in the coal pile. The coal backup web is about one-sixteenth of an inch thick.

**Type III** Same as Type II, but the coal backup web is thicker, about one-eighth of an inch thick. It was probably thickened to prevent it from breaking.

**Type IV** Same as Type II, but one large lump of coal covers the whistle hole; this is a crude mold modification for late non-whistle tenders.

**Type V** Same as Type IV, but the tender has a typical coal pile over the whistle opening.

**Type VI** Same as Type I, but the die for the four small holes was ground off and was used to manufacture a non-whistle tender for low-priced locomotives; it has no opening in the front.

| | | OPTIONAL PUNCHINGS |
|---|---|---|
| **Type I** | | |
| 2466W Early | | |
| | Oval Hole B | Punchings E |
| | Tabs D | |
| **Type II** | | |
| 2466W Late | 671W | Tabs D | Punchings E |
| 2466WX | 2020W | Hole A | |
| **Type III** | | |
| 2466T | 6066T | None | |
| 6466T | | | |
| **Type IV** | | |
| 6466WX Early | 6020W Early | Tabs D | Punchings E |
| | | Hole A | |
| **Type V** | | |
| 6466WX Late | | Tabs D | Punchings E |
| **Type VI** | | |
| 6020W Late | | Tabs D | Hole A |
| 6466W | | Tabs C | Punchings E |

---

| | 2466W TYPES* 1 2 3 4 5 6 | 2466W/671W/2020W TYPES 1 2 | 6466WX TYPES 1 2 | 6020W TYPES 1 2 | 6466W TYPES 1 2 3 | 6066T TYPES 1 2 3 4 |
|---|---|---|---|---|---|---|
| **Mold Number** | | | | | | |
| I Closed | X | | | | | |
| I Punched | X X X X X X | X X | | | | X |
| II Punched | | X | X X | X | X X X | X X |
| III Punched | | | | | X X X | X X |
| IV Punched | X | | | X | | X |
| V Punched | | | | | | X |
| VI Punched | | X | | X X | | |
| **Plastic Color** | | | | | | |
| Black | X | X X X X X | X | X X | X X X | X X |
| Pastel | X | | | | | |
| Clear | | | | X | | |
| **Body Paint** | | | | | | |
| Flat Black | X | X X X X X X | X | X X | X X X | X X X X X |
| Unpainted | X | | | | | |
| **Lettering** | | | | | | |
| Silver, small | X X | X | X | X X | X | X X X |
| White, small | X | X X | X | X X | X X X | X X X |
| White, large | X | | | X X | | |
| **Railings** | | | | | | |
| Dull top rail | X | | | | | |
| Nickel top rail | X X X X X | X X | X X | X X | X X X | X X |
| (4) vertical nickel | X | | | | | X X X |
| **Frames** | | | | | | |
| I | X | | | | | X |
| II | X X X X X X | X X | | X | | X X X |
| III | | | X | | | X X X |
| IV | X | | X | | | |
| V | | | | | | |
| VI | | | | | | |
| **Frame Finish** | | | | | | |
| Black paint | X | X X X X X X | X X | X X | X X X | X X X |
| Oxide | X X X X X X | X X | X X | X X | X X X X | X X X |
| **Trucks** | | | | | | |
| Staple-end, dish | X | | | | X | |
| Staple-end, normal wheel, thick axle | X X | X X | X X | X | X | X |
| Staple-end, normal wheel, thin axle | X X | X X X | X X | X X | X X | X X |
| Bar-end | | | | | | X X |
| Scout frame, magnetic coupler | | B | | | | |
| **Coupler** | | | | | | |
| Early coil | X | X X X X | | | | |
| Late coil | X X | | X X | X X | X X | X X |
| Magnetic | X X X X X X | X X | X X | X X | X X X | X X X |
| Metal whistle | | | | | X X | X X X |
| Plastic "housing" | | | | | X X | X X X |

40

**THE FIVE STAR GENERAL MEETS ITS HALLOWEEN BROTHER**
1872 Five Star General with three passenger cars
1882 Sears Special General with two passenger cars
This brightly colored set is sometimes called the "Halloween Special."
Shempp Collection

# Chapter II
# DIESEL AND ELECTRIC ENGINES
# AND MOTORIZED UNITS

First, last and always, Joshua Lionel Cowen was a steam engine man. To be sure, he thought that electrics like the big GG-1 "sort of slide along, like a big, pretty snake", but he had an instinctive dislike for any locomotive which didn't feature the spinning, flashing rods of his beloved "iron horses". Shortly after World War II, however, Cowen realized that he had to modernize his line, just as the real railroads were doing. And so began the long and prestigious run of Lionel's diesels, electrics and charming, little self-propelled auxiliary units.

### DIESELS

One factor which convinced Joshua Lionel Cowen to modernize his line was cost-sharing for the expensive dies used to make the first of the great diesels, the F-3. The Santa Fe and New York Central Railroads, as well as General Motors, the makers of the F-3, knew that Lionel's locomotives were billboards in miniature which would pay off in advertising for them. Therefore, they agreed to underwrite part of the cost for the F-3 dies.

When the F-3 emerged in 1948, it wasn't prominently displayed in the catalogue, but sales figures soon had Cowen wondering why he hadn't produced the locomotive earlier. A big, twin-motored double-A unit, the F-3 broke all sales records. It couldn't be produced fast enough to meet the demand! The Santa Fe version of this locomotive became Lionel's all-time top seller, lasting for 18 years through four different numbers. Many other road names joined the originals in time, and B units were soon produced. When the locomotive was equipped with magnetraction in 1950, there wasn't a load the twin-motored giant couldn't haul.

Other diesels were, of course, produced soon after the F-3 emerged from Lionel's miniature erecting shops. In 1949, a fine model of the NW-2 switcher was produced. Before this locomotive was cheapened in 1955, it had a die-cast frame and, in the minds of many operators, the finest electric motor ever made by Lionel. (The editor's 30 year old 2023 Union Pacific Alco with this motor pulled 42 Fundimensions freight cars all by itself at a recent Greenberg train show!) In 1950, a shortened model of the Alco FA was made to give 027 railroaders their own powerful diesel. This locomotive also featured the excellent switcher motor and a die-cast base before it was cheapened.

In 1955, production of the GP-7 and GP-9 "road switchers" began to replace the "premium" Alcos and switchers. These were good models of the popular all-purpose locomotive made by General Motors, even if Lionel's designation was not totally accurate. Lionel simply turned a GP-7 into a GP-9 by adding a plastic fan shroud to the roofs of the GP-7. In the real world, GP-7 locomotives came both ways.

In 1954, Lionel produced an awesome model of the boxy Fairbanks-Morse Trainmaster diesel. These magnificent locomotives are all highly-prized and sought by collectors and operators - with reason. All these locomotives had two motors and were fearsome pullers. In addition, they were built to scale, which meant that they were the longest single locomotives Lionel ever produced.

The only diesel which was not very close to accuracy was the strange 44 ton switcher series made only for a few years, beginning in 1956. Lionel apparently wanted an inexpensive switcher engine for its low-end market which would still be of a bit better quality than its least expensive switchers and Alcos. The attempt was not very successful because the 44-ton engine

0000 Alaska GP-9 prototype. Elliott Smith Collection.

was rather unattractive and far too large to represent its prototype.

The Lionel diesels represent good opportunities for collectors at both ends of the financial scale. All of the Fairbanks-Morse locomotives and the better F-3 AA pairs command very high prices, even for the more common versions. The better NW-2 switchers and Alcos also are somewhat costly, as well as the GP-7 and GP-9 locomotives. However, the collector operating on a budget can accumulate a fascinating collection of less expensive Alcos and NW-2 switchers at bargain prices, since these were made in huge numbers.

### ELECTRICS

The Lionel Corporation has always been justly famous for its models of electric engines. In prewar years, its models of the Olympian bi-polar electric in Standard Gauge were seldom matched by competitors. It was, therefore, fitting that Lionel should begin its postwar production of electrics with a real thoroughbred - the Pennsylvania Railroad's magnificent GG-1. The handsome prototype, styled by Raymond Loewy, had a service life of half a century and was an excellent subject for a Lionel model. The first GG-1, the single-motored 2332, was produced in 1947. Later models of this locomotive added magnetraction and a second motor, and they were selected to pull some of Lionel's best passenger consists, such as the Congressional Limited. Although Lionel's model was too short to be a true scale model, it was an excellent "runner", and many operators still use it as their Number One engine today.

The GG-1 was not the only electric produced; others soon followed. In 1956, Lionel produced a fine model of the General Electric EP-5 rectifier, which the firm erroneously called a "Little Joe". (The real "Little Joe" was originally built for export to the Soviet Union; hence the nickname for Joseph Stalin. It never got to Russia, but it did serve for many years on the South Shore Line near Chicago.) Engineers on the New Haven gave the prototype the nickname "Jet" because of its quick acceleration with commuter trains. The Lionel model had four-wheel trucks instead of the prototype's six-wheel units, but otherwise it was a good model with Lionel's best features. It was made in New Haven, Pennsylvania, Milwaukee and Great Northern markings.

Another electric "brute" was produced in 1958, but it did not meet with public success, so it was only made in Virginian markings. This was the homely but powerful General Electric EL-C Rectifier. The prototype was built to haul heavy coal trains over mountain territory - certainly not for beauty! Lionel's model was faithful to its prototype, but in a small model the result was a rather boxy, ungainly locomotive despite its attractive blue and yellow markings. This is now an engine prized by collectors.

One other electric deserves mention - the odd 520 Box Cab electric, made in 1956. This was a model of a General Electric 80 ton box cab which was made without any of Lionel's premium features for the low end of the market. It was not very successful, but can be regarded as a "sleeper" by collectors, since it is not too common and there is no real interest in it.

Except for the 520 Box Cab locomotive, all the electrics are sought by collectors, with the GG-1 getting the most attention and the best prices. The common New Haven EP-5 can be a good buy for the collector who is in the right place at the right time.

## MOTORIZED UNITS

Real railroads featured much more than main line locomotives and rolling stock, and so should Lionel Land, in the eyes of its administrators. In the postwar years, Lionel produced a dazzling array of self-propelled auxiliary equipment, featuring clever engineering and great charm. These were first produced in 1955, when the 41 U.S. Army Switcher, the 50 Gang Car and the 60 Trolley initiated a long and highly successful line of these little wonders. The Army Switcher had a normal three-position reversing switch, but the others changed direction when their bumpers struck an object. A little man sitting atop the Gang Car changed his seating position when the locomotive reversed, and the trolley reversed its pole. Many variations of these units soon followed, among them two snow plows (both plow and rotary types), a stylish station wagon called an "Executive Inspection Car", a "Fire Fighting Car" and a "Ballast Tamper".

Perhaps the most cleverly engineered and certainly the most complicated of these units was the 3360 Burro Crane of 1956-1957. This crane could propel itself and a few cars, just like any locomotive. However, through an ingenious slip clutch, it could also swivel its cab, lower its hook and lift loads.

The Gang Car is very common, easily affordable and a great deal of fun to operate. Beyond that, however, the motorized units are prized by collectors and bring high prices, especially the Mining Switcher and the AEC Switcher, which are true rarities. Other common units are the 41 and 51 Army and Navy Switchers. These units added considerable color and action to the Lionel line, and they are only rivaled by the better accessories for operating fun.

## LIONEL'S GM-EMD SWITCHERS: SW-1 OR NW-2?
### By William Meyer

The Electromotive Division of General Motors produced 1,144 NW-2 switchers beginning in 1939. These 12-cylinder, 1,000 horsepower switchers are probably the most commonly spotted locomotives in any freight yard. The "W" in the model designation means that the locomotives' frames were welded, not die-cast. A comparison of the two most popular EMD switchers, the SW-1 and the NW-2, reveals significant differences.

The prototype SW-1 is 600 horsepower, while the more powerful NW-2 has 1,000 horsepower. The NW-2 has two exhaust stacks, but the SW-1 has only one. The bell for the NW-2 is located just forward of the front stack, and the bell of the SW-1 is located at the front of the hood. The "brake wheel" radio antenna appears on some prototypes, but not on others. As far as the body goes, the NW-2's hood is longer, extending to the edge of the front stairwell, while the SW-1's hood is two feet shorter and contains a sandbox in the stairwell area.

Clearly, the NW-2 and the SW-1 are two very different locomotives. Just as clearly, Lionel's diesel switcher is a model of the NW-2, not the SW-1. However, a reading of the Lionel catalogues demonstrates that the differences between the two switcher prototypes are sometimes lost upon the Lionel Corporation and its successor, Fundimensions.

Lionel introduced the NW-2 GM switcher in 1949, but it wasn't until 1955 that the catalogue referred to it incorrectly as the "1,000 horsepower SW-1", effectively combining the right horsepower designation with the wrong locomotive - or vice versa! The error was corrected in the next catalogue, 1956, when Lionel correctly identified its diesel switcher as a "1,000 horsepower NW-2". This correct designation is also found in the 1957 and 1958 catalogues, but in 1961 the model designation was not present and the 616 Santa Fe switcher was merely referred to as a "diesel switcher".

Unfortunately, the copywriters for Fundimensions must have read the 1955 catalogue, because they seem to have forgotten everything Lionel learned about its switcher. In the 1970 MPC catalogue, the switcher is mis-identified as an SW-2 (!) model, and from 1971 to 1974 its designation is SW-1. In 1975, the catalogue simply refers to these locomotives as "diesel switchers", but the error reappears in 1976: SW-1. In 1977, they were "diesel switchers" again, and in 1978 they are called SW-1 again. The error persists through 1981, and in 1982 they are once more demoted to "diesel switchers". In 1983 and 1984, they are once more erroneously labeled as "SW-1 switchers". No wonder collectors are confused!

Despite Lionel's consistent misnomers, the model Lionel and Fundimensions have produced for 35 years is clearly the NW-2 General Motors EMD Switcher. So remember: Whatever the catalogues may call these locomotives, they are NW-2 switchers, not SW-1 locomotives! "By their features, ye shall know them...".

### DIESEL POWER TRUCK TYPES

Lionel diesels came with four basic motors. The study of these units shows Lionel's continuing concern with cost and quality considerations.

#### TYPE I MOTOR
Die-cast truck frame
Five exposed gears
Lettered: "THE LIONEL CORPORATION NEW YORK"
Four axle depressions
One screw
Axles not visible

#### TYPE II MOTOR
Built-up power truck with attached side frames to suit prototype
Sheet metal bottom

# SMALL MOTORIZED UNITS

3360 BURRO CRANE

3927 Track Cleaning Car

68 EXECUTIVE INSPECTION CAR

51 NAVY YARD

53 Rio Grande

65 HANDCAR

60 Trolley

42 PICATINNY ARSENAL

57 A E C

50 Gang Car

55 TIE-JECTOR

60[A] Trolley

59 MINUTEMAN

58 GREAT NORTHERN

69 MAINTENANCE CAR

52 FIRE CAR

54 BALLAST TAMPER

41 U.S. ARMY

56 M St L

205 Missouri
   Pacific AA
208 Santa Fe AA

209 New Haven
   AA
210 Texas Special
   AA

226 Boston &
   Maine AB
218 Santa Fe AA

227 Canadian
   National A,
221 Santa
   Fe A

45

Five external gears

Lettered: "LIONEL DIESEL SWITCHER, "OIL",* THE LIONEL CORPORATION NY MADE IN U.S. of AMERICA"

Four axle bearings, all visible

Two axles visible — either one or two magnetic axles

Unpainted side frames

Three-position reverse

Three-part pickup assembly

There are seven subcategories to Type II

## TYPE II SUBCATEGORIES

| Type II Subcategories | A | B | C | D | E | F | G |
|---|---|---|---|---|---|---|---|
| Oil hole with valve | | | | X | X | | X |
| No oil hole | | X | X | | | | |
| Oil hole, no valve | | | X | | | X | |
| One magnetized axle | | X | | X | | X | X |
| Two magnetized axles | X | | X | | X | | |
| Round axle bushings | X | X | X | | | X | X |
| Axle bushing with swage marks | | | | X | X | | |

## TYPE III MOTOR

No bottom plate

Five external gears

Exposed worm and spur gears only, worm is relatively centered between axles

No magnetraction

No axle bearings

## TYPE III SUBCATEGORIES

(A) No tires, front spring mounted motor

(B) Two tires on non-geared side, non-spring mounted motor, examples: 213, 215

## TYPE IV MOTOR

No bottom plate

Motor has only worm and spur gears; both visible

No axle bearings, axles visible, spacers added to axle on one side

Rubber tire traction with grooved wheels to hold tire (no magnetraction)

Black motor side frames

**Bold print** indicates that the name appears on the side of the item. When it does not appear on the side or where its name is abbreviated, the item's popular designation, i.e., **HANDCAR**, appears in bold and its omission from the item's side is noted in the text.

|  | Gd | VG | Exc | Mt |
|---|---|---|---|---|

**0000 ALASKA** GP-9 prototype. Elliott Smith Collection. **NRS**

**41 U.S. ARMY** Switcher, 1955-57, 2-4-2, gas turbine, black with white-lettered "TRANSPORTATION CORPS", three-position E-unit, no light. Several pieces have been reported with a red, white and blue triangle above the center window on both sides. One report says this was a post-factory addition. However, we need to learn if this variety was indeed factory produced. Reports from original owners would be very helpful. Breslin comment. Price for usual variety. 35 60 90 120

**42 PICATINNY ARSENAL** Switcher, 1957, 2-4-2, gas turbine, olive drab with white handrails and lettering, three-position E-unit, no light.
90 150 225 300

**44 U.S. ARMY** Mobile Missile Launcher, 1959-62, blue with white lettering, gray missile launcher with four missiles, blue man sits at control panel, red light on roof, three-position E-unit, one fixed die-cast coupler, magnetraction Type IIF motor, Type III pickups. Ambrose comment.

(A) Dark gray missile launcher, blue man with face and hands painted flesh color. Algozzini Collection. 40 75 100 150

(B) Light gray missile launcher, unpainted blue man. Algozzini Collection. 40 75 100 150

**45 U.S. MARINES** Mobile Missile Launcher, 1960-62, olive drab with white lettering, gray center unit on frame, gray launch unit, red light on roof, magnetraction Type IIF motor, Type III pickups, one fixed die-cast coupler, Ambrose Collection. 50 100 150 200

* It is not clear if "OIL" appears on all Type II motors, particularly Type IIA, IIB

**50 LIONEL** Gang Car, 1955-64, orange body with blue bumpers, two fixed blue men, one gray rotating man, bump reverse, no light.

(A) Dummy horn in center of armature plate; V-shaped bumper bracket.
15 35 45 65

(B) Same as (A), but horn on right side of armature plate.
15 35 45 65

(C) Same as (B), but L-shaped bumper bracket. 15 35 45 65

(D) Same as (A), but two gray bumpers, two fixed gray men and one rotating blue man. Very difficult to confirm men as original, but gray bumpers are unique to this version. Ocilka and Niedhammer observations.
30 70 90 130

**51 NAVY YARD** Switcher, 1956-57, 2-4-2, Vulcan, light blue with white lettering, three-position E-unit, no light, window struts often broken.
45 75 100 150

**52 FIRE CAR** 1958-61, red with white lettering, gray pump and hose reel, red light, bump reverse, man with fire nozzle turns. 75 100 150 225

**53 RIO GRANDE** Snow Plow, 1957-60, 2-4-2, Vulcan, black body and lettering, yellow cab sides, handrails and snow plow, three-position E-unit, no light, one coupler, window struts often broken.

(A) Lettering "Rio Grande" has letter "a" printed backwards.
95 150 225 300

(B) Same as (A), but "a" printed correctly. 120 200 275 400

**54 BALLAST TAMPER** 1958-61, 1966, 1968-69, yellow with black lettering, blue man in cab, one fixed coupler, shift lever for tamper action, unit is geared to half-speed while tamping, two activator track clips to operate shift lever, no reverse, no light, antenna on rear easily damaged.
70 100 135 180

**55 TIE-JECTOR** 1957-61.

(A) Red with white lettering, number on side "5511", switch lever for ejector action on side, two activator track clips to operate switch lever, no reverse, one coupler on rear, no light, pulling more than one car could damage gears or cause the motor to overheat. 70 100 135 180

(B) Same as (A), but slot similar to savings bank car behind rubber man. Algozzini Collection. 100 130 165 210

(C) Same as (A), but orange tint to red plastic body. Algozzini Collection.
100 130 165 210

See also Factory Errors.

**56 M St L MINE TRANSPORT** 1958, 2-4-2, Vulcan, white cab sides and railing, red body and lettering, three-position E-unit, no light, window struts often broken. 150 225 300 450

**57 AEC** Switcher, 1959-60, 2-4-2, Vulcan, three-position E-unit, no light, white body, red cab sides, window struts often broken. It is the consensus of opinion that a cream-colored variety is entirely due to aging. Salamone observation. 175 300 400 600

**58 GREAT NORTHERN** Rotary Snowplow, 1959-61, 2-4-2, Vulcan, green body and logo, white cab, sides and handrails, snow blower rotates when moving, three-position E-unit, no light, window struts often broken.
180 300 400 600

See also Factory Errors.

**59 MINUTEMAN** Switcher, 1962-63, 2-4-2, gas turbine.

(A) White body with blue and red-lettered "U.S. AIR FORCE" "MINUTE-MAN", three-position E-unit, no light, black handrails. 90 180 265 400

See also Factory Errors.

**60 LIONELVILLE** Trolley, 1955-58, four-wheel Birney style, yellow plastic body with red roof, lettered "60 BLT 8-55 LIONEL", "LIONELVILLE RAPID TRANSIT" AND "SAVE TIME HAVE FARE READY". Trolley pole rotates according to direction of operation, bump reverse, interior light. Models without roof vents are believed to be earlier. Roof vents and an aluminized paper reflector on the roof underside were added to prevent roof damage due to the combination of bulb and motor heat.

(A) Two-piece spring bumper, black lettering, no roof vents.
60 125 175 250

(B) Two-piece spring bumper, blue lettering, no roof vents, orange cast to red roof, frame has six-sided threaded bushing at attachment end of frame, Phillips-head screws, trolley pole insulator has square top (part 60-41), orange motor brush holder. Rankin Collection. 60 100 140 200

(C) Two-piece bumper, black lettering, people on strips in door, front and back window, "PERRY ST. - EAST" in one end window on top and "NEAL ST. - LOCAL" in other top end window. Klassen Collection.    **NRS**

(D) Same as (A), except dark red lettering, no roof vents, orange-red roof, six-sided threaded bushing attachment to end of frame, one Phillips screw, pole insulator has splines on top, orange motor brush holder. Brill and Ranker Collections.    **NRS**

(E) Same as (A), except two motor men silhouettes rotate to show in front window according to direction car is moving.    100  175  275  400

(F) One-piece bumper, blue lettering, roof vents.    85  150  200  300

(G) One-piece bumper, blue lettering, no roof vents, bright red roof, frame does not have six-sided threaded bushing, slotted screws, trolley pole insulator (part 60-41) has splines on top, black motor brush holder. Rankin and Alvatrain Collections.    **NRS**

**65 HANDCAR** 1962-66, "HANDCAR NO.65" appears embossed on side of plastic body, Friedman comment. Red pump, two vinyl men pump, one in a red and one in a blue shirt, the vinyl often causes a chemical reaction with the plastic body which damages the body where the men stand, no light, no reverse. Two different bodies are found:

TYPE I: The five-laminate rectifier is exposed and visible from the underside. It is mounted through a 3/8" x 9/16" slot in the frame end. The rectifier is numbered "G16542". The plastic body base is filled at the end center to cover the rectifier. The middle rail collector passes through a spring and a hole in the collector slide. It is soldered to the slide bottom. Griesbeck Collection.

TYPE II: The rectifier is not visible from the underside, and a stamped metal clip holds the rectifier in place. The rectifier is thin and mounts inside the frame. There is no slot. The plastic body is open at the end center. The middle rail collector slide has a vertical post through the spring to which the collector wire is attached. Griesbeck Collection.

(A) Dark yellow body.    75  100  150  225

(B) Light yellow body.    90  125  175  250

**68 EXECUTIVE INSPECTION CAR** 1958-61, DeSoto 1958 station wagon **without** name on side, red with cream side panel and roof, knob on roof is E-unit cutoff switch, two-position E-unit, operating head and taillight

(A) Red with cream striping.    75  100  150  225

(B) All red with no striping, top knob for E-unit is a non-operating dummy, factory prototype in TCA Museum. Geller observation.    **NRS**

(C) Blue with cream stripe, probable pre-production prototype; Bohn observation. Algozzini Collection.    — — — 800

**69 MAINTENANCE CAR** 1960-62, self-powered signal service car, "MAIN-TENANCE CAR" does not appear on side, dark gray and black body with light gray platform, blue bumpers, L-shaped bumper bracket, one blue man, sign reverses when direction reverses, "DANGER" on one side and "SAFETY FIRST" on the other.    90  185  225  325

**202 UNION PACIFIC** 1957, Alco A unit, 0-27, orange body with black lettering, sheet metal frame, opening where front coupler would be is closed off, dummy coupler on rear, one-axle magnetraction, two-position E-unit, headlight, Type IID motor, Type II pickups, no horn, no weight.

15  30  50  75

**204 SANTA FE** 1957, Alco AA units, 0-27, Santa Fe freight paint scheme, blue body with yellow cab roof, upper stripe and lettering, red and yellow lower stripe, sheet metal frame, front and rear dummy couplers, two-axle magnetraction, three-position E-unit, light in both units, Type IIE motor, Type II pickup, no horn, no weight.    35  75  100  150

**205 MISSOURI PACIFIC** 1957-58, Alco AA units, 0-27, blue body with white lettering, sheet metal frame, front and rear dummy couplers, two-axle magnetraction, three-position E-unit, light in powered unit, Type IIE motor, Type II pickup, no horn, no weight.    30  45  100  150

**208 SANTA FE** 1958-59, Alco AA units, 0-27 Santa Fe freight paint scheme, blue body with yellow cab roof, upper stripe and lettering, red and yellow lower stripe, sheet metal frame, front and rear dummy couplers, two-axle magnetraction, three-position E-unit, light in powered unit, Type IIE motor, Type II pickup, horn, no weight.    35  60  90  120

**209 NEW HAVEN** 1958, Alco AA units, 0-27, black body with orange and white stripes and lettering, sheet metal frame, front and rear dummy couplers, two-axle magnetraction, three-position E-unit, light in powered unit, Type IIE motor, Type II pickup, horn, no weight.    50  100  150  200

**210 The Texas Special** 1958, Alco AA units, 0-27, red body and lettering with white stripe, sheet metal frame, front and rear dummy couplers, two-axle magnetraction, three-position E-unit, light in powered unit, Type IIE motor, Type II pickup, no horn, no weight.    40  75  100  150

**211 The Texas Special** 1962-66, Alco AA units, 0-27, red body and lettering with white stripe, sheet metal frame, front and rear dummy couplers, two rubber traction tires on drive wheels, weight in body, two-position E-unit, light in powered unit, Type IIIB motor, Type II pickup, no horn, with weight.    30  50  70  100

**212 U.S. MARINE CORPS** 1958-59, Alco A unit, 0-27, box labeled "212T". Ambrose comment.

(A) Blue body with white stripes and lettering, sheet metal frame, opening where front coupler would be is closed off, dummy coupler on rear, one-axle magnetraction, two-position E-unit, light, Type IID motor, Type II pickup, no horn, no weight.    30  60  90  120

(B) Same as (A), except slightly lighter blue, much brighter white lettering and trim, die-cast dummy coupler on front, operating coupler on rear, no reverse unit, Type IIA motor, no tires, no magnetraction.

30  60  90  120

**212 SANTA FE** 1964-66, Alco AA units, 0-27, Santa Fe war bonnet passenger paint scheme, silver body with red cab, nose, and stripe; yellow and black trim, black lettering, sheet metal frame, front and rear dummy couplers, two rubber traction tires on drive wheels, two-position E-unit, light in powered unit, Type IIIB motor, Type III pickup, horn, with weight, E-unit lever has slot in roof. I.D. Smith observation.    25  50  75  100

**213 MINNEAPOLIS & ST. LOUIS** 1964, Alco AA units, 0-27, red body with white stripe and lettering, sheet metal frame, front and rear dummy couplers, two rubber traction tires on drive wheels, two-position E-unit, light in powered unit, Type IIIB motor, no horn, with weight.

35  75  100  150

**215 SANTA FE** Uncatalogued, 1965, Alco, AB units, gray plastic body painted silver and red with black and yellow stripes and black lettering, Type IIIB motor, with weight, two-position E-unit. Also came with 212T dummy A unit instead of 218C B unit in set 19444, tire traction. I.D. Smith and Ambrose observations.    35  50  70  100

**216(A) BURLINGTON** 1958, Alco A unit, 0-27, silver body with red stripes and lettering, sheet metal frame, front and rear dummy couplers, two-axle magnetraction, three-position E-unit, light, Type IIE motor, no horn, no weight.    38  75  100  150

**216(B) MINNEAPOLIS & ST. LOUIS** Uncatalogued, lighted, Alco A unit, 0-27, gray plastic body painted red, with weight, white lettering, Type IIIA motor, three-position E-unit, open pilot, no front couplers.

40  75  100  150

**217 BOSTON & MAINE** 1959, Alco AB units, 0-27, letters B and M **only** on unit's side, black body with large blue stripe, thin white stripe at roof line, black and white lettering, sheet metal frame, front and rear dummy couplers, two-axle magnetraction, three-position E-unit, light in A unit, Type IIC motor, Type III pickup, no horn, no weight.    35  75  100  150

**218 SANTA FE** 1959-63, Alco, 0-27, Santa Fe war bonnet passenger paint scheme, silver body with red cab, nose and stripe; yellow and black trim, black lettering, sheet metal frame, front and rear couplers, two-axle magnetraction, three-position E-unit, light in powered unit, Type IIC motor, Type III pickup, horn, no weight.

(A) Double A units (Type IIC motors).    35  50  70  100

(B) AB units.    35  50  70  100

**219 MISSOURI PACIFIC** Uncatalogued, c. 1959, Alco AA units, blue with white lettering, sheet metal frame, front and rear dummy couplers, two-axle magnetraction, three-position E-unit, light in powered unit, Type IIC motor, Type III pickup, no horn, no weight.    40  75  100  150

**220 SANTA FE** 1961, Alco A unit, 0-27, Santa Fe war bonnet passenger paint scheme, silver body with red cab, nose and stripe, yellow and black trim, black lettering, sheet metal frame, front and rear couplers, three-position E-unit, two-axle magnetraction light. Corrugated box for power unit. Box dummy A says "220T Tender". Rohlfing and Ambrose comments. Also available with 220T dummy A unit in uncatalogued set X568 in 1960; advance dealer catalogue shows this dummy. Ambrose comment. Price for powered A only.    25  50  70  100

202

212

216

221[B]

221[A]

228

230

231

232

1055

1066

2024

# ALCO DIESELS

219 MISSOURI PACIFIC

224 UNITED STATES NAVY

229 MINNEAPOLIS & ST LOUIS

2041 ROCK ISLAND

2041 [ROCK ISLAND] - FACTORY ERROR

2031 ROCK ISLAND

204 SANTA FE

211 The Texas Special

212 SANTA FE

213 MINNEAPOLIS & ST LOUIS

215 SANTA FE

217 BOSTON & MAINE

**221** Alco A unit, 0-27, sheet metal frame, opening where front coupler would be is closed off, dummy coupler on rear, rubber traction tire on one drive wheel, two-position E-unit, no light, Type IVA motor, Type III pickup, no horn, no weight.

(A) **Rio Grande,** 1963-64, yellow with black stripes and lettering.

|  |  |  |  |
|---|---|---|---|
| 20 | 30 | 40 | 60 |

(B) **U.S. MARINE CORPS,** uncatalogued, olive drab with white stripes and lettering, 2 position E-unit, 1 axle magnetraction. Light, no weight. Part of uncatalogued set 19334 made for J.C. Penney. Ambrose comment.

|  |  |  |  |
|---|---|---|---|
| 40 | 75 | 100 | 150 |

(C) **SANTA FE,** uncatalogued, olive drab with white stripes and lettering, two-position E-unit, tire traction, no light or weight. Ambrose comment.

|  |  |  |  |
|---|---|---|---|
| 40 | 75 | 100 | 150 |

**222 Rio Grande** 1962, Alco A unit, 0-27, yellow with black stripes and lettering, sheet metal frame, opening where front coupler would be is closed off, dummy coupler on rear, rubber traction tire on one drive wheel, no reverse, light, Type IVA motor, Type III pickup, no horn, no weight.

(A) As described above.

|  |  |  |  |
|---|---|---|---|
| 15 | 30 | 40 | 60 |

(B) Same as (A), but die-cast dummy coupler in front. Ambrose Collection.

|  |  |  |  |
|---|---|---|---|
| 12 | 17 | 25 | 35 |

**223, 218C SANTA FE** 1963, Alco AB units, 0-27, Santa Fe war bonnet passenger paint scheme, silver body with red cab, nose and stripe, yellow and black trim, black lettering, A unit numbered 223; B unit numbered 218, sheet metal frame, front and rear dummy couplers, rubber traction tires on drive wheel, two-position E-unit, light in A unit, horn.

|  |  |  |  |
|---|---|---|---|
| 40 | 75 | 100 | 150 |

**224 U.S. NAVY** 1960, Alco AB units, 0-27, blue body with white lettering, sheet metal frame, front and rear dummy couplers, two-axle magnetraction, three-position E-unit, light in A unit, Type IIC motor, Type III pickup, no horn, no weight.

|  |  |  |  |
|---|---|---|---|
| 40 | 75 | 100 | 150 |

**225 CHESAPEAKE & OHIO** 1960, Alco A unit, 0-27, dark blue with yellow lettering, sheet metal frame, front and rear dummy couplers, two-axle magnetraction, two-position E-unit, light, Type IIC motor, Type III pickup, no weight.

|  |  |  |  |
|---|---|---|---|
| 30 | 60 | 90 | 120 |

**226 BOSTON & MAINE** Uncatalogued, 1960, only "BM" on sides, Alco AB units, 0-27, black body with large blue stripe, thin white stripe at roof line, black and white lettering, sheet metal frame, front and rear dummy couplers, two-axle magnetraction, three-position E-unit, light in A unit, Type IIC motor, Type III pickup, horn, no weight.

|  |  |  |  |
|---|---|---|---|
| 35 | 60 | 100 | 120 |

**227 CANADIAN NATIONAL** Uncatalogued, 1960, Alco A unit, 0-27, green body with yellow trim and lettering, sheet metal frame, opening where front coupler would be is closed off, dummy coupler on rear, no reverse, light, Type IIIA motor, Type III pickup, no horn, made for Canadian market, with weight.

|  |  |  |  |
|---|---|---|---|
| 30 | 45 | 80 | 125 |

**228 CANADIAN NATIONAL** Uncatalogued, 1960, Alco A unit, 0-27, green body with yellow trim and lettering, sheet metal frame, front and rear dummy couplers, two-axle magnetraction, two-position E-unit, light, Type IIC motor, Type III pickup, no horn, made for Canadian market, no weight.

|  |  |  |  |
|---|---|---|---|
| 30 | 45 | 80 | 125 |

**229 MINNEAPOLIS & ST. LOUIS** 1961-62, Alco A unit in 1961 and Alco AB units in 1962, 0-27, red body with white stripes and lettering, sheet metal frame and front and rear dummy couplers. A unit has one-axle magnetraction, two-position E-unit, headlight, Type IIB motor, Type III pickup, horn, no weight. We do not know if the 1961 A unit differed from the 1962 version. Both have the same catalogue specifications (horn, headlight and magnetraction), but the 1961 catalogue showed the lettering "M St L" interrupting the side stripe. We do not know if this version was made. Our color photograph shows the 229 as illustrated in the 1962 catalogue. Ambrose comment.

(A) A unit only.

|  |  |  |  |
|---|---|---|---|
| 25 | 50 | 70 | 100 |

(B) A and B units.

|  |  |  |  |
|---|---|---|---|
| 50 | 75 | 100 | 150 |

**230 CHESAPEAKE & OHIO** 1961, Alco A unit, 0-27, blue body with yellow stripe and lettering, sheet metal frame, opening where front coupler would be is closed off, dummy coupler on rear, two-axle magnetraction, two-position E-unit, light, Type IID motor, Type II pickup, no horn.

|  |  |  |  |
|---|---|---|---|
| 25 | 35 | 50 | 75 |

**231** Alco A unit, 1961-63, 0-27, sheet metal frame, front and rear dummy couplers, two-axle magnetraction, two-position E-unit, light, no horn.

(A) **ROCK ISLAND,** black body with red middle stripe, white upper stripe and lettering, Type IIA motor, Type III pickup.

|  |  |  |  |
|---|---|---|---|
| 35 | 50 | 70 | 100 |

(B) Same as (A), but without lettering and white upper stripe, motor type not known.

|  |  |  |  |
|---|---|---|---|
| 35 | 50 | 70 | 100 |

(C) Same as (A), but without red stripe, with white upper stripe, Type IIC motor, Type III pickup, 1963.

|  |  |  |  |
|---|---|---|---|
| 15 | 30 | 55 | 80 |

**232 NEW HAVEN** 1962, Alco A unit, 0-27, orange body with black stripe and black and white lettering, sheet metal frame, opening where front coupler would be is closed off, dummy coupler on rear, magnetraction, two-position E-unit, light, Type IIE motor, Type II pickup, no horn, no weight.

|  |  |  |  |
|---|---|---|---|
| 25 | 30 | 50 | 75 |

**400 BALTIMORE AND OHIO** 1956-58, Budd RDC passenger car, silver body with blue lettering, operating couplers at both ends, magnetraction, three-position E-unit, lights, horn, single motor.

|  |  |  |  |
|---|---|---|---|
| 100 | 150 | 200 | 250 |

**404 BALTIMORE AND OHIO** 1957-58, Budd RDC baggage - mail car, silver body with blue lettering, operating couplers at both ends, magnetraction, three-position E-unit, single motor, light, horn.

|  |  |  |  |
|---|---|---|---|
| 100 | 175 | 225 | 300 |

**520** Box Cab Electric, 1956-57, GE 80 ton, 0-4-2, 0-27, red body with white lettering "LIONEL LINES", sheet metal frame, single pantograph, dummy coupler on one end, operating coupler on the other end, three-position E-unit, no light, no horn, check pantograph for damage. Same body used for 3535 Security Car.

(A) Black pantograph.

|  |  |  |  |
|---|---|---|---|
| 28 | 48 | 65 | 85 |

(B) Copper-colored pantograph.

|  |  |  |  |
|---|---|---|---|
| 28 | 48 | 65 | 85 |

See also Factory Errors.

520 Box Cab Electric

## NW-2 SWITCHERS

**600 MKT** 1955, NW-2 Switcher, 0-27, red body with white lettering, sheet metal frame, operating couplers at both ends, one-axle magnetraction, three-position E-unit, no light, Type IID motor, Type II pickup, no horn.

(A) Black frame with black end rails, Type IID motor.

|  |  |  |  |
|---|---|---|---|
| 50 | 75 | 100 | 150 |

(B) Gray frame with yellow end rails, Type IIE motor, Type II pickup*.

|  |  |  |  |
|---|---|---|---|
| 60 | 90 | 125 | 175 |

(C) Gray frame with black end rails, Type IID motor, Type II pickup. Lower Collection.

**NRS**

**601 SEABOARD** 1956, NW-2 Switcher, black and red body with red stripes and white lettering, black sheet metal frame, operating couplers at both ends, axle magnetraction, three-position E-unit, light, Type IIE motor, Type II pickup, horn.

|  |  |  |  |
|---|---|---|---|
| 50 | 75 | 100 | 150 |

**602 SEABOARD** 1957-58, NW-2 Switcher, 0-27, black and red body with red stripes and white lettering, sheet metal frames, dummy couplers at both ends, two-axle magnetraction, three-position E-unit, light, Type IIE motor, Type II pickup, horn.

|  |  |  |  |
|---|---|---|---|
| 40 | 60 | 90 | 120 |

* Much easier to find on the West Coast than the East Coast.

2330 PENNSYLVANIA

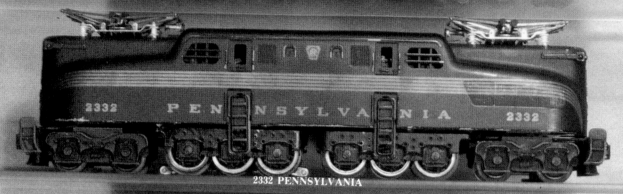

2332 PENNSYLVANIA

2340 PENNSYLVANIA

2360[B] PENNSYLVANIA

2360[C] PENNSYLVANIA

**610 ERIE** 1955, NW-2 Switcher, black body, yellow lettering, operating couplers, axle magnetraction, three-position E-unit, light, Type IIE motor, Type II pickup, no horn.

| | | | |
|---|---|---|---|
| (A) Black frame. | 50 | 75 | 100 | 150 |
| (B) Yellow frame. Lebo Collection. | | | | NRS |
| (C) Same as (A), but no light. Lahti Collection. | 50 | 75 | 100 | 150 |
| (D) Same as (B), but no light. Giroux Collection. | | | | NRS |

(E) Same as (A), but early production with two-axle magnetraction, no light, reportedly only a few thousand made, Yeckel observation. We do not know if this is the same as (C).    **NRS**

**611 JERSEY CENTRAL** 1957-58, NW-2 Switcher, 027, orange and blue body with blue and white lettering, sheet metal frame, one-axle magnetraction, three-position E-unit, light, Type IID motor, Type II pickup, no horn.

| | | | |
|---|---|---|---|
| (A) Dummy couplers front and rear. Weiss Collection. | 50 | 75 | 100 | 150 |

(B) Dummy coupler on front, operating coupler on rear.    Confirmation requested.    50    75    100    150

**613 UNION PACIFIC** 1958, NW-2 Switcher, 0-27, yellow with gray hood top and cab roof, red lettering, "ROAD OF THE STREAMLINERS", sheet metal frame, dummy couplers, both ends, magnetraction, three-position E-unit, light, Type IIE motor, Type II pickup, no horn, bell, non-operating couplers.    75    100    150    225

**614 ALASKA** 1959-60, NW-2 Switcher, 0-27, blue body with yellow-orange lettering, yellow dynamic brake super-structure on top of motor hood, sheet metal frame, dummy couplers at both ends, one-axle magnetraction, two-position E-unit, light, Type IIG motor, Type II pickup, no horn, appears to be the only example of IIG motor.

(A) No dynamic brake unit, Niedhammer observation. This is a legitimate variation, not a simple omission. This version came with a plastic bell situated in such a way that the dynamic brake unit could not be installed. Catalano observation.    50    75    100    150

(B) With yellow dynamic brake unit atop hood.    75    100    150    225

**616 SANTA FE** 1961-62, NW-2 Switcher, black body with black and white safety stripes front and rear, white lettering, dummy horn and bell are omitted, sheet metal frame, operating couplers at both ends, two-axle magnetraction, three-position E-unit, light, Type IID motor, Type II pickup, horn. Arpino comment.    50    75    100    150

**617 SANTA FE** 1963, NW-2 Switcher, black body with black and white safety stripes front and rear, white lettering, sheet metal frame, dummy couplers both ends, dummy horn, bell and radio antenna trim pieces, axle magnetraction, marker lights, headlight lens, three-position E-unit. light, Type IIE motor, Type II pickup, horn.    Arpino and Ambrose comments.

75    100    150    225

**621 JERSEY CENTRAL** 1956-57, NW-2 Switcher, 0-27, blue body with orange lettering, sheet metal frame, operating couplers at both ends, one-axle magnetraction, three-position E-unit, no light, Type IID motor, Type II pickup, horn.    40    60    90    120

**622 SANTA FE** 1949-50, uncatalogued as Santa Fe. Catalogued but never made as Lionel (1949) and New York Central (1950), NW-2 Switcher, first magnetraction engine, black body with white lettering, die-cast frame, coil-operated couplers at both ends, three-position E-unit, light both ends, Type I motor, Type I pickup, no horn, operating bell, excellent runner, 6220 is similar except numbered for 0-27.

(A) 1949, large GM decal on cab.    90    125    175    250

(B) 1950, small GM decal on lower front side of motor hood, no weight in cab.    75    100    150    200

(C) 1950 late, same as (B), but weight cast in cab frame.

75    100    150    200

(D) "LIONEL" not "SANTA FE", catalogued but not made.    **Not Manufactured**

(E) "NEW YORK CENTRAL" not "SANTA FE", catalogued but not made.    **Not Manufactured**

**623 SANTA FE** 1952-54, NW-2 Switcher, 0-27, black body with white lettering, die-cast frame, coil-operating couplers at both ends, magnetraction, three-position E-unit, no horn, Type I motor, Type I pickup, no horn, excellent runner. Suggestion has been made that color variations in the decals are entirely due to aging, since blue is particularly susceptible to fading.

Reader comments invited.    Weisskopf comment.

| | | | |
|---|---|---|---|
| (A) Ten stanchions hold handrail to side. | 50 | 75 | 100 | 150 |
| (B) Three stanchions hold handrail to side. | 35 | 60 | 85 | 125 |

**624 CHESAPEAKE & OHIO** 1952-54, NW-2 Switcher, 0-27, blue body with yellow stripe and lettering, die-cast frame, coil-operating couplers at both ends, magnetraction, three-position E-unit, lights, at both ends, Type I pickup, no horn, excellent runner.

| | | | |
|---|---|---|---|
| (A) Ten stanchions hold handrail to side. | 75 | 125 | 175 | 250 |
| (B) Three stanchions hold handrail to side. | 75 | 100 | 150 | 225 |

**625 LEHIGH VALLEY** 1957-58, GE 44 ton switcher, 0-27, red and black body with white stripe and lettering, black sheet metal frame, dummy couplers at both ends, magnetraction, three-position E-unit, light, Type IID motor, Type II pickup, no horn.    60    90    125    175

**626 BALTIMORE AND OHIO** 1959, GE 44 ton center-cab switcher, yellow lettering and frame, 027.

(A) Blue body and yellow frame.    75    125    175    250

(B) Lavender body and black frame. Niedhammer Collection.    **NRS**

**627 LV** 1956-57, GE 44 ton switcher, 0-27, Lehigh Valley paint scheme, red body with white stripe and lettering, black sheet metal frame, operating couplers at both ends, one-axle magnetraction, three-position E-unit, no light, Type IID motor, Type II pickup, no horn.    40    60    90    120

**628 NORTHERN PACIFIC** 1956-57, GE 44 ton Switcher, 0-27, black body with yellow stripe, yellow sheet metal frame, operating couplers at both ends, one-axle magnetraction, three-position E-unit, light, Type IID motor, Type II pickup, no horn.

(A) Yellow lettering.    50    75    100    150

(B) White lettering. Hudzik Collection.    **NRS**

**629 BURLINGTON** 1956, GE 44 ton Switcher, 0-27, silver body with red stripe and lettering, black sheet metal frame, operating couplers at both ends, one-axle magnetraction, three-position E-unit, light, Type IID motor, Type II pickup, no horn. The silver finish on most pieces is not attractive. Hence a substantial premium for excellent and better.    75    125    200    300

**633 SANTA FE** 1962, NW-2 Switcher, 0-27, blue body with blue and yellow safety stripes and yellow lettering, sheet metal frame, dummy coupler on rear only, two-position E-unit, light but no lens on light, Type IVA motor, Type III pickup, no horn, traction tires.    40    75    95    150

**634 SANTA FE** 1963, 65-66, NW-2 Switcher, 0-27, blue body with yellow lettering, sheet metal frame, plastic dummy front coupler, metal dummy rear coupler, two-position E-unit, light, Type IVA motor, Type III pickup, no horn.

(A) 1963, 1965, yellow and blue safety stripes on front of motor hood and on cab, with lens.    25    40    60    100

(B) 1966, same as (A), but no safety stripes, without lens.

25    40    60    100

(C) 1970, very early MPC, used old Lionel number. No safety stripes, but lens. Silver plastic bell and silver plastic brake wheel. Red end marker lights. Listed here for user's convenience.    15    20    40    50

**635 UNION PACIFIC** 1965, uncatalogued, NW-2 Switcher, 0-27, yellow plastic body painted yellow, red striping and trim, red "NEW 7-58", white "U.P." and "635" on front of cab, no bell, no horn, Type IVA motor, Type III pickup, light but no headlight lens, dummy couplers front and rear, weight on underside of hood, came in 1965 uncatalogued set 19440. Ambrose and Niedhammer observations.    30    50    70    125

See also Factory Errors.

**645 UNION PACIFIC** 1969, NW-2 Switcher, 0-27, black frame, yellow unpainted plastic body with red heat-stamped lettering and stripes, weight attached to hood underside, headlight with lens, two-position reverse, two fixed couplers, Type IVB motor, Type III pickup.    30    50    70    110

See also Factory Errors.

**1055 TEXAS SPECIAL** 1959-60, not shown in the consumer catalogue but listed as part of a special set "To meet the needs of the low-price mass toy market" in the 1959 and 1960 Advance Catalogues. In 1959, it was described as No. 1105 Texas Special set and in 1960 as the No. 1107 Sportsman Diesel set. In 1959, the catalogue illustration does not show some of the car numbers: unnumbered box, unnumbered plug door box, unnumbered single-dome tank, 6012 gondola with two canisters and an unnumbered caboose. In 1960, it was shown with an unnumbered 6042

# NW-2 SWITCHERS

621 Jersey Central

601 Seaboard

611 Jersey Central

613 Union Pacific

614 Alaska

623 Santa Fe

624 Chesapeake & Ohio

6250 Seaboard

600 MKT

610 Erie

SEABOARD

601

JERSEY CENTRAL

UNION PACIFIC

ROAD OF The Streamliners

ALASKA RAILROAD

614

A.T.&S.F.

623

CHESAPEAKE & OHIO

624

6250

SEABOARD

MKT 600

610

**NW-2 SWITCHERS**

622 Santa Fe

634 Santa Fe

645 UNION PACIFIC

616 Santa Fe

633 Santa Fe

635 UNION PACIFIC

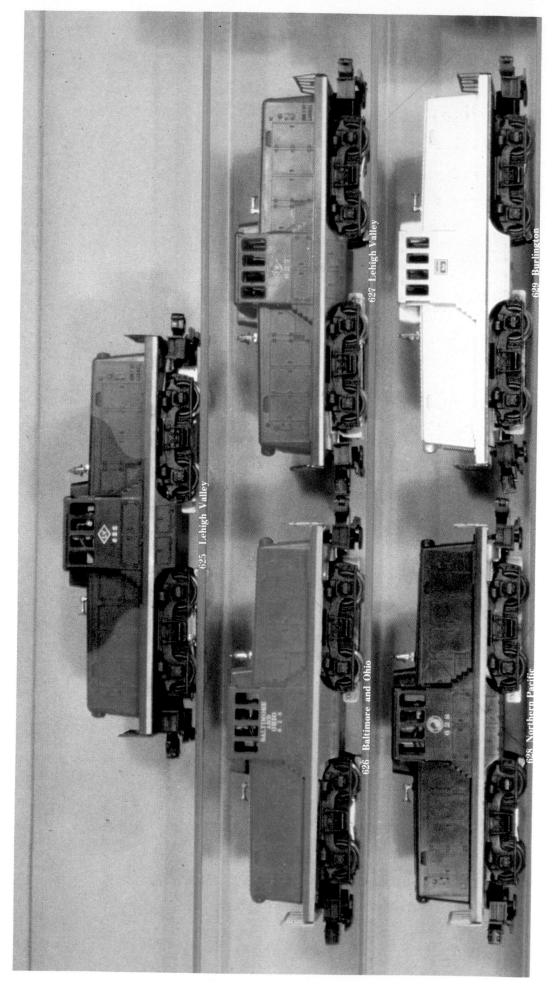

625 Lehigh Valley

627 Lehigh Valley

629 Burlington

626 Baltimore and Ohio

628 Northern Pacific

black gondola with two canisters, a 6044 teal blue AIREX boxcar and unnumbered 6047 caboose. Rohlfing Collection. We hope that our readers will verify this information. The locomotive is an Alco A unit, 0-27, red body with white lettering, sheet metal frame, opening where front coupler would be is closed off, dummy coupler on rear, no magnetraction or rubber tires, no reverse, Type IIIA motor, no horn, light and weight. At this time, Lionel apparently felt that such "stripped-down units", because of their low quality, did not belong in their regular line and would reflect badly on the line. Yet, paradoxically, the mass marketers could readily sell these in quantity because of their obvious low price (probably $15 or less) while trading on the Lionel Line's quality reputation. Unfortunately, consumers got what they paid for and the Lionel Line's reputation declined.

(A) Alco A unit, 0-27, red body with white lettering, sheet metal frame, opening where front coupler would be is closed off, dummy coupler on rear, no magnetraction or rubber tires, no reverse, Type IIIA motor, no horn, light with weight.     **15   25   40   75**

**1065 UNION PACIFIC** 1961, uncatalogued, Alco A unit, 0-27, yellow body with red lettering and red stripe, sheet metal frame, opening where front coupler would be is closed off, dummy coupler on rear, no magnetraction, no traction tires, no reverse, Type IIIA motor, Type III pickup, no horn, with weight.
(A) With light.     **15   25   40   75**
(B) No light. I.D. Smith observation.     **15   25   40   75**

**1066 UNION PACIFIC** 1964, uncatalogued, Alco A unit, 0-27, yellow body with red stripe and lettering, sheet metal frame, opening where front coupler would be is closed off, dummy coupler on rear, no magnetraction, no reverse, Type IVA motor, Type III pickup, no horn or weight.
    **15   25   40   75**

**2023 UNION PACIFIC** 1950-51, Alco AA units, 0-27, die-cast frame, coil-operated couplers on cab ends, dummy middle couplers, magnetraction, three-position E-unit, light in both units, Type I motor, Type I pickup, horn, excellent runner.
(A) 1950, yellow body with gray roof and frame, red stripes and lettering.     **75   100   175   300**
(B) 1950, same as (A), but gray nose, and gray painted truck side frames.     **200   300   500   650**
(C) 1951, silver body and frame with black stripes and lettering, gray roof.     **65   95   150   250**
NOTE: The Anniversary Set from the year 1950 consisted of the 2023 Union Pacific Alco AA with the yellow and gray paint scheme and a gray nose top, the 2481 Plainfield coach, the 2482 Westfield coach and the 2483 Livingston observation car. The gray-nosed 2023 represents the earliest stage of this locomotive's production and was supposedly included only with the Anniversary Set. However, some collectors maintain that a few gray-nosed 2023 Alcos were sold separately. In any case, this set is highly prized by collectors.

**2024 CHESAPEAKE & OHIO** 1969, Alco A unit, 0-27, blue body with yellow stripe and lettering, sheet metal frame, front and rear dummy couplers, one rubber traction tire, two-position E-unit, light, Type IVB motor, Type IV pickup, no horn or weight.     **15   25   35   60**

**2028 PENNSYLVANIA** 1955, GP-7 Road Switcher, 0-27, tuscan body, light in cab end only. Ambrose comment.
(A) Yellow rubber-stamped lettering, riveted railing.     **90   150   200   350**
(B) Yellow rubber-stamped lettering, welded railing, rivet holes.     **90   150   200   350**
(C) Gold lettering, welded rails, no rivet holes.     **80   140   180   300**
(D) Welded rails, tan frame. Catalano and Algozzini Collections.     **125   200   275   400**

**2028 UNION PACIFIC** 1955 GP-7, shown in Advance Catalogue, but not manufactured. We illustrate the prototype from the La Rue Shempp Collection in this chapter.     **NRS**

**2031 ROCK ISLAND** 1952-54, Alco AA units, 0-27, black body with white stripe and lettering, red middle stripe, die-cast frame, coil-operated couplers on cab ends, dummy middle couplers, magnetraction, three-position E-unit, light in both units, Type I motor, Type I pickup, horn, excellent runner.
    **75   100   175   275**

**2032 ERIE** 1952-54, Alco AA units, 0-27, black body with yellow stripes and lettering, die-cast frame, coil-operated couplers on cab ends, dummy middle couplers, magnetraction, three-position E-unit, light in both units, Type I motor, Type I pickup, horn, excellent runner.     **70   95   160   250**

**2033 UNION PACIFIC** 1952-54, Alco AA units, 0-27, silver body and frame with black lettering, die-cast frame, coil-operated couplers on cab ends, dummy middle couplers, magnetraction, three-position E-unit, light in both units, Type I motor, Type I pickup, horn, excellent runner. Very hard to obtain in excellent or better condition because the silver paint is highly susceptible to mildew. LaVoie comment.
(A) Smooth roof over motor.     **60   100   150   225**
(B) Dime-sized round bump over motor.     **60   100   150   225**

**2041 ROCK ISLAND** 1969, Alco AA units, 0-27, black body with white stripe and lettering, red middle stripe, sheet metal frame, front and rear dummy couplers, light, Type IIB motor, Type IIIB pickup, two-position E-unit, no horn, with weight, catalogued with nose emblem but production pieces lack emblem.     **40   60   90   125**
See also Factory Errors.

**2240 WABASH** 1956, F-3 AB units, 0-27, gray and blue body with white side panels and trim, yellow heat-stamped $^2$ lettering, blue frame with black trucks, louvered roof vents, filled in portholes, operating coupler on front of A unit, all other couplers are dummys, magnetraction, three-position E-unit, light in A unit, single vertical motor, horn.     **150   200   280   400**

**2242 NEW HAVEN** 1958-59, F-3 AB units, checkerboard paint scheme, silver roof and frame, black nose, black, white, silver and red sides, lettering heat-stamped $^3$ on nose and sides, silver frame with black pilot and trucks, louvered roof vent, filled in portholes, operating coupler on front of A unit, all others are dummys, magnetraction, three-position E-unit, light in A unit, single vertical motor, horn, often referred to as an 0-27 engine because of its single motor, although it is shown only as a Super 0 engine in the catalogue.     **175   250   325   450**

**2243 SANTA FE** 1955-57, F-3 AB units, 0-27 & 0, Santa Fe war bonnet passenger paint scheme, silver body with red cab, nose and stripe, yellow and black trim, black heat-stamped lettering, silver frame with black trucks, louvered roof vent, filled in portholes, operating coupler on front of A unit, all other couplers are dummys, magnetraction, three-position E-unit, light in A unit, single vertical motor, horn, this unit is often referred to as an 0-27 engine due to its single motor and its 0-27 listing in 1955-56 but in 1957 it was catalogued in 0 Gauge only.     **75   125   175   250**

**2243C SANTA FE** 1955-57, F-3 B unit, came as part of 2243 and not catalogued separately; it matches 2383 AA units for which no B was made.
    **30   50   65   100**

**2245 TEXAS SPECIAL** 1954-55, F-3 AB units, 0-27, red body and pilot with white lower panel and silver frame and trucks.
(A) As described above.     **100   150   225   300**
(B) Red body with black trucks and silver pilot. O'Brien Collection, Catalano observation. More common in Midwestern states than in other areas.     **100   150   225   300**

**2321 LACKAWANNA** 1954-56, FM Trainmaster, gray body with yellow trim and maroon mid-stripe and lettering, side trim stripe and lettering are rubber-stamped, two operating couplers, magnetraction, three-position E-unit, light both ends, twin vertical motors, horn, excellent runner.
(A) Factory prototype shown on cover of 1954 Lionel Advance Catalogue, screens on roof vent, very elaborate paint scheme. LaRue Shempp Collection.     **NRS**
(B) Reddish-maroon roof and striping with interior lights mounted horizontally on a riveted bracket shaped like an inverted "L". Ocilka Collection.     **200   275   375   525**
(C) Dull maroon roof and striping, interior lights mounted vertically on riveted bracket which is just an upright piece. Ocilka Collection.     **NRS**
(D) Gray roof and body.     **175   225   275   425**

**2322 VIRGINIAN** 1965-66, FM Trainmaster, operating couplers at both ends, magnetraction, three-position E-unit, light at both ends, twin vertical motors, horn, excellent runner.
(A) Orange yellow body with blue stripe and roof.     **215   275   325   475**

$^2$ Silk-screened on reproduction bodies.

$^3$ Silk-screened side lettering with nose decal on reproduction bodies.

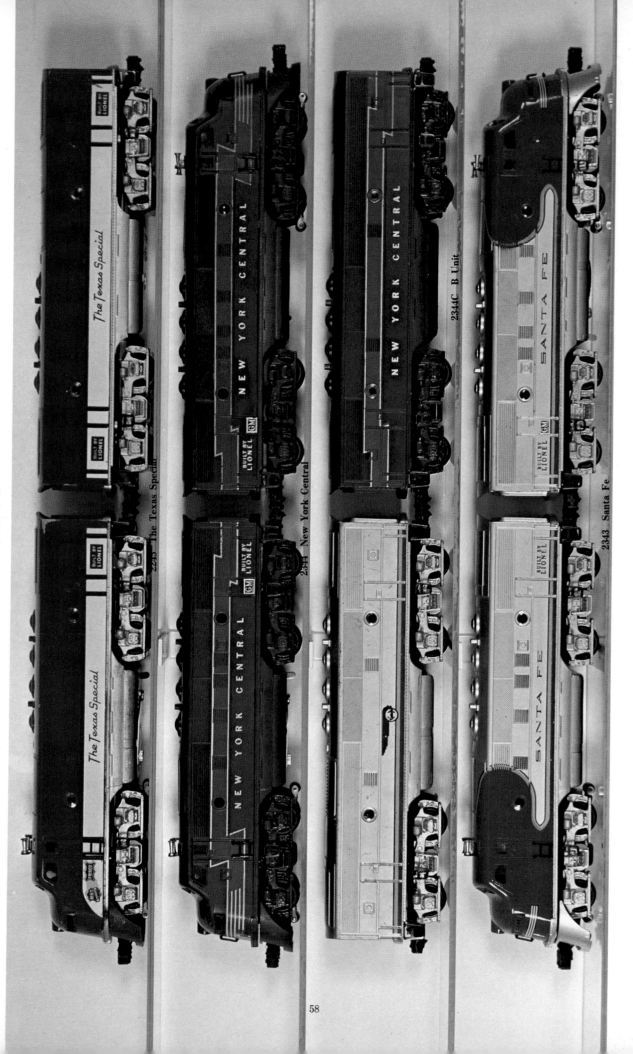

**G.M. F-3**

2245 The Texas Special

2344 New York Central

2344C B Unit

2343 Santa Fe

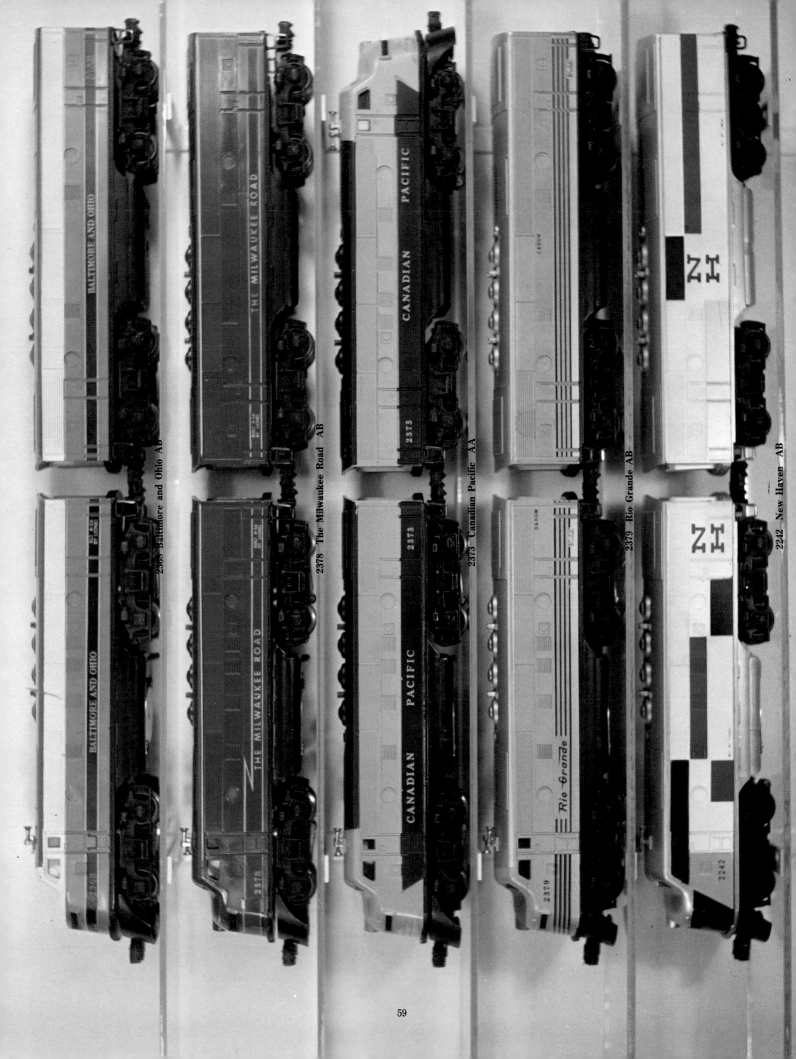

2300 Baltimore and Ohio AB

2378 The Milwaukee Road AB

2373 Canadian Pacific AA

2379 Rio Grande AB

2242 New Haven AB

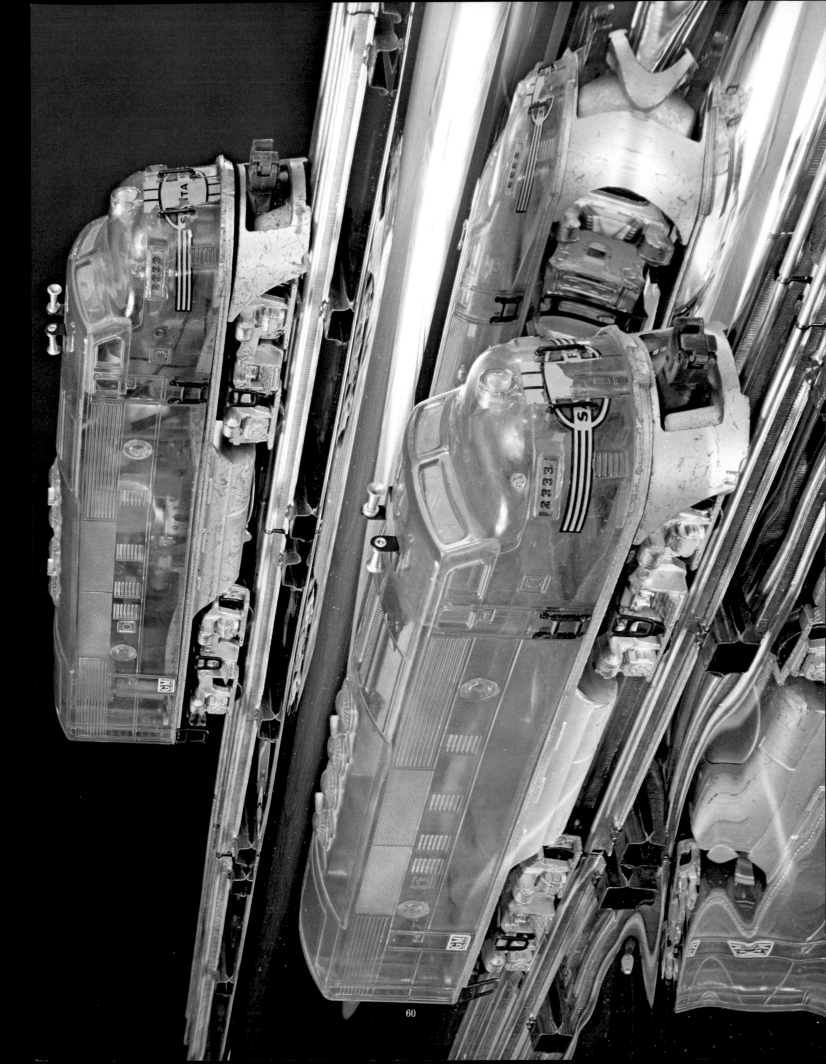

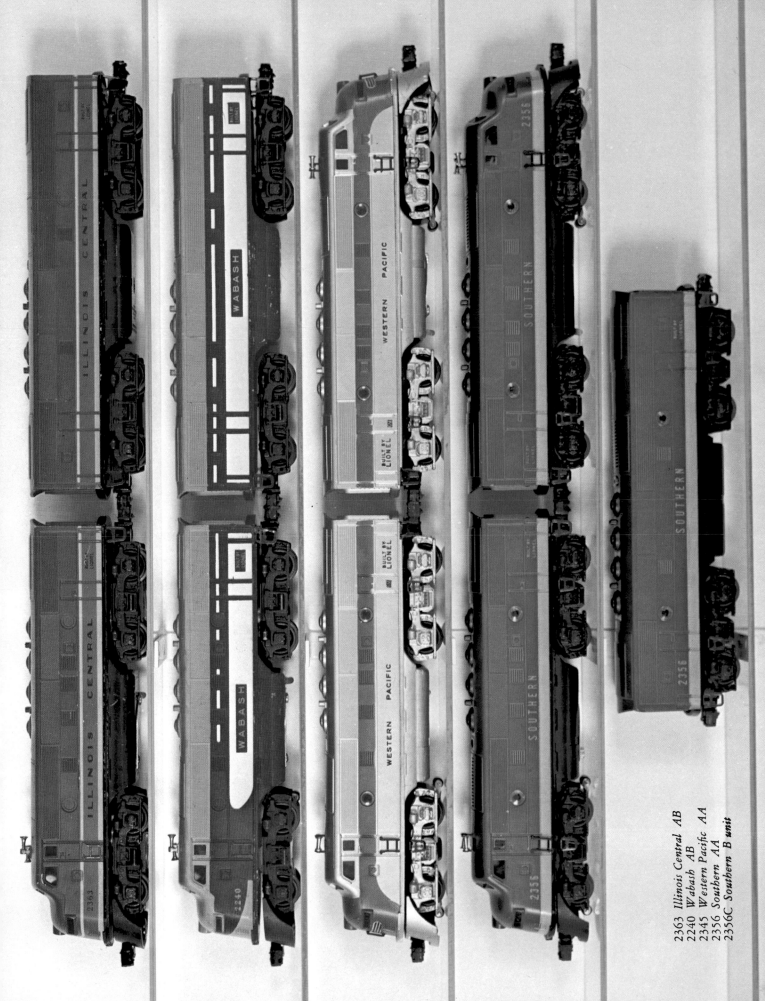

2363 *Illinois Central AB*
2240 *Wabash AB*
2345 *Western Pacific AA*
2356 *Southern AA*
2356C *Southern B unit*

2321[A]  Lackawanna FM Trainmaster

2321[B]  Lackawanna FM Trainmaster

2331[A]  Virginian FM Trainmaster

2331[C]  Virginian FM Trainmaster

2322[A]  Virginian FM Trainmaster

2341  Jersey Central FM Trainmaster

(B) Yellow body with black stripe. Question as to existence. Confirmation requested. **NRS**

(C) Same as (A), but decal number and logo on cab sides under windows rather than on both ends. Ambrose comment. **215 275 325 475**

**2328 BURLINGTON** 1955-56, GP-7 Road Switcher, 0-27, silver body with black lettering, red frame and handrails, words and emblem rubber-stamped, operating couplers both ends, magnetraction, three-position E-unit, light at both ends, horn. **80 125 200 300**

**2329 VIRGINIAN** 1958-59, GE EL-C Rectifier electric, blue body with yellow stripe, lettering, handrail and frame, heat-stamped, single metal pantograph, operating couplers both ends, magnetraction, three-position E-unit, light both ends, single vertical motor, pickup, horn, wiring easily adapted for overhead catenary operation, illustrated page 32.
**150 225 325 475**

**2330 PENNSYLVANIA** 1950, GG-1 Electric, green with five gold stripes and red Keystone decal, five stripes rubber-stamped, three twin metal pantographs, coil-operated couplers at both ends, magnetraction, three-position E-unit, light at both ends, twin vertical motors, horn, wiring easily changed for overhead catenary operation, excellent runner.
**225 325 450 650**

**2331 VIRGINIAN** 1955-58, FM Trainmaster, rubber-stamped lettering and end crisscross,[1] operating couplers at both ends, magnetraction, three-position E-unit, light at both ends, twin vertical motors, horn, excellent runner.

(A) 1955, yellow body with black stripe and gold lettering.
**300 400 550 750**

(B) 1956-58, yellow body with blue stripe and yellow lettering.
**275 350 425 600**

(C) 1957, same as (B), but dull blue stripe **300 375 450 700**

**2332 PENNSYLVANIA** 1947-49, GG-1 Electric, five stripes rubber-stamped, twin metal pantographs, operating couplers both ends, no magnetraction, three-position E-unit, light at both ends, single-angle mounted motor, AC vibrator box horn, wiring easily adapted for overhead catenary operation, hard to find with stripes and lettering in good condition[2].

(A) Very dark green (almost black) body with silver stripes, Keystone is rubber-stamped. **250 325 450 625**

(B) Dark green body with gold stripes, Keystone decal. **150 200 250 350**

(C) Flat black body with gold stripes, Keystone decal. **250 350 600 900**

(D) Flat black body with silver stripes, Keystone rubber-stamped.
**250 375 650 1000**

**2333 F-3 AA units,** 1948-49, screened roof vent, open portholes with lenses, grab-irons on nose, ladder on cab door, coil-operated couplers on cab ends, dummy middle couplers, no magnetraction, three-position E-unit, light in both units, twin horizontal motors, horn.

(A) **SANTA FE,** Santa Fe war bonnet passenger paint scheme, silver body with red cab, nose and stripe, yellow and black trim, black heat-stamped lettering, silver frame and trucks. **90 150 200 300**

(B) **NEW YORK CENTRAL,** dark gray body with gray center stripe outlined with white trim, rubber-stamped trim, heat-stamped lettering, red and white GM decal on rear side door, gray frame and trucks, this item is catalogued as #2333 but it is referred to in the service manual as #2334; since the engine number-boards show 2333 we use that number.
**100 175 250 350**

(C) 1948, same as (B), but rubber-stamped lettering. **100 175 250 350**

(D) Same as (B), but GM decal is black and white. Schwartzel Collection.
**100 175 250 350**

(E) SANTA FE, clear body with Santa Fe nose decal and red and white GM decal, a few of these were made for display use. **NRS**

(F) Same as (A), but black not silver body, shown in 1948 catalogue but not made. **Not Manufactured**

(G) Same as (E), no striping on side, paste-on road name on side. Lower Collection. **750**

(H) Same as (A), but red and white GM decals are above "BUILT BY LIONEL" at rear of cab, not on rear side doors, rubber-stamped Santa Fe lettering. We would appreciate reader ownership reports so we can evaluate how common or rare this version is. Breslin, Michel, Uptegraft and Algozzini Collections. **NRS**

2333C F-3B unit not made but a 2343C looks like it. **Not Manufactured**

**2334** Number listed in Service Manual for 2333(B)

**2337 WABASH** 1958, GP-7 Road Switcher, 0-27, blue and gray body with white stripes and lettering, black frame and handrails, heat-stamped[2] lettering, dummy couplers at both ends, magnetraction, three-position E-unit, light at both ends, horn. Arpino comment. **90 140 200 275**

**2338 MILWAUKEE** 1955-56, GP 7 Road Switcher, catalogued as both 0 and 0-27, black and orange body with white and/or black lettering, black frame and handrails, operating couplers at both ends, magnetraction, three-position E-unit, light at each end, horn.

(A) Orange translucent plastic shell that is painted black, unpainted orange band goes completely around shell, decal does not adhere well to orange shell, the orange plastic of the shell is very shiny, black lettering; believed to have been made for Sears. **500 700 1000 1500**

(B) Orange translucent plastic shell that is painted black both inside and out, orange band goes as far as cab and starts again after cab, black lettering on orange band, white lettering on orange area.
**100 150 225 300**

(C) Black plastic shell painted with dull orange band that goes as far as cab and starts again after cab, black lettering on orange band, white lettering on black area. **75 100 150 200**

(D) Same as (C), but "BUILT BY LIONEL" missing from orange stripe and Milwaukee logo on cab is white on black background. Heid Collection.
**NRS**

**2339 WABASH** 1957, GP-7 Road Switcher, blue and gray body with white stripes and lettering, black frame and handrails, heat-stamped [3] lettering, operating couplers at both ends, magnetraction, three-position E-unit, light at both ends. **90 140 200 300**

**2340 PENNSYLVANIA** 1955, GG-1, Electric, five gold stripes, red Keystone decal, stripe rubber-stamped, lettering heat-stamped, three twin metal pantographs, coil-operated couplers at both ends, magnetraction, three-position E-unit, light at both ends, twin vertical motors, horn, wiring easily changed for overhead catenary operation, excellent runner[4].

(A) Tuscan red, special Pennsylvania paint scheme used on a few GG-1s for the "Congressional" and the "Senator",[1] shown in the 1955 catalogue as #2340-1.
**250 325 450 625**

(B) Dark green, standard Pennsylvania paint scheme for freight and passenger service, shown in the 1955 catalogue as 2340-25.
**225 300 425 600**

**2341 JERSEY CENTRAL** 1956, FM Trainmaster, orange body with blue stripe and roof, white heat-stamped lettering, different spacing between "Jersey" and "Central" on each side, operating couplers at both ends, magnetraction, three-position E-unit, light at both ends, twin vertical motors, horn, excellent runner, came with orange decal as well as white. Ambrose comment.

(A) High gloss orange. Rubin observation. **500 650 800 1000**

(B) Dull orange. **400 500 600 900**

**2343 SANTA FE** 1950-52, F-3 AA units, Santa Fe war bonnet passenger paint scheme, silver body with red cab, nose and stripe, yellow and black trim, black heat-stamped [2] lettering, rubber-stamped [2] top and side stripes, silver frame and trucks, screened roof vents, open portholes with lenses, grab-irons on nose, ladder on cab door, coil-operated couplers on cab ends, dummy middle couplers, magnetraction, three-position E-unit, light in both units, twin horizontal motors, horn, excellent runner. **100 150 200 350**

**2343C SANTA FE** 1950-55, F-3 B unit, dummy B unit, silver body with red, yellow and black trim.

(A) 1950-52 screen roof vents, matches 2343. **40 65 90 125**

(B) 1953-55 louver roof vents, matches 2353. **40 65 90 125**

**2344 NEW YORK CENTRAL** 1950-52, F-3 AA units.

(A) Dark gray body with gray center stripe outlined with white trim, rubber-stamped trim with heat-stamped lettering,[2] gray frame and trucks, screened roof vents, open portholes with lenses, grab-irons on nose, ladder on cab door, coil-operated couplers on cab ends, dummy middle couplers,

[1] Silk-screened words and end criss-cross, words are slightly higher on repro-duction bodies.

[2] Silk-screened on reproduction bodies.

[3] Silk-screened or decal on repainted bodies

[4] Refer to **The Remarkable GG-1** by Karl Zimmermann, Quadrant Press Inc.

[1] Silk-screened words and end criss-cross, words are slightly higher on repro-duction bodies.

[2] Silk-screened on reproduction bodies.

2339  Wasbash  GP-7

2347  Chesapeake & Ohio  GP-7

2346  Boston and Maine  GP-9

2346  Boston and Maine  [Preproduction sample]

2350[B]  New Haven G.E.  EP-5

2365  Chesapeake & Ohio  GP-7

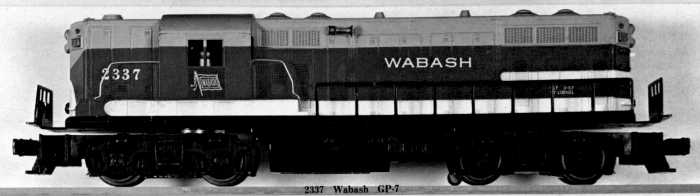

2337  Wabash  GP-7

2328  Burlington  GP-7

2338  Milwaukee Road  GP-7

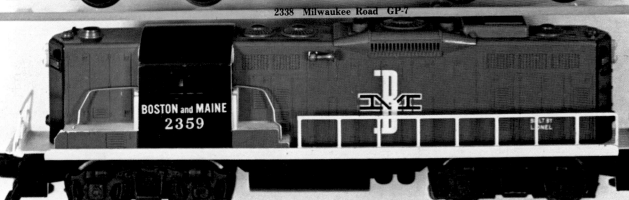

2359  Boston and Maine  GP-9

magnetraction, three-position E-unit, light in both units, twin horizontal motors, horn, excellent runner.                125 200 275 400

(B) Same as (A), but decals for GM logo are orange and white, as pictured in 1952 catalogue, pp. 18-19. Algozzini Collection.                **NRS**

**2344C NEW YORK CENTRAL** 1950-55, F-3 B unit, dummy B unit, dark gray body with gray center stripe and white trim.

(A) 1950-52, screen roof vents, matches 2344.          60  90 125 175

(B) 1953-55, louver roof vents, matches 2354.          60  90 125 175

**2345 WESTERN PACIFIC** 1952, F-3 AA units, silver and orange body with black heat-stamped lettering,[2] silver frame and trucks, screened roof vents, open portholes with lenses, grab-irons on nose, ladder on cab door, coil-operated couplers on cab ends, dummy middle couplers, magnetraction, three-position E-unit, light in both units, twin horizontal motors, horn, excellent runner, no B unit made. Substantial premium for fresh and bright silver paint.                200 300 450 650

**2346 BOSTON & MAINE** 1965-67, GP-9 Road Switcher, heat-stamped lettering, operating couplers at both ends, magnetraction, three-position E-unit, headlight, horn.

(A) Glossy blue body, black cab, white trim, lettering, frame and handrails.
                                                         75 100 150 200

(B) Black body, red ends, silver and red heat-stamped lettering, black MPC frame, without GP-9 roof blister, pre-production sample made after 1970. Listed here for user convenience. Eddins Collection.                **NRS**

**2347 CHESAPEAKE & OHIO** 1962, uncatalogued, GP-7 Road Switcher, made for Sears Roebuck, blue body with yellow heat-stamped lettering, frame and handrails, operating couplers at both ends, magnetraction, three-position E-unit, headlight, horn, very hard to find.
                                                        600 900 1400 2000

See also Uncatalogued Sets.

**2348 MINNEAPOLIS & ST. LOUIS** 1958-59, GP-9 Road Switcher, red body with blue roof and white stripe, heat-stamped lettering, black frame and handrails, operating couplers at both ends, magnetraction, three-position E-unit, headlight, horn.

(A) As described above.                          100 150 225 300

(B) Same as (A), but black-painted rectifier base. (Factory original.) Rohlfing Collection.                **NRS**

**2349 NORTHERN PACIFIC** 1959-60, GP-9 Road Switcher, black body with gold and red striping, heat-stamped [2] gold leaf lettering, gold frame and handrails, operating couplers at both ends, magnetraction, three-position E-unit, headlight, horn.

(A) Gold heat-stamped lettering, as above.          100 150 225 300

(B) Gold heat-stamped "BUILT BY LIONEL", but gold rubber-stamped "NORTHERN PACIFIC" and "2349". Fleming Collection.
                                                        100 150 225 300

### General Electric EP-5 Rectifiers

**2350 NEW HAVEN** 1956-58, G.E. EP-5 Rectifier Electric, black plastic body with heat-stamped [3] lettering, white and orange stripes, twin metal pantographs, operating couplers at both ends, magnetraction, three-position E-unit, light at both ends, single vertical motor, horn, wiring easily changed for overhead catenary operation.

(A) Gray "N", orange "H", painted nose trim. Gray New Haven lettering.
                                                        100 200 275 400

(B) Orange "N", black "H", painted nose trim, orange New Haven lettering.                                    200 350 500 700

(C) Same as (A), but nose trim is decal.            90 125 175 250

(D) Same as (B), but nose trim is decal.           200 300 400 600

(E) Same as (C), but orange and white paint, stripes go completely through door.                                           100 150 225 300

(F) Same as (C), but body is yellow plastic painted black. Rohlfing Collection.
                                                        100 200 275 400

**2351 MILWAUKEE ROAD** 1957-58, G.E. EP-5 Rectifier Electric, yellow unpainted plastic body [4] with heat-stamped lettering, black roof and red stripe, twin metal pantographs, operating couplers at both ends, magnetraction, three-position E-unit, light at both ends, single vertical motor, horn, wiring easily changed for overhead catenary operation.
                                                        150 225 275 400

**2352 PENNSYLVANIA** 1958-59, GE. EP-5 Rectifier Electric, tuscan red or brown body with single gold stripe, heat-stamped 6 gold leaf [2] lettering, twin metal pantographs, operating couplers, magnetraction, three-position E-unit, light both ends, single vertical motor, horn, wiring easily changed for overhead catenary operation.          175 250 350 500

**2353 SANTA FE** 1953-55, F-3 AA units, Santa Fe war bonnet passenger paint scheme, silver body with red cab, nose and stripe, yellow and black trim, black heat-stamped [1] lettering, rubber-stamped [1] top and side stripes, silver frame and trucks, louvered roof vents, open portholes with lenses, ladder on cab door, coil-operated couplers on cab ends, dummy middle couplers, magnetraction, three-position E-unit, light in both units, twin horizontal motors, horn, excellent runner, for B unit see 2343C.

(A) Notch cut out below coupler at bottom of pilot, 1953 production. LaVoie Collection.                                   100 150 225 300

(B) Smooth bottom on pilot, 1954-55 production.   100 150 225 300

**2353C SANTA FE** F-3 B unit, not made; for B unit to match 2353 see #2343C (B).                                          **Not Manufactured**

**2354 NEW YORK CENTRAL** 1953-55, F-3 AA units, dark gray body, gray center stripe outlined with white trim, rubber-stamped trim with heat-stamped [1] lettering, gray frame with gray trucks, louvered roof vents, open portholes with lenses, ladder on cab door, coil-operated couplers on cab ends, dummy middle couplers, magnetraction, three-position E-unit, light in both units, twin horizontal motors, horn, excellent runner.
                                                        110 175 250 350

**2354C NEW YORK CENTRAL** F-3 B unit not made; for B unit to match 2354 see 2344C (B).                            **Not Manufactured**

**2355 WESTERN PACIFIC** 1953, F-3 AA units, silver and orange body with black heat-stamped [1] lettering, silver frame and trucks, louvered roof vents, open portholes with lenses, ladder on cab door, coil-operated couplers on cab ends, dummy middle couplers, magnetraction, three-position E-unit, light in both units, twin horizontal motors, horn, excellent runner, no B unit made. Substantial premium for fresh and bright silver paint.

(A) As described above.                          200 300 450 650

(B) Nose decal on dummy unit. Blotner Collection.   200 300 450 650

See also Factory Errors.

**2356 SOUTHERN** 1954-56, F-3 AA units, green body with light gray lower stripe and yellow trim and lettering, lettering is rubber-stamped, [2] black frame and trucks, louvered roof vents, open portholes with lenses, ladder on cab door, coil-operated couplers on cab ends, dummy middle couplers, magnetraction, three-position E-unit, light in both units, twin horizontal motors, horn, excellent runner.          175 250 350 500

**2356C SOUTHERN** 1954-56, F-3 B unit, dummy B unit, green body with gray lower stripe and yellow trim, matches 2356.   75 100 150 200

**2358 GREAT NORTHERN** 1959-60, G.E. EP-5 Rectifier Electric, orange and green body with yellow stripes and lettering, lettering is heat-stamped, [2] twin metal pantographs, operating couplers at both ends, magnetraction, three-position E-unit, light at both ends, single vertical motor, horn, wiring easily changed for overhead catenary operation. Original GN end decals are almost always flaking.          175 250 350 500

**2359 BOSTON & MAINE** 1961-62, GP-9 Road Switcher, flat blue body, black cab and white trim, lettering, frame and handrails, lettering is heat-stamped, operating couplers at both ends, magnetraction, three-position E-unit, headlight, horn.          75 100 150 225

**2360 PENNSYLVANIA** 1956-58, 1961-63, GG-1 Electric, twin metal pantographs, coil-operated couplers at both ends, magnetraction, three-position E-unit, light at both ends, twin vertical motors, horn, wiring easily changed for overhead catenary operation, excellent runner.

(A) 1956, tuscan body with five rubber-stamped [2] gold stripes, catalogue #2360-1.                                225 450 650 900

(B) 1956-58, same as (A) but dark green body, catalogue #2360-25.
                                                        200 300 450 650

---

[2] Silk-screened on reproduction bodies.

[3] Silk-screened or decal on repainted bodies

[4] Refer to **The Remarkable GG-1** by Karl Zimmermann, Quadrant Press Inc.

[1] Silk-screened words and end criss-cross, words are slightly higher on reproduction bodies.

[2] Silk-screened on reproduction bodies.

(C) Tuscan body with single gold stripe, heat-stamped [1] lettering and numbers. This version made 1957, 1958, 1961 and 1962. Ambrose comment.     **175 275 425 600**

(D) Same as (C), but decal [2] lettering and numbers, 1963 production. Ambrose comment.     **200 300 450 650**

(E) Same as (C), but rubber-stamped lettering and numbers, probably pre-production sample.     **NRS**

(F) Black body with one large gold stripe, decal lettering, rough surface on body casting shows through paint, repainted and lettered by Lionel for William Vagell.     **NRS**

(G) Same as (C), but rubber-stamped lettering and stripe, early production. Tom Collection.     **NRS**

(H) Same as (A), but very glossy tuscan finish, two pieces known to exist. Rubin Collection.     **NRS**

(I) Semi-gloss medium chocolate brown-painted body, five rubber-stamped stripes, rubber-stamped lettering, large Keystone decals applied over stripes as used for single-striped version. Probably transition piece; scarce. Bratspis Collection.     **— — 800 —**

**2363 ILLINOIS CENTRAL** 1955-56, F-3 AB units, brown body with orange stripe and yellow trim, rubber-stamped [2] lettering and lines, black frame, trucks, and lettering, louvered roof vents, filled in portholes, operating coupler on front of A unit, all other couplers are dummys, magnetraction, three-position E-unit, light in A unit, twin vertical motors, horn, excellent runner.

(A) Black lettering.     **175 250 350 500**

(B) Brown lettering. Degano Collection.     **225 325 450 650**

**2365 CHESAPEAKE & OHIO** 1962-63, GP-7 Road Switcher, blue body with yellow frame, handrails and lettering, heat-stamped [1] lettering, dummy couplers at both ends, magnetraction, three-position E-unit, light, no horn, no battery box fuel tank.     **80 125 175 250**

**2367 WABASH** 1955, F-3 AB units, gray and blue body with white side panels and trim, yellow heat-stamped [1] lettering, blue frame, black trucks, louvered roof vents, filled-in portholes, operating coupler on front of A unit, all other couplers are dummys, magnetraction, three-position E-unit, light in A unit, twin vertical motors, horn, excellent runner.     **175 300 400 600**

**2368 BALTIMORE & OHIO** 1956, F-3 AB units, blue unpainted plastic body with white, black and yellow trim, rubber stamped lettering, black frame and trucks, louvered roof vents, filled in portholes, operating coupler on front of A unit, all other couplers are dummys, magnetraction, three-position E-unit, light in A unit, twin vertical motors, horn, excellent runner.     **225 350 500 750**

**2373 CANADIAN PACIFIC** 1957, F-3 AA units, gray and maroon with yellow trim and lettering, heat-stamped [1] top and sides, black frame and trucks, louvered roof vents, filled in portholes, operating couplers on cab ends, dummy middle couplers, magnetraction, three-position E-unit, light in both units, twin vertical motors, horn, no B unit made, excellent runner.

(A) Black frame.     **300 575 650 950**

(B) Silver frame. Trentacoste Collection. Additional reports requested.     **NRS**

**2378 MILWAUKEE ROAD** 1956, F-3 AB units, gray plastic body with orange lower stripe trimmed in yellow, yellow heat-stamped trim and lettering, louvered roof vents, filled in portholes, operating coupler on front of A unit, all other couplers are dummys, magnetraction, three-position E-unit, light in A unit, twin vertical motors, horn, excellent runner.

(A) Yellow stripe along roof line.     **325 500 650 950**

(B) Without yellow stripe along roof line.     **275 425 575 850**

(C) A unit without stripe, B unit with yellow stripe along roof line. This is a legitimate pair.     **200 300 400 600**

**2379 RIO GRANDE** 1957-58, F-3 AB units, yellow body with silver roof and lower stripe, black trim and lettering, green panel in front of windshield, black frame and trucks, heat-stamped trim and lettering, decal nose, louvered roof vents, filled in portholes, operating coupler on front of A unit, all other couplers are dummys, magnetraction, three-position E-unit, light in A unit, twin vertical motors, horn, excellent runner.     **175 250 350 500**

See also Factory Errors.

**2383 SANTA FE** 1958-66, F-3 AA units, Santa Fe war bonnet passenger paint scheme, silver body with red cab, nose and stripe, yellow and black trim, black heat-stamped [1] lettering, rubber-stamped [2] top and side stripes, silver frame and black trucks, louvered roof vents, filled in portholes, operating couplers on cab ends, dummy middle couplers, magnetraction, three-position E-unit, light in both units, twin vertical motors, horn, excellent runner, for B unit see 2243C.

(A) Red cab, nose and stripe.     **85 125 200 275**

(B) Orange red cab, nose and stripe. Lebo Collection. Additional reports requested.     **NRS**

**2383C SANTA FE** F-3 B unit not made, for B unit to match 2383 see 2243C.

    **Not Manufactured**

**2550 BALTIMORE AND OHIO** 1957-58, Budd RDC baggage-mail car, dummy unit to match #400, silver body with blue lettering, operating couplers at both ends. Was sold separately and came with 400 and 2559 in 1958 set. Lord comment.     **120 200 250 350**

**2559 BALTIMORE AND OHIO** 1957-58, Budd RDC passenger car, dummy unit to match #400, silver body with blue lettering, operating couplers at both ends. Was sold separately with second 2559 in 1957 set; Lord comment.     **100 150 200 250**

**3360 BURRO** Crane, 1956-57, self-propelled operating crane, yellow body with red lettering, dummy couplers at both ends, reverse lever on side can be operated by hand or by a track trip, a very interesting operating unit.

(A) Yellow boom.     **60 110 175 250**

(B) Yellow boom with small decal "danger".     **80 150 225 300**

(C) Brown cab, probable factory prototype. Bohn observation.     **NRS**

**3927 LIONEL LINES** 1956-60, track cleaning car, orange body with blue lettering. Motor drives cleaning brush and does not drive wheels. Hence unit must be pulled by strong engine. A complete unit has two bottles, a brush and a wiper. Replacement brushes and wipers available. Original bottles marked "LIONEL".

(A) As described above.     **25 60 100 125**

(B) With red running light. Kaim Collection. Additional sightings requested.     **NRS**

(C) Unpainted dark green plastic body, white rubber-stamped lettering. The plastic pellets used in the injection mold machines are available in different colors. Lionel was consistent in using the same color pellets for its production runs. This unusual car was likely produced by the factory before its major production run, to compare alternative color schemes. Otten Collection.     **NRS**

**4810 SOUTHERN PACIFIC** 1954, FM Trainmaster, black body, red stripe, preproduction prototype, La Rue Shempp Collection, illustrated in this text; general design utilized by Fundimensions in 1979 for 8951.     **NRS**

**6220 SANTA FE** 1949-50, uncatalogued as SANTA FE. Catalogued but never made as LIONEL (1949), and NEW YORK CENTRAL (1950) NW-2 Switcher, 0-27 versions of #622, first magnetraction engine, black body with white lettering, die-cast frame, coil-operated couplers at both ends, three-position E-unit, light at both ends, Type I motor, Type I pickup, no horn, operating bell, excellent runner.

(A) **SANTA FE** with large GM decal on cab, 1949. Ely observation.

    **90 150 200 275**

(B) **SANTA FE** with small GM decal on lower front side of motor hood, 1950, no weight in cab. Ely observation. Came in set 1457B in 1949. Rohlfing observation.     **90 150 200 275**

(C) Same as (B), but weight cast in cab frame, late 1950. Ely observation.

    **90 150 200 275**

(D) **LIONEL** (1949) catalogued but not made.     **Not Manufactured**

(E) **NEW YORK CENTRAL** (1950), catalogued but not made.

    **Not Manufactured**

**6250 SEABOARD** 1954-55, NW-2 Switcher, 0-27, blue and orange body with blue and white lettering, die-cast frame, coil-operated couplers at both ends, magnetraction, three-position E-unit, light at both ends, Type I pickup, no horn, excellent runner.

(A) 1954, SEABOARD is a decal with closely spaced lettering. Foss comment.     **100 150 225 300**

(B) 1955, SEABOARD is rubber-stamped with widely spaced lettering. Foss comment.     **90 125 175 250**

---

[1] Silk-screened words and end criss-cross, words are slightly higher on reproduction bodies.

[2] Silk-screened on reproduction bodies.

---

[1] Silk-screened words and end criss-cross, words are slightly higher on reproduction bodies.

[2] Silk-screened on reproduction bodies.

SO RARE

Four surviving factory prototypes:
2321 Lackawanna Trainmaster with screen roof vents
4810 Southern Pacific Trainmaster
2028 Union Pacific GP-7
8561 Union Pacific Caboose

Not so rare but hard to get are the 2321 maroon top Lackawanna
Trainmaster and two TCA special 6464 Box Cars

Shempp Collection

2329 *Virginian Rectifier*
2358 *Great Northern*
2352 *Pennsylvania*
2351 *Milwaukee Road*
2350 *New Haven*

# Chapter III
# BOXCARS

By Roland LaVoie

Like the real railroads, Lionel's railway operations used the boxcar and its variants as the most common rolling stock in its roster. These cars were made in so many variations that the only way to classify a Lionel boxcar is to define it as any car with a roof which is not a passenger car or caboose! These cars were made in all kinds of colors and featured a myriad of railroad markings. No Lionel railroad could be complete without at least a few of these cars obediently following their locomotives in freight trains.

The earliest "pure" boxcars were essentially all-metal prewar carry-overs equipped with postwar trucks and couplers. Soon after these first cars were produced, Lionel updated its lineup of boxcars with three basic body types. One type, used in Scout and other inexpensive sets, was the short type with non-opening doors. These boxcars are sometimes referred to as "plug-door" boxcars, but they are not really plug door cars at all. (See the article by Norman Anderson for definitions and details.) Another type used a short body which had opening doors. The third type, easily the best of them, was the 6464-type boxcar, which was quite a bit longer than the other two types and had opening doors. These boxcars were highly realistic; they featured many different colors and road markings. So complex is the 6464 series that train scholars have identified several **hundred** variations!

All these cars were modified heavily as needed for different uses. Some had a bank slot added to the roof. Others had clear plastic inserts and circular grates added for the fanciful mint and aquarium cars. The 6464-type was changed into a double-door "automobile" car. Mechanisms of all descriptions were fitted, shoehorned or crammed into their interiors. One exotic type of boxcar had a pointed roof which parted to launch a missile, cannon shell or helicopter. Another type contained a big generator and had portholes on its sides. Workmen popped out of spring-loaded doors to survey the area or toss mail sacks out the door.

The stock cars followed a similar evolution. Three basic types were produced in the postwar years. The long, well-detailed 6356 two-level stock car made its debut in 1954. Several different road names followed in subsequent years. Lionel also produced a much shorter stock car with non-opening doors for operating purposes; this car was found in giraffe and sheriff-outlaw variations. Finally, Lionel made a short stock car which had opening doors; this car was used for the operating cattle car as well as several non-operating cars.

These cars varied in a similar fashion to their boxcar analogues. The 6356 was modified for the operating horse car and the poultry dispatch cars. One of the poultry cars featured a spring-operated "chicken sweeper" who swept the floor of the car when the door popped open. The horse and circus cars were changed to accommodate single doors and swing-down livestock ramps.

The refrigerator cars were not made in very many variations or numbers. The milk cars, of course, were the most numerous; they had opening hatches and sprung doors. A non-operating version of the short white milk car was also produced. A longer 0 Gauge milk car featured an entirely different method of construction; the car roof and ends were cast in one piece, while the base and sides were separate. It is a pity that the design of Lionel's 6672 refrigerator car was not produced earlier in the postwar years, because it was a rather handsome car. As it was, Lionel only made Railway Express and Santa Fe versions of this refrigerator car. It was made with plug doors and little metal mechanism plates, and it was extremely well detailed. The roof and ends were one piece, while the base and sides were another piece.

It is no accident that the listings for the box, stock and reefer cars are so long. Lionel produced a large number of these cars because they offered an opportunity to use real railroad markings better than any other type of car. They were always popular with the train-buying public, but acquiring a complete collection of them is a task requiring extreme patience - not to mention extensive financial resources! With the exception of the flatcars, no other type of rolling stock served Lionel so well for so long.

## LOOKING AT THE LIONEL OPERATING MILK CARS
### By David Fleming
### Art: Jerry Schuchard

Ask a person who remembers a childhood of the early and middle fifties what he or she remembers about Lionel trains, and you will likely be told one of two things: the "little white pills you would drop down the stack to make the engine smoke" or "the little white car that delivered the milk cans". That "little white car" was the Lionel Automatic Refrigerated Milk Car, which became the most popular accessory ever made by the Lionel Corporation. Although it was produced in such huge quantities that it is common today and sometimes overlooked by collectors, in its heyday the Automatic Refrigerated Milk Car was "most everybody's grocery-getter", delivering its contents on demand with the simple touch of a small red button.

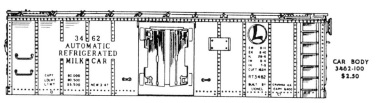

The 1947-49 Milk Car had metal doors.

Despite the omnipresence of the milk car even today on train sellers' tables, certain variations of the car are not very well known at all. In a recent examination of the milk cars in my own train collection, I turned up an early 1947 brass-base mechanism model which had not been described by anyone up to that time. For that matter, Lionel never documented the first form of this car, the 3462 early production model, or the last form of the car, the 3482, in any of its service literature. Therefore, a close examination of all the varieties of this car can turn up some interesting variations.

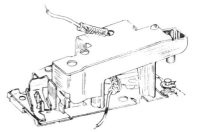

The 1947 car had the Type I brass base mechanism.  J. Schuchard illustration.

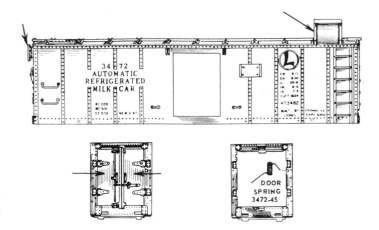

The 1950 model featured a new plastic door assembly.

The Automatic Refrigerated Milk Car was introduced in 1947 with a 3462 number designation and a clear plastic body painted cream, with a first-run variation in glossy cream paint. The car was equipped with a brass-base mechanism, Type I, from which the milkman slid out on a small square slide. The brass base was attached to the car frame by three (and later, four) tabs which fit through slots. This was probably the design concocted by inventor Richard G. Smith, a carpenter in upstate New York, who invented many of the accessories marketed by both Lionel and American Flyer. Other accessories credited to Smith are the Lionel barrel car, log dump car, log loader, icing station and forklift platform. For American Flyer, Smith invented a flatcar which unloaded a vehicle and a baggage car which picked up or dropped off a mail sack.

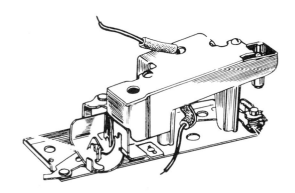

The 1948 car had a revised mechanism which we call Type II.

In 1948, the milk car received its most significant design change of its nine-year run with the Type II mechanism, which was made of parts less delicate than the original brass-base model, with fewer folds and shapes. Thicker metal was used, and the overall design was simpler. Instead of being guided by a square slide, the milkman now pivoted out of the car on a swinging plate. The sweep arm which moves the man out of the car now had a large triangular hole behind him. This version kept its 3462 number designation; it retained its original coil couplers.

In 1949, when Lionel introduced magnetic couplers for most of its rolling stock, the milk car number changed to 3472. Additional holes of no significance are found in the frame, and when one compares this frame to the 3464 Operating Boxcar, it is apparent that 3464 frame blanks were used to form the frames of the 1949 and 1950 milk cars. The first versions of the 3472 retained the short hatch on the roof and the aluminum doors of the 3462, but the car body was either painted eggshell or, more commonly, was made of unpainted white plastic.

In 1950, the milk car received the most visible changes of its evolution. It had new plastic doors (along with a new method of attaching them to the body), a larger loading hatch and a slightly revised mechanism, Type III. The Type III mechanism used a coil spring return to pull the man back inside the car and better load the next can out of the chute leading from the loading hatch. The sweep arm to which the man was attached now had an L-shaped slot which replaced the triangular hole. Additionally, a cast boss was formed on the can rack to hold the can sweep arm, which had been previously riveted to the solenoid bracket. Lionel also began the production of plastic doors which clipped onto the body rather than being folded onto it. These plastic doors were so easily broken or lost that they currently represent one of the big markets for replacement parts manufactured today. Changed along with the doors was the frame, which now had side cutouts instead of side indentations. These allowed the car frame to clear the door frame. It is of minor note that some of these frame alterations appear as variations of the 6454 boxcars, which used the same frame blanks.

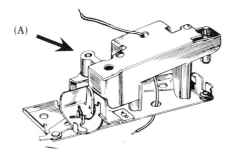

The 1950 mechanism with the new cast boss to hold the can sweep arm (A).

In 1951, the milk car ran unchanged from the preceding year. It also reached the apex of its popularity; the incredible total of 180,000 units were sold at $11.50 per copy. Lionel earned about a million dollars from gross sales of nearly $2,700,000, and inventor Smith, who earned two percent of the wholesale gross, realized a tidy $20,000 royalty from Lionel - a considerable sum in those days. In the 1951 catalogue, a full page was devoted to the milk car, and in thousands of American homes, the milkman, immaculately dressed in white, was "getting his job done". In these postwar years, Lionel

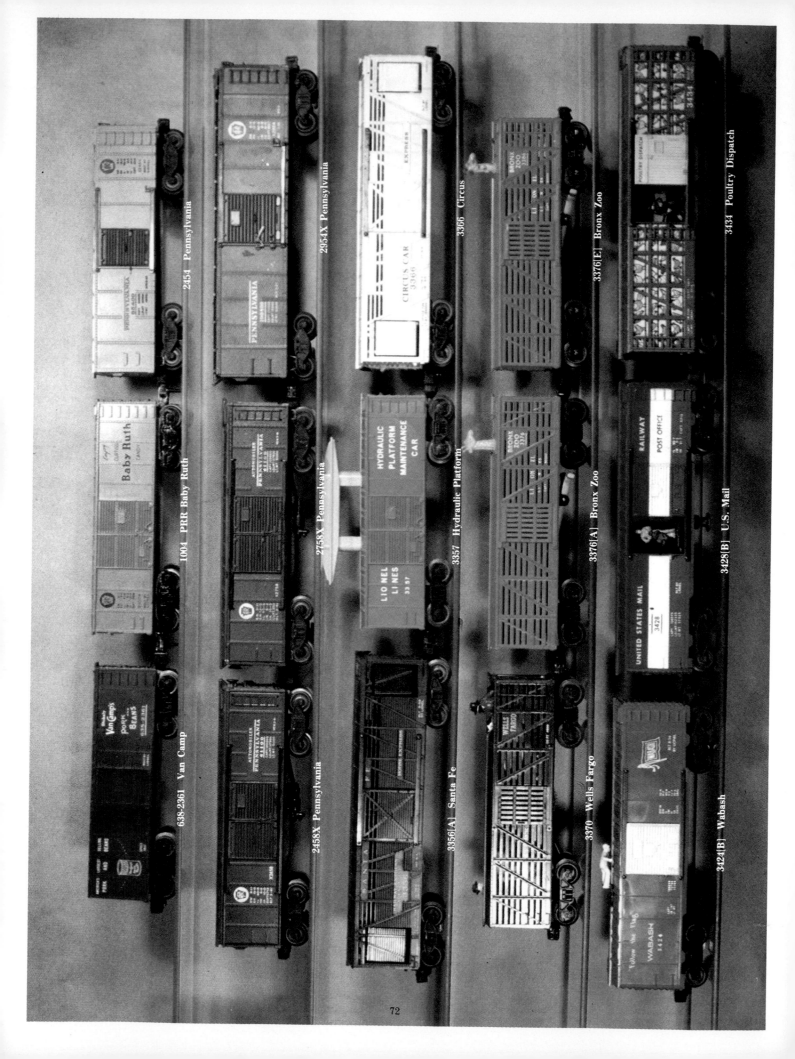

2454 Pennsylvania

2954X Pennsylvania

3366 Circus

3376[E] Bronx Zoo

3434 Poultry Dispatch

1004 PRR Baby Ruth

2758X Pennsylvania

3357 Hydraulic Platform

3376[A] Bronx Zoo

3428[B] U.S. Mail

638-2361 Van Camp

2458X Pennsylvania

3356[A] Santa Fe

3370 Wells Fargo

3424[B] Wabash

3462 Milk Car

3472 Milk Car

3484-25 A.T. & S.F.

3494-275 State of Maine

3530[D] Electro Mobile Power

3454 PRR Merchandise

3464X N.Y.C.

3484 Pennsylvania

3494-150 M-P-Eagle

3494-625 SOO

3435 Traveling Aquarium

3464 A.T. & S.F.

3474 Western Pacific

3494-1[A] N Y C Pacemaker

3494-550 Monon

# LIONEL 3462-72-82 MILK CAR
## VARIATION CHRONOLOGY
### by David Fleming

| YEAR | 1947 | 1948 | 1949 | 1950 | 1951 | 1952-53 | 1954 | 1955 |
|---|---|---|---|---|---|---|---|---|
| **CAR NUMBER / BODY** | 3462 | | | 3472 | | | 3482 | |
| COLOR | Gloss | Flat White or Cream Paint | | White or Eggshell Plastic | | | White Plastic | |
| DOORS | Aluminum | | | White or Eggshell Plastic | | | White Plastic Notched Opening | |
| HATCH | Small Painted Cream | | | Large White or Eggshell Plastic | | | Large White Plastic | |
| **MISCELLANEOUS / MECHANISM** | RT 3462 | | | RT 3472 | | | RT 3482 | |
| TYPE | 1947 Type 1 | 1948 Type 2 | | 1950 Type 3 | | | 1954 Type 4 | |
| MISCELLANEOUS | Has Slide | Swing Plate Has Triangle Hole In Arm | | L-Shape Hole In Arm Boss For Can Sweep | | | Large Plunger, Removable Coil, Large Solonoid | |
| RETURN | Hair Pin Spring | | | Small Coil Spring | | | Large Coil Spring | |
| **MATERIAL / FRAME** | Brass Base | Nickel Plate Steel | | Cadmium Plate Steel | | | | |
| TYPE | 3462 Side Dents | | 3464 Operating Holes | | 3472 and 6472 | | 3482 Ribed w/ Cutouts | |
| MISCELLANEOUS / TRUCKS | Has Tab Slots | No Slots | Side Dents | Door Frame Cutouts | | | Tab & Screw Mount | |
| SIDES | Staple Sides | | | | | Bar Sides | | |
| COUPLER / MISCELLANEOUS | Coil | | Magnetic No Tabs | | | | | |
| MAJOR VARIANTS | 1947 2 Var | 1948 | 1949 | 1950-53 | | | 1954-55 | |
| CATALOG PRICE | $8.95 | $9.95 | | $11.50 | | | $10.50 | |

rode the crest of toy train technology with this "state-of-the-art" product.

Only one change was made in 1952; the staple-end metal trucks on the milk car were replaced by bar-end metal trucks. This change provides collectors with a means of differentiating the very similar cars made between 1950 and 1953.

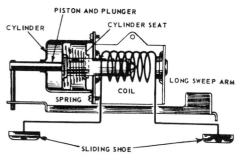

The 3662 had a new mechanism with a cylinder and piston to provide a smoother action.

In its final development, as Lionel's corporate attention was being diverted to the design of the larger 11-inch pneumatically operated 3662-1 0 Gauge milk car, the company saw fit to revise its little white marvel one more time. The Type IV mechanism employed in this revision incorporated a larger solenoid plunger, probably for a different and smoother action in the operation of the milkman. In addition, all previous versions had attached the body to the frame by means of two spring clips on the car underside. In the 1954 final revision, this method of attachment changed to the more common slot and tab on one end and screw on the other. To designate cars with these changes, the car was renumbered 3482.

In the 1954 change, Lionel had forgotten to renumber the small reporting marks on the side of the car; they remained 3472 while the large number read "3482". This oversight was corrected in the 1955 run of the 3482. Production of the small white milk car ceased after 1955 in favor of the bigger 3662-1 0 Gauge milk car, which had its own variations. This big and very attractive car came with dull brown and bright brown roofs; in its last years, it had the cheaper Timken plastic trucks instead of bar-end metal trucks.

A chart of variations is included with this article for the 1947-1955 production of the milk car. Readers are requested to write to us if any further changes are discovered.

These, then, are the developmental details of the most popular car of Lionel's operating fleet. The Automatic Refrigerated Milk Car kept many fumble-fingered youths of the 1950s busy learning the significance of the push button. It even gave Joshua Lionel Cowen himself the excuse to pretend he was a mere spectator in his own showroom. This man-boy, who had been making trains for over half a century, would enthrall himself for hours with his little white wonder, telling his customers, "Marvelous, isn't it?"

## REEFERS AND INSULATED PLUG-DOOR BOXCARS: SIMILARITIES AND DIFFERENCES

### By Norman E. Anderson

NOTE: The author is affiliated with Diesel-Electric Locomotive Services, Inc. of Meridian, Idaho.

Hobbyists who take part in the world of scale model railroading are usually very careful with the terminology they use to identify rolling stock, in keeping with the philosophy of realism they strive to achieve. The world of tin-plate railroads and toy trains is, however, not so precise at times, and misunderstandings can result when various types of rolling stock are given erroneous designations. Therefore, in an attempt to clarify terms for tinplaters, I will try to define the characteristics of two frequently mismodeled and misnamed types of cars - plug-door insulated boxcars and refrigerator cars, or "reefers".

There are some similarities between reefers and insulated plug-door boxcars in that both cars have insulated sides and ends for temperature and environment control and flush-fitting, or "plug" doors. However, reefers differ in that they have either ice bunkers or refrigeration units to keep the inside temperature low to preserve the produce, etc. being shipped in the car. Insulated plug-door boxcars do not have these features.

Basically, there are three types of reefers: (1) Original design wood-sided reefers with ice bunkers; (2) Steel smooth-sided reefers with ice bunkers; and (3) Steel smooth-sided reefers which have mechanical (diesel-driven) refrigeration units. Visually, the first two types should have plug doors and four ice hatches in the four corners of the roof. The mechanical reefer should have plug doors, louvered side doors at one end of the car on both sides (for air entry to the refrigeration unit and maintenance) and a roof exhaust stack.

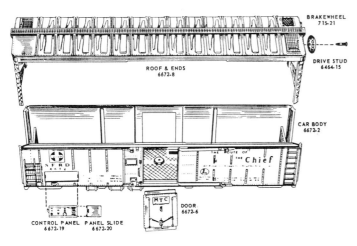

6672 Refrigerator Car.

The recent 5700 wood-sided reefers produced by Fundimensions are close to correct for Type 1 reefers, except that they lack the roof ice hatches. A check of Athearn or other H0 reefers will show this missing detail. The 6352-1 Pacific Fruit Express reefer built by Lionel (and its Fundimensions 6700 revival) is the Lionel attempt at a Type 2 reefer. This car totally misses the mark, however, since it has a standard boxcar door and no correctly positioned roof ice hatches - even though it is set up to receive ice blocks from the icing station accessory.

The 6464(T) New York Central mechanical reefer, 6572 Railway Express and 6672 Santa Fe reefers are similar to a Type 3 reefer. Louvered doors are indeed present, and the underframe-mounted items, which could be diesel fuel tanks, might qualify it as a Type 3 reefer. These reefers represent the closest Lionel gets to detailing a Type 3 reefer. As far as I can tell, Fundimensions has not duplicated this car exactly, although I notice that the 9800 Billboard Reefer Series appears to have the same underframe detail - which would be incorrect. In summary, although attempts have been made to produce reefers, these cars appear to be the most poorly reproduced examples from prototypes made by either Lionel or Fundimensions.

Insulated or plug-door boxcars have been made in various lengths, with 40, 50 and 60-foot versions being the most popular, both in single and double-door versions. Usually, these cars are equipped with some sort of inside load-restraining gates or bars. In the early days of these cars, large markings advertised these special load-protecting features, such as DF Load Dividers or DF ("Damage-Free") or PC ("Protected Cargo"). However, more recently these features have become so commonplace that mention of them is less conspicuous, if it is mentioned at all. Probably part of the confusion resulting in these cars being mistaken for reefers is brought about by the Association of American Railroads' car designation "RBL". Since the cars are different from ordinary boxcars, they carry a special designation code so that they were thrown into the general category with reefers, since both types were insulated. The "RBL" designation stands for Refrigeration Box with Load dividers, even though the cars are not actually refrigerated, just insulated. The Standard "O" "refrigerator" cars produced by Fundimensions appear to be this type of insulated boxcar, but they should not be called "reefers".

Hopefully, the foregoing explanations will clear up the problems associated with the naming of these Lionel and Fundimensions products. Even if liberties are taken with the names of these cars, one must remember that Lionel and Fundimensions, being makers of **toy** trains, should be held accountable only to a certain degree and no more.

**638-2361 VAN CAMP'S PORK & BEANS** 1962, Uncatalogued, Type II red body with white and yellow lettering, coin slot, 8-1/2" long, non-opening door, part of set 19142. Bohn and Rohlfing comments. **7  15  20  30**

**1004 PRR Baby Ruth** 1949-51, orange with blue lettering, 8" long, non-opening door, Scout trucks and couplers. Rohlfing and Breslin comments.

(A) "Baby Ruth" in solid blue lettering. **2  3  4  6**
(B) "Baby Ruth" in outlined blue lettering. **2  3  4  6**
NOTE: 2454 appears with two different road names.

**2454 PENNSYLVANIA** 1945-46, orange with black lettering, numbered "65400", 9-1/4" long.

(A) 1945, orange doors, clear shell painted orange, metal trucks with early coil couplers, reported without whirly wheels. Foss and Clark Collections. **20  30  40  60**

(B) 1946, brown door, metal trucks with late coil couplers. Foss Collection. **20  30  40  70**

(C) Same as (A), but early coil couplers. Arpino Collection. **20  30  40  60**

**X2454 BABY RUTH** 1946, orange-painted orange plastic body, brown unpainted plastic doors, "Enjoy Curtiss Baby Ruth Candy" to left of door in black script, PRR logo in black to right of door, black reporting marks: EW 9-11; EH 13-0; IL 40-6; IW 9-2; IH 10-4: CU FT 3936, X2454 BUILT BY LIONEL in black below reporting marks, one large and one small hole in

3665[B] Minuteman

3665[A] Minuteman

3619 Helicopter Reconnaissance

3672 Bosco

3662-1 Milk Car

3656 Armour

6004 Baby Ruth

4454 Baby Ruth PRR

3854 PRR Merchandise

6014[B] Bosco PRR

X6014[B] Baby Ruth

X6014[A] Baby Ruth

6014[A] Frisco

6014 Frisco

6014 Chun King

76

6024 RCA Whirlpool

6050 Lionel Savings Bank

6352-1 Pacific Fruit Express

6428 U.S. Mail

6448 Target Car

6024 Nabisco Shredded Wheat

6044 Airex

6050 Swift

6376 Lionel Circus

6445 Fort Knox Gold

6014 Wix

X6034[A] Baby Ruth PRR

6050 Libby's Tomato Juice

6356-1 NYC two level stock

6434 Poultry Dispatch

77

middle of frame, steps at corners, frame held to body by screws at corners, staple-end metal trucks, late coil couplers.

(A) Same as above.      **4   8   10   15**

(B) Silver-painted plastic body and doors, black sans-serif lettering "Baby Ruth" to right of door, PRR logo to right of door, reporting marks below PRR logo, bar-end metal trucks with late coil couplers. Operating merchandise car with five black cubes stamped "BABY RUTH" and one red cube stamped "BABY RUTH", very rare, Roberts Collection.    **NRS**

**2458X PENNSYLVANIA** 1947, double-door automobile car, brown with white lettering, compressor assembly on underframe, metal body, continuation of prewar 2758, not illustrated.    **7   11   15   30**

**X2758 PENNSYLVANIA** 1945-46, double-door automobile car, brown metal body with white lettering, compressor assembly on underframe and steps and brakewheels. A similar car was produced in 1941-42 which had automatic box couplers. Kotil reports the following variations:

(A) Staple-end trucks, whirly wheels, early coil couplers.   **8   12   15   30**

(B) Staple-end trucks, early dish wheels.    **8   12   15   30**

(C) Staple-end trucks, regular wheels, late coil couplers.   **8   12   15   30**

**X2954 PENNSYLVANIA** Not catalogued, Bakelite painted tuscan, white lettering, metal trucks, coil-operated coupler, same body as 2954, made in 1941-42. It is unlikely that this car was produced by the factory with postwar trucks. In some cases service stations and individuals removed prewar trucks and replaced them with postwar trucks.   **100   200   250   350**

**3356 SANTA FE RAILWAY EXPRESS** 1957-60 and 1964-66, operating car from horse corral set, horses move by vibrator action from car to pen and back; green car, yellow lettering, brakewheel to right of operating doors, galvanized metal bottom. Price does not include corral. For corral add $15, $20, $25, $35.

(A) Lettered "BLT. 5-56", metal trucks with bar-ends, magnetic couplers with tabs.    **20   30   40   65**

(B) No built date, Timken trucks with disc-operating couplers.    **20   30   40   65**

**3357 HYDRAULIC PLATFORM MAINTENANCE CAR** Cop and hobo move to special gray plastic on-off platform, blue plastic Type II plug-door body with white lettering, Timken trucks, disc-operating couplers, price includes platform. Reissued by Fundimensions in 1982.

(A) Medium blue plastic.    **15   25   35   60**

(B) Darker blue plastic.    **15   25   35   60**

**3366 CIRCUS CAR** 1959-62, operating car with nine white rubber horses and 3356-150 corral. Vibrator coils under the car, corral vibrates and miniature rubber "fingers" on base of horse causes it to move forward. (Same mechanism as found on 3356.) Unpainted ivory plastic car, 10-3/8" long, metal trucks with bar-ends, magnetic couplers with tabs, one black sliding shoe, red roof and catwalk. White corral with white fence, gray walkway and red inner section. As operating car faces the viewer brakewheel is on left end and "BLT BY LIONEL" appears in red, heat-stamped lettering on lower right.

(A) Set.    **85   125   175   250**

(B) Car only.    **50   75   100   150**

**3370 WESTERN & ATLANTIC** 1961-64, sheriff and outlaw bob and shoot at each other, green with yellow lettering.

(A) Timken trucks, disc-operating couplers.   **10   15   25   45**

(B) Arch bar trucks, disc-operating couplers, Hutchinson Collection.    **10   15   25   45**

**3376 BRONX ZOO** 1960-69, giraffe lowers head to pass under bridge unit, action caused by special rail unit with overhead section. (See accessory chapter, 3424-100, for discussion). Timken plastic trucks with disc-operating couplers. We have also had reports of both blue and green cars with gold lettering instead of yellow; Niedhammer observation. We need to know which of the varieties listed below have this lettering. Reader comments are requested. Price for set.

(A) Blue car, white lettering, brown-spotted giraffe.   **10   12   17   25**

(B) Blue car, white lettering, solid yellow giraffe.   **10   12   17   25**

(C) Green car, yellow lettering, solid yellow giraffe.   **20   35   50   75**

(D) Blue car, yellow lettering, brown-spotted giraffe.   **15   25   35   45**

(E) Blue car, yellow lettering, solid yellow giraffe.   **15   25   35   45**

(F) Green car, yellow lettering, brown-spotted yellow giraffe. Lord and Weingart Collections. Came in box marked 3376-160. Ambrose comment.

Also has dummy couplers, 561-1 "General"-type trucks. I.D. Smith Collection.    **20   30   50   75**

(G) Same as (A), but no lettering. Breslin Collection.    **NRS**

**3386 BRONX ZOO** 1960, shown in the 1960 Advance Catalogue as part of set No. 1109 with 1060 locomotive (see 1060 locomotive for details). Also came with uncatalogued set X568NA, which included 220P and 220T in 1960. See Uncatalogued Set chapter for full contents. Shown in 1961 advance catalogue with 1065 Union Pacific Alco. Ambrose comment. Light blue body, white lettering. Price includes rail/overhead unit.

(A) Solid yellow giraffe, arch bar trucks, dummy couplers.    **20   35   50   75**

(B) Yellow giraffe with brown spots, Timken trucks, dummy couplers.    **20   35   50   75**

(C) Yellow giraffe with brown spots, arch bar trucks, dummy couplers, came with 1060 set cited above. Fleming and I.D. Smith Collections.    **20   35   50   75**

(D) Prototype: Bongo and Bobo car, "World's Only Performing Giraffes", illustrated on page 39 in LIONEL: A Collector's Guide and History, Volume IV. Catalano Collection.    **—   —   1000   —**

(E) Same as (B), but aqua body. Halverson Collection.    **NRS**

**3424 WABASH** 1956-58, operating brakeman, Type IIB blue plastic body with white lettering, white unpainted five-panel plastic door, "8-56", metal trucks with tab magnetic couplers, sliding shoe. Price includes rail trip and overhead unit.

(A) White man, medium blue plastic body, blue sliding shoe.    **20   30   40   60**

(B) White man, lighter blue plastic body, white sliding shoe.    **20   30   40   60**

(C) White man, darker blue plastic body, blue sliding shoe.    **25   35   50   75**

(D) Man with dark blue pants, gray shirt, flesh-colored skin, red cap.    **25   35   50   75**

**3428 UNITED STATES MAIL** 1959, operating door, Type III blue plastic body, red plastic five-panel door painted red, white and blue, Timken trucks, disc-operating couplers.

(A) Blue man carries gray mailbag.   **20   35   50   75**

(B) Gray man carries blue bag.   **20   35   50   75**

(C) Same as (A), but Type IIIB body.   **20   35   50   75**

**3434 POULTRY DISPATCH** 1959-60 and 1965-66, operating sweeper, activated by remote control track, illuminated. Reissued by Fundimensions in 1983.

(A) Gray plastic body painted brown with white lettering, gray man, Timken trucks, disc-operating couplers.   **30   60   90   120**

(B) Gray plastic painted slightly darker brown, blue man with flesh-colored hands, face and broom; metal trucks with magnetic tab couplers.    **30   60   90   120**

(C) Same as (B), but gray man.   **30   60   90   120**

**3435 TRAVELING AQUARIUM** 1959-62, lighted with "swimming" tropical fish; clear plastic car painted green with gold or yellow lettering; Timken trucks with disc-operating couplers and two pickup shoes. Aquarium windows appear wave-like; car interior painted black to control light reflection; vibrator motor moves continuous belt creating illusion of swimming fish. This car, rather an exotic piece, was greeted with derision by collectors at its issue, but today it is considered a highly desirable item. Reissued by Fundimensions in 1981.

(A) Large "L" with gold circle and gold lettering: "Tank No. 1", "Tank No. 2".    **60   80   150   250**

(B) Same as (A), but no circle around large "L".   **60   80   150   250**

(C) Yellow lettering, no tank designations, no circle around large "L".    **40   60   80   110**

(D) Similar to (C), but heavier and brighter lettering.   **40   60   80   110**

(E) Same as (A), but no circle, no tank designation. Degano Collection    **50   70   140   240**

**3454 PRR AUTOMATIC MERCHANDISE CAR** 1946-47, car throws out six plastic "Baby Ruth" cubes which resemble merchandise containers. Reproduction cubes do not read "Baby Ruth" and are medium brown. The car is 8-1/2" long measured from one end of the catwalk to the other along the top of the body, and 3-1/8" high measured from the flange of the wheels sitting on a flat surface to the top of the catwalk, and 2" wide. Lettering on the car is as follows: "AUTOMATIC/MERCHANDISE CAR/3454/CAPY 100000/LDLMT 120800/LTWT 48200 NEW 6-46" to left of door and "EW 9-11/EH 13-0/IL 40-6/IW 9-2/IH 10-4/CUFT 3836/x3454/BUILT BY/ LIONEL" to right of door. On the right above the lettering is a 1/2" diameter circle with a PRR Keystone logo in its center. Steps are at corners as part of stamped sheet metal frame; staple-end metal trucks, later coil couplers with sliding shoes, and brakewheel fastened to one end only by a rivet. The mechanism for this car can toss the cubes over a foot. On a prototype scale, that would mean a heavy carton thrown 50 feet, which certainly would qualify the prototype railroad worker for Olympic competition!

(A) Flat silver paint on clear plastic shell, dark blue (almost black) lettering and logo, lettering is heat-stamped cleanly and evenly, body is fastened to frame by four 1/4" self-tapping black roundhead screws; operating mechanism wired to sliding shoes on trucks by flexible light blue wires; mechanism fastened to frame by two black roundhead screws, six dark brown plastic cubes. Sattler, Falter, Davis and LaVoie Collections.

30    50    80    100

(B) Same as (A), but medium blue lettering and logo, lettering and numbering not as crisply heat-stamped into body as (A); many numbers and some letters filled in with color. Body fastened to frame by four 5/8" self-tapping black roundhead screws. Operating mechanism wired to sliding shoes on trucks by one flexible black wire and one flexible blue wire. Came with six black plastic cubes. Sattler and Davis Collections.

30    50    80    100

(C) Same as (A), but red letters and numbers; heat stamping not as crisp as (A); for example, the 8 in "120800" and the 8 in "48200" are filled in with color. Body fastened to frame by four 5/8" black self-tapping roundheaded screws; operating mechanism wired to sliding shoes on truck by two black flexible wires; operating mechanism fastened to frame by two plated roundheaded screws; came with six red plastic cubes. This car probably represents a limited production run or a very early production color sample, and it was most likely made shortly after the built date on the car (6-46). Extremely rare; possibly only six in existence. Sattler Collection.

—    —    1000    —

(D) Same as (A), but method of mounting hatchway to roof differs, letters and numbers rubber-stamped instead of heat-stamped. Davis Collection.

NRS

See also Factory Errors.

**3462 AUTOMATIC REFRIGERATED MILK CAR** 1947-48, operating car, man delivers milk cans, cream white paint on clear plastic with black lettering including "RT3462", staple-end metal trucks with coil couplers, sliding shoes and metal doors. The car body is attached to the base by two metal springs; remove springs to access jammed cans. This is the most popular type of operating car made by Lionel. Price includes platform and five cans.

(A) 1947, early brass-base mechanism with thinner metal stock and more folding than later mechanism. The base mechanism is attached to the car frame by three and, later, four brass tabs twisted 90 degrees. The 1947 base is one inch shorter than the 1948 base, as the earlier base does not include the pivot plate found on later models. A square sheet metal plate slides out under the milkman, carrying him with it. This plate is placed within a track in the brass base under the milkman's right foot. Considerably more scarce than later versions. Fleming Collection. **NRS**

(B) 1948, later, more common mechanism with milkman attached to swinging can sweep arm.

15    20    30    40

**3464 A T & S F** 1949-50, 52, operating car, "X3464" on side; man appears as door opens, plunger mechanism, orange appearance, black lettering, marked "X3464" on side, metal trucks, magnetic couplers, metal or plastic doors, usually painted orange. The underlying paint varies in color. On some pieces the man is missing so that his color is unknown. The following observations are primarily owed to Joseph Kotil:

(A) Clear plastic, staple trucks, steps, blue and white man, brown metal door.

6    9    12    15

(B) Same as (A), but black metal door.

6    9    12    15

(C) Same as (A), but opaque blue-gray plastic, black metal door.

6    9    12    15

(D) Same as (A), but blue plastic, black metal door (missing man).

6    9    12    15

(E) Marbled black plastic, staple-end trucks, no steps, blue man, black metal door.

6    9    12    15

(F) Same as (E), but green plastic (missing man).

6    9    12    15

(G) Same as (E), but clear plastic (missing man).

6    9    12    15

(H) Same as (E), but clear plastic, emblem with red and yellow coloring, rare.

NRS

(I) Clear plastic, bar-end trucks, no steps, blue man, black metal door

6    9    12    15

(J) Same as (I), but black plastic door.

6    9    12    15

(K) Same as (I), but orange plastic, black plastic door.

6    9    12    15

(L) Orange-brown body, black metal doors. Same color as 3464X NYC, but with AT & SF lettering and numbering. Three examples known to exist. Niedhammer, Stewart and Sattler Collections.

NRS

**3464X N Y C 159000** 1952, operating car, "X3464" on side, man emerges as door opens, plunger mechanism, orange-brown body, white lettering "NEW 9-44" on left of black door, metal trucks with staple or bar-ends and magnetic couplers; door on operating side has single large panel, door on non-operating side has no panels.

(A) Staple-end trucks, semi-gloss orange-brown, man with flesh-colored face, steps, metal doors.

6    9    12    15

(B) Staple-end trucks, flatter orange-brown, all blue man, no steps, metal doors. Kotil Collection.

6    9    12    15

(C) Bar-end trucks, no steps, metal doors. Kotil Collection.

6    9    12    15

(D) Bar-end trucks, no steps, plastic doors. Kotil Collection.

6    9    12    15

**3472 AUTOMATIC REFRIGERATED MILK CAR** Man delivers milk cans, "RT 3472" on side.

(A) Pink and gray marble plastic body painted cream white, black lettering, short metal roof hatch, tin-plated door frame with aluminum doors, black underframe/floor with four steps; indentations on underframe for door frames; indentation visible from bottom; early operating mechanism, metal trucks with staple-ends, magnetic couplers, spring clips hold body and frame together.

10    15    25    45

(B) Same as (A), but white unpainted plastic.

10    15    25    45

(C) White unpainted plastic body, staple-end or bar-end trucks, magnetic couplers, long loading hatch with two simulated ice hatches and portion of catwalk; no holes in body for door frame tabs; plastic doors, base now cut out for new door assembly, four steps.

10    15    25    45

(D) Same as (C), but pure white unpainted plastic body which contrasts with cream white hatch loading door and grayish-white plastic doors and frame.

10    15    25    45

(E) Same as (C), but grayish-white body, hatch and doors, (whiter than (C).

10    15    25    45

**3474 WESTERN PACIFIC** 1952-53, operating car, man appears as door opens, silver body with orange feather, metal trucks with bar-ends, magnetic couplers.

(A) Medium density lettering.

25    50    70    100

(B) Lighter density lettering.

25    50    70    100

**3482 AUTOMATIC REFRIGERATED MILK CAR** 1954-55 operating car, man delivers milk cans. This is the most popular type of operating car made by Lionel. White unpainted plastic, black lettering, body fastened to frame by Phillips head screw at one end and sliding bar at other; frame base has two ridges, plastic doors, metal trucks with bar-ends and magnetic uncouplers. Price includes stand and five cans.

(A) Large numerals "3482" on upper left and small "RT 3472" on lower right.

10    25    40    60

(B) Large numerals "3482" on upper left and small "RT 3482" on lower right.

10    25    40    60

**3484 PENNSYLVANIA** 1953, operating car with plunger mechanism, man appears as door opens, Type I clear plastic body painted tuscan, 1953-type black plastic door painted tuscan, bar-end metal trucks with magnetic couplers.

(A) Body and door painted tuscan-brown.

12    25    40    60

(B) Body and door painted tuscan-red, appears lighter than (A).

12    25    40    60

**3484-25 A.T.&S.F.** 1954, operating car with plunger mechanism, man appears as door opens, found with Types I, IIA and IIB bodies, bar-end metal trucks, magnetic tab couplers*.

* See Lionel 6464 Boxcar Variations for type definitions.

# 6454 BOXCARS

6454[B] N.Y.C.

6454[B] Erie

6454 Unpainted Body

6454 Pennsylvania

6454[A] N.Y.C.

6454 SP

6454 A.T. & S.F.

6454[C] N.Y.C.

(A) 1954, Type I clear plastic body painted glossy or flat orange, white rubber-stamped lettering, Santa Fe herald, 1/2" long.  20  50  90  120

(B) 1954, Type I clear plastic body painted flat orange, 1953 Type black plastic doors painted shiny orange, heat-stamped white lettering, Santa Fe herald 7/16" long.  20  50  90  120

(C) Type IIA clear plastic body painted shiny orange, 1953-type black plastic door painted shiny orange, heat-stamped white lettering, 7/16", Santa Fe herald.  20  50  90  120

(D) Same as (C), Type IIA but heat-stamped black lettering, 7/16" long, Santa Fe herald.  —  600  900  1200

(E) 1954, Type IIB red plastic body painted flat orange, 1953-type black plastic door painted shiny orange, heat-stamped white lettering, 7/16" long, Santa Fe herald.  20  50  90  120

(F) Same as (E), but door painted flat orange.  20  50  90  120

(G) Type I clear plastic body painted shiny orange, 1953-type black plastic door painted shiny orange, heat-stamped black lettering, very rare.  NRS

**3494-1 N Y C PACEMAKER** 1955, operating car with plunger mechanism, man appears as door opens, bar-end metal trucks with magnetic couplers.
(A) Type IIA red plastic body with gray-painted areas, white rubber-stamped lettering, with a comma under the second "s" of System.  20  50  90  120

(B) Type IIB dark blue plastic body painted pastel blue, 1956-type red plastic door painted buttercup yellow, black heat-stamped lettering, no comma under second "s" of System. See picture in prototype section for this one of a kind boxcar.  NRS

**3494-150 M.P.** 1956, operating car with plunger mechanism, man appears as door opens, Type IIB gray plastic body with blue-painted areas, "Eagle" on left is 5/8 of an inch long, "XME" and "Merchandise Service" on lower right, no grooves, 1956-type yellow unpainted plastic door, bar-end metal trucks with magnetic tab couplers.  25  50  90  120

**3494-275 STATE OF MAINE** 1956-58, operating car with plunger mechanism, man appears as door opens, Type IIB blue plastic body with painted white and red stripes and black heat-stamped lettering; bar-end metal trucks with magnetic couplers; letters "O", "F", "D" and "U" are placed on door sign boards. Lionel redesigned its boxcar door in 1956 to accommodate these letters and the new door is known as the 1956-type door, blue plastic door painted white and red.
(A) "B.A.R."is under and overscored, dark red stripes.  30  40  55  75

(B) Same as (A), but medium red stripes.  30  40  55  75

(C) "B.A.R." is neither under nor overscored, "3494275" is omitted.  50  75  125  200

See also Factory Errors.

**3494-550 MONON** 1957-58,, operating car with plunger mechanism, blue man appears as door opens, Type IIB plastic body with white-painted stripe and heat-stamped white lettering (except (C), lettered "BLT 6-57", bar-end metal trucks with magnetic tab couplers 11" long, 1956-type maroon plastic door with white-painted stripe (except (C).
(A) Maroon plastic body and doors.  70  125  175  250

(B) Same as (A), but missing "BLT 6-57" on one side. This is a collectible factory error. Numerous examples show the progressive fading of the "BLT 6-57" as the stamp deteriorated.  75  125  175  250

(C) Blue plastic body and orange plastic doors painted maroon with decal lettering, prototype.  NRS

**3494-625 SOO** 1957-58, operating car with plunger mechanism, blue man with flesh-colored face appears as door opens, Type IIB maroon plastic body painted tuscan-brown with white heat-stamped lettering, 1956-type maroon plastic door painted tuscan-brown, bar-end metal trucks with magnetic tab couplers, 11" long.
(A) As described above.  70  125  175  250

(B) Gray body painted tuscan; maroon door painted tuscan. Hessler Collection.  70  125  175  250

**3530 ELECTRO MOBILE POWER** or "Operating GM Generator Car", 1956-58, operating car; opening the door completes the circuit for the accompanying floodlight through the lighting pole. The pole, 3530-30, has

two leads which hook into the car roof and two leads that run from the pole to the 3530-12 searchlight. The searchlight has a magnet on the bottom. Inside the car is a large plastic generator, strictly for looks (the same generator is used on the searchlight car). Fuel tanks are found under the car and appear identical to the ones on the 1047 Switchman but not on the diesels. Blue plastic car body with white and blue lettering. Popovich reports two types of pole-transformer base units. One unit has a light blue base, the other a black base, but both utility poles are brown and the riser pipes are gray. We do not know which of the following car variations came with which pole types.
(A) Orange generator, black fuel tank.  15  25  50  75
(B) Gray generator, black fuel tank.  15  25  50  75
(C) Same as (A), but white stripe extends through ladder to car end.  15  25  50  75

(D) Orange generator, blue fuel tank, white stripe extends through ladder to car end.  15  25  50  75
(E) Same as (A), but blue fuel tank, short white stripe. Kotil Collection.  15  25  50  75
(F) Same as (A), but bluish-green body. Ocilka Collection.  15  25  50  75

**3619 HELICOPTER RECONNAISSANCE CAR** 1962-64, operating car with red helicopter, black propeller and black landing gear. The helicopter, stored inside, is launched by a spring-loaded device which is pressed to cock. The spring is released by a magnetic section of uncoupling track. Yellow or yellow-orange plastic car sides and ends with red and black lettering, Timken trucks with two disc-type couplers.
(A) Yellow.  17  23  45  70
(B) Yellow-orange. Degano Collection.  22  28  50  100
(C) Same as (A), but yellow helicopter. Shanfeld Collection.  25  30  50  100

**3656 ARMOUR** 1949-55, operating cattle car with cattle and corral. Cattle sometimes need prodding but move more or less continuously from corral to car and back. Orange car with white or black lettering and brown paper decal on door; metal trucks, magnetic couplers, two sliding shoes. Price includes cattle and corral. (A) and (B) are less common than (C) and (D).
(A) ARMOUR in white lettering.  18  35  48  60
(B) ARMOUR in black lettering.  18  45  60  100
(C) Circa 1949-1950, LIONEL LINES in black lettering, orange-painted clear plastic body, orange-painted clear plastic doors, staple-end metal trucks, magnetic couplers. Budniak Collection.  14  25  30  50
(D) 1952-53, LIONEL LINES in white lettering, orange-painted yellow-white opaque plastic, orange-painted orange plastic double door, orange-painted die-cast sliding door, bar-end metal trucks, magnetic couplers, Kaiser Collection.  14  25  30  50

**3662-1 AUTOMATIC REFRIGERATED MILK CAR** 1955-60, 1964-66, operating car, man delivers late milk cans without weighted magnets. White car with brown top and doors, "L" in circle, metal trucks with magnetic tab couplers. Price includes five cans and stand.
(A) Lettered "NEW 4-55", bright brown roof and ends.  15  25  38  55
(B) Same as (A), but dull, chalky brown roof and ends.  15  25  40  55
(C) Same as (A), but later production: Timken plastic trucks, disc-operating couplers. LaVoie Collection.  15  25  40  55
(D) Same as (A), but without built date.  18  27  48  65

**3665 MINUTEMAN** 1961-64, operating car, fires either rocket or shells, white plastic sides, blue plastic roof that opens, Timken trucks.
(A) Red, white and blue rocket with blue tip on black firing unit, two disc-couplers.  12  16  30  45
(B) Green-olive drab marine cannon that fires silver-painted, 1-3/4" long wooden shells (shells came in plastic bag inside car), one disc coupler, one fixed coupler. Eddins Collection.  15  22  35  55

NOTE: It may seem incredible, but apparently there actually was a prototype for the 3665 and 3666 missile cars. According to a report by Steve Solomon in LCCA's The Lion Roars (December 1983, p. 2), the chassis and body for the real car were built by American Car and Foundry in Berwick, Pa. and the launching mechanism by American Machine and Foundry in Stamford, Ct. The car was 85-90 feet long and had launch control panels in the nose cone end of the car. Stability problems with the tie-down system apparently defeated the car's purpose because the track and the roadbed

---

* See Lionel 6464 Boxcar Variations for type definitions.

6464-50 Minneapolis & St. Louis

6464-25 Great Northern

6464-1 Western Pacific

6464-100 Western Pacific-b

6464-100 Western Pacific-a

6464-175 Rock Island

6464-125 New York Central

6464-150 Missouri Pacific-b

6464-150 Missouri Pacific-a

6464-150 Missouri Pacific-c

6464-200 Pennsylvania

6464-75 Rock Island

6464-225 Southern Pacific

6464-275 State of Maine-a

6464-250 Western Pacific

6464-275 State of Maine-b

6464-300 Rutland-b

6464-300 Rutland-a

6464-375 Central of Georgia

6464-425 New Haven-b

6464-500 Timken

6464-525 Minneapolis & St. Louis

6464-725 New Haven-a

6464-900 New York Central

6464-350 Missouri, Kansas & Texas

6464-425 New Haven-a

6464-475 Boston & Maine

6464-515 Missouri, Kansas & Texas

6464-700 Santa Fe

6464-825 Alaska

6464-325 Baltimore & Ohio Sentinel

6464-400 Baltimore & Ohio Timesaver

6464-450 Great Northern

6464-510 New York Central

6464-650 Denver & Rio Grande

6464-725 New Haven-b

couldn't handle the strain of the launch. In addition, fixed tie-downs along the roadbed were not cost-effective. The car was built some time in 1960 or 1961.

**3666 MINUTEMAN,** circa 1964, uncatalogued by LIONEL but offered by Sears as part of set 3-9820. Car has operating cannon which fires gray wooden shells 1-3/4" long. The car has white plastic sides with blue lettering and a blue plastic roof which opens. It came with the following set components: (1) a 240 locomotive; (2) an un-numbered gray flatcar with a green tank; (3) a 6470 "EXPLOSIVES" boxcar; (4) a 6814(C) Rescue caboose without stretchers; (5) a 1249 ALLSTATE TOY TRANS-FORMER with a pink top, apparently made by Marx; and (6) 10 plastic soldiers. (A jeep has been mentioned in some reports, but not all.) The set box side reads as follows: SEARS SET 39820 ALLSTATE BY LIONEL/STEAM LOCOMOTIVE WITH LIGHT AND SMOKE/BOX CAR EXPLODES WHEN SHELL HITS/ROOF OF CANNON CAR OPENS AND SHELL IS FIRED AUTOMATICALLY/45 WATT TRANS-FORMER WITH CIRCUIT BREAKER. Jarman, Vergonet and Bohn Collections. Price for 3666 car only. **75 125 150 200**

**3672 BOSCO** 1959-60, operating milk car with yellow "BOSCO" milk cans; "Corn Products Co." on side, yellow sides, tuscan ends, roof door and lettering, metal trucks, magnetic couplers. Price includes platform and five cans.

(A) With Bosco decal. **70 125 175 250**
(B) 1960, without Bosco decal. **70 125 175 250**
(C) No lettering, Bosco decal on operating boxcar body and frame, prototype of an operating boxcar. **— — — 750**

**3854 AUTOMATIC MERCHANDISE CAR** 1946-47, operating boxcar, tuscan with white lettering, 11" long, marked "3854" and "X3854", two sliding shoes on each truck; probably the rarest of all postwar freight and passenger cars, prewar car with modern trucks. **150 200 250 350**

**4454 BABY RUTH PRR** 1946, from electronic set with control receiver inside car (see Locomotive 4471), orange with black lettering, brown doors, brown electronic control decal with white lettering; metal trucks with staple-end, center rail pickups, coil-operated couplers.

(A) Same as above. **20 30 40 60**
(B) Same as (A), except door has hollow interior side pin stop, rather than solid pin door stop. Hutchinson observation. **20 30 40 60**

**6004 BABY RUTH PRR** Non-operating doors, 8-1/2" long.
(A) 1950, orange, Type I body with blue lettering. **1 2 3 8**
(B) 1951, yellow with black lettering. **2 3 5 10**
(C) Blue plastic car, paper decal on one side only; decal reads "McCall's Readers Buy Carloads Of Cocoa". Decal also pictures coffee cup and container of Nestle's Sweet Milk Cocoa. Algozzini Collection. **NRS**

**X6004 BABY RUTH PRR** 1951, non-operating doors, 8-1/2" long, Scout couplers, part of set 1461S (see 6110 locomotive for details), orange unpainted Type I plastic body with blue lettering. Came in box numbered "6004" as part of set 1461S; I.D. Smith and Rohlfing comments.
**2 3 5 10**

**6014 AIREX** Uncatalogued, red Type I body with yellow lettering. Roskoski Collection. **NRS**

**X6014 BABY RUTH PRR.**
(A) 1957, white with black lettering. **2 3 4 7**

**6014-335 FRISCO** Type III, snow-white body, black lettering, numbered "6014" but came in a box numbered "6014-335'. We suspect that the other white cars listed under "6014 Frisco" probably came in boxes marked "6014-335".

(A) Same as above. Halverson Collection. **2 4 6 10**
(B) 1955-56, red Type I body with white lettering. **3 4 6 8**
(C) Same as (B), but lighter red with metal trucks with bar-ends and magnetic tab couplers. **3 4 6 8**
(D) 1951, white body, black lettering, bar-end metal trucks, magnetic couplers. Rohlfing Collection. **3 4 6 8**

**6014 BOSCO PRR** 1958.
(A) White with black lettering. **15 20 30 50**
(B) Orange Type I body with brown lettering. **4 7 9 11**
(C) Red Type I body with white lettering. Timken trucks. **4 7 9 11**
(D) Orange Type I body, black lettering. Kotil Collection. **4 7 9 11**

**6014** 6014 came in numerous product or road names, colors and body types. For convenience 6014s are listed alphabetically (by road or product name) with our letters. All 6014 cars have non-operating doors and are 8-1/2" long. The chart listing the body types follows:

# 0-27 Plug Door Box Car Types

Type I

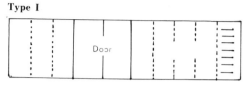

Type II

Type III

Type IV

(E) Same as (C), but bar-end trucks. Kotil Collection. **4 7 9 11**
(F) Same as (D), but has raised black lettering. Blotner Collection. **4 7 9 11**

**6014 CAMPBELL SOUP** 1969, uncatalogued, red with white lettering, question as to existence. Confirmation requested. **NRS**

**6014 CHUN KING** Uncatalogued, red Type I body with white lettering. **50 75 100 150**

**6014 FRISCO.** Also see 6014-335.
(A) 1969, orange Type I body with blue lettering. **2 4 6 8**
(B) 1964-66, 1968, white Type III body with black lettering. **2 4 6 8**
(C) 1969, white Type III body with very heavy black lettering. **2 4 6 8**
(D) White Type I body with black lettering, hole for bank, Timken trucks, one disc-operating coupler, one fixed coupler. **10 15 20 35**
(E) Red Type I body with white lettering. **2 4 6 8**
(F) Cream unpainted Type I body with black lettering, Timken trucks, two disc-operating couplers. **5 6 9 12**
(G) Same as (A), but Type III body, Rohlfing Collection. **2 4 6 8**
(H) Same as (B), but Type II body. **2 4 6 8**
(I) Same as (B), but has LCCA Meet overstamp. Rohlfing Collection. **NRS**

**6014 PILLSBURY** Prototype, not manufactured. Elliott Smith Collection. **— — — 200**

**6014 WIX** Uncatalogued, cream white Type I body with red lettering. **50 75 100 150**

**6024 NABISCO SHREDDED WHEAT** 1957, orange Type I body with black lettering, 8-1/2" long, non-opening doors. **7 10 15 20**

**6024 RCA WHIRLPOOL** 1957, uncatalogued, red Type I body with white lettering, 8-1/2" long, non-opening doors, Type I body. Rohlfing Collection. **30 40 55 85**

**X6034 Baby Ruth PRR** 1953, 8-1/2" long, non-opening doors.

| | | | | |
|---|---|---|---|---|
| (A) Orange, Type I body with black lettering. | 2 | 3 | 5 | 7 |
| (B) Red with white lettering. | 2 | 3 | 5 | 7 |
| (C) Same as (A), but blue lettering, Rohlfing Collection. | 2 | 3 | 5 | 7 |

**6044 AIREX** Uncatalogued, 8-1/2" long, non-opening doors.

| | | | | |
|---|---|---|---|---|
| (A) Purple Type I body with white/bright yellow lettering. | — | 15 | 22 | 30 |
| (B) Medium blue Type I body with white and yellow lettering. | 2 | 4 | 7 | 9 |
| (C) Light blue Type I body with white and yellow lettering. | 2 | 4 | 7 | 9 |
| (D) Teal blue Type I body with white and orange lettering. | 40 | 60 | 80 | 110 |

(E) Dark blue body, white and yellow lettering. Wilson and Halverson Collections. Very rare. **NRS**

**6050 LIBBY'S TOMATO JUICE** 1961, special Libby's promotional car, Type III body with coin slot, 8-1/2" long, non-opening doors, Timken trucks, fixed couplers.

| | | | | |
|---|---|---|---|---|
| (A) Green stems on vegetable decal. | 9 | 13 | 18 | 25 |
| (B) Green stems missing from decal. | 50 | 75 | 100 | 150 |

**6050 LIONEL SAVINGS BANK** 1961, coin slot, white with green, 8-1/2" long, Type I body, non-opening doors. Rohlfing Collection.

(A) White body, red lettering, green bank and windows, letters and logos all decals, Timken trucks, two operating couplers, large "BUILT BY LIONEL". Hudzik Collection. 9 13 18 25

(B) Same as (A), but letters and logos are heat-stamped. Hudzik Collection. 9 13 18 25

(C) Same as (B), but brighter white body, small "BUILT BY LIONEL", one operating and one dummy coupler. Hudzik Collection. 9 13 18 25

**6050 SWIFT REFRIGERATOR** 1962, coin slot, usually red with white lettering.

| | | | | |
|---|---|---|---|---|
| (A) Type II body. | 4 | 7 | 9 | 15 |
| (B) Type III body, lettering high on car. | 40 | 60 | 80 | 100 |
| (C) White with red lettering. Gay Collection. | | | | **NRS** |

(D) Type III body, red with white lettering, white S in scroll between second and third step. Blotner Collection. **NRS**

**6352-1 PACIFIC FRUIT EXPRESS** 1955-57, Union Pacific logo, "63521" on car sides, operating ice car, Type IIB unpainted orange plastic body with unpainted light brown doors, metal trucks with bar-ends and magnetic couplers. Came with ice house and five ice cubes; original cubes have bubble found in middle, reproductions do not. Price for car only. Reissued by Fundimensions in 1982.

(A) Unpainted light brown doors, four lines of medium density lettering: "IL, IW, IH, CU.FT." on lower right ice house door side. 25 40 55 75

(B) Same as (A), but heavier lettering. 25 40 55 75

(C) Same as (A), but three lines of lettering: "IL, IW, IH" on lower right car door. For set add 30, 55, 95, 115. 40 55 75 100

(D) Same as (A), but peach tint to orange body. Algozzini Collection. 25 40 55 75

**6356-1 N Y C** 1954-55, two-level stock car, 11-1/4" long, metal trucks, magnetic couplers, small or large lettering.

| | | | | |
|---|---|---|---|---|
| (A) Flat yellow with black lettering. | 10 | 15 | 25 | 40 |
| (B) Medium yellow with black lettering. | 10 | 15 | 25 | 40 |

(C) White-painted body (reported as ivory, but probable color fade), unpainted black doors. Algozzini Collection. **NRS**

(D) Gold-painted body, silver-painted roof with unpainted black doors, possible factory prototype. Algozzini Collection. **NRS**

**6376 LIONEL LINES** 1956-57, "CIRCUS CAR", two levels, white unpainted plastic with red lettering, 11-1/4" long, "BLT 4-56", red catwalk, metal trucks with bar-ends, magnetic tab couplers. 35 50 65 90

**6428 UNITED STATES MAIL** 1960-61, "RAILWAY POST OFFICE", Type IV gray plastic body painted red, white and blue, 1956-type deep red plastic door painted red, white and blue, heat-stamped white and black lettering, Timken trucks, disc-operating couplers.

| | | | | |
|---|---|---|---|---|
| (A) Shiny red paint. | 15 | 25 | 40 | 60 |
| (B) Flat red paint. | 15 | 25 | 40 | 60 |

(C) Flat red paint without lettering on one side. Examples are well known and collectible. 30 40 55 75

**6434 POULTRY DISPATCH** 1958-59, illuminated car showing three rows of fowl on the way to market, without a "working man". Black plastic body painted red with white lettering, gray plastic doors with black lettering, bar-end metal trucks with magnetic tab couplers. 30 40 55 75

**6445 FORT KNOX GOLD RESERVE** 1961-63, very unusual Lionel bank modeled on the aquarium car. Clear plastic car painted silver, but with unpainted windows for viewing gold bullion inside, black lettering. Differs from the 3435 aquarium car in that there are nickel-sized circular screens at car ends, (these were open areas on aquarium car), bank slot on top.

| | | | | |
|---|---|---|---|---|
| (A) Silver-painted plastic, gold bullion. | 40 | 60 | 85 | 115 |
| (B) Gold-painted plastic with silver bullion, one of a kind. | | | | **NRS** |

**6448 TARGET CAR** 1961-64, this car from the missile/space period is spring-loaded and designed to be shot at with a missile. When hit the car "explodes". Each car is different - one side is the "target" with two bulls' eyes, the other has "DANGER" warnings. It is quite an unusual Lionel car and is based on a modification of the Type II boxcar body, but rivet rows end to provide space for lettering "TARGET RANGE CAR". Ladder sections omitted on both sides to allow space for a red stripe that only appears on one side. The color of the sides and roof is unpainted plastic, with Timken trucks and two disc-operating couplers unless otherwise indicated. The car has a metal post and rubber sleeves to hold the car together. It comes with and without side slots and these slots differ in their locations - on one side they are closer to the end than on the other side.

| | | | | |
|---|---|---|---|---|
| (A) Flat red sides, white roof and ends, white lettering, no slots in sides | 4 | 6 | 8 | 15 |
| (B) Same as (A), but slots on one side. | 4 | 6 | 8 | 15 |
| (C) Same as (A), but shiny red sides, slots on one side. | 4 | 6 | 8 | 15 |
| (D) Shiny red sides, ends, roof, white lettering, no side slots. | 4 | 6 | 8 | 15 |
| (E) White sides, flat red ends and roof, white lettering. | 4 | 6 | 8 | 16 |
| (F) White sides, shiny red roof and ends, white lettering, slots on both sides. | 4 | 6 | 8 | 16 |
| (G) White sides, roof, ends, red lettering, slots on both sides | 4 | 6 | 8 | 16 |

**6454 A.T.&S.F.** 1948, "63132" and "X6454" on sides, orange paint on plastic body with black lettering, brown metal doors, single panel door on one side and no panel door on other, steps, staple-end metal trucks with magnetic couplers, two small holes in frame in addition to truck mounting holes.

| | | | | |
|---|---|---|---|---|
| (A) Orange-painted clear plastic. | 10 | 15 | 20 | 30 |
| (B) Orange-painted black plastic. Kotil Collection. | 10 | 15 | 20 | 30 |
| (C) Orange-painted green marble plastic. Kotil Collection. | 10 | 15 | 20 | 30 |
| (D) Same as (A), but black-painted doors. Arpino Collection. | 10 | 15 | 20 | 30 |

**6454 PENNSYLVANIA** 1949-53, "65400" and "X6454" on sides, tuscan paint on clear plastic with white lettering, magnetic couplers, brown or black metal doors, Hutchinson comment. We need to know which of the varieties listed below have which doors. Reader comments invited.

| | | | | |
|---|---|---|---|---|
| (A) Slightly shinier tuscan than (B), two large and two small holes in floor in addition to truck mounting holes, staple-end trucks. | 10 | 15 | 20 | 30 |
| (B) Slightly duller tuscan than (A), two small holes on floor, steps, staple-end trucks. | 10 | 15 | 20 | 30 |
| (C) One large and five small frame holes, steps, staple-end trucks. Kotil Collection. | 10 | 15 | 20 | 30 |
| (D) One large and three small frame holes, no steps, staple-end trucks. Kotil Collection. | 10 | 15 | 20 | 30 |
| (E) Same as (D), but bar-end trucks. Kotil Collection. | 10 | 15 | 20 | 30 |

**6454 N.Y.C.** 1951, "159000" and "X6454" on sides, metal doors, steps, staple-end metal trucks with magnetic couplers, floor has two small holes plus truck mounting holes.

| | | | | |
|---|---|---|---|---|
| (A) Brown paint on clear plastic with white lettering. | 10 | 15 | 20 | 30 |
| (B) Brown-orange paint on clear plastic with white lettering. | 10 | 15 | 20 | 30 |
| (C) Orange paint on clear plastic with black lettering, maroon doors. | 15 | 25 | 35 | 50 |
| (D) Same as (C), but six frame holes. Kotil Collection. | 15 | 25 | 35 | 50 |

**6454 ERIE** 1949-53 "81000" and "X6454" on sides.

| | | | | |
|---|---|---|---|---|
| (A) Brown with white lettering, bar-end metal trucks, no steps. | 10 | 15 | 25 | 40 |

THE GIRL'S SET

2037-500 Loco 6464-515 Box Car 6436-500 Hopper

6464-510 Box Car 6462-500 Gondola 6427-500 Caboose

# PROTOTYPE AND RARE 6464 BOX CARS

3494-1[B] NYC

3494-1[A] NYC

6464[T] NYC

6464 W.P.

6464 W.P.

6464[E] Clemco

6464-375 Central of Georgia

6464-375 Central of Georgia

6464 Parker Kalon

6464[G] M. Steinthal

6464[F] Hathaway Denver

6464 Western Pacific

6464-650 Denver & Rio Grande

6464-650 Denver & Rio Grande

6464-825 Alaska [258A]

# LIONEL 6464 BOX CAR VARIATIONS

by Dr. Charles Weber*

Dr. Charles Weber wrote the section on 6464 box cars. His study, completed several years ago and recently updated, introduced a new level of sophistication to the study of Lionel variations. It should be noted, however, that Dr. Weber did not contribute the prices listed for the 6464 box cars. It is his strongly held conviction, that the concern with prices detracts from the essential enjoyment of toy train collecting. His willingness to contribute to this volume is most appreciated.

**Type I Side**
Note placement and absence of rivets

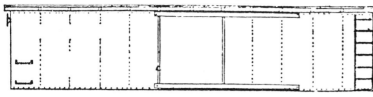

**Type IIA and IIB Side**

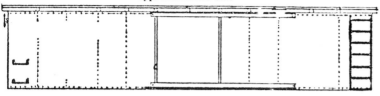

**Type IIB Top**
Type IIa has same top as Type I.
Type IIb is the same as IIa except ice hatch markings are present

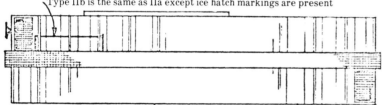

**1953 Door**
(two panels)

**1956 Door**
(five panels)

**Type IV Side**
(Part not shown, same as Type III)

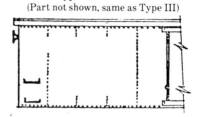

Drawings by Bob Fox

* Dr. Weber gratefully acknowledges the assistance of the following people without whose assistance this research could not have been carried forth: Sid Brown, Ron Niedhammer, Allan Stewart, Ernie Davis, Dick Meerly, Joe Ryan, Lee Stuhl, Joe Ranker, Elliott Smith and Bill Fryberger.

**Type III Side / B Type IV Side**
Type III and IV are noticeably lighter in weight and roof ribs can be seen on the inside

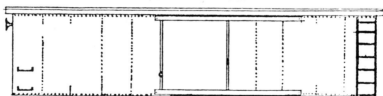

(B) Slightly lighter brown than (A), staple-end metal trucks, steps.

| | | | |
|---|---|---|---|
| 10 | 15 | 25 | 40 |

(C) Same as (A), except has black plastic doors. Hutchinson comment. **NRS**

(D) Same as (A), but staple-end metal trucks. Budniak Collection.

| | | | |
|---|---|---|---|
| 10 | 15 | 20 | 30 |

**6454 S P** 1950-53, white lettering as follows: "SP 96743; CAPY 10000; LD LMT 12410; LT WT 44900; NEW 3-42" on left. "SOUTHERN PACIFIC LINES" in circular herald, "RXW10-5; H-13-4; EW-9-4; IL40-6; IW9-2; IH10-6; CU FT 3713" on right. "X6454" and "BUILT BY LIONEL" on right. Staple or bar-end metal trucks, steps. Schmaus observation.

(A) Brown with white lettering, no steps, staple-end trucks.

| | | | |
|---|---|---|---|
| 10 | 15 | 20 | 30 |

(B) Lighter brown than (A), steps.

| | | | |
|---|---|---|---|
| 10 | 15 | 20 | 30 |

(C) Dark red, staple-end truck. Kotil Collection.

| | | | |
|---|---|---|---|
| 20 | 30 | 40 | 60 |

(D) Dark red, bar-end truck. Kotil Collection.

| | | | |
|---|---|---|---|
| 20 | 30 | 40 | 60 |

(E) Black-painted clear plastic shell, white heat-stamped lettering, prototype. This color scheme was later used for the 6464-225, Degano Collection.

| | | | |
|---|---|---|---|
| — | — | — | 750 |

(F) Brown body and doors, smaller S P herald (rare). Niedhammer Collection.

**NRS**

(G) Dark red body and doors, smaller S P herald. Niedhammer Collection.

**NRS**

**6454 BABY RUTH PRR** 1948, orange body, brown metal doors with hollow door stop pin, black lettering and PRR logs, two small holes in frame, staple-end metal trucks, late coil couplers. Hutchinson observation.

(A) Same as above.

| | | | |
|---|---|---|---|
| 50 | 75 | 100 | 200 |

(B) Same as (A), but darker orange and bar-end betal trucks with magnetic couplers. Arpino Collection.

| | | | |
|---|---|---|---|
| 50 | 75 | 100 | 200 |

**6464-1 WESTERN PACIFIC** 1953-54, usually silver with blue letters, Type I body painted silver, body mold color varies, 1953-type door, black door mold painted silver, no decals, heat-stamped lettering, letter color varies.

| | | | | |
|---|---|---|---|---|
| 1 Opaque white body mold, bright blue lettering. | 12 | 18 | 30 | 50 |
| 2 Clear body mold, bright blue lettering. | 12 | 18 | 30 | 50 |
| 3 Light gray body mold, bright blue lettering. | 12 | 18 | 30 | 50 |
| 4 Black body mold, medium blue lettering. | 12 | 18 | 30 | 50 |
| 5A Clear body mold, medium blue lettering. | 12 | 18 | 30 | 50 |
| 5B Transparent blue body mold, medium blue lettering. | 12 | 18 | 30 | 50 |
| 6 Light green body mold, medium blue lettering. | 12 | 18 | 30 | 50 |
| 7 Light green body mold, dark blue lettering. | 12 | 18 | 30 | 50 |

8A Blue-black body mold, dark blue lettering. **12 18 30 50**

8B Black body mold, black lettering, one-of-a-kind. **NRS**

9 Clear body mold, dark blue lettering. **12 18 30 50**

10 Bluish-opaque body mold, red lettering, rare. **500 — 1200 2000**

11A Clear body mold, red lettering, rare. **— — 1200 2000**

11B Clear body mold painted orange, door painted orange, white lettering, one-of-a-kind. **— — — 2000**

11C Dark orange body and doors, silver lettering, rare. Caplan Collection. **NRS**

**6464-25 GREAT NORTHERN** Type I body painted glossy or flat orange, except 23B, body mold color varies, 1953 type door, black door mold painted glossy or flat orange, no decals, except 21-23A, heat-stamped white lettering.

12 Opaque-white body, glossy orange body and door paint. **10 15 20 45**

13 White body, glossy orange body and door paint. **10 15 20 45**

14 Clear body, glossy orange body and door paint. **10 15 20 45**

15 Black-marble body, glossy orange body and door paint. **10 15 20 45**

16 Gray body, glossy orange body and door paint. **10 15 20 45**

17A White body, flat orange body and door paint. **15 20 35 55**

17B White body, glossy orange body paint, flat orange door paint. **15 20 35 55**

18A Clear body, flat orange body and door paint. **15 20 35 55**

18B Clear body, glossy orange body and door paint. **15 20 35 55**

19 Black body, flat orange body and door paint. **15 20 35 55**

20 Gray body, flat orange body and door paint. **15 20 35 55**

21 Clear body, flat orange body and door paint, red and green decals. **100 200 250 400**

22 Black body, flat orange body and door paint, red and green decals. **100 200 250 400**

23A Black body, glossy orange body paint, flat orange door paint, red and green decals. **100 200 250 400**

23B Clear body painted tuscan, no information on door mold color, paint, decal, one-of-a-kind. **— — 1500 —**

**6464-50 MINNEAPOLIS & ST. LOUIS** 1953-56, Type I body, painted flat or glossy tuscan, except 29B, 1953-type door painted flat or glossy tuscan, black door mold, no decals, white heat-stamped lettering.

24 Opaque-white body, flat tuscan body and door paint. **15 20 30 45**

25 Clear body, flat tuscan body and door paint. **15 20 30 45**

26 Black body, flat tuscan body and door paint. **15 20 30 45**

27 White body, flat tuscan body and door paint. **15 20 30 45**

28 Opaque-white body, glossy tuscan body and door paint. **15 20 30 45**

29A Light gray body, glossy tuscan body and door paint. **15 20 30 45**

29B Gray body, flat tuscan over copper-colored paint, glossy, tuscan door, one-of-a-kind. **NRS**

30 Clear body, glossy tuscan body and door paint. **15 20 30 45**

**6464-75 ROCK ISLAND** 1953-54, 1969, Type I body, except 36A-B (Type IV), painted in shades of green or gray, mold color varies, 1953-type door, except 36A-B (1956-type door), door painted glossy, flat or light green, black door mold, except 36A-B (green), no decals, heat-stamped gold lettering, except 36A-B (bright gold lettering).

31A Clear body, glossy green body and door paint. **15 22 35 55**

31B Same as 31A, except body painted light gray. **15 22 35 55**

31C Same as 31A, except body painted green. **15 22 35 55**

32 Gray body, glossy green body and door paint. **15 22 35 55**

33 Clear body, light flat green body paint, flat green door paint. **15 22 35 55**

34 Opaque-white body, flat green body and door paint. **15 22 35 55**

35 Gray body, medium flat green body paint, flat green door paint. **15 22 35 55**

36A Type IV green body, flat green body and door paint, 1956-type green door, bright gold lettering. **10 15 30 50**

36B Same as 36A, except light green door paint. **10 15 30 50**

**6464-100 WESTERN PACIFIC** 1954-55, Type IIA body, except 37 and 40 (Type I), opaque-white body mold (37-39) and clear body mold (40-46), orange or silver (40-46) body paint, 1953-type door painted orange or silver (40-46), black door mold, white, gray-white or black (40-46) rubber-stamped lettering, no decals.

37 Type I opaque-white body, flat orange body and door paint, white lettering, blue feather numbered "1954", not 6464-100, three known copies. **— — 2000 3000**

38A Type IIA opaque-white body, orange body and door paint, white lettering, lighter blue feather. **100 175 250 400**

38B Same as 38A, except darker orange body and door paint, blue feather, large WP, small "BUILT BY LIONEL", similar to 6464-250. **— — 1000 —**

39 Type IIA opaque-white body, orange body and door paint, gray-white lettering, blue feather. **125 200 275 450**

40 Type I clear body, silver body and door paint, black lettering, short yellow feather (18.5cm) **45 75 90 125**

41-46: All have: Type IIA clear bodies, silver body and door paint, black lettering, but feather color and length vary.

41 Long yellow feather (18.7cm). **30 40 70 100**

42 Long yellow-orange feather, doors regular yellow. **30 40 70 100**

43 Short yellow feather. **30 40 70 100**

44 Long yellow-orange feather. **30 40 70 100**

45 Short yellow-orange feather. **30 40 70 100**

46 Yellow feather, doors yellow-orange. **30 40 70 100**

**6464-125 NEW YORK CENTRAL** 1954-56, Type IIA body except 47 (Type I), 1953-type door, except 55, 56A, 57A and B, no decals, white lettering, except 47 and 57A (black), other characteristics vary as described.

47 Type I clear body painted light yellow, white door mold painted red, black rubber-stamped, one-of-a-kind. **NRS**

48 Clear body painted glossy gray and flat red, red unpainted door, heat-stamped lettering, gray top row of rivets, no cedilia. **20 30 40 65**

49 Same as 48, except rubber-stamped lettering. **20 30 40 65**

50 Red body painted gray, red unpainted door, heat-stamped lettering, gray top row of rivets, no cedilia. **20 30 40 65**

51 Red body painted gray, red unpainted door, heat-stamped lettering, red top row of rivets, half gray, no cedilia. **20 30 40 65**

52A Red-black marble body painted shiny red and glossy gray, red unpainted door, heat-stamped lettering, gray top row of rivets, no cedilia. **20 30 40 65**

53A Red body painted shiny gray, white door painted shiny red, rubber-stamped, red top row of rivets, no cedilia. **20 30 40 65**

53B Same as 53A, except dull red and gray paint. **20 30 40 65**

54 White body painted red and glossy gray, white door painted red, rubber-stamped, red top row of rivets, cedilia. **20 30 40 65**

55 White body painted gray and red, 1956-type unpainted door, red door mold, rubber-stamped, top row of rivets red, cedilia. **20 30 40 65**

56A Red body painted flat gray, 1956-type red unpainted door, rubber-stamped, top row of rivets red, cedilia. **20 30 40 65**

56B Red body painted flat gray and flat red, 1953-type white door painted red, rubber-stamped, half of top row of rivets red, half with cedilia. **40 60 80 110**

57A Red body painted gray, 1956-type maroon door painted red, black rubber-stamped lettering, red top row of rivets, cedilia. **20 30 40 65**

57B Red body painted glossy gray, 1956-type white unpainted door, rubber-stamped, red top row of rivets, cedilia. **20 30 40 65**

**6464-150 MISSOURI PACIFIC** Catalogued 1954-55 and 1957. This car has several interesting variations. First, the word "Eagle" comes in three sizes: large, 3/4" high, medium, 5/8" high and small, 1/2" high. Second, "Eagle" is found either to the left or right of the door. Third, the gray stripe on the car's side may be painted on a blue unpainted or blue-painted shell, or it may be the body color itself. In the latter case, blue paint creates the gray stripe effect. Fourth, the door may or may not have a painted gray stripe.

The following characteristics apply to all Missouri Pacifics except as noted: no decals, except 58 and black and white rubber-stamped lettering.

59-67C: Have Type IIA bodies and 1953-type doors.

58 Type I clear body painted blue and gray, 1953-type yellow unpainted door with gray-painted stripe, decal, right 3/4" Eagle, XME, preproduction sample, reportedly one-of-a-kind. **NRS**

# PROTOTYPE AND RARE 6464 BOX CARS

6464[U] Pillsbury

6464[K] Tidewater

6464[N] DSSA

6464[Q] Burlington

6352-1[D] PFE

6464[C] Hotpoint

6464[J] Cookie Box

6464[M] Wabash

6464[P] Louisville & Nashville

6464[S] NYC

6464[B] Hotpoint

6464[I] M & SL

6464[L] Norfolk Southern

6464[O] Louisville & Nashville

6464[R] Great Northern

See description on page 205.

59 Navy blue body with painted gray stripe, yellow unpainted door with gray-painted stripe, right 3/4" Eagle, XME.    25  35  50  80
60 Same as 59, except no XME.    25  35  50  80
61 Same as 59, except body painted navy blue with painted gray stripe, no XME.    25  35  50  80
62 Gray body painted royal blue to create the effect of a gray stripe, yellow door with painted gray stripe, right 3/4" Eagle, XME, "3-54" on left.    25  35  50  80
63 Royal blue body with painted gray stripe, yellow door with painted gray stripe, right 3/4" Eagle, no XME.    25  35  50  80
64 Violet body with painted gray stripe, light yellow door with gray stripe only, right 3/4" Eagle, XME.    25  35  50  80
65A Same as 64, except no XME.    25  35  50  80
65B Same as 65A, except faded violet body mold.    25  35  50  80
66 Royal blue body with painted gray stripe, white door painted plain dark yellow, no door stripe, right 3/4" Eagle, no XME, seal on first panel.    40  65  80  125
67A Royal blue body with painted gray stripe, yellow door with painted gray stripe, right 3/4" Eagle.    25  35  80  80
67B Same as 67A, except navy body paint and no XME.    25  35  50  80
67C Same as 67A, except navy body paint.    25  35  50  80
68 Type IIA navy blue body with painted gray stripe, 1956-type dark yellow door mold unpainted, no door stripe, right 3/4" Eagle, no XME.    40  65  80  125
69 Type IIA white body painted royal blue and gray, 1956-type light yellow unpainted door, no stripe, right 5/8" Eagle, XME and grooves.    40  65  80  125
70 Same as 69, except dark yellow door mold.    40  65  80  125
71 Type IIA white body painted royal blue and gray, 1953-type white door with stripe, right 5/8" Eagle, XME and grooves, left "3-54".    40  65  80  125
72 Type IIA royal blue body painted gray, 1953-type light yellow door unpainted, right 5/8" Eagle, XME and grooves.    40  65  80  125
73 Type IIA navy blue body with painted gray stripe, 1953-type yellow door unpainted, right 5/8" Eagle, XME and grooves.    40  65  80  125
74A Type IIA royal blue body with painted gray stripe, 1953-type yellow door with gray stripe, right 5/8" Eagle, XME and grooves.    25  35  50  80
74B Same as 74A, except violet body mold and MP Lines circular logo is in first panel to left of door.    200  350  450  550
75 Type IIA royal blue body with painted gray stripe, 1953-type yellow unpainted door, no stripe, right 5/8" Eagle, XME, grooves and seal on panel.    30  45  75  110
76 Type IIB royal blue door with painted gray stripe, 1953-type dark yellow door with gray stripe, right of 5/8" Eagle, XME and grooves.    30  45  75  110
77 Same as 76, except white door painted dark yellow, no stripe.    30  45  75  110
78 Type IIA light gray body painted royal blue to produce gray stripe effect, 1956-type yellow unpainted door, no stripe, left 5/8" Eagle, XME.    30  45  75  110
79 Type IIB gray body painted royal blue and gray, 1956-type yellow unpainted door, no stripe, left 1/2" Eagle, XME.    30  40  75  110
80 Type IIB gray body painted royal blue and gray, 1956-type dark yellow unpainted door, no stripe, left 1/2" Eagle, XME.    30  45  75  110
81 Type IIB gray body painted royal blue to produce gray stripe appearance, 1956-type yellow unpainted door, no stripe, left 1/2" Eagle, XME.    30  45  75  110
82 Same as 81, except door has gray stripe and no XME.    25  35  50  80

**6464-175 ROCK ISLAND** Catalogued 1954-55, Type I body, except 87 (Type IIA), silver body and door paint, 1953-type black door, no decals, heat-stamped lettering in various colors.
83 Clear body mold, light blue lettering.    25  35  60  85
84 Black body mold, medium blue lettering.    25  35  60  85
85 Clear body mold, medium blue lettering.    25  35  60  85
86 Opaque-white body mold, black lettering.    —  —  —  750
87 Type IIA gray body, medium blue lettering.    NRS

**6464-200 PENNSYLVANIA** Catalogued 1954-55, most characteristics vary but all are without decals and have white heat-stamped lettering.
88 Type I clear body painted tuscan brown, 1953-type black door painted tuscan brown.    30  45  75  105
89 Same as 88, except body and door painted glossy tuscan red.    30  45  70  105
90 Type I opaque-white body painted tuscan red, 1953-type black door painted tuscan red.    30  45  70  105
91 Type IIA clear body painted tuscan red, 1953-type black door painted tuscan red.    30  45  75  105
92 Same as 91, except opaque-white body mold.    30  45  75  105
93A Type IV body, tuscan brown and 1956-type tuscan brown door painted tuscan brown, no "New 5-53" designation.    20  30  45  75
93B Same as 93A, except door mold and paint are tuscan red.    20  30  45  75
94 Type IV tuscan brown body, 1956-type tuscan brown door painted tuscan brown, with "New 5-53" built date.    NRS

**6464-225 SOUTHERN PACIFIC** Catalogued 1954-56, Type IIA body except 95 (Type I), flat black (95-97) or glossy black (98A-99) or black (100) paint body, all with 1953-type black door molds, no decals, red, white and yellow rubber-stamped lettering.
95 Type I black body painted flat black, black-painted door, one of three.    NRS
96 Opaque-white body painted flat black, flat black-painted door.    15  30  45  70
97 Same as 96, except black body mold.    15  30  45  70
98A Black body painted glossy black, flat black-painted door, lighter stamping.    15  30  45  70
98B Opaque-white body painted glossy black, flat black-painted door    195  —  340  400
99 Red body painted glossy black, doors painted silver, then glossy black.    15  30  45  70
100 Black body painted black with silver roof, black-painted doors.    NRS

**6464-250 WESTERN PACIFIC** Catalogued 1966-67, Type IV orange body mold, 1956-type gray door mold, no decals, white rubber-stamped lettering.
101 Light orange body paint, dark orange door paint, medium blue feather.    15  30  40  60
102 Orange body and door paint, light blue feather.    15  30  40  60
103 Same as 102, except medium blue feather.    15  30  40  60
104 Same as 102, except dark blue (purple-blue) feather.    15  30  40  60

**6464-275 STATE OF MAINE** Catalogued 1955, 1957-59, 1956-type door, no decals, white and black lettering, characteristics vary considerably but are identified by groups when possible.
106A - 111C have Type IIA bodies and grooves and are rubber-stamped.
106A White body painted red and navy blue, red unpainted door.    30  60  90  150
106B Same as 106A, except royal blue body.    30  60  90  150
107 White body and door molds, red and navy blue body and door paint.    21  37  55  75
108A White body and door molds, red and royal blue body and door paint.    21  37  55  75
108B Same as 108A, except blue body mold.    21  37  55  75
109 Navy blue body painted red and white, white door painted red and navy blue.    15  30  40  60
110 Same as 109, except red and royal blue door paint.    15  30  40  60
111A Royal blue body painted red, white and royal blue, white door painted red and light royal blue.    15  30  40  60
111B Same as 111A, except red and dark royal blue door paint.    15  30  40  60
111C Royal blue body painted red, white and navy blue, white door painted red and royal blue.    15  30  40  60
112A Type IIB body, royal blue body and door, red and white body and door paint, no grooves, white heat-stamped black rubber-stamped.    15  30  40  60
112B Same as 112A, except lettered BAR only, on 6464.    NRS
113 Type IIB blue-violet body painted red and white, royal blue door painted red and white, no grooves, white heat-stamped black rubber-stamped.    15  30  40  60

114-120B have Type III bodies, no grooves, heat-stamped white and rubber-stamped black lettering.

114 Royal blue body and door molds, red, white and navy blue body paint, red and white door paint.
15 30 40 60

115 Navy blue body and door molds, red, white and light blue body paint, red and white door paint.
15 30 40 60

116 Royal blue body and door molds, red, white and light blue body paint, red and white door paint.
15 30 40 60

117 Royal blue body painted red, white and light blue, navy blue door painted red and white.
15 30 40 60

118 Royal blue body and door molds, red, white and light blue body paint, red, white and royal blue door paint.
15 30 40 60

119 Royal blue body and door molds, red and white body and door paint.
15 30 40 60

63120A Marble (red, white and black) body painted red, white and light blue; light whitish-blue door painted red, white and lighter blue.
15 30 40 60

120B Same as 120A, except red, white and royal blue body paint and navy door mold.
15 30 40 60

6464-300 RUTLAND Catalogued 1955-56; yellow door molds; no decals; 1955 cars have rubber-stamped lettering; 1956 cars are heat-stamped.

NOTE: Some Rutlands have shown up with repainted doors because of the high Rutland prices. Three ways to distinguish a Rutland with a repainted door from one that has not been repainted are:

(A) Green paint on door bottom should match the body's paint perfectly.
(B) Where colors abut there should be some irregularity (i.e., beading, blurring or barely palpable ridge).
(C) On the bottom half of the back of the doors there should be a faint green, mist-like speckle caused by paint backspray.

122-128B have Type IIA bodies; 1953-type doors except 127 (1956-type door).

121 Yellow body and door molds; dark green body paint; door unpainted; dark green and yellow-orange rubber-stamped lettering; "R" on left.
15 35 55 75

122 Yellow body and door molds; very glossy dark green body paint; door unpainted; dark green and yellow-orange rubber-stamped lettering; "R" on left.
15 30 40 60

123 Yellow body and door molds; dark green body paint; "split door" has dark green bottom; dark green and yellow-orange rubber-stamped lettering; "R" on left.
150 200 300 450

124 Gray body painted dark green and yellow; door unpainted; dark green and yellow-orange rubber-stamped lettering; "R" on left.
15 30 40 60

125 Clear and white marble body painted dark green and yellow; unpainted door; dark green and yellow rubber-stamped lettering; "R" on left.
15 30 40 60

126 Yellow body and door molds; dark green body paint; unpainted door; light green and yellow rubber-stamped lettering; "R" on left.
15 30 40 60

127 Yellow body and door molds; dark green body paint; 1956-type unpainted door; light green and yellow heat-stamped lettering; "R" on right.
12 25 35 70

128A Yellow body and door molds; super glossy dark green body paint; door unpainted; dark green and yellow rubber-stamped lettering; "R" on left; solid shield herald.
— — 1000 1200

128B Same as 128A, except dark green paint on body and bottom of "split door".
— — 1750 —

129-131B Type IIB body; light green and yellow heat-stamped lettering; "R" on right.

129 Yellow body and door molds; dark green body paint; 1956-type unpainted door.
12 25 35 70

130A Yellow body and door molds; flat green body paint; 1956-type unpainted door.
12 25 35 70

130B Same as 130A, except "split door" with dark green bottom.
150 225 300 475

131A Blue body; 1953-type door; dark green and flat yellow body and door paint.
150 225 300 475

131B Same as 131A, except yellow marble body mold. 150 225 300 475

131C IIA Type body, brown paint; 1953-type door with gold lettering; one of three.
NRS

6464-325 B&O SENTINEL Catalogued in 1956 only; IIB gray body painted aqua-blue and silver; 1956-type gray door painted aqua-blue and silver; yellow, green and silver decals; navy blue and silver heat-stamped lettering.
80 130 200 275

6464-350 MKT [KATY] Catalogued in 1956 only; IIB Type body; 1956-type door; no decals; heat-stamped white lettering except 137 (black lettering).

133 Maroon body painted tuscan red; dark cherry red unpainted doors.
60 90 130 175

134 Maroon body painted tuscan brown; dark cherry red doors painted tuscan brown; doors and sides almost match.
60 90 130 175

135 Maroon body painted tuscan brown; maroon unpainted doors.
60 90 130 175

136 Tuscan red unpainted body; dark cherry red unpainted doors.
60 90 130 175

137 Girl's Set pink body, white door paint (?); black lettering; one-of-a-kind.
NRS

138 Maroon unpainted body; dark cherry unpainted doors.
65 85 135 175

139A Shiny maroon unpainted body; maroon unpainted doors.
65 85 135 175

139B Same as 139A, except flat maroon body and door molds.
65 85 135 175

140 Maroon (?) unpainted body, black unpainted door.
65 85 135 175

6464-375 CENTRAL OF GEORGIA Catalogued 1956-57 and 1966-67; 1956-type gray door painted silver; yellow and red decals except 149A; heat-stamped lettering.

141-145B have Type IIB body molds and Blt. 3-56 dates.

141 Maroon body; silver-painted roof and oval; maroon and white lettering.
20 35 55 85

142 Same as 141, except mottled oval. 20 35 55 85

143 Duller maroon body; silver-painted roof and gray oval; maroon and white lettering.
20 35 55 85

144 Maroon body; silver-painted roof and gray oval; red and white lettering.
20 35 55 85

145A Bright maroon body; silver-painted roof and gray oval; red and white lettering.
20 35 55 85

145B Same as 145A, except maroon and white lettering.
20 35 55 85

146-149B Type IV body mold; silver roof and gray oval.

146 Darker maroon body; red and white lettering; no built date.
20 35 55 85

147 Same as 146, except maroon and white lettering. 20 35 55 85

148 Gray body mold; red-painted body; red and white lettering; with "BLT 3-56".
— — 2500 3000

149A Maroon body; maroon and white lettering; no built date or decal.
200 300 400 550

149B Same as 149A, except has "BLT 3-56". 200 300 400 550

6464-400 B&O TIMESAVER 1956-57, 1969, 1956-type door; heat-stamped lettering; other characteristics vary as described.

150A - 156A have Type IIB body molds; orange, black and white decals; blue and white lettering except 152B (black and white lettering).

150A Navy blue body and door molds, orange and silver body paint; orange painted door stripe; "BLT5-54".
15 30 45 75

150B Same as 150A, except light navy blue body mold. 15 30 45 75

151 Light navy blue body painted orange and silver; royal blue door with painted orange stripe, "BLT5-54".
15 30 45 75

152A Royal blue body painted orange and silver; royal blue door with painted orange stripe; "BLT 5-54".
15 30 45 75

152B Same as 152A, except black and white lettering. 15 30 45 75

153 Dark blue body and door molds; orange and silver body paint; orange door stripe; "BLT2-56".
25 50 85 130

154 Same as 153, except navy blue body and door molds.
25 50 85 130

155 Same as 153, except royal blue body and door molds.
25 50 85 130

156A Blue (?) body with orange stripe; blue (?) door with brown-orange stripe, "BLT 2-54", unpainted roof.
NRS

**156B** Same as 156A, except medium blue body and door molds; door stripe (?); no mention of unpainted roof; black and white lettering.

          **25   50   85  130**

**156C** No body or door mold color or paint information; only that "BLT 5-54" on one side and "BLT 2-56" on other.     **NRS**

**157 - 162** have Type IV medium bright blue body and door molds and no built date.

**157** Body painted lighter blue, dull orange and silver; door painted lighter blue with bright orange; black and white lettering; dull point.

          **10   15   30   45**

**158** Same as 157, except dull orange door paint and sharp point.

          **10   15   30   45**

**159** Lighter blue, bright orange and silver body paint; lighter blue and dull orange door paint; black and white lettering; sharp point.

          **10   15   30   45**

**160** Same as 159, except dull point.   **10   15   30   45**

**161** Dark blue; bright orange and silver body paint; lighter blue and bright orange door paint; blue and white lettering; sharp point.

          **10   15   30   45**

**162** Same as 161, except dull point.   **10   15   30   45**

**163** Yellow body painted light yellow and white; yellow door painted light yellow and white; blue or black and white lettering; no information as to decals or lettering application; no built date; 1969 "Timken" colored paint; one-of-a-kind.     **—   —  1200  —**

**6464-425 NEW HAVEN** Catalogued 1956-58; black body paint, except 164B (glossy black); 1956-type unpainted door, except 168 (orange); no decals; white heat-stamped lettering; with full serif except for 164A and 164B (partial serif).

**164A - 170** have Type IIB black body molds, except 169 (gray).

**164A** Light orange door mold; partial serif.   **10   20   30   45**

**164B** Glossy black body paint; light orange door mold; partial serif

          **10   20   30   45**

**165** Dark orange door mold.     **8   15   25   37**

**166** Light orange door mold.     **8   15   25   37**

**167** Dark orange door mold.     **8   15   25   37**

**168** Black door with orange paint.   **8   15   25   37**

**169** Gray body painted black; light orange door mold.   **8   15   25   37**

**170** Black unpainted door.     **8   15   25   37**

**171-175** have Type III black-painted bodies; and unpainted doors.

**171** Gray body mold and dark orange door molds.   **8   15   25   37**

**172** Black body mold; light orange door mold.   **8   15   25   37**

**173** Marble body mold; light orange door mold.   **8   15   25   37**

**173A** Same as entry 173, but Type IIA body. Budniak Collection.

          **8   15   25   37**

**174** Same as 173, except dark orange door mold.   **8   15   25   37**

**175** Same as 173, but orange (?) door mold.   **8   15   25   37**

**6464-450 GREAT NORTHERN** Catalogued 1956-57 and 1966-67; 1956-type door; except 182 (1953-type); red, white and black decals, except 183 (without black); yellow and olive heat-stamped lettering.

**176** Type IIB dark olive body painted dark olive, orange and dark yellow; dark olive door painted dark olive, orange and light yellow; "BLT 1-56".

          **15   30   50   80**

**177** Same as 176, except door painted dark olive and orange only, does not have yellow lines.   **25   50   75  100**

**178** Type III blue body painted dark olive, orange and dark yellow; light olive door painted light olive, orange and light yellow; "BLT 1-56".

          **30   55   85  125**

**179** Type IV light olive body painted light olive, light orange and light yellow; light olive door painted light olive, light orange and light yellow; no built date.   **15   30   42   70**

**180** Same as 179, except dark orange body and door paint.

          **15   30   40   70**

**181** Type IV light olive body painted light olive, orange and light yellow; light olive unpainted door no built date.

          **15   30   40   70**

**182** Type IV light olive body painted light olive and (?); 1953-type black door painted flat orange; no built date.   **15   30   45   70**

**183** Type IV light olive body painted light olive, orange and light yellow; light olive door painted light olive, orange and light yellow; red decal only; no built date.   **15   30   45   75**

**6464-475 BOSTON & MAINE** Catalogued 1957-60 and 1967-68; 1956-type black unpainted except 194-195B (see text descriptions); no decals; black and white heat-stamped lettering.

**184** Type IIB medium blue unpainted body; "BLT2-57".

          **10   20   25   40**

**184A** Same as entry 184, but Type IIA body. Budniak Collection.

          **10   20   25   40**

**185** Same as 184, except lighter blue body mold.   **10   20   25   40**

**186** Type III black body painted flat blue; "BLT 2-57".   **10   20   25   40**

**187A** Type III unpainted light blue body; "BLT2-57".   **10   20   25   40**

**187B** Same as 187A, except marble body mold.   **10   20   25   40**

**187C** Type III marble body mold painted medium blue; no built information.   **10   20   25   40**

**187D** Type III light green body painted medium blue; "BLT 2-57".

          **10   20   25   40**

**187E** Same as 187D, except very light blue body paint.   **10   20   25   40**

**187F** Type III marble body painted light blue; "2-57" date.

          **10   20   25   40**

**188** Type IV dark blue body painted blue-purple; "BLT 2-57".

          **8   15   20   32**

**189** Type IV unpainted light blue body mold; "BLT 2-57".

          **8   15   20   32**

**190** Same as 189, except no built date.    **8   15   20   32**

**191** Type IV unpainted medium blue body mold; "BLT 2-57".

          **8   15   20   32**

**192A** Type IV gray body painted darker blue; "BLT 2-57".

          **8   15   20   32**

**192B** Same as 192A, except light blue body mold.   **8   15   20   32**

**193** Type IV gray body painted darker blue; no built date.

          **8   15   20   32**

**194** Same as 193, except white unpainted door mold; no built date; unblackened door runner rivets.   **8   15   20   32**

**195A** Type IV yellow body painted darker blue; white door painted black; no built date; unblackened door runner rivets.   **8   15   20   32**

**195B** Same as 195A, except light blue body paint.   **8   15   20   32**

**196** Type IV gray body painted blue-green; color similar to 2346 GP-9 diesel.   **8   15   20   32**

**6464-500 TIMKEN** Catalogued 1957-58 and 1969; 1956-type door; heat-stamped lettering.

**197 - 205** Type IIB body; charcoal lettering; except 204 (shades of black); orange, black and white decal, except 204 (yellow).

**197** Yellow body and door molds painted white.   **12   24   40   65**

**198** Same as 197, except door painted golden yellow and white.

          **12   25   40   65**

**199** Same as 197, except door painted yellow and white.

          **12   25   40   65**

**200** Yellow body painted white; white door painted yellow and white.

          **12   25   40   65**

**201** Yellow body and door molds painted yellow and white.

          **12   25   40   65**

**202** Yellow-orange body and door molds painted white.   **20   35   50   70**

**203** Orange-tinted body painted white; yellow door painted white.

          **12   25   35   65**

**204** Dark blue body painted yellow and white; yellow door painted white; all decal lettering in shades of black; 6464-000.   **12   25   35   65**

**205** Light gray body painted yellow and white; yellow door painted white.

          **12   25   35   65**

**206** Type III yellow body painted white; yellow door painted white; orange, black and white decal; charcoal lettering.   **12   25   35   65**

**207** Same as 206, except orange-tinted door body.   **12   25   35   65**

**208 - 212B** have Type IV yellow body and door molds; orange, black and white decals; charcoal lettering, except 210 - 212 B (see text) and no built dates.

**208** Darker yellow and white body paint; lighter yellow and white door paint.   **12   25   35   55**

**209** Lighter yellow and white body paint; darker yellow and white door paint.   **12   25   35   55**

**210** Darker yellow and white body and door paint; glossy black lettering.

          **12   25   35   55**

**211** Darker yellow and white body paint; lighter yellow and white door paint.   **12   25   35   55**

| | | | | |
|---|---|---|---|---|
| 212A | Darker-yellow and white body and door paint. | 12 | 25 | 35 | 55 |
| 212B | Yellow body paint; red heat-stamped lettering. | — | — | 1200 | — |
| 212C | Green body paint; white heat-stamped lettering. | — | — | 750 | — |
| 212D | Green body paint; gold heat-stamped lettering. | — | — | 750 | — |
| 212E | Same as 212D, except red lettering. | — | — | 850 | — |

**NOTE:** Boxcars 213A - 215 were made by MPC in 1970 for Glen Uhl. The cars carried a unique identification, "BLT 1-71 BY LIONEL MPC". These cars are listed here because of their 6464-500 numbers. All yellow cars came with metal trucks as did 200 of the orange cars. It is reported that 500 yellow and 1,300 orange cars were manufactured.

**213A** Blank number-boards, yellow body painted yellow; yellow door painted yellow; light orange, black and gray decals; glossy black lettering.

    15  30  40  75

**213B** Same as 213A, except light yellow body and door paint.

    15  30  40  76

**214A** Blank number-boards, orange body and door molds painted orange; light orange, black and gray decals; glossy black lettering; plastic trucks.

    15  30  40  80

**214B** Same as 214A, except metal trucks.

    15  30  40  80

**215** "9200" number-boards; unpainted orange body; orange door painted orange; glossy black lettering; fifty made, plastic trucks. Halvenson Collection.

    70  125  250  300

**6464-510 NEW YORK CENTRAL PACEMAKER** Catalogued 1957-58; light green-blue body paint; 1956-type dark yellow door mold painted light flat yellow; no decals; black heat-stamped lettering, from Girl's Train, no cedilia or built date.

**216A** Type IIB royal blue body mold.    100  150  300  380

**216B** Same as 216A, except gray body mold.    100  150  350  425

**216C** Type IIA royal blue body.    **NRS**

**6464-515 KATY** Type IIB dark yellow body painted light flat yellow; except 218B and C; 1956-type navy blue door painted light green-blue, except 218B and C; no decals; dark brown-charcoal heat-stamped lettering, except 218B and C, from Girl's Train set.

**217** Same as above.    100  150  250  400

**218A** Overstamped with 6464-150 lettering.    **NRS**

**218B** Tan body paint; sky blue door paint; beige lettering.

    —  —  1500  —

**218C** Light yellow body paint; sky blue door paint.    110  —  285  325

**6464-525 MINNEAPOLIS & ST. LOUIS** 1956-type door, except 221 and 222 (1953-type); no decals; white heat-stamped lettering.

**219** Type IIB unpainted red body and door molds.    10  20  25  40

**220** Type IIB red body and door molds painted flat red.    10  20  25  40

**221** Type IIB red door painted red; 1953-type white door painted red; doors and body paint match.    10  20  25  40

**222** Type IIB red body painted flat red, 1953-type unpainted red door.

    10  20  25  40

**223** Type III gray body painted red; red door painted red.

    10  20  25  40

**224** Same as 223, except black body mold.    10  20  25  40

**225** Same as 223, except marble body mold.    10  20  25  40

**226** Type IV gray body painted red; red unpainted doors.

    10  20  25  40

**227** Same as 226, except maroon door mold painted red on outside only.

    10  20  25  40

**228** Type IV gray body painted red; black unpainted door.

    10  20  25  40

**229** Type IV gray body painted maroon; unpainted white door mold; color similar to 6464-375.    —  —  750  —

**229(B)** Same as 219, but yellow lettering. Algozzini Collection.    **NRS**

**6464-650 DENVER & RIO GRANDE WESTERN** Catalogued 1957-58 and 1966-67, usually found with silver-painted band on lower side and lower door and silver-painted roof. A black stripe usually separates the yellow and silver areas. The car has yellow-painted body and doors with silver-painted bands across the body and doors and a silver-painted roof. The car also comes with an unpainted yellow body, but with silver-painted bands and a silver roof. Rare variations include cars without silver-painted roofs. The following items have 1956-type yellow doors, except 239B; no decals and black heat-stamped lettering.

**230** Type IIB light orange-tinted body, with silver-painted side band and roof; unpainted yellow door with silver-painted band; built date.

    22  40  60  85

**231** Type IIB yellow body with silver-painted side band and roof; yellow unpainted door with silver-painted door band.    22  40  60  85

**232** Type IIB light yellow body painted yellow with silver side band and roof; yellow unpainted door with silver-painted band.    22  40  60  80

**233** Same as 232, but without black stripe on door separating yellow and silver areas.    25  50  75  100

**234** Type IIB light yellow body with silver-painted side band and roof; unpainted yellow door with silver-painted door band; no black door stripe or built date.    **NRS**

**235** Type IIB yellow body painted light buttery yellow with silver-painted side band only; yellow doors painted light buttery yellow with silver-painted door band; built date.    **NRS**

**236** Type IIB yellow unpainted body with silver-painted side bands only; yellow unpainted doors with silver bands; built date.    **NRS**

**237** Type IV unpainted yellow body with silver-painted side bands and roof; yellow unpainted doors with silver-painted bands; no built date.

    20  30  40  60

**238** Type IV lighter yellow body with silver-painted side bands only, no silver paint on roof; yellow unpainted doors with silver-painted bands; no built date.    **NRS**

**239A** Same as 238, but yellow body.    **NRS**

**239B** Type IV gray body with yellow-painted body including roof and with silver-painted side bands; gray door painted yellow with gray-painted band; built date.    —  500  750  1000

**6464-700 A.T. & S.F.** Catalogued 1961 and 1967; Type IV gray body, except 240 (Type III); 1956-type gray door mold, except 240 (red door mold); no decals; white heat-stamped lettering, except 243 (see text).

**240** Type III body with red paint; red unpainted door mold.

    300  450  600  —

**241A** Red body and door paint.    18  32  65  80

**241B** Same as 241A, except medium red body paint.    18  32  65  80

**242** Medium red body paint; silver door paint.    18  32  65  80

**243** Medium red body paint; red door paint; "FORD" lettering rubber-stamped on right.    **NRS**

**244** Lighter red body and door paint.    18  32  55  80

**6464-725 NEW HAVEN** Catalogued 1962-68 and 1969 and 6464-735; Type IV gray body mold, except 247C (black); 1956-type unpainted door; no decals; heat-stamped lettering.

**245A** Lightest orange body paint; black door mold; black shiny lettering.

    8  15  20  35

**245B** Same as 245A, except lighter orange body paint; black not shiny lettering.    8  15  20  35

**246A** Lighter orange body paint; black door mold, dull black lettering.

    8  15  20  35

**246B** Medium orange body paint; black door mold; high gloss black lettering (shinier than 245).    8  15  20  35

**247A** Medium orange body paint; black door mold; glossy black lettering.

    8  15  20  35

**247B** Black body paint; orange door mold; white lettering.

    11  22  40  70

**247C** Black body painted black; orange door painted orange; white lettering; Type VII trucks. McCormack Collection.    **NRS**

**6464-825 ALASKAN** Catalogued 1959-60; 1956-type door; no decals; heat-stamped lettering.

248 - 252 have Type III bodies.

**248** Gray body painted dark blue and yellow, gray doors painted blue; doors slightly lighter blue than body, yellow and orange lettering.

    70  90  120  170

**249** Same as 248, but dark yellow and orange lettering.    70  90  120  170

**250** Dark blue body painted with yellow stripes; dark blue unpainted doors; yellow and orange lettering, doors and body match.    70  90  120  170

**251** Dark blue body painted dark blue and yellow; gray doors painted dark blue; yellow and orange lettering.    70  90  120  170

**252** Royal blue body painted dark flat blue and yellow; white doors painted glossy dark blue; yellow and orange lettering.    50  75  100  140

**253** Type III body, black unpainted door mold, other information unknown.
                                                                                    **NRS**

**254** Type IV body, yellow unpainted door mold, other information unknown.
                                                                                    **NRS**

**255** Type IV royal blue body painted dark blue and yellow; dark blue doors painted dark blue, light yellow and orange lettering; doors and body match.
                                                                 **80   110   150   200**

**256** Type IV gray body painted dark blue and yellow; gray doors painted dark blue; yellow and light orange lettering.
                                                                 **80   110   150   200**

**257** Type IV royal blue body painted dark blue and yellow; white door painted dark blue; yellow and orange lettering; doors and body match.
                                                                 **80   110   150   200**

**258A** Type IV light gray body painted dark blue and yellow; white door painted dark blue; yellow and orange lettering.
                                                                 **80   110   150   200**

**258B** Type IV light gray body painted dark blue and yellow; white unpainted door; white lettering.
                                                                 **—   —   1200   —**

**6464-900 NEW YORK CENTRAL** Catalogued 1960-67; Type IV gray body, except 259 (Type III black body); 1956-type door; no decals; red, black and white heat-stamped lettering.

**259** Type III black body painted light jade green; gray door painted light jade green; thinner red lettering.
                                                                                    **NRS**

**260** Light jade green-painted body and door; gray door mold; thinner red lettering.
                                                                 **15   25   40   70**

**261** Dark jade green body and door paint; gray door mold; thicker red lettering.
                                                                 **15   25   40   70**

**262A** Light jade green body paint; black unpainted door mold, thicker red lettering.
                                                                 **15   25   40   70**

**262B** Same as 262A, except gray door mold.
                                                                 **15   25   40   70**

**6464-1965 TCA SPECIAL** (Pittsburgh) Uncatalogued but made in 1965 for TCA National Convention; Type IV gray body painted blue; 1956-type gray door, except 265 (black door); blue door paint, except 265 (unpainted); no decals; white heat-stamped lettering.   800 Produced.

**263** 6464-1965 on bottom.
                                                                 **—   —   250   300**

**264** 6464-1965X on bottom. Only 74 produced.
                                                                 **—   —   275   325**

**265** Unpainted black door; no number on bottom.
                                                                                    **NRS**

**266** On bottom, "Presented to Joe Ranker".
                                                                                    **NRS**

**6464-TCA SPECIALS** In 1967, as they had in other years, TCA asked Lionel to make their special convention car. Lionel was unable to do so, and TCA therefore purchased a number of 6464 series boxcars and specially labeled them for the conventions. Each car was rubber-stamped "12th T.C.A. NATIONAL CONVENTION BALTIMORE MD. JUNE - 1967" on the bottom. They were also rubber-stamped with sequential numbers on the bottom. In addition, an extra brass door was supplied with each car. The brass doors were silk-screened in blue "TRAIN COLLECTORS ASSOCIATION ORGAN-IZED 1954 INCORPORATED 1957" and showed a railroad crossing signal lettered "NATIONAL CONVENTION BALT MD JUNE 67". It is believed that several hundred convention cars were distributed. It is reported, but not verified, that brass door reproductions have been made and that cars have been rubber-stamped to appear as if they were 1967 Convention cars. The following is a sampling of convention cars:

**267A** 6464-250 **WESTERN PACIFIC** Type IV light orange body painted dark orange, 1956-type gray door painted dark orange; no decals; white heat-stamped lettering, stamped 547.
                                                                 **—   —   —   275**

**267B** Similar to 267A but stamped "548"; dark blue feather.
                                                                 **—   —   —   275**

**267C** Similar to 267A but stamped "178"; unblackened rivets.
                                                                 **—   —   —   275**

**268** 6464-375 **CENTRAL of GEORGIA** Type IV maroon body painted with silver oval, 1956-type gray door painted silver; yellow and red decals; white and red heat-stamped lettering; no built date, rubber-stamped "411".
                                                                 **—   —   —   275**

**269** 6464-450 **GREAT NORTHERN** Type IV light olive body painted light olive, 1956-type olive door painted light olive, orange and yellow, red, white and black decals, yellow heat-stamped lettering, rubber-stamped "228" or "254".
                                                                 **—   —   —   275**

**270** 6464-475 **BOSTON & MAINE** Type IV dark blue unpainted body, 1956-type black unpainted door, no decals, black heat-stamped lettering, "BLT 2-57", rubber-stamped "580".
                                                                                    **NRS**

**271** 6464-525 **MINNEAPOLIS & ST. LOUIS** Type IV gray body painted red, 1956-type red unpainted doors, no decals, white heat-stamped lettering, "BLT 6-57", rubber-stamped "588".
                                                                                    **NRS**

**272** 6464-650 **DENVER & RIO GRANDE WESTERN** Type IV yellow unpainted body with silver-painted band and roof, 1956-type yellow unpainted door with silver-painted band, no decals, black heat-stamped lettering, rubber-stamped "387" or "483".
                                                                 **—   —   —   275**

**273** 6464-700 **A.T. & S.F.** Type IV gray body painted red, 1956-type gray door painted red, no decals, white heat-stamped lettering, rubber-stamped "220" or "360".
                                                                 **—   —   —   275**

**274** 6464-735 **NEW HAVEN** Type IV body, 1956-type door, no decals, black heat-stamped lettering, other details unknown.
                                                                                    **NRS**

**275** 6464-900 **NEW YORK CENTRAL** Type IV body, 1956-type door, no decals, white, black and red heat-stamped lettering, other details unknown.
                                                                                    **NRS**

**276** 6464-000 **BOSTON & MAINE** Type IV body, 1956-type door, black lettering, specially numbered "6464-000" rather than 6464-475, other details unknown, one-of-a-kind.
                                                                                    **NRS**

**6464-1970 TCA SPECIAL** (Chicago) Uncatalogued but made in 1970, TCA National Convention car, Type V yellow body painted slightly darker yellow, 1956-type red door mold, no decals, white heat-stamped lettering, 1,100 produced.

**277** Unpainted door.
                                                                 **—   —   90   110**

**278** Red door paint.
                                                                 **—   —   90   110**

**6464-1971 TCA SPECIAL** (Disneyland) Uncatalogued but made in 1971, TCA National Convention car, 1,500 produced.

**279** Type VII white body painted white, 1956-type dark orange-yellow door painted yellow, no decals, red, black and blue heat-stamped lettering.
                                                                 **—   —   160   200**

**6468-1 BALTIMORE & OHIO** 1953-55, double-door automobile car, Type A body,* white heat stamped lettering.

(A) Tuscan brown-painted black plastic body and doors.
                                                                 **75   110   150   250**

(B) Shiny blue-painted black plastic body and doors.   **9   12   18   30**

(C) Shiny blue-painted clear plastic body, shiny blue-painted black plastic door.
                                                                 **9   12   18   30**

(D) Flat blue-painted clear plastic body, flat blue-painted black plastic door.
                                                                 **9   12   18   30**

(E) Shiny blue-painted off-white opaque body. Kotil Collection.
                                                                 **9   12   18   30**

(F) Flat blue-painted off-white opaque body. Kotil Collection.
                                                                 **9   12   18   30**

**6468-25 NEW HAVEN** 1956-58, double-door automobile car, Type B orange unpainted plastic body,* black plastic door, bar-end metal trucks, magnetic couplers, "BLT 3-56".

(A) Full serif lettering with large black N and large white H.
                                                                 **8   13   17   30**

(B) Same as (A), but N missing serifs at top on right.   **8   13   17   30**

(C) Same as (A), but brown-painted doors, magnetic tab couplers.
                                                                 **20   30   50   80**

(D) Full serif lettering with large white N and large black H.
                                                                 **70   110   140   190**

(E) Same as (D), but half serif lettering. Blotner Collection.
                                                                 **70   110   140   190**

**6470 EXPLOSIVES** 1959-60, Type III red plastic body** with white lettering, Timken trucks with disc-operating couplers, spring-loaded car that explodes when hit by a missile.

(A) Red.                                                         **2   3   5   15**

(B) Orange-red.                                                  **2   3   5   15**

* There are two types of automobile bodies:
Type A does not have an ice hatch, as on 6352-1.
Type B has a faint line across the roof nearer brakewheel end, as on 6352-1.

** A modification of a Type III body:  rivet rows are short to leave "TARGET RANGE CAR" lettering on No. 6446.

**6472 REFRIGERATOR** 1950, white unpainted plastic, black lettering, "4-50", "RT 6472", plastic doors, spring clips hold body to frame, magnetic couplers.

| | | | |
|---|---|---|---|
| (A) Staple-end metal trucks. | 5 | 7 | 10 | 18 |
| (B) Bar-end metal trucks. | 5 | 7 | 10 | 18 |
| (C) Same as (B), but steps added. Rohlfing Collection. | 5 | 7 | 10 | 18 |

**6473 HORSE TRANSPORT** 1962-64, unpainted dark yellow body, heads bob as car rolls.

(A) Heavily stamped maroon-brown lettering, one operating and one dummy coupler, later Timken plastic trucks. Vagner Collection.

          5 7 10 18

(B) Same as (A), but lightly stamped maroon-brown lettering. Vagner Collection.

          5 7 10 18

(C) Lightly stamped red lettering.

          5 7 10 18

(D) Lighter yellow body, red lettering, two operating couplers, late Timken plastic trucks. Popovich and Vagner Collections.  **NRS**

(E) Same as (B), but pale yellow body and tuscan lettering. Halverson Collection.  **NRS**

**6480 EXPLOSIVES** Type III body**, white lettering.

(A) Flat red roof, ends and sides, side grooves, Timken trucks.

          2 3 5 18

(B) Shiny red roof, ends and sides, side grooves, Timken trucks.

          2 3 5 18

(C) Flat red roof, ends and sides, no side grooves, arch bar trucks.

          2 3 5 18

(D) Shiny red roof, ends and sides, side grooves on both sides, arch bar trucks.  2 3 5 18

**6482 REFRIGERATOR** 1957, white unpainted plastic car, non-operating versions of 3482, black "L" in double circle, "EW 9-11 EH 8-10 IL 29-6 IW 8-4 IH 7-5 CU.FT. 1834 RT 6482", opening doors with springs, body held to frame by frame tab at one end and Phillips-head screw at other, four non-operating ice hatches on roof, no brakewheels, sheet metal floor with two lengthwise ribs protruding outward for almost two-thirds of car length, but no holes for mechanism, Timken trucks, disc-operating couplers. Popovich and Jackson Collections.  15 30 50 75

**6530 FIRE FIGHTING INSTRUCTION CAR** 1960-61, white lettering and doors, Timken trucks with disc-operating couplers. This car came without fire fighting instructions!

| | | | |
|---|---|---|---|
| (A) Unpainted red plastic body. | 10 | 20 | 35 | 50 |
| (B) Black plastic body. | — | — | 750 | — |

**6556 KATY M-K-T** 1958 only, stock car, red plastic body paintd red, white lettering, white doors, two-level stock car, bar-end metal trucks, magnetic couplers. Came in only one set, 251W, Super 0, with 2329 Virginian. This is the most scarce stock car. Lord Collection.  60 90 120 170

** A modification of a Type III body: rivet rows are short to leave "TARGET RANGE CAR" lettering on No. 6446.

**6572 RAILWAY EXPRESS** 1958-59, 1963, refrigerator, red and white express decal, instrument panel on side with sliding cover, flat brown spring inside door guide shuts door. This car and its close match, 6672, come with plug-doors, as did their prototype. The plug-door fits into the car body side so that when it is shut, it fits flush with the side, unlike the overlapping doors found with most boxcars. The plug-door seals the interior more effectively. Griggs observation.

(A) 1958-59, blue plastic roof and green plastic sides painted dark green with dull gold lettering, bar-end metal trucks, magnetic tab couplers.

          25 35 50 80

(B) 1958-59, gray plastic painted light green, shiny gold lettering, bar-end metal trucks, magnetic tab couplers.  15 22 30 50

(C) 1963, gray plastic body painted light green, dull gold lettering, Timken trucks, disc-operating couplers.  10 15 25 40

(D) Green plastic roof and sides painted light green, dull gold lettering, Timken trucks, magnetic tab couplers.  12 18 25 40

(E) Dark green plastic roof and green plastic sides painted flat dark green, dull gold lettering, 2400-series passenger trucks. This version was found in the 216 Burlington Alco set of 1958. Ambrose Collection.

          25 35 55 77

(F) Same as (D), but shiny gold lettering similar to that found on (B). Fleming Collection.  15 22 30 50

**6646 LIONEL LINES** 1957, stock car, plastic body, black "L" in circle, 9" long.

| | | | |
|---|---|---|---|
| (A) Orange-painted clear plastic body. | 3 | 10 | 15 | 25 |
| (B) Orange unpainted plastic body. Kotil Collection. | 3 | 8 | 10 | 20 |

**6656 LIONEL LINES** 1949-55, stock car, black lettering, 9" long.

(A) Bright yellow, 1949, large black "L" in circle above car number, "LIONEL LINES CAPY. 800000" in black, one brakewheel, metal door guides, staple-end metal trucks, magnetic couplers. Warnick Collection.

          3 5 10 14

(B) Same as (A), but orange body and bar-end metal trucks. Warnick Collection.  3 5 10 14

(C) Bright yellow body, "ARMOUR" decal, black "L" in circle, "6656", brown decal, yellow lettering, red star, staple-end trucks, magnetic couplers, two oval holes on base. Like the 3656, the decal was used only in the 1950 production; Lord comment. Brooks Collection.

          35 60 85 125

**6672 SANTA FE** 1954-56, refrigerator car, white body with brown roof, instrument panel on side with sliding aluminum cover, brown spring inside door guide shuts doors, bar-end metal trucks, magnetic tab couplers. Griggs observations.

(A) 1955, black lettering with Lionel "L" in circle, chocolate brown roof.

          15 25 35 55

(B) 1956, same as (A), but without "L" and circle.  20 30 40 65

(C) 1954, same as (A), but with blue lettering.  12 18 25 35

(D) 1954, same as (C), but with three lines of data to right of door; much scarcer that other varieties.  30 40 50 70

**See prototype Boxcars in the Factory Errors Chapter.**

# Chapter IV
# CABOOSES

Note: Middle row cabooses have been modified with stacks, ladders and tool boxes.

By Roland LaVoie

No freight train looks complete without one of those homes on wheels for the train crew, the caboose. Lionel made sure that its cabooses were among the most colorful of all its freight cars. Lighted or unlighted, these cars have always been of interest to collectors and operators.

Lionel began its caboose production in the postwar years with a prewar carry-over, the Pennsylvania all-metal N5. Both lighted and unlighted versions were produced, and this little red caboose was extremely well detailed. It looks especially good when it is used with the 675/2025 Lionel K-4 Pacific steamer and since it is quite common, it is a favorite with operators.

By far, the most common of all the caboose styles was the Southern Pacific square cupola caboose with its cupola towards the rear of the car. It was produced in many different road names and levels of trim; some were lighted and elaborately detailed with metal battery boxes, smokestacks and ladders. Others had virtually no trim at all, and a few were even produced without lettering for the cheaper sets of the late postwar years. The most common of these cabooses is the maroon one lettered for Lionel Lines, carrying a 6257, 6357 or 6457 number. The better ones are easy to acquire and rather attractive in full trim. One unusual version of this caboose, highly prized today, was produced with a smoke unit. When the caboose was at rest and the current turned up, a thin wisp of smoke would come from the stack, as if the crew was cooking breakfast.

In the early fifties, Lionel began production of a beautifully detailed and handsome Pennsylvania Railroad N5C "Porthole" caboose. This caboose had a centered cupola, four round windows on each side and two round windows at each end. It was also produced in Virginian and Lehigh Valley markings, although the Pennsylvania was the only road to use this caboose.

Late in the postwar period, Lionel produced its most modern caboose in Lionel Lines and Erie markings, the Bay Window caboose. This long, slender-bodied caboose had no cupola. Instead, an alcove was built into each side of the car at the center, and the onlooker watched the train from the side rather than the top of the car. This caboose was outfitted with deluxe passenger trucks and couplers at both ends. One particularly rare version of the Lionel Lines caboose and all of the Erie cabooses are much sought after by collectors.

Of course, Lionel also produced a fine series of work cabooses. Basically, these were flatcars outfitted with a caboose cab and tool boxes or bins. The earliest of these cabooses were extremely well detailed cars built onto a die-cast frame; they were usually gray and had Delaware, Lackawanna and Western markings. Two of them even had a small searchlight mounted between the tool boxes, though Lionel finally discontinued its production because of the expense. Later versions were somewhat cheaper. The die-cast frame was replaced by a stamped-steel frame, and the tool boxes gave way to one large bin. None of the later work cabooses were lighted, but they were produced in many colors and road markings. Most of the later work cabooses are quite common, while some of the early ones are highly desirable and scarce.

97

Cabooses have always been interesting to operators and collectors alike. In fact, through a careful study of these cars, much information has been gathered concerning Lionel's construction practices. (See Joseph Kotil's analysis of caboose dies.) Many collectors specialize in the collection of cabooses. As is the case with most other types of Lionel freight cars, a collector can build a fine collection on a modest budget.

In this chapter, we list cabooses by catalogue number. Usually the catalogue number appears on the car's sides. The exceptions almost always involve a suffix. For example, one caboose is catalogued as a 6017-100; the 100 is the suffix, but it only has the number 6017 on its sides. In the text for this item, we explain that only 6017 is found on the car's sides. Any item whose catalogue number does not correspond to the number on the car's sides is identified.

Prior to 1970 Lionel made five basic caboose body types: the Southern Pacific (SP), work caboose, Pennsylvania C-5, Pennsylvania N5C and the bay window caboose. Each came with various add-ons, including lights, operating couplers at both ends, window inserts, smoke stacks, tool boxes, etc. The Southern Pacific (SP) was by far the most popular style and the majority of Lionel's cabooses were based on the SP prototype.

In the first edition of the postwar Lionel Price Guide, two basic SP molds were identified: Type I and Type II. Since that time, further analysis by Joseph Kotil has uncovered significant new information about these cabooses. As a consequence, the information on caboose types has been expanded in the following manner. Type I is subdivided into Dies 1, 1A, 2, 2A, 3, 3A, 3B and 3C. Mold Type II is now called Die 4. Type I cabooses in this section have been reclassified as being Die 1 through Die 3C, whenever possible.

## SP CABOOSE DIES
### By Joseph Kotil

The major elements of caboose construction as they relate to die identification are listed below as are the definitions of Dies 1 through 4.

**A. Window Frames, Front and Rear Cupola Windows**
1. No window frames   Dies 1, 1A, 2, 2A, 3, 3A, 3B and 3C
2. Window frames   Die 4

**B. Step Construction**
1. Thin, early type   Dies 1, 1A, 2, 2A, 3, 3A, 3B and 3C
2. Thick, later type   Die 4

**C. Reinforced Stack Plug Opening**
1. Present   Dies 1, 1A, 2, 2A, 3C and 4
2. Not present   Dies 3, 3A and 3B

**FIGURE 1**

**D. Stack Plug (where no stack)**
1. Above -- plug raised parallel to roof slope   Die 3
2. Rim -- rim raised parallel to catwalk with recessed center   Dies 1, 1A, 2 and 2A
3. Below -- plug below roof line, parallel to catwalk   Die 4

**E. Vertical Rivets Below Side Windows 3 and 4**
1. 8 rivets   Dies 1, 2, 3, 3A, 3B and 4
2. 4 rivets   Dies 1A, 2A, 3C and 4

**F. Ladder Slot**
1. Present   Dies 1, 2 and 4
2. Not present   Dies 3, 3A, 3B and 3C

**G. Wedges along Catwalk, Roof Panel 4**
1. Present   Dies 3B and 3C
2. Not present   Dies 1, 1A, 2, 2A, 3, 3A and 4

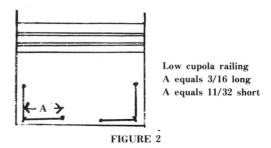

Low cupola railing
A equals 3/16 long
A equals 11/32 short

**FIGURE 2**

**H. Cupola Roof Railings**
1. High roof railings   Dies 1, 1A, 2 and 2A
2. Low, short roof railings (11/32")   Die 3
3. Low, long roof railings (3/16")   Die 3A, 3B and 3C
4. Curved roof railings   Die 4

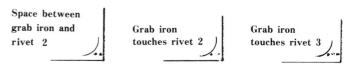

Space between grab iron and rivet 2

Grab iron touches rivet 2

Grab iron touches rivet 3

**FIGURE 3**

**I. Grab Rail at Corner**
1. Grab rail touches rivet 2   Dies 1 and 1A
2. Grab rail clears rivet 2   Dies 2 and 2A
3. Grab rail touches rivet 3   Die 4

**J. Extra Rivet Between Door Rivet Row and Roof Rivet Row, at End**
1. No extra rivet   Dies 1, 1A, 2 and 2A
2. Extra rivet   Dies 3, 3A, 3B, 3C, 3D and 4

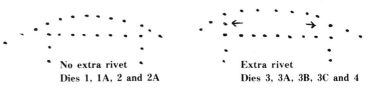

No extra rivet
Dies 1, 1A, 2 and 2A

Extra rivet
Dies 3, 3A, 3B, 3C and 4

**FIGURE 4**

**K. Three Extra Rivets on Panel 2**
(Rivets and lines faintly seen reveal repair of damaged die on panels 1 and 2)
1. No damage and repair   Dies 1, 1A, 2, 2A, 2B and 4
2. Damaged and repaired   Dies 3, 3A, 3B and 3C

**L. Catwalk Overhang Supports**
1. No supports   Dies 1, 1A, 2, 2A, 3, 3A, 3B and 3C.
2. Supports   Die 4

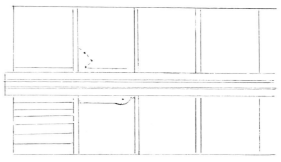

**FIGURE 5**

## SP DIE CHARACTERISTICS

| | **Die 1** | **Die 2** | **Die 3** | **Die 4** |
|---|---|---|---|---|
| A. | No window frame on front and rear cupola windows | No window frame | No window frame | Window frame |
| B. | Thin steps | Thin steps | Thin steps | Thick steps |
| C. | Reinforced stack opening | Reinforced stack opening | Stack opening not reinforced | Reinforced stack opening |
| D. | Rim-type stack plug | Rim - type stack plug | Raised plug | Lower plug |
| E. | 8 rivets below windows 3 and 4 | 8 rivets below windows 3 and 4 | 8 rivets below window 3 and 4 | 4 rivets below windows 3 and 4 |
| F. | Ladder slots | Ladder slots | No ladder slots | Ladder slots |
| G. | No wedges by catwalk | No wedges by catwalk | No wedges by catwalk | No wedges by catwalk |
| H. | High cupola roof detail | High cupola roof detail | Low cupola roof detail | Curved cupola roof detail |
| I. | Side grab rail touches rivet 2 | Space between side grab rail and rivet 2 | Space between side grab rail and rivet 2 | Side grab rail touches rivet 3 |
| J. | No extra rivet on ends above door | No extra rivet on ends above door | Extra rivets on ends above door | Extra rivets on ends above door |
| K. | No die crack on roof | No die crack on roof | Die crack on roof | No die crack on roof |
| L. | No supports for catwalk overhang | No supports for catwalk overhang | No supports for catwalk overhang | Brackets support catwalk overhang |

| **Die 1A** | **Die 2A** | **Die 3A** | **Die 3C** |
|---|---|---|---|
| Same as above except (E.) 4 rivets below windows 3 and 4 | Same as above except (E.) 4 rivets below windows 3 and 4 | Same as above except (H.) low, long cupola roof railing | Same as 3 except (C.) reinforced roof (plug for the 6557 Smoking Caboose and the 6017-100 B&M (1959) and possibly others); (E.) 4 rivets below windows 3 and 4; (G.) wedges present; (H.) low, long cupola roof railing |

**Die 3B**

Same as 3 except

(G.) wedges are present

(H.) low, long cupola roof railing.

|  | Gd | VG | Exc | Mt |
|---|---|---|---|---|

**1007 LIONEL LINES** SP Die 3, 1948-52, Scout caboose with Scout trucks, "1007" behind "LIONEL LINES" on left side, "1007" in front of "LIONEL LINES" on right side. These locations imply that the same stamp was used on both sides.

| | | | | |
|---|---|---|---|---|
| (A) Red with white lettering. | 1 | 1.50 | 2 | 3 |
| (B) Lighter red with white lettering. | 1 | 1.50 | 2 | 3 |
| (C) Orange-red with white lettering. | 1 | 1.50 | 2 | 3 |

**2257 LIONEL** SP Die 1, 1948, metal trucks with two operating coil couplers, two brakewheels, "2257" centered on side under cupola.

| | | | | |
|---|---|---|---|---|
| (A) Not illuminated, no stack, red with white lettering, no tool boxes. | 2 | 3 | 4 | 6 |
| (B) Illuminated, stack, tuscan with white lettering, and tool boxes. | 5 | 7 | 10 | 12 |
| (C) Same as (A), but tuscan. Kotil Collection. | 2 | 3 | 4 | 6 |
| (D) Same as (B), but red. Kotil Collection. | 5 | 7 | 10 | 12 |
| (E) Same as (A), but only one coil coupler. Budniak Collection. | 2 | 3 | 4 | 6 |

**2357 LIONEL** SP Die 1 or 2, 1948, metal trucks with two operating coil couplers, two brakewheels, two ladders, brown stack, tool boxes, illuminated, window inserts, "2357" centered under cupola.

| | | | | |
|---|---|---|---|---|
| (A) Red with white lettering. | 5 | 7 | 10 | 15 |
| (B) Tuscan with white lettering. | 5 | 7 | 10 | 15 |
| (C) Same as (B), but brakewheels mounted towards platform, not towards outside. Fleming Collection. | 5 | 7 | 10 | 15 |
| (D) Same as (B), but black metal stack instead of brown. Budniak Collection. | 4 | 7 | 10 | 15 |

**2419 D. L. & W.** Work Caboose 1946-47, gray with black lettering, die-cast frame; handrails, ladders, two tool boxes, brakewheels, die-cast smoke stack.

| | | | | |
|---|---|---|---|---|
| (A) 1946, metal trucks with open-type early coil couplers | 15 | 22 | 30 | 50 |
| (B) 1947, metal trucks with regular coil couplers. | 15 | 22 | 30 | 50 |

**2420 D. L. & W.** Work Caboose 1946-49, gray with black lettering, die-cast frame; handrails, ladders, two tool boxes, brakewheels, die-cast smokestack and searchlight.

| | | | | |
|---|---|---|---|---|
| (A) 1946, metal trucks with open-type early coil couplers. | 20 | 30 | 40 | 75 |
| (B) 1946-49, metal trucks with regular coil couplers. Shown in 1946 catalogue set no. 2111WS with 671 locomotive. Gray body, black serif or sans-serif lettering on die cast gray frame, staple-end metal trucks, coil couplers. Rohlfing Collection. | 20 | 30 | 40 | 75 |
| (C) Darker gray cab and tool boxes on light gray frame. Ocilka Collection. | 20 | 30 | 40 | 75 |

**2457**

**2457 PENNSYLVANIA** N5, 1946-47, metal body with white lettering, black frame, usually semi-gloss red-painted body, black window frames, smokestack, illuminated, window inserts, metal couplers, "477618" appears on car sides, pierced cupola end windows. Some lettered "Eastern Division". Ely comment. (We need to know which are and which are not.)

| | | | | |
|---|---|---|---|---|
| (A) Glossy red body, black window frames, whirly wheels, steps, front and rear cupola windows, rivet detail on roofwalk, two operating coil couplers. Foss observation. | 7 | 10 | 15 | 20 |
| (B) Same as (A), but plain wheels, one operating coil coupler. | 7 | 10 | 15 | 20 |
| (C) Semi-gloss red paint, black window frames, plain wheels, steps, no cupola end windows, no rivet detail on roofwalk, two operating coil couplers. Foss observation. | 7 | 10 | 15 | 20 |

# N5C CABOOSE

(D) Brown body, red window frames, whirly wheels, no steps, front and rear cupola windows, no roofwalk rivet detail, underscored "2457" on bottom. Foss observation.

| | 7 | 12 | 15 | 18 |

(E) Glossy red body, black window frames, no "EASTERN DIV.", front and rear cupola windows, plain wheels, no steps, staple-end metal trucks, one late coil coupler, no rivet detail on catwalk, "2457" on bottom in silver, "BLT. 4.41 N5 P.R.R." on lower right of car side, white heat-stamped lettering, battery box on frame, plastic air compressor mounted on metal channel. LaVoie Collection.

| | 7 | 10 | 15 | 18 |

(F) Same as (C), but only one coil coupler; cupola end windows present. Rohlfing Collection.

| | 7 | 10 | 15 | 20 |

(G) Same as (A), but plain wheels. Budniak Collection.

| | 7 | 10 | 15 | 20 |

(H) Same as (G), but staple-end metal trucks, two magnetic couplers. Budniak Collection.

| | 7 | 10 | 15 | 20 |

2472

**2472 PENNSYLVANIA** N5, 1945-47, red metal body with white lettering, black frame, no window inserts, no stack, metal trucks, one operating coil coupler, "477618" on car sides.

(A) Pierced cupola end windows, lettered "EASTERN DIV." Lemieux Collection.

| | 4 | 6 | 8 | 12 |

(B) Unpierced cupola end windows, lettered "EASTERN DIV.", late coil couplers, bottom rubber-stamped "2472". Kotil and Lemieux Collections.

| | 4 | 6 | 8 | 12 |

**2857 N Y C** 1946, scale detailed caboose, catalogued, but not manufactured.

**Not Manufactured**

**2957 N Y C** Circa 1946, originally manufactured 1940-42, refitted with postwar staple-end trucks with coil couplers by either Lionel service stations or owner.

| | 100 | 200 | 300 | 400 |

**4357 PENNSYLVANIA** N5, 1948-50, red metal body with white lettering, black frame, green and white "ELECTRONIC CONTROL" decal, electronic control receiver.

| | 25 | 37 | 50 | 75 |

**4457 PENNSYLVANIA** 1946-47, N5, red metal body with white lettering, black frame, green and white "ELECTRONIC CONTROL" decal, electronic control receiver.

| | 25 | 37 | 50 | 75 |

**6007 LIONEL LINES** 1950, SP Die 3, Scout caboose with Scout trucks, only trim is front and rear railings, screws fasten body and frame.

| | 1 | 1.50 | 2 | 3 |

**6017 LIONEL LINES** SP Dies, 1951-61, only trim is front and rear railings.

(A) Die 2, gray-painted black plastic with black lettering, black frame, plastic Timken trucks, tab fasteners, "6017" on rear left side and front right side, one operating disc coupler. Came in box marked "6017-85". Ambrose comment.

| | 7 | 11 | 15 | 20 |

(B) Red with white lettering, black frame, staple-end metal trucks, Die 3A. Rohlfing Collection.

| | 1 | 1.50 | 2 | 3 |

(C) Light tuscan, painted black plastic, white lettering, black frame, Timken trucks with one magnetic tab coupler, Die 1. Came with 1958 set No. 1595. Ambrose Collection.

| | 1 | 1.50 | 2 | 3 |

(D) Light tuscan-painted mustard plastic; lighter tuscan than (C), Timken trucks, one magnetic tab coupler.

| | 1 | 1.50 | 2 | 3 |

(E) Same as (C), but very light tuscan-painted orange plastic, Die 1A. Rohlfing Collection.

| | 1 | 1.50 | 2 | 3 |

(F) Same as (C), but dark tuscan-painted orange plastic.

| | 1 | 1.50 | 2 | 3 |

**Top Row: Bay Window Cabooses, lower rows: Work Cabooses**

**6017-225 A.T.**
frame with ta
operating fron
front sides. S
(A) Red-painte
(B) Bright red

**6017-235 A.T.**
lettering, one
frame, with en
coupler. Koti
needed. Ambr

**6027 ALASKA**
tab body faste
on rear left and

**6037 LIONEL**
screw body fa
Scout couplers
Gondola for a
(A) Brown wit

(B) Reddish-b

(C) Same as (B
(D) Same as (A
(E) Same as (A

**6047 LIONEL**
(A) SP Die 2
coupler.
(B) SP Die 2A
coupler, one Ti
(C) SP Die 4, li

(D) Dark red
set of 1959-60.

**6057 LIONEL**
(A) SP Die 1A

(B) Same as (
(C) SP Die 4,
coupler.
(D) Brown wit
(E) Red, die 4,

**6057-50 LION**
frame with tab

**6058 C & O 19**
body fasteners

**6059-50 M St**
coupler, one f
(A) Dark mar
(B) Lighter m

**6059-60 M St**
Timken truck
(A) Unpainte
coupler.
(B) Unpainte

(C) Red-paint

**6067 NO LET**
requested.

**6119 D.L.& W**
(A) Stamped
tool bin; metal
(B) Same as (
(C) Stamped
bin, metal tru

(G) Die 4, dark tuscan-painted black plastic, black frame with tab fasteners

| | 1 | 1.50 | 2 | 3 |

(H) Dark tuscan-painted tuscan plastic, black frame with tab fasteners, Timken trucks, two couplers, one operating coupler. 1.50 2 2.50 3

(I) Die 4, dark tuscan-painted red plastic, Timken trucks, one operating disc coupler, black frame with tab fasteners — 1.50 2 3

(J) Flat maroon-tuscan paint, bar-end metal trucks, magnetic coupler, black frame with screw fasteners for body. 1 1.50 2 3

(K) Same as (J), but shiny maroon-tuscan paint, Die 3A. Rohlfing Collection. 1 1.50 2 3

(L) "LIONEL" rather than "LIONEL LINES", "6017" underscored, bar-end metal trucks, one operating coupler, black frame with screw body fastener, shiny maroon-tuscan paint, Die 3B. Rohlfing Collection.
2 3 4 6

(M) Brown plastic body, metal trucks. Pauli Collection. 1 1.50 2 3

(N) Die 3B, unpainted shiny maroon plastic; white "LIONEL LINES" between third and fourth windows and "6017" between first and second windows on lower half of one side; on other side "LIONEL LINES" between windows one through three and "6017" below second cupola window, on lower half; screw fasteners, bar-end metal trucks, magnetic couplers at both ends (second coupler may have been added). Edmunds Collection.
1 1.50 2 3

(O) Die 1A, flat tuscan-painted black plastic, same lettering as (N), tab fasteners, Timken trucks, operating couplers, truck has small "4" embossed, rear coupler may have been added. Edmunds Collection.
1 1.50 2 3

(P) Die 1A, brown-painted black plastic, same lettering as (N) Timken trucks, one disc-operating coupler. Stem Collection. 1 1.50 2 3

(Q) Same as (O), but red plastic body painted tuscan. Rohlfing Collection.
1 1.50 2 3

(R) Tuscan-painted body, Timken trucks, one disc coupler, Die 1. Rohlfing Collection. 1 1.50 2 3

(S) Same as (L), but two operating couplers, one with tab and the other without. Budniak Collection. 1 1.50 2 3

(T) Die 2: flat maroon-painted marbled gray plastic, lettered as in (N), tab fasteners, plastic trucks, one disc coupler. NOTE: Marbled plastic is usually scrap material melted down and re-molded. Several colors produce the marbled look. This practice was common in the early postwar years and during the Korean War, when plastic was scarce. Budniak Collection.
1 1.50 2 3

**6017-50 UNITED STATES MARINE CORPS** 1958, SP Die 1A, dark blue with white lettering, black frame with tab body fasteners, "601750" on front left side and rear right side, Timken trucks, one operating coupler.
12 17 25 50

**6017-85** See 6017 (A).

**6017-100 BOSTON AND MAINE** 1959, 1964-65, SP Dies 3C and 4, blue with white lettering, "6017" under cupola on both sides, black frame with tab body fasteners, Timken trucks, one operating coupler; catalogued as 6017-100 but only "6017" appears on car. Powell Collection. Came as part of uncatalogued Sears set; Beavin comment. Information needed about following variation types:
(A) Medium blue. 7 11 15 30
(B) Lighter blue. Pauli Collection. 7 11 15 25
(C) Purplish blue. Pauli Collection. 40 65 120 175

**6017-185 A.T. & S.F.** 1959, SP Die 4, light gray with red lettering, galvanized frame, tab body fasteners, no end rails, no cupola window frames, thin steps, stack plug flush with roof, four rivets below 3rd and 4th side windows, wedges along roof catwalk, low cupola roof railings, grab-rails at corners clear second rivet, extra rivet between door rivets and roof rivet row, three extra rivets on roof panel, low profile square handrails at each end, "6017" on rear left and front right sides, catalogued as "6017-185", but "6017" appears on car. Kotil comment.
(A) Timken trucks, one fixed coupler. 5 7 15 25
(B) Front Timken truck with operating coupler, rear arch bar truck with fixed coupler. 5 7 15 25
(C) Timken trucks, one operating coupler, one fixed coupler, SP Die other than 4. 5 7 15 25
(D) Same as (C), but black frame, square end railings, stack plug flush with roof and reinforced from below, Timken trucks, one disc coupler, Die 4. George Cole and Rohlfing Collections. 5 7 15 25
(E) Die 1A: bar-end metal trucks, one magnetic coupler, black frame, screw fastener, gray-painted black plastic, end rails. Budniak Collection. **NRS**
See also 6017-225 and 6017-235.

**6017-200 UNITED STATES NAVY** 1960, SP Die 4, light blue with white lettering, black frame with tab body fasteners, Timken trucks, one operating coupler; catalogued as "6017-200", but "6017" appears on car.
(A) As described above. 15 22 30 50
(B) Light blue body with aqua tint, blue platform and steps, tall stack, metal ladders and platform ends, battery boxes, clear plastic window inserts, bar-end metal trucks, two magnetic couplers. Hopper Collection. **NRS**

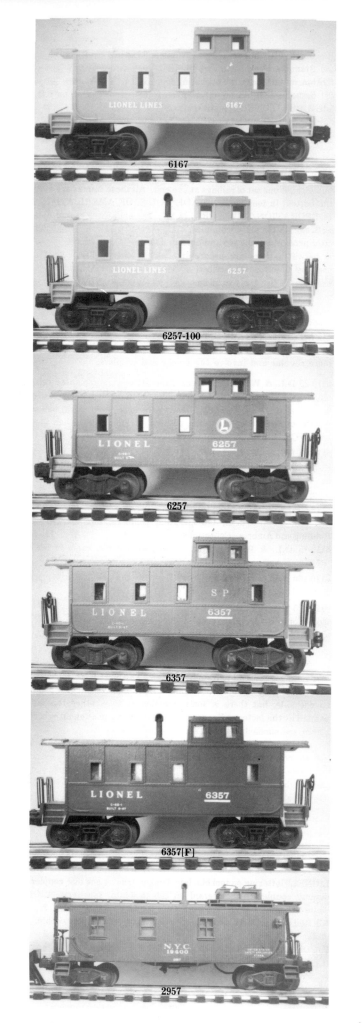

6167

6257-100

6257

6357

6357[F]

2957

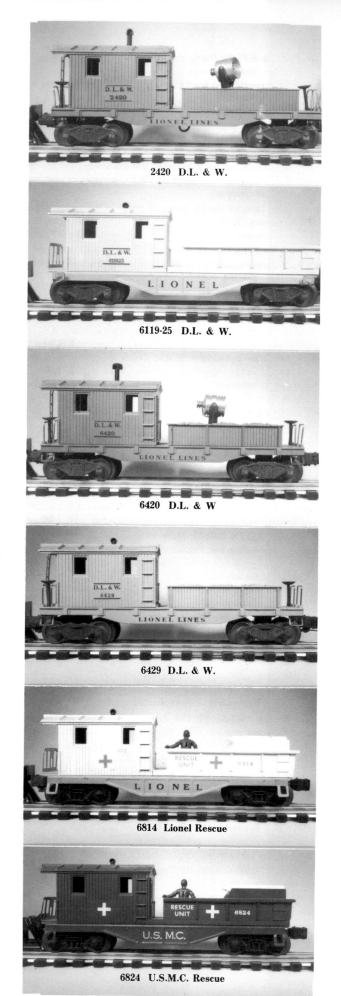

2420 D.L. & W.

6119-25 D.L. & W.

6420 D.L. & W

6429 D.L. & W.

6814 Lionel Rescue

6824 U.S.M.C. Rescue

(F) Orange-red cab and tool bin, lettering on tool bin, "LIONEL" on frame. Pauli Collection. **6 9 12 15**

(G) Same as (B), but no "LIONEL" on frame. LaVoie Collection. **6 9 12 15**

**6157** Reported but not verified, more information needed.

## UNLETTERED & UNNUMBERED CABOOSES

Lionel made a number of unlettered and unnumbered cabooses. These often came with inexpensive sets and the omission of letters and numbers probably can be explained by cost reduction. We have had difficulty in matching the catalogue numbers as they appear in the Service Manual with these unnumbered cabooses. Numbers do appear on their boxes. We would appreciate very much your assistance in matching cabooses with numbers. We have made some matches below. Known numbers are: 6167-25 (red) body, body mold number 6059-2; 6167-50 (yellow) body, body mold number 6167-52; 6167-100 (body color unknown), body mold number 6167-102; 6167-125 (red) body, body mold number 6059-2 and 6167-150 (body color unknown), body mold number 6167-102.

**6167 LIONEL LINES** 1963, SP Die 4, galvanized frame with tab-fastened body, Timken trucks.

(A) Red plastic body, white lettering, one disc-operating coupler, one fixed coupler, no end rails. Budniak Collection. **1 1.50 2 3**

(B) Flat red plastic body, white lettering, one disc-operating coupler, one fixed coupler. **1 1.50 2 3**

(C) Same as (A), but only one disc coupler. Kotil Collection. **1 1.50 2 3**

**6167-25 NO LETTERING,** SP Type 4 red unpainted plastic body, galvanized underframe, Timken trucks with one dummy coupler, frame with tab-fastened body, no end rails, came with set No. 11420 (1964) with 1061 locomotive and 6112 gondola in box probably numbered 6042-50, confirmation requested. Light Collection. **1 2 3 5**

**6167-50 NO LETTERING** 1964, SP Die 4, yellow unpainted plastic body, galvanized underframe, Timken trucks, fixed couplers, frame with tab-fastened body, no end rails. **1 1.50 4 8**

**6167-85 UNION PACIFIC** 1964-69, SP Die 4, unpainted yellow plastic body, black lettering, Timken trucks, one disc-operating coupler, one fixed coupler; frame with tab-fastened body, only "6167" appears on car.

(A) One disc-operating coupler, one fixed coupler. **6 9 15 25**

(B) Only one disc-operating coupler. Kotil Collection. **6 9 15 25**

**6167-100 NO LETTERING** 1964, SP Die 4, light red unpainted body, Timken trucks, one fixed coupler, galvanized frame with tab body fasteners and no end rail. **1 1.50 2 3**

**6167-125 NO LETTERING** 1964, SP Die 4, arch bar trucks, one fixed coupler, frame with tab body fasteners, with end rail.

(A) Dark brown unpainted plastic. **1 1.50 2 3**

(B) Medium red unpainted plastic. **1 1.50 2 3**

(C) LIONEL LINES, 6167 only on caboose, SP-4 die, Timken plastic trucks, one disc and one dummy coupler, part of set No. 11430. Winton Collection. **1 1.50 2 3**

**6167-150 NO LETTERING.** More information requested.

**6219 C&O** 1960, Work Caboose, stamped flat black frame, blue cab with yellow lettering, blue tool bin, Timken trucks, one disc-operating coupler. **10 15 25 50**

**6257 LIONEL** 1948-56, SP Dies, metal trucks, one operating coupler, frame fastened to body with screws.

(A) "6257" is underscored, partially filled double circle around "L", red, painted black plastic brakewheel, Die 2. **1 1.50 2 3**

(B) Same as (A), but unpainted red plastic body, one brakewheel, original box stamped "25 LIONEL 25". Kotil Collection. **1 1.50 2 3**

(C) Same as (A), but unpainted red plastic body and partially filled double circle. **1 1.50 2 3**

(D) Same as (A), but circle not filled in. **1 1.50 2 3**

(E) Same as (A), but black plastic painted duller red. **1 1.50 2 3**

(F) Same as (A), but black plastic painted brownish-red. **1 1.50 2 3**

(G) "6267" is underscored, no "L". **1 1.50 2 3**

(H) "SP" above underscored "6257", black plastic painted red. **1 1.50 2 3**

(I) "SP" above underscored "6257", clear plastic painted flat red (compared to (H)), lighted, light may have been added after piece left factory. **1 1.50 2 3**

(J) "SP" above underscored "6257", clear plastic painted brownish-red as compared to (K), (L) and (M). **1 1.50 2 3**

(K) "SP" above underscored "6257", black plastic painted brownish-red, "S" is thicker than on other 6257s. **1 1.50 2 3**

(L) Same as (K), but regular "S". **1 1.50 2 3**

(M) "SP" above underscored "6257", black plastic painted shiny brownish-red when compared to (J), (K) and (L). **1 1.50 2 3**

(N) Same as (B), but no brakewheel, box stamped "50 LIONEL 50". Kotil Collection. **1 1.50 2 3**

(O) Red-painted black plastic, white "SP" above underscored "6257" between third and fourth windows, "LIONEL" beneath first and second windows, "C 40-1 BUILT 9-47" beneath "LIONEL". Edmunds Collection. **1 1.50 2 3**

(P) Same as (O), but lighter red-painted black plastic body, Die 2 (sample observed had one staple-end and one bar-end metal truck). Rohlfing Collection. **1 1.50 2 3**

(Q) Same as (P), but Die 1, staple-end metal trucks, magnetic couplers. Rohlfing Collection. **1 1.50 2 3**

(R) Light red-painted black plastic body, white "SP" above underscored "6257" between third and fourth windows, "C-40-1 BUILT 9-47" below "LIONEL", bar-end metal trucks, magnetic couplers, Die 2. Rohlfing Collection. **1 1.50 2 3**

**6257-25 LIONEL** Die 3A, "L" in double circle, underscored "6257", unpainted bright red plastic body, metal trucks, one brakewheel, "6257-25" on box end, car marked only "6257". Kotil Collection. **1 1.50 2 3**

**6257-50 LIONEL** Die 1 or 3A, box end marked "6257-50", car marked only "6257".

(A) "L" in double circle, "6257" underscored, unpainted bright red plastic body, no brakewheel, metal trucks, Die 1. Kotil Collection. **1 1.50 2 3**

(B) No "L" in circle, "6257" underscored, unpainted bright red plastic body, no brakewheel, metal trucks, Die 3A. Kotil Collection. **1 1.50 2 3**

(C) Same as (A), but Die 3A. Rohlfing Collection. **1 1.50 2 3**

**6257-100 LIONEL LINES** 1956-63, SP Die 4, red unpainted plastic, stack, Timken trucks, one disc-operating coupler, tabs fasten black frame and body, "6257-100" catalogue number, only "6257" on car. **1 1.50 2 3**

**6257X LIONEL LINES** 1948 catalogue, page 5; came with two couplers instead of the usual one with the 6257 because it was part of the 1656 switcher outfit. Foss and Hutchinson observations. **NRS**

**6357 LIONEL** 1948-57, SP Dies, smoke stack, bar-end metal trucks, "6357" underscored, "SP" above "6357" underscored, lighted, screws fasten black base to body, one operating coupler, "C-40-1" and "BUILT 9-47", brakewheel, except as noted.

(A) Brownish-red-painted black plastic, two operating couplers, no stack. **4 6 8 12**

(B) Shiny maroon-painted black plastic, one operating magnetic coupler. **4 6 8 12**

(C) Duller maroon-painted black plastic, Die 1. Rohlfing Collection. **4 6 8 12**

(D) Black plastic painted maroon, Timken trucks. **4 6 8 12**

(E) 1963 only, SP Die 4, gray plastic-painted maroon, Timken trucks, one disc-operating coupler, ladder, without "SP". Ambrose Collection. **10 20 30 40**

(F) Black plastic painted maroon, without "SP". **4 6 8 12**

(G) Black plastic painted bright red, Die 1, staple-end trucks. Pauli Collection. **4 6 8 12**

(H) 1948, Same as (A), but staple-end trucks, one wire wound coupler. Hutchinson Collection. **4 6 8 12**

(I) Light red-painted black plastic body, staple-end metal trucks, one magnetic coupler, no stack, Die 1. Rohlfing Collection. **4 6 8 12**

**6357-25 LIONEL** SP Die 2, "L" in double circle over underscored "6357", ("6357-25" does not appear on car sides), lighted, stack, brakewheel, black base, screws fasten body to frame, bar-end metal trucks, one operating magnetic coupler.

| | | | | |
|---|---|---|---|---|
| (A) Reddish-maroon-painted; black plastic. | 4 | 6 | 8 | 12 |
| (B) Maroon-painted black plastic. | 4 | 6 | 8 | 12 |
| (C) Brownish-maroon-painted black plastic. | 4 | 6 | 8 | 12 |
| (D) Gray with red lettering. | — | — | 1000 | — |

(E) Same as (B), but description matches general heading of 6357; only the color differs. Box marked "6357-25"; came as part of set 2201WS. Budniak Collection. **NRS**

**6357-50 A.T. & S.F.**, SP Die 4, (not LIONEL), "6357" not underscored, black plastic-painted red, Timken trucks, one disc-operating coupler. Usually screw fasteners came only with tab frame body fasteners. Without "C-40-1", "BUILT 9-47", and "SP". This caboose is probably as scarce as the tuscan Lehigh Valley, but it has not received the publicity. Came in "over and under" set only, box marked "6357-50", 1960. Stein, Ambrose and Degano observations. **150 250 350 500**

## N 5 C CABOOSE CATALOGUE NUMBERS

We are following the recommendation of Joseph Kotil and are recataloguing the 6417-N5C cabooses. The following numbers come from **GREENBERG'S REPAIR AND OPERATING MANUAL FOR LIONEL TRAINS,** Third Edition, page 309, and represent a change from the previous Price Guides.

**6417 PENNSYLVANIA** 1953-57, N5C, "536417" on side, tuscan with white lettering, lights, bar-end metal trucks (PT-1 and 479-1), two operating couplers, lettered "BLT 2-53". (The part number for the caboose body is 6417-3.)

| | | | | |
|---|---|---|---|---|
| (A) With "NEW YORK ZONE". | 7 | 11 | 15 | 25 |
| (B) Without "NEW YORK ZONE". | 10 | 15 | 20 | 30 |

(C) Gray-painted black plastic shell, dark maroon "NEW YORK ZONE" in sans-serif, "BLT 2-53", "L" in circle, plug in light unit, bar-end metal trucks, operating tab couplers. Degano Collection. **NRS**

(D) Lime green-painted black plastic shell, dark maroon "NEW YORK ZONE" in sans-serif,"BLT 2-53", one operating coupler, no tabs. Degano Collection. **NRS**

(E) Same as (A), but shiny reddish tuscan-painted black plastic body. Budniak Collection. **7 11 15 25**

**64173** See 6417-25.

### 6417-25 LIONEL LINES

**6417-25 LIONEL LINES** 1954, N5C, "64173" on side, tuscan with white lettering, lettered "BLT 11-53". In previous editions, this car was numbered 6417-53. (The part number for the caboose body is 6417-26.)

| | | | | |
|---|---|---|---|---|
| (A) Magnetic couplers with tabs. | 7 | 11 | 15 | 25 |
| (B) Magnetic couplers, no tabs. Kotil Collection. | 7 | 11 | 15 | 25 |

**6417-50 LEHIGH VALLEY** 1954, N5C, numbered on side "641751", lettered "BLT 6-54", Lionel "L" in circle on lower right car side, bar-end metal trucks (PT-1), magnetic couplers, apparently not lighted. (Listed as 6417-51 in last edition but changed to correspond to Service Manual entry which lists the body part number as 6417-50.)

| | | | | |
|---|---|---|---|---|
| (A) Tuscan with white lettering, tab couplers. | — | — | 1000 | — |
| (B) Gray with red lettering. | 20 | 30 | 40 | 60 |
| (C) Tuscan with gold lettering, Degano Collection. | — | — | 1200 | — |

(D) Gray-painted clear plastic shell, blue heat-stamped lettering "BLT 6-54", "L" in circle on lower right, plastic window inserts, press in light unit, bar-end trucks, magnetic operating couplers without tabs. Degano Collection. **— — 1000 —**

**6417-51** See 6417-50.

**6419 DL&W** 1949-50, 1956-57, Work Caboose, bar-end metal trucks, two magnetic couplers, die-cast frame (#2419), "D L & W 6419" on cab side and black "LIONEL LINES" lettering on frame side, smokestack on roof, brakewheel at each end, steps at each corner. In 1950, Lionel also offered a deluxe version of the 6419, the 6420 with searchlight (see below). In 1956, after a five year absence, the 6419 was offered as part of the Virginian set whose number is believed to be 2267W. The 6419 was also offered for separate sale. In 1957, the caboose was again offered as part of Set 2281W headed by a single motor 2243 Santa Fe F-3 AB catalogued as 0 Gauge. (See 2243 for this interesting tale.) The caboose was also offered for separate sale again in 1957. Lord comment.

| | | | | |
|---|---|---|---|---|
| (A) Black marble plastic painted dark gray. | 10 | 15 | 20 | 30 |
| (B) Pink plastic painted light gray. | 10 | 15 | 20 | 30 |
| (C) Orange plastic, catalogued but not manufactured. | | | **Not Manufactured** | |
| (D) Same as (B), but clear plastic painted light gray. Budniak Collection. | 10 | 15 | 20 | 30 |

(E) Same as (D), but light gray-painted die-cast base, staple-end metal trucks, magnetic couplers, high stack, came in 1949 set 1457B. Rohlfing Collection. **10 15 20 30**

(F) Same as (E), but bar-end metal trucks, light gray-painted marbled purple plastic. Rohlfing Collection. **10 15 20 30**

(G) Same as (F), but short stack. Rohlfing Collection. **10 15 20 30**

**6419-57 N & W** 1957, Work Caboose, bar-end metal trucks, one magnetic tab coupler, low stack, medium gray die-cast frame, "LIONEL LINES" in black letters, light gray boxes, light gray cab with "576419" in black.

| | | | | |
|---|---|---|---|---|
| (A) As described above. | 25 | 35 | 45 | 80 |
| (B) Same as (A), but ladder on cab. Abraham and Alvatrain Collections. | 25 | 35 | 45 | 80 |

**6420 D.L. & W.** 1949-50, Work Caboose, staple-end metal trucks, coil couplers, dark gray die-cast frame with black "LIONEL LINES", dark gray cab, searchlight, tall stack, two brakewheels, dark gray tool boxes. **37 50 75 125**

**6427 LIONEL LINES** 1955-60, N5C, numbered "64273" on side, lights, tuscan with white lettering, "BLT 11-53", bar-end metal trucks, single tab magnetic coupler. "6427", the "official" Lionel number, is used in the Service Manual and 6427-3 is the part number for the body. Numbering in this edition now corresponds to Lionel's. **6 9 15 25**

**64273** See 6427.

**6427-60 VIRGINIAN** 1958, N5C, dark blue with yellow lettering, "6427" on side, "BLT 8-58", lighted, bar-end metal trucks, one tab magnetic coupler. (Body is part number 6427-63.). **50 75 110 175**

### 6427-500 PENNSYLVANIA

**6427-500 PENNSYLVANIA** 1957-58, N5C, from "Girl's Set", numbered "576427" on side, lighted, bar-end metal trucks, one coupler. Reproductions have been made and are reportedly marked.

(A) Sky blue with white lettering, production model. **50 75 100 200**

(B) Flat yellow finish on black plastic body, extremely heavy white heat-stamped letters and numbers, one brakewheel, preproduction Lionel color sample not produced. Degano Collection. **— — 1000 —**

(C) Semi-gloss yellow paint on black plastic body and black heat-stamped lettering which is heavier nearer the A and lighter nearer the P; tab-operating coupler, roller shows considerable wear; preproduction Lionel color sample not produced. Degano Collection. **— — 1000 —**

(D) Pink-painted black plastic body, very heavily heat-stamped in white, bar-end metal trucks, one magnetic operating coupler, plastic window inserts, preproduction color sample for Girl's Set not produced. Degano Collection.                                    — — 1000 —

**6427 A.T. & S.F.** 1960, N5C, catalogued but not manufactured.
**Not Manufactured**

**6429 D.L. & W.** 1963, Work Caboose, light gray cab, medium gray tool boxes, light gray die-cast frame, bar-end metal trucks, one tab, magnetic coupler, two brakewheels, short stack, came in one set only. Ambrose comment.                    **20    30    40    60**

**6437-25 PENNSYLVANIA** 1961-68, N5C, tuscan with white lettering, "BLT 2-53", lighted, Timken trucks, one operating coupler; "6437" on side.
(A) Timken trucks.                           **6    9    15    25**
(B) Metal trucks.                            **6    9    15    25**

6447

**6447 PENNSYLVANIA** 1963, N5C, tuscan with white lettering, "BLT 2-53", non-illuminated, used in one Super 0 set, Timken trucks, one coupler.
                                            **30    40    60    120**

**6457 LIONEL** 1949-52, SP type, "L" in double circle over underscored "6457", "LIONEL" under first two windows, "C-40-l" and "BUILT 9-47" centered in two lines under "LIONEL", lighted, smokestack, ladders, battery box, two brakewheels, two operating couplers, black box fastens with screws to body, "blt. 9-47". Schmaus observation.
(A) Gloss brown-painted black plastic; staple-end metal trucks, black stack, ladders, brakewheels and battery boxes, Die 1. Rohlfing Collection.
                                            **6    9    12    17**
(B) Brownish-maroon-painted black plastic, bar-end metal trucks, black stack.                                      **6    9    12    18**
(C) Brown-painted black plastic, staple-end metal trucks, brown stack, Die 1.                                       **6    12    25    45**
(D) Same as (A), but red plastic mold. Rohlfing Collection.
                                            **6    9    12    18**
(E) Same as (C), but Die 2. Kotil Collection.  **6    9    12    18**
(F) Flat maroon-painted black plastic, bar-end metal trucks, two magnetic couplers, black trim, Die 2. Rohlfing Collection.   **6    9    12    18**
(G) Same as (F), but brown-painted black plastic. Rohlfing Collection.
                                            **6    9    12    18**

**6517 LIONEL LINES** 1955-59, Bay Window, red with white lettering, lighted, stack, 0-27 passenger trucks, two operating couplers.
(A) "BLT 12-55" and "LIONEL" underscored.    **25    35    60    90**
(B) "BLT 12-55" and "LIONEL" not underscored. **20    30    50    75**
See also Factory Errors.

**6517-75 ERIE** 1966, Bay Window, with white lettering, stack, lighted, 0-27 passenger trucks, two operating couplers.
(A) Flat medium red-painted body.         **135    190    275    350**
(B) Dull brick red-painted body, clearly different from (A). Budniak Collection.                                 **135    190    275    350**
(B) Orange-painted black plastic, one of three Lionel preproduction color samples; car base rubber-stamped "6517-75" and "LIONEL" in silver. Degano Collection.                          — — 1500 —

**6517-1966 T.C.A.** Convention bay window caboose, 1966, dull orange-painted body with white "TCA" on caboose bay, white TCA logo at left of bay, octagonal convention data lettering to right of bay in white, Timken

**6517-1966 T.C.A.**

four-wheel passenger die-cast trucks, two magnetic couplers. 700 produced for convention in Santa Monica. It has been reported that Lionel mistakenly produced the first 500 cars in red and had to repaint them orange.
                                            — — — 250

**6557 LIONEL** 1958-59, SP Die 3C, with smoke unit, black plastic painted brown, white lettering, "BUILT 9-47", bar-end metal trucks, tab magnetic coupler.
(A) Regular catwalk.                       **50    75    100    175**
(B) Slightly raised hump on catwalk.       **50    75    100    175**
(C) Black plastic body painted dark tuscan, white lettering, bar-end metal trucks, tab magnetic couplers at both ends, regular catwalk, brown plastic smoke deflector instead of usual black, lettering and numbering reversed so that "6557" is under cupola and "LIONEL" is at front of caboose, white smoke unit, no brakewheel, possible prototype or very limited run, extremely rare. Klaassen and Powell Collections.   — — — 1000

**6657 Rio Grande** 1957-58, SP Die 1 or 2, yellow body with silver lower band, black lettering, bar-end metal trucks, tab magnetic coupler, smokestack, lighted.
(A) Without smoke unit.                     **50    75    100    125**
(B) With brown smoke unit.                           **NRS**
(C) With white smoke unit. Powell Collection.        **NRS**

**6814-1 LIONEL** 1959-61, Work Caboose, "RESCUE UNIT", short stack, white cab and tool boxes, red lettering, light gray base, man, two stretchers, oxygen tank unit, Timken trucks, two couplers, "6814" appears on car.
(A) As described above.                     **20    30    40    60**
(B) Same as (A), but with Red Cross emblem on plastic yard-type stand.
                                            **50    75    100    130**
(C) Black frame, no stretchers, man or oxygen tanks, "LIONEL" in white sans-serif lettering on frame side, no brakewheels, Timken trucks, one disc-operating coupler, one fixed coupler, made by Lionel for Sears set No. 9820, circa 1964. For background, see 3666 boxcar and 240 locomotive and tender, made by Lionel for Sears with No. 240 steamer, circa 1968. Lebo and Powell Collections.                **30    40    50    100**
(D) Same as (A), but only one disc coupler. Rohlfing Collection.
                                            **20    30    40    60**

**6824 U.S.M.C.** 1960, Work Caboose, "RESCUE UNIT", short stack, olive drab cab, tool boxes, white lettering, man, two stretchers, oxygen tank unit, Timken trucks, two couplers.        **25    37    50    75**

**6824 RESCUE UNIT** Circa 1960, Work Caboose, no number on car, short stack, olive drab cab and tool boxes, white cross, black frame with white serif "LIONEL", Timken trucks, tab front coupler, no rear coupler; Catalano observation. Probably came in box with suffix mark after number; reader comments requested.                             **15    25    40    75**

**NO NUMBERS**

(A) SP Die 4, olive drab unpainted plastic, galvanized base, tabs fasten base to body, one fixed coupler, open on top, Timken trucks, no lettering, no back railing, resembles olive drab hopper, gondola and turbo missile cars. Wilson Collection. We need to learn this car's catalogue number and set number.                                     **NRS**

(B) SP Die 4, yellow unpainted body, black-painted frame, tab fasteners, end handrails only, one dummy coupler, arch bar trucks. Could be 6067, 6167-25, 6167-125(C) or 6167-150; reader comments invited. Budniak Collection.                             **NRS**

SP Types: See 6067, 6167-50, 6167-100 and 6167-125.

Work Caboose: See 6119-25, 6120, 6824.

# Chapter V
# CRANES AND SEARCHLIGHTS

Note differences in the width and spacing of the word Lionel on the frames
of the 2460 and 6560-25 on the bottom row.

Real railroads called them "Big Hooks" - those huge steam-powered cranes which any self-respecting railroad kept on hand for the inevitable derailment or more serious emergency. They could lift the heaviest locomotives and put them back on the tracks. If an emergency were to occur at night, these big machines could be sent out in a work train with powerful searchlights mounted on flatcars.

Lionel made excellent models of both of these cars in the postwar years. Many an operator's layout had a train composed of a searchlight car, crane and work caboose on a siding, just in case. Some operators carried things to extremes. It is reported that playwright Ben Hecht, a big Lionel fan, liked to stage wrecks on his main lines and untangle them with the crane car.

Lionel began its postwar cranes by carrying the metal prewar crane into 1946 and 1947. This rather small crane operated well, but lacked realism. It was dwarfed by some of Lionel's newer rolling stock, so Lionel soon began to produce a very attractive model of the big Bucyrus-Erie cranes used for many years by prototype railroads. The first of these cranes had die-cast frames and six-wheel trucks; they were indeed impressive! Early models were, like their prototypes, black with white lettering, but as production went on Lionel also made gray and red-bodied cranes.

The Bucyrus-Erie crane operated by means of two wheels. The wheel at the rear of the cab raised or lowered the boom, while the wheel at the side raised and lowered the hook. The crane was strong enough to lift any freight car, but it could not lift a heavy die-cast locomotive very easily. It wasn't equipped with outrigger booms to keep from turning over, unlike American Flyer's excellent Industrial Brownhoist crane car.

Lionel cheapened later models of the Bucyrus-Erie by changing from six-wheel to four-wheel trucks and by replacing the die-cast base with a plastic base. Later models also added a smokestack towards the rear of the crane cab.

Lionel also produced a flatcar with a derrick in the later postwar years. This car was made with a red flatcar body and a yellow boom. There was a small crank which allowed the operator to lift loads with the derrick's hook. It was not a bad car to have in one's collection, but it lacked the massive quality which was so appealing in the Bucyrus-Erie crane car.

The last postwar run of the 6560 Bucyrus-Erie figured in a tin plate mystery which still has not been totally resolved. It was made in Hagerstown, Maryland as part of a freight set with a 2029 steam engine in 1969, the last year of postwar production before the takeover of Lionel trains by General Mills. Apparently the new owners found themselves with a considerable quantity of leftover 6560 cranes at the Hagerstown facility, so they had boxes made for them and catalogued them as their own production. It is still not clear whether or not Fundimensions actually produced any of these cars in 1970 or 1971, though the firm was certainly distributing them.

The searchlight cars were extremely well made; all but one model had gray die-cast depressed-center bases. The depression in the base usually held a plastic generator, strictly for appearance, while the searchlight was mounted on one end of the car. Production began with the 6520 car in 1949. On this car, the operator could turn the searchlight on and off by means of a remote track. A metal strip was connected to a slender pawl hidden inside the plastic generator. Each time the metal strip beneath the car was pulled down by a magnet in a remote track, the contact was either broken or restored.

Two variations of this car used a searchlight housing mounted on a vibrator motor so that the light would rotate. The earliest version retained the on-off pawl switch of the 6520, while the later version lacked this feature. A third conversion of the 6520 became the Extension Searchlight Car, first made in 1956. The searchlight was attached to the car base by a magnet instead of a rivet. Wires led from the light housing to a reel of wire mounted at the center depression of the flatcar, while a small generator was attached to the other end. The operator could unreel the light, unwind the cord and place the searchlight quite some distance from the car itself.

The final version of the searchlight car, sometimes referred to as the "Night Crew" car, was made from 1961 to the end of the postwar period. This searchlight was mounted on a superstructure attached to a standard Lionel plastic flatcar. A blue rubber man stood guard over the assembly. Although reasonably well made, it lacked a great deal of the massiveness of the earlier searchlight cars, and thus was not as appealing.

The crane and searchlight cars were a colorful and important part of Lionel's postwar rolling stock. It was a badge of honor for a young boy to own one of the Bucyrus-Erie cranes and re-rail a freight car in the bright light of a searchlight car. Of such elements was the great play value of Lionel Trains composed.

A comparison of the bold, serif, expanded lettering on 6460(A) on top, and the thin, serif, condensed lettering on 6460(B). Griesbeck Collection and photograph.

|  | Gd | VG | Exc | Mt |
|---|---|---|---|---|

**2460 BUCYRUS ERIE** Crane, 1946-50, black with white lettering with serifs, "LIONEL LINES" in single arch on cab, Irvington-type six-wheel trucks with coil couplers, die-cast frame.

| | Gd | VG | Exc | Mt |
|---|---|---|---|---|
| (A) "LIONEL LINES" in single arch on black cab. | 20 | 30 | 40 | 75 |
| (B) "LIONEL LINES" in single arch on gray cab. | 30 | 45 | 60 | 100 |
| (C) "LIONEL LINES" in two arched lines, factory production. Latina observation. | 10 | 15 | 20 | 60 |
| (D) "LIONEL LINES" with top line arched and bottom line straight; red cab on black base, no cab smokestack and no cutout for stack. Catalano observation. | 20 | 30 | 40 | 75 |
| (E) Same as (D), but black cab on black base. Latina Collection. | 20 | 30 | 40 | 75 |

**2560 LIONEL LINES** Crane, 1946-47, continuation of prewar 2660 design with modification, light yellow metal cab with red roof, "2560" rubber-stamped on cab, staple end metal trucks, coil-operated couplers.

| | Gd | VG | Exc | Mt |
|---|---|---|---|---|
| (A) Brown boom. | 10 | 15 | 20 | 40 |
| (B) Green boom. | 10 | 15 | 20 | 40 |
| (C) Black boom. | 10 | 15 | 20 | 40 |
| (D) Brown cab, catalogued but not manufactured. | | | | Not Manufactured |

**3360 BURRO CRANE** See Chapter II.

**4460 BUCYRUS ERIE** Crane car, shown in 1950 Advance Catalogue for Electronic Set, but never made. **Not Manufactured**

**6460 BUCYRUS ERIE** Crane, 1952-54, bar-end metal four-wheel trucks, die-cast frame.

(A) Black with white cab lettering, "LIONEL LINES" without serifs in two lines; bold serif expanded "LIONEL LINES" on frame in white letters, data lines read "WT-375,000-2-18 NM". Griesbeck Collection.

| | 12 | 17 | 25 | 40 |
|---|---|---|---|---|

(B) Same as (A), but thin condensed letters on frame, data lines read "WT-375,000 2 18 NH" (note absence of dashes and "H" instead of "M"). Griesbeck Collection.

| | 12 | 17 | 25 | 40 |
|---|---|---|---|---|

(C) Gray plastic painted red with white lettering, "LIONEL LINES" without serifs in two lines.

| | 20 | 30 | 40 | 60 |
|---|---|---|---|---|

(D) Black with white lettering, "LIONEL LINES" with serifs in one arched line, not factory production.

| | 10 | 15 | 20 | 28 |
|---|---|---|---|---|

(E) Same as (C), but black plastic cab painted red. Budniak Collection.

| | 20 | 35 | 50 | 90 |
|---|---|---|---|---|

**6460-25 BUCYRUS ERIE** Crane, listed in 1954 catalogue with red cab, but never made. **Not Manufactured**

**6560 BUCYRUS ERIE** Crane, 1955-58, black plastic frame, large smokestack, "LIONEL LINES" in two lines, top line arched, bottom line straight, crank wheel with short handle, cab fastened to base with clips, four-wheel trucks.

(A) 1955 only, gray cab, black lettering, bar-end metal trucks, magnetic couplers, came with set 1527 with 1615 steam switcher. Ambrose Collection.

| | 15 | 22 | 30 | 50 |
|---|---|---|---|---|

(B) Red cab, white lettering, bar-end metal trucks with magnetic tab couplers (Type VI). Box end flags marked: "No. 6560 OPERATING WORK CRANE LIONEL 25". This is clearly a different unit than 6560-25 shown below variety (E) as the next entry. That car is marked "656025" on its frame, while this car is marked "6560" only. We would appreciate reader comments about the dating of both units and the explanation for this odd numbering situation. Yeckel Collection.

| | 10 | 15 | 20 | 40 |
|---|---|---|---|---|

(C) Red-orange cab, strikingly different from usual red, bar-end metal trucks, magnetic couplers, no number on frame side, attached by screws instead of clips, very early production. Griesbeck and Ambrose Collections.

| | 50 | 75 | 125 | 200 |
|---|---|---|---|---|

(D) Same as (B), but solid wheel on cab side. LaVoie Collection.

| | 10 | 15 | 20 | 40 |
|---|---|---|---|---|

(E) Same as (B), but no 6560 number on frame, frame mold 2460-5. Griesbeck, Grossano and Lord Collections. **NRS**

(F) Same as (C), but black cab with stack. Ambrose Collection.

| | 50 | 75 | 125 | 200 |
|---|---|---|---|---|

### THE HAGERSTOWN SET AND THE 6560 CRANE

Among collectors, there has always been contention about the 6560 crane made in Hagerstown, Maryland as part of set No. 11600 in 1969 (see 2029 locomotive for details). The problems have come about because collectors could not distinguish the postwar 6560 crane in the Hagerstown set from the 6560 marketed by Fundimensions in 1970 and 1971. There is no question that these cranes did, indeed, come in Fundimensions boxes after 1969 - but Fundimensions did not actually manufacture these cranes. When General Mills leased the rights to Lionel production in 1969, it of course inherited all existing rolling stock. After an inventory at the Hagerstown facility, Fundimensions found that a considerable number of 6560 cranes were left over - much more than the remaining components of the Hagerstown set. Fundimensions then had boxes made so that these leftovers could be marketed under the MPC name. The 6560 crane with the dark blue base found in Fundimensions boxes is identical to the crane included in the Hagerstown set. Earlier production runs of the 6560 have also been found in the Hagerstown set. The following is a list of all varieties known to be part of that set. Reader confirmation on thse varieties is requested.

(A) Very dark blue frame, red cab, "LIONEL/LINES" and "BUCYRUS/ERIE/CLASS 280/RAILROAD CRANE" heat-stamped in white on cab, "LIONEL LINES" and "WT 275,000-2-18 NH" heat-stamped on frame in white, Timken trucks, disc couplers, solid wheel on cab side. Catalano observation.

| | | | |
|---|---|---|---|
| | 12 | 17 | 25 | 40 |

(B) Same as (A), but dull black plastic frame.   12  17  25  40
(C) Same as (B), but no lettering on frame.   **NRS**
(D) Same as (A), but one operating and one dummy coupler.
   12  17  25  40
(E) Same as (A), but both couplers are non-operating.   12  17  25  40
(F) Same as (A), but orange-red cab.   12  17  25  40

NOTE: The above observations were made by Philip Catalano, I.D. Smith, Ron Griesbeck and Glenn Halverson.

**6560-25 BUCYRUS ERIE** Crane, 1956, red cab with white lettering, plastic frame numbered "6560-25", four-wheel trucks, "LIONEL LINES" in two lines, stack.   22  30  50  100

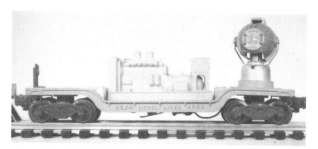

3520

## SEARCHLIGHTS

**3520 SEARCHLIGHT** 1952-53, "LIONEL LINES" on gray die-cast frame, orange diesel generator unit, steps, bar-end metal trucks, one brakewheel, die-cast searchlight revolves by vibrator mechanism, remote control on-off switch for searchlight.

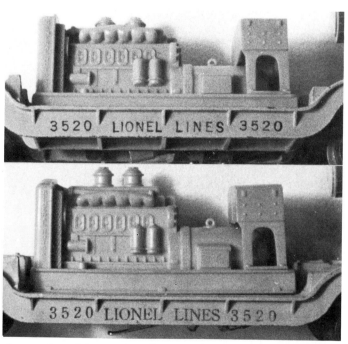

A comparison of the 3520(A) with sans-serif lettering and numbering (top) with 3520(B) with serif lettering and numbering. Griesbeck Collection and photograph.

(A) "3520 LIONEL LINES 3520" on frame in plain sans-serif numbering and lettering. Griesbeck Collection.   15  22  30  50
(B) Same as (A), but lettered in larger serif letters and numbers. See photo for comparison. Griesbeck Collection.   **NRS**

**3530 GENERATOR** See Boxcars.

3620

**3620 SEARCHLIGHT** 1954-56", LIONEL LINES" in sans serif lettering on gray die-cast frame (lettering is found in both light and heavy faces), orange diesel generator, steps, bar-end metal trucks, one brakewheel, searchlight revolves by vibrator mechanism, no remote control on-off switch. Parvin observation.

(A) Thin lettering, bright orange plastic generator. Stekoll Collection.
   12  17  25  40
(B) Same as (A), but thicker lettering, later production. Stekoll Collection.
   12  17  25  40
(C) Thin lettering, dull orange plastic generator, orange plastic searchlight hood painted gray. Hood is same shade of orange as generator; however, gray paint does not match gray paint on flatcar or the gray shade of the normal gray plastic searchlight hood. Possibly, the factory ran out of gray plastic and molded the searchlight hoods out of the same plastic used for the generator for a time. They then painted the hood gray. This may explain entry (D) below as well. Stekoll Collection.   12  17  25  40
(D) Gray die-cast flatcar base, "3620 LIONEL LINES 3620" rubber-stamped in black sans serif letters, bright red-orange generator and bright red-orange searchlight housing. NOTE: A detachable variation such as the searchlight housing raises the inevitable question of substitution. In this case, however, the color of the housing and the generator are perfectly matched. This car is probably genuine. Art Tom Collection.   **NRS**

3650

**3650 EXTENSION SEARCHLIGHT** 1956-59, gray die-cast base, black lettering, "LIONEL LINES" without serif, gray plastic searchlight unit on red base held by magnet to steel plate in die-cast frame, gray generator, red reel with green cord and crank supported on black frame, bar-end metal trucks, magnetic tab couplers.
(A) Light gray die-cast frame, two brakewheels.   10  15  25  60
(B) Dark gray die-cast frame, one brakewheel.   10  15  25  60
(C) Same as (A), but olive tint to paint on gray frame. Blotner Collection.
   **NRS**

6520

**6520 SEARCHLIGHT** 1949-51, gray die-cast base, die-cast searchlight, staple-end metal trucks, magnetic couplers, on-off switch, manual rotation of light, one brakewheel, steps.

(A) Green diesel generator, shiny smooth gray light housing.

|  |  |  |  |
|---|---|---|---|
| 37 | 50 | 75 | 125 |

(B) Green diesel generator, crinkle gray light housing.

|  |  |  |  |
|---|---|---|---|
| 37 | 50 | 75 | 125 |

(C) Green diesel generator, glossy smooth black light housing. Breslin Collection.

|  |  |  |  |
|---|---|---|---|
| 37 | 50 | 75 | 125 |

(D) Orange diesel generator, gray crinkle light housing.

|  |  |  |  |
|---|---|---|---|
| 15 | 22 | 30 | 50 |

(E) Maroon diesel generator, gray crinkle light housing.

|  |  |  |  |
|---|---|---|---|
| 15 | 22 | 30 | 50 |

(F) Maroon diesel generator, smooth gray light housing.

|  |  |  |  |
|---|---|---|---|
| 15 | 22 | 30 | 50 |

(G) Tan diesel generator, gray metallic enameled light.

|  |  |  |  |
|---|---|---|---|
| 75 | 115 | 150 | 225 |

6822

**6822 SEARCHLIGHT** 1961-69, red frame with white lettering, blue man, Timken trucks, disc-operating couplers.

(A) Black lighting unit base, gray searchlight housing.

|  |  |  |  |
|---|---|---|---|
| 7 | 10 | 15 | 30 |

(B) Gray lighting unit base, black searchlight housing.

|  |  |  |  |
|---|---|---|---|
| 7 | 10 | 15 | 30 |

# Chapter VI
# FLATCARS

In prototype railroading, the lowly flatcar has a rich and varied history. In fact, during the early days of railroading, nearly every car was essentially a flatcar with a structure built onto it. For example, early tank and vat cars were really wooden decks with the tank or vat superstructures attached to them in some way. (An excellent example of this construction can be found at the Strasburg Railroad near Lancaster, Pennsylvania, where a tank car made in 1906 features a wooden deck with a steel tank atop it.) However, as the needs of railroads changed, so did the flatcars. Bulkheads were mounted onto the flatcar ends to hold loads in place. Modern flatcars often have facilities for mounting highway trailers. Truly, the flatcar has been an all-purpose car for America's railroads.

It should come as no surprise, then, that Lionel's postwar flatcars reflected the same changes and the same functions. These cars carried everything from transformers to Christmas trees for Lionel. Since the flatcar was very inexpensive for Lionel to make, it made economic sense to promote these cars, especially within train sets. It is no accident that this chapter is as long as it is.

The earliest postwar flatcars were well detailed, with scribing to suggest wooden decks - except that they were die cast. All of them were painted gray, as the real ones often were, and if they were not merely decks with railings, they were adapted to other purposes. With a cab and two tool boxes, they became work cabooses. A variant of this casting had a depressed center. This flatcar then became the carrier for transformers, cable reels and other loads; in modified form, it was the base for the die-cast searchlight cars. An extra-long variant of this car had four trucks and carried a transformer or two plastic bridge girders.

Lionel's first plastic flatcars came with four dies, one of which had at least four die variations. The article on flatcar molds and dies by Michael Ocilka, contained in this chapter, gives a complete breakdown of these construction variations. These cars proved to be most versatile for the Lionel Corporation. In the early postwar years, there was not a bulk load which could not be found carried in miniature on these cars. Later on, the Lionel flat cars became the carriers of the structures for the Military and Space loads. Some carried atomic waste canisters; others carried rocket, cannon, helicopter and satellite launching mechanisms. Automobiles, trucks and cranes were frequent travelers upon Lionel's flatcars, not to mention numerous pieces of construction equipment.

In the late fifties, a shorter plastic flatcar was made. Originally intended as a base for the horse car of the "General" set, this car, most often unmarked, was found in many an inexpensive set in Lionel's last years. A stamped metal short flatcar was also made and adapted readily to loads with stakes such as pipes and logs. Finally, a plastic flatcar with an upward arch in its center became the base for the Allis-Chalmers radioactive condenser car, the Mercury Space Capsule car and a missile firing car.

In spite of the fact that Lionel's chief reason for making so many flatcars may have been economic, it must be remembered that these cars also had considerable play value. If a child didn't like Lionel's load, he could substitute his own very readily. Many a "foreign" toy car, tank or truck has made circuits around a Lionel layout. Collectors are just beginning to realize the variability and interest of these cars, and one might expect that values for some of the scarcer varieties will change accordingly. It is still quite possible to acquire a large collection of flatcars at very nominal prices.

# LIONEL FLATCAR MOLD VARIATIONS
## By Michael J. Ocilka

During the postwar period, the Lionel Corporation produced many flatcars with a wide variety of loads. Most of these flatcars can be identified by a mold mark embossed into the plastic body on the underside of the car. Such marks, usually expressed in the form of numbers, would help assembly workers identify the correct metal mold to use in producing the particular car so that the load would fit properly, among other reasons.

Basically, there are four solid plastic flatcar molds. Three of these molds do not show any significant variations in construction. These are the 1877 mold, originally used for the General sets and widely used in inexpensive sets thereafter; the 3419 mold used for operating helicopter and satellite launching flatcars; and the full-sized 6511-2 flatcar mold.

The major exception to this lack of variation is the 6424-11 flatcar mold. Apparently, the Lionel Corporation chose to minimize its expenses by devoting all necessary construction changes to only one of the four basic types of flatcars. This particular mold, in several different die forms, has been used on over 30 differently numbered postwar flatcars and is still being used by Fundimensions for its flatcars today.

In 1954, Lionel introduced the 6511-2 flatcar mold with 13 stake holes around the body perimeter. However, the company ran into a problem when it wanted to produce the 6424 automobile flatcar and the 6262 wheel car in 1956. These two flatcars needed a different mold than the 6511-2 because they required mounting holes for the metal racks which held the loads onto the cars. They did not need the 13 stake holes. Lionel's answer was to develop a new flatcar mold, the 6424-11.

This mold, which we will designate as Die 1, was made with only two stake holes, one across from the brakewheel and the other on the diagonally opposing end of the car. These two stake holes were probably needed for the injection molding process. Two other holes were made at each end of the car on the center line for mounting the racks for the loads with a screw. These screws were later replaced with rivets. Both of these cars, the 6424 and the 6262, are found with metal trucks for the 1956 production period with the Die 1 variation of the 6424-11 mold.

Die 2 with 13 stake holes. Ocilka Collection, Bartelt photograph.

So far, so good. Then, in 1957, Lionel decided to produce the 6801 Flatcar With Boat. This car necessitated a further change to the 6424-11 mold. More stake holes had to be added so that the cradle holding the boat could be snapped onto the car. All 13 stake holes were molded into the car so that the cradle could be placed almost anywhere on the car. This is evidence of Lionel's planning for future use of the car, as the later 6823 confirms. The 6424-11 mold with evidence of two center holes and all 13 stake holes is known as the Die 2 variation. In fact, since the 6424 and 6262 were still in production, they are found in a Die 2 configuration.

There are two interesting points to be made here. First, the 6424 and 6262 cars with the Die 2 mold were equipped with Timken plastic trucks instead of bar-end metal trucks. Because of this truck change, the racks were held in place with rivets instead of screws. Second, since the 6801 Flatcar With Boat did not need the screw/rivet holes for any type of load support, the holes were "plugged", although visible circles remained on this car where the holes would have been tapped. Die 2, therefore, has 13 stake holes and two small "plugs" where the rack holes used to be on Die 1.

In 1958, the 6805 Atomic Disposal Flatcar (known better to collectors as the "Radioactive Waste" car) necessitated a second mold change to the 6424-11 flatcar mold. Four new holes were added to this car to accept four clips with a dual purpose. These clips not only held the Super 0 rails to the flatcar body, but also supplied a power connection from the roller pickup on the trucks to the blinking lights in the radioactive canisters.

Die 3 with 13 stake holes and 4 6805 holes. Ocilka Collection, Bartelt photograph.

Strangely enough, both Die 1 and Die 2 were changed by the addition of these four holes. Die 2 with these four holes becomes the Die 3 variation, and Die 1 with the four holes becomes the Die 4 variation. It would at first seem that the Die 3 and Die 4 nomenclature should be reversed, but there is a simple explanation. As far as is known, every 6805 Atomic Disposal flatcar has the body with 13 stake holes, not the version with two stake holes. I am not sure why Die 1 also had the four extra holes added, unless it was planned to use this mold for the 6805 as well. This hypothesis would be proved if a 6805 Atomic Disposal Car turns up in the two stake-hole variation.

Die 4 with 2 stake holes, open circular holes and 4 added rectangular holes. Ocilka Collection, Bartelt photograph.

I specifically omit a possible fifth die variation because only one flatcar has used it. The 6469 Liquified Gas Car, first made in 1963, has a Die 4 mold with extra holes added to accommodate bulkheads at each end. I am not aware of any other production car with the bulkhead holes, the 6424-11 mold and a Die 4 designation, so it is best to call the 6469 car a modified Die 4 variation.

Some words of caution are in order to prevent misidentification of some cars. Quite a few cars were made with the unvarying 6511-2 mold, which should not be confused with the Die 2 variation of the 6424-11 mold. When looking from the underside of these cars, the observer will spot all 13 stake holes in both cases. However, in the Die 1 and Die 4 6424-11 mold variations, 11 of these holes are filled in from the top to look like a solid flatcar. Make sure to check all cars from the top as well as the bottom; this is particularly important for flatcars 3512, 6262 and 6424.

A summary of the 6424-11 mold variations is as follows:

DIE 1: Two stake holes on the sides of the car at diagonally opposing ends, two small circular holes on the center line of the car.

DIE 2: 13 stake holes instead of two; circular holes on center line are plugged, but detectable.

DIE 3: 13 stake holes, plugged center holes and four rectangular holes added.

DIE 4: Two stake holes, open circular holes and four added rectangular holes.

The prototype of the No. 44 Missile Launcher as photographed by Frank Edgcombe.

## LIONEL SPACE AND MILITARY ACTION TRAINS
By Gordon L. Wilson

### S.A.M.A.T.

Hong Kong Fly-Apart! Cheap plastic! Rinky-dink trash! Garbage! Scrap heap rejects! Which derogatory term did you use to describe the Lionel movement into the Space Age? Regardless of what you said or thought, one fact is very clear: Lionel's military rockets got further off the ground than some of the early real rockets at Cape Canaveral. The variety of gadgetry was endless. It included everything from a pencil sharpener to a two-stage rocket that actually worked.

Many of the items produced, if used by the real railroads, would today result in massive marches and protest rallies. For instance, how would you respond to a flatcar going through your town carrying radioactive waste material, flaunting that fact by having viewing windows so you could watch the fission process? Many a Lionel layout was certainly contaminated for all time by the #6805 flatcar with radioactive waste disposal canisters. Or how about a boxcar full of highly volatile explosives parked on a siding near your home? Nervous breakdown time, huh?

Conversely, Lionel engineers did manage to manufacture a few railroad military items which were reasonably close to believable. The #6651 "Big Bertha" cannon car was similar to a German World War I and II weapon of the same name. It also resembled the U.S. Army's "Atomic Cannon" of the 1950s. The United States Army did transport many military vehicles from place to place via the rails during World War II. The 6800 series military flats did likewise. The United States Navy, however, was a different story. It is somewhat hard to believe that a submarine ever found its way atop a railroad flatcar, except on a Lionel layout.

Why did a quality toy train company deviate from the standard line of relatively realistic toys to inexpensive plastic gadgetry? There is probably no single answer, but rather many contributing factors, not the least of which is the date October 4, 1957. How often have we heard "It's a Communist plot"? Well, if you are familiar with history, you will know that on that date Sputnik I went into orbit around the third planet in our solar system. American public school curricula changed overnight to an emphasis on the sciences. The movie industry began to turn out countless films on invasions from outer space. People everywhere built bomb shelters, for "doomsday" was

now a reality. Plastic model corporations, such as Aurora and Revell, switched their marketing from model cars to model rockets. To compete in an already declining market, Lionel had little choice but to enter the "space race". Coupled with the fact that the basic Lionel philosophy for years had been to provide action toys as a part of their train outfits, it was only natural to develop rocket and satellite launching cars. In 1961, to further ensure the development and exploitation of this military-space marketing campaign, Lionel hired General John B. Medaris, as President of the Corporation, whose background was totally geared to the military.

Unfortunately for all concerned, there were some serious drawbacks to this program. Much like the ill-fated "Girl's Set", which was produced in 1957 to attract the female element into trains, the military items, because of their unrealistic quality, bombed just as miserably. Everyone knew that satellites and rockets were not launched from railroad flatcars, but rather from elaborate complexes at Cape Kennedy. (There was a prototype for the minutemen rocket-launching boxcar, but it was abandoned as impractical.) Another drawback fell into the area of safety. Lionel's marketing philosophy stated unequivocally that they were making "sane" toys that did not kill or maim. Perhaps they didn't kill, but the sharp tips of the plastic rockets could certainly wreak havoc on one's eyes if a person were not careful.

Undoubtedly another reason for the decline in sales can be attributed to the fact that the children who grew up during the "Golden Age" of Lionel were now entering college, the service or the business community. Consequently, their change in life styles dictated a change in their buying habits. Electric trains were toys; toys were for kids, and they were no longer kids. Nonetheless Lionel persisted in manufacturing gadgets. The few serious collectors disdained the items and refused to buy the cheapened-quality product.

The many persons who did purchase Lionel military/space material did so, in all likelihood, strictly for inexpensive play value. As a result many of the items, when located today, are missing their loads. However, despite the high mortality rate of the military units, most of them are surprisingly easily collected today. Unlike other areas of Lionel, there are very few truly rare and super-expensive items. The military trucks made for Lionel by Pyro are hard to find unbroken. The balloons for the #3470 Target Launcher Car also suffered. Over the years the rubber has fused together, causing the balloons to be non-inflatable. The truly "rare" pieces are the #229 khaki-colored Minneapolis and St. Louis Alco Diesel and the

Top row: 6806 with khaki Army trucks on the left and gray U.S. Marine Corps trucks on the right. The trucks were made by Pyro. Only the gray trucks were sold with Lionel equipment. Second row: 6413 Mercury Project car in rare aquamarine color on left and in usual powder blue color on the right. Third row: A unnumbered gray unpainted plastic flat car, possibly a prototype with helicopter and a 3429 U.S.M.C. flat car with helicopter. Fourth row: An khaki color amphibious vehicle made by Pyro and not sold by Lionel and the gray Pyro amphibious vehicle that came with the Lionel 6807 flatcar. Fifth row: Two unnumbered gray flatcars. The car on the left has the moss green tank with swivel turret that came with the 240 Sears set. The origins of the tank on the left flatcar are not known. The cars on the first four shelves are from the Gordon Wilson Collection. The Pyro tanks and Canteen truck on the bottom shelf are from the Robert Boero Collection. Lionel did not sell the items on the bottom shelf.

USMC helicopter which properly belongs on the #3429 Helicopter Car. Some items, such as the Sears Military Set with the #3666 Cannon Car and #347 Cannon Launching Platform, are hard to find, BUT they are findable if one will look hard enough.

Even more fascinating than the produced material were the items which appeared in the advance catalogues, but were never produced. A few of the items with more obvious changes are the #6175 Rocket Carrying Car, the helicopters, the #44 Mobile Missile Launcher, the #470 IRBM Missile Launching Platform and the #462 Derrick Platform set. The #6175 Rocket Carrying Car first appeared in the 1958 Advance Catalogue. It is missing the "US NAVY" identification, but has instead some unintelligible printing near its base. It also looks more like a high-powered rifle shell (bullet) than it does an intercontinental rocket. Strangely, in 1959 and later years, in the catalogues the missile is pictured just as it was in the 1958 Advance Catalogue, despite the fact that it was produced in a different shape. The helicopters first produced in 1958 look like real Chinook helicopters used later in Viet Nam for rescue missions. There is no clear plastic bubble on the front. They all have four rotors, as well as what appears to be an operating rear blade. The rear sections are raised in a graceful curve. There are no markings to identify which branch of service the 'copter is from. On the flatcar, the support piece for the tail is not notched to accept the tail, but rather is flat and protruding. Perhaps the item most altered between the Advance Catalogue and actual production was the 44 Mobile Missile Launcher. First, it is not identified with any branch of the service—it didn't even have a number other than the one under the picture. It is pictured with a whip antenna on the right front and a radar-scanning disc on top of the cab. On the rear quarter of the unit is a large five-point white star, which presumably identifies it as American, since the Russians use a red star. Finally, to the rear of the control panel man is a seat and what appears to be a clear plastic shield held on with a bar parallel to the railroad tracks. The 470 IRBM Missile Launching Platform also changed radically from the 1959 Advance Catalogue. The launch mechanism is totally different. The original one is streamlined and sleek, while the actual one has a lattice-work configuration. Instead of a Quonset hut building, it is shown as a complete wall-like "block house" with two microwave discs on top. These are the same discs that appear on the 199 Microwave Tower. Beginning at each end of the block building is a single-rail fence that surrounds the entire missile-firing area. Finally there is the 462 Derrick Platform Set which is pictured with the boom derrick hoisting a radioactive canister magnetically. The description even makes reference to a magnetically-operated hoist. When it finally appeared, the derrick boom assembly was exactly the same as that on the 6670 Boom Derrick Car. This military equipment was less than realistic, but Lionel continued to make the material. Yet on the rear of the 1959 Advance Catalogue a major step in railroad realism was made—all the unrealistic military items appear on realistic two-rail track. There's a message there somewhere.

What many persons do not realize is that the military units are essentially both a beginning and an end of the old Lionel Corporation. Nearly everyone attributes the demise of the Lionel Toy Corporation to the cheapened and unrealistic quality of the trains and accessories of the 1960s. In 1917, as the "Great War" was taking place on the European continent,

Lionel got into the military business. In World War II they manufactured instruments for the United States armed forces, while in World War I they were making toy trains for the public. The #203 self-propelled armored gray locomotive with a two-gun turret pulling two #900 ammunition cars marked Lionel's entry into the military train market. This particular set, and a more expensive version with two #702 Supply Cars, was one of Lionel's best selling sets between 1917 and 1921. First catalogued in 1918, the promotional hype read, "Play war! Bring up siege guns on tracks". Not very subtle for a toy company! Today, it is one of the most difficult to obtain and desirable to own of all the prewar sets.

When Fundimensions began Lionel production in 1970, they catalogued a Satellite Launching Car. It, along with many other non-military/space items, was not produced in that year. It was not until 1980 that vestiges of the past started to reappear, with the reissuing of the Allis Chalmers Car and the Radioactive Waste Disposal Car.

On the surface, 1981 appears to be Lionel's "plunge" back into space and military items, as they vigorously promoted their Land and Space Early Reaction set, L. A. S. E. R. for short. Only time will tell.

Next is a checklist of Lionel space and military items manufactured between 1917 and 1969. It is divided into four areas: motorized and locomotive units, operating/action cars, non-operating cars and accessories. Finally, there is a year-by-year listing of all predominantly military sets.

## POWER UNITS

41 - US Army Turbine Switcher
42 - Picatinny Arsenal Turbine Switcher
44 - US Army Mobile Missile Launcher
45 - US Marine Corps Mobile Missile Launcher
51 - US Navy Turbine Switcher
52 - Fire Car
57 - AEC Turbine Switcher
59 - Minuteman Vulcan Diesel
203 - Gray Armored Locomotive with rotating two-gun turret, 1917-21
212 - USMC Alco Diesel
212D - USMC Alco Diesel
221 - USMC Alco Diesel
221 - AT & SF Alco Diesel
224 - US Navy Alco Diesel and non-powered "B" unit
229 - M & St. L Alco Diesel A unit
240 - 2-4-2 Scout-type locomotive with smoke
1625 - 0-4-0

## OPERATING ROLLING STOCK

3309 - Turbo Missile Firing
3330 - Blue Flatcar with Submarine Kit
3349 - Turbo Missile Firing Car
3349 - Same as above
3409 - Blue Flat with yellow Helicopter
3410 - Blue Flat with Helicopter
3413 - Mercury Capsule Launching Car

3419 - Royal blue Flat with Operating Two-blade Helicopter
3419 - Dark blue Flat with Four-blade gray Helicopter
3429 - USMC Automatic Helicopter Car
3470 - Target Launching Car
3509 - Satellite Car
3509 - Satellite Car
3510 - Red Satellite Car
3510 - Dark Red Satellite Car
3512 - Fire Extension Ladder Car
3512 - Same as above, but with black extension ladder
3519 - Automatic Satellite Launching Car
3535 - AEC Security Car
3540 - Operating Radar Car
3619 - Helicopter Reconnaisance Car
3619 - Same as above, except dark golden yellow body
3665 - Minuteman Missile Car
3665 - Same as above, except yellow body
3665 - Same as above, except for light blue split roof
3666 - Minuteman Cannon Car

3820 Flat with submarine.

3820 - Same as 3830
3830 - Blue Flat with removable US Navy submarine
6448 - Exploding Boxcar
6470 - Exploding Boxcar
6480 - Exploding Boxcar
6512 - Cherry Picker Car
6544 - Missile Firing Car
6630 - IRBM Launcher
6640 - IRBM Launcher
6650 - IRBM Launcher
6651 - Cannon Car
6805 - Atomic Disposal Flatcar

### MANUAL ROLLING STOCK

702  - Gray Supply Car
900  - Gray Ammunition Car
1877 - Three small gray flatcars
6017 - Plain Gray Caboose
6017 - Type Caboose
6017 - 50 USMC Caboose
6017 - 200 US Navy
6076 - Type Hopper
6112 - Scout-type Gondola
6175 - Red Flatcar with 175 rocket

6175 - Black Flatcar with 175 rocket
6407 - Red Flat
6413 - Mercury Capsule Carrying Car
6413 - Same as above, except aqua-green plastic, no brake-wheels, one operating coupler and one fixed coupler
6463 - Two-dome Rocket Fuel Tank
6500 - Red Flatcar with Bonanza Plane
6500 - Black unnumbered Flat with Bonanza Plane
6519 - Allis Chalmers Car
6519 - Same as above, except dark orange color
6530 - Fire Safety Car
6651 - USMC Flatcar with Stakes
6800 - Red Flatcar with Bonanza Plane
6800 - Red Flatcar with Bonanza Plane
6803 - Military Unit - USMC
6804 - Military Unit - USMC
6806 - Military Unit - USMC
6806 - Military Unit - USMC
6807 - Military Unit - USMC
6808 - Military Unit - USMC
6809 - Military Unit - USMC

Note: These trucks are gray with USMC ensignia. They were NOT made by Lionel but for Lionel by the Pyro Manufacturing Company, Union, New Jersey. All the same trucks, in olive green with a white star on the sides, were issued separately well before Lionel came out with them in 1958.

6814 - Rescue Unit Caboose
6814 - Same as above, except black base and no load
6819 - Red Flat with gray helicopter

6820 Flat with helicopter.

6820 - Blue Flat with gray helicopter
6823 - Red Flat with IRBM Missiles
6824 - Same as 6814 except color is olive with white letters USMC
6844 - Black Flat with six "Little John" Missiles
6830 - Blue Flat with gray Submarine.

### ACCESSORIES

175   - Remote Control Rocket Launcher
175-50- Rocket for Rocket Launcher
197   - Rotating Radar Antenna
199   - Microwave Relay Tower
347   - Cannon Launching Platform

| | | | | |
|---|---|---|---|---|
| 394 | - Rotary Beacon | | | |
| 413 | - Countdown Control Panel | | | |
| 419 | - Heliport Control Tower | | | |
| 448 | - Missile Launching Platform | | | |
| 462 | - Derrick Platform Set with Radioactive Waste Containers | | | |
| 470 | - Missile Launching Platform | | | |
| 494 | - Rotary Beacon | | | |
| 943 | - Exploding Ammo Dump | | | |

## MILITARY/SPACE SETS

The following is a listing of set numbers for military-related sets of trains marketed by Lionel between 1917 and 1965. For a listing of set contents see our chapter on Lionel sets.

1917 & 1918:   Outfit 213, 214 and 215.

1919, 1920, 1921:   Outfit 214 and 215.

1958:   Nos. 1595, 1591, 1505W and 2717W.

No. 1595 - Marine Battlefront Special: 1625LT, 6804, 6808, 6806, 6017 (Gray)

No. 1591 - US Marine Land and Sea Limited: 212, 6809, 6807, 6803, 6017-50

No. 2505W - Super "O" Virginian Rectifier Freight: 2329, 6805, 6519, 6800, 6464-500, 6357

No. 2717W - Super "O" Rio Grande Diesel Freight: 2379 A & B, 6519, 6805, 6800, 6434, 6657

1959:   No set No.: 212, 6803, 6804, 6806, 6807, 6808, 6809, 1625WS, 2527, 2545WS

1960:   Nos. 1629, 1633, 1805, 2527, 2549W

1961:   Nos. 1643, 1647, 1650, 1810, 2572, 2574, uncataloged - Sears Roebuck Military Set

1962:   Nos. 11212, 11232, 11252, 11268, 11288, 11298, 12512, 13008, 13018, 13028, 13058 and Uncatalogued Sears Roebuck Marine Corps Military Set

1963:   11341, 11361, 11385, 13108, 13128

1964:   No. 11440

1965:   No sets cataloged - Military/Space items for separate sale only.

| | Gd | VG | Exc | Mt |
|---|---|---|---|---|
| **1877 FLAT WITH FENCE AND HORSES** 1959-62, brown unpainted plastic body, white lettering, six horses. | 20 | 30 | 40 | 60 |

**(1877) NO NUMBER** circa 1960-65, 1877 Type. Car catalogue number does not appear on car, hence appears in parentheses.

| | Gd | VG | Exc | Mt |
|---|---|---|---|---|
| (A) Flatcar with logs, unpainted gray plastic, three logs, no stakes, Timken trucks, one disc-operating coupler, one fixed coupler. | 1 | 2 | 3 | 5 |
| (B) Flat without stakes or load, unpainted brown plastic, arch bar trucks, fixed couplers. | 1 | 1.50 | 2 | 4 |
| (C) Flat without stakes or load, unpainted gray plastic, arch bar trucks, fixed couplers. Edmunds Collection. Used for Sears military tank car flat; Bohn comment. | 1 | 1.50 | 2 | 4 |
| (D) Flat with yellow auto, part of set 19142-100. Dupstet Collection. | | | | NRS |

| | Gd | VG | Exc | Mt |
|---|---|---|---|---|
| **1887 FLAT WITH FENCE AND HORSES** 1959, tuscan with yellow lettering and fence, six horses, part of uncatalogued Sears 0-27 set. | 60 | 85 | 125 | 170 |

**2411 FLAT WITH BIG INCH PIPES** 1946-48, same gray die-cast frame as 2419 Work Caboose, three black metal pipes with grooves at end, or three wood logs; staple-end metal trucks, coil coupler, black serif-lettered "LIONEL LINES", six black stakes, four steps, two sets of end rails.

| | Gd | VG | Exc | Mt |
|---|---|---|---|---|
| (A) 1946, metal pipes. Foss comment. | 3 | 6 | 10 | 15 |
| (B) 1947-48, wood logs. Foss comment. | 3 | 6 | 10 | 15 |

**2461 TRANSFORMER CAR** 1947-48, gray die-cast depressed-center belly frame with black serif-lettered "LIONEL LINES", staple-end metal trucks, coil couplers with sliding shoes, two brakewheels.

| | Gd | VG | Exc | Mt |
|---|---|---|---|---|
| (A) Black transformer, small white decal on one side with "Transformer" and "L" in circle. | 11 | 17 | 25 | 35 |
| (B) Red transformer, same decal as (A). | 11 | 17 | 25 | 35 |
| (C) Red transformer, same decal as (A), no lettering on frame. | 11 | 17 | 25 | 35 |
| (D) Red transformer, no decals or lettering, center insulators same length as side insulators (usually they are shorter). Rohlfing Collection. | 11 | 17 | 25 | 35 |

**(3309) TURBO MISSILE LAUNCHING CAR** circa 1960. Also see 3349.

| | Gd | VG | Exc | Mt |
|---|---|---|---|---|
| (A) Light red plastic car, no number or lettering, blue launch mechanism, red missile, blue missile holder, arch bar trucks, fixed couplers; Royer comment. Note that 3309 does not have an extra missile rack while 3349 does. | 12 | 25 | 35 | 50 |
| (B) Same as (A), but cherry red. Royer comment. | 12 | 25 | 35 | 50 |
| (C) Same as (A), but light blue launcher, Timken trucks. Royer comment. | 12 | 25 | 35 | 50 |
| (D) Same as (A), except gray "General"-type flatcar. Blotner Collection. | | | | NRS |
| (E) Same as (B), but has extra missile rack like 3349; came with 3309 instruction sheet which showed extra missile rack. Budniak Collection. | | | | NRS |

**3330 FLAT WITH OPERATING SUBMARINE KIT** 1960-61, flat (6511-2 mold) with disassembled submarine requiring assembly, blue car, white-lettered "LIONEL" with serifs, Timken trucks, disc-operating couplers, gray submarine lettered "U.S. Navy, No.3830".

| | Gd | VG | Exc | Mt |
|---|---|---|---|---|
| | 20 | 35 | 50 | 75 |

**3349 TURBO MISSILE LAUNCHING CAR** Circa 1960, also see 3309. Note that 3349 has an extra missile rack that 3309 usually does not have. 3349 came with set 19142-100. It also came with other sets. No number or lettering, light red or olive drab plastic car with blue launch mechanism, red and white missiles, blue missile holder, Timken trucks. No mold number on car. Operating couplers. Royer and Ocilka comments.

| | Gd | VG | Exc | Mt |
|---|---|---|---|---|
| (A) Light red body. | 10 | 15 | 25 | 50 |
| (B) Olive drab body, Marine Corps markings. | 10 | 15 | 25 | 50 |
| (C) Red body, no lettering, aqua blue launcher and missile rack (blue with a slight green tinge), one fixed and one operating coupler, Timken plastic trucks. Halverson Collection. | | | | NRS |

**3361-55 LOG DUMP** 1955-58, unpainted gray plastic with black lettering, bar-end metal trucks, magnetic tab couplers, metal channel runs car length and holds operating mechanism.

| | Gd | VG | Exc | Mt |
|---|---|---|---|---|
| (A) "LIONEL LINES" with heavy 7/32" serif letters, 336155 on right in large serif numbers, car dimensions to left in sans-serif lettering, drive gear for operating mechanism is white plastic. Backus and Ocilka Collections. | 8 | 15 | 20 | 30 |
| (B) "LIONEL LINES" with lighter serif letters than (A), 336155 on left, dimensions data to right, drive gear is solid black plastic. Backus and Ocilka Collections. | 8 | 15 | 20 | 30 |
| (C) "LIONEL LINES" in 1/8" sans-serif letters, darker gray plastic body, car number to right and dimensions data to left, drive gear is medium orange plastic. Backus Collection. | 8 | 15 | 20 | 30 |
| (D) Same as (A), but original box marked "3361X". Reader comments requested. Budniak Collection. | | | | NRS |

**3362/64 FLAT WITH HELIUM TANKS or LOGS** 1961-63, dumps three silver-painted wooden tanks or three large dark-stained logs, unpainted dark green plastic body, mold No. 2, with LIONEL LINES serif lettering, "LD LMT 128800, LT WT 40200, CAPY 100000" in white sans-serif lettering, metal channel runs length of car, magnetic operation, Timken plastic trucks, one disc and one dummy coupler. Some reports say that although all of these cars were stamped 3362, this car was referred to as 3364 when it was equipped with logs instead of helium tanks; Rohlfing, Ambrose and I.D. Smith comments. However, the nomenclature of this car may not be so simple; see Entry (C) below.

| | Gd | VG | Exc | Mt |
|---|---|---|---|---|
| (A) With helium tanks. | 8 | 15 | 25 | 40 |
| (B) With logs, Popp Collection. | 8 | 15 | 25 | 40 |

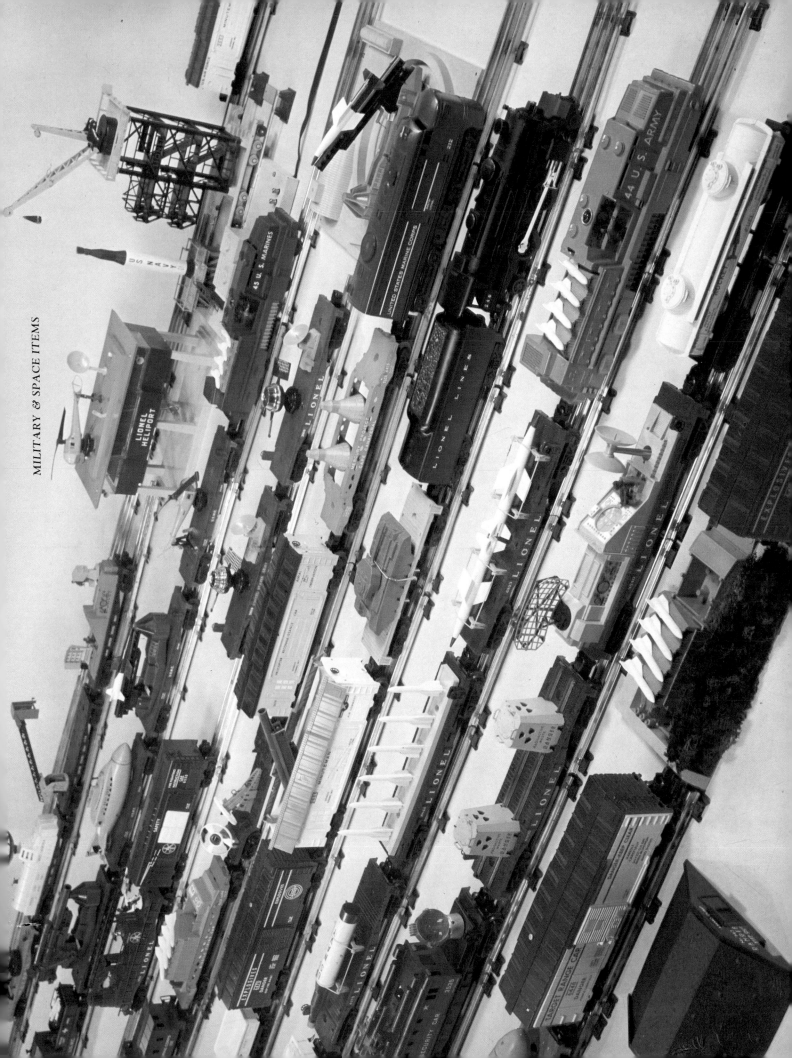

(C) No lettering on car; box (1969-type) has "3362/3364" and "OPERAT-ING UNLOADING CAR". Came with two helium tanks and instruction sheet for "3362-15 Lionel Helium Tank Unloading Car". Algozzini and G. Wilson Collections.

        **10   20   30   50**

**3364 LOG DUMP** 1965-69, dumps three large dark-stained logs, mechanism similar to 3362; not illustrated.     **7   10   15   20**

**3409 HELICOPTER LAUNCHING CAR** 1961-62, helicopter with black plastic spring-wound launch mechanism, manually cocked and released; light blue unpainted flatcar, white lettering; gray "Navy" plastic helicopter with simulated door, black lettering, clear plastic front bubble, black plastic skid, single propeller, yellowish tail end piece and rotor, arch bar trucks, fixed couplers, mold 3419-30. Pauli Collection.

        **14   25   35   60**

**3409 SATELLITE CAR** Circa 1961, uncatalogued, light blue flat, white lettering, manual release, black and silver satellite, yellow microwave disc on gray superstructure, Timken trucks, operating disc couplers. Wilson Collection.     **NRS**

**3410 HELICOPTER LAUNCHING CAR** 1961-62, same as 3409 but with Timken trucks, disc-operating couplers.    **13   20   30   40**

**3413 MERCURY CAPSULE CAR** 1962-64, car launches rocket into air, Mercury capsule separates and returns via parachute. Red plastic frame, white-lettered "LIONEL", no numbers, gray superstructure with red rocket launcher; gray Mercury capsule nose with parachute inside of rocket, red rocket base; Timken trucks, one disc-operating coupler, one fixed coupler.

        **20   35   45   75**

**3419 REMOTE CONTROLLED HELICOPTER LAUNCHING CAR** 1959-65, similar to 3409 in function but with two slots on top and large 2" black winder designed to be released (after manually cocked) by UCS magnet track; with alternate manual lever and lock lever on car top near black plastic piece which holds copter tail assembly rigid prior to flight, flatcar mold number 3419-30.

(A) Light blue body, same helicopter as 3409.   **13   25   35   50**
(B) Medium blue body, 1-1/4" diameter winder, Timken trucks, disc couplers, same helicopter as 3409.   **13   25   35   50**
(C) Royal blue body, gray helicopter with two top rotors and four tips, 2" winder.     **13   25   40   65**
(D) Dark blue, almost purple, two control levers on car's top surface, all yellow helicopter (see 3429 for copter description).   **13   25   40   65**
(E) Aqua blue body, helicopter with two top rotors and four tips.

        **13   25   35   50**
(F) Same as (C), but helicopter as in (E). Mitarotonda comment.

        **13   25   35   50**
(G) Same as (B), but purple body. Rohlfing Collection. **13   25   35   50**

**3429 U.S.M.C.** 1960, U.S. MARINE CORPS operating helicopter car, olive drab paint over blue plastic car, white lettering, same mechanism as 3419, all-yellow helicopter with three windows behind bubble, one porthole in rear section, one blade, same as 3419(D). One control lever on car's top surface, other on car's side; winder could be remotely released. **14   25   35   50**

**3451 LOG DUMP** 1946-47, black die-cast base, white lettering, staple-end metal trucks, coil couplers.
(A) 1946, shaft retainers for the swivel movement are riveted with round-head rivets from the top and swaged from the bottom; nickel-sized hole between second and third set of stakes; heat-stamped lettering.

        **10   15   20   35**
(B) 1947, shaft retainer rivets are integral to casting and swaged from top, hole about size of half dollar on frame, heat-stamped lettering.

        **10   15   20   35**
(C) Same as (B), but rubber-stamped lettering. Latina Collection.

        **10   15   20   35**
(D) Same as (A), but rubber-stamped lettering. Rohlfing Collection.

        **10   15   20   35**

**3460 FLAT WITH TRAILERS** 1955, red unpainted plastic flatcar, mold number 6511-2, white lettering, metal strip holds trailers, bar-end metal trucks, magnetic tab couplers, trucks fastened to frame by metal plate; metal plate slides into two slots at each end of car; trailers are dark green with aluminum sign reading "LIONEL TRAINS", end decal reads "FRUEHAUF DURAVAN", lower right-hand decal reads "FRUEHAUF", van with single axle, four wheels.  **10   20   25   40**

**3461 LOG DUMP** 1949-55, five logs stained dark brown, white lettering, "LIONEL LINES", one brakewheel.
(A) 1949-53, black die-cast frame and dump unit; staple-end metal trucks, magnetic couplers.      **10   20   25   40**
(B) 1954-55, green die-cast frame, black dump unit, bar-end metal trucks, magnetic couplers, box marked either 3461-25 or 3461X. Budniak Collection.        **14   20   35   50**
(C) 1952-55, black die-cast frame and dump unit, bar-end metal trucks, magnetic couplers. Kaiser Collection.   **10   20   25   40**

**3470 TARGET LAUNCHER** 1962-64, dark blue unpainted flatcar, mold No. 6511-2, no lettering; white superstructure with red letters, red lever on top activates motor; blue balloon carriage on top; car came with Lionel balloons, which when inflated and motor was turned on would raise the balloon approximately 1" above the balloon carrier, the balloon would then follow the moving car; with two dry cell batteries for operation; Timken trucks, disc couplers, clear plastic blower nozzle. Diggle Collection.
(A) As described above.      **12   25   40   60**
(B) Same as (A), but light blue unpainted flatcar. Blotner Collection.

        **12   25   40   60**
(C) Same as (A), but red plastic blower nozzle. Diggle Collection.

        **12   25   40   60**
(D) Same as (A), but light gray blower nozzle. Diggle Collection.

        **12   25   40   60**

**3509 MANUALLY OPERATED SATELLITE CAR** 1961, not catalogued, green car, white lettering, black and silver satellite, gray superstructure holds yellow microwave disc; manually-operated by side lever, Timken trucks, disc couplers, mold 3419-30.
(A) As described above.      **9   15   22   30**
(B) Blue flatcar body from 3419 helicopter car; "3419" oversprayed with blue paint and water-release "3509" decal applied over number. White "LIONEL" heat-stamped on car after this overprint process (the heat-stamp overrides the blue paint). Remote control winding spool same as 3419, except that an extension for the spool neck is apparently glued onto winding spool. This extension is slightly smaller than the base of the neck. Antenna pedestal is 1/2" shorter than on 3519 and has no panel or rivet detail cast in. We would like to hear from others who possess this car. This is a fascinating manufacturing variation; it would appear that the folks at the Lionel factory were not above doing a little "kitbashing" from time to time! Stekoll Collection.     **NRS**

**3510 RED SATELLITE CAR** 1961-62, black and silver satellite, arch bar trucks, fixed couplers.
(A) Darker red car, gray superstructure, yellow microwave disc.

        **13   25   35   50**
(B) Red car, no superstructure.      **9   20   27   40**
(C) Red body, mold 3419-30, flatcar bottom has molded solid "box" between "New York" and "N.Y." of corporate identification, gray superstructure, yellow microwave dish, small black winder manually operated by lever, arch bar trucks, fixed couplers, no load came with sample observed. Halverson Collection.  **13   25   35   50**

**3512 LADDER CO.** 1959-61, red unpainted plastic body, 6424-11 mold Die 4, white lettering, truck mechanism causes light shield to rotate causing light rotation, man rotates at other car end; mechanism uses rubber belt which almost always deteriorates; Timken trucks, disc couplers, three small metal nozzles, two ladders. Ocilka comment.
(A) Black ladder.      **22   35   50   70**
(B) Silver ladder.      **32   45   65  120**

**3519 REMOTE CONTROL SATELLITE CAR** 1961-64, green base, white letters, gray superstructure with yellow microwave disc, black and silver satellite, Timken trucks, disc couplers; car activated manually by lever on side or by remote control track, mold #3419-30. **8   15   25   35**

**3535 AEC SECURITY** 1960-61, black base, mold No. 6511-2, red building, white letters, gray gun on roof, gray rotating-type searchlight with vibrator motor, Timken trucks, disc couplers, one pickup roller. Same body used for 520 Box Cab Electric (page 51).   **19   35   50   90**

**3540 OPERATING RADAR CAR** 1959-60, red car base, mold No. 6511-2, white letters, gray superstructure with yellow microwave disc; black and silver radar antenna; blue seated man with flesh-colored hands and face; radar unit panel similar to 44 Rocket Launcher with dials and gauges;

# FLAT CARS

3330

3349[A]

3361-55

3362

3362

3410

3413

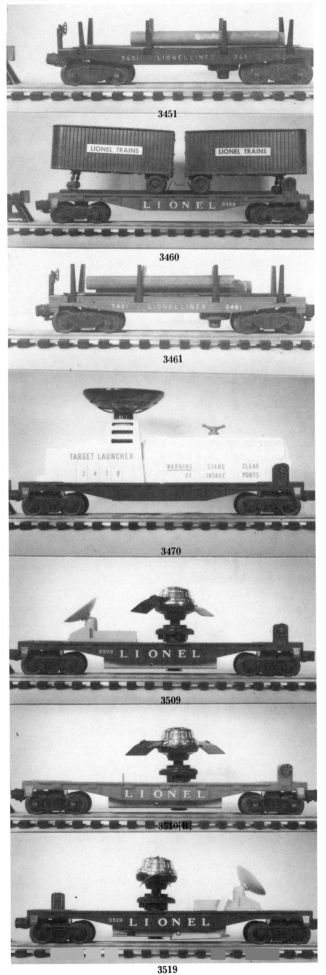

3451

3460

3461

3470

3509

3510[B]

3519

2461　6461

6561　6561

6418

lighted green radar screen with black lines and white dots; rotating radar tower powered by rubber band drive attached to disc and axle; rubber band usually deteriorates; one roller pickup for radar screen light.

|  |  |  |  |
|---|---|---|---|
| 22 | 55 | 75 | 125 |

**3545 LIONEL TV CAR** 1961-62, black base, white letters, blue superstructure with blue TV camera and base; 6511-2 mold, blue man with flesh-colored face and hands in seated position looking into TV projection screen; screen shows a Santa Fe diesel coming and an open railroad track in the direction the car is moving; to the rear of seated figure is a movable light structure that "illuminates" the cameraman's subject; TV cameraman rotates by rubber band drive attached to disc and axle; rubber band usually deteriorates. Ocilka comment.

|  |  |  |  |
|---|---|---|---|
| 20 | 45 | 65 | 115 |

**3820 FLAT WITH OPERATING SUBMARINE** 1960-62, olive drab car, mold No. 6511-2, white-lettered "USMC", gray submarine marked "U.S. NAVY 3830", Timken trucks, disc couplers.

|  |  |  |  |
|---|---|---|---|
| 17 | 25 | 35 | 65 |

**3830 FLAT WITH OPERATING SUBMARINE** 1960-63; blue car, mold No. 6511-2, white-lettered "LIONEL", gray submarine with black-lettered "U.S. NAVY 3830", Timken trucks, disc couplers.

|  |  |  |  |
|---|---|---|---|
| 12 | 25 | 35 | 60 |

**NOTE:** There are three different 6111 flatcars.

**6111 FLAT WITH LOGS** 1955, yellow-painted stamped-steel car, black serif lettered "LIONEL", three logs, bar-end metal trucks.

|  |  |  |  |
|---|---|---|---|
| 1 | 1.50 | 2 | 4 |

6111(A) LIONEL flatcar. Note sans-serif lettering. Pro Custom Hobbies Collection.

**6111 FLAT WITH PIPES OR LOGS** Circa 1955-56, painted stamped-steel frame; frame similar to preceding 6111, probably held pipes or logs, pipe or log holders.

(A) Gray-painted frame "LIONEL" in sans-serif lettering, Timken trucks, disc couplers. Schreiner and Light Collections. **NRS**

(B) Light gray-painted frame, aluminum-finished pipes, "LIONEL" in white serif lettering, bar-end metal trucks, tab couplers. White and Kotil Collections. **NRS**

(C) Dark gray-painted frame, "LIONEL" in serif lettering, Timken trucks, came with log load. Rohlfing and Kotil Collections. **NRS**

(D) Same as (C), but "LIONEL" in sans-serif lettering. Kotil Collection. **NRS**

(E) Dark blue-gray-painted frame, "LIONEL" in serif lettering, Timken trucks. Kotil Collection. **NRS**

**6111 FLAT WITH PIPES** 1957, red-painted stamped-steel car, white-lettered "LIONEL", pipes.

(A) Lettering with serifs.

|  |  |  |  |
|---|---|---|---|
| 1 | 1.50 | 2 | 4 |

(B) Lettering without serifs, bar-end metal trucks, magnetic tab couplers. Budniak Collection.

|  |  |  |  |
|---|---|---|---|
| 1 | 1.50 | 2 | 4 |

(C) Same as (A), but cherry red body, Timken trucks, two disc couplers. Budniak Collection.

|  |  |  |  |
|---|---|---|---|
| 1 | 1.50 | 2 | 4 |

**6121 FLAT WITH PIPES** 1955, yellow-painted stamped steel, black-lettered "LIONEL", three pipes.

(A) Lettering with serifs.

|  |  |  |  |
|---|---|---|---|
| 1 | 1.50 | 2 | 4 |

(B) Lettering without serifs.

|  |  |  |  |
|---|---|---|---|
| 1 | 1.50 | 2 | 4 |

**6151 FLATCAR WITH PATROL TRUCK** 1958, yellow stamped-steel car, black serif lettering, steps, bar-end metal trucks, magnetic couplers.

(A) White plastic patrol truck cab lettered "LIONEL RANCH", in black, with longhorns insignia; black plastic body lettered "RANGE PATROL", truck made by PYRO.

|  |  |  |  |
|---|---|---|---|
| 12 | 25 | 40 | 60 |

(B) Orange steel car. Degano Collection.

|  |  |  |  |
|---|---|---|---|
| 17 | 25 | 40 | 50 |

(C) Same as (A), but Timken trucks with two disc couplers; shown on page 2 of 1958 catalogue. Budniak Collection.

|  |  |  |  |
|---|---|---|---|
| 12 | 25 | 40 | 60 |

**6175 FLATCAR WITH ROCKET** Red and white rocket with blue letters, gray rocket rack, Timken trucks, disc couplers.

(A) Black plastic car, die 2 No. 6424-11 mold, white lettering. Ocilka Collection.

|  |  |  |  |
|---|---|---|---|
| 19 | 35 | 55 | 75 |

(B) Same as (A), but die 3 6424-11 mold. Ocilka Collection.

|  |  |  |  |
|---|---|---|---|
| 12 | 25 | 40 | 50 |

(C) Red plastic car, mold No. 6511-2, white lettering.

|  |  |  |  |
|---|---|---|---|
| 10 | 15 | 20 | 40 |

(D) Same as (A), but red car. Ocilka comment.

|  |  |  |  |
|---|---|---|---|
| 19 | 35 | 55 | 75 |

**6262 FLAT WITH WHEELS** 1956-57, white lettering, gray superstructure with eight sets of Lionel wheels and axles; magnetic tab couplers.

3535

3540

3545

6121[A]

6151[A]

6175 [note wrong load]

6262

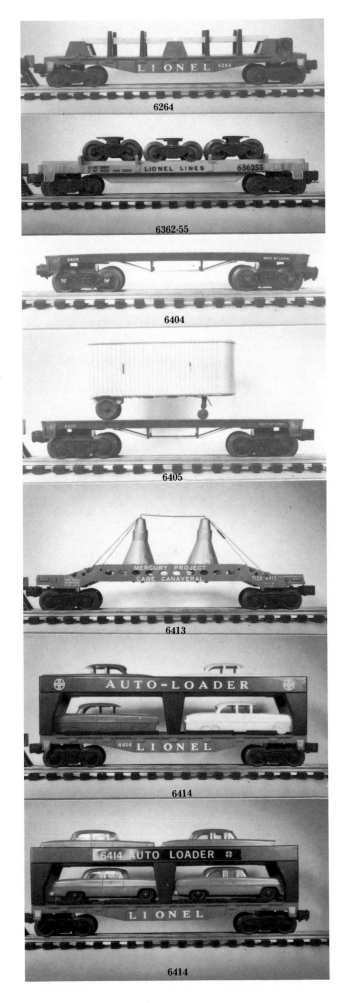

6264

6362-55

6404

6405

6413

6414

6414

(A) 1956, black flatcar, mold No. 6424-11 die 1, bar-end metal trucks. Ocilka Collection. **9 18 25 40**

(B) 1957, black flatcar, mold #6424-11 die 2, plastic Timken trucks. Ocilka comment. **9 18 25 40**

(C) Red flatcar. G. Wilson Collection. **20 40 65 100**

**6264 FLAT WITH LOG LOAD** 1957, lumber for fork lift car, red plastic car, mold No. 6511-2, white lettering, brown lumber rack, black stakes, one brakewheel, bar-end metal trucks, magnetic couplers; truck mounting plates that fit into car grooves. **12 25 35 60**

**6311 FLAT** 1955, reddish-brown plastic body with metal pipes, mold No. 6511-2; bar-end metal trucks, magnetic tab couplers, truck mounting plates that fasten with screws. Pauli Collection. Came with 2028 PRR GP-7 set and was also available as a separate item. Included seven stakes and three pipes. Much harder to find than 6511. Ambrose comments.
**7 15 20 30**

**6343 BARREL RAMP CAR** 1961-62, red with white lettering, 6424-11 mold, die 4, Timken trucks disc couplers with six stained brown barrels, part of set No. 11222. **8 15 20 40**

**6361 FLAT WITH TIMBER** 1960-61, 64-69; green plastic, three wooden sticks with bark held by chains with spring on underside; metal channel provides support for car; Timken trucks, disc couplers.

(A) White lettering. **9 17 25 40**

(B) No lettering, gold chains. Degano Collection. **11 20 35 75**

(C) Lighter green flatcar, no lettering, black timber chains. Halverson Collection. **NRS**

**6362-55 TRUCK CAR** 1956, carries three Lionel trucks without couplers, bar-end trucks. Mitarotonda comment.

(A) Clear plastic painted orange, magnetic tab couplers, serif lettering.
**7 14 30 45**

(B) Orange plastic, magnetic couplers, sans-serif lettering.
**7 14 30 45**

(C) Orange unpainted plastic, serif lettering, magnetic couplers. Kotil Collection. **8 15 20 40**

(D) Same as (B), but sans-serif lettering. Mitarotonda and Kotil Collections. **8 15 20 40**

**6401-50 FLATCAR** Circa 1960?, olive drab plastic car, probably mold No. 1877-3 although Service Manual cites part number 6401-51 as frame. Probably has no number or lettering, Timken trucks, one operating coupler, one fixed coupler. Confirmation requested: car number probably appears on box end.

**6401 FLAT WITH VAN** Light gray car with gray two-wheel van, mold No. 1877-3, Timken trucks, one disc coupler, one fixed coupler. Pauli Collection. **3 7 12 20**

**6402 FLAT WITH REELS OR BOAT** medium gray plastic car, mold No. 1877-3.

(A) 1964, orange reels marked "LIONEL", elastic bands hold reels in place. **3 6 9 15**

(B) 1969, blue boat. **4 8 12 20**

(C) Same as (A), but two orange cable reels on brown flatcar. Arpino Collection. **NRS**

**6402-50 FLATCAR WITH CABLE REELS,** 1964, medium gray plastic car, mold No. 1877-3 from General flatcar, although Service Manual calls for part number 6402-51. "6402" on car side. Orange reels marked "LIONEL", elastic bands hold reels in place, Timken trucks, one operating coupler, one fixed coupler. **2 3 5 11**

**6404 FLATCAR** not catalogued in 1960 Consumer catalogue, but shown in 1960 Advance Catalogue. Black body with struts, 1877-3 mold, arch bar trucks, dummy couplers. Came with brown auto with gray bumpers. Part of special low-price set No. 1109, "The Huntsman Steamer... designed for the toy market and ... not ... included in the Lionel consumer catalogue". For more information about this set, see the entry for 1060 in the steam locomotive section. Car was possibly also offered as a Merchants' Green Stamp premium car, and possibly by other mass merchandisers as a low-price "leader". We would like information from the 1960 Merchants' Green Stamp catalogue. Fleming Collection and observations.
**14 22 35 60**

**6405 FLAT WITH TRAILER** 1961, brown plastic flat, mold No. 1877-3 with struts; Timken trucks, disc couplers; yellow trailer marked "Made in the U.S. of America, The Lionel Corporation, New York, New York", trailer has single axle with two wheels while Piggyback outfit trailer has single axle with four wheels. **7 10 15 30**

**6406 FLAT WITH AUTO** 1961, mold 1877-3, tuscan unpainted plastic General-style flatcar, Timken trucks, two dummy couplers, no struts. Came in set 1123 "Pacemaker" in 1961 with 1060 locomotive. No lettering or numbering; no load on sample observed. Powell Collection. **NRS**

**6407 FLAT WITH ROCKET** 1963, red flatcar, no numbers, white letters, gray superstructure holds large white and red rocket with blue nose.

(A) Nose is a pencil sharpener that can be removed and used; rocket does not launch. **45 90 160 275**

(B) Nose is not a pencil sharpener. Catalano comment.
**42 80 140 250**

**6409-25 FLAT** With unknown load, if any. Red body, body mold number 6511-2, no number, no brakewheel, white-lettered "LIONEL", arch bar trucks, fixed couplers believed to be from Set 11311, 1963 Catalogue, page 3; confirmation of item and set number requested. Schreiner Collection.
**NRS**

**6411 FLAT WITH LOGS** 1948-50, gray die-cast frame rubber-stamped "6411" on underside, black "LIONEL LINES" serif lettering, two brakewheels, end railings, logs. Not illustrated.

(A) 1948, staple-end metal trucks, coil couplers. I. D. Smith Collection.
**3 5 6 10**

(B) 1949-50, same as (A), but magnetic couplers. I. D. Smith and Schmaus Collections. **3 5 6 10**

**6413 MERCURY PROJECT CAPE CANAVERAL** 1962-63, blue plastic car, does not have mold number, white letters, two gray Mercury capsules held by bands with cloth coating; metal plates hold capsules, Timken trucks, disc couplers. Ocilka comment.

(A) Powder blue car. Wilson Collection. **10 20 25 50**

(B) Aquamarine car. Wilson Collection. **10 20 25 50**

**6414 AUTO LOADER** 1955-57, red base, 6511-2 mold, white letters, black metal superstructure, white letters. NOTE: The autos for this car are readily available for about $5.00 each in premium versions.

(A) Premium cars with windshields, bumpers, rubber tires; car colors vary; most are yellow, red, blue and white. "6414" on right side of car, bar-end metal trucks, magnetic tab couplers. **10 20 30 50**

(B) Premium cars with windshields, bumpers, rubber tires; colors of cars vary, "6414" on left side. **10 20 30 50**

(C) Four red premium cars with gray non-chrome bumpers, bar-end metal trucks, magnetic tab couplers, "6414" on right. **10 20 30 50**

(D) Four cheap cars without bumpers, wheels or windshields, two red cars and two yellow cars; simulated wheels on the exterior with an interior space where the axle would have been attached; red cars have attachment for axle, yellow cars do not, "6414" on left side; Timken trucks, disc couplers, box marked "6414-85", cars with axle attachment stamped "4" under roof, while cars without axles attached are stamped "1" under roof. "PT. No. 6068-3" stamped under all four autos. Algozzini Collection.
**8 15 20 40**

(E) Decal version made for Glen Uhl by Lionel; 200 reportedly made with black decals, yellow letters, red autos; have gray plastic bumpers, black wheels, Timken trucks, one disc coupler, one fixed coupler; "6414" on decal, not on flatcar. **20 40 50 75**

(F) 1966, four red premium cars with gray non-chrome bumpers, Timken trucks with disc operating couplers, "6414" on left. Hutchinson Collection.
**10 20 30 50**

(G) Four dark brown premium cars with chrome bumpers, 6414 to right, bar-end metal trucks, magnetic couplers. Art Tom Collection. **NRS**

(H) Four medium green premium cars with chrome bumpers, 6414 to left, Timken plastic trucks, one disc-operated and one fixed coupler. Art Tom Collection. **NRS**

(I) Four yellow premium cars with gray bumpers, "6414" on left, two operating couplers. Savage Collection. Brown autos with gray bumpers have also been reported; Stekoll comment. **12 20 30 50**

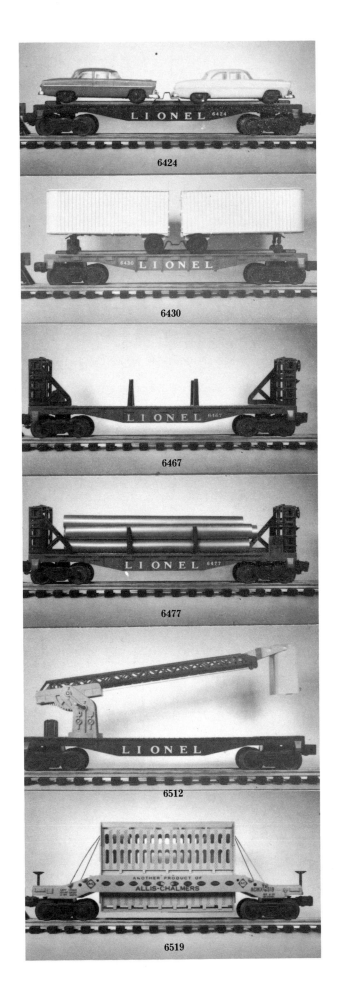

6424

6430

6467

6477

6512

6519

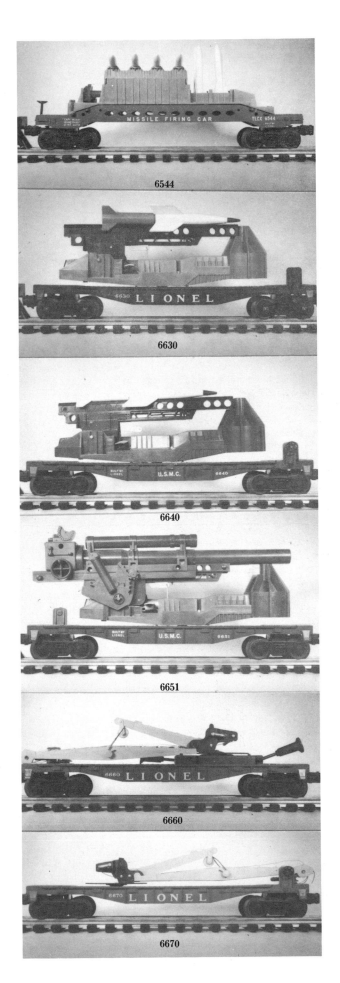

6544

6630

6640

6651

6660

6670

**6416 BOAT LOADER CAR** 1961-63, red base, 6511-2 mold, white letters, black metal superstructure with white letters, four boats, Timken trucks, disc couplers.

(A) Boats with white hull, blue top, brown interior.   25   40   60   125
(B) All red boats. Wilson Collection.   23   37   50   100
(C) Boats with white hull, blue top and red inner shells. Blotner Collection.
   25   40   60   125
(D) Boats with white hull, red top, black inner shells. This could be (B). Ocilka comment.   23   37   50   100
(E) Boats with red hulls with white decks and inner shells. Ocilka Collection.   23   37   50   100

**6418 FLAT WITH U.S. STEEL GIRDERS** 1955, depressed-center, die-cast gray body, four trucks with bar-ends, magnetic tab couplers. For 0 Gauge only, will not pass through 0-27 switches. Knight comment.

(A) All orange "LIONEL" girder. Catalano comment.   17   30   40   75
(B) Pinkish-orange girders with black "U.S. STEEL" lettering. Catalano comment.   17   30   40   75
(C) Black girders with white "U.S. STEEL" lettering, and numbered "6418" on lower right. Degano comment.   25   37   50   85
(D) Red girders with white "U. S. STEEL" lettering. Blotner Collection.
   25   37   50   85

**6424 FLAT WITH TWO AUTOS** 1956-59, black plastic flatcar with white lettering, black metal superstructure to keep autos from falling off; bar-end metal trucks, magnetic tab couplers.

(A) Mold No. 6424-11 die 1, 1956 bar-end metal trucks, magnetic tab couplers, number on right. Kotil Collection.   8   15   20   40
(B) Mold No. 6424-11 die 2, 1957 Timken trucks, disc couplers, number on right. Kotil Collection.   8   15   20   40
(C) Mold No. 6511-2, Timken trucks, disc couplers, number on left. Kotil Collection.   8   15   20   40
(D) Same as (A), but red flatcar.   12   25   50   90
(E) Same as (C), but red flatcar. Algozzini Collection.   12   25   50   90
(F) Same as (C), but mold 6424-11, Die 1. Ocilka Collection.
   8   15   20   40

**6430 FLATCAR WITH COOPER-JARRETT VANS** 1955-58, red plastic base, mold No. 6511-2, white lettering; trucks are fastened to plate, plate slides into car.

(A) "6430" appears on right side of car, trailer mounting unit is screwed onto car; COOPER-JARRETT VAN is gray plastic with an aluminum sign with an orange arrow and black lettering.   7   15   20   35
(B) "6430" appears on the left side of car, mold 6424-11, see next entry, 6431.   7   15   20   35
(C) COOPER-JARRETT VAN in white plastic.   7   15   20   35
(D) 1955-58, Two dark green plastic trailers, metal signs on sides lettered "Lionel Trains", small decal on right front of each trailer lettered "fruehauf", also decal center top front of each trailer lettered "FRUEHAUF Dura-Van", trailers with four rubber tires, bar-end metal trucks, magnetic tab couplers, one brakewheel. Powell Collection.   7   15   20   35
(E) Same as (A), except Cooper-Jarrett signs are copper-colored, not aluminum. Blotner Collection.   7   15   20   35

**6431 FLAT WITH VANS** 1965, red plastic flat, mold No. 6424-11, with white lettering and numbers; "6430" appears on left side; 6431 is a special with a Midge Toy tractor and two white unlettered trailers; the red die-cast tractor is marked: "Midge Toy, Rockford, Illinois, U.S.A., Patent 2775847", tractor has fifth wheel, a plug that fits into an enlarged hole in the trailer; the trailer mounting bracket and the flatcar trucks are riveted to the car; Timken trucks, disc couplers, one brakewheel. The vans used on this car were also possibly used with accessories 460 and 461; verification requested. Vagner comment.

(A) As described above.   20   40   50   75
(B) Same as (A), but mold 6511-2. Algozzini Collection.
   20   40   50   75
(C) Same as (B), but vans are bright yellow instead of white. Algozzini Collection.   **NRS**

**6440 FLAT WITH VANS** red unpainted plastic flatcar, mold 6511-2, white LIONEL lettering and "6440" to left, Timken plastic trucks.

(A) 1960, no van mounting units, two gray unpainted plastic vans with side slots for nameplates, but nameplates are absent, bottom of vans embossed "MADE IN U.S. OF AMERICA/THE LIONEL CORPORATION/NEW YORK, N.Y." in three lines, trailers have one two-wheel axle each, two disc-operating couplers, box marked "No. 6440 FLATCAR WITH PIGGY BACK VANS". Blotner, Landry, Marshall, Shewmake, Surratt and Toone Collections.   15   25   40   60
(B) 1961, same as (A), except vans have "COOPER-JARRETT" nameplates and car has one disc-operating and one dummy coupler. Ocilka Collection.   15   25   40   60
(C) Same as (B), except two disc-operating couplers. Sykes Collection.
   15   25   40   60

**6461 TRANSFORMER CAR** 1949-50, gray die-cast depressed-center base, black lettering, black plastic transformer with white decal, two brakewheels, steps, staple-end metal trucks, magnetic couplers, see color illustration. Lord observation.   12   22   30   45

**6467 BULKHEAD CAR** 1956, red flat with black bulkheads with stakes and white lettering, mold 6511-2, called "Miscellaneous Car", bar-end metal trucks, magnetic tab couplers.   13   25   35   50

**6469 LIONEL LIQUIFIED GASES** 1963, red car, mold 6424-11, Die 4, white letters, no numbers, large liquified gas cylinder lettered "Lionel", "ERIE", and "6469". 6467 is often found with this liquified gas cylinder but it did not come with it; Timken trucks, disc couplers, see color illustration. Ocilka Collection.   16   30   45   75

**6475** Vat Cars. See Chapter XII, Vat Cars.

**6477 BULKHEAD CAR WITH PLASTIC PIPES** 1957-58, red base, black bulkheads, white letters, stakes, called "Miscellaneous Car".

(A) Bar-end metal trucks, 6511-2 mold, magnetic couplers.
   13   25   35   60
(B) Timken trucks, disc couplers. Pauli Collection.   13   25   35   60

**6500 FLAT WITH BONANZA PLANE** 1962, 1965, black flatcar, white lettering, no number on car, 6511-2 mold, Timken trucks, disc couplers, red and white plane, one wing lettered "N2742B", see color illustration.

(A) Plane has red top and white bottom. Catalano comment.
   32   65   85   145
(B) Plane has white top, red bottom. Catalano comment.
   37   75   100   175
(C) Same as (B), but gray "General" flatcar. Blotner Collection.
   37   75   100   175

**6501 FLAT WITH JET BOAT** 1963, red base, white-lettered "LIONEL", mold 6511-2, Timken trucks, disc couplers, boat with white hull, brown top, brown deck, no lettering, boat uses baking soda mixed with water to create a gas given off at nozzle.   17   30   40   70

**6502-50 FLAT WITH BRIDGE GIRDER** 1962, No number, blue unpainted plastic car, mold 6511-2, orange unpainted Lionel 214 bridge side, Timken trucks, fixed couplers.

(A) Blue unpainted plastic.   1   1.50   2   4
(B) Deeper blue unpainted plastic.   1   1.50   2   4
(C) Same as (A), but one disc coupler, one fixed coupler.   1   1.50   2   4

**6502-75 FLAT WITH BRIDGE GIRDER** 1962

(A) Blue car with white lettering and orange girder, mold 6511-2, Morse observation.   **NRS**
(B) Black flatcar with orange girder, mold 6511-2, no number on car, car has "LIONEL" in white serif lettering, arch bar plastic trucks with two non-operating couplers. Bratspis Collection.   10   25   40   60

**6511 FLAT WITH PIPES** 1953-56, 6511-2 mold, white lettering, black stakes, three aluminum-colored plastic pipes, bar-end metal trucks, steel truck mounting plate.

(A) Brown flatcar, white lettering, magnetic tab couplers.
   3   7   9   12
(B) Dark red flatcar, white lettering, magnetic couplers.   3   7   9   12
(C) 1953, same as (B), but die-cast truck mounting bracket. Rohlfing Collection.   3   7   9   12

**6512 CHERRY PICKER CAR** 1962-63, black or blue base, mold 6511-2, white letters, no number on car, orange structure at end of ladder with gray man inside, structure swivels to outside, black metal ladder extends twice the length of unextended ladder, gray superstructure holds ladder, Timken trucks, disc couplers.

6801

6803

6804

6805

6806

6807

6808

6810

6816

6817

6819

6821

| | | | | |
|---|---|---|---|---|
| (A) Black base. | 19 | 35 | 50 | 85 |
| (B) Blue base. | | | | NRS |

**6518 TRANSFORMER CAR** 1956-58, gray die-cast depressed-center car, black transformer, four trucks, for 0 Gauge only, will not pass through 0-27 switches. Knight comment.

| | | | | |
|---|---|---|---|---|
| | 18 | 35 | 55 | 85 |

**6519 ALLIS CHALMERS** 1958-61, condenser car, orange base, blue letters, gray condenser held by metal bars, two brakewheels, often broken, Timken trucks, disc couplers.

| | | | | |
|---|---|---|---|---|
| (A) Orange base. | 11 | 18 | 25 | 40 |
| (B) Darker orange base. | 11 | 20 | 30 | 50 |

**6544 MISSILE FIRING CAR** 1960-64, blue frame, gray launcher, red firing knob, four white small rockets, Timken trucks, disc couplers, two brakewheels.

| | | | | |
|---|---|---|---|---|
| (A) White-lettered console. Degano comment. | 14 | 23 | 33 | 55 |
| (B) Black-lettered console. Degano comment. | 20 | 35 | 70 | 110 |

**6561 REEL CAR WITH DEPRESSED CENTER** 1953-56, die-cast gray frame, black lettering, two plastic reels marked "LIONEL", wound with aluminum coil, same base as searchlight car with modification to hold reels, steps, two brakewheels, bar-end metal trucks, see color illustration. We have had reports of reels for this car in several different configurations, but this car originally only came with the wide aluminum wire. Lionel also sold these reels with wire for layouts; that is why some cars show up with insulated wire on these reels, or even reels which are empty. Cars from original sets apparently always have the wide aluminum wire. The gray plastic reels with this wire are much more difficult to find with the car than are the orange reels. G. Wilson and Ambrose comments.

| | | | | |
|---|---|---|---|---|
| (A) Gray plastic reels. | 10 | 20 | 30 | 40 |
| (B) Orange plastic reels. Pauli Collection. | 8 | 15 | 20 | 30 |

**6630 IRBM LAUNCHER** 1960-64, black car, white letters, blue superstructure with black missile firing ramp, pushing levers cock launching unit, ramp rises to a 30 to 45 degree angle prior to takeoff due to air pressure generated by bellows at front end, red and white missile with blue tip, arch bar trucks with fixed couplers; made for Sears set. G. Wilson comment.

| | | | | |
|---|---|---|---|---|
| | 17 | 35 | 45 | 65 |

**6640 U S M C LAUNCHER** 1960, olive drab car and superstructure, black firing ramp, same mechanism as 6630, white rocket with blue tip.

| | | | | |
|---|---|---|---|---|
| | 20 | 35 | 50 | 85 |

**6650 I R B M LAUNCHER** 1959-63, red car base, mold 6424-11, Die 2, blue superstructure, white letters, black firing ramp, white and red missile with blue nose, same mechanism used for 6630, Timken trucks, disc couplers.

| | | | | |
|---|---|---|---|---|
| | 13 | 25 | 35 | 60 |

**6651 U S M C CANNON** Circa 1960-61, not catalogued, olive drab car, gun and superstructure, mold 6511-2, white lettering, fires four projectiles, Timken trucks, disc-operating couplers.

| | | | | |
|---|---|---|---|---|
| | 17 | 35 | 50 | 75 |

**6660 FLATCAR WITH CRANE** 1958, dark red flat, mold 6424-11, white lettering, two black metal bases, outriggers, ochre boom, Timken trucks, disc couplers.

(A) Silver crank handles, hook on cable end. Catalano comment.

| | | | | |
|---|---|---|---|---|
| | 17 | 35 | 55 | 70 |

(B) Black crank handles, round bar magnet inside of red plastic housing on cable end. Catalano comment.

| | | | | |
|---|---|---|---|---|
| | 17 | 35 | 55 | 70 |

**6670 FLATCAR WITH BOOM** 1959-60, red unpainted body, yellow boom, no outriggers, Timken trucks, disc-operating couplers. Note that two varieties follow. We would like to learn which of these types came with which sets.

(A) Darker red body, mold 6511-2, "6670" to right of "LIONEL". Fleming Collection.

| | | | | |
|---|---|---|---|---|
| | 13 | 25 | 35 | 50 |

(B) Brighter red body, mold 6424-11, Die 2, "6670" to left of "LIONEL". Fleming Collection.

| | | | | |
|---|---|---|---|---|
| | 13 | 25 | 35 | 50 |

**6800 FLAT WITH AIRPLANE** 1957-60, red car, black and yellow Beechcraft Bonanza airplane.

(A) Plane with black upper and yellow lower fuselage, 6424-11 mold, Die 2 or Die 3, Timken trucks, disc couplers, "6800" to left of "LIONEL".

| | | | | |
|---|---|---|---|---|
| | 16 | 25 | 38 | 55 |

(B) Plane with yellow upper and black lower fuselage, 6424-11 mold, Die 1, metal trucks attach via metal plates and slots and screws, "6800" to right of "LIONEL".

| | | | | |
|---|---|---|---|---|
| | 16 | 25 | 38 | 55 |

(C) Same as (A), but lighter red flatcar body, mold 6424-11, Die 2. Ocilka Collection.

| | | | | |
|---|---|---|---|---|
| | 16 | 25 | 38 | 55 |

**6801 FLAT WITH BOAT** 1957-60, red plastic body, white lettering, boat usually with cream deck and clear windshield, boat numbered 6801-60, Timken trucks, disc couplers, "6801" usually left of "LIONEL".

| | | | | |
|---|---|---|---|---|
| (A) Turquoise boat hull, flatcar mold 6511-2. | 12 | 22 | 35 | 55 |
| (B) Same as (A), but mold 6424-11, Die 2 or Die 3. Warswick Collection. | 12 | 22 | 35 | 55 |
| (C) Medium blue hull, flatcar mold 6511-2. | 12 | 22 | 35 | 55 |
| (D) Brownish-yellow hull. | 12 | 22 | 35 | 55 |

(E) White hull, brown deck, bar-end metal trucks, metal plates fasten trucks to base, "6801" to right of "LIONEL", flatcar mold 6511-2.

| | | | | |
|---|---|---|---|---|
| | 12 | 22 | 35 | 55 |

(F) Same as (A), but mold 6424-11, Die 2. Ocilka Collection.

| | | | | |
|---|---|---|---|---|
| | 12 | 22 | 35 | 55 |

(G) 1956, Type 2 die, metal trucks mounted with screw. Ocilka Collection.

| | | | | |
|---|---|---|---|---|
| | 12 | 22 | 35 | 55 |

**6802 FLAT WITH BRIDGE** 1958-59, red flat, white lettering, black plastic bridge sides lettered in white "U.S. STEEL", one brakewheel, "6802" to left of "LIONEL", Timken trucks, disc couplers.

| | | | | |
|---|---|---|---|---|
| (A) Flatcar mold 6424-11, Die 2. | 4 | 7 | 11 | 17 |
| (B) Flatcar mold 6511-2. Pauli Collection. | 4 | 7 | 11 | 17 |

**6803 FLATCAR WITH TANK AND TRUCK** 1958-59, two gray U.S.M.C. vehicles, tank and truck with microwave disc, flatcar mold 6424-11, Die 2, Timken trucks, disc couplers.

| | | | | |
|---|---|---|---|---|
| | 20 | 35 | 45 | 70 |

**6804 FLAT WITH U.S.M.C. TRUCKS** 1958-59, red plastic flat, mold 6424-11, Die 2, white lettering, 6804 to left of "LIONEL", gray U.S.M.C. trucks, one with microwave disc, one with two guns.

| | | | | |
|---|---|---|---|---|
| | 22 | 35 | 45 | 70 |

**6805 ATOMIC DISPOSAL FLATCAR** 1958-59, red plastic car, mold 6424-11, Die 3, white letters, "6805" on left side, two Super 0 rails run car length, two removable grayish-tan or gray disposal containers with red and black-lettered "RADIOACTIVE WASTE" in black and "DANGER" in red, each letter of "DANGER" is underlined, containers have red flashing lights, bar-end metal trucks, magnetic tab couplers. The Fundimensions reissue comes with gray canisters. However, they can be differentiated from the Lionel canisters rather easily. The Lionel canisters are black plastic painted gray; the mold number inside is 6805-6 with either a 1 or a 2 opposite the mold stamping. (The mold made two canisters at a time, and these numbers showed which side of the mold made the individual canister. The same process is used with gondola cars.) The words "RADIOACTIVE WASTE" are slightly larger than those found on Fundimensions reproductions. In addition, the Fundimensions canisters are unpainted gray plastic, rather than black plastic painted gray. I.D. Smith, Lebo and LaVoie Comments.

| | | | | |
|---|---|---|---|---|
| (A) Gray canisters. | 13 | 25 | 35 | 60 |
| (B) Grayish-tan canisters. | 13 | 25 | 35 | 60 |

(C) Unpainted bright red plastic body, mold 6424-11, "LIONEL" in white serif lettering, no number on car, black plastic canisters painted light gray, black and red lettering on containers, arch bar trucks, one operating and one dummy coupler. Shanfeld Collection.

| | | | | |
|---|---|---|---|---|
| | 13 | 25 | 35 | 60 |

**6806 FLAT WITH U.S.M.C. TRUCKS** 1958-59, red plastic flat, mold 6424-11, Die 2, white lettering, "6806" on left side, Timken trucks, disc couplers.

(A) Two gray plastic U.S.M.C. trucks: one with radar disc truck, other a hospital truck with U.S. Navy insignia on van rear. The U.S.M.C. trucks on this and other similar cars are lettered "PYRO". Ambrose comment.

| | | | | |
|---|---|---|---|---|
| | 21 | 35 | 45 | 75 |

(B) Gray U.S.M.C. radar disc truck, and gray plastic open-windowed snack bar truck with lettering "MOBILE USO CANTEEN" with small chimney, door with white anchor. Lionel Train & Seashell Museum comment. **NRS**

**6807 LIONEL FLAT WITH BOAT** 1958-59, red plastic flat.

(A) Mold 6511-2, white lettering, "6807" on left, large gray amphibious-type boat, known as DKW, Timken trucks, disc couplers.

| | | | | |
|---|---|---|---|---|
| | 21 | 35 | 50 | 80 |

(B) Same as (A), but 6424-11 mold, Die 2. Savage Collection.

| | | | | |
|---|---|---|---|---|
| | 21 | 35 | 50 | 80 |

**6808 LIONEL FLAT WITH U.S.M.C. TRUCKS** 1958-59, red plastic flat, mold 6424-11, Die 2, "6808" on left, Timken trucks, disc couplers, one

U.S.M.C. gray mobile searchlight truck, one gray two-gun tank.

|  | 21 | 35 | 50 | 80 |

**6809 LIONEL FLAT WITH U.S.M.C. TRUCKS** 1958-59, red plastic flat, mold 6424-11, Die 2, white lettering, "6809" on left, Timken trucks, disc couplers, gray U.S.M.C. trucks: one with cannon, other hospital van with U.S. Navy insignia.

| (A) Hospital van with Navy insignia on one side. | 21 | 35 | 45 | 75 |
| (B) Hospital van with Navy insignia on both sides. | 21 | 35 | 45 | 75 |

**6810 LIONEL FLAT WITH TRAILER** 1958, red plastic flat, mold 6424-11, white lettering, "6810" on left, Timken trucks, disc couplers, white trailer, black-painted plate with copper-colored arrow, black and white-lettered "COOPER JARRETT INC".

|  | 9 | 15 | 20 | 30 |

**6812 TRACK MAINTENANCE CAR** 1959, red plastic flat, white lettering "6812" on left, 6511-2 mold, Timken trucks, disc couplers, superstructure with blue men, platform cranks up and if cranked up far enough will come out.

| (A) All-dark yellow-gold superstructure. Algozzini Collection. | 9 | 17 | 25 | 40 |
| (B) Superstructure with black base and gray top, flatcar mold 6511-2. Algozzini Collection. | 9 | 17 | 25 | 40 |
| (C) Gray base, black top. | 9 | 17 | 25 | 40 |
| (D) All-cream base and top. | 25 | 40 | 60 | 100 |
| (E) Dark yellow base, gray top. Askensis comment. | | | | NRS |
| (F) Black base, black top. Askensis comment. | | | | NRS |
| (G) Black base, dark yellow top. Askensis comment. | | | | NRS |
| (H) Light yellow base and top. Askensis comment. | | | | NRS |
| (I) All-gold superstructure. Algozzini Collection. | | | | NRS |

**6816 FLAT WITH ALLIS-CHALMERS BULLDOZER** 1959-60, red or black plastic flat, white letters, "6816" on left, Timken trucks, disc couplers, orange plastic Allis-Chalmers bulldozer, black rubber treads, lettered "HD 16 Diesel" and "Torque Converter".

| (A) Red plastic car, mold 6511-2. | 15 | 30 | 45 | 70 |
| (B) Black plastic car. Wirtz Collection. | | | | NRS |
| (C) Same as (A), but 6424-11 mold, Die 2. Ocilka Collection. | 15 | 30 | 45 | 70 |
| (D) Same as (A), but lighter orange bulldozer. Algozzini Collection. | 15 | 30 | 45 | 70 |

See also Factory Errors.

**6817 FLAT WITH ALLIS-CHALMERS SCRAPER** 1959-60, red plastic flat, white letters, "6817" on left, Timken trucks, disc couplers, orange plastic scraper with black rubber tires.

| (A) 6424-11, Die 2. | 16 | 30 | 45 | 70 |
| (B) 6511-2 mold. Ocilka observation. | 16 | 30 | 45 | 70 |

**6818 TRANSFORMER CAR** 1958, red plastic base, white lettering, one brakewheel, black plastic transformer with heat-stamped lettering on one side, Timken trucks, disc couplers.

| (A) Base mold 6424-11, Die 2. | 5 | 10 | 12 | 25 |
| (B) Base mold 65ll-2. | 5 | 10 | 12 | 25 |

**6819 FLAT WITH HELICOPTER** 1959-60, red plastic car, mold 6424-11, Die 3, white lettering, "6819" on left, Timken trucks, disc couplers, gray helicopter with separate yellow plastic tail section, single black rotor, clear plastic nose, operating-type helicopter without launching mechanism, Ocilka Collection.

|  | 9 | 17 | 24 | 40 |

**6820 FLAT WITH HELICOPTER** 1960-61, light blue-painted black plastic flatcar, white letters, "6820" on left, mold 6424-11, Die 4, Timken trucks, disc couplers, gray Navy helicopter, separate yellow plastic tail section, single black rotor, clear plastic nose, with "Little John" missiles, operating-type helicopter without launching mechanism.

| (A) As described above. Bratspis Collection. | 16 | 35 | 45 | 60 |
| (B) Same as (A), except darker blue flatcar. Blotner Collection. | 16 | 35 | 45 | 60 |

**6821 FLAT WITH CRATES** 1959-60, red unpainted plastic flatcar, mold 6424-11, Die 3 or Die 4, white lettering "6821" on left side. Ocilka Collection. The same crate structure had been used on the 3444 Animated Gondola, except that here there is no slot for the operating lever, and the two screw holes in the crate structure are plugged. Additionally, these crates have no lettering. Wilson and Ambrose comments.

|  | 7 | 15 | 19 | 25 |

6823

6825

6826

**6822 SEARCHLIGHT CAR** See "Cranes and Searchlights".

**6823 FLAT WITH IRBM MISSILES** 1959-60, red plastic car, mold 6424-11, Die 3, white lettering, "6823" on left, Timken trucks, disc couplers, two red and white missiles with blue tips, front of one missile fits into rear of other missile, same missiles as on 6630 and 6640 missile launching cars.

|  | 12 | 22 | 31 | 45 |

**6825 FLAT WITH TRESTLE BRIDGE** 1959-60, red plastic car, mold 6511-2, white lettering, "6825" on left side, Timken trucks, disc couplers, with bridge designed for H0 rolling stock. G. Wilson comment.

| (A) Black bridge. | 8 | 15 | 20 | 30 |
| (B) Gray bridge. | 8 | 15 | 20 | 30 |

**6826 FLAT WITH CHRISTMAS TREES** 1959-60, red plastic base, mold 6511-2, "6826" on left, Timken trucks, disc couplers, several scrawny trees.

|  | 14 | 25 | 32 | 50 |

**6827 FLAT WITH P & H STEAM SHOVEL** 1960-63, black plastic car, mold 6424-11, Die 4, white lettering, "6827" on left side, Timken trucks, disc couplers, came as kit, shown assembled. Ocilka Collection.

|  | 14 | 30 | 45 | 70 |

**6828 FLAT WITH P & H CRANE** 1960-63, 68, black or red plastic flatcar, mold 6424-11, Die 4, "6828" on left, Timken trucks, disc couplers, crane with black chassis, yellow or yellow-orange cab, lettered "HARNISCHFEG-ER MILWAUKEE WISCONSIN" and "P & H" embossed on cab and on boom near top.

| (A) Yellow cab, black flatcar. | 16 | 25 | 38 | 60 |
| (B) Yellow-orange cab, red flatcar. Mold number for this car needed. | 16 | 25 | 38 | 60 |

**6830 FLAT WITH NON-OPERATING SUBMARINE** 1960-61, blue plastic car, mold 6511-2, white letters, "6830" on left, Timken trucks, disc couplers, "U.S. NAVY SUBMARINE 6830", gray with black letters. The winding nose on this sub did not turn, and there was no attachment inside for any rubber band. Ambrose comment.

|  | 16 | 25 | 38 | 60 |

**6844 FLAT WITH MISSILES** Circa 1960, black plastic flatcar, mold 6424-11, Die 1, also Die 4, white lettering, "6844" to left, Timken trucks, disc couplers, gray superstructure holds six white Lionel missiles.

| (A) As described above. Ocilka and Smith Collections. | 16 | 25 | 35 | 60 |
| (B) Same as (A), but red unpainted plastic flatcar, light gray missile superstructure. Tom Art Halverson Collections. | 20 | 40 | 75 | 100 |

6828

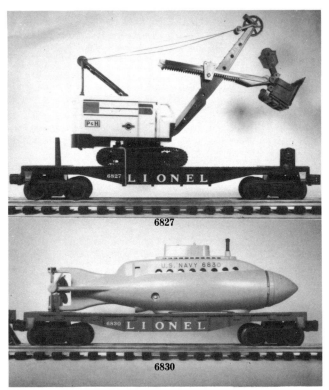

6844

6827

6830

**NO NUMBER** See 1877, 3309, 3349.

One of the areas for future research is determining the catalogue numbers and loads of the no-number flatcars, gondolas, cabooses and hoppers produced by Lionel. The following is a listing of reported cars. One method of identification is from original boxes and/or original set components. If you have "no number" cars in original boxes or with original sets, we would appreciate very much your assistance.

(A) Red plastic flatcar, mold 6511-2, white-lettered "LIONEL" (serif or sans-serif?), Timken trucks, one disc coupler, one fixed coupler. Pauli Collection.                                                          **1  1.50  2  3**

(B) Same as (A), but two fixed couplers.             **1  1.50  2  3**

(C) Olive drab flatcar. See 6401-50.                  **1  1.50  2  3**

(D) Flat with yellow autos. See 6406.                 **1  1.50  2  3**

(E) Red plastic flatcar, mold 6511-2, white-lettered "LIONEL" (serif or sans-serif?), arch bar trucks, two fixed couplers, no brakewheel. Kotil Collection.                                                          **1  1.50  2  3**

(F) Same as (E), but no lettering, Timken trucks.    **1  1.50  2  3**

(G) Black plastic flatcar, mold 6511-2, white-lettered "LIONEL" (serif or sans-serif?) arch bar trucks, two fixed couplers, no brakewheel. Kotil Collection.                                                          **1  1.50  2  3**

(H) Blue plastic flatcar, mold 6511-2, no lettering, arch bar trucks, two fixed couplers, no brakewheel. Kotil Collection.                      **1  1.50  2  3**

(I) Same as (H), but Timken trucks. Kotil Collection.  **1  1.50  2  3**

(J) Gray flatcar with green tank. The flatcar is embossed with mold 1877-3 and also embossed "MADE IN U.S. OF AMERICA/THE LIONEL CORPORATION/NEW YORK, N.Y." on its underside. No other lettering or numbering is present. Car has Timken plastic trucks with one disc-operating and one dummy coupler. The moss-green tank has a swivel turret and two molded green plastic wheel/axle sets. The tank is lettered "Q" inside the turret. This car came in a military set made for Sears with a 240 locomotive. For details of this set, see the entries for the 240 steam locomotive and the 3666 cannon-firing boxcar. Vergonet, Bohn and Jarman Collections.                                          **50  100  150  200**

(K) 6511-type flat, all red, white "LIONEL", no number, arch bar trucks, fixed couplers, no brakewheel, no load, 6511-2 mold, may be 6409-25 from set 11311 in 1963 catalogue, page 3, reader comments invited. Schreiner Collection.                                                            **NRS**

# Chapter VII
# GONDOLAS

## INTRODUCTION
### By Roland LaVoie

There probably isn't a collector who possessed Lionel trains as a youngster who cannot recall at least one New York Central gondola car in the consist of a busy freight train. The gondola car was one of Lionel's staples, just as it was - and still is - on real railroads. These versatile cars could carry loose bulk material such as ore or coal, but they could also convey scrap iron, barrel drums or almost anything else which was not suitable for a flatcar. There are even reports of some enterprising party hosts using them to convey snacks and hors d'oeuvres around a table! (This editor confesses to doing this at his school's Christmas party among his teaching colleagues last year - along with dumping pretzel logs from a dump car!)

Lionel recognized the value of the humble gondola car from its earliest years. Although its prewar Standard and 0 Gauge gondolas were metal, Lionel made all of its postwar cars from plastic. The first postwar gondola was a short black Pennsylvania car with white lettering. It was quite well detailed and was nearly always included in the early sets. It featured a plastic body mounted to a metal base - as would most of the gondolas made up to the mid-fifties.

In 1949, the Pennsylvania short gondola was joined by another eight-inch gondola which would replace it entirely the next year, the 1002. This short gondola was first used with the Scout sets, but it was also equipped with regular trucks and couplers in later years. This car and its renumbered mates in

the 6000 Series were always lettered "LIONEL" with the car's number - when they carried markings at all. The cars were entirely plastic, with no metal base as its predecessor had.

The 1002 and its stablemates were not the only gondolas introduced in 1949. A longer (9-9/16-inch) gondola was introduced as well. More often than not, this car was marked for the New York Central. The earliest of these long gondolas featured plastic bodies mounted upon metal bases, but later on the car was made entirely of plastic. The New York Central gondolas were made in huge quantities, and most varieties are easy to acquire today. The car could be found in black, red, green or blue versions in NYC markings. For a complete study of the variations of this car, consult the excellent article by Richard Vagner, which can be found in this chapter.

The short and long gondola cars were so popular with Lionel that they continued in their basic form right through postwar production. However, some of the long gondolas were adapted for operation. The 6362 Culvert Car had a metal channel mounted inside the body to hold steel culvert sections. One of the most amusing of all Lionel's animated cars was an adaptation of the gondola. The 3444 Animated Gondola featured a cop-and-hobo chase around packing crates when the vibrator motor was activated. A radio receiver was mounted to the base of the early Pennsylvania short gondola for use in the famous Electronic Set. (See Pat Scholes' article in the steam locomotive section of this book.) Finally, a special plastic mold was used to produce Lionel's 3562 Operating Barrel Car, a gondola which used a vibrator motor to dump wooden barrels into a trackside bin or an activated ramp.

The gondola cars, whether they were short or long, were an integral part of anybody's train set. Even though most of them are very common, they make an interesting study for the variations collector. In fact, the construction practices of the Lionel Corporation can best be traced through the evolution of the gondola. This interesting car does not deserve to be ignored by any collector or operator.

## The New York Central Gondolas — 1949-1969
### By Richard Vagner

In 1949, the Lionel Corporation introduced a new longer gondola which carried the New York Central markings in every year it was made. The new car was 10-3/8 inches long and had a very realistic appearance. The detailing included rivets, steps, brakewheels, brakewheel chains and good interior detailing. The car was included in the majority of the better freight sets produced during the remaining 21 years of Lionel's history. During the production run of this car 13 different number/color combinations were produced which are all relatively easy to find. In addition a large number of visual variations were produced including herald position, number of lines of weight data, presence or absence of built date, brakewheels and steps. Finally, there were variations in truck types. Other changes include die modifications, coupler changes, truck connections, color differences, frame changes and various combinations of the above. Using only the visual variations which can be seen with the car sitting on the shelf, about 30 different combinations can be found and if the manufacturing changes are included, over 50 different variations can be found.

If a matrix is constructed using the year in which various changes were made on one axis and each number/color combination produced on the other axis, these gondolas can be dated to certain time spans. The matrix can be used to insure the correct gondola is in a set for a given year; it can tell the year a set was manufactured as a result of manufacturing changes and if the car has been altered. These production changes can also be used to date other Lionel cars to definite time periods.

Most of the information as to when certain rolling stock was produced comes from the Lionel catalogues. There are some gondolas not shown in the catalogues in certain years which show manufacturing details clearly dating them to years in which production is not indicated in the catalogue. There are gondolas shown in the catalogues in colors in which they have never been found. Any gondola can be compared with the matrix and placed into a time frame depending on the known dates of various manufacturing changes.

The NYC gondolas introduced in 1949 are 10-3/8 inches from coupler centers or 9-5/8 inches outside body length. (In prototype practice, railroad cars are measured from coupler center to coupler center, rather than coupler end to coupler end, as the former measurement will actually provide accurate information on train length because it compensates for overlapping within the couplers.) There are five distinct mold variations which separate the cars into distinct time frames. The first was body mold Type Ia. This was only found in the black 6462 gondola which was produced in 1949. On the floor, inside the gondola, in the center panel, were three round marks. The center mark was the result of injecting the plastic into the mold and was either raised or depressed. The other two marks were from round plugs on a diagonal in the same panel.

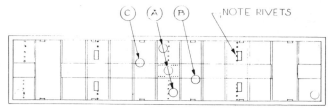

Type I molds.
Ia: center only (three a's plus b)
Ib: center plus right (three a's plus b)
Ic: all (three a's, b, c)                   Drawing by Trip Riley

The next was body mold Type Ib. Type Ib is identified by the addition of another round plug in the panel to the right of the center panel. To find the right-hand side of the gondola, examine the four rectangular holes holding the metal tabs which hold the frame to the body. On the floor inside the car on the left side of one pair of these holes will be found three rivets on the edge of the hole. This goes to the right. To identify a Type Ib mold look in the panel to the right of the center panel for the round plug. This is only found on the black and tuscan red 6462 gondolas produced in early 1950.

The next was body mold Type Ic which first appeared in mid-1950. Type Ic is identified by the addition of another round plug in the panel to the left of the center panel. This Type Ic mold is found on the black and tuscan red 6462s and the 6002 black gondola with Scout trucks. This mold continued into 1953 in the tuscan red and black 6462 gondolas.

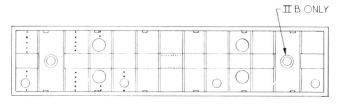

Type IIa: plastic molded clips hold frame
Type IIb: metal frame not used, trucks riveted directly to body

Next is body mold Type IIa, beginning in 1954. This was a completely new mold, and the machine, with its dual dies, produced two cars at one time. On the floor of the car were now four round plug marks in panels 1, 5, 9 and 13. Under the body hidden by the metal frame was a part identification number. It is a 6462-2 and underneath it is a 1 or 2 indicating which of the two molds the car was formed in. This body mold is used on the light red-painted, red plastic, black, green and pink 6462s, the grey, red and black 6562s and the red 6342 culvert gondola. This mold was used from 1954 to 1958.

The final mold Type IIb, was introduced in 1959. This mold is changed to eliminate the metal frame and allow the trucks to be riveted directly to the gondola floor. This body mold is used on the black 6062, the blue and red 6162, the yellow 6162 Alaska gondola and the 6342 red culvert gondola produced from 1966 to 1969. The Type IIb mold was used from 1959 to 1969. The mold numbers 6462-2/1 or 6462-2/2 are readily visible since the frame was eliminated. It appears that equal numbers of both mold 1 and 2 are found.

The black 6462 is the only gondola found in the first four mold types: Types Ia, Ib, Ic and IIa. The tuscan red 6462 gondola is found only in mold Type Ib and Ic. The painted red and red unpainted plastic 6462 is found only in mold Type IIa. The red 6342 is the only gondola found in both mold Types IIa and IIb. The green and pink 6462s and the grey, red and black

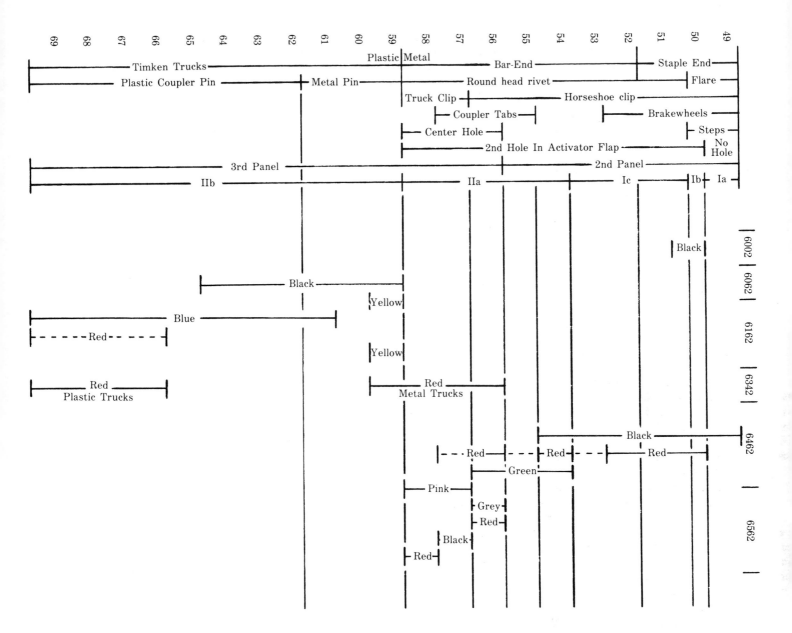

6562s are only found in mold Type IIa. The 6062 and 6162s are only found in mold Type IIb.

The next major distinguishing feature is the position of the the N in NYC and the style of lettering used for the herald. From 1949 to 1955, the N is found in the second panel. From 1956 to 1969, the N is found in the third panel. The lettering style changes from the early-serif to the later-block type.

The black 6462 and black 6002 are only found with the N in the second panel. The tuscan red 6462 is found only with the N in the second panel. The light red cars are found with the N in the second or third panel and the red unpainted plastic are only found with the N in the third panel. The green 6462s are found with the N in the second or third panel. The pink 6462, the gray, red and black 6562s, the red 6342 and the 6062 and 6162s are all found with the N in the third panel.

The third major distinguishing feature is the type of car truck. There are two major types of trucks with two variations of each type. From 1949 to 1958, the 10-3/8 inch gondolas had metal trucks with die-cast sides. From 1949 to 1951, these trucks were the staple-end variation and from 1952 to 1958, they were the bar-end variation. From 1959, all 10-3/8 inch gondolas were manufactured with plastic Timken trucks. From 1959 to 1961, these had a metal knuckle pin on the operating trucks and from 1962 to 1969, the knuckle pin was part of the plastic knuckle.

If the bar graph is examined it will be seen that the 1949 black 6462 is the only 1949 car and the only car found in mold Ia. In 1950, the black 6462 was made with both molds Ib and Ic. Then, in 1952, the trucks were changed from staple-end to bar-end while the body was still in mold Ic. In 1954, the black 6462 was found in body mold Type IIa with bar-end trucks. We consequently have five variations with only three manufacturing changes.

The tuscan red 6462 is slightly different from the black in that although all tuscan red bodies seem to have been painted during 1950, they were assembled as needed into at least 1952. Thus the tuscan red is found in body molds Ib and Ic in both staple-end and bar-end trucks.

The green and light red-painted 6462s started in 1954 and are only found in body mold Type IIa. In 1954 and 1955, these cars have the N in the second panel and in 1956, the N is found in the third panel.

133

During 1956 the red 6462 changed again to a self-colored red plastic. It seems to have been made in this red plastic into 1958.

There are other variations in the 1950 black and tuscan red 6462s including the presence or absence of steps and the brakewheels. The early 1950 black and tuscan red 6462s had both steps and brakewheels. The 6002, produced later in 1950, did not have steps and had no hole in the body for the brakewheels. The steps had been part of the metal frame and used much more metal as part of the frame, since the steps protrude out and require a substantially larger piece of metal to be stamped for the frame. Assuming that Lionel made 500,000 gondolas and each gondola frame required an extra half inch of steel, a considerable amount of money was involved over the production run. Thus, early 1950 black and tuscan red gondolas have steps and Type Ib and Ic molds. Later 1950 and 1951 black and tuscan red gondolas have brakewheels but no steps because the frame die had been changed when the 6002 was made. During 1951 the brakewheels were eliminated from the black 6462. Some time later in 1951 the "built date" was dropped from this car. The tuscan red 6462 retained its brakewheel and "built date" into 1952 and probably 1953.[1]

Thus, the black 6462 shows several other variations. First, one other variation in the black 6462 needs to be mentioned. Sometime during 1950 the third line of weight data found on the 1949 and early 1950 models was eliminated. The three lines of weight data are found on mold Types Ia and Ib and on cars with brakewheels, steps and the built date. The black 6462 from 1950 has two more variations with the two lines of weights being found with and without steps. All 1951 cars came with staple-end trucks and are found with and without the built date and with and without brakewheels.

There are eight recognizable variations in the black 6462 which can readily be found. If two other criteria are added the number of variations increases again. The 1950 black plastic car had the beginning of a die break visible in the floor of the car. This die break can be traced through the black plastic 6002, with the Scout trucks, into the 1951 and 1952 cars, until finally, in 1953, the end posts of the car deform and the die was abandoned. The die break is progressive through the other production changes. However the die break is not found in the tuscan red 6462s which confirms these bodies were produced in 1950 and assembled into 1952. The other source of variations were the mold colors. Clear, blue, gray, green, brown, pink and black mold colors have been reported. The 1954 black 6462s have been reported in pink and black molds. Other mold colors are possible and the number of possible combinations using the existing breakdowns based on other criteria is not known.

Coupler variations are another means of classifying years of production. The 1949 black 6462 has the Type IV mechanical coupler which has no hole in the activator flap and has the flared end of the rivet showing. In 1950, the hole in the activator flap appears and during the late 1950 production of the 6002 the end of the rivet appears as round. There is no other change until 1955 when the tab coupler was introduced. During 1957 the tab coupler was phased out and the cars produced during this time may or may not have tab couplers.

Dating based on coupler type is not highly reliable since couplers broke and were changed.[2]

During 1956 a number of new gondolas were introduced with different loads. From 1949 through 1956, the 6462 gondolas probably came with a load of six wooden barrels. The 6002 Scout seems to have been produced without any load. In 1956, the 6562 red and gray gondolas came with a load of four round plastic LCL canisters. A new special gondola, the red plastic 6342, was introduced with the 342 culvert loader which carried a load of seven metal culverts on a sloping metal ramp.

In 1957, another 6562 in black was introduced and the pink 6462 came as part of the Girl's Train. Both carried a load of four canisters. The 6342 was continued with the 342 culvert loader. One significant 1957 change was in the method used to fasten the trucks to the metal frame. Previously a metal pin was swaged to the truck and a metal horseshoe clip fitted to the pin to retain the truck. In 1957, Lionel went to a sheet metal clip made from spring steel to hold the truck to the frame. This creates a variation in the 6342 gondola. It seems the cars that came with the early 342 culvert loader use the early style pin and the cars which came with the later 345 unloader came with the sheet metal clip. During the overlap of these two accessories during 1958 the 342 may have come with a 6342 using either method of truck fastening.

During 1958 there is some uncertainty as to what gondolas were produced. A red 6562 is stated to have been produced while there is some evidence a red plastic 6462 was made also. Information relative to this is needed. The 6342 continued and the pink 6462s were available as leftovers from the previous year.

A new gondola was produced in 1959 when the Type IIa mold was modified to eliminate the metal frame and allow the trucks to be fastened directly to the frame. The final two numbers in the series were introduced. The 6062 was catalogued in red but was probably only produced in the black in which it has been found. The load for the 6062 gondola at the start of production was probably two wire reels. If this load was continued throughout the production run confirmation would be appreciated. The yellow 6162 Alaska was part of the Alaska set of that year. While it is the only 10-3/8 inch which does not carry the NYC herald, it does belong in this series. The 6162 Alaska seems to have come with a load of four white canisters. These are reports of 6162 Alaska gondolas with four dark blue cannisters. Confirmation of canisters color would be appreciated. These cars have the new plastic Timken trucks which appeared earlier on many cheaper cars. Technically, these are not Timken trucks as Timken did not make trucks but only bearings. Actually these are A.A.R. trucks with Timken bearings. See Greenberg's Repair and Operating Manual. These trucks have the coupler cast in plastic as part of the truck. The early plastic trucks before 1962 have a metal knuckle pin which in 1962 was changed to plastic which was part of the knuckle.

In 1961, the last regular production run number/color combination was introduced. This 6162 was catalogued in red or black but it was actually produced as a blue. This blue 6162

---

[1] We assume that these were painted at one time because of the unusuallyhigh color consistency and that all variations are found inboth Ib and Ic molds.

[2] Coupler dating is much more reliable when the car is obtained from the original purchaser, as the principal source of confusion would be repairs. However, in the case of goods obtained at collector meets, less reliance should be placed on coupler dating.

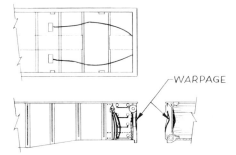

WARPAGE

The top drawing shows the die break. Drawings by Trip Riley.

continued until the end of the Lionel production in 1969. The blue 6162 comes in a number of color variations and with "built dates" and without "built dates". The colors range from very light blue to dark blue. This car was produced with the same features as the black 6062 which was also produced this year. It had a load of four canisters in red or white and possibly other colors.

In 1962, the final changes were made which produced the last variations in this series. This is the change to the late plastic trucks. The plastic knuckle pin has already been mentioned. The trucks were modified so the axles are visible from the bottom and the dummy couplers are mounted on arch bar trucks from the General rolling stock of 1959-1962. One significant visual variation created with this change is the dropping of the built date.

In 1966, a 6342 culvert gondola was introduced without the metal frame under the car. It is the same as the 6162 except for the metal ramp for the culverts and the different color and number. It ran until 1969 along with the blue 6162.

One other gondola was made in 1969 or 1970 using leftover culvert gondola bodies. It was a red 6162 boxed as 6162-110. It came without a load and had the 3/16 inch hole in the center of the floor for the rivet which held the ramp in the 6342. It is not known if this car was made by Lionel or MPC.

Two other 6462s are known from single examples and there are unconfirmed reports of other variations. An orange 6462 is known which has the N in the third panel and bar-end trucks and a yellow-cream color gondola similar to the 6464-515 Katy box-car from the Girl's Set! This car was the IIa mold with bar-end trucks and the N is in the third panel.

We would be most appreciative of your comments, additions and corrections to this essay.

|  | Gd | VG | Exc | Mt |
|---|---|---|---|---|
| **1002 LIONEL** 1949, white lettering, from the Scout set, with Scout couplers, 8" long. Reader confirmation requested for other examples. | | | | |
| (A) Blue unpainted plastic. | 1 | 1.50 | 2 | 3 |
| (B) Black unpainted plastic. | 1 | 1.50 | 2 | 3 |
| (C) Silver with black lettering. | 40 | 60 | 100 | 150 |
| (D) Yellow with black lettering. | 30 | 60 | 100 | 150 |
| (E) Red with white lettering. Oswald Collection. | 30 | 60 | 100 | 150 |
| (F) Light blue with black lettering. | | | | NRS |

**2452 PENNSYLVANIA** 1945-47, black body, white lettering, black metal underframe held to body by four filister-head screws in corners of body floor, steps at corners, built date "NEW 12-45", usually brakewheels; always found with staple-end trucks.

Body Mold Type Ia, rectangular opening approximately 2" x 2" in center of floor in body does not go through metal frame. The opening was designed to fit a frame supporting the electronic control unit found in No. 4452.
(A) 1945, whirly wheels, thick axles, early coil couplers with fiber bar showing on bottom, one pickup shoe on each end, 2452 stamped in silver on bottom. Vagner Collection.    2    3    5    8

(B) 1945, same as (A), except dished wheels, without raised area around axles on back of wheels. Kotil and Vagner Collections.    2    3    5    8
(C) 1946, same as (A), except thin axles and regular wheels. Vagner Collection.    2    3    4    7
(D) 1947, regular wheels, late coil couplers with pickup shoe on metal plate which is fastened to axles, otherwise same as (A). Kotil and Rohlfing Collections.    2    3    4    7
(E) 1947, same as (D), except stamped 2452X on bottom indicating no brakewheels were installed. Kotil Collection.    2    3    4    7
Body mold Type Ib, round opening approximately 1" in diameter in center of floor in body does not go through metal frame.
(F) 1947, regular wheels, late coil couplers, brakewheels and steps, not stamped on bottom, otherwise same as (D). Vagner Collection.    2    3    5    7
(G) 1947, same as (F), except stamped 2452X on bottom indicating no brakewheels were installed. Vagner Collection.    2    3    5    7
(H) Same as (D), but magnetic couplers. Budniak Collection.    2    3    4    7

**3444 ERIE** 1957-59, cop chases hobo, vibrator motor, unpainted red plastic body with white lettering, on-off switch, "BLT 2-57".
(A) Tan-colored crates.    17    30    40    55
(B) Clear unpainted plastic crates. Piker Collection.    NRS

**3562-1 A.T.&.S.F.** 1954, operating barrel car, man "unloads" barrels, black with white lettering, "Built 5-54", six wooden barrels, plastic unloading bin.

(A) Black body with black central barrel trough. Catalano observation.    25    50    75    100
(B) Black body with yellow trough.    25    50    75    100

**3562-25 A.T.&.S.F.** 1954, operating barrel car, man "unloads" barrels, "NEW 5-54", six wooden barrels, plastic unloading bin.
(A) Gray-painted plastic body with dark blue lettering, bar-end metal trucks, magnetic couplers, body has molded plastic tab to hold base upon which a man is attached so that barrels are not dumped in transit. A metal tab fits into the gap between the plastic tab and the side edge to lock the man into place. Lemieux Collection.    10    15    20    40
(B) Same as (A), but does not have molded plastic tab. Lemieux Collection.    10    15    20    40
(C) Same as (A), but royal blue lettering, considerably brighter color than dark blue version. Halverson Collection.    15    20    25    45
(D) Gray with red lettering    40    60    80    150

**3562-50 A.T.&.S.F.** 1955-57, operating barrel car, man "unloads" barrels, "NEW 5-54", six stained wooden barrels, plastic unloading bin, plastic tab to lock metal base holding man into place, bar-end metal trucks, magnetic couplers with tabs.
(A) Bright yellow unpainted plastic, black lettering.    10    15    25    50
(B) Darker yellow-painted gray plastic body, black lettering, only one tab coupler, box stamped 3562-25Y. Probably first run using 3562-25 body shells and boxes. LaVoie and Ambrose Collections.    20    35    50    70

**3562-75 A.T.&.S.F.** 1958, operating barrel car, man "unloads" barrels, "NEW 5-54", six wooden barrels, plastic unloading bin, orange with black lettering.    16    30    40    70

**4452 PENNSYLVANIA** 1946-48, special black gondola with white lettering for electronic control set with electronic control unit.    30    45    60    80

**6002 N.Y.C.** 1949, black unpainted plastic body with white lettering, "BLT 2-49", 9-9/16" long, Scout trucks with magnetic couplers.    2    6    8    15

**6012 LIONEL** 1951-56, black unpainted plastic with white lettering, 8" long, no brakewheel.
(A) 1951, staple-end metal trucks, magnetic couplers; from set 1477S. Rohlfing Collection.    1    1.50    2    3
(B) 1956, bar-end metal trucks, magnetic tab couplers; came in set with 520 boxcab electric. Cole, Kruelle and Rohlfing Collections.    1    1.50    2    3
(C) Same as (B), except no tabs on couplers. Budniak Collection.    1    1.50    2    3

**6032 LIONEL** 1952-53, black unpainted plastic, Scout trucks, operating magnetic couplers, 8" long, no brakewheel, white lettering.    1    1.50    2    3

**6042 LIONEL** Uncatalogued, 8-1/8" long, detailed undercarriage and box interior, unpainted plastic, white lettering, fixed couplers open at top, brakewheel embossed in plastic car sides, red or white canisters.
(A) Black unpainted plastic, arch bar trucks. Kotil Collection.

|  | 1 | 1.50 | 2 | 3 |

(B) Blue unpainted plastic, arch bar trucks. Kotil Collection.

|  | 1 | 1.50 | 2 | 3 |

(C) Blue unpainted plastic, Timken trucks. Kotil Collection.

|  | 1 | 1.50 | 2 | 3 |

**6042-125 LIONEL** same as 6042 but blue unpainted plastic, numbered "6042".
(A) Blue unpainted plastic.  1  1.50  2  3
(B) Shinier blue unpainted plastic.  1  1.50  2  3

**6062 N.Y.C.** 1959-64, glossy black plastic body, white lettering, "N.Y.C" overscored, "6062" underscored, "NEW 2-49", Timken trucks, disc-operating couplers.
(A) Detailed plastic undercarriage similar to 6042, "6462-2" mold. Schreiner Collection.  3  7  10  15
(B) Stamped metal undercarriage similar to 6462. Schreiner Collection.

|  | 3 | 7 | 10 | 15 |

(C) Same as (A), but 6462-2 mold with no detail of any kind on plastic undercarriage. Budniak and Rohlfing Collections.  3  7  10  15

**6062-50 N.Y.C.** circa 1968-69, glossy black unpainted plastic, "N.Y.C." overscored, "6062" underscored (not 6062-50), no "NEW 2-49", (compare with 6062 previously), 9-9/16" long, detailed plastic undercarriage, no brakewheels molded on side, body mold "6462-2" on base underside, 6062-50 appears only on the box end. Car has Timken plastic trucks, one disc-operating coupler and one fixed coupler, two red unpainted plastic canisters with "LIONEL" molded on top. This car came in an orange and white box lettered "LIONEL" in large white letters and then "LIONEL TOY CORPORATION/HAGERSTOWN, MARYLAND". Talley and Falter Collections.  2  4  8  14

**6112 LIONEL** Circa 1956-58, 8" long, plain undercarriage and box interior, disc-operating couplers. Truck undersides come with many different numbers, for example, 5 and 3, 7 and 2, 2 and 0, 4 and 8 etc., appear on blue cars. Griesbeck comment.
(A) White unpainted plastic body, black lettering, four red canisters, early Timken trucks. Vagner Collection.  4  7  11  15
(B) Blue unpainted plastic body, white lettering. Early Timken trucks, three black-lettered white canisters, hard to find. Bohn and Vagner comments.  1  1.50  6  9
(C) Black with white lettering, early Timken trucks, four red canisters rubber-stamped "LIONEL AIR ACTIVATED CONTAINER/CAPY. 20000/Lt.Wt.4400/61125". Schreiner and Rohlfing Collections.  1  1.50  2  3
(D) Same as (C), but bar-end metal trucks, sheet metal clip holds truck to frame. Kotil and Vagner Collections.  1  1.50  2  3

**(6112) LIONEL** Circa 1960, olive drab or blue, 8" long, plain undercarriage and box interior, brakewheels molded on side, body mold number "6112-86" molded into base underside, Timken trucks, catalogue number uncertain, parentheses indicate number does not appear on car, original box will probably provide catalogue number.
(A) Unpainted blue plastic, one tab and one fixed coupler. Schreiner Collection.  1  2  3  4
(B) Unpainted olive drab plastic, disc-operating couplers, came with olive drab flat (3349) and olive drab work caboose (6824), set number unknown. Source: Catalano and Wilson.  7  11  18  29
(C) Same as (A), but two non-operating couplers. This car was apparently sold in set No. 11420 (1964) with a 1061 locomotive and 6167-25 caboose. The gondola box was probably numbered 6042-250, but confirmation of this is requested. Light Collection.  1  2  3  4

**6112-135 LIONEL** Black plastic body, 8" long, operating tab couplers, three white "LIONEL AIR ACTIVATED CONTAINER", numbered "6112" on car although box numbered "6112-135". Catalano observation.

|  | 1 | 2 | 3 | 4 |

**6142 LIONEL** 1961-66, 1970, 8-1/8" long, detailed undercarriage, box interior and sides, unpainted plastic, white lettering, Timken trucks, one disc-operating coupler, one fixed coupler.
(A) Black unpainted plastic.  1  1.50  2  3
(B) 1970, Black unpainted plastic, with Bettendorf trucks (introduced by MPC about 1970), one manual-operating coupler with plastic tab, one fixed coupler with open top, with "old" Lionel number, probably from leftover bodies. (Similar combinations are also seen with hoppers.)

|  | 1 | 1.50 | 2 | 3 |

**6142-50 LIONEL** 1956, 1961-63, Unpainted shiny green plastic, white lettering "LIONEL" and "6142", Timken plastic trucks with one disc-operating and one dummy coupler, one molded brakewheel each side, body mold 6112-86, no built date, two red canisters. Possibly included in 1065 diesel set in 1961. Additional information requested. Came in set 11560 in 1956. I. D. Smith and Rohlfing observations.  1  1.50  2  3

**6142-75 LIONEL** 1961-63, Same as 6142 but unpainted blue plastic, numbered "6142", with white canisters, 6112-88, mold 6112-86, Timken plastic trucks, disc couplers. Rohlfing Collection.  1  1.50  2  3

**6142-100 LIONEL**
(A) Light green unpainted plastic body, no lettering, mold No. 6112-85. Molded brakewheels, Timken plastic trucks, one disc-operating and one dummy coupler, two white 6112-88 canisters, part of set No. 11430. Further confirmation requested. Winton Collection.  1  1.50  2  3
(B) Green body, 6142 only on car, Timken trucks, two disc couplers, mold 6112-86, came with four white canisters with "61125" printed on canister. Budniak Collection.  1  1.50  2  3

**6142-150 LIONEL** Circa 1961-63?, Same as 6142 above but unpainted blue plastic, with "6142" numbered cable reels. Need information as to whether 6142-150 has a body mold number.  1  1.50  2  3

**6142-175 LIONEL** Circa 1961-63?, probably similar to 6142 above although body's part number differs from previous entries numbered "6142". Need information as to whether 6142-175 has a body mold number.

|  | 1 | 1.50 | 2 | 3 |

**6162 N.Y.C.** 1961-69, unpainted plastic body, white lettering, 9-9/16" long, "N.Y.C." overscored, "6162" underscored.
(A) 1969, red, no "new" date, one Timken truck and one arch bar truck, one disc-operating coupler, one fixed coupler, heavy heat-stamped letters. Vagner Collection.  2  5  7  10
(B) 1961, blue, "NEW 2-49", Timken trucks, two disc-operating couplers. Came in set 1609; box imprinted "6162-1 GONDOLA CAR WITH CANISTERS", three unlettered white canisters. Budniak Collection.  2  5  7  10
(C) 1961, aqua blue, "NEW 2-49", Timken trucks, two disc-operating couplers, two brakewheels. Pauli Collection.  2  5  7  10
(D) 1962, blue, no "new" date, Timken trucks, disc-operating couplers. Griesbeck Collection.  3  5  7  10
(E) Same as (C), but no brakewheels. Gordon Collection.  3  5  7  10
(F) Same as (D), but one disc and one dummy coupler, box marked 6162-110, came with two red canisters. Budniak Collection.

|  | 3 | 5 | 7 | 10 |

**6162-60 ALASKA** 1959, bar-end metal trucks, magnetic tab couplers, four white canisters with set No. 1611, 10-3/8" long.
(A) Yellow unpainted plastic body, dark blue lettering.  25  37  50  75
(B) Same as (A), but Timken plastic trucks, two disc couplers. Vagner Collection.  25  37  50  75
(C) Same as (A), but cream-colored plastic body. Algozzini Collection.  NRS

**6342 N.Y.C.** 1956-58, 1966-69, special gondola for culvert loader with black metal channel, culverts fall down channel, 9-9/16" long, red unpainted plastic, white lettering, "N.Y.C." overscored, three lines of weights, "6342" not overscored, came with 348 culvert unloader.
(A) No "new" date, Timken trucks, 1965-69; Hutchinson observation. Came with 348 manual culvert unloader; Ambrose comment.  7  10  15  25
(B) "NEW 2-49", bar-end metal trucks, magnetic tab couplers.  7  10  15  25
(C) "NEW 2-49", orange-red plastic body.  7  10  15  25
(D) Same as (B), but dull brick red. Halverson Collection.  NRS

2452

2452[B or C]

2452[F]

3444

4452

6002

6012

6032

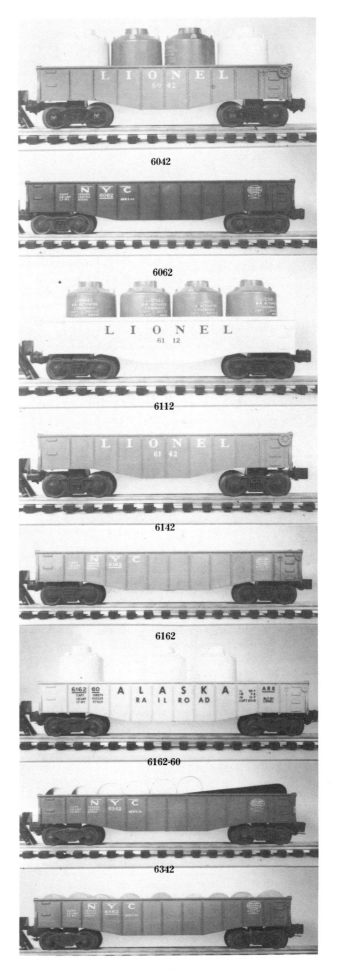

6042

6062

6112

6142

6162

6162-60

6342

6462

3562-1

3562-25        3562-25

3562-50        3562-75

**6452 PENNSYLVANIA** 1948-49, short gondola, 8", white plastic body painted black, white lettering, quarter-sized hole in bottom of body, holes and embossings in base, no brakewheels, staple-end magnetic trucks, "PENNSYLVANIA" overscored by line on top, numbered "347000", reporting marks on left in two lines: "CAPY 140000 LT WT 56500/LD LMT 153500 NEW 12-45". Reporting marks on right in four lines: "6452 LIONEL/IL 56-2/CU FT 1745/BLT 12-45 G27". No number stamped on bottom. Also see next entry. Dixon, Vagner and Budniak Collections.

                                       1  1.50  2  5

**6462 PENNSYLVANIA** 1947-48, short, 8" long, dark maroon plastic body painted black, white lettering, quarter-sized hole in center of plastic body, metal underframe, stamped "6452" but "6462" on car sides, brakewheel disc with center holes, without brakewheel, staple-end metal trucks, late coil couplers, sliding shoes. Vagner Collection.    1  1.50  2  5

**6462 N.Y.C.** 1949, 9-9/16" long. Note that variation letters differ from those in the last edition. The cars are now arranged by color, although some varieties are found under 6462-25, 6462-75 and 6462-125. Note: Black cars come with 6 straight-sided solid wooden drums. Other colors came with six brown-stained turned-wood barrels with ribs. Bohn comment.

### BLACK CARS: 1949-54

(A) Unpainted black plastic body, "N" in second from left panel, "6462" underscored, staple-end metal trucks, "NEW 2-49", three lines of weights, high gloss metal underframe, brakewheels and steps.    2  3  5  8
(B) Same as (A), but black-painted opaque-blue plastic. Kotil Collection
                                       2  3  5  8
(C) Same as (A), but black-painted gray plastic. Kotil Collection.
                                       2  3  5  8
(D) Same as (A), but black-painted green plastic. Kotil Collection.
                                       2  3  5  8
(E) Same as (A), but flat black-painted brown plastic. Dorn Collection.
                                       2  3  5  8
(F) Same as (A), but only two lines of weights, no brakewheels.
                                       2  3  5  8
(G) Flat black-painted shiny black plastic body, "N" in second from left panel, "6462" underscored, "NEW 2-49", two lines of weights, no brakewheels, bar-end metal trucks, magnetic couplers.  2  3  5  8
(H) Same as (G), but unpainted black plastic. Kotil Collection.
                                       2  3  5  8
(I) Flat black-painted shiny black plastic, "N" in second from left panel, "6462" underscored, no "new" date, two lines of weights, no brakewheels, Type VI bar-end metal trucks, magnetic couplers. Crile and Clark Collections.               2  3  5  8
(J) Same as (I), but unpainted black plastic body. Kaiser Collection.
                                       2  3  4  6

(K) Same as (A), but black-painted red marbled plastic, no brakewheels. Rohlfing Collection.                 2  3  5  8
(L) Same as (I), but flat black-painted pink plastic. Budniak Collection.
                                       2  3  5  8

### RED CARS: 1950-52, 1954, 1956

(M) Dark-painted light-colored plastic body, metal underframe, no lines over "N.Y.C.", "N" in second panel from left, line under "6462", no "new" date, two lines of weights, no brakewheel, no steps, bar-end metal trucks.              2  5  8  10
(N) Same as (M), but shiny red-painted clear plastic. Kotil Collection.
                                       2  5  8  10
(O) Same as (M), but shiny red-painted light blue plastic. Kotil Collection.
                                       2  5  8  10
(P) Bright red paint over black plastic, white lettering, metal underframe, no lines over "N.Y.C.", "N" in second panel from left, line under "6462", no "new" date, two lines of weights, no brakewheel, no steps, bar-end metal trucks.              2  5  8  10
(Q) "General" red paint over dark gray plastic body, white lettering, "N" in second panel from left, line under "6462", "NEW 2-49", staple-end metal trucks, two lines of weights, two brakewheels. Pauli Collection.
                                     2  5  8  10
(R) Same as (M), but same maroon color as 6456 Lehigh Valley hopper. Sipple Collection.                     2  4  8  10
(S) Dark red paint over clear plastic, white lettering, metal underframe, no line under "6462", "NEW 2-49", staple-end metal trucks, three lines of weights, steps and two brakewheels. Falter Collection.  2  4  8  10
(T) Same as (R), except medium red paint and two lines of weights. Lahti Collection.                             2  4  8  10
(U) Same as black (A), but clear plastic painted gloss red. Budniak Collection.                            2  4  8  10
(V) Same as (P), but dark red paint. Rohlfing Collection.  2  4  8  10

### GREEN CARS: 1954-56

(W) Green paint over black plastic body, white lettering, metal underframe, lines over "N.Y.C.", "N" in third panel from left, line under "6462", "NEW 2-49", bar-end metal trucks, three lines of weights, no brakewheel, no steps.                        3  5  9  14
(X) Darker green body than (S), white lettering, dull black metal underframe, no lines over "N.Y.C.", "N" in second panel from left, line under "6462". no "new" date, bar-end metal trucks, tab magnetic couplers, two lines of weights, no brakewheels, no steps, 3/16" diameter hole in underframe center.         3  5  9  14
(Y) Flat medium green paint over black plastic body, white lettering, metal underframe, no lines over "N.Y.C.", line under "6462", no "new" date,

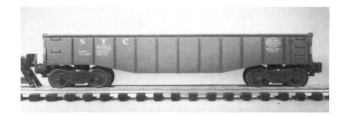

6462 "N" in second panel from left, "NYC" in serif letters, line under "6462" two lines of weights, no brakewheel, no steps, no "new" date, magnetic tab couplers, bar-end trucks.

6562 "N" in third panel, "NYC" in sans-serif lettering, no line under or over "6562", three lines of weights, no brakewheels, no steps, "NEW 2-49", magnetic tab couplers, bar-end trucks.

Catalogue number not known.  Note molded brakewheel.

metal trucks, magnetic couplers, two lines of weights.   Warswick Collection.                                                                     3      5      9    12

(Z) Same as (U), but no tabs on couplers, no hole in underframe, dark cream lettering, two brakewheels. Pauli Collection. This version may not have originally come with brakeweels. We would appreciate it if our readers would provide additional confirmation.                        3      5      9    12

(AA) Gold-painted car, two brakewheels.  Reader comments requested. Algozzini Collection.                                                          **NRS**

**6462-25** Green-painted black plastic body, very white lettering, metal underframe, no lines over "N.Y.C", "N" in second panel from left, line under "6462", no "new", two lines of weights, no hole in underframe, no steps, no brakewheels, bar-end metal trucks, magnetic couplers without tabs, numbered "6462" only, "6462-25" is catalogue number that appears on box.

(A) Green-painted black plastic body. Kotil Collection.    3      5      9    12
(B) Darker green, than (A). Pauli Collection.              3      5      9    12

**6462-75** Red-painted black plastic body, white lettering, lines over "N.Y.C", "N" in third panel from left, "NEW 2-49", three lines of weights, bar-end metal trucks, magnetic couplers, numbered "6462", "6462-75" is catalogue number that appears on box.

(A) Bright red paint. Pauli Collection.                    3      5      9    14
(B) Shiny darker red. Kotil Collection.                    3      5      9    14
(C) Dull red. Kotil Collection.                            3      5    12    20

**6462-100** Circa 1951-52, Red unpainted plastic body, metal trucks, no brakewheels, reader confirmation requested. Ambrose comment.        **NRS**

**6462-125** 1954-57, Red unpainted plastic body, white lettering, metal underframe, lines over "N.Y.C.", "N" in third panel, line under "6462", "NEW 2-49", three lines of weights, no brakewheel, no steps, bar-end metal trucks, magnetic tab couplers, only "6462" appears on car, "6462-125" is catalogue number that appears on box.  Came with 1615 steam switcher in 1955. Ambrose and Vagner comments. Came with 1956 set No. 1553W as well. Rohlfing comment. Also see 6562. Kotil Collection.

(A) Dull red. Kotil Collection.                            3      5      9    14
(B) Shiny red, no line under 6462. Griesbeck Collection.
                                                           3      5      9    14
(C) Same as (B), but "6462" is underscored. Rohlfing Collection.
                                                           3      5      9    14

**6462-500 N.Y.C.** 1957-58,  pink-painted body, black lettering, from Girl's Set, lines over "N.Y.C.", "N" in third panel from left, line under "6462", "NEW 2-49", bar-end metal trucks, magnetic tab couplers, three lines of weights, no brakewheel, no steps, note that 6462, not 6462-500, appears on car. Vagner comment.                              **40    75  100  150**

**6562 N.Y.C.** 1956-58, metal underframe, lines over "N.Y.C.", "N" in third panel from left, no line under "6562", "NEW 2-49", bar-end metal trucks, magnetic tab couplers, three lines of weights, no brakewheels, no steps, 9-9/16" long, 3/16" hole in center of metal base.  Degano observation.

(A) 1956, unpainted gray plastic, maroon lettering, gray plastic is lighter and less shiny than (D), magnetic couplers with tabs, no mold number, metal base. Fleming Collection.                        7    13    25    40
(B) 1956 and 1958, red unpainted plastic body, white lettering.
                                                           7    13    25    40
(C) 1957, black unpainted plastic body, white lettering.   7    13    25    40
(D) Unpainted gray plastic, red lettering, gray plastic is darker and more shiny than (A), magnetic couplers without tabs, no mold number, metal base. Fleming Collection.                           7    12    25    40

**6562-1** Red unpainted plastic body, white lettering, metal underframe, lines over "N.Y.C.", "N" in third panel, line under "6462", "NEW 2-49", bar-end metal trucks, magnetic tab couplers, three lines of weights, no brakewheel, no steps, came with four red canisters, box marked "6562-1" and "25" rubber-stamped after "LIONEL" on box end, although only "6462" appeared on car. This car with an unknown load also came in a box marked "6462-125". Kotil Collection.

(A) As described above.                                    3      5      9    14
(B) Same as (A), but gray body, box marked 6562-1. Ambrose Collection.
                                                           3      5      9    14
(C) Same as (A), but came in box marked "6562-25 CANISTER CAR", four red canisters. Ambrose and Budniak Collections.        3      5      9    14
(D) Same as (A), but black body; came in box marked 6562-50. Ambrose Collection.                                                3      5      9    14
(E) Same as (A), but medium light red. Rohlfing Collection.
                                                           3      5      9    14

NOTE:  Cars marked 6462 coming in boxes marked 6562-1 may be the result of packaging errors. Before we list any of the 6562-1 cars above as separate entries, we will need more detailed descriptions of each of these cars from readers.  Sorting these cars out may be an intricate puzzle.

**NO NUMBER** 8-1/8" long, detailed undercarriage and box interior, blue unpainted plastic, no lettering, Timken trucks, fixed couplers, "61 12-86" mold number embossed in bottom, catalogue number not known. Schreiner Collection.                                              1  1.50    2      3

**NO NUMBER** Green unpainted plastic, short gondola, length unknown, interior detail unknown, Timken trucks, one fixed coupler, one disc-operating coupler, mold number and catalogue number not known. Schreiner Collection.                                            1  1.50    2      3

NOTE:  On those 9-9/16" cars with a metal underframe, the mold number (part number) is under the metal under frame.

# Chapter VIII
# HOPPERS AND DUMP CARS

For the transportation of loose loads in bulk quantities, nothing is quite so handy as the hopper car, either in its open or closed versions. In the coal mining regions of the country, long trains of black hopper cars carrying "black diamonds" to power plants are a familiar sight. In the Midwest, equally long trains of covered hopper cars carry grain to market with ease. The Lionel Corporation's freight consists would have been incomplete without at least a few of these handy freight carriers.

The 3559 with red bin.

In the first postwar years, Lionel was content to manufacture the operating dump car from prewar years with its red bin, and the company soon made another dump car with a longer body and rectangular bin. The first of Lionel's hopper cars appeared in late 1947 or (more likely) early 1948. This was the car marked "LEHIGH VALLEY 25000", which was a familiar sight throughout all of postwar production. The first versions of this car had metal plates holding the trucks, but later versions were all plastic - the same developmental history as the gondola cars. They came with Lehigh Valley markings in black, maroon, red, gray and yellow colors. The short hopper car carried other railroad markings such as the 6076 Santa Fe in gray.

The 3459 dump car replaced the 3559.

The short hopper car was adapted into an operating version in Norfolk and Western markings for use with an overhead coal ramp. The operator would fill the car with coal (preferably from a coal loader). Then, the train would back up a ramp until the hopper car at the end would hook onto a coupler mounted at the rear of the ramp. At the touch of a button, the car's hatches would open and dump the coal into a waiting trough below the ramp. Then, the operator would press another button, and the car would uncouple and roll down the ramp to await pickup by the train.

In 1954, Lionel began its production of a large covered hopper; the first version of this "Cement Car", as Lionel called

it, was made in Norfolk and Western markings. The roof cover had 12 hatches which could open - although operators had to be very careful of their fragility. Later cars were produced in other road markings, and some were made without covers. In the uncovered versions, Lionel usually included a center spreader bar which fit into two holes high up on the car sides. Real railroads had this bar attached to the car sides to keep the sides from bulging outwards with a heavy load. Lionel put it there to keep the thin plastic sides from cracking when squeezed by an over-enthusiastic child. These big cars were extremely well detailed and handsome additions to a layout.

Lionel produced several varieties of coal dumping cars throughout the postwar years. The firm kept making its Marx-like 3659 prewar dump car (renumbered 3559); this car was very short, with a V-shaped red bin and black ends. The bin tilted when the car was activated by a special track. This dump car was only made in 1946. In that year, Lionel began production of another all-metal dump car, the 3459/3469. This car had a rectangular bin which tilted so that the side of the bin opened and dumped the car's load. Most of these cars were made in black, but green versions are also found, and early aluminum and yellow versions are rare and highly prized.

The 3359-55 had two gray bins.

The last coal dumping hopper made by Lionel was the strange 3359-55 Twin Bin dumping car of 1955-1957. This car featured two gray plastic bins which operated in sequence instead of simultaneously. The action was accomplished by means of a rotating cam beneath the bins which advanced in steps. About 10 pushes of the operating button would dump both bins. Lionel claimed that this car had a prototype which was used by the City of New York for gravel-dumping purposes, but nobody has ever described the prototype.

Considering the quantities produced, it is rather surprising that Lionel did not make its hopper cars in more road names. The small hoppers are almost always found in Lehigh Valley markings, and there are only six road markings for the 50 ton "quad" hopper (though there are more varieties than that). Perhaps Lionel was familiar with the concept of "unit trains" which would carry merchandise in the cars of only one rail line. More likely, Lionel did not feel the need to change the road markings to sell the cars, since the short hoppers especially were mostly included in sets rather than sold separately. Whatever the case, most of the hopper and dump cars are quite easy to obtain today, although it is difficult to build a collection of all the varieties. A full study of the Lehigh Valley hopper cars is needed to match the one Richard Vagner has done for the New York Central gondolas.

# Hopper Body Types

**All trucks attached with metal plates have steps on side**

Raised posts with screws for trucks

**Type I**

Trucks attached with metal plate, 2 screws

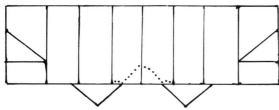

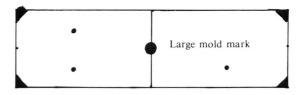

Large mold mark

**Type II** Same as I, but cutout for operating dump

Same as I, but cutout for operating dump

**Type III**

Raised posts with screws for trucks; metal plate, 2 screws

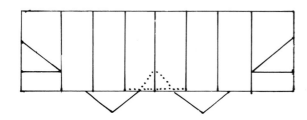

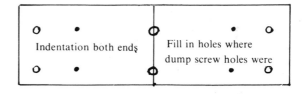

Indentation both ends

Fill in holes where dump screw holes were

**Type IV** Same as III, but cutout for operating dump

Same as II, but cutout for operating dump

**Type V** Same as III

Raised posts, no screws; metal plate with tub

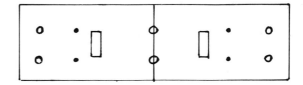

**Type VI.**

Rivet to post

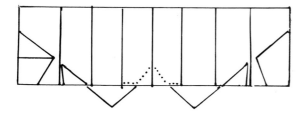

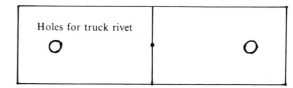

Holes for truck rivet

6456            6456

6456            6456

3456            2856-2956

|  | Gd | VG | Exc | Mt |
|---|---|---|---|---|

**2456 LEHIGH VALLEY** Type I body, white lettering, "NEW 1-48", and "BLT-I-48", two brakewheels, staple-end metal trucks, coil couplers, steps, 8-9/16" long.

| | | | | |
|---|---|---|---|---|
| (A) Flat black. | 5 | 7 | 12 | 20 |
| (B) Shiny black paint over marbled plastic. | 5 | 7 | 12 | 20 |
| (C) Same as (A), but only one brakewheel. Budniak Collection. | | | | |
| | 5 | 7 | 12 | 20 |

**2856 B & O** 1946, scale-detailed hopper car; catalogued but not manufactured.      **Not Manufactured**

**2956 B & O** Circa 1946, scale-detailed hopper car from 1940-42; black die-cast body, white lettering, "BLT 3-27", "532000", "2956", working die-cast bottom hatches, staple-end metal trucks, coil couplers, apparently not manufactured after 1942; car most likely converted from tin-plate trucks to staple-end trucks by service station or owner.    **90   160   200   320**

**3359-55 LIONEL LINES** 1955, twin gray bins which tilt, red simulated power unit mounted on black bar-end metal trucks, magnetic tab couplers, came with two OTC contactors, cam rotates and dumps bins in alternation, long receiving bin and 96C controller.    **9   15   20   30**

**3456 N & W** 1951-55, black with white lettering, "BLT 8-50", "NEW 8-50", operating bottom hatches, steps, brakewheels, 8-9/16" long.

| | | | | |
|---|---|---|---|---|
| (A) Black paint on colored plastic, Type II body, staple-end metal trucks. | | | | |
| | 12 | 20 | 25 | 40 |
| (B) Black paint on brown plastic, Type IV body. | 12 | 20 | 25 | 40 |
| (C) Black paint on blue plastic, Type IV body. | 12 | 20 | 25 | 40 |
| (D) Light blue with red lettering. | | | | NRS |
| (E) Black paint on white plastic, Type IV body. Kotil Collection. | | | | NRS |

**3459 LIONEL LINES** 1946-48, "AUTOMATIC DUMP CAR", bin dumps, black frame and simulated dump mechanism, two brakewheels, staple-end metal trucks.

| | | | | |
|---|---|---|---|---|
| (A) 1946, unpainted aluminum bin with blue lettering, staple-end metal trucks. | | | | |
| | 40 | 60 | 80 | 100 |
| (B) 1946-47, black-painted bin, white lettering, staple-end metal trucks. | | | | |
| | 9 | 15 | 20 | 30 |
| (C) 1948, green-painted bin, white lettering. | 20 | 25 | 35 | 50 |
| (D) Yellow-painted body with black heat-stamped lettering, rare. We would like to observe this car for further study. | | | | NRS |
| (E) Same as (B), 1946, but receiving bin which came with car is made of a black dump car body bin fabricated of steel instead of aluminum. Came in set 1415WS. Rohlfing Collection. | 12 | 18 | 25 | 35 |

**3469 LIONEL LINES** 1949-55, "AUTOMATIC DUMP CAR", bin dumps, black frame and simulated dump mechanism, two brakewheels, bar-end metal trucks. Original box marked 3469X. Budniak comment.

| | | | | |
|---|---|---|---|---|
| | 9 | 12 | 20 | 30 |

**3559 COAL DUMP CAR** 1946, rerun of 3659 prewar car with new staple-end metal trucks, black frame and end unit, red bin, silver/white "3559" rubber-stamped on underside.

| | | | | |
|---|---|---|---|---|
| (A) Early coil couplers, open truck underside. | 7 | 10 | 15 | 25 |
| (B) Regular coil couplers. | 7 | 10 | 15 | 25 |

**5459 LIONEL LINES** 1946, "AUTOMATIC DUMP CAR" with green and white "ELECTRONIC CONTROL" decal, black car with white lettering, electronic control receiver hidden inside frame of car; staple-end metal trucks, coil-operated couplers.    **22   35   50   80**

**546446** See 6446-1 or 6446-25.

**6076 (A-C) A T S F** 1963, Type VI body, gray plastic, black lettering, "BUILT BY LIONEL", no date, no brakewheels, special promotional set for Libby (No. 19263) 8-9/16" long.

| | | | | |
|---|---|---|---|---|
| (A) Timken trucks, one disc coupler, one fixed coupler. | 9 | 15 | 20 | 30 |
| (B) Arch bar trucks, fixed couplers. | 9 | 15 | 20 | 30 |
| (C) One Timken truck with disc coupler; one arch bar truck with fixed coupler. | 9 | 15 | 20 | 30 |

**6076 (D-J) LEHIGH VALLEY** Type VI body, 8-9/16" long, no brakewheels.

| | | | | |
|---|---|---|---|---|
| (D) Gray body, black lettering, "BUILT 1-48", no "new" date, Timken trucks, one disc coupler, one fixed coupler. | 4 | 6 | 8 | 12 |
| (E) Black body, white lettering, "BUILT 1-48", "NEW 1-48", Timken trucks, one disc coupler, one fixed coupler. | 4 | 6 | 8 | 12 |
| (F) Same as (E), but arch bar trucks, fixed couplers. | 4 | 6 | 8 | 10 |
| (G) Same as (E), but without "new" dates. | 4 | 6 | 8 | 10 |
| (H) Same as (E), but without "built" and "new" dates. Pauli Collection. | | | | |
| | 4 | 6 | 8 | 10 |
| (I) Red with white lettering, "Built 1-48 " "NEW 1-48", arch bar trucks fixed couplers. | 4 | 6 | 8 | 10 |
| (J) Same as (E), but fixed couplers. Kotil Collection. | 4 | 6 | 8 | 10 |

(K) Dull yellow-painted Type VI gray body, black lettering, "NEW 1-48", "BUILT 1-48", "CAPY 100000; LO LMT 128300; CU. FT. 1860". Timken plastic trucks, one disc-operating and one dummy coupler, no brakewheel. Sekely Collection.    **2   3   5   6**

(M) NO LETTERING, Type VI body, unpainted olive drab, Timken trucks, one disc coupler, one fixed coupler, with open top. Wilson Collection. Part of J.C. Penney set.    **1.50   2   3   5**

(N) NO LETTERING, Type VI unpainted gray plastic body, Timken trucks, fixed couplers. Griesbeck and Kotil Collections.    **1.50   2   3   5**

(R) NO NUMBER LEHIGH VALLEY, black Type VI body, white-lettered "CAPY 100000 LD LMT 128300 CU FT 1860", no "BLT" date, no "NEW" number, Timken trucks, Schreiner Collection. (We need assistance in identifying Lionel's number for this car. The original box probably bears the Lionel catalogue number.)    **NRS**

NOTE: The Lionel Service Manual lists three 6176 varieties: 6176-25 with 6176-2 body, 6176-50 with 6076-88 body and 6176-75 with 6176-76 body. All have Timken trucks, one disc and one fixed coupler. We believe that these Lionel numbers correspond to one or another of our body types and descriptions. Of particular help would be information corroborating box numbers and body mold numbers with our descriptions and body types.

**6176(A-J) LEHIGH VALLEY** Type VI body, no brakewheel.

(A) Dark yellow, blue lettering, "NEW 1-48", "BUILT 1-48", "LIONEL 6176", Timken trucks, one disc coupler, one fixed coupler.

|  |  |  |  |
|---|---|---|---|
| 3 | 5 | 7 | 10 |

(B) Same as (A), but without "new" date. 

|  |  |  |  |
|---|---|---|---|
| 3 | 5 | 7 | 10 |

(C) Same as (A), but medium yellow.

|  |  |  |  |
|---|---|---|---|
| 3 | 5 | 7 | 10 |

(D) Light yellow, black lettering, "new" not present, "BUILT 1-48" and "LIONEL 6176" both present, Timken trucks, disc couplers.

|  |  |  |  |
|---|---|---|---|
| 3 | 5 | 7 | 10 |

(E) Same as (D), but one disc coupler, one fixed coupler.

|  |  |  |  |
|---|---|---|---|
| 3 | 5 | 7 | 10 |

(F) Light yellow, black lettering, "NEW 1-48", "BUILT 1-48" and "LIONEL 6176" all missing. Pauli Collection.

|  |  |  |  |
|---|---|---|---|
| 3 | 5 | 7 | 10 |

(G) Gray with black lettering, "NEW 1-48" not present, "BUILT 1-48" present, Timken trucks, one disc coupler, one fixed coupler.

|  |  |  |  |
|---|---|---|---|
| 3 | 5 | 7 | 10 |

(H) Same as (A), but black lettering. Part of set No. 11430. Kotil and Winton Collections.

|  |  |  |  |
|---|---|---|---|
| 3 | 5 | 7 | 10 |

(I) Same as (G), but with "NEW 1-48". Kotil Collection.

|  |  |  |  |
|---|---|---|---|
| 3 | 5 | 7 | 10 |

(J) 1966, black body, white lettering, Timken trucks, one disc and one fixed coupler, no number, built date or new date on car, came in set 11560 in 1966. Rohlfing Collection.

|  |  |  |  |
|---|---|---|---|
| 3 | 5 | 7 | 10 |

**6176(P)** NO LETTERING, deep bright yellow, Type VI body, Timken trucks, one disc coupler, one fixed coupler, from set No. 11430. Edwards Collection.

|  |  |  |  |
|---|---|---|---|
| 2 | 4 | 7 | 10 |

**6346-56 ALCOA** 1956, 50 ton quad hopper, aluminum with blue lettering, "NEW 6-56", hatch covers, Alcoa labels, no center brace hole, brakewheel, bar-end metal trucks, magnetic couplers. See also Factory Errors.

|  |  |  |  |
|---|---|---|---|
| 12 | 25 | 30 | 45 |

**6436-1 LEHIGH VALLEY** 1955, uncatalogued, 50 ton quad hopper, gray plastic painted black, white lettering, "NEW 3-55", no covers, bar-end trucks, magnetic tab couplers, one brakewheel. Cummings comment.

(A) Center spreader bar holes.

|  |  |  |  |
|---|---|---|---|
| 8 | 15 | 20 | 30 |

(B) Without center spreader bar holes.

|  |  |  |  |
|---|---|---|---|
| 15 | 30 | 40 | 55 |

**6436-25 LEHIGH VALLEY** 1955-57, 50 ton quad hopper, no covers, maroon with white lettering, "NEW 3-55", brakewheels, bar-end metal trucks, magnetic couplers.

|  |  |  |  |
|---|---|---|---|
| 8 | 15 | 20 | 30 |

**6436** See 6436-110.

**6436-100** - see 6436-110.

**6436-110 LEHIGH VALLEY** 1963-68, 50 ton quad hopper, red-painted gray plastic with white lettering, spreader, no covers, Timken trucks, magnetic couplers, brakewheel. Car may be numbered 6436 or 6436-100. See variations below. Car may or may not have lettering "NEW 3-55". All cars have "BLT BY LIONEL", but we do not know if all varieties have built dates.

(A) Numbered only "6436", no new or built dates, came in box numbered 6436-110. Fleming Collection.

|  |  |  |  |
|---|---|---|---|
| 10 | 22 | 30 | 55 |

(B) Numbered "6436-100", has "NEW 3-55", no built date, came in box numbered 6436-110. Kotil Collection.

|  |  |  |  |
|---|---|---|---|
| 40 | 60 | 90 | 125 |

(C) Numbered "6436-100" without new or built date, came in box numbered 6436-110. Kotil Collection.

|  |  |  |  |
|---|---|---|---|
| 10 | 22 | 30 | 55 |

**6436-1969 TCA** 1969, uncatalogued, 50 ton quad hopper, special 1,000 run for 1969 TCA Convention, "BLT BY LIONEL 4-69" spreader bar, no cover, red-painted body with white convention data and lettering, white palm tree and white TCA logos. Timken plastic trucks, disc-operating couplers.

|  |  |  |  |
|---|---|---|---|
| — | — | 100 | 135 |

**6436-500 LEHIGH VALLEY** 1957-58, 50 ton quad hopper from Girl's Set, numbered "643657" and "NEW 3-55".

(A) Lilac car with maroon lettering.

|  |  |  |  |
|---|---|---|---|
| 45 | 90 | 125 | 170 |

(B) Burgundy-painted black plastic shell, white heat-stamped lettering, "NEW 3-55", one metal spreader bar; Lionel preproduction paint sample. Degano Collection.

|  |  |  |  |
|---|---|---|---|
| — | — | 1000 | — |

(C) Same as (A), but no center spreader bar holes. Darasko Collection.

|  |  |  |  |
|---|---|---|---|
| 45 | 90 | 125 | 170 |

**6446-1 N & W** 1954-55, 50 ton quad hopper, "NEW 6-54", "546446" on side, bar-end metal trucks, roof with 12 covers, brakewheel. (In earlier editions this item was catalogued as a 54-6446 and variations had different letter designations.)

(A) Gray plastic body painted gray, black lettering, covers, "BLT BY LIONEL".

|  |  |  |  |
|---|---|---|---|
| 13 | 25 | 35 | 60 |

(B) Light gray, black lettering.

|  |  |  |  |
|---|---|---|---|
| 13 | 25 | 35 | 60 |

(C) Gray plastic body painted gray, black lettering, without center brace hole, magnetic couplers.

|  |  |  |  |
|---|---|---|---|
| 13 | 25 | 35 | 60 |

(D) Gray body, brace holes and brace, no roof, plastic trucks, 1963 couplers.

|  |  |  |  |
|---|---|---|---|
| 13 | 25 | 35 | 60 |

**6446-25 N & W** 1955-57, 50 ton quad hopper, numbered "546446", and "NEW 6-54", roof with 12 covers. (Note: We have changed hopper classifications from previous editions so that our numbers correspond to Lionel's cataloguing system.)

(A) Black-painted gray plastic, white lettering, 6446-25 on car sides, no center brace hole, bar-end metal trucks, magnetic couplers, brakewheel "BLT BY LIONEL NEW 6-54;" box end lettered "6446 CEMENT CAR 25 LIONEL 25". Kotil and Ambrose Collections.

|  |  |  |  |
|---|---|---|---|
| 9 | 15 | 25 | 45 |

(B) Same as (A), but center brace hole with brace, tab magnetic couplers.

|  |  |  |  |
|---|---|---|---|
| 9 | 15 | 25 | 45 |

(C) 1963, Gray unpainted plastic, black lettering. Center brace hole, no brace, Timken trucks, disc-operating couplers, box end marked "6446 CEMENT CAR", part of set 13098. Powell, Ambrose and Kotil Collections.

|  | 10 | 20 | 35 | 50 |

(D) Gray plastic painted gray, no cover, no center brace hole, bar-end metal trucks, car sides stamped 6446-25. Ambrose Collection.

|  | 10 | 20 | 35 | 50 |

(E) 1970-71, Royal blue, white lettering, produced by MPC; only 400 produced, MPC's smallest regular production run. Made for Glen Uhl. Listed here for your convenience.

|  | 30 | 60 | 100 | 175 |

(F) Same as (A), but no brakewheel. Budniak Collection.

|  | 9 | 15 | 25 | 45 |

(M-Q) Specials made for N & W that are rare and very desirable, but are not catalogued.
(M) Gold with white lettering.  — — 1000 —
(N) Pink with black lettering.  — — 1000 —
(O) Light blue plastic painted light blue, white lettering.

|  | — | — | 1000 | — |

(P) Same as (G), but with covers and center brace holes.

|  | — | — | 1000 | — |

(Q) Silver with white lettering.  — — 1000 —

**6446-60 LEHIGH VALLEY** 1963 only, lettered "6436" and "NEW 3-55". The catalogue used this number to differentiate this car from 6436-110, which was an open hopper. Box ends are stamped 6446-60; this car identical to 6436-110 except for cover and lack of spreader bar.
(A) Red body and covers, "NEW 3-55" on both sides, Timken trucks, original box reads "6446-60/LIONEL/COVERED HOPPER/CAR". Algozzini and Ambrose Collections.  20 35 45 65
(B) Same as (A), but black body and covers. Ambrose Collection.

|  | 20 | 35 | 45 | 65 |

**54-6446 N&W** 1954, 50 ton quad hopper, "NEW 6-54", bar-end metal trucks, brakewheel.
(A) Gray plastic body painted black, white lettering, center brace hole with brace, tab magnetic couplers.  20 35 45 65
(B) Gray plastic body painted black, white lettering, without center brace hole, with covers, magnetic couplers.  16 25 35 50
(C) Gray plastic body painted gray, black lettering, without center brace hole, with covers, magnetic couplers. Kotil Collection.  16 25 35 50

6456 Lehigh Valley.

**6456 LEHIGH VALLEY** 25000 "NEW 1-48", "BUILT 1-48", steps, brakewheels, except as noted.
**Type I Bodies**
(A) Maroon with white lettering, staple-end trucks.  5 7 9 12
(B) Black with white lettering, bar-end metal trucks.  5 7 9 12
(C) Faded brown with white lettering, staple-end metal trucks.

|  | 5 | 7 | 9 | 12 |

(D) Same as (B), staple-end trucks. Kotil and Rohlfing Collections.

|  | 5 | 7 | 9 | 12 |

(E) Maroon with cream lettering, staple-end trucks. Griesbeck Collection.

|  | 5 | 7 | 9 | 12 |

**Type III Bodies**
(H) Gray with maroon lettering, bar-end metal trucks.  5 7 9 12
(I) Shiny red paint over opaque body, yellow lettering, bar-end metal trucks.  15 22 40 70
(J) Maroon with white lettering, bar-end metal trucks.  5 7 9 12
(K) Dark maroon with white lettering, staple-end metal trucks.

|  | 5 | 7 | 9 | 12 |

(L) Black with white lettering, bar-end metal trucks.  5 7 9 12
(M) Reddish-maroon with white lettering, bar-end metal trucks.

|  | 5 | 7 | 9 | 12 |

(N) Same as (I), but white lettering. Degano Collection.  **NRS**

**Type V Bodies**
(S) Shiny black unpainted plastic, white lettering, bar-end metal trucks, no brakewheel.
(T) Shiny black unpainted plastic, white lettering, Timken trucks, disc-operating couplers.  5 7 9 12
(U) Flat black unpainted plastic, white lettering, Timken trucks, disc-operating couplers.  5 7 9 12
**Type VI Bodies**
(X) Shiny black unpainted plastic, white lettering, Timken trucks, disc-operating couplers, no brakewheels.  5 7 9 12

**6476 LEHIGH VALLEY** 25000 "NEW 1-48", "BUILT 1-48",.
(A) Type V red plastic body, white lettering, bar-end metal trucks, magnetic tab couplers, brakewheels, steps.  5 7 9 12
(B) Type V gray plastic body, black lettering, Timken trucks, disc-operating couplers, steps.  5 7 9 12
(C) Type V red plastic body, white lettering, Timken trucks, disc-operating couplers, steps, no brakewheels.  5 7 9 12
(D) Type V darker red plastic body, white lettering, Timken trucks, disc-operating couplers.  5 7 9 12
(E) Type VI red plastic body, white lettering, Timken trucks, disc-operating couplers.  5 7 9 12
(F) Type VI pale red plastic body, white lettering, Timken trucks, disc-operating couplers.  5 7 9 12
(G) Type VI black unpainted plastic body, white lettering, Timken trucks, disc-operating couplers. Maher Collection.  5 7 9 12
(H) Type V black unpainted plastic body, white lettering, steps, Timken trucks, disc-operating couplers. Kotil Collection.  5 7 9 12

**6476-125 LEHIGH VALLEY** Listed in Service Manual, probably with "6476" on side and "6476-125" on original box; more information requested.  **NRS**

**6476-135 LEHIGH VALLEY** Light yellow, black lettering, "new" not present, "BUILT 1-48" and "LIONEL 6176" both present, Timken trucks, disc couplers. Came in box marked 6476-135. Ambrose and Halverson Collections.  3 5 10 15

**6536 M St L** 1958-59, 1963, 50 ton quad hopper, red-painted black plastic, white lettering, center brace, no covers, "BLT 6-58", no brakewheel. Ambrose comment.
(A) 1958, bar-end metal trucks, magnetic couplers. Powell Collection.  12 17 25 40
(B) 1959, Timken plastic trucks, two operating couplers. Powell Collection.  12 17 25 40
(C) 1963, Timken plastic trucks, one operating and one dummy coupler, no brakewheel, unpainted red plastic. Powell Collection.  12 17 25 40

**6636 ALASKA** 1959, 50 ton quad hopper, black plastic body with orange-yellow lettering, does not have Eskimo shown in catalogue, no covers, center brace, Timken trucks, disc-operating couplers.
(A) No brakewheel  17 25 35 60
(B) Brakewheel. Patton Collection.  17 25 35 60

6736 Detroit & Mackinac.

**6736 DETROIT & MACKINAC** 1960, 50 ton quad hopper.
(A) Red plastic, white lettering, no covers, center brace, Timken trucks, disc-operating couplers.  17 25 35 60
(B) Same as (A), but face of figure on Mackinac Mac logo obliterated by white blotch caused by die flaw; a common variation and thus not listed in Factory Error section, even though technically it is a factory error. Algozzini Collection.  20 30 40 70

**546446** See 6446-1 or 6446-25.

**NO LETTERING:** See 6076 (J-K).

3459          3459

3469          3559

3359

Lionel made three basic dump cars: the intermediate size car had two
different catalogue numbers, 3459 and 3469.

6076

6076[N]

6176

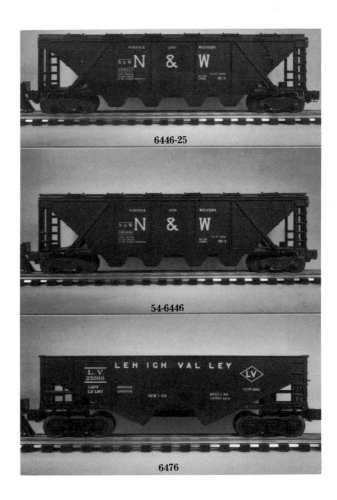

6446-25

54-6446

6476

# Chapter IX
# PASSENGER CARS

Lionel has always possessed a reputation for making fine models of passenger cars. In fact, it is possible that the "State Set" cars of the twenties have no peer for construction quality and detail. Lionel continued this tradition into the postwar era with some truly beautiful examples of passenger cars. To have all the room lights out so that the operator's crack Lionel "express" could come by, headlight on the locomotive and lights shining through the passenger car windows, was an inspirational sight in the postwar years.

2625 Irvington from the Madison Series.

Lionel continued the production of two noteworthy passenger cars from the prewar period in the early postwar years. One was the all-metal 027 short passenger car; this car was made in brown, green and blue versions with contrasting colors on the roofs and window inserts. The other was much more significant. For its first postwar 0 Gauge trains, Lionel kept producing the heavyweight "Madison" Pullman cars. These magnificent cars were made of heavy Bakelite plastic with lights in the interior and opening metal doors. Today, they are among the most prized of all Lionel's rolling stock, and it is doubtful that Lionel will ever revive them, for a specific and tragic reason. In 1952, the government was soliciting scrap metal for the Korean War effort. Lionel contributed a large number of obsolete dies for this effort; unfortunately, through a regrettable slip-up, the Madison passenger car dies were included in Lionel's contribution. (It must be noted that the Williams firm has made an excellent reproduction of the Madison heavyweight car.)

2400 Maplewood.

The first passenger car which was original to the postwar period emerged in 1948. This short 027 passenger car was first made in green with a gray roof and yellow window edges and letters. Two different Pullman coaches and an observation car were made for a 1948 set pulled by the 671 Turbine. These passenger cars soon became the mainstay of Lionel's passenger car fleet. They were made in yellow and gray for the highly-prized Anniversary Set in 1950, pulled by a special gray-nosed Union Pacific 2023 Alco AA diesel locomotive.

These cars were also made in silver with gray roofs and all-silver versions, and a Vista Dome car joined the observation and Pullman cars in 1954. Most were lettered for "LIONEL LINES", although a Santa Fe series with blue striping was also produced.

Lionel's best passenger car came as a response to an unexpected challenge in the marketplace. In 1951, the American Model Toy Company, virtually unknown for trains until that time, came out with a series of attractive extruded aluminum long passenger cars which were more attractive than anything Lionel had made up to that time. The cars had ridged aluminum sides, a smooth metal roof, metal trucks and metal couplers (though the couplers were dummies). When pulled by an F-7 GM Diesel locomotive produced by AMT, these cars made a magnificent train, and they sold extremely well.

Lionel was, of course, quick to respond to the challenge of AMT with all of its corporate resources. In the next year, 1952, Lionel was ready with a spectacular new train set which featured its own line of extruded aluminum passenger cars.

Canadian Pacific Skyline 500 Vista Dome.

The old reliable 2343 Santa Fe F-3 AA, with its superior motors and design, pulled cars which were a significant advance over even the AMT cars. Lionel subcontracted the aluminum extrusions for the bodies and inserted its own plastic ends, trucks and detailing. The cars were considerably longer and better detailed, with massive metal trucks and operating couplers. They included a baggage car, a Pullman, a Vista Dome and an observation car which were lettered after cars used by the crack Burlington Zephyr. The AMT cars were never a factor in the toy train marketplace after the Lionel cars emerged. Later versions of these cars were lettered for the Santa Fe, Canadian Pacific and Pennsylvania Railroads. The Canadian Pacific set is highly prized by collectors, and the Pennsylvania cars were headed by a GG-1 locomotive to form Lionel's magnificent Congressional Limited set.

1875 Western Atlantic from the Gerneral Set. Eddins Collection, Bennett photograph.

Lionel made one other type of passenger car during the postwar years. In 1959, Lionel included an entirely new car for its "General" old-time steam locomotive. This was an old-fashioned, open-vestibule passenger car appropriate to those used around the time of the Civil War. It featured lights in some versions, authentic period trucks and ornately scribed sides to resemble wood construction. These cars were made in both baggage and coach-styles, and one of the coaches in blue rather than the usual yellow is a scarce collector's item. One of the yellow coaches concealed a whistle, since the General locomotive's tender did not have room for a whistle casing.

The Lionel postwar passenger cars are very popular with collectors today, even the most common 027 varieties. It is sometimes difficult to acquire a set of three or four cars in the same general condition, although it is relatively easy to find many of the individual cars. The big aluminum passenger cars always command a good market, especially since the aluminum extrusions suffer dullness of finish and corrosion after a long period of improper storage. The Blair Manor and Craig Manor coaches and the Banff Park observation from the Canadian Pacific set are especially prized pieces. Any of these cars would make a handsome addition to an operating layout.

1866 Western & Atlantic.

| | Gd | VG | Exc | Mt |
|---|---|---|---|---|
| **1865 WESTERN & ATLANTIC** 1959-62, 1860-type coach, yellow with brown roof and lettering, unlighted, fixed couplers. | | | | |
| (A) As described above. | 13 | 17 | 25 | 35 |
| (B) Same as (A), except has interior illumination. Klaassen Collection. | | | | NRS |
| **1866 WESTERN & ATLANTIC** 1959-62, 1860-type mail-baggage. | | | | |
| (A) Yellow with brown roof and lettering. | 17 | 20 | 25 | 35 |
| (B) Unpainted lemon yellow, no lettering. | | | | NRS |
| (C) Same as (A), except has interior illumination. Klaassen Collection. | | | | NRS |
| **1875 WESTERN & ATLANTIC** 1959-62, coach, yellow with tuscan roof and lettering, offered separately, similar to 1865. | 40 | 60 | 90 | 120 |

**1875W WESTERN & ATLANTIC** 1959-62, coach with whistle; yellow with tuscan roof and lettering, lights, came with Five Star General Set, lighted, operating couplers.    40   60   80   100

**1876 WESTERN & ATLANTIC** 1959-62, mail-baggage, lights, came with Five Star General Set; similar to 1866.    25   40   60   90

**1885 WESTERN & ATLANTIC**, 1959, blue with white lettering, brown top, lighted, uncatalogued by Lionel. Offered by Sears as part of set 79 N 0966 with 1875 W coach car, 1887 flatcar with horses and 1882 engine. Weiss Collection.    75   150   250   350

2401 Hillside.

**2400 MAPLEWOOD** 1948-49, Pullman, "LIONEL LINES", green sides, yellow window outlines, white lettering, gray roof, lights.

| | 15 | 20 | 35 | 50 |
|---|---|---|---|---|
| **2401 HILLSIDE** 1948-49, observation, matches 2400. | 15 | 20 | 35 | 50 |
| **2402 CHATHAM** 1948-49, Pullman, matches 2400. | 15 | 20 | 35 | 50 |

2404 Santa Fe.

**2404 SANTA FE** 1964-65, Vista Dome, aluminum paint on plastic with blue lettering, not illuminated.    12   18   22   30

**2405 SANTA FE** 1964-65, Pullman, matches 2404.    12   18   22   30

**2406 SANTA FE** 1964-65, observation, matches 2404.    12   18   22   30

2408 Santa Fe.

**2408 SANTA FE** 1966, Vista Dome, aluminum paint on plastic, blue lettering, window inserts, lighting. Came with only one set, No. 11590, with 212 Santa Fe Alco AA, 2409 and 2410. Ambrose Collection.

   12   18   22   30

**2409 SANTA FE** 1966, Pullman, matches 2408. Ambrose Collection.

   12   18   22   30

**2410 SANTA FE** 1966, observation, matches 2408. Ambrose Collection.

   12   18   22   30

2412 Santa Fe.

**2412 SANTA FE** 1959-63, Vista Dome, silver with blue stripe through windows, lights.    12   20   30   40

**2414 SANTA FE** 1959-63, Pullman, matches 2412.    12   20   30   40

**2416 SANTA FE** 1959-63, observation, matches 2412.    12   20   30   40

**2421 MAPLEWOOD** 1950-53, Pullman, "LIONEL LINES", aluminum-painted sides.

(A) 1950-51, Gray roof, black stripe. Ambrose comment.

   15   20   30   40

(B) 1952-53, Aluminum-painted roof and no stripes. Ambrose comment.

   20   22   34   40

(C) Black roof with orange stripe. Lord Collection. Further sightings requested.    **NRS**

# SMALL PASSENGER SETS

Fourth set from the front is the 1950 U.P. Anniversary Set with yellow, red and gray paint scheme: 2023AA, 2481, 2482 and 2483. Fifth set from the front is the 1951 U.P. passenger set with 2422, 2421 and 2423.

2422 Chatham.

**2422 CHATHAM** 1950-53, Pullman, "LIONEL LINES".

| | | | | |
|---|---|---|---|---|
| (A) Matches 2421 (A). | 15 | 20 | 30 | 40 |
| (B) Matches 2421 (B). | 20 | 22 | 34 | 50 |

**2423 HILLSIDE** 1950-53, observation.

| | | | | |
|---|---|---|---|---|
| (A) Matches 2421 (A). | 15 | 20 | 30 | 40 |
| (B) Matches 2421 (B). | 20 | 22 | 34 | 50 |

**2429 LIVINGSTON** 1952-53, Pullman.

| | | | | |
|---|---|---|---|---|
| (A) A match for 2421(A), was not made. | | | **Not Manufactured** | |
| (B) Matches 2421 (B). | 20 | 22 | 34 | 50 |

NOTE: We have also had a report of the 2421, 2422, 2423 and 2429 made with silver-painted roofs with the black stripe. Arpino observation. Further confirmation of this variation is requested.

2430 Pullman in blue and silver.

**2430 PULLMAN** 1946-47, blue and silver sheet metal.

| | | | | |
|---|---|---|---|---|
| (A) Silver letters, staple-end trucks, early coil couplers. | 12 | 15 | 25 | 40 |
| (B) White letters, staple-end trucks, later coil couplers. | 12 | 15 | 25 | 40 |

**2431 OBSERVATION** 1946-47, blue and silver sheet metal, matches 2430.

| | | | | |
|---|---|---|---|---|
| (A) Silver letters, staple-end trucks, early coil couplers. | 12 | 15 | 25 | 40 |
| (B) White letters, staple-end trucks, later coil couplers. | 12 | 15 | 25 | 40 |

**2432 CLIFTON** 1954-58, Vista Dome, "LIONEL LINES", aluminum paint with red lettering, lights.  12  20  30  40

**2434 NEWARK** 1954-58, Pullman, matches 2432.  12  22  30  40

**2435 ELIZABETH** 1954-58, Pullman, matches 2432.  12  22  30  40

NOTE: There are two different passenger cars numbered 2436.

**2436 SUMMIT** 1954-58, observation, "LIONEL LINES", silver with red lettering, lights, matches 2432.  12  20  30  48

2436 Mooseheart with red lettering.

**2436 MOOSEHEART** 1957-58, observation, "LIONEL LINES", aluminum-painted plastic, red-lettered "Mooseheart", came as part of a conventional passenger set, 1608W in 1958, as well as part of an unusual set with a

Railway Express refrigeration car REX6572 in green with gold lettering and 2400-series passenger trucks and a 215 Burlington Alco A unit in red trim. Price for Mooseheart only.  25  40  60  80

2440(B) Pullman in green.

**2440 PULLMAN** 1946-47, sheet metal body, staple-end metal trucks, coil couplers. Ervin observation.

(A) 1946, Blue with silver roof and lettering, early coil trucks.  15  22  30  45

(B) 1947, Green with dark green roof, yellow window inserts, white lettering.  15  22  30  45

**2441 OBSERVATION** 1946-47, matches 2440.

| | | | | |
|---|---|---|---|---|
| (A) Matches 2440 (A). | 15 | 22 | 30 | 45 |
| (B) Matches 2440 (B). | 15 | 22 | 30 | 45 |

NOTE: Lionel used "2442" for two different passenger cars.

**2442 PULLMAN** 1946-47, brown sheet metal, gray windows, lights, staple-end metal trucks, coil couplers. Ervin observation.

| | | | | |
|---|---|---|---|---|
| (A) 1946, Silver letters. | 15 | 22 | 30 | 45 |
| (B) 1947, White letters. | 15 | 22 | 30 | 45 |

2445 Elizabeth with red window stripe.

**2442 CLIFTON** 1956, Vista Dome, "LIONEL LINES", aluminum paint, red window stripe, lights. Ambrose Collection.  15  25  40  60

**2443 OBSERVATION** 1946-47, matches 2442 PULLMAN.

| | | | | |
|---|---|---|---|---|
| (A) 1946, Silver letters. | 15 | 22 | 30 | 45 |
| (B) 1947, White letters. | 15 | 22 | 30 | 45 |

**2444 NEWARK** 1955-56, matches 2442 CLIFTON.  15  25  40  60

**2445 ELIZABETH** 1955-56, matches 2442 CLIFTON.  15  25  40  60

**2446 SUMMIT** 1955-56, matches 2442 CLIFTON.  15  25  40  60

2482 Westfield in yellow with red stripes.

**2481 PLAINFIELD** 1950, Pullman, "LIONEL LINES", yellow with red stripes, part of 1950 Anniversary Set with 2482, 2483 and 2023(A) diesel. Price for 2481 only.  40  60  90  125

**2482 WESTFIELD** 1950, Pullman, matches 2481.  40  60  90  125

# Chapter X
# TANK AND VAT CARS

2855    6415

2855    6425

6555    6315

## TANK AND VAT CARS
By Roland LaVoie

Tank cars of all descriptions were a common sight in the New York area, since the North Jersey chemical refineries were close at hand. Since it is a general rule that model train manufacturers imitate what they see around them, it would have been expected that Lionel would produce a large variety of these cars; in the postwar era, they did just that.

The first Lionel tank cars in the postwar era were exquisitely detailed large single-dome cars which had been designed in the late 1930s. These cars had separate metal caps on the tank ends and metal railings and ladders, as well as a die-cast frame. One early version had decals and lettering for the Shell Oil Company, but all the other versions were decaled and lettered with Sunoco markings.

Lionel also began the production of the most common of its postwar tank cars in 1946. This was the short double-dome Sunoco tank car. This car had a plastic body without metal trim which was mounted upon a stamped sheet metal base. The 2465 version of this car had Sunoco markings, but the later 6465 version had Gulf, Cities Service and Lionel Lines markings as well. Rare indeed was the postwar layout without at least one silver Sunoco two-dome tank car in a train or on a siding. This car, the New York Central gondola and the Lehigh Valley hopper car are easily the most common of all the Lionel postwar freight cars.

In the middle 1950s, three more types of tank cars joined Lionel's postwar fleet. In 1953, a plastic three-dome tank car on a long plastic frame was made. The domes had realistic plastic safety valve extensions, and later in the 1950s the Sunoco version was joined by a Gulf version. In 1952, a short single-dome tank car on a sheet metal frame was made. This car had a tank body without much detailing; it was made for inexpensive sets. The first of these tank cars was made for Scout sets, but a later version had a yellow Sunoco tank body and regular trucks and couplers. Finally, a single-dome chemical tank car was produced in 1956. This car was very nicely detailed, with metal handrails and ladders and a metal catwalk around the tank dome. It was first produced in burnt-orange Gulf markings; later, a Lionel Lines version in orange was produced.

These tank car designs provided Lionel operators with a tank car for every purpose during the postwar years. The Sunoco two-dome tank cars seem to be everywhere, and although they are inexpensive, they have enough variation to make a very interesting study all by themselves. For a detailed analysis of tank car construction and variation, see William Schilling's article on the Lionel tank cars in this chapter.

The Lionel vat cars are a whimsical, yet highly interesting design which has always attracted the attention of collectors. Only three versions of the car were produced, beginning in the late 1950s. One car featured vats labeled for Libby's Pineapple, another for Heinz and the most common one simply for "pickles". There are many variations and factory errors for the Pickle Car, some of dubious origin. This car was made as a low-slung girder car with a roof on a metal frame. Inside the girderwork, four round vats were arranged beneath simulated hatches in the roof. We would be interested in learning whether Lionel modeled this car from a prototype or from its sometimes rich (if not realistic) corporate imagination.

## TANK CARS
### By William Schilling

Lionel's tank car line had three basic types by 1948. An inexpensive single-dome car, an intermediate two-dome car and a premium price single-dome car. The single-dome, inexpensive car, the 1005, was made without applied trim and utilized inexpensive Scout couplers and trucks. The Scout couplers were a simple design and had fewer parts than did the staple-end coil couplers found on the more expensive cars. Metal tabs formed as part of the frame fastened the body to the frame. The inexpensive cars' frames were usually finished by chemical blackening rather than enamel painting. The body consisted of a tank with an integrally cast dome with the separate tank ends cemented in place.

The second type, the 2465, was a two-dome car with railings on each side, and considerably more expensive trucks. The trucks had wound coil couplers and consisted of many small pieces which were probably tediously hand-assembled. The trucks probably cost as much to make as the rest of the car. The tank was fastened by screws to the sheet metal frame. The two-dome car had a tank with the domes and ends cemented in place. If you examine a tank body interior, you will see that the dome cavities are closed off by the tank shell itself. We assume that the tank shell was cast with the dome cavities closed off and walls protruding upward to make the cavities. A cap was then glued in place.

The most expensive car in 1948 was the single-dome 2555 car with a metal tank, plastic dome, separate metal ends and a die-cast frame. A single screw fastened the tank to the frame. The car was decorated with a handrail along each side, a ladder on each side, a brakewheel and a diamond warning placard. The car had an air tank on the bottom.

The 1005 Sunoco was sold as part of the Scout set, Lionel's least expensive set in the late 1940s.

The first series of inexpensive tank cars, the 1005 Scout cars, was introduced in 1948 and offered until 1950. In 1952, Lionel introduced the 6035. This car continued the Scout frame, Scout truck side frames and single-dome simple tank without trim. The lettering and diamond design were silk-screened. The lettering was blue and the diamond was yellow with red arrow and blue "SUNOCO" extending beyond the diamond.

The next inexpensive single-dome car was the 6015 Sunoco catalogued from 1954 through 1955. The car was shown in the 1954 catalogue with the plastic side frame trucks that were used with the 6035. The illustrated car also had a black ladder extended to the frame. We assume that Lionel painted a 6035 in yellow for the catalogue illustration and that the production models came with the bar-end trucks. We can not explain the ladder shown in the catalogue.

The 6015 continued the double indented frame of the 6035 which is 7-3/4 inches (19.7 cm.) long. All four observed

examples were painted with black enamel. All four cars had the small round-head rivet. All have the large offset hole which is 13/32 inches (10 mm.) from one side and 7/32 inches (5 mm.) from the other.

In 1956 Lionel apparently dropped the SUNOCO logos from most if not all of its tank cars and utilized the GULF logo in its place. We assume that Lionel had a licensing agreement with Sunoco for Lionel use of the Sunoco trademark. We wonder why this relationship ended. Consequently Lionel produced an inexpensive GULF single-dome tank car in black and numbered this car as 6025. This car was offered again in 1957 and 1958. We hope to be able to identify the year by year differences in this car.

A closeup view of the Scout truck, Schilling collection. Bartelt photograph.

**NOTE:** The listings and variation definitions in this chapter have been substantially changed from the 1983 edition of this book.

**Gd VG Exc Mt**

**1005 SUNOCO** 1948-50, single-dome, gray unpainted plastic tank, tank fastened to frame by metal tabs on frame bent over tank, from Scout set with Scout couplers. We have three different versions of this car. We would appreciate reader assistance in dating these. We may be able to date these from sets with known dates or other cars with differences in frame finish.
(A) Chemically-blackened frame with steps (chemically-blackened frame will not produce paint chips when scraped). Schilling Collection.

|  | 1 | 2 | 3 | 6 |

(B) Same as (A), but without steps. Schilling Collection.

|  | 1 | 2 | 3 | 6 |

(C) Black enamel-painted frame with steps (enameled frame will produce paint chips when scraped). Schilling Collection.

|  | 1 | 2 | 3 | 6 |

2465(A) Sunoco was illustrated, as shown above, in the 1946 Lionel catalogue on pages 2 and 12. Note the unusual decal placement. It is a scarce car. Struhltrager Collection.

The intermediate series of tank cars began with the two-dome 2465 Sunoco tank cars. We have identifed seven major steps in the development of the 2465 during the three years it was catalogued. We can not currently date these steps. We assume that the cars had the following chronological order. However, we cannot date them as to year at this time.

**2465 SUNOCO** 1946-48, two domes, silver-painted plastic tank with black or blue decal lettering or blue rubber-stamped lettering. The car had either one of two different diamond decals or silk-screened diamond, staple-end metal trucks, coil couplers, steps, two wire handrails and "2465" rubber-stamped in silver on the underside of the frame. All known 2465 cars have frames with similar hole patterns and four steps. There are two versions of the frame, however. One has a plain side and the other has an indent centered on each side. The indents are 15/16" long (24 mm.)

The 2465 tank cars had a single large plastic tank casting (usually clear plastic) to which was added two end pieces and two domes. The four additional pieces were glued in place. The tank in turn was fastened to the metal frame by two screws. The type of screws varied over the years. Either the car or the frame was put in a jig and the other piece fastened to it. In comparison, the 1005 Scout tank included lineup plugs in the frame for the tank. Screw fasteners were more expensive than folded metal tabs.

**2465(A)** Type I trucks with early coil couplers, no lettering and a "GAS SUNOCO OILS" decal with all three words within the diamond. The car is illustrated in the 20-page version of the 1946 catalogue on pages 2 and 12. This car was first reported by David Dunn and confirmed by Phillip Stuhltrager, who graciously supplied the photograph.  **10    20    40    80**

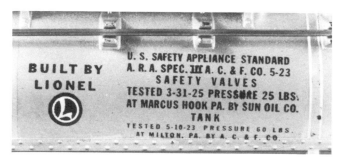

The 2465(B) has eight lines of technical information. Schilling Collection. Bartelt photograph.

**2465(B)** Type II trucks with early coil couplers with thin axles and dish wheels, black decal lettering; "SUNOCO" is within the diamond. There are eight lines of technical information on the right side of the car: "U.S. SAFETY APPLIANCE STANDARD/A.R.A SPEC. III A. C. & F. CO. 5-23/SAFETY VALVES/TESTED 3-31-25 PRESSURE 25 LBS./AT MARCUS HOOK PA. BY SUN OIL CO./TANK/TESTED 5-10-23 PRESSURE 60 LBS./AT MILTON, PA BY A.C. & F.CO." The last two lines are in much smaller type.  **4    6    10    16**

The 2465(B) has "SUNOCO" within the diamond.

**2465(C)** Type III trucks with late coil couplers and the same decal lettering and diamond as in the earliest cars.  **4    6    10    16**

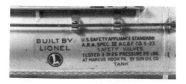

THe 2465(D) has only six lines of technical information. Schilling Collection. Bartelt photograph.

**2465(D)** Type III trucks with late coil couplers and blue decal lettering. "SUNOCO" extends beyond the diamond. The technical data on the right side was changed by eliminating the last two lines of data which were in much smaller type.  **4    6    10    16**

**2465(E)** Same as (D), but with an indent on the side of the frame.  **NRS**

2465(D) and later cars have "SUNOCO" extending beyond the diamond. Schilling Collection.

**2465(F)** Type III trucks with late coil couplers with silk-screened lettering and diamond. "SUNOCO" extends beyond the diamond.

**4    6    10    16**

2465(G) frame with indent on the side.

**2465(G)** Same as the 2465(F), but has an indent on the frame sides.  **4    6    10    16**

In addition to the seven major varieties that we have observed, there is also variation in the screws that fasten the tank to the frame. We would expect that with enough data we can date the changes in screw fasteners.

We do not know the type of screw that came with the 2465(A).

2465(B) came with a white slotted-round-head screw.

2465(C) came with either white slotted-round-head screws or black slotted-round-head screws.

2465(D) came with white pan-head-slotted screws or black round-head-slotted screws.

2465(E) same as 2465(D) but with indent on the side.

2465(F) came with black Phillips screws.

2465(G) came with black round-head-slotted screws.

2555 Sunoco, Bennett photograph.

**2555 SUNOCO** 1946-48, single-dome, silver tank, yellow diamond, staple-end metal trucks, coil couplers, one brakewheel, screws fasten frame and tank.

(A) Staple-end trucks, early coil couplers, thick axles, black decal lettering: "GAS/SUNOCO/OILS" all within diamond, technical data decal on left has rectangular corners, "S.U.N.X. 2555/CAP'Y-100,00 LBS. LT.WT 42,000/LIONEL LINES", Schilling Collection.  **10    15    26    35**

(B) Same as (A), but thin axles. Schilling Collection.     **10  15  26  35**
(C) Staple-end trucks, late coil couplers, rubber-stamped on frame "2555", otherwise same as (A). Schilling Collection.     **10  15  26  35**
(D) Staple-end trucks, late coil couplers, black decal lettering: "SUNOCO" extends beyond diamond, technical data decal on left has rounded corners. (6555(C) also has rounded decal corners.) Lettering on right matches right lettering on (A). Schilling Collection.     **10  15  26  35**
(E) Staple-end trucks, late coil couplers, black decal lettering: "GAS/ SUNOCO/OILS" all within diamond, does not have bold lettering found on right of earlier models, only technical data with L logo on right. Data reads: "U.S. SAFETY APPLIANCE STANDARD / A.R.A. SPEC. III A. C. & F. CO.5-23 / SAFETY VALVES / TESTED 3-31-25 PRESSURE 25 LBS. / AT MARCUS HOOK PA. BY SUN OIL CO. / TANK". Silver rubber-stamped "2555" on underside of frame. Schilling Collection.     **10  15  26  35**
(F) Staple-end trucks, magnetic couplers, with flared rivet and no hole on activator plate, diamond markers at each end, otherwise same as (E). Car is not marked 2555 at any place on the car. At least one sample came in a box marked "6555" obliterating original "2555" box marking, came with Set 2151 from 1949, Schilling and Donangelo Collections.   **10  15  26  35**

2755 Sunoco, Bennett photograph.

**2755 S.U.N.X.** 1945, single-dome, silver tank, black decal lettering, "GAS SUNOCO OILS" all within diamond, staple-end metal trucks, early coil couplers without bottom plate, black brakewheel, screws fasten frame and tank, four steps on frame. This was the premium Lionel tank car.
**NOTE:** 2755 was made before World War II and is found with a gray tank and box couplers.
(A) Whirly wheels.     **20  30  60  85**
(B) Dish wheels, thick axles. Kotil Collection.     **20  30  60  85**
(C) Same as (B), but frame 955-6, later coil couplers with bottom plate. Budniak Collection.     **20  30  60  85**

**2855 S.U.N.X.** 1946, single-dome, black tank, white decal lettering, staple-end metal trucks, coil couplers, black brakewheel, four steps, screws fasten tank and frame.
(A) "GAS SUNOCO OILS" within diamond, see color illustration.     **40  60  80  150**
(B) "GAS OILS" omitted from diamond, "SUNOCO" goes beyond diamond.     **40  60  80  150**
(C) Same as (B), but gray tank, see color illustration.   **45  70  90  165**

The 2955 was a prewar car apparently made in very small quantities after World War II with postwar trucks.

**2955 S.U.N.X.** 1940-42, 1946, single-dome, black die-cast tank and frame.
(A) 1940-42, stamped-steel tin plate trucks, box coupler.     **110  175  300  460**

(B) Circa 1946, staple-end metal trucks, coil couplers.   **110  175  275  375**
(C) Same as (B), but "SHELL".     **75  125  175  275**

6015 Lionel Lines, Bennett photograph.

**6015 SUNOCO** 1954-55, single-dome, 8" long, "LIONEL LINES", bar-end metal trucks, body fastened to frame by tabs, frame has two indentations on each side.
(A) Yellow-painted gray plastic, magnetic couplers with small round-head rivet and offset hole. Schilling and Kotil Collections.   **2  4  6  8**
(B) Dark yellow tank, black lettering, magnetic tab couplers. Schilling Collection.     **2  4  6  8**
(C) Yellow unpainted plastic tank, black lettering, magnetic tab couplers. Schilling and Kotil Collections.     **2  4  6  8**

6025(E) Gulf, Bennett photograph.

**6025 GULF** 1956-57, single-dome, 8" long, "LIONEL LINES", body fastened to black frame with tabs.
(A) Black shiny tank, white lettering, orange Gulf emblem, bar-end metal trucks with off-center holes in bottom plate, magnetic tab couplers.     **2  5  7  10**
(B) Gray tank, blue lettering, bar-end metal trucks with off-center holes in bottom plate, magnetic tab couplers.   **2  4  7  10**
(C) Gray tank, blue lettering, AAR trucks with Timken bearings, disc couplers, orange Gulf emblem, Schilling Collection.
(D) 1957, orange tank, thin blue lettering, AAR trucks with Timken bearings, disc couplers, Schilling Collection.   **2  4  6  8**
(E) Same as (C) and (D), but thick lettering, Schilling Collection.     **2  4  6  8**

**6035 SUNOCO** 1952-53, single-dome, unpainted gray plastic dome, continuation of Scout 1005 with Scout truck side frames but magnetic couplers, very dark blue silk-screened lettering and yellow, dark blue and red silk-screened diamond. The body was fastened to the frame with metal tabs which are part of the frame. The frame has two indents each, 7/32 inches(5 mm.) wide on each side, and has no steps. All observed samples had chemically-blackened frames.

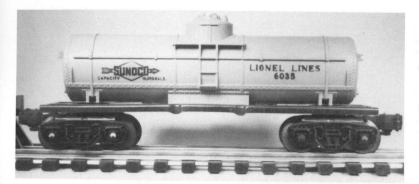

6035 Sunoco, Bennett photograph.

Two different versions of the plastic Scout side frame truck were used for the 6035 tank. The centered-hole version is on the left, the offset on the right. Schilling Collection.

Two different kinds of plastic side frame trucks were used. Both trucks have the small round-head rivet as shown above. One truck however has the large hole centered on the truck bottom plate while the other has the hole 3/8 inches (10 mm.) from one side and 3/16 inches (5 mm.) from the other.

| | | | | |
|---|---|---|---|---|
| (A) Centered hole. Schilling Collection. | 1 | 2 | 3 | 4 |
| (B) Off-center hole. Schilling Collection. | 1 | 2 | 3 | 4 |

6045 Cities Service, Bennett photograph.

**NOTE:** There are two different 6045 tanks.

**6045 CITIES SERVICE** 1960, not catalogued, two domes, green tank, white lettering "CSOX 6045", body fastened to gunmetal frame with tabs. We would like to learn the set(s) that the 6045 CITIES SERVICE came with.

| | | | | |
|---|---|---|---|---|
| (A) Arch bar trucks, fixed couplers. Eddins Collection. | 6 | 9 | 12 | 20 |
| (B) AAR trucks with Timken bearings, one fixed and one disc coupler, Schilling Collection. | 6 | 9 | 12 | 20 |

**6045 LIONEL LINES** 1958, 1963, two domes, "L" in circle, body fastened to frame with tabs. Plastic knobs line up casting and frame.

| | | | | |
|---|---|---|---|---|
| (A) 1958, light gray tank, blue lettering, AAR trucks with Timken bearings, disc couplers, "BLT 1-58". | 2 | 4 | 6 | 8 |
| (B) Same as (A), but fixed couplers, Schilling Collection. | 2 | 4 | 6 | 8 |
| (C) Same as (A), but arch bar trucks, fixed couplers. Strong Collection. | 2 | 4 | 6 | 8 |

6045 Lionel Lines, Bennett photograph.

| | | | | |
|---|---|---|---|---|
| (D) 1963, orange tank, black lettering, AAR trucks with Timken bearings, disc couplers, no built date. | 2 | 5 | 7 | 10 |
| (E) Similar to (D), but black tank ends, "BLT BY LIONEL" in two lines, fixed couplers, Schilling Collection. | 2 | 5 | 7 | 10 |

**NOTE:** There are three different 6315 tanks.

**6315 GULF** 1956-59, chemical single-dome, metal catwalk around dome; screws fasten tank and frame, "BLT 1-56"; see color illustration.

| | | | | |
|---|---|---|---|---|
| (A) Burnt-orange and black tank, bar-end metal trucks, magnetic tab couplers. | 15 | 22 | 30 | 40 |
| (B) Same as (A), but redder-orange. | 15 | 22 | 30 | 40 |
| (C) All orange tank, AAR trucks with Timken bearings, disc couplers. | 8 | 12 | 15 | 25 |
| (D) Same as (C), but no built date. | 8 | 12 | 15 | 25 |
| (E) Same as (C), but no tabs on couplers. Budniak Collection. | 8 | 12 | 15 | 25 |

6315 Lionel Lines, Bennett photograph.

**6315 LIONEL LINES** 1963-66, chemical single-dome, metal catwalk around dome, ladder, screws fasten tank and frame, orange tank, black lettering, AAR trucks with Timken bearings, disc couplers.   7  12  15  25

6315 - 1972 TCA, Bennett photograph.

**6315-1972 TCA 18th NATIONAL CONVENTION** 1972, chemical single-dome, special for TCA, limited run of 2,000, bar-end metal trucks, magnetic tab couplers; manufactured by Fundimensions, but listed here because of number.   —  —  50  80

**6415 SUNOCO** 1953-55, three domes, silver tank, body fastened to black frame with one screw; black plastic frame with steps and four warning panels, white brakewheel, plastic air tank, wire railing around tank, see color illustration. This was the premium tank car in the Lionel line for 1953-55.

(A) Black lettering "6600 GALS", "6415" to right of dome, bar-end metal trucks, magnetic tab couplers, silver brakewheel, "L" in circle with extra line, Schilling Collection.     5   7   10   15

(B) Same as (A), but no tabs, 3-1/2" long metal strip to center, off center hole on truck pickup plate, Schilling Collection    5   7   10   15

(C) Same as (A), but "6415" not on tank.    5   7   10   15

(D) Same as (A), but "6415" not on tank, no tabs, Schilling Collection.
    5   7   10   15

(E) Same as (A), but blue lettering, AAR trucks with Timken bearings, disc couplers, black brakewheel. Schilling Collection.    6   8   12   20

(F) Black lettering, "8000 GALS", "6415" to right of dome, bar-end metal trucks, magnetic tab couplers, silver brakewheel. "L" in circle, no extra line. Kotil Collection.    5   7   10   15

(G) Same as (F), but no tabs, Schilling Collection.    5   7   10   15

(H) Same as (F), but "TANK", instead of "6415". Schreiner Collection.
    5   7   10   15

(I) Same as (H), but no tabs, Schilling Collection.    5   7   10   15

(J) Same as (F) but no brakewheel, one-piece plastic frame without metal strip from trucks, arch bar trucks, disc couplers with tabs, numbered "6415-T-10A" on the bottom of the frame, Schilling Collection.    **NRS**

(K) Same as (E), but blue lettering, "TANK" appears on right, one silver brakewheel. I. D. Smith Collection.    5   7   10   15

**6425 GULF** 1956-58, three domes, silver tank, orange GULF circle, blue lettering, "BLT 2-56", black frame, bar-end metal trucks, magnetic tab couplers; see color illustration. In 1956 Gulf replaced Sunoco in the Lionel tank car fleet. Consequently the three-dome car number was changed from 6415 to 6425.    7   11   18   30

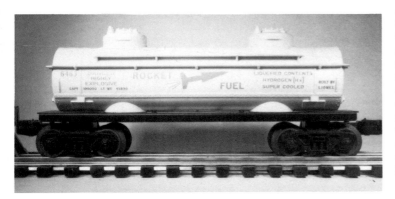

6463 Rocket Fuel, Bennett photograph.

**6463 ROCKET FUEL** 1962-63, two domes, body fastened to black frame with tabs, AAR trucks with Timken bearings, disc couplers.

(A) Blue tank, white lettering. Eddins Collection. We would like to learn if other blue tanks exist.    **NRS**

(B) White tank, red lettering.    6   8   15   25

**NOTE:** There are four different road names found on 6465s: SUNOCO, LIONEL LINES, CITIES SERVICE and GULF. The catalogues show the following progression of manufacture: 1948-55: "SUNOCO"; 1956: no name; 1957: not catalogued; 1958-59: "LIONEL LINES"; 1960-62: "CITIES SERVICE"; 1963: "LIONEL LINES" listed as 6465-150, no color shown in catalogue; 1964: "LIONEL LINES" listed as 6465-150, no color shown in catalogue; 1965: "LIONEL LINES" listed as 6465; 1966: "LIONEL LINES" in orange with black ends; 1968-69: uncatalogued. Ambrose comment.

**6465 SUNOCO** 1948-56, two domes, silver-painted plastic tanks with blue or black silk-screened or rubber-stamped lettering. Staple-end or bar-end trucks, coil couplers or magnetic couplers, several different frames, different colors of plastic. The 1956 production is of special interest since the catalogue illustrations show the car without the "SUNOCO" lettering. We would like to learn what 1956 production actually looked like.

6465 Sunoco tank without steps.

The long run of the 6465 tank car makes it an ideal candidate for the study of year to year mechanical changes in the Lionel line. As with the gondolas analyzed by Richard Vagner, we find that changes in trucks, truck mounting and couplers are very important to our analysis.

When I initially studied tank cars, I found a 6465 tank car with the staple-end trucks with late coil couplers using the same frame as the 2465. Since it was believed that the change from the 2400 series freight cars to the 6400 series freight cars reflected the change in couplers and trucks, I assumed either an isolated use of leftover parts by the factory or a change in frames by a later owner. However, being very curious, I kept looking for this variation and have to my delight found five more identical pieces. We therefore have revised our thinking about the number system and the truck coupler usuage. However, the variation is useful in that it clearly dates the earliest 6465 lettering schemes and the latest 2465 lettering schemes. I expect that similar situations exist in other early 6400 series freight cars. We look forward to hearing from other collectors.

All observed 6465 tank cars have a stud riveted to the truck and are fastened to the frame by a horseshoe clip. The earlier 6465 tank cars with staple-end trucks and magnetic couplers have the activator flap fastened by a flared rivet. We believe that the rounded rivet was first used on 1951 production and consequently would not be found with a 6465 Sunoco tank car with staple-end trucks. The identification of the year change from flared to round rivet was the result of research by Richard Vagner. In our data collection we discovered a 6465 tank car with Type II frame, staple-end trucks and magnetic couplers. The activator flaps were fastened by a round-head rivet which we believed was not used until 1951 and which is inconsistent with the other characteristics. Consequently we took the car apart and found evidence that the trucks had been changed. There were scratches where the horseshoe rivets had been removed and reinstalled.

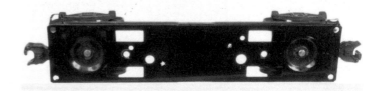

Type I frame, Schilling Collection. Greenberg photograph.

**FRAME TYPES**

1. 2465 type, circa 1948, four steps with a 5/32" hole by each step, indent 15/16" long centered on the side, four rectangular holes each 1" x 5/16", two larger round holes, one is 9/32" in diameter, the other is 7/32" in diameter, two small round holes each 1/8" in diameter and two round stampings, punched from the top 1/8" in diameter with sharp flange protruding from the bottom and usually filled with paint. There are two holes each 5/32" in diameter for mounting the tank. The truck depressions are 1-1/8" in diameter measured at the widest point. Came with staple-end trucks with late coil couplers.

2. Circa 1949, four steps with a 5/32" hole by each step, indent 15/16" long centered on each side, four rectangular openings each 1" x 5/16", one hole

Type 2 frame, Schilling Collection, Greenberg photograph.

1/16" from the side which is 3/16" in diameter, one hole centered equal distance from each side which is 1/16" in diameter. There is an elongated hole 1/4" x 9/32" which is 1/16" from the side. At the same end of the frame there is a slot which is 3/8" long and 1/16" wide. There are two mounting holes 5/32" in diameter. The staple-end trucks do not have a hole in the activator flap which indicates that the truck was made in 1949.

Type 3 frame, Schilling Collection, Greenberg photograph.

3. Circa 1950, same as Type 2, but with four additional holes. One large hole, 3/8" diameter in the center, three smaller holes, one 1/4" from the frame side and 1/16" diameter, one 1/8" from the other side of the frame and 1/16" diameter, one 1/4" from the indentation and 3/32" in diameter. The staple end trucks had a hole in the activator flap which indicates that the trucks were made in 1950 or later. We would like to learn the purpose of the large hole and the three small holes. These were likely made for another piece of rolling stock.

4. Same as Type 3, but without steps. The steps were apparently cut off at the factory since the frame paint covers the cut off area. In the 1950 Lionel Advance Catalogue on page 5 the 6465 is shown without steps as part of set 1463W. It is also shown without steps on page 6.

Type 5 frame, Schilling Collection, Greenberg photograph.

5. No steps with a 5/32" hole in each corner, no side indent but cutout 1-3/16" long by 1/16" high centered on the side, (same as one version of 3472 milk car, four rectangular openings each 1" x 5/16", one hole 1/16" from the side which is 3/16" in diameter, one hole centered equal distance from each side which is 1/8" in diameter. There is an elongated hole 1/4' x 9/32' which is 1/16" from the side. At the same end of the frame there is a slot which is 3/8" long and 1/16" wide. There are two mounting holes 5/32" in diameter. There are four additional holes as on Types 3 and 4: one large hole, 3/8" diameter in the center, three smaller holes, one 1/4" from the frame and 1/16" diameter, 1/8" from the other side of the frame and 1/16" diameter, 1/4" from the indentation and 1/8" in diameter. We should be able to learn the purpose of the large hole and the three small holes. These were likely made for another piece of rolling stock. We have found Type 5 frames most frequently with staple-end trucks. We have found one sample with bar-end trucks. We assume that the bar-end truck version is original but would appreciate reader confirmation.

Probably in 1951, Lionel redesigned the tank car frame. The new frame differed in several significant ways from the earlier models. First the steps permanently disappeared. Lionel at the same time ended the use of steps on

its gondolas. Second, the dish for fastening the trucks was made deeper and smaller in diameter. The deeper dish permitted the trucks to swivel 360 degrees. This in turn permitted the use of a box which was 8-1/8" long rather than 10" as previously used. A smaller box meant savings not only on packaging each car but on smaller set boxes and less warehouse space. Joe Kotil points out that the material savings were significant with at least 11/16" inches in width. With the steps gone, Lionel could have used coil stock of the finished width. Another advantage was the reduction of die maintenance costs due to the steps. However we do not know that our reasoning was Lionel's reasoning! At the same time that the new frame was introduced, Lionel also introduced its new bar-end trucks. There may also be a relationship between the new frame and the new trucks.

The following frames except for Type 6 all came with bar-end trucks with magnetic couplers and round rivets on the activator flap. Consequently these were made from 1951 through 1956. At the present time we do not have enough information for a more detailed chronology. The frame order that follows is based on the assumption that the frame when first made had very few holes and that more holes were added as production continued and new uses for the frames were devised.

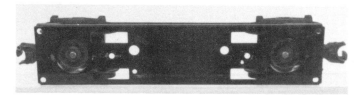

Type 6 frame, Schilling Collection. Greenberg photograph.

6. Type 6 frame, circa 1951, no steps with a 5/32" hole in each corner, no indent or cutout on the side, rectangular openings each 1" x 5/16", one 7/32" hole adjacent to rectangular hole and one 9/32" diameter hole adjacent to rectangular hole, two 3/32" diameter holes with one adjacent to a mounting hole and the other adjacent to a rectangular hole, two mounting holes each 5/32" in diameter. The frame was painted shiny black or satin black.

Type 7 frame, Schilling Collection. Greenberg photograph.

7. Type 7 frame, circa 1951, no steps with a 5/32' hole in each corner, no indent or cutout on the side, rectangular holes each 1' x 5/16", one large hole, 3/8" in diameter in the center of the frame and two mounting holes each 5/32" in diameter. The frame was painted shiny black, satin black or oxidized black.

Type 8 frame, Schilling Collection.

8. Type 8 frame, same as Type 7, but with three very small additional holes: two holes are 1/16" in diameter and the third hole is slightly larger. The frame was painted shiny black or glossy black. We would like to learn what use, if any, Lionel made of these small holes.

**NOTE:** Joe Kotil believes that Frame 8 preceeded Frame 7, reader comments invited.

9. Type 9 frame, six rectangular openings, oval openings for tank tabs, introduced in 1958.

## 6465 PRODUCTION LISTING

(A) Type 1 frame, black round-head-slotted screws, silver rubber-stamped "6465" on the underside of the frame, aluminum-painted clear plastic, staple-end trucks mounted by a steel stud with a ring for a horseshoe clip. The stud is fastened to the truck by a rounded flared end which sometimes splits, later coil couplers, silk-screened lettering and logo, "SUNOCO" extends beyond diamond, "CAPACITY 8000 GALS." On the right "U.S. SAFETY APPLIANCE STANDARD/A.R.A. SPEC. III A.C & F. CO. 5-23/SAFETY VALVES/TESTED 3/31/25 PRESSURE 25 LBS./AT MARCUS HOOK PA. BY SUN OIL CO./TANK." Schilling Collection.

2   4   6   10

**NOTE:** The following cars follow the (A) entry, but we do not have enough information to date these. Hopefully we will learn more about these tanks cars and be able to chronologically organize them. Reader reports on original sets containing these cars will help us date them.

(B) Type 2 frame, silver or black round-head-slotted screws, same lettering on frame and tank as (A), staple-end trucks mounted by a brass stud with a ring for a horseshoe clip. The stud is fastened to the the truck by a flared star end. This change in stud material and flaring design from (A) probably was due to breakage problems with the steel stud. Brass has considerably more flexibility. Magnetic couplers.

2   4   6   10

(C) Type 3 frame with steps, silver or black round-head slotted screws, same lettering on frame and tank as (A), staple-end trucks mounted by a brass stud with a ring for a horseshoe clip. The stud is fastened to the truck by a flared star end. The dome caps are made from red, white, blue or yellow plastic which is painted to match the tank. The domes on most other tank varieties are consistently clear plastic. The tanks on this variation are found with clear plastic painted silver and multicolored plastic painted silver. Schilling Collection.

2   4   6   10

(D) Type 4 frame, same as Type 3 but without steps. In the 1950 Lionel Advance Catalogue on page 5 the 6465 is shown without steps as part of set 1463W. It is also shown without steps on page 6. Black round-head slotted screws, same lettering on frame and tank as (A), staple-end trucks mounted by a brass stud with a ring for a horseshoe clip. The stud is fastened to the truck by a flared star end. The activator flap as fastened by a flared rivet. There is a hole in the activator flap as well as a hole in the truck bottom plate. The dome caps are made from clear plastic which is painted to match the tank. The tanks on this variation are found with clear plastic painted silver and multicolored plastic painted silver. Schilling Collection.

2   4   6   10

(E) Same as (D), but with dark gray tank. When the tank car is held to the light, many pin holes are evident. One of the samples had a paint run. Schilling Collection.

2   4   6   10

(F) Type 5 frame, black round-head-slotted screws, same lettering on frame tank as (A), staple-end trucks mounted by a brass stud with a ring for a horseshoe clip. The stud is fastened to the truck by a flared star end. The activator flap was fastened by a flared rivet. There is a hole in the activator flap as well as a hole in the truck bottom plate. The dome caps are made from clear plastic which is painted to match the tank. The tanks on this variation are found with clear plastic painted silver. Schilling Collection.

2   4   6   10

(G) Same as (F), but Type 6 frame. Schilling Collection.

2   4   6   10

(H) Type 7 frame, four different kinds of screws: black round-head slotted, silver round head-slotted, black round-head Phillips, silver round-head Phillips. Same lettering as (A). Bar-end trucks mounted by a brass stud with a ring for a horseshoe clip. The stud was fastened to the truck by a flared star end. The activator flap was fastened by a round-head rivet and had a hole in it. There is also a hole in the truck bottom plate. Schilling Collection.

2   4   6   10

(I) Same as (H), but with last line of data on right side of tank changed to "6465" from "TANK". Lionel omitted the silver rubber-stamped "6465" which had previously been stamped on the underside of each car. We presume that this was a cost reduction measure. We do not know the date of this change. However, readers who have original sets with this tank car may be able to assist us. We may be able to precisely date their sets and

consequently date the change from TANK to 6465 lettering on the side. Schilling Collection.

2   4   6   10

(J) Same as (I), but with tab magnetic couplers. Schilling Collection. We would appreciate reader reports on original sets containing this variation.

2   4   6   10

(K) Same as (H), but Type 8 frame. Schilling Collection.  2  4  6  10

1956 marked the end of Sunoco tank cars in the Lionel line. Thereafter Lionel produced Gulf, Cities Service, Rocket Fuel and Lionel Lines. We wonder why this change occurred.

In 1958 Lionel introduced a new model of the two-dome tank car. The car was redesigned to substantially reduce manufacturing and assembly costs. First the applied hand railing was replaced by a cast-in plastic railing. Second, the tank was mounted by two tabs to the newly designed Type 9 frame. This reduced the need to fasten two screws. The redesigned frame had substantially more visible openings which was an improvement.

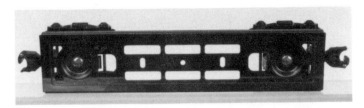

Note the new Type 9 frame with its six rectangular openings. However only one of the two original tabs remain. The other tab broke in the disassembly of the car. We do not recommend disassembling the car and its frame. Schilling Collection.

The new Type 9 frame had six rectangular openings, 1/4" x 1" with round corners, two tab hole openings about 1/2" x 1/2" and triangular openings at each corner. To securely fasten the tank to the frame, tabs from the tank fitted into new aligning slots in the frame. This method had been used earlier with the inexpensive Scout tank car. Lionel also provided a 1/8" diameter screw hole in the frame center which was not used for this car. The car continued the cemented ends and domes of the previous models but with revamping of the dies for the end pieces. The tank proper was substantially redesigned with underside openings centered under each dome.

Plastic trucks which are properly known as AAR trucks with Timken bearings replaced the bar-end die-cast trucks of the earlier tank cars. The magnetic couplers were replaced by the much simplier disc coupler. The trucks were fastened by rivets rather than horseshoe clips and are nearly impossible to remove.

The changes reflected sophisticated engineering efforts and produced a very attractive car for substantially lower cost.

**6465 GULF** 1958, two domes, black plastic tank, dark gun-metal frame, plastic simulated handrails around the tank, tank fastened to frame by two tabs, no frame indentation, Type 9 frame with six rectangular slots, white lettering: "BLT 1-58/BY LIONEL" centered on the side and "LIONEL LINES/6465" to the right. Orange, blue and white "GULF" logo on the left, no rubber-stamping on bottom, AAR trucks with Timken bearings, disc couplers.

(A) Black painted plastic tank, Foss and Schilling Collections.

23   35   50   100

(B) Unpainted black plastic tank, Mueller and Schilling Collections.

23   35   50   100

(6465-60) GULF 1958, two domes, gray-painted black plastic tank, dark gun-metal frame, plastic simulated handrails around the tank, tank fastened to frame by two tabs, no frame indentation, frame with six rectangular slots, blue lettering: "BLT 1-58/BY LIONEL" centered on the side and "LIONEL LINES/6465" to the right. Orange, blue and white "GULF" logo on the left, no rubber-stamping on bottom, AAR trucks with Timken bearings, disc couplers, "6465-60" appears on box ends while "6465" appears on car. Schilling and Rohlfing Collections.

6   9   12   20

6465-60 Gulf, Bennett photograph.

6465(C) LIONEL LINES has an unpainted orange tank with black ends. Schilling Collection.

**6465 LIONEL LINES** 1958-59, two domes, "L" in circle, plastic simulated handrails around the tank, Type 9 frame with six rectangular openings and no steps and no indentations, AAR trucks with Timken bearings.
(A) Black unpainted plastic tank, white lettering, "BLT 1-58", disc couplers, Schilling Collection. **4 7 10 15**
(B) Orange unpainted plastic tank, black lettering, no built date, one disc coupler, one fixed coupler, confirmation requested. **NRS**
(C) Orange unpainted plastic tank, black ends, "BLT/BY LIONEL" varies in height, centered on car, one fixed coupler, one disc coupler, Smith and Schilling Collections. **4 7 10 15**
(D) Same as (C), but two disc couplers, Schilling Collection.
**4 7 10 15**

The 6465 CITIES SERVICE comes in various shades of green. Schilling Collection.

**6465 CITIES SERVICE** 1960-62, two domes, various shades of green, plastic simulated handrails around the tank, Type 9 frame with six rectangular openings and no steps and no indentations, AAR trucks with Timken bearings, white lettering "CSOX/6465/CAPY 80000/P. I. WT. 50000" on the left, "CITIES SERVICE" in the center and "A.R.A./SPEC III/BLT BY/LIONEL" on the right.
(A) Green-painted black plastic, disc couplers, Schilling Collection.
**6 10 15 25**
(B) Green-painted gray plastic, disc couplers, Schilling Collection.
**6 10 15 25**
(C) Same as (B), one disc coupler, one fixed coupler, Schilling Collection.
**6 10 15 25**

6555 Sunoco, Bartelt photograph.

**6555 SUNOCO** 1949-50, single-dome, silver tank, staple-end metal trucks, magnetic couplers, brakewheel, ladders, handrails. This was the updated version of the premium single-dome 2555.
(A) "SUNOCO" goes beyond diamond. **9 15 20 30**
XX(B) "GAS SUNOCO OILS" all within diamond, bold black lettering, decal-shaped. Kotil Collection. **8 15 20 30**
(C) "SUNOCO" beyond diamond, less bold blue-black lettering, round corner decal. Kotil Collection. **8 15 20 30**

## VAT CARS

6475 Libby's.

**NOTE:** There are three different vat cars numbered 6475.

**6475 LIBBY'S CRUSHED PINEAPPLE** Light or aqua car with white and silver labels and red and blue letters.
(A) AAR trucks with Timken bearings, disc couplers. **20 30 40 65**
(B) Arch bar trucks, fixed couplers. **20 30 40 65**
(C) Aqua, AAR trucks with Timken bearings, fixed couplers. Kotil Collection. **20 30 40 65**
(D) Light blue, AAR trucks with Timken bearings, fixed couplers. Kotil Collection. **20 30 40 65**

6475 Heinz 57.

**6475 HEINZ 57** Tan car with brown roof, green lettering, green vat labels with red lettering. A reliable informant has suggested that the HEINZ 57 cars were "the product of a lark and not genuine Lionel". More information is needed about this car. **40 60 80 100**

6475 Pickles.

**6475 PICKLES**  Tan car body, brown roof, metal frame, AAR trucks with Timken bearings, disc couplers, dark green lettering on frame: "TLCX CAPY 135575 LD LMT 115225 BLTBY LIONEL 6475".

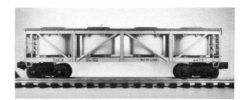

6475(B) no slats.

(A) Yellow vats with black slats, red lettered "PICKLES".

                                         **10   15   25   40**

(B) Four dark yellow vats with brown barrel slats both vertically and horizontally; vats are labeled "PICKLES" in red serif lettering. Breslin Collection.                         **10   15   25   40**

(C) Same as (A), but light brown vats. Blotner Collection.      **NRS**

(D) Same as (A), but red vat lettering is missing. Blotner Collection.      **NRS**

**NOTE:**  See also Factory Errors entry with note concerning reproduction vats without slats.

# Chapter XI
# ACCESSORIES

By Roland LaVoie

The battle for the toy train market was a ferocious struggle in the postwar years. Lionel, American Flyer and Marx all tried to carve out their own particular niches within the industry, and when one of these companies felt feisty enough, it would try to muscle in on the other's territory. In the highly competitive toy train industry, the advantage always went to the most innovative producer. All of these trains had their particular advantages and disadvantages, but when the smoke of battle had cleared, the Lionel Corporation reigned supreme.

It is well recognized that Lionel achieved this supremacy through superior marketing techniques, fine quality control (at least most of the time) and great engineering. However, it is not generally recognized that Lionel's three-rail track put the company in a much better position than American Flyer to exploit its strengths. American Flyer's two-rail track meant that both rails had to supply power and be insulated. This meant that any wiring for switches and accessories had to be somewhat complex. On the other hand, Lionel's three-rail track meant that the company had two ground rails to work with. Therefore, the Lionel Corporation was in a far better position, electrically speaking, to design special operating tracks, cars and accessories. The company also possessed brilliant engineers to take advantage of this electrical flexibility.

The result of Lionel's exploitation of its electrical abilities was an array of operating cars and accessories which has never been equaled. These amazingly diverse operating devices added big profits to the company and, perhaps more importantly, strengthened the illusion for children that they were creating their own little world which they could control. In the postwar years, busy little workmen swarmed all over Lionel Land, tossing milk cans, dumping barrels or coal, dispatching train orders or flipping mail sacks out of doors. Lionel Land later became a little more sinister as missiles, satellites and rockets arched above plywood boards everywhere, but that was only a reflection of the times, for the late fifties and early sixties saw an ominous escalation of the arms race.

The first operating cars continued some of the principles perfected in the late prewar years. Die-cast coal and log dump cars dumped their commodities into trackside trays, while a little silver boxcar tossed packing crates haphazardly out of its doors. They were only preludes for some incredibly clever cars to follow. In 1947, the most popular of all these accessories, the "Automatic Refrigerated Milk Car", began a long run. (See the article in the boxcar chapter by David Fleming and Jerry Schuchard.) Children (and adults) never tired of seeing a little man, dressed in immaculate white, fling the doors of the car open to heave a little metal can of milk onto a platform. This car was soon accompanied by the popular cattle car, which featured little rubber cows tramping along runways of a stock pen and moving (somewhat reluctantly) into and out of a short orange stock car.

As the years went by, Lionel refined its engineering techniques to produce other clever operating cars. A brakeman standing atop the Automatic Brakeman Car ducked when he hit a telltale and stood up again after he cleared the tunnel or bridge. Did it matter that this was 19th Century railroading applied to a 20th Century car? Not at all! In another amusing car, a giraffe sticking his head out of the roof of a boxcar ducked his head when he approached a telltale. A little blue workman standing atop a gondola kicked wooden barrels off the car and (perhaps) onto another ramp, where another workman sent them up an incline to a second car. In a funny recreation of railroad melodrama, a policeman chased a hobo around and around the packing crates of a gondola, never catching him. A spring-loaded boxcar "blew up" quite harmlessly when hit by a missile. Helicopters flew somewhat erratically either from a flatcar or a launching tower, as did satellites or rockets.

The trackside accessories were, if possible, even more clever than the operating cars. All kinds of action took place on the Lionel layout equipped with many accessories. Beacons revolved, searchlights shone, towers blinked and oil wells bubbled. Little baggage carts scurried into and out of a freight station. A busy worker pushed plastic ice cubes into a refrigerator car, while coal towers and loaders clanked and whirred under the burden of their plastic loads (only Lionel No. 206 Coal, if you please). Turntables and engine transfer tables were available for the truly ambitious railroaders, and crossing signals of all kinds flashed miniature red warnings to avoid mock disasters at grade crossings. Semaphores moved and signals winked; water tower spouts descended and, at a little newsstand, a puppy ran around a fire hydrant while his paperboy master turned to offer a newspaper. It was all calculated to create the illusion of a busy, innocent and idealized world - and it succeeded beyond anyone's expectations!

Among train collectors and operators, these accessories retain their charm even today. Although many accessories bring high prices, a good number of them were made in such quantities that they will always be reasonably priced. For example, it is quite possible to buy an original Lionel milk car, complete with stand and milk cans, in excellent condition for thirty dollars or less. When one considers that the car sold new for $11.95 in 1952, that is a real bargain in today's toy train marketplace.

There is much more to these accessories than price, however. Today's world of video games and computers are dynamic and clever beyond anything Lionel ever invented, but the user of these devices is always utilizing somebody else's creativity. With Lionel's accessories, one could create a whole world in miniature - a world infinitely more certain than the real one, and a world which is ruled by the operator as a benevolent dictator. Perhaps the wish to create those worlds, however unrealistic, is responsible for the phenomenal growth in popularity of toy train collecting. Such creativity may not be very "practical", but it tends to bring out the artist and idealist in each of us. In an age of technology, that is a truly welcome endeavor.

30(A)

30(B)

30(B)

025          026

36

37

38

38

41,153C, 145C

56

70

71

75

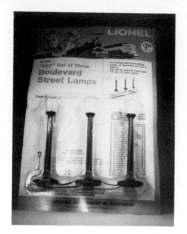

76

89

92

93

97

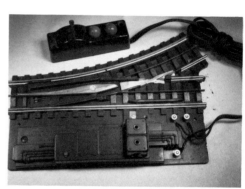

112

114

115

118

120

125

164

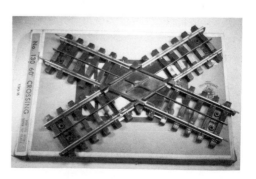

130

| | Gd | VG | Exc | Mt |
|---|---|---|---|---|

**011-11 INSULATING PINS** 1940-60, for 0 Gauge, white or black, each.

| | .03 | .05 | .05 | .05 |
|---|---|---|---|---|

**011-43 INSULATING PINS** 1961, for 0 Gauge, per dozen.

| | .40 | .75 | 1 | 1.50 |
|---|---|---|---|---|

**T011-43 INSULATING PINS** 1962-66, for 0 Gauge, per dozen.

| | .50 | .75 | 1 | 1.50 |
|---|---|---|---|---|

**020X 45 DEGREE CROSSOVER** 1946-59, for 0 Gauge:
(A) Black base, brown Bakelite center stamped "LIONEL CORP./020X/ CROSSING/NEW YORK", red center insulation. LaVoie Collection.

| | 1.50 | 2 | 4 | 10 |
|---|---|---|---|---|

(B) Same as (A), but black Bakelite center and black insulation. LaVoie Collection.

| | 1.50 | 2 | 4 | 10 |
|---|---|---|---|---|

**020 90 DEGREE CROSSOVER** 1945-61, for 0 Gauge.
(A) Black base, indented center with cross-shaped projection, solid metal rail connector under base, center held with visible rivet, red insulators, aluminum and black plate reads "MADE IN U.S. AMERICA/No. 020/CROSSING/THE LIONEL CORP./N.Y." LaVoie Collection.

| | 1.50 | 2 | 4 | 8 |
|---|---|---|---|---|

(B) Same as (A), but later version: rail connector under base has punched circular hole, black insulators, no plate, larger center with square projection heat-stamped "No. 020/CROSSING/MADE IN/U.S. OF AMERICA/ LIONEL CORP./N.Y." LaVoie Collection.

| | 1.50 | 2 | 4 | 8 |
|---|---|---|---|---|

**T020 90 DEGREE CROSSOVER** 1962, 1966, 1969, for 0 Gauge.

| | 1.50 | 2 | 4 | 8 |
|---|---|---|---|---|

**022 REMOTE CONTROL SWITCHES** 1945-49, new curved control rails, new long curved rails, new auxiliary rails, new long straight rail, new location for screw holes holding bottom. For more information see Lionel Service Manual.

| | 25 | 40 | 50 | 75 |
|---|---|---|---|---|

**022LH REMOTE CONTROL SWITCH** 1950-61, left-hand switch for 0 Gauge, with controller.

| | 10 | 15 | 25 | 35 |
|---|---|---|---|---|

**022RH REMOTE CONTROL SWITCH** 1950-61, right-hand switch for 0 Gauge, with controller.

| | 10 | 15 | 25 | 35 |
|---|---|---|---|---|

**022-500 0 GAUGE ADAPTER SET** 1957-61, combines Super 0 with 0 track.

| | 1 | 1.50 | 2 | 3 |
|---|---|---|---|---|

**T022-5000 0 GAUGE ADAPTER SET** 1962-66, combines Super 0 with 0 track.

| | 1 | 1.50 | 2 | 3 |
|---|---|---|---|---|

**022A REMOTE CONTROL SWITCH**, reported as a standard 022 switch issued from the factory with an 027 controller. Reader comments requested.

| | | | | NRS |
|---|---|---|---|---|

**025 BUMPER** 1946-47, 0 Gauge illuminated black bumper with a piece of track, late prewar carry-over. Bohn comment.

| | 3 | 5 | 8 | 14 |
|---|---|---|---|---|

**026 BUMPER** 1948-50, die-cast bumper with spring-loaded gray metal energy absorber, bayonet bulb socket, four wide feet, center rail pickup with notch.
(A) 1948, Gray only. Rohlfing comment.

| | 5 | 10 | 15 | 20 |
|---|---|---|---|---|

(B) 1949-50, Red.

| | 3 | 5 | 8 | 14 |
|---|---|---|---|---|

**027C-1 TRACK CLIPS** 1947, 1949, for 0 track, per dozen.

| | .50 | .75 | 1 | 2 |
|---|---|---|---|---|

**30 WATER TOWER** 1947-50, with operating spout.
(A) Single-walled plastic tank, solenoid makes spout move; gray die-cast base, brown plastic frame, translucent amber tank with two binding nuts on gray roof. 6-1/8" x 10-1/8" high.

| | 25 | 45 | 60 | 90 |
|---|---|---|---|---|

(B) Double-walled plastic tank without place for hose connections, gray die-cast base, black metal frame, unusual variation.

| | 40 | 75 | 130 | 220 |
|---|---|---|---|---|

**31 CURVED TRACK** 1957-66, Super 0, 36" diameter.

| | .30 | .50 | .60 | .80 |
|---|---|---|---|---|

**31-7 POWER BLADE CONNECTOR** 1957-61, Super 0.

| | — | — | — | .25 |
|---|---|---|---|---|

**31-15 GROUND RAIL PIN** 1957-66, Super 0, per dozen.

| | — | — | — | .75 |
|---|---|---|---|---|

**31-45 POWER BLADE CONNECTION** 1961-66, Super 0, per dozen.

| | — | — | — | .75 |
|---|---|---|---|---|

**32 STRAIGHT TRACK** 1957, Super O.

| | .35 | .50 | .75 | 1 |
|---|---|---|---|---|

**32-10 INSULATING PIN** 1957-60, Super 0, per dozen.

| | — | — | — | .50 |
|---|---|---|---|---|

**32-20 POWER BLADE INSULATOR** 1957-60, Super 0.

| | — | — | — | .10 |
|---|---|---|---|---|

**32-25 INSULATING PIN** Part of 1122-500, 0-27 adapter set.

| | — | — | — | .10 |
|---|---|---|---|---|

**32-30 GROUND PIN** Part of 922-500 0 Gauge adapter set.

| | — | — | — | .10 |
|---|---|---|---|---|

**32-31 POWER PIN** Part of 022-500 0 Gauge adapter set.

| | — | — | — | .10 |
|---|---|---|---|---|

**32-32 INSULATING PIN** Part of 022-500 0 Gauge adapter set.

| | — | — | — | .10 |
|---|---|---|---|---|

**32-33 GROUND PIN** Part of 1122-500 0-27 adapter set.

| | — | — | — | .10 |
|---|---|---|---|---|

**32-34 POWER PIN** Part of 1122-500 0-27 adapter set.

| | — | — | — | .10 |
|---|---|---|---|---|

**32-45 POWER BLADE INSULATION** 1961-66, per dozen, for Super 0.

| | — | — | — | .75 |
|---|---|---|---|---|

**32-55 INSULATING PIN** 1961-66, for Super 0, per dozen.

| | — | — | — | .75 |
|---|---|---|---|---|

**33 HALF CURVED TRACK** 1957-66, Super 0, 4-1/2".

| | .25 | .50 | .85 | 1 |
|---|---|---|---|---|

**34 HALF STRAIGHT TRACK** 1957-66, Super 0, 5-3/4".

| | .25 | .50 | .75 | 1 |
|---|---|---|---|---|

**35 BOULEVARD LAMP** 1945-49, 6-1/8" high, finial top.

| | 3 | 4 | 6 | 10 |
|---|---|---|---|---|

**36 OPERATING CAR REMOTE CONTROL SET** 1957-66, for Super 0.

| | 1 | 2 | 4 | 8 |
|---|---|---|---|---|

**37 UNCOUPLING TRACK SET** 1957-66, for Super 0.

| | 1 | 2 | 4 | 7 |
|---|---|---|---|---|

**38 WATER TOWER** 1946-47, water put in amber double-walled tank; then by gravity, water flows to base, after which it is pumped by motor back up; solenoid-operated spout. Water does not come out of the spout. Tan die-cast tank base "No. 38", brown die-cast frame, amber-tinted plastic double-walled tank with two rubber hoses subject to deterioration. Roof with metal center post for water plug in center, two binding posts for roof with rubber gaskets and speed nuts. Came with little funnel. Also came with envelope of water tank coloring tablets, 38-70; when these tablets were used, the water showed much better within the tank walls. Powell Collection.

| (A) Brown roof. | 50 | 150 | 225 | 300 |
|---|---|---|---|---|
| (B) Red roof. | 60 | 175 | 250 | 350 |

**38 ACCESSORY ADAPTER TRACKS** 1957-61, pair, for adapting 55, 154, 497, 3360 and 3414 to Super 0.

| | 1 | 2 | 4 | 8 |
|---|---|---|---|---|

**39 SUPER 0 OPERATING SET** 1957.

| | 1 | 2 | 4 | 8 |
|---|---|---|---|---|

**39-25 OPERATING SET** 1961-66, Super 0, uncoupling and operating units.

| | 1 | 2 | 4 | 8 |
|---|---|---|---|---|

**40 HOOK UP WIRE** 1950-51, 1953-63, with cable reel, insulated 18 Gauge wire.

| | 1 | 2 | 3 | 4 |
|---|---|---|---|---|

**40-50 CABLE REEL** 1960-61, 15" of three conductor wire.

| | 1 | 2 | 3 | 4 |
|---|---|---|---|---|

**40-25 CONDUCTOR WIRE** 1956-59, 15" of four conductor wire.

| | 1 | 3 | 4 | 5 |
|---|---|---|---|---|

**41 CONTACTOR.**

| | .40 | .60 | .80 | 1 |
|---|---|---|---|---|

**42 042 MANUAL SWITCHES** 1947-59, pair for 0 Gauge, change in 1950 from screw-type lamp socket to bayonet-type lamp socket.

| | 10 | 20 | 25 | 40 |
|---|---|---|---|---|

**43 POWER TRACK** 1959-66, 1-1/2" track section with ground and power terminals.

| | 1.50 | 2 | 3 | 4 |
|---|---|---|---|---|

**44-80 MISSILES** 1959-60, set of four for No. 44, 45, 6544 and 6844.

| | 1.50 | 2 | 3 | 5 |
|---|---|---|---|---|

**45 GATEMAN** 1946-49, door opens, gateman comes out with lantern, with contactor.

| | 7 | 12 | 20 | 30 |
|---|---|---|---|---|

**45-N GATEMAN** 1945, door opens, gateman comes out with lantern, with contactor.

| | 7 | 12 | 20 | 30 |
|---|---|---|---|---|

**48 INSULATED STRAIGHT TRACK** 1957-66, Super 0.

| | .75 | 1 | 1.50 | 2 |
|---|---|---|---|---|

**55-150 TIES** 1957-60, 24 ties for No. 55 Tie Jector.

| | 1.50 | 2 | 3 | 7 |
|---|---|---|---|---|

**56 LAMP POST** 1946-49, 7-3/4" high.

| | 10 | 20 | 35 | 50 |
|---|---|---|---|---|

**58 LAMP POST** 1946-50, ivory, 7-1/2" high. Powell Collection.

| | 8 | 12 | 20 | 35 |
|---|---|---|---|---|

**61 GROUND LOCK ON** 1957-66, Super 0.

| | .25 | .40 | .50 | 1 |
|---|---|---|---|---|

**62 POWER LOCK ON** 1957-66, Super 0.

| | .25 | .40 | .50 | 1 |
|---|---|---|---|---|

**64 STREET LAMP** 1945-49, green, 6-3/4" high.

| | 6 | 9 | 16 | 20 |
|---|---|---|---|---|

**70 YARD LIGHT** 1949-50, black, 4-1/2" high, swivel die-cast head.

| | 6 | 20 | 35 | 50 |
|---|---|---|---|---|

**71 LAMP POST** 1949-59, gray, die-cast 6" high.

| | 2 | 5 | 10 | 20 |
|---|---|---|---|---|

132

133

138

140

142-125

145

148

150

151

151

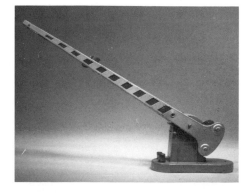

152

153

**75 GOOSE NECK LAMPS** 1961-73, set of two black lamps, each 6-1/2" high, base 1-3/4" x 1-1/2". Young Collection. Revived by Fundimensions in 1980.　　　　　　　　　　　　　**5　10　15　25**

**76 BOULEVARD STREET LAMPS** 1955-66, 1968-69, set of three plastic light fixtures with two-pin base bulbs.　　　**2　3　4　6**

**88 CONTROLLER** 1946-60, normally "on" button used for direction reversing.　　　　　　　　　　　　**.50　.75　1　2**

**89 FLAGPOLE** 1956-58, fabric American flag in red, white and blue with purple Lionel pennant with white lettering, white shaft, tan plastic base with four green corner plots made from sponge, 11" high, reissued by Fundimensions in 1983, original hard to find. Bohn comment.
　　　　　　　　　　　　　　　**6　10　20　30**

**90 CONTROLLER**, large red button embossed with "L".
(A) Plain black plastic case without notches.　**.25　.50　.75　1.00**
(B) Same as (A), but flat surface above button is covered by a thin aluminum plate over cardboard for labeling the accessory to be operated. The plate folds over and attaches to the bottom of the plastic casing by two indentations which fit into cutouts in the casing. Earlier models lack these cutouts, and this version is easy to find without the aluminum plate. LaVoie Collection.　　　　　　　**.50　1.50　2　3**

**91 CIRCUIT BREAKER** 1957-60, electro-magnetic action, adjustable from 1 to 6 amps, 4-3/4" x 1-3/8".　　　　　　**1　2　3　5**

**92 CIRCUIT BREAKER CONTROLLER** 1959-66, 1968-69, fixed load breaker.　　　　　　　　　　　**.50　.75　1　2**

**93 WATER TOWER** 1946-49, aluminum finish, black spout, red base, "LIONEL TRAINS" decal with red letters outlined in black and a black line around decal edge, Lord observation.　**7　12　20　35**

**96C CONTROLLER**, all metal, two binding posts, red push button. Binding posts are closer together than on 88 controller, which looks similar. I.D. Smith and Rohlfing observations.　　**.25　.50　.75　1.00**

**97 COAL ELEVATOR** 1946-50, coal carried from tray to bunker by endless chain with buckets; switch controls bunker exit chute; yellow bunker with red metal roof, black Bakelite base, aluminum-colored metal frame; two binding posts on one side; three posts other side, with controller.
　　　　　　　　　　　　　**50　75　150　200**

**100 MULTIVOLT - DC/AC** Power Pack, 1958-66.　　　　**NRS**

**109 TRESTLE SET** Sold with set #2574 in 1961 catalogue. Pages 40 & 41, additional sightings requested. Hutchinson comment.　　**NRS**

**110 TRESTLE SET** 1955-69, set of 22 or 24 graduated piers. Piers are gray or black; black are more desirable.
(A) Plain brown box labeled on one of the long sides, "110-23" which is Lionel's part number for the box. Note that 110-22 parts envelope comes with variation A. The box was manufactured by Densen Banner. The box is 23" long by 17" wide. Came with 110-22 parts envelope. Came with gray trestles. Halverson Collection. Note that values for excellent and mint require the complete packaging.　　　　**3　8　15　25**
(B) Plain brown box labeled on one of long sides: "110-35" which is Lionel's part number for the box. Box was manufactured by Express Container Corp. Plain brown box with red and blue lettering. A manilla parts envelope marked "110-35" came inside box; Halverson Collection.
　　　　　　　　　　　　　　**1　2　5　10**
(C) Same as (B), but black trestles and yellow box labeled "110-35" manufactured by Star Corrugated Box Company Inc. Came with parts envelope "110-26". Black trestles. Halverson Collection.
　　　　　　　　　　　　　　**2　3　8　15**
(D) Box labeled "Lionel No. 110 22-piece Graduated Trestle Set". Came in orange and blue box 11" long, 8" wide and 4" high. Gray trestles. Box labeled "110-38 Manufactured by United Container Co." Hillside box. Later production. Halverson Collection.　　　　**NRS**
(E) Same as (C), but gray trestles and orange box with black lettering.
　　　　　　　　　　　　　　**2　3　8　15**
Note that the first three variations come with 24 piers while the last one has only 22: Variation (D) has a 1061 Scout Set illustrated on the box cover. The set is on a trestle moving to the right of the box.

**111 TRESTLE SET** 1956-69, set of 10 large piers.　**2　3　5　7**

**111-100 TRESTLE PIERS** 1960-63, two 4-3/4" piers.　**1　2　3　5**

**112 SUPER 0 SWITCHES** 1957-66, remote control, pair with controllers.
　　　　　　　　　　　　　　**20　40　75　95**

**112LH SUPER 0 SWITCH** 1962-66, left-hand with controller.
　　　　　　　　　　　　**10　20　35　45**

**112RH SUPER 0 SWITCH** 1962-66, right-hand with controller.
　　　　　　　　　　　　**10　20　35　45**

**112-125 SUPER 0 SWITCH** 1957-61, left-hand, with controller, remote control.　　　　　　　　　　**10　20　35　45**

**112-150 SUPER 0 SWITCH** 1957-61, right-hand, with controller, remote control.　　　　　　　　　　**10　20　35　45**

**114 NEWSSTAND WITH HORN** 1957-59, brown plastic base with bench on right side, yellow plastic building, gray roof, diesel horn operated by battery, battery circuit completed through controller, four connecting clips on base, bayonet-type lamp socket.　　**20　30　50　75**

**115 LIONEL CITY STATION** 1946-49, with automatic train control stop, red metal base, cream side with red window and door trim, red roof, two aluminum-finished die-cast external lights and one interior light, three binding posts, 13-5/8" long, 9-1/4" wide, 8-1/2" high, carry-over from prewar production. Ocilka and I. D. Smith comments.　**75　110　175　300**

**118 NEWSSTAND WITH WHISTLE** 1958, brown plastic base with three mounting plates, building is yellow-sided with gray plastic roof, whistle unit and light inside, bench is flanked on left side by two green "sponge" bushes.　　　　　　　　　**20　30　50　75**

**119 LANDSCAPED TUNNEL** 1957, 14" long, 10" wide, 8" high.
　　　　　　　　　　　　　　**2　3　5　7**

**120 90 DEGREE CROSSING** 1957-66, Super 0.　**1　2　3　7**

**121 LANDSCAPED TUNNEL** 1959-66, 14" long, 12" wide, 12" high.
　　　　　　　　　　　　　　**2　3　5　7**

**123 LAMP ASSORTMENT** 1955-59, orange box with 48 assorted bulbs, 13-3/4" x 7-3/4" x 1-3/4", with white simulated steam locomotive headlight beam and five oversized pictures of lamps on box cover. Box lid has "LIONEL" in white on blue field, "REPLACEMENT LAMP ASSORT-MENT" in orange, and "No. 123" and "FOR MODEL TRAINS & ACCESSORIES" in blue. Salamone Collection.　　　**NRS**

**123-60 LAMP ASSORTMENT** 1960-63, same configuration as No. 123, but larger box with 120 assorted lamps. Curiously, these lamps show less variation by type than did those in the earlier set. Salamone Collection.
　　　　　　　　　　　　　　　　**NRS**

**125 WHISTLE SHACK** 1950-55, similar to 145 Gateman, but contains whistle, not lighted, medium red roof, medium red tool box top, roof and tool box lid easily interchanged with other units, white building, red windows and door, red sticker with gold-lettered "LIONELVILLE" over door, frosted plastic window in door; other windows without plastic. Rohlfing and Halverson comments.
(A) Dark gray base.　　　　　　**7　10　30　50**
(B) Light gray base.　　　　　　**7　10　30　50**
(C) Green base. Ambrose comment. This is a legitimate variation which belongs to the postwar period, not early Fundimensions.　**NRS**
NOTE: Several collectors have reported that the green base 125 represents the earliest production of Fundimensions. A sample of the early Fundimensions 2125 has shown that this is not so. The greenbase 125 is identical in every other way to its postwar counterparts. The Fundimensions version is a strange hybrid; it has the postwar motor, but it is found with a dark brown base, green roof, white sides, red tool box lid and red main door. On the sample observed, a light clip was attached between the two wiring posts; this clip, similar to that used in the late postwar N5C cabooses, appears to be a factory product. That's interesting, because a light wired in that way would only work when the whistle was blown! Halverson and LaVoie comments.

**128 ANIMATED NEWSSTAND** 1957-60. Newsdealer moves, newsboy turns, pup runs around hydrant, 8-1/2" long, 6-1/4" wide, 4-1/4" high. Green building, red roof, tan base, red hydrant. Revived by Fundimensions in 1982.　　　　　　　　　　**20　60　85　150**

**130 60 DEGREE CROSSING** 1957-61, Super 0.　**1　2　4　8**

**131 CURVED TUNNEL** 1959-66, 28" long, 14" wide, 12" high.
　　　　　　　　　　　　　　**2　3　5　10**

**132 PASSENGER STATION** 1949-55, maroon plastic base, white building, green trim and roof, illuminated with stop feature, 6-1/2" high, 12-1/8"

**154(A)**

**154(B)**

**154**

**154C, OTC**

**155**

**156**

**157(A)**

**157(B)**

**160**

**161**

**163**

**164**

long, 8-1/4" wide, three binding clips, train stop control lever controls length of pause, base plastic is shinier than 133 base plastic.

|  | 11 | 20 | 30 | 50 |

**133 PASSENGER STATION** 1957-66, illuminated, maroon base, white building with green doors and windows, green roof, two binding clips on bottom. Similar to 132 but without train stop control. **11 15 25 35**

**137 PASSENGER STATION** 1946 catalogued but only made prewar. **NRS**

**138 WATER TOWER** 1953-57, brown plastic single-walled tank with operating spout, orange plastic roof without screw posts and without holes, differs from roofs on 30 and 38, gray plastic base, brown plastic frame, 10-1/8" high, base 6-1/8" x 6-1/8". **30 35 60 90**

**140 AUTOMATIC BANJO SIGNAL** 1954-66, warning sign with moving arm, flashing moving arm causes light flashing, contactor 7-1/2" high, shown in original box. **5 10 20 30**

**142 MANUAL SWITCHES** 1957-66, Super 0, pair. **10 15 20 30**

**142-125 LEFT-HAND SWITCH** 1957-61, Super 0, manual.
**5 7 10 15**

**142-150 RIGHT-HAND SWITCH** 1957-61, Super 0, manual.
**5 7 10 15**

**142LH MANUAL SWITCH** 1962-66, Super 0, left-hand. **5 7 10 15**

**142RH MANUAL SWITCH** 1962-66, Super 0, right-hand. **5 7 10 15**

**145 AUTOMATIC GATEMAN** 1950-66, blue-suited watchman with flesh-colored face and hands carrying lantern, emerges as train passes; lighted white plastic shed with red door, frosted plastic window material in door and window, red toolbox lid, green metal base, black die-cast base on crossing sign, white plastic crossing sign No. 309-29 with black lettering. Variations in roof color and toolbox lid covers, base 6-3/4" x 7" high.

|  | 10 | 15 | 20 | 30 |

**145C CONTACTOR** 1950-60. **.50 .75 1 1.50**

**147 WHISTLE CONTROLLER** 1961-66, also known as horn controller. Uses one "D" size battery. **.50 .75 1 1.50**

**148 DWARF TRACKSIDE LIGHT** 1957-60, buff-colored plastic body, black lens unit, red and green bulbs, pin-type bulbs, three binding clips on bottom, require 148C DPDT switch for operation, hard to find. Bohn comment. **15 35 50 80**

**150 TELEGRAPH POLE SET** 1947-50, set of six brown plastic poles with metal base clips. **5 10 20 30**

**151 SEMAPHORE** 1947-69, moving plastic blade with yellow-painted tip with red and green translucent plastic inserts, black die-cast base, silver-painted metal shaft, red ladder, metal bulb assembly, three binding posts on base top, with contactor. **5 10 15 25**

**152 AUTOMATIC CROSSING GATE** 1945-49, red-painted die-cast base, large metal gate with black paper strip, small pedestrian gate, bayonet-base bulb, two screw posts on base top, with contactor. This gate was made with a small pedestrian gate on the opposite side of the base. Many examples are found without this gate. We need to know if this accessory was ever made without the pedestrian gate or if observed samples have lost it. Spitzer observation. **7 10 15 30**

**153 AUTOMATIC BLOCK CONTROL** 1945-69, two position with contactor for controlling two trains on single track, green die-cast base, aluminum shaft, orange ladder, black metal ladder holder, black die-cast lamp shell; common ground post is center post, 9" high.
(A) 1945-49, base contains resistor in series with ground for using 6-8 volt screw-base bulbs. I.D. Smith and Rohlfing comments. **6 10 15 25**
(B) 1950-69, no resistor, uses 12-14 volt bayonet-base bulbs. I.D. Smith and Rohlfing comments. **6 10 15 25**

**153C CONTACTOR** single pole, double throw. **.50 1 1.50 2**

**154 AUTOMATIC HIGHWAY SIGNAL** 1945-69, crossbuck with two alternately flashing red bulbs, operating by 154C contactor, 8-3/4" high, three screw posts, black base.
(A) White-painted die-cast X-shaped sign with black raised lettering, "STOP" in white lettering on black die-cast part, screw socket bulbs.
**7 10 15 20**
(B) White plastic X-shaped sign with white raised lettering, "STOP" in raised white lettering on black plastic, bayonet socket bulbs.
**7 10 15 20**

(C) 1950, same as (A), but orange-painted metal base, rare. Bohn comment. **NRS**
(D) 1950, same as (A), but metal base painted red on interior and exterior, rare. Bohn comment. **NRS**

**155 BLINKING LIGHT SIGNAL WITH BELL** 1955-57, similar to No. 154, but with large base containing bell. Black and white plastic base, black shaft, black plastic railroad crossing sign with white lettering, "STOP" raised white lettering, bayonet-type bulbs.
(A) 1955, early mechanism with copper blade contacts, small screw holes in metal fastening tabs on base. LaVoie comment. **6 12 20 30**
(B) 1956-57, later mechanism with spring contacts and rubber grommets on metal fastening tabs on base; works better than early version. LaVoie Collection. **6 12 20 30**
NOTE: 155 was also used by Lionel to refer to the Prewar Station Platform.

**156 STATION PLATFORM** 1946-51, two lights, miniature billboards, green plastic base, metal uprights, red plastic roof, 12" long, 3-1/4" wide, 5-1/8" high, includes four signs. **5 15 25 40**

**157 STATION PLATFORM** 1952-59, lighted with miniature billboards, maroon plastic base, black metal post, green plastic roof, 12" long, 5-1/8" high, 3-1/4" wide, at least 11 different signs exist, Bohn comment.
(A) Campbell Soup, Switch to Rival Dog Food, Baby Ruth and Sunoco; signs can be interchanged, some are less common. **6 10 20 30**
(B) Same as (A), but with different signs: Dogs Prefer Rival, Airex, Baby Ruth and Sunoco. **6 10 20 30**
(C) Red plastic base, Airex, Gulf, Rival and Baby Ruth signs. Ocilka Collection. **15 25 40 60**

**160 UNLOADING BIN** 1952.
(A) Short. **.25 .50 1 2**
(B) Long (for 3359-55 twin-bin dump car). **.25 .50 1 2**

**161 MAIL PICKUP SET** 1961-63, the mail bag transfers from stand to car, tan plastic base contains coil, red shaft with red and white semaphore, red plastic bag holder, red plastic bag painted gray, hollowed out, contains a magnet. The accessory came with a second magnet which is glued to the car. **20 50 75 100**

**163 SINGLE TARGET BLOCK SIGNAL** 1961-69, as train approaches, signal light changes from green to red automatically, can be wired to control a second train in a two-train operation; contactor and wires.
**7 15 20 30**

**164 LOG LOADER** 1946-50, logs unloaded from car to bin and carried to top by chain, then fall into stake-ended platform. Upon command the stakes move from a vertical to horizontal position, the logs then roll into a waiting car. Two-button controller, on/off black button on left side. Orange "Unload" button on right side, 9" high, 11-1/4" wide, 10-3/4" long, with controller and logs, base and roof painted black, molded phenolic plastic.
(A) Green metal base, yellow die-cast frame, red plastic roof.
**65 85 150 200**
(B) Same as (A), but green roof. **NRS**

**167 WHISTLE CONTROLLER** 1945-46, with two buttons: one for whistle, one for direction. (Several different types have been made.)
**.50 1.00 1.25 2.00**

**175 ROCKET LAUNCHER** 1958-60, tan metal base track, boxes cover part of motor unit, white and red rocket, black plastic superstructure on gray plastic base, gray crane with gray plastic base, gray top and yellow boom, crane lowers satellite onto missile; countdown apparatus, firing button. Tower crane approximately 17" tall; crane with boom, cable and magnet; magnet meets magnet at end of rocket, crane lifts rocket from car or other location and locates it on missile launching platform, rocket controller launches missile; crane track fits 282R Gantry Crane. **50 85 150 225**

**175-50 EXTRA ROCKET** 1959-60, for 175. **1.50 2 3 5**

**182 MAGNET CRANE** 1946-49, winch raises and lowers block and tackle, spoked-wheel control knob, differs from solid wheel of 282R, derrick revolves 360 degrees, includes one 165C controller that came with earlier prewar crane; plastic base, aluminum-painted crane, 2460(A) crane car black plastic cab. "LIONEL LINES" (two lines), "Lionel" in arched line, higher gray stack than on 282R; Electro-magnet has black plastic case with ridges; 282R has simple sheet metal "hat" containing magnet; "Cutler Hammer" on magnet case on 182, red metal ladder. Arpino Comment.
(A) As described above. **70 90 150 200**

175

182

192

193

195

197

199

206, 207

214

252(A)

252(B)

253

256

(B) Same as (A), but black stack instead of gray. Rohlfing Collection.

|  | 70 | 90 | 150 | 200 |

**192 OPERATING CONTROL TOWER** 1959-60, illuminated control room, rotating anemometer, vibrator-powered. Does not come with radar antenna, gray plastic base, green frame, yellow tower room, green roof, orange ladders, two binding clips on bottom. Reissued by Fundimensions in 1984.

|  | 75 | 125 | 185 | 275 |

**193 INDUSTRIAL WATER TOWER** 1953-55, gray plastic base, green shed, metal red frame, black plastic pipe, gray plastic top with red flashing light, two binding clips on bottom, 14-3/4" high.

(A) Red metal frame.

|  | 15 | 30 | 45 | 75 |

(B) Black-painted metal frame. Salamone, Trentacoste and Weise Collections.

|  | 20 | 35 | 50 | 85 |

**195 FLOODLIGHT TOWER** 1957-69, eight lights on one side; optional second eight lights may be affixed to other side using 195-75 extension, illustration barely shows second light on unit; tan plastic base, gray and silver plastic tower with red "LIONEL" metal and plastic eight-light unit; two clips on bottom, 12-1/2" high.

(A) As described above.

|  | 7 | 10 | 20 | 30 |

(B) Medium tan base embossed "199 MICROWAVE TOWER" in capitals and red rubber-stamped "195 FLOOD LIGHT". Breslin Collection. **NRS**

**195-75 EIGHT BULB EXTENSION** 1958-60, for 195, not illustrated.

|  | 2 | 3 | 6 | 8 |

**196(A) SMOKE PELLETS** 1946, 100 pellets in a package for bulb-type smoke unit only.

|  | — | — | — | 10 |

**196(B) SMOKE PELLETS** 1947, 100 pellets in bottle for bulb-type smoke unit only.

|  | — | — | — | 10 |

**197 ROTATING RADAR ANTENNA** 1958-59, plastic base; black plastic frame with orange letters, "LIONEL", orange platform, vibrator mechanism rotates radar screen. 12" high, base 3" x 4-1/2". Antenna is missing from sample illustrated.

(A) Gray base.

|  | 12 | 25 | 50 | 75 |

(B) Orange base.

|  | 12 | 35 | 65 | 100 |

**199 MICROWAVE RELAY TOWER** 1958-59, two parabolic antennae, three blinking lights, two binding clips on bottom; very dark gray plastic base, gray plastic tower, white antenna, "199 MICROWAVE TOWER" embossed on underside, top piece of plastic on gray tower is tan. I.D. Smith observation.

|  | 18 | 40 | 65 | 95 |

**206 ARTIFICIAL COAL** 1946-68, half-pound burlap bag with red-lettered "No. 206" "ARTIFICIAL COAL" "The Lionel Corporation, New York" "Made in U.S. of America".

|  | — | — | 6 | 8 |

**207 ARTIFICIAL COAL** Considerably smaller bag than 206, same lettering, except "Corp." rather than "Corporation".

|  | — | — | 4 | 7 |

**209 BARRELS** 1946-50, set of four.

|  | — | 1.50 | 3 | 5 |

**213 RAILROAD LIFT BRIDGE** Shown in 1950 catalogue only; prototype made, MPC archives has crude mock-up, collector owns engineering sample. Bohn comment. **Not Manufactured**

**214 PLATE GIRDER BRIDGE** 1953-69, 10" x 4-1/2"; center sheet metal base thinner than 314, black plastic sides.

(A) "LIONEL" on both sides, "BUILT BY LIONEL" in small letters in rectangular box.

|  | 1.50 | 2 | 3 | 4 |

(B) "U S STEEL" on both sides instead of "LIONEL", "BUILT BY LIONEL" in small letters in rectangular box, "USS" within white-edged circle on both sides. Spitzer Collection. **NRS**

**252 CROSSING GATE** 1950-62, black plastic base with two binding posts on underside, clip-in bulb assembly with bayonet base; plastic gate with black metal counterweights; lucite strip with two red markers; gate 9-3/4" long, with contactor.

(A) White plastic boom.

|  | 7 | 10 | 15 | 25 |

(B) Cream-colored boom.

|  | 7 | 10 | 15 | 25 |

**253 BLOCK CONTROL SIGNAL** 1956-59, 7" high, signal halts train automatically; tan plastic base 4" x 2" with black signal control box, white plastic lamp shell, pin-type bulbs, variation duration stop, level controls length of stop, three binding posts on bottom, hard to find intact with original lamp shell. Bohn comment.

|  | 10 | 20 | 30 | 45 |

**256 FREIGHT STATION** 1950-53, maroon platform, white house with green windows, green door and roof; picket fence with billboard; lighted, two clips on bottom, 15" long, 5" wide, 5-1/2" high.

|  | 6 | 12 | 20 | 30 |

**257 FREIGHT STATION WITH DIESEL HORN** 1956-57, matches 256 but with battery-powered horn and control button.

|  | 12 | 20 | 35 | 50 |

**260 BUMPER** 1951-69, red die-cast body with spring-loaded black plastic energy absorber, illuminated with bayonet bulb, spring-loaded clips for outside rails.

(A) Four wide feet, center rail pickup with notch.

|  | 3 | 6 | 10 | 15 |

(B) Four narrow feet, center rail pickup without notch.

|  | 3 | 6 | 10 | 15 |

(C) 1968, Black plastic bumper with black plastic energy absorber, center rail pickup without notch, came with Hagerstown set No. 11600. I.D. Smith Collection and observation. Made specifically for Super 0 track; red metal varieties do not fit Super 0; very difficult to find. Ocilka Collection and comment.

|  | 9 | 18 | 30 | 45 |

(D) Same as (C), but bottom plate made of Bakelite not stamped "260 Illuminated bumper". Plate held on by hex screw instead of regular Phillips screw. Halverson Collection. **NRS**

**262 HIGHWAY CROSSING GATE** 1962-69, combination flashing light and gate, black plastic base, shaft and light unit, black plastic railroad crossing sign with metal counterweight, does not have lucite strips or lenses as does 152, flashing lights have pin base.

(A) As described above.

|  | 6 | 10 | 20 | 30 |

(B) Earliest production did not have flashing lights because device was not produced with solenoid coil which activates flashing, used L19R bulbs. Reader comments requested. Arpino Collection. **NRS**

**264 OPERATING FORK LIFT PLATFORM** 1957-60, lift truck goes to loaded lumber car 6264, brings lumber back to platform. Includes platform with black metal base, brown deck area, white crane, orange lift truck with blue man, red flatcar 6264 with timbers, platform 10" long, 10-5/8" wide, 5-1/2" high.

|  | 50 | 85 | 140 | 225 |

**282 GANTRY CRANE** 1954, gray plastic crane with metal base black cab with white lettering, "LIONEL" arched, "LINES" straight across, smoke-stack on cab, magnet on end of hook, cab turns clockwise or counter-clockwise, "cable" raises or lowers, magnet turns off and on, three-lever controller 282C, cab sits on maroon plastic base with simulated metal plate, cab turns on maroon plastic drum. Does not come with track that fits wheels on base, however rocket launcher track is right size.

(A) Same as above.

|  | 60 | 90 | 150 | 275 |

(B) Same as (A), but red crane cab, Klaassen Collection. **NRS**

**282R GANTRY CRANE** 1956, similar to 282 in appearance and function but with changes in the mounting and gearing of the motor and a modified platform casting and platform assembly.

|  | 60 | 90 | 150 | 275 |

**299 CODE TRANSMITTER BEACON SET** 1961-63, black transmitting kit with three binding clips and silver-printed decal showing Morse Code Tower, black plastic base, gray recording unit, black top, elongated flashing bulb with unusual filament. Top is gray plastic searchlight with white scored plastic lens, metal bracket.

|  | 15 | 25 | 45 | 75 |

**308 RAILROAD SIGN SET** 1945-49, five die-cast white enameled metal signs with black lettering.

|  | 3 | 6 | 10 | 15 |

**309 YARD SIGN SET** 1950-59, nine plastic signs with die-cast metal bases, orange box with blue lettering, blue cardboard interior box liner with silver lettering.

|  | 3 | 6 | 8 | 10 |

**310 BILLBOARD** 1950-68, unpainted green plastic frame with cardboard Campbell Soup advertisement, Campbell boy in red, with yellow background, red lettering; red, yellow and black soup can. This is one of probably 50 different billboard designs that Lionel made over the years; set of five frames, 1957 frames with yellow base squares, hard to find. Bohn comment.

|  | 1.00 | 1.50 | 2.00 | 5.00 |

Beginning in 1950 Lionel offered a billboard assortment, the No. 310. The assortment usually consisted of five green unpainted plastic frames with an uncut sheet of eight different billboards. The billboards made through 1956 included the word "STANDARD" in black letters. Thereafter "STANDARD" was dropped from the sign. Over 50 different billboard advertisements were offered. See Chapter 13 for a listing of billboards.

**313 BASCULE BRIDGE** 1946-49, green Bakelite bridge base, die-cast metal base underneath motor, sheet metal superstructure on bridge, red light on

257

262

264

282

299

308

309

310

313

314

315

317

321

332

334

bridge top, pale yellow bridge tender building with orange windows and red roof, five binding posts, black metal alignment frame with permanently affixed lockon, 21-1/2" long, 9-1/4" high when bridge is level. Prewar version has gray-painted superstructure, while postwar version has unpainted aluminum superstructure. Ocilka observation.

|  | 150 | 200 | 300 | 425 |
|---|---|---|---|---|
| **313-82 FIBER PINS** 1946-60, each. | .05 | .05 | .05 | .08 |
| **313-121 FIBER PINS** 1961, per dozen. | — | — | — | 1.50 |

**314 SCALE MODEL GIRDER BRIDGE** 1945-50, single span, 10" long, heavy sheet metal plate for base, die-cast sides fastened by rivets, "LIONEL" rubber-stamped in black on both sides; also lettered in small box with rounded corners "BUILT BY LIONEL". Carry-over from prewar silver version.

(A) 1946, dark gray, 11/32" high lettering upwards of bridge center line. Rohlfing and Algozzini Collections.     2   5   7   10

(B) 1947-50, lighter gray, 3/8" high centered lettering. Rohlfing and Algozzini Collections.     2   5   7   10

**315 TRESTLE BRIDGE** 1946-47, silver-painted sheet metal, illuminated with binding posts in center of span on top, 24-1/2" long.   15   25   40   60

**316 TRESTLE BRIDGE** 1949, 24" x 6-1/8".

(A) Painted gray, rubber-stamped "316 TRESTLE BRIDGE" on bottom. Rohlfing Collection.     2   4   7   10

(B) Unpainted aluminum, no rubber-stamping. C. Rohlfing Collection.
    2   4   7   10

**317 TRESTLE BRIDGE** 1950-56, gray-painted sheet metal, 24" by 6-1/8" wide.     2   4   7   10

**321 TRESTLE BRIDGE** 1958-64, sheet metal base, gray plastic sides and top, 24" long, 7" high, 4-1/2" wide.     5   7   10   15

**332 ARCH UNDER BRIDGE** 1959-66, came unassembled, gray plastic sides and black metal deck.     10   20   30   40

**334 OPERATING DISPATCHING BOARD** 1957-60, blue attendant with white face and hands hurries across catwalk and appears to change information in illuminated slots, green board, white lines, plastic lettered material inside unit changes "information". Tan plastic base with three binding clips, clock on top and two speaker units, reverse side shows large billboard "AIREX" "REEL ROD REELS", color picture of man fishing, lower section Lionel Travel Center, 9-7/8" long, 4-1/8" wide, 7-1/2" high.
    50   100   125   175

**342 CULVERT LOADER** 1956-58, culvert pipes stored on sloping ramp, picked up by pincher unit and transferred to car, loaded into special gondola car 6342, length of unit is 11-1/2" x 10" x 6", includes loading station with black metal base and tan plastic box-like unit; red building, dark gray roof; 6342 controller, connecting wires and culvert section; illustration shows 342 and 345 arranged for operation. Price includes car, very difficult to keep in proper adjustment. Bohn comment.     50   75   125   175

**345 CULVERT UNLOADING STATION** 1958-59, traveling crane controlled by remote control, lowers magnet to gondola car, magnet picks up culvert section and transports it onto station, unit has black metal base, gray ramp, red tower building with gray roof, orange post on crane, black horizontal piece; 12-1/2" long, 9-1/2" wide and 7" high; includes gondola designed for use with 342. Culverts roll from 345 across special bridge onto 342, very difficult to keep in proper adjustment. Bohn comment.
    70   150   200   300

**346 CULVERT UNLOADER** Circa 1965-66, hand-operated. Made for Sears, same as 345, except lacks motor mechanism; hand crank extends through platform top, Hutchinson observation. This accessory was included as part of Sears No. 9836 set, which also included the extremely rare 2347 C & O GP-7 Diesel locomotive. This manual version of the regular issue 345 culvert unloader has a base which is lettered as such. A large metal crank protrudes from the base of the unloader. Black metal base and tower ladders; gray superstructure; tuscan tower and mechanism stanchions; gray roof. "LIONELVILLE/CULVERT PIPE/CO." in gold sans-serif letters on tower side surrounded by gold rectangle. Embossing on side of superstructure reads: "No. 345 CULVERT UNLOADER/THE LIONEL CORPORATION, NEW YORK/MADE IN THE U.S. OF AMERICA". (Note number.) Came in box labeled "No. 346/OPERATING CULVERT UNLOADER". Lionel later issued this unloader outside of the Sears set. In

doing so, the company pasted a "No. 348" label on the box over the 346 number, despite the fact that the unloader itself was identical to the one included in the Sears set. This accessory included a 6342 gondola with Timken trucks and dummy couplers. Beavin Collection.     **NRS**

**347 CANNON FIRING RANGE SET,** Circa 1962-64. Olive drab plastic battery with four cannon barrels and four silver shells. Each barrel has a firing pin which is set prior to use. A silver shell is placed in each cannon. The firing wheel is then rotated slowly, firing the shells in sequence. Came with uncatalogued Sears set. Instructions 347-10(8/64) came with unit. (We need to learn the Sears set number and its contents.) Jarman Collection.
    50   75   100   125

**348 CULVERT UNLOADER** 1966-69, manual loader, with car. See entry for 346. Beavin Collection.     30   40   60   90

**350 ENGINE TRANSFER TABLE** 1957-60, motorized table moves train from one track to another, 17-1/2" long and 10-3/8" wide, black sheet metal with plastic tie, fastened through bottom by rails fastened through holder, control unit with three yellow buttons and one red button; yellow building with red light on top; building lifts off motor underneath; illustration shows one original and one extension unit.     65   130   175   300

**350-50 TRANSFER TABLE EXTENSION** 1957-60, metal base with plastic ties, metal rails.     25   40   65   90

**352 ICE DEPOT** 1955-57, white shed, red roof, blue man with orange arms and paddle, cubes put in end with chute that raises; chute has a cube permanently fastened at end. Another version had five cubes fastened at end, operating mechanism moves, opens car hatch, cubes come out at end with man; came with 6352-1 car, depot, cubes, station 11-3/4" long, 4" wide, 8-1/2" high, two binding posts. Reissued by Fundimensions in 1982.

(A) Brown plastic base.     100   120   160   250

(B) Red plastic base.     100   120   160   250

**353 TRACK SIDE CONTROL SIGNAL** 1960-61, signal changes from green to red as train passes, can be wired to control two trains; 9" high, tan plastic base and control box; white plastic shaft, black plastic lamp housing, black metal ladder, three control posts, three binding posts on top of base
    5   10   15   20

**356 OPERATING FREIGHT STATION** 1952-57, maroon plastic base, white shed with green windows, door and roof, picket fence with billboard signs; two baggage men with carts run out onto platform and back into station powered by vibrator motor; one cart is orange with blue man, rubber feet for vibrator on bottom; other cart is green with blue man, two pads on bottom, bayonet light socket inside, 15" long, 5" wide, 5-1/2" high. Early production featured one cart with lithographed metal baggage and one without baggage. Reproduction baggage units are available. The baggage-equipped cart was discontinued early in production because the extra weight of the baggage caused erratic operation of the carts, forcing the operator to make continual voltage adjustments. Original Lionel baggage-equipped carts are probably very scarce. Reissued by Fundimensions in 1984. Bohn, Weiss and LaVoie comments.

(A) As described above.     30   45   70   120

(B) Same as (A), but light green unpainted plastic roof, approximately Penn Central green, Lapan Collection     **NRS**

**362 BARREL LOADER** 1952-57, barrels move up the ramp by vibrator action, gray plastic base, yellow ramp, brown plastic fence, 19" long, 4-1/8" wide, 4" high. Car not included in price, came with 6 brown-stained wooden barrels, 364C controller, rubber track spacers, metal platform extension and metal track spacing guides.

(A) Cream-colored man.     30   45   60   100

(B) Blue-colored man; this version came with model packed with 4-55 instruction sheet. Salamone Collection.     30   45   60   100

**362-78** Box of six small wooden barrels for barrel car or platform. Halverson Collection.     2   4   6   9

**364 CONVEYOR LUMBER LOADER** 1948-57, gray crackle finish, red belt conveys logs; red ladder; two green, one red spotlight lens; three blue binding posts. "LIONEL ATOMIC MOTOR", 27-7/8" long, 3-3/16" wide, 4-1/8" high, came with logs, controller switch.

(A) As described above.     30   45   60   100

(B) Shiny gray paint with later Lionel motor similar to that used on 397 Coal Loader. Ocilka Collection.     30   45   60   100

342

342,345

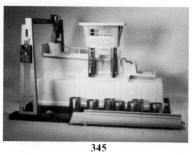

345

348

350

352(A)

353

356

362

364

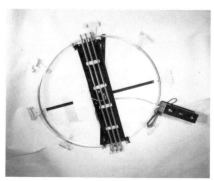

375

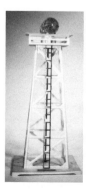

394(A)

**364C ON-OFF SWITCH** 1959-64. Some samples have a red slide instead of a black one; these are somewhat scarcer than the all-black variety. I. D. Smith comment.　　.25　.50　1.00　1.50

**365 DISPATCHING STATION** 1958-59, elevated control room shows dispatchers at work, simulated radio antenna, loud speakers; 11" long, 5" wide, 6-1/2" high; not illustrated.　　35　50　75　100

**375 TURNTABLE** 1962-64, rotates track, powered by two D cells, black metal table rotates on 0 Gauge curve rail, friction drive.
　　50　100　145　225

**390C SWITCH** 1960-64, double pole, double throw switch, for H0 reversing loop layouts, hard to find. Bohn comment. As with the 364C switch, some samples came with a red slider instead of a black one. I. D. Smith comment.　　.50　1.00　2.00　3.00

**394 ROTARY BEACON** 1949-53, light bulb heat drives beacon, bulb has dimple 11-3/4" high, base 5" x 5".
(A) Unpainted aluminum tower with black lettering.　8　12　20　30
(B) Green-painted steel tower.　　8　12　20　30
(C) Red-painted steel tower.　　8　12　20　30

**395 FLOODLIGHT TOWER** 1949-56, tower with four black die-cast floodlight units, ladders, two binding clips on bottom.
(A) Green-painted tower. This is a common variety of the tower. However, one example has been reported by Michael Ocilka which has been rubber-stamped "APR 20, 1955" on the underside of the base. We wish to know if other towers have been similarly stamped with dates and what those dates might be.　　8　12　20　30
(B) Silver-painted tower.　　8　12　20　30
(C) Yellow-painted tower, hardest of all versions to find.
　　15　25　35　50
(D) Unpainted aluminum tower. Keith, Budniak and Cusumano Collections. The easiest way to distinguish this version from the silver-painted tower is to note the lighter weight of this version. LaVoie comment.
　　10　15　25　35
(E) All red-painted tower with black ladder and lights. Lahti and LaVoie Collections; hard to find.　　15　25　35　50
NOTE: The production sequence of the 395 Floodlight Tower is apparently quite complex. We are not sure which of the five versions was produced first, although we now have good information about the relative scarcity of these towers. The yellow tower is extremely hard to find and is the most scarce of the versions. Next is the painted silver tower, followed by the red tower. The unpainted aluminum tower appears to be the second most common version, and the green one the most common of all. We have also had reports of factory conglomerations of these varieties. The 394 and 494 Rotating Beacons have similar construction variations, although nowhere near as complex as this tower. We would appreciate comments from our readers about the relative dates and scarcity of each of these versions.

**397 DIESEL OPERATING COAL LOADER** 1948-57, car dumps coal into large tray, tray vibrations (more or less!) move coal to conveyor, conveyor carries coal up and fills car; 10-1/2" long, 7-7/16" wide, 6" high.
(A) Early model with yellow diesel cover, yard light mounted on gray die-cast metal base, red coal holding unit, two motor binding posts, wires hooked directly to lamp post.　　100　150　225　350
(B) Same as (A), but no yard light.　　90　140　200　325
(C) Later model with blue diesel motor cover and without yard lights.
　　30　40　75　125
(D) Similar to (C), but has shiny red plastic tray, later type motor and rubber coupling. Ocilka Collection.　　30　40　75　125

**410 BILLBOARD BLINKER** 1956-58, green plastic billboard unit similar to 310 but with black sheet metal base; black metal back with two binding posts; die-cast metal light unit for bayonet-base bulbs, timing via metallic strip. Reissued by Fundimensions in 1982. Original very hard to find. Bohn comment.　　10　15　20　30

**413 COUNTDOWN CONTROL PANEL** 1962, controls rocket launching, gray plastic with black lettering; red dial, countdown set lever, and start and fire buttons; on the underside are two mounting posts, through which the circuit (between the two posts) is completed by depressing the "fire" button.　　6　9　12　20

**415 DIESEL FUELING STATION** 1955-67, man comes out of building; fuel pipe moves to fueling position; gray metal base, white building with red trim and roof and gray metal base, yellow base on fueling pipe and on diesel sand tank, blue tank with white lettering, three binding posts on top side of base; 9" wide, 9" long, and almost 10" high. Reissued by Fundimensions in 1983.　　30　50　100　150

**419 HELIPORT CONTROL TOWER** 1962, helicopter launched by spring mechanism, red control tower with gray roof, clear windows, with spring mechanism visible inside, pull ring for spring release protrudes from base of tower. Yellow radar disc, yellow helicopter with black blades, white lettering on tower "LIONEL HELIPORT", not lighted, terminal base 11" x 5" x 5-1/2" high.　　75　100　135　250

**443 MISSILE LAUNCHING PLATFORM** 1960-62, includes platform, missile and exploding ammo dump, 11" x 12".　　10　15　20　30

**445 SWITCH TOWER** 1952-57, blue towerman runs up and down stairs with red lantern, other blue towerman comes in and out of building; white building, green windows, balcony and roof; maroon plastic base; three binding clips on bottom. Reissued by Fundimensions in 1984.
　　18　25　35　60

**448 MISSILE FIRING RANGE SET** 1961-63, with camouflage and exploding target range car, tan plastic base; 9" x 5-1/2", gray plastic launching unit 6544-5, (launching unit also came on flatcar). Small white rockets, 6448 Target Range Car with Timken trucks, two disc-operating couplers, black metal frame, white and red side, white side with red lettering, ends and roof
　　25　35　50　75

**450 SIGNAL BRIDGE** 1952-58, spans two tracks, gray plastic base, black metal frame, two sets of red and green lights, inside width 7-1/2", inside height 6", three binding posts on each side　　15　20　32　50

**450L SIGNAL BRIDGE HEAD**, black replacement hood for this and other signal accessories; fastens to accessory by spring clips. Rohlfing comment.
　　3　5　7　10

**452 SIGNAL BRIDGE** 1961-63, also known as "Overhead Gantry Signal", Signal changes from green to red as train approaches, bridge 7-3/4" high, gray plastic base with metal grip for fastening unit, black-painted metal frame ladder, black plastic light unit, direction of light unit can be reversed.
　　40　60　80　150

**454 CONSTRUCTION SET**, listed on page 27 of 1948 catalogue. Further details needed, reader comments invited.　　NRS

**455 OIL DERRICK** 1950-54, pumping motion, bulb heat causes bubbling action in tube, four aluminum oil barrels, 9-1/4" long, 5-1/2" wide and 14-1/2" high, orange diesel unit. Reissued by Fundimensions in 1981.
(A) Red metal base, apple green metal tower, red tower top.
　　75　100　175　250
(B) Dark green metal base and tower.　　NRS
(C) Same as (A), but green tower top; slightly more common than (A). Juenemann Collection.　　75　100　175　250

**456 COAL RAMP** 1950-55, with operating hopper 9-1/2" long, not shown, gray metal ramp with red light, 35" long, 3-3/16" wide and 6-3/16" high, shown with 397 Operating Coal Loader for continuous action, price for 456 with special hopper car, red coal receiving tray, steel support rods to hold tray over 397 coal loader, special controller. Bohn comment.
(A) Light gray ramp. Rohlfing comment.　　48　60　90　150
(B) Dark blue-gray ramp; service manual denotes darker color with "X" after part numbers. Rohlfing comment.　　48　60　90　150

**460 PIGGYBACK TRANSPORTATION** 1955-57, hand crank and lever on platform (visible in illustration) cause lift truck to move 360 degrees and cause truck platform to raise and lower, flatcar and two trailers not illustrated.　　20　30　40　65

**460P PIGGYBACK PLATFORM** Carton lettered "PLATFORM", made for those already having a piggyback flatcar with vans; red lift truck, white rubber-stamped lettering "ROSS TRAILOADER". Catalano observation.
　　20　30　40　65

**460-150 TWO TRAILERS FOR FLATCARS.**
(A) Box label has "No.460-150/TWO TRAILERS". Two white Cooper-Jarrett vans with copper signs, four rubber tires on one axle for each van. Halverson Collection.　　NRS
(B) Same as (A), but pre-1958 box, two green Fruehauf vans. Ambrose Collection.　　NRS

**394(B)**

**395(A)**

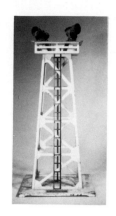

**395(B)**

**395(C)**

**397(A)**

**397(B)**

**410**

**413**

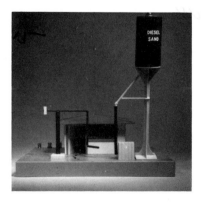

**415**

**419**

**445**

**448**

**450**

452

455

456

460

461

462

464

465

470

494

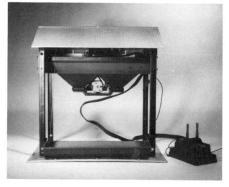

497

703-10

177

909

919

920

927

943

950

970

971

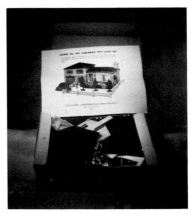

982

1045(A)

1045(B)

1047

3366-100, 362-78
3356-100, 3656-9

3356-150(A)

3356-150(B)

3110

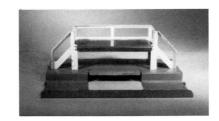

3462(A)

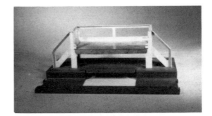

3462(B)

3530

3656(A)

3656(B)

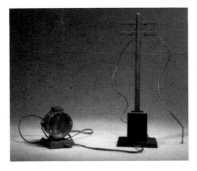

3957-50

6418

CTC Lockon

SP Smoke Pellets

**461 PLATFORM WITH TRUCK AND TRAILER** Red lift truck with blue man and black steering wheel, gray plastic base, white trailer with single axle and two wheels, tractor marked "MIDGE TOY, ROCKFORD, ILL. U.S.A. PATENT 2775847".                                25 40 60 90

**462 DERRICK PLATFORM SET** 1961-62, derrick handles "radioactive" waste containers, lifts containers from car to platform, platform has three black cranks similar to those on the 6560 Crane, one crank rotates crane unit, one moves lifts, raises and lowers boom, a third raises and lowers table, plastic radioactive containers similar to those found on flatcars but without lighting assembly, 8-1/2" long, 11" wide, 1-3/4" high, buff plastic base, yellow crane boom.                  25 40 60 100

**464 LUMBER MILL** 1956-60, simulates the transformation of logs into dressed lumber, vibrator mechanism inside moves finished lumber, gray plastic base; white mill building with red door, gray shed, length 10-1/2", width 6", height 6", logs, lumber, controller and mill. Reissued by Fundimensions in 1980.                      50 75 100 175

**465 SOUND DISPATCHING STATION** 1956-57, operator speaks into microphone, voice comes out of 4" loudspeaker in station; battery-powered, buff-colored plastic base, red room, gray roof, yellow microwave tower on roof, gray microphone with left red button for train, right red button for talk, gray plastic ladder into station, also includes lockon insulating pins, wires and four batteries, length 11", width 5", height 5", antenna 3".
                                                 30 45 60 100

**470 MISSILE LAUNCHING PLATFORM** 1959-62, missile tilts and flies, tan plastic base, blue missile launching unit base, black cradle, white, red and blue missile, includes target car; 6470 in set; note Quonset hut-type building on platform.                   12 17 25 35

**480-25 CONVERSION COUPLER** 1950-60, converts Scout coupler to remote control operation.                       .50 1.00 1.50 2.00

**480-32 CONVERSION MAGNETIC COUPLER** 1961-69, converts Scout coupler to remote control operation, has finger tab which is not present on 480-25. I. D. Smith observation.          .50 1.00 1.50 2.00

**494 ROTARY BEACON** 1954-66, vibrator-driven rotating light, 11-3/4" high, base 5" x 5", bayonet-type bulb; two binding clips on bottom.
(A) Red-painted tower with silver-lettered black metal plate on base. LaVoie Collection.                           7 12 20 30
(B) Unpainted aluminum tower, tabbed metal nameplate on base as in (A). Switzer Collection.                          7 12 20 30
(C) Silver-painted metal tower and top. Cummings and Rohlfing Collections. This version considerably heavier in weight than (B).
                                                 7 12 20 30

**497 COALING STATION** 1953-58, bin carries coal to top of structure, coal empties into overhead storage area, released from storage area into waiting car, gray metal base, black metal posts, red metal bin, green plastic roof, with controller with one lever for up and down, other lever dumps load, 10" high, 6" x 9-1/2" base. Reissued by Fundimensions in 1983.
(A) Medium green roof, same as above.       50 75 100 200
(B) Very dark green roof, Trentacoste Collection      NRS

**565 CONSTRUCTION SET**, listed on page 36 of 1948 catalogue. Further details needed; reader comments invited.           NRS

**703-10 SPECIAL SMOKE BULB** 1946, box shows 671-75.
                                                 — — 3 6

**760 072 TRACK** 1954-57, 16 sections of 0 curved track with 72" diameter, each section 14" long (Note: reproduction track available).
                                                 15 20 35 45

**868 ACCESSORY PROMOTION** 1958; Lionel offered an unusual boxed set of accessories to Service Stations. The cost to these stations was substantially below wholesale. This set included a 494 rotary beacon in a pre-1959 box, a 128 animated newsstand, a 252 crossing gate with cellophane see-through packaging, 310 billboards with 1958 billboards, a set of three 76 Boulevard Lamps in cellophane packaging, a 260 bumper, a folded 950 Railroad Map and a sheet of 12 railroad trading cards, each of which showed a locomotive from a different railroad with a quiz question. Ambrose Collection.   NRS

**902 ELEVATED TRESTLE SET**, 1960, came as part of uncatalogued set X568NA (see also Uncatalogued Sets). Came packed in paper bag which was factory stamped "902 ELEVATED TRESTLE SET" in large letters with pictures for assembly. The trestles themselves had to be punched out from

heavy cardboard sheets. Ambrose Collection. Another version of this accessory came in a cardboard container which reads "MADE 1959 THE LIONEL CORPORATION". The container held 10 cardboard punch-out trestles, 10 railroad signs, a girder bridge and a tunnel. Algozzini Collection.                                          NRS

**909 SMOKE FLUID** 1957-68, two ounces for 746, 1872, 243, etc.
                                                 — — — 2

**919 ARTIFICIAL GRASS** 1946-64, half-pound bag of artificial grass, red lettering on bag.                         — — 3 5

**920 SCENIC DISPLAY SET** 1957-58, includes four feet of mountain paper with two tunnel portals, black and gray plastic portals with "HILLSIDE" embossed on top, "L" in circle, and "1967" in lower right, came as set of two.                                    10 15 20 30

**920-2 TUNNEL PORTALS** 1957, pair of realistically molded cut stone tunnel portals. Part of 920 Scenic Display Set of 1957; also sold separately. Portals have "1957" molded on them. Bohn Collection. Reissued by Fundimensions in 1984.                   8 15 28 40

**920-3 GREEN GRASS**, 1957; bag is printed "GREEN GRASS/FOR/MODEL TRAIN LAYOUTS/L/THE LIONEL CORPORATION/NEW YORK/ N.Y./ Made In U.S. of America 920-17". Bag is 11" high by 5" wide. Part of 920 Scenic Display Kit. LaRue Collection.         .50 1 3 5

**920-4 YELLOW GRASS**, 1957; bag is printed "Yellow Grass for Model Train Layouts/L/The Lionel Corporation/New York, N.Y./Made In U.S. of America 920-18". Bag is 7" high and 5" wide. Came with 920 Scenic Display Kit with 920-2, 920-3, 920-5 and 920-8. LaRue Collection.
                                                 .50 1 5 9

**920-5 ARTIFICIAL ROCK** 1958, expanded mica-type mineral.
                                                 50 1 2 3

**920-8 LICHEN** 1958, treated and colored for realistic shrubbery.
                                                 50 1 2 3

**925 LIONEL LUBRICANT** 1946-69, large tube.     .50 1 2 3

**926 LIONEL LUBRICANT** 1955.               .25 .50 1 2

**926-5 INSTRUCTION BOOKLET** 1946-48.        .25 .50 1 2

**927 LUBRICATING AND MAINTENANCE KIT** 1950-53, tube of lubricant, vial of lubricating oil, can of track-cleaning solvent, cleaning sticks, etc.
                                                 2 4 5 7

**928 MAINTENANCE AND LUBRICANT KIT** 1960-63, includes oil, lubricant, "Track Clean".                        2 3 4 6

**943 AMMO DUMP** 1959-61, target "explodes" on impact, spring-loaded mechanism inside, gray metal base, green plastic body, 3" long, 5" wide, 4" high, four plastic parts; one each labeled "B" "A", two unlabeled ends.
                                                 4 6 8 12

**950 U.S. RAILROAD MAP** 1958-66, by Rand McNally, full color 52" x 37".
                                                 3 5 7 10

Items #951 to #969 and #980 to #988 were produced for Lionel by Bachmann Bros., Inc. of Philadelphia, Pa., manufacturers of Plasticville buildings. The sets contain regular Plasticville items, although sometimes in different quantities or combinations than Bachmann Plasticville sets.
According to Dick Reddles, Bachmann Vice President, Lionel shipped its traditional orange and blue boxes to Bachmann in Philadelphia and Bachmann packed the boxes with Plasticville and shipped them back to Lionel.
To be "Mint" or "Excellent" the following items must include the Lionel box with the Lionel number.

**951 FARM SET** 1958, 13 pieces: truck, tractor, jeep, horses, cows, harrow, plow, wagon and footbridge.              3 7 20 30

**952 FIGURE SET** 1958, 30 pieces: people, fire plug, fire alarm box and metal boxes.                             3 7 15 25

**953 FIGURE SET** 1960-62, 32 pieces including paint brush, not illustrated.
                                                 2 7 15 25

**954 SWIMMING POOL AND PLAYGROUND SET** 1959, 30 pieces: 12 fence pieces, six trees, slide, swing, teeter-totter, roundriding, bench, table with umbrella, two chairs, two chaise lounges, pool. Hemmert Collection.
                                                 3 7 15 30

**955 HIGHWAY SET** 1958, 22 pieces; two buses, auto, seven telegraph poles, 10 yellow street signs, seven green street indicators 3 7 15 30

**956 STOCKYARD SET** 1959, 18 pieces: corral, cows, railroad signs.

| | | | |
|---|---|---|---|
| 3 | 7 | 15 | 30 |

**957 FARM BUILDING AND ANIMAL SET** 1958, 35 pieces: four farm structures, fence, gate, pump, horse, fowl and domestic animals.

| | | | |
|---|---|---|---|
| 3 | 7 | 15 | 30 |

**958 VEHICLE SET** 1958, 24 pieces: three autos, two fire trucks, ambulance, bus, street signs, fire alarm box, mailbox, fire plug, traffic light.

| | | | |
|---|---|---|---|
| 3 | 7 | 15 | 30 |

**959 BARN SET** 1958, 23 pieces: dairy barn, horses, fowl and domestic animals; orange and blue traditional box, not illustrated.

| | | | |
|---|---|---|---|
| 3 | 7 | 15 | 30 |

**960 BARNYARD SET** 1959-61, 29 pieces: three farm buildings, dog house, tractor, truck, wagon, hoe, fowl, domestic and farm animals.

| | | | |
|---|---|---|---|
| 3 | 7 | 15 | 30 |

**961 SCHOOL SET** 1959, 36 pieces: school, flagpole, two buses, street signs, fence pieces, shrubs and benches.

| | | | |
|---|---|---|---|
| 3 | 7 | 15 | 30 |

**962 TURNPIKE SET** 1958, 24 pieces: interchange, stanchions, five telegraph poles, four autos, ambulance, bus and street signs.

| | | | |
|---|---|---|---|
| 3 | 7 | 18 | 35 |

**963 FRONTIER SET** 1959-60, 18 pieces: cabin, windmill, fences, cows and pump.

| | | | |
|---|---|---|---|
| 3 | 7 | 15 | 30 |

**964 FACTORY SITE SET** 1959, 18 pieces: factory with water tower, auto, four telegraph poles, railroad signs.

| | | | |
|---|---|---|---|
| 3 | 7 | 18 | 35 |

**965 FARM SET** 1959, 36 pieces: dairy barn, three farm buildings, farm equipment, fowl, domestic and farm animals.

| | | | |
|---|---|---|---|
| 3 | 7 | 15 | 30 |

**966 FIRE HOUSE SET** 1958, 45 pieces: firehouse, fire engines, alarm box, hydrant, ambulance, bus, autos, traffic light, street signs, street post, bench, mailbox, people, telegraph poles and pine trees.

| | | | |
|---|---|---|---|
| 3 | 7 | 15 | 30 |

**967 POST OFFICE SET** 1958, 25 pieces: post office, mailbox, people, benches, street lights, street post, traffic lights, truck and autos.

| | | | |
|---|---|---|---|
| 3 | 7 | 15 | 30 |

**968 TV TRANSMITTER SET** 1958, 28 pieces: TV station, fence, gate, people, mailbox, fire plug, jeep, two autos and trees.

| | | | |
|---|---|---|---|
| 7 | 10 | 20 | 35 |

**969 CONSTRUCTION SET** 1960, 23 pieces: house construction materials, workers and autos.

| | | | |
|---|---|---|---|
| 10 | 18 | 30 | 45 |

Lionel Plasticville continues at 980

**970 TICKET BOOTH** 1958-60, 46" high, 22" wide, 11" deep, simulated blackboard on front, green roof with "LIONELVILLE" sign, trimmed in red, clock on roof reads 7:07; trimmed in green and red, came packed flat in carton; carton has label with "3592-1" and manufactured by United Container Corporation, Philadelphia, PA., "United for Strength".

| | | | |
|---|---|---|---|
| 25 | 37 | 50 | 75 |

**971 LICHEN** 1960-64, box with green, yellow and brown lichen, 4-1/2 ounces.

| | | | |
|---|---|---|---|
| 2 | 3 | 4 | 6 |

**972 LANDSCAPE TREE ASSORTMENT** 1961-64, four evergreens, three flowering shrubs, lichen.

| | | | |
|---|---|---|---|
| 2 | 3 | 4 | 6 |

**973 COMPLETE LANDSCAPING SET** 1960-64, includes 4" x 8" roll of grass mat, one 16" x 48" roll of earth, ballast and road mats.

| | | | |
|---|---|---|---|
| 3 | 4 | 6 | 8 |

**974 SCENERY SET** 1962-63, 4" x 8" grass mat, two 3-D background mountains, bag of lichen, nine assorted trees.

| | | | |
|---|---|---|---|
| 4 | 6 | 8 | 10 |

Lionel Plasticville continues

**980 RANCH SET** 1960, 14 pieces: loading pen, cattle, pigs, sheep and farm implements.

| | | | |
|---|---|---|---|
| 3 | 7 | 15 | 30 |

**981 FREIGHT YARD SET** 1960, 10 pieces: loading platform with carts, switch tower, telephone poles and railroad men.

| | | | |
|---|---|---|---|
| 3 | 7 | 15 | 30 |

**982 SUBURBAN SPLIT LEVEL SET** 1960, 18 pieces: split level house, pine trees, auto, ranch and fence.

| | | | |
|---|---|---|---|
| 3 | 7 | 15 | 30 |

**983 FARM SET** 1960-61, seven pieces: dairy barn, windmill, Colonial house, horse, cows and auto.

| | | | |
|---|---|---|---|
| 10 | 20 | 35 | 50 |

**984 RAILROAD SET** 1961-62, 22 pieces: switch tower, telegraph poles, loading platform, figures, R.R. signs and accessories.

| | | | |
|---|---|---|---|
| 3 | 7 | 15 | 30 |

**985 FREIGHT AREA SET** 1961, 32 pieces: water tower, work car, loading platform, switch tower, watchman's shanty, telegraph poles, autos, R.R. signs and accessories.

| | | | |
|---|---|---|---|
| 7 | 11 | 18 | 35 |

**986 FARM SET** 1962, 20 pieces: farm house, barn and 18 domestic animals.

| | | | |
|---|---|---|---|
| 5 | 11 | 15 | 32 |

**987 TOWN SET** 1962, 24 pieces: church, gas station, auto, street signs, bank and store.

| | | | |
|---|---|---|---|
| 10 | 18 | 35 | 50 |

**988 RAILROAD STRUCTURE SET** 1962, 16 pieces: railroad station with freight platform, water tank, work car, hobo shacks, bench, figures, crossing gate and shanty.

| | | | |
|---|---|---|---|
| 6 | 11 | 15 | 32 |

**1008 UNCOUPLING UNIT** 1957, plastic clip-on uncoupler which works by spring-loaded tangs which grab disc on Timken-equipped trucks. Does not, as a rule, work very well.

| | | | |
|---|---|---|---|
| .50 | 1 | 1 | 2 |

**1008-50 UNCOUPLING TRACK SECTION** 1948, Scout type, manual uncoupler unit is permanently fastened to track piece.

| | | | |
|---|---|---|---|
| .25 | .50 | 1 | 1.50 |

**1013 CURVED TRACK** 1958-69, 0-27, 9-1/2" long.

| | | | |
|---|---|---|---|
| .10 | .15 | .20 | .40 |

**1013-17 STEEL PINS** 1946-60, 0-27, each.

| | | | |
|---|---|---|---|
| — | .05 | .05 | .05 |

**1013-42 STEEL PINS** 1961-68, per dozen.

| | | | |
|---|---|---|---|
| — | — | .60 | .80 |

**1018-1/2 STRAIGHT TRACK** 1955-69, 0-27 Gauge, 1/2 section.

| | | | |
|---|---|---|---|
| .10 | .15 | .30 | .50 |

**1018 STRAIGHT TRACK** 1945-69, 0-27, 8-7/8" long.

| | | | |
|---|---|---|---|
| .10 | .15 | .30 | .40 |

**1019 REMOTE CONTROL TRACK SET** 1946-50, for 0-27 Gauge, with controller.

| | | | |
|---|---|---|---|
| 1.50 | 2 | 5 | 8 |

**1020 90 DEGREE CROSSING** 1955-69, 0-27 track.

| | | | |
|---|---|---|---|
| 1.50 | 2 | 3 | 6 |

**1021 90 DEGREE CROSSING** 1945-54, 0-27 track, 7-3/8" square.

| | | | |
|---|---|---|---|
| 1.50 | 2 | 3 | 6 |

**1022 MANUAL SWITCH** 1953-69, pair, for 0-27 track.

| | | | |
|---|---|---|---|
| 2 | 4 | 6 | 10 |

**1023 45 DEGREE CROSSING** 1956-69, for 0-27.

| | | | |
|---|---|---|---|
| 1.50 | 2 | 3 | 6 |

**1024 MANUAL SWITCHES** 1946-52, pair 0-27, directional wiring, same moving rails as 1121 Remote Switches, circular metal red and green-painted direction markers, wide keystone-shaped aluminum and black plate reads "No. 1024/THE LIONEL CORPORATION/MADE IN U.S./OF AMERICA".

| | | | |
|---|---|---|---|
| 1 | 2 | 4 | 10 |

**1025 ILLUMINATED BUMPER** 1946-47, with lamp and one section of 0-27 track.

| | | | |
|---|---|---|---|
| 1 | 2 | 4 | 6 |

**1045 OPERATING WATCHMAN** 1946-50, large blue Bakelite man with flesh-colored hands and face, white flag, aluminum-colored post, two binding posts on bottom, red base. A very popular accessory in its time despite being ludicrously out of scale (the man is much taller than the trains!).

(A) Nickel warning sign with black letters.

| | | | |
|---|---|---|---|
| 8 | 12 | 20 | 30 |

(B) Brass sign with black lettering.

| | | | |
|---|---|---|---|
| 8 | 12 | 20 | 30 |

**1047 OPERATING SWITCHMAN** 1959-61, switchman waves flag as train approaches, green metal case, blue switchman with red flag, flesh-colored face and hands, five railroad ties with clip holding three, blue diesel fuel tank unit on base, two binding posts, black die-cast base on rail crossing sign, white plastic sign with black letters, 4-1/2" high. Reissued by Fundimensions in 1983.

| | | | |
|---|---|---|---|
| 30 | 50 | 70 | 125 |

**1121 REMOTE CONTROL SWITCHES** 1946-51, pair of 0-27 switches, each with two indicator lenses and rounded motor cover, single controller 1121-C-60 with two levers and four indicator light lenses, switches are 9-3/8" x 6-7/8" and came with either bright or satin rail finish. Units used screw-type bulbs to 1950; bayonet-type bulbs thereafter. Also produced in prewar period from 1937-42 with metal switch cover box and metal controller cover with red-painted levers. Reliable operation, La Voie comment.

(A) Flat plastic direction indicator lenses on switches.

| | | | |
|---|---|---|---|
| 7 | 10 | 20 | 30 |

(B) Protruding rubber direction indicator lenses on switches, rivet location on bottom differs from (A).

| | | | |
|---|---|---|---|
| 7 | 10 | 20 | 30 |

**1122 REMOTE CONTROL SWITCHES** 1952, early production: pair of 0-27 switches, each with rotating direction indicator and a single controller 1122-100 with two levers and four indicator light lenses, non-derailing design. Five notches on switchbox cover, insulated rails on outside with insulating break in rail itself so that no insulated pins were needed. The moving rails were fastened to the drive rod with a large circular rivet. A light was mounted on a separate socket which plugs into a notch accessible through an arch-shaped hole in cover. Came at first with swiveling directional lenses with exposed surfaces which broke easily; later versions have recessed lenses. Flat frog point and wide frog rail. Operational problems and "teething" troubles led to a substantial redesign in 1953; see 1122E entry. LaVoie comment.

(A) 1952, direction indicator with exposed lenses.    10   20   30   40

(B) 1953, direction indicator with recessed lenses.    10   20   30   40

**1122E REMOTE CONTROL SWITCHES** 1953-69, pair of 0-27 switches, each with rotating direction indicator and a single controller, 1122-100 with two levers and four indicator light lenses.

(A) Three notches on redesigned rounded switch cover which allowed clearance for larger locos. (Note: Lionel also sold this rounded cover to retrofit the older switches; this version had the arched cutout for the light socket.) Light clip redesigned to be completely internal, thus eliminating the arched cutout and separate light socket. The insulated rails were moved to the two inside short rails which branch from a rounded frog point; insulating pins now required. The long curved and straight rails were made solid without any breaks, and a metal track insert was placed on the frog to prevent premature wear of the plastic base by wheel flanges. This switch had its moving rails fastened to the drive rod by a large clover-shaped rivet. The rack in the mechanism was redesigned and the frog rail made much narrower. The bracket for the directional indicator was reinforced. Stamped "MODEL 1122 (E)" on galvanized base bottom; reliable operation. LaVoie comment.    10   20   30   40

(B) Same as (A), but later production: small circular rivet fastens moving rails to drive rod instead of clover-shaped rivet.    10   20   30   40

**1122LH SWITCH** 1955-69, 0-27, remote control, left-hand with controller.    5   9   13   18

**1122RH SWITCH** 1955-69, 0-27, remote control, right-hand with controller.    5   9   13   18

**1122-234 FIBER PINS** 1958-60, 0-27 each.    .03   .05   .05   .05

**1122-500 0-27 GAUGE ADAPTER** 1957-66, For combining 0-27 and Super 0, four ground rail pins, two insulating pins, three power rail pins.    .25   .50   1   2

**1640-100 PRESIDENTIAL KIT** 1960, car decals, whistle stop audience, Presidential candidate.    3   7   12   15

**2003 TRACK "MAKE-UP" KIT FOR "027 TRACK"** 1963, box has black over print: "MAKE THIS EXCITING 'LOOP-TO-LOOP' LAYOUT!" Contains eight No. 1013 curved track, two No. 1018 straight track and one No. 1023 45-degree crossover. Griesbeck Collection.    **NRS**

**3330-100 OPERATING SUBMARINE KIT** 1960-61, kit that after assembly operates under water.    5   10   15   20

**3356-150 HORSE CAR CORRAL** Horse moves by vibrator action, galvanized metal base; white plastic frame.

(A) Green and brown interior plastic liners, black horses, came with matching car; price for corral only.    10   15   20   35

(B) Same as (A), but with gray and red interior liners and white horses, price for corral only.    15   20   30   40

(C) Red watering trough instead of gray. Trentacoste Collection.    **NRS**

**3366-100 NINE WHITE HORSES** 1959-60, extra horses for 3356.    5   7   10   20

**3376 GIRAFFE ACTIVATOR UNIT.**    2   3   4   6

**3424-75** See next entry.

**3424-100 LOW BRIDGE SIGNAL SET** Operated giraffe and brakeman car.    2   3   4   6

NOTE: Every box for the above accessory is marked "3424-100 Low Bridge Signal Set". However, there were two distinct combinations for this accessory, one for the 3424 Wabash Brakeman Car and one for the 3376-86 Giraffe Car. The Lionel Service Manual refers to the giraffe car version as 3424-75, although no box is known to be marked that way. The differences are as follows: the 3424 Brakeman Car came with two boxed 3424-100 telltale poles. Each box included the telltale and a base with spring-mounted track clips. Four two-rail grounding rails came with the brakeman car, two for 0 and two for 027 track. This ground rail was fastened to the base by twisting its metal tangs into holes in the bottom of the base. The 3376-86 Giraffe Cars also came with the telltale pole and track base, but the ground rails were replaced by a long, spring-loaded bar which fastened outside the rails to a small indentation in the track clip and pressed

against the outside rail sides at its ends. We need to hear from a reader who has a 3376 Bronx Zoo Giraffe Car in its original packing box to be sure of the designation of this accessory for the giraffe car; reader comments are requested. Roskoski and LaVoie comments.

**3462P MILK CAR PLATFORM** All metal unit.

(A) Green base, white platform frame, gray steps, unpainted platform, came with milk car, price for platform only.    2   3   5   10

(B) Brown base, gray steps, unpainted platform, yellow railing, came with Bosco car, price for platform only.    20   28   35   50

SPECIAL NOTE: Research of several 3462P platforms shows that this number was stamped on the bottom base of all milk car platforms. All samples observed (TOY TRAIN STATION, about 6 or 7) were from original 3472 and 3482 boxes. It's safe to conclude that 3462P is the only existing number for this platform. R.E. LaVoie.

**3530 SEARCHLIGHT WITH POLE AND BASE** Came with blue generator car marked 3530, searchlight has red base with magnet, gray plastic housing, plastic lens, green wire and bayonet-type bulb, telegraph pole is brown unpainted plastic; black unpainted plastic base is marked "SERVICE TRANSFORMER THE LIONEL CORPORATION NEW YORK, N.Y." with aluminum metal tube, two green wires emerge from the aluminum tube, hook into the female receptacles on the boxcar. Price with car.    15   25   50   75

**3656 STOCKYARD WITH CATTLE** Cattle powered by vibrator motor march through pen into car and out, stockyard is a metal unit with plastic gates, loading ramp, came with 3656 operating cattle car, price for pen only.

(A) Early version with two rubber grommets at each end, chain on right-hand side (as unit faces camera), does not have decal in center, operates better than later unit.    7   10   15   25

(B) Later model with metal plate on center of unit visible in illustration, binding post right side, rubber supporting pads underneath platform, platform lifts out, not permanently fastened, yellow metal frame and gate, shiny metal platform, green base with ramp for cows.    5   7   12   20

(C) No chain or holes for chains, but base has nameplate. Appears to be a factory conglomeration of versions (A) and (B). Cummings Collection.    **NRS**

**3672-79 SEVEN BOSCO CANS** 1960, for 3672 car.    5   7   9   15

**3927-50 COTTON TRACK CLEANING PADS** 1957-60.    .50   1   2   4

**3927-75 TRACK CLEAN FLUID** 1957-69, non-flammable detergent.    .50   1   2   3

**5159 MAINTENANCE AND LUBRICANT KIT** 1964-68.    1   2   3   4

**5159-50 MAINTENANCE AND LUBRICANT KIT** 1969.    1   2   3   4

**6019 REMOTE CONTROL TRACK** 1948-66, for 0-27 track, unloading and uncoupling.    1   2   3   4

**6029 UNCOUPLING TRACK SET** 1955-63, 0-27, uncoupling only.    .25   .50   1   2

**6149 REMOTE CONTROL UNCOUPLING TRACK** 1964-69.    .25   .50   1   2

**6418 BRIDGE** sheet metal base painted black, black plastic sides with white lettered "U.S.STEEL 6418"; sides are marked "6418" in box to lower right side, but metal base is embossed "214" Switzer observation.    1   2   3   7

**6650-80 MISSILE** 1960, for 6650, 6823, 443 and 470.    1   2   4   6

**6816-100 ALLIS CHALMERS TRACTOR DOZER** 1956-60.    4   6   8   15

**6817-100 ALLIS CHALMERS MOTOR SCRAPER** 1959-60.    4   6   8   15

**6827-100 HARNISCHFEGER TRACTOR SHOVEL** 1960.    5   7   9   17

**6828-100 HARNISCHFEGER MOBILE CONSTRUCTION CRANE** 1960    5   7   9   17

**OC CURVED TRACK** 1945-61, 10-7/8", 0 Gauge.    .15   .25   .40   .70

**TOC CURVED TRACK** 1962 66, 1968-69, 10-7/8", 0 Gauge.    .15   .25   .40   .70

**OS STRAIGHT TRACK** 1945-61, 0 Gauge.    .20   .30   .40   .70

**TOS STRAIGHT TRACK** 1962-69, 0 Gauge.    .20   .30   .40   .70

**1/2OC HALF SECTION CURVED TRACK** 1945-66, 0 Gauge.    .20   .30   .40   .70

| | | | | |
|---|---|---|---|---|
| **TOC1/2 HALF SECTION STRAIGHT TRACK** 1962-66, 0 Gauge. | | | | |
| | .20 | .30 | .40 | .70 |
| **OTC LOCKON** See illustration of 154 contractor. | .15 | .20 | .30 | .50 |
| **OC18 STEEL PINS** 1945-59, each. | .02 | .03 | .05 | .05 |
| **OC51 STEEL PINS** 1961, dozen. | .20 | .30 | .50 | .75 |
| **TOC51 STEEL PINS** 1962-69, dozen. | .20 | .30 | .50 | .75 |
| **011-11 FIBER PINS** 1946-50, each. | .03 | .03 | .05 | .05 |
| **T011-43 FIBER PINS** 1962-66, dozen. | .20 | .30 | .40 | .60 |
| **UTC LOCKON** 1945, fits 0-27, 0 and standard Gauge track. | | | | |
| | .25 | .50 | .75 | 1.25 |

**RCS REMOTE CONTROL TRACK** 1945-48, for 0 Gauge, five rails, does not have electromagnet.  1  2  2  3

**ECU-1 ELECTRONIC CONTROL UNIT** 1946.  10  15  20  40

**CTC LOCKON** 1947-69, for 0 and 0-27 track.  .10  .20  .30  .40

**UCS REMOTE CONTROL TRACK** 1948-69, for 0 Gauge.  3  5  8  15

**LTC LOCKON** 1950-69, with light, for 0 and 0-27 track.  1  2  3.50  5

**SP SMOKE PELLETS** 1948-69, 50 tablets per bottle.  —  —  —  10

## TRANSFORMERS

Transformers are usually bought to operate trains and related items. Hence if a transformer is not operating it has little if any value. (If a transformer is repairable, after it is repaired, it will yield the values indicated.) Several of the larger models such as the KW, V, VW, Z or ZW have some minimal value - even if completely burned out - for knobs, plates and nuts. In the listing that follows, we report only Good, Excellent and Mint conditions and the value assigned assumes that the transformer is in operating condition.

**1010** 1961-1966, 35 watts, circuit breaker.  1  1.50  3

**1011** 1948-1949, 25 watts.  1  1.50  3

**1012** 1950-54, 40 watts.  1  1.50  3

**1014** 40 watts, handle colors either red, black or silver. Rohlfing observation.  1  1.50  3

**1015** 1956-1960, 45 watts.  1  1.50  3

**1016** 1959-1960, 35 watts.  1  1.50  3

**1025** 1961-1969, 45 watts, circuit breaker.  1  1.50  3

**1026** 1961-1964, 25 watts, made as early as 1961; came with set 1123 made in that year. Rohlfing comment.  1  1.50  3

**1032** 1948, 75 watts, reverse and whistle controls.  9  14  18

**1033** 1948-1956, 90 watts, whistle control. Very good reputation for reliability. LaVoie comment.  10  15  20

**1034** 1948-54, 75 watts.  6  9  15

**1037** 1946-1947, 5-17 volts, 40 watts.  1  1.50  3

**1041** 1945-1946, 60 watts, whistle control, circuit breaker.  5  7  11

**1042** 1947-1948, 75 watts, whistle control, circuit breaker.  9  14  18

**1043**

(A) 1953-1957, 50 watts, black case.  2  3  5

(B) 60 watts, ivory case with gold-plated speed control and binding post for Girls' Set. Black base, embossed in stylized letters "SA".  15  20  40

**1044** 1957-1969, 90 watts, whistle control, direction control.  10  15  20

**1053** 1956-1960, 60 watts, whistle control.  5  8  11

**1063** 1960-1964, 75 watts, whistle control, circuit breaker.  9  14  18

**1073** 1962-1966, 60 watts, circuit breaker.  3  5  17

**1101** 1948, 25 watts.  1  1.50  3

**A** 1947-1948, 90 watts, circuit breaker, 14-24 volts.  8  10  18

**KW** 190 watts, operates two trains with whistle control, circuit breaker. Favored by many operators due to separate 14 volt fixed circuit.  35  60  100

**LW** 1955-1966, 125 watts, green power "on light", buttons for direction and horn, circuit breaker.  15  20  35

**Q** 1946, 75 watts, 6-24 volts, whistle control.  8  12  18

**R** 1946-1947, two independent circuits, 100 watts, 6-24 volts.  11  15  30

**RW** 1948-1954, 110 watts, circuit breaker, whistle control.  8  15  25

**S** 1947 only; catalogued as 75 watt but produced as 80 watt; dial-type rheostat, whistle and reversing controls. Rohlfing Collection.  8  12  18

**SW** 1961-1966, 130 watts, two-train operation, whistle.  18  35  50

**TW** 1953-1960, 175 watts, whistle control.  18  40  70

**V** 1946-1947, 150 watts, four independent circuits.  18  30  60

**VW** 1948-1949, 150 watts, four independent circuits.  30  50  125

**Z** 1945-1947, 250 watts, four independent circuits, 6-25.  25  50  75

**ZW** 1948-1949, 250 watts, four independent circuits.  65  75  145

**ZW** 275 watts, four independent circuits. Excellent examples in great demand. Earlier examples with Bakelite circuit breakers which hold up much better than later wafer-type; replacement Bakelite circuit breakers are available for about $10. Original box brings $5.00 premium. LaVoie comment.  75  95  160

## LIONEL METAL TRUCKS

Lionel produced at least seven major types of metal trucks, each of which described below:

I. Metal Trucks with Early Coil Coupler, Whirly Wheels (1945). Type I has the first postwar trucks, a remotely-operated knuckle coupler with a coil on the coupler shank and a shaft that is moved by the coil to open the knuckle. A sliding shoe contacts the special remote control uncoupling section and is mounted on a jury-rigged bracket. The bracket is readily visible on the underside of the truck. The truck side frames are fastened by a rivet swaged over resembling a "staple-end". The wheels have a whirl pattern on the inside back surface and ride on thickened axles.

Bottom view of Type 1 trucks

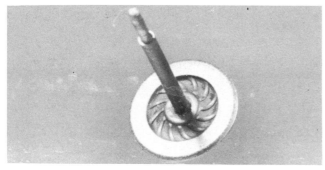

Whirly wheel with thick axle

II. Metal Trucks with Early Coil Coupler, Regular Wheels (1945-1946). This is similar to Type I but has wheels with regular back inside surfaces and axles of usual thickness.

III. Metal Trucks with Late Coil Coupler (1946-1947). This coupler also uses an opening knuckle activated by a coil and plunger and the truck side frames have the "staple end" fastening. However, the mounting bracket for the sliding shoe is integral with the metal plate that covers the bottom of the truck.

IV. Metal Trucks with Magnetic Coupler, Staple-End and No Hole on Activator Flap (introduced 1948). Lionel found that it could produce a highly reliable coupling action without the expense and complication of a coil plunger unit. Lionel designed a coupler that opens by pulling down a flap on the underside of the truck. To move the flap Lionel modified the remote control track and added an electromagnet to the center of that track. The electromagnet pulls the flap which is connected to the coupler by a lever arrangement so that the knuckle opens. The flap has a rivet swaged on the underside and no hole on the flap with the rivet. Type IV is a highly successful design.

V. Metal Trucks with Magnetic Coupler, Staple-End and Hole on Activator Flap (introduced circa 1950). This type is the same as Type IV but a hole

has been added to the activator flap behind the rivet. The rivet on the flap is swaged on the truck's top surface.

Side and bottom views of two versions of the bar-end truck. The left truck hs a magnetic coupler, the right has the late coil coupler.

VI. Metal Trucks with Magnetic Coupler, Bar-End and Hole on activator Flap (introduced circa 1952). Lionel modified Type V by changing the method of fastening the side frames to the bolster with a bar fitting into the side frames. The top of the bolster is embossed.

VII. Metal Trucks with Magnetic Coupler, Bar-End Hole on Activator Flap and Tab (circa 1955). Lionel modified Truck Type VI by adding a tab to facilitate hand uncoupling. This design change made the trains easier for children to play with at some slight sacrifice of realism.

Side and bottom views of Type VI and Type VII.

# Chapter XII
# CATALOGUED SETS

### CATALOGUED SETS

By Cindy Floyd

Our report is based on the consumer catalogue illustrations, advance catalogues and wholesale sheets. We urge our readers to check their equipment against these lists and report to us when the equipment deviates. We do not know if all sets were actually made. We would appreciate reader confirmation of original boxed sets in their possession and reader information on uncatalogued sets not listed here.

All Lionel catalogued sets are listed in the order in which they appeared in the catalogue.

### 1945

**LIONEL CATALOGUE SETS**

**463W:** 224 Locomotive, 2224, 2458, 2452, 2555, 2457, eight OCs, three OSs, RCS, 167, UTC.

### 1946

**LIONEL CATALOGUE SETS**

**4109WS:** 671R Locomotive, 4424W, 4452, 4454, 5459, 4457, eight OCs, four OSs, UTC, ECU, 926-5.

**1401:** 1654 Locomotive, 1654T, 2452, 2465, 2472, eight 1013s, 1018, 1019,UTC, 926-5, 1037.

**1401W:** Same as above, but with built-in whistle in tender and 1041.

**1400:** 221 Locomotive, 221T, two 2430s, 2431, eight 1013s, three 1018s, 1019, UTC, 926-5, 1037.

**1400W:** Same as above, but with built-in whistle in tender and 1041.

**1403:** 221 Locomotive, 221T, 2411, 2465, 2472, eight 1013s, three 1018s, 1019, UTC, 926-5, 1037.

**1403W:** Same as above, but with built-in whistle and 1041.

**1402:** 1666 Locomotive, 2466T, two 2440s, 2441, eight 1013s, three 1018s, 1019, UTC, 926-5, 1037.

**1402W:** Same as above, but with built-in whistle and 1041.

**1405:** 1666 Locomotive, 2466T, 2452, 2465, 2472, eight 1013s, three 1018s, 1019, UTC, 926-5, 1037.

**1405W:** Same as above, but with built-in whistle and 1041.

**1407B:** 1665 Locomotive, 2403B, 2419, 2560, 2452X, eight 1013s, five 1018s, 1019, UTC, 926-5, 1037.

**1409:** 1666 Locomotive, 2466T, 3559, 2465, 3454, 2472, eight 1013s,five 1018s, 1019, UTC, 926-5, 1037.

**1409W:** Same as above, but with built-in whistle and 1041.

**1411W:** 1666 Locomotive, 2466WX, 2452X, 2465, 2454, 2472, eight 1013s, three 1018s, 1019, UTC, 926-5, 1041.

**1413WS:** 2020 Locomotive, 2466WX, 2452X, 2465, 2454, 2472, eight 1013s, three 1018s, 1019, UTC, 926-5, 1041.

**1417WS:** 2020 Locomotive, 2020W, 2465, 3451, 2560, 2419, eight 1013s, five 1018s, 1019, UTC, 926-5, 1041.

**1415WS:** 2020 Locomotive, 2020W, 3459, 3454, 2465, 2472, ten 1013s, five 1018s, 1019, 1121, UTC, 926-5, 1041.

**1419WS:** 2020 Locomotive, 2020W, 3459, 2452X, 2560, 2419, 97, ten 1013s, five 1018s, 1019, two 1121, UTC, 926-5, 1041.

**1421WS:** 2020 Locomotive, 2020W, 3451, 2465, 3454, 2472, 164, ten 1013s, five 1018s, 1019, two 1121, UTC, 926-5, 1041.

**2100:** 224 Locomotive, 2246, two 2442s, 2443, eight OCs, three OSs,RCS, UTC, 926-5.

**2100W:** Same as above, but with built-in whistle and 167.

**2101:** 224 Locomotive, 2466, 2555, 2452, 2457, eight OCs, three OSs, RCS, UTC, 926-5.

**2101W:** Same as above, but with built-in whistle and 167.

**2103W:** 224 Locomotive, 2466W, 2458, 3559, 2555, 2457, eight OCs, three OSs, RCS, UTC, 926-5, 167.

**2105WS:** 671 Locomotive, 2466W, 2555, 2454, 2457, eight OCs, three OSs, RCS, UTC, 926-5, 167.

**2110WS:** 671 Locomotive, 2466W, three 2625s, eight OCs, five OSs, RCS, UTC, 926-5, 167.

**2111WS:** 671 Locomotive, 2466W, 3459, 2411, 2460, 2420, eight OCs, five OSs, RCS, UTC, 926-5, 167.

**2113WS:** 726 Locomotive, 2426W, 2855, 3854, 2857, eight OCs, seven OSs, RCS, UTC, 926-5, 167.

**2114WS:** 726 Locomotive, 2426W, three 2625s, eight OCs, five OSs, RCS, UTC, 926-5, 167.

**2115WS:** 726 Locomotive, 2426W, 2458, 3451, 2460, 2420, eight OCs, three OSs, RCS, UTC, 926-5, 167.

**2116WS:** 703 Locomotive, 2703W, four 2625s, eight OCs, seven OSs, RCS, UTC, 926-5, 167. Not manufactured.

**2117WS:** 703 Locomotive, 2703W, 2856, 3854, 2855, 2857, eight OCs, seven OSs, RCS, UTC, 926-5, 167. Not manufactured.

### 1947

**LIONEL CATALOGUE SETS**

**1431W:** 1654 Locomotive, 1654W, 2452X, 2465, 2472, eight 1013s, 1018, 1019, CTC, 1042, 926-5.

**1431:** Same as above, but without whistle and 1035.

**1432W:** 221 Locomotive, 221W, two 2430s, 2431, eight 1013s, three 1018s, 1019, CTC, 1042, 926-5.

**1432:** Same as above, but without whistle and 1035.

**1433W:** 221 Locomotive, 221W, 2411, 2465, 2457, eight 1013s, three 1018s, 1019, CTC, 1042, 926-5.

**1433:** Same as above, but without whistle and 1035.

**1434WS:** 2025 Locomotive, 2466WX, two 2440s, 2441, eight 1013s, three 1018s, 1019, CTC, 926-5, S transformer.

**1435WS:** 2025 Locomotive, 2466WX, 2452X, 2454, 2457, eight 1013s, three 1018s, 1019, CTC, 926-5, S transformer.

**1439WS:** 2025 Locomotive, 2466WX, 3559, 2465, 3454, 2457, eight 1013s, five 1018s, 1019, CTC, 926-5, S transformer.

**1437WS:** 2025 Locomotive, 2466WX, 2452X, 2465, 2454, 2472, eight 1013s, five 1018s, 1019, CTC, 926-5, S transformer.

**1441WS:** 2020 Locomotive, 2020W, 2419, 2560, 2461, 3451, eight 1013s, five 1018s, 1019, CTC, 926-5, S transformer.

**1443WS:** 2020 Locomotive, 2020W, 3459, 3462, 2465, 2457, ten 1013s, five 1018s, 1019, 1121, CTC, 926-5, S transformer.

**2120WS:** 675 Locomotive, 2466WX, two 2442s, 2443, eight OCs, three OSs, RCS, CTC, 167, 926-5.

**2120S:** Same as above, but with 2466T and without 167, but with 88.

**2121WS:** 675 Locomotive, 2466WX, 167, 2555, 2452, 2457, eight OCs, three OSs, RCS, CTC, 926-5.

**2121S:** Same as above, but with 2426T and without 167, but with 88.

**2123WS:** 675 Locomotive, 2466WX, 2458, 3559, 2555, 2457, eight OCs, three OSs, RCS, CTC, 167, 926-5.

**2125WS:** 671 Locomotive, 671W, 2411, 2454, 2452, 2457, eight OCs, five OSs, RCS, CTC, 167, 926-5.

**2126WS:** 671 Locomotive, 671W, three 2625s, eight OCs, five OSs, RCS, CTC, 167, 926-5.

**2124W:** 2332 Locomotive, three 2625s, eight OCs, five OSs, RCS, CTC, 167, 926-5.

**2127WS:** 671 Locomotive, 671W, 3459, 2461, 2460, 2420, eight OCs, five OSs, RCS, CTC, 167, 926-5.

**2129WS:** 726 Locomotive, 2426W, 3854, 2411, 2855, 2457, eight OCs, seven OSs, RCS, CTC, 167, 926-5.

**2131WS:** 726 Locomotive, 2426W, 3462, 3451, 2460, 2420, eight OCs, seven OSs, RCS, CTC, 167, 926-5.

**4109WS:** 671R Locomotive, 4671W, 4452, 4454, 5459, 4457, eight OCs, six OSs, CTC, ECU-50, ECU-1, 926-5.

## 1948
### LIONEL CATALOGUE SETS

**1111:** 1001 Locomotive, 1001T, 1002, 1005, 1007, eight 1013s, 1018, 1009, 1011, CTC.

**1112:** 1001 Locomotive, 1001T, 1002, 1004, 1005, 1007, eight 1013s, three 1018s, 1009, CTC-10, 1011, 926-5.

**1423W:** 1655 Locomotive, 6654, 6452, 6465, 6257, eight 1013s, three 1018s, 6019, CTC, 1042, 926-5.

**1425B:** 1656 Locomotive, 6403B, 6456, 6465, 6257X, eight 1013s, three 1018s, 6019, CTC, 1034, 926-5.

**1427WS:** 2026 Locomotive, 6466WX, 6465, 6454, 6257, eight 1013s, three 1018s, 6019, CTC, 1032, 926-5.

**1426WS:** 2026 Locomotive, 6466WX, two 6440s, 6441, eight 1013s, three 1018s, 6019, CTC, 1032, 926-5.

**1429WS:** 2026 Locomotive, 6466WX, 3451, 6465, 6454, 6357, eight 1013s, five 1018s, 6019, CTC, 1033, 926-5.

**1430WS:** 2025 Locomotive, 6466WX, 2400, 2402, 2401, eight 1013s, seven 1018s, 6019, CTC, 1033, 926-5.

**1445WS:** 2025 Locomotive, 6466WX, 3559 with 206, 6465, 6454, 6357, eight 1013s, five 1018s, 6019, CTC, 1033, 926-5.

**1447WS:** 2020 Locomotive, 6020W, 3451, 2461, 2460, 6419, eight 1013s, five 1018s, 6019, CTC, 1033, 926-5.

**1449WS:** 2020 Locomotive, 6020W, 3462, 6465, 3459 with 206, 6411, 6357, eight 1013s, eleven 1018s, 6019, CTC, 1033, 926-5.

**2135WS:** 675 Locomotive, 2466WX, 2456, 2411, 2357, eight OCs, three OSs, RCS, CTC, 926-5.

**2136WS:** 675 Locomotive, 2466WX, two 2442s, 2443, eight OCs, three OSs, RCS, CTC, 926-5.

**2137WS:** 675 Locomotive, 2466WX, 2458, 3459, 2456, 2357, eight OCs, three OSs, RCS, CTC, 926-5.

**2140WS:** 671 Locomotive, 2671W, 2400, 2402, 2401, eight OCs, five OSs, RCS, CTC.

**2141WS:** 671 Locomotive, 2671W, 3451, 3462, 2456, 2357, eight OCs, five OSs, RCS, CTC.

**2143WS:** 671 Locomotive, 2671, 3459, 2461, 2460, 2420, eight OCs, five OSs, RCS, CTC.

**2145WS:** 726 Locomotive, 2426W, 3462, 2411, 2460, 2357, eight OCs, seven OSs, RCS, CTC.

**2146WS:** 726 Locomotive, 2426W, 2625, 2627, 2628, eight OCs, seven OSs, RCS, CTC.

**2139W:** 2332 Locomotive, 3451, 2458, 2456, 2357, eight OCs, five OSs, RCS, CTC, 926-5.

**2144W:** 2332 Locomotive, 2625, 2627, 2628, eight OCs, five OSs, RCS, CTC, 926-5.

**2133W:** 2333 Santa Fe Twin Diesel, 2458, 3459, 2555, 2357, eight OCs, seven OSs, RCS, CTC.

**2133W:** 2333 New York Central Twin Diesel, 2458, 3459, 2555, 2357, eight OCs, seven OSs, RCS, CTC.

## 1949
### LIONEL CATALOGUE SETS

**1115:** 1110 Locomotive, 1001T, 1002, 1005, 1007, 1011, CTC, 1009, eight 1013s, 1018.

**1117:** 1110 Locomotive, 1001T, 1002, 1005, 1004, 1007, 1011, CTC, 1009, eight 1013s, three 1018s.

**1423W:** 1655 Locomotive, 6654W, 6452, 6465, 6257, eight 1013s, three 1018s, 6019, 1033, CTC, 027C-1.

**1425B:** 1656 Locomotive, 6403B, 6456, 6465, 6257, eight 1013s, three 1018s, 6019, 1034, CTC, 127C-1.

**1451WS:** 2026 Locomotive, 6466WX, 6462, 3464, 6257, eight 1013s, three 1018s, 6019, 1033, SP, CTC, 027C-1.

**1426WS:** 2026 Locomotive, 6466WX, two 6440s, 6441, eight 1013s, CTC, three 1018s, SP, 6019, 1033, 027C-1.

**1453WS:** 2026 Locomotive, 6466WX, 3464, 6465, 3461, 6357, eight 1013s, CTC, five 1018s, SP, 6019, 1033, 027C-1.

**1455WS:** 2025 Locomotive, 6466WX, 6462, 6465, 3472, 6357, eight 1013s, CTC, five 1018s, SP, 6019, 1033, 027C-1.

**1475B:** 622 Diesel, 6462, 3464, 6520, 6419, eight 1013s, 027C-1, five 1018s, CTC, 1034, 6019.

**1430WS:** 2025 Locomotive, 6466WX, 2402, 2400, 2401, eight 1013s, 027C-1, seven 1018s, CTC, 1033, SP, 6019.

**1447WS:** 2020 Locomotive, 6020W, 6461, 3461, 2460, 6419, eight 1013s, CTC, five 1018s, 027C-1, 1033, 6019, SP.

**1459WS:** 2020 Locomotive, 6020W, 6411, 3656, 6465, 3469, 6357, eight 1013s, CTC, eleven 1018s, 027C-1, 6019, 1033, SP.

**2135WS:** 675 Locomotive, 6466WX, 6456, 6411, 6457, eight OCs, three OSs, UCS, CTC, CO-1, SP.

**2136WS:** 675 Locomotive, 6466WX, two 6442s, 6443, eight OCs, three OSs, UCS, CTC, CO-1, SP.

**2147WS:** 675 Locomotive, 6466WX, 3472, 3465, 3469, 6457, eight OCs, three OSs, UCT, CTC, CO-1, SP.

**2149B:** 622 Diesel, 6520, 3469, 2460, 6419, eight OCs, five OSs, UCS, CTC, CO-1.

**2139W:** 2332 Locomotive, 6456, 3464, 3461, 6457, eight OCs, five OSs, UCS, CTC, CO-1.

**2141WS:** 671 Locomotive, 2671W, 3472, 6456, 3461, 6457, eight OCs, five OSs, UCS, CTC, CO-1, SP.

**2140WS:** 671 Locomotive, 2671W, 2400, 2402, 2401, eight OCs, five OSs, UCS, CTC, CO-1, SP.

**2153WS:** 671 Locomotive, 2671W, 3469, 6520, 2460, 6419, eight OCs, five OSs, UCS, CTC, CO-1, SP.

**2151W:** 2333 Santa Fe Twin Diesel, 3464, 6555, 3469, 6520, 6457, eight OCs, nine OSs, UCS, CTC, CO-1.

**2151W:** 2333 New York Central Twin Diesel, 3464, 6555, 3469, 6520, 6457, eight OCs, nine OSs, UCS, CTC, CO-1.

**2144W:** 2332 Locomotive, 2625, 2627, 2628, eight OCs, five OSs, UCS, CTC, CO-1.

**2155WS:** 726 Locomotive, 6426W, 6411, 3656, 2460, 6457, eight OCs, seven OSs, UCS, CTC, CO-1, SP.

**2146WS:** 726 Locomotive, 2426W, 2625, 2627, 2628, eight OCs, seven OSs, UCS, CTC, CO-1, SP.

**4110WS:** 671 Locomotive, 4671W, 4452, 4454, 5459, 4357, 97, 151, VW transformer, ECU-1, ten OCs, eighteen OSs, two-1/2 OSs, 022, CTC, CO-1, SP, ECU-50.

## 1950
### LIONEL CATALOGUE SETS

**1113:** 1120 Locomotive, 1001T, 1002, 1005, 1007, eight 1013s, 1018, 1009, 1011, CTC.

**1461S:** 6110 Locomotive, 6001T, 6002, 6004, 6007, eight 1013s, three 1018s, 6019, 1012, CTC, SP.

**1463W:** 2036 Locomotive, 6466W, 6462, 6465, 6257, eight 1013s, three 1018s, 6019, 1033, CTC.

**1469WS:** 2035 Locomotive, 6466W, 6462, 6465, 6456, 6257, eight 1013s, three 1018s, 6019, 1033, CTC, SP.

**1457B:** 6220 Diesel, 6520, 3464, 6462, 6419, eight 1013s, five 1018s, 6019, 1034, CTC.

**1473WS:** 2046 Locomotive, 2046W, 3464, 6465, 6520, 6357, eight 1013s, five 1018s, 6019, 1033, CTC, SP.

**1464W:** 2023P Twin Diesel, 2481, 2482, 2483, eight 1013s, five 1018s, 6019, 1033, CTC.

**1467W:** 2023P Twin Diesel, 6656, 6465, 6456, 6357, eight 1013s, five 1018s, 6019, 1033, CTC.

**1471WS:** 2035 Locomotive, 6466W, 3469X, 6465, 6454, 3461X, 6357, eight 1013s, seven 1018s, 6019, 1033, CTC, SP.

**1475WS:** 2046 Locomotive, 2046W, 3656, 3461X, 6472, 3469X, 6419, eight 1013s, seven 1018s, 6019, 1033, CTC, SP.

**2167WS:** 681 Locomotive, 2671W, 6462, 3464, 6457, eight OCs, five OSs, UCS, CTC, SP.

**2163WS:** 736 Locomotive, 2671WX, 6472, 6462, 6555, 6457, eight OCs, seven OSs, UCS, CTC, SP.

**2173WS:** 681 Locomotive, 2671W, 3472, 6555, 3469X, 6457, eight OCs, seven OSs, USC, CTC, SP.

**2159W:** 2330 Locomotive, 3464, 6462, 3461X, 6456, 6457, eight OCs, seven OSs, USC, CTC.

**2150WS:** 681 Locomotive, 2671W, 2421, 2422, 2423, eight OCs, five OSs, UCS, CTC, SP.

**2165WS:** 736 Locomotive, 2671WX, 3472, 6456, 3461X, 6457, eight OCs, seven OSs, UCS, CTC, SP.

**2175W:** 2343P Twin Diesel, 6456, 3464, 6555, 6462, 6457, eight OCs, seven OSs, UCS, CTC.

**2185W:** 2344P Twin Diesel, 6456, 3464, 6555, 6462, 6457, eight OCs, seven OSs, UCS, CTC.

**2161W:** 2343P Twin Diesel, 3469X, 3464, 3461X, 6520, 6457, eight OCs, seven OSs, UCS, CTC.

**2171W:** 2344P Twin Diesel, 3469X, 3464, 3461X, 6520, 6457, eight OCs, seven OSs, UCS, CTC.

**2148WS:** 773 Locomotive, 2426W, 2625, 2627, 2628, eight OCs, seven OSs, UCS, CTC, SP.

**2169WS:** 773 Locomotive, 2426W, 3656, 6456, 3469X, 6411, 6457, eight OCs, seven OSs, UCS, CTC, SP.

## 1951

### LIONEL CATALOGUE SETS

**1119:** 1110 Locomotive, 1001T, 1002, 1004, 1007, eight 1013s, 1018, 1009, 1011, CTC.

**1477S:** 2026 Locomotive, 6466T, 6012, 6014, 6017, eight 1013s, three 1018s, 6019, 1034, CTC, SP.

**1463WS:** 2026 Locomotive, 6466W, 6462, 6465, 6257, eight 1013s, three 1018s, 6019, 1033, CTC, SP.

**1469WS:** 2035 Locomotive, 6466W, 6462, 6465, 6456, 6257, eight 1013s, three 1018s, 6019, CTC, SP.

**1464W:** 2023 Twin Diesel, 2421, 2422, 2423, eight 1013s, five 1018s, 6019, 1033, CTC.

**1467W:** 2023 Twin Diesel, 6656, 6465, 6456, 6357, eight 1013s, five 1018s, 6019, 1033, CTC.

**1471WS:** 2035 Locomotive, 6466W, 3469X, 6465, 6454, 3461X, 6357, eight 1013s, seven 1018s, 6019, 1033, CTC, SP.

**1481WS:** 2035 Locomotive, 6466W, 3464, 6465, 3472, 6462, 6357, eight 1013s, seven 1018s, 6019, 1033, CTC, SP.

**2163WS:** 736 Locomotive, 2671WX, 6472, 6462, 6465, 6457, eight OCs, seven OSs, UCS, CTC, SP.

**2167WS:** 681 Locomotive, 2671W, 6462, 3464, 6457, eight OCs, five OSs, UCS, CTC, SP.

**2173WS:** 681 Locomotive, 2671W, 3472, 6465, 3469X, 6457, eight OCs, seven OSs, UCS, CTC, SP.

**2175W:** 2343 Twin Diesel, 6456, 3464, 6465, 6462, 6457, eight OCs, seven OSs, UCS, CTC.

**2185W:** 2344 Twin Diesel, 6456, 3464, 6465, 6462, 6457, eight OCs, seven OSs, UCS, CTC.

## 1952

### LIONEL CATALOGUED SETS

**1119:** 1110 Locomotive, 1001T, 1002, 1004, 1007, eight 1013s, 1018, 1009, 1011, CTC.

**1465:** 2034 Locomotive, 6066T, 6032, 6035, 6037, eight 1013s, three 1018s, 6019, 1012, CTC.

**1477S:** 2026 Locomotive, 6466T, 6012, 6014, 6017, eight 1013s, three 1018s, 6019, 1034, CTC, SP.

**1485WS:** 2025 Locomotive, 6466W, 6462, 6465, 6257, eight 1013s, three 1018s, 6019, 1033, CTC, SP.

**1479WS:** 2056 Locomotive, 2046W, 6462, 6465, 6456, 6257, eight 1013s, three 1018s, 6019, 1033, CTC, SP.

**1467W:** 2032 Diesel, 6656, 6456, 6465, 6357, eight 1013s, five 1018s, 6019, 1033, CTC.

**1464W:** 2033 Diesel, 2421, 2422, 2423, eight 1013s, five 1018s, 6019, 1033.

**1483WS:** 2056 Locomotive, 2046W, 3472, 6462, 3474, 6465, 6357, eight 1013s, seven 1018s, 6019, 1033, CTC, SP.

**1484WS:** 2056 Locomotive, 2046W, 2421, 2422, 2429, 2423, eight 1013s, seven 1018s, 6019, 1033, CTC, SP.

**2177WS:** 675 Locomotive, 2046W, 6462, 6465, 6457, eight OCs, five OSs, UCS, CTC, SP.

**2179WS:** 671 Locomotive, 2046WX, 3464, 6465, 6462, 6457, eight OCs, five OSs, UCS, CTC, SP.

**2183WS:** 726 Locomotive, 2046W, 3464, 6462, 6465, 6457, eight OCs, seven OSs, UCS, CTC, SP.

**2187WS:** 671 Locomotive, 2046WX, 6462, 3472, 6456, 3469, 6457, eight OCs, seven OSs, UCS, CTC, SP.

**2189WS:** 726 Locomotive, 2046W, 3520, 3656, 6462, 3461, 6457, eight OCs, seven OSs, UCS, CTC, SP.

**2191W:** 2343 SANTA FE Diesel, 2343C, 6462, 6656, 6456, 6457, eight OCs, seven OSs, UCS, CTC.

**2193W:** 2344 New York Central Diesel, 2344C, 6462, 6656, 6456, 6457, eight OCs, seven OSs, UCS, CTC.

**2190W:** 2343 Twin Diesel, 2533, 2532, 2534, 2531, eight OCs, nine OSs, UCS, CTC.

### OTHER 1952 SETS

**NOTE:** Number in parentheses indicates Lionel catalogued equivalent set. We would appreciate reader assistance.

**Sears 79N09651T:** (1465), 2034 Locomotive, 6066T, 6032, 6035, 6037, eight 1013s, three 1018s, 6019, 1012, CTC.

**Sears 79N09654T:** (1485WS), 2025 Locomotive, 6466W, 6462, 6465, 6257, eight 1013s, three 1018s, 6019, 1033, CTC, SP.

**Sears 79N09655T:** (1479WS), 2056 Locomotive, 2046W, 6462, 6465, 6456, 6257, eight 1013s, three 1018s, 6019, 1033, CTC, SP.

**Sears 79N09656T:** (1467W), 2032 Diesel, 6656, 6456, 6465, 6357, eight 1013s, five 1018s, 6019, 1033, CTC.

**Sears 79N09673T:** (2187WS), 681 Locomotive, (Lionel catalogue shows a 671 engine with this set), 2046WX, 6462, 3472, 6456, 3469, 6457, eight OCs, seven OSs, UCS, CTC, SP.

## 1953

### LIONEL CATALOGUE SETS

**1500:** 1130 Locomotive, 6066T, 6032, 6034, 6037, eight 1013s, 1018, 6009, 1012.

**1501S:** 2026 Locomotive, 6066T, 6032, 6035, 6037, eight 1013s, three 1018s, 6009, 1043.

**1511S:** 2037 Locomotive, 6066T, 6032, 3474, 6035, 6037, eight 1013s, three 1018s, 6019, 1043.

**1503WS:** 2055 Locomotive, 6026W, 6462, 6465, 6456, 6257, eight 1013s, three 1018s, 6019, 1033.

**1505WS:** 2046 Locomotive, 2046W, 6464-1, 6462, 6415, 6357, eight 1013s, five 1018s, 6019, 1033.

**1502WS:** 2055 Locomotive, 2046W, 2421, 2422, 2423, eight 1013s, five 1018s, 6019, 1933.

**1467W:** 2032 Twin Diesel, 6656, 6465, 6456, 6357, eight 1013s, five 1018s, 6019, 1033.

**1464W:** 2033 Twin Diesel, 2421, 2422, 2423, eight 1013s, five 1018s, 6019, 1033.

**1507WS:** 2046 Locomotive, 2046W, 3472, 6415, 6462, 6468, 6357, eight 1013s, five 1018s, 6019, 1033.

**1509WS:** 2046 Locomotive, 2046W, 3520, 6456, 3469, 6460, 6419, eight 1013s, five 1018s, 6019, 1033.

**2201WS:** 685 Locomotive, 6026W, 6462, 6464-50, 6465, 6357, eight OCs, five OSs, UCS.

**2203WS:** 681 Locomotive, 2046WX, 3520, 6415, 6464-25, 6417, eight OCs, five OSs, UCS.

**2205WS:** 736 Locomotive, 2046W, 3484, 6415, 6468, 6456, 6417, eight OCs, seven OSs, UCS.

**2211WS:** 681 Locomotive, 2046WX, 3656, 3461, 6464-75, 6417, eight OCs, five OSs, UCS.

**2213WS:** 736 Locomotive, 2046W, 3461, 3520, 3469, 6460, 6419, eight OCs, seven OSs, UCS.

**2207W:** 2353 Santa Fe Diesel, 2343C, 3484, 6415, 6462, 6417, eight OCs, seven OSs, UCS.

**2209W:** 2354 New York Central Diesel, 2344C, 3484, 6415, 6462, 6417, eight OCs, seven OSs, UCS.

**2190W:** 2353 Twin Diesel, 2533, 2534, 2532, 2531, eight OCs, nine OSs, UCS.

## OTHER 1953 SETS

**Sears 79N09662T:** (1501S), 2026 Locomotive, 6066T, 6032, 6035, 6037, eight 1013s, three 1018s, 6009, 1043.

**Sears 79N09664T:** (1503WS), 2055 Locomotive, 6026W, 6462, 6465, 6456, 6257, eight 1013s, three 1018s, 6019, 1033.

**Sears 79N09665T:** (1505WS), 2046 Locomotive, 2046W, 6464-1, 6462, 6415, 6357, eight 1013s, five 1018s, 6019, 1033.

**Sears 79N09656T:** (1467W), 2032 Diesel, (The Sears catalogue shows a photo of the 2023 Locomotive, which we believe is in error), 6656, 6465, 6456, 6357, eight 1013s, five 1018s, 6019, 1033.

**Sears 79N09682T:** (2211WS), 681 Locomotive, 2046WX, 3656, 3461, 6464-75, 6417, eight OCs, five OSs, UCS.

## 1954
### LIONEL CATALOGUE SETS

**1500:** 1130 Locomotive, 1130T, 6032, 6034, 6037, eight 1013s, 1018, 6009, 1012.

**1513S:** 2037 Locomotive, 6026T, 6012, 6014, 6015, 6017, eight 1013s, three 1018s, 6009, 1043.

**1503WS:** 2055 Locomotive, 6026W, 6456, 6462, 6465, 6257, eight 1013s, three 1018s, 6019, 1033.

**1515WS:** 2065 Locomotive, 2046W, 6415, 6462, 6464-25, 6456, 6357, eight 1013s, five 1018s, 6019, 1033.

**1523:** 6250 Diesel, 6511, 6456, 6460, 6419, eight 1013s, five 1018s, 6019, 1034.

**1516WS:** 2065 Locomotive, 2046W, 2434, 2432, 2436, eight 1013s, five 1018s, 6019, 1033.

**1517W:** 2245P Diesel, 2245C, 6464-225, 6561, 6462, 6427, eight 1013s, five 1018s, 6019, 1033.

**1519WS:** 2065 Locomotive, 6026W, 3461, 6462, 6356, 3482, 6427, eight 1013s, five 1018s, 6019, 1033.

**1521WS:** 2065 Locomotive, 2046W, 3620, 3562, 6561, 6460, 6419, eight 1013s, five 1018s, 6109, 1033.

**1520W:** 2245P Diesel, 2245C, 2432, 2435, 2436, eight 1013s, five 1018s, 6019, 1033.

**2201WS:** 665 Locomotive, 6026W, 6464-50, 6462, 6357, eight OCs, five OSs, UCS.

**2217WS:** 682 Locomotive, 2046WX, 3562, 6464-175, 6356, 6417, eight OCs, five OSs, UCS.

**2219W:** 2321 Diesel, 6415, 6462, 6464-50, 6456, 6417, eight OCs, five OSs, UCS.

**2223W:** 2321 Diesel, 3482, 3461, 6464-100, 6462, 6417, eight OCs, seven OSs, UCS.

**2221WS:** 646 Locomotive, 2046W, 3620, 3469, 6468, 6456, 6417, eight OCs, seven OSs, UCS.

**2222WS:** 646 Locomotive, 2046W, 2530, 2532, 2531, eight OCs, seven OSs, UCS.

**2225WS:** 736 Locomotive, 2046W, 3461, 3620, 3562, 6460, 6419, eight OCs, seven OSs, UCS.

**2227W:** 2353 Santa Fe Diesel, 2353 Dummy, 3562, 6356, 6456, 6468, 6417, eight OCs, seven OSs, UCS.

**2229W:** 2354 New York Central Diesel, 2354 Dummy, 3562, 6356, 6456, 6468, 6417, eight OCs, seven OSs, UCS.

**2231W:** 2356P Diesel, 2356C, 2356T, 6561, 6511, 3482, 6415, 6417, eight OCs, seven OSs, UCS.

**2234W:** 2353P Diesel, 2353T, 2530, 2532, 2533, 2531, eight OCs, nine OSs, UCS.

## OTHER 1954 SETS

**Sears 79N09659T:** (1513S), 2037 Locomotive, 6026T, 6012, 6014, 6015, 6017, eight 1013s, three 1018s, 6009, 1043.

**Sears 79N09664T:** (1503WS), 2055 Locomotive, 6026W, 6456, 6462, 6465, 6257, eight 1013s, three 1018s, 6019, 1033.

**Sears 79N09670T:** (1523), 6250 Diesel, 6511, 6456, 6460, 6419, eight 1013s, five 1018s, 6019, 1034.

**Sears 79N09671KT:** (1517W), 2245P Diesel, (The Sears catalogue shows a photo of the 2355 Locomotive, which we believe is in error), 2245C, 6464-225, 6561, 6462, 6427, eight 1013s, five 1018s, 6019, 1033.

**Sears 79N09683T:** (2217WS), 682 Locomotive, 2046WX, 3562, 6464-175, 6356, 6417, eight OCs, five OSs, UCS.

**Sears 79N09687T:** (2225WS), 736 Locomotive, 2046W, 3461, 3620, 3562, 6460, 6419, eight OCs, seven OSs, UCS.

## 1955
### LIONEL CATALOGUE SETS

NOTE: All set numbers for 1955 are unknown. Sets are listed by engine numbers only. We would appreciate reader assistance.

600 Diesel, 6012, 6015, 6017, 1014, CTC.

610 Diesel, 6014, 6111, 6017, 1014, CTC.

1615LT Locomotive, 6311, 6462, 6560, 6119, 1014, eight 1013s, 1018, CTC.

2028 Pennsylvania Diesel, 6111, 6462, 6560, 6119, 1014, eight 1013s, 1018, CTC.

2037 Locomotive & Tender, 6105, 6014, 6012, 6017, 1043, eight 1013s, three 1018s, CTC.

2016 Locomotive & Tender, 6105, 6014, 6012, 6017, 1033, eight 1013s, three 1018s, CTC.

2328 Diesel, 6456, 6462, 6465, 6357, 1033, eight 1013s, three 1018s, CTC.

2328 Diesel, 2436, 2432, 2435, 1033, eight 1013s, three 1018s, CTC.

2055 Locomotive & Tender, 3562, 6436, 6465, 6357, 1033, CTC.

2243 Double-Unit Diesel, 6446, 6561, 3620, 6560, 6419, 1033, eight 1013s, five 1018s, CTC.

2245 Double-Unit Diesel, two 2432s, 2436, 1033, eight 1013s, five 1018s, CTC.

2065 Locomotive & Tender, 3562, 6464-275, 3469, 6357, 1033, eight 1013s, five 1018s, 1033, CTC.

2065 Locomotive & Tender, 2435, 2434, 2432, 2436, 1033, eight 1013s, five 1018s, CTC.

2065 Locomotive & Tender, 3662, 6415, 3494, 3461, 6427, 1033, eight 1013s, five 1018s, CTC.

2338 Diesel, 6561, 6436, 3562, 6362, 6560, 6419, CTC.

682 Locomotive & Tender, 6561, 6436, 3562, 6362, 6560, 6419, 1033, CTC.

665 Locomotive & Tender, 3359, 6415, 3620, 3562, 6464-275, 6446, 6417, eight OCs, five OSs, UCS, CTC.

646 Locomotive & Tender, 3359, 6415, 3620, 3562, 6464-275, 6446, 6417, eight OCs, five OSs, UCS, CTC.

2363 Double-Unit Diesel, 6672, 6414, 6464-125, 3662, 3361, 6517, CTC.

2367 Double-Unit Diesel, 2530, UCS, CTC.

736 Locomotive & Tender, 6464-275, 3562, 6414, 3359, 6517, eight OCs, seven OSs, UCS, CTC.

2331 Diesel, 6464-275, 3562, 6464-300, 3662, 6511, 3359, 6414, 6517, eight OCs, OS, UCS, CTC.

2321 Diesel, 6464-275, 3562, 6464-300, 3662, 6511, 3359, 6414, 6517, eight OCs, OS, UCS, CTC.

2340-1 Twin-Motor Locomotive, 2544, 2543, 2541, 2542, CTC.

2340-25 Twin-Motor Twin Locomotive, 3361, 6414, 3620, 6464-300, 6417, CTC.

## OTHER 1955 SETS

**NOTE:** In 1956 and 1957, Sears sets were substantially different from the Lionel catalogued sets. This difference reflecting differences in trade practices was greater than it had ever been previously.

**Sears 49NU9601:** 610 Diesel, 6014, 6012, 6015, 6017, 1014, eight 1013s, 1018.

**Sears 79N09651:** 1615LT Locomotive & Tender, crane car, gondola, caboose, eight sections curved track, one section straight.

**Sears 79N09653:** 2055 Locomotive & Tender, 3562, 6436, 6465, 6357, 1033, CTC. (Duplicate of Lionel Set with 2055 Locomotive.)

**Sears 79N09652:** 2338 Diesel, boxcar, hopper car, oil car, caboose, 90-watt transformer, eight curved track, three straight.

## 1956

### LIONEL CATALOGUE SETS

**Unknown Set Number:** 520 Locomotive, X6014, 6012, 6017, 1015, CTC.

**1552:** 629 Diesel, 2434, 2432, 2436, eight 1013s, three 1018s, 6029, 1015, CTC.

**1545:** 628 Deisel, 6424, 6014, 6025, 6257, eight 1013s, three 1018s, 6029, 1015, CTC.

**1543:** 627 Diesel, 6121, 6112, 6017, eight 1013s, 1018, 6029, 1015, CTC.

**1551W:** 621 Diesel, 6362, 6425, 6562, 6257, eight 1013s, three 1018s, 6029, 1053, CTC.

**1557W:** 621 Diesel, 3620, 6436, 6511, 6560, 6119, eight 1013s, three 1018s, 6019, 1053, CTC.

**1549:** 1615 Locomotive, 1615T, 6262, 6560, 6119, eight 1013s, three 1018s, 6029, 1015, CTC.

**1547S:** 2018 Locomotive, 6026T, 6121, 6014, 6112, 6257, eight 1013s, 1018, 6029, 1015, CTC.

**1555WS:** 2018 Locomotive, 6026W, 3361X, 160, 6464-400, 6462, 6257, eight 1013s, three 1018s, 6019, 1053, CTC.

**1553W:** 2338 Diesel, 6464-425, 6430, 6462, 6346, 6257, eight 1013s, three 1018s, 6019, 1053, CTC.

**Unknown Set Number:** 2338 Diesel, 3494-275, 3562, 6414, 6362, 6357, eight 1013s, three 1018s, 6109, 1053, CTC.

**1562W:** 2328 Diesel, 2444, two 2442s, 2446, eight 1013s, three 1018s, 6019, 1053, CTC.

**1561WS:** 2065 Locomotive, 6026W, 3424, 6262, 6430, 6562, 6257, eight 1013s, three 1018s, 6109, 1033, CTC.

**1565WS:** 2065 Locomotive, 6026W, 3662, 3650, 6414, 6346, 6357, eight 1013s, five 1018s, 6019, 1033, CTC.

**1567W:** 2243P Diesel, 2243C, 3424, 3356;, 6430, 6672, 6357, eight 1013s, five 1018s, 6019, 1033, CTC.

**1563W:** 2240P Diesel, 2240C, 6467, 3562, 6414, 3620, 6357, eight 1013s, five 1018s, 6019, 1033, CTC.

**2255W:** 601 Diesel, 3424, 6362, 6560, 6119, eight OCs, three OSs, UCS, CTC.

**Unknown Set Number:** 2331 Diesel, 3359, 3562, 6560, 3361X, 160, 6419, eight OCs, seven OSs, UCS, CTC.

**Unknown Set Number:** 2341 Diesel, 2533, 2532, 2531, eight OCs, seven OSs, UCS, CTC.

**2259W:** 2350 Locomotive, 6464-425, 6511, 6430, 3650, 6427, eight OCs, five OSs, UCS, CTC.

**2263W:** 2350 Locomotive, 6468, 6414, 3359, 3662, 6517, eight OCs, seven OSs, UCS, CTC.

**Unknown Set Number:** 646 Locomotive, 2046W, 3562, 6414, 6436, 6376, 6417, eight OCs, five OSs, UCS, CTC.

**2257WS:** 665 Locomotive, 2046W, 3361X, 160, 6346, 6467, 6462, 6427, eight OCs, three OSs, UCS, CTC.

**2265WS:** 736 Locomotive, 2046W, 3424, 3620, 6430, 6467, 6517, eight OCs, seven OSs, UCS, CTC.

**Unknown Set Number:** 2378P Diesel, 2378C, 342, 3359, 3662, 3562, 6517, eight OCs, seven OSs, UCS,CTC.

**2269W:** 2368P Diesel, 2368C, 6315, 6518, 3356, 3361X, 160, 6517, eight OCs, seven OSs, UCS, CTC.

**2271W:** 2360-25 Locomotive, 3424, 3662, 6418, 6414, 6417, eight OCs, seven OSs, UCS, CTC.

**2274W:** 2360-1 Locomotive, 2544, 2543, 2542, 2541, eight OCs, eleven OSs, UCS, CTC.

## OTHER 1956 SETS

**Sears 79N09606:** (Unlike any Lionel catalogue set.) 20?? Locomotive with whistle, but no smoke, operating boxcar, gondola, tank car, caboose. We do not know the complete engine number or the car numbers.

**Sears 79N09602:** 628 Diesel, gondola, boxcar, crane car, caboose, twelve curved track, three straight track, transformer. We do not know the car numbers.

**Sears 49N9668:** (1543), 627 Diesel, 6121, 6112, 6017, eight 1013s, 1018, 6029, 1015, CTC.

**Sears 79N09613:** (1553W), 2338 Diesel, 6464-425, 6430, 6462, 6346, 6257, eight 1013s, three 1018s, 6019, 1053, CTC.

## 1957

### LIONEL CATALOGUE SETS

**1569:** 202 Diesel, 6014, 6111, 6112, 6017, eight 1013s, two 1018s, 1008, 1015. (Set also shown with X6014 boxcar.)

**1571:** 625 Diesel, 6424, 6476, 6121, 6112, 6017, eight 1013s, two 1018s, 1008, 1015.

**1573:** 250LT Locomotive, 6112, 6025, 6464, 6476, 6017, eight 1013s four 1018s, 1008, 1015.

**1575:** 205P Diesel, 205T, 6121, 6112, 6111, 6560, 6119, eight 1013s, three 1018s, 6029, 1015.

**Unknown Set Number:** 204 Twin Diesel, two 2432s, 2436.

**1578S:** 2018LT Locomotive, 1130T, 2434, 2432, 2436, eight 1013s, three 1018s, 6029, 1015.

**1577S:** 2018LT Locomotive, 1130T, 6014, 6121, 6464-475, 6111, 6112, 6017, eight 1013s, three 1018s, 6029, 1015. (Set also show with X6014 Boxcar.)

**1587S:** 2037-500LT Locomotive, 1130T-500, 6462-500, 6464-510, 6436-500, 6464-515, 6427-500, eight 1013s, five 1018s, 6029, 1043.

**1579S:** 2037LT Locomotive, 1130T, 6476, 6111, 6468, 6121, 6112, 6025, 6017, eight 1013s, three 1018s, 6029, 1043.

**1585W:** 602 Diesel, 6014, 6111, 6464-525, 6025, 6121, 6112, 6476, 6024, 6017, eight 1013s, five 1018s, 6029, 1053. (Set was described as having a 601 Diesel on the customer's order form. We believe this was a typing error.)

**1581:** 611 Diesel, 6024, 6424, 6464-650, 6025, 6476, 6560, 6119, eight 1013s, three 1018s, 6029, 1043.

**1589WS:** 2037LTS Locomotive, 6026W, 6424, 6464-450, 6025, 6024, 6111, 6112, 6017, eight 1013s, five 1018s, 6029, 1044.

**1586:** 204P Diesel, 204T, two 2432s, 2436, eight 1013s, five 1018s, 6029, 1043.

**1583WS:** 2037LTS Locomotive, 6026W, 6482, 6112, 6646, 6121, 6476, 6017, eight 1013s, three 1018s, 6029, 1053.

**2275W:** 2339 Diesel, 3444, 6464-475, 6425, 6427, eight OCs, five OSs, UCS.

**2276W:** 404 Diesel, two 2559s, eight OCs, seven OSs, UCS.

**2277WS:** 665LTS Locomotive, 2046W, 6446, 3650, 6560, 6119, eight OCs, five OSs, UCS.

**2283WS:** 646LTS Locomotive, 2046W, 3424, 3361, 6464-525, 6562, 6357, eight OCs, seven OSs, UCS.

**2279W:** 2350 Locomotive, 6464-425, 6424, 3424, 6477, 6427, eight OCs, seven OSs, UCS.

**2287W:** 2351 Locomotive, 342, 6464-500, 3650, 6315, 6427, eight OCs, nine OSs, UCS.

**2285W:** 2331 Twin Diesel, 6418, 6414, 6425, 3662, 6517, eight OCs, seven OSs, UCS.

**2281W:** 2243P Diesel, 2243C, 6464-150, 3361, 3562, 6560, 6119, eight OCs, seven OSs, UCS.

**2289WS:** 736LTS Locomotive, 2046W, 6430, 3359, 3494-275, 3361, 6427, twelve 31s, three 32s, 48, 39.

**2293W:** 2360-1 Locomotive, 3662, 3650, 6414, 6518, 6417, twelve 31s, three 32s, 48, 39.

**2291W:** 2379 Diesel, 2379C, 3444, 3530, 3562, 6464-525, 6657, twelve 31s, three 32s, 48, 39.

**2292WS:** 646LTS Locomotive, 2046W, 2530, 2533, 2532, 2531, twelve 31s, three 32s, 48, 39.

**2295WS:** 746LTS Locomotive, 746W, 342, 3530, 3361, 6560, 6419, twelve 31s, three 32s, 48, 39.

**2296W:** 2373P Diesel, 2373T, three 2552s, 2551, twelve 31s, seven 32s, 48, 39.

**2297WS:** 746LTS Locomotive, 746W, 345, 3356, 264, 3662, 6517, twelve 31s, five 32s, 48, 39.

### OTHER 1957 SETS

**Sears 79N09643:** 2339 Diesel, searchlight car, flatcar with autos, flatcar with lumber, refrigerator car, hopper, miscellaneous car, stock car, work caboose, eight curved track, seven straight track, 90-watt transformer.

**Sears 79NH09642:** Locomotive with whistle and smoke, tender, operating crane car, gondola with four canisters, boxcar, flatcar with logs, oil car, work caboose, eight curved track, five straight track, 50-watt transformer.

**Sears 79N09641:** Locomotive, two boxcars, wheel car, stock car, gondola with four canisters, flatcar with three pipes, caboose, eight curved track, three straight track, 45-watt transformer.

**Sears 49N9668:** Diesel, flatcar with pipes, gondola with canisters, caboose, eight curved track, one straight track, 45-watt transformer.

### 1958
### LIONEL CATALOGUE SETS

**1590:** 249LT Locomotive, 6014, 6151, 6112, 6017, eight 1013s, two 1018s, 1008, 1015, CTC.

**1595:** 1625LT Locomotive, 6804, 6808, 6806, 6017, eight 1013s, 1018, 6029, 1015, CTC.

**1591:** 212 Diesel, 6809, 6807, 6803, 6017-50, eight 1013s, two 1018s, 1008, 1015, CTC.

**1593:** 613 Diesel, 6476, 6813, 6660, 6113, 6119, eight 1013s, two 1018s, 1008, 1015, CTC.

**1597S:** 2018LT Locomotive, 6014, 6818, 6476, 6025, 6112, 6017, eight 1013s, three 1018s, 6029, 1015, CTC.

**1599:** 210 Twin Diesel, 6801, 6014, 6424, 6112, 6465, 6017, eight 1013s, three 1018s, 6029, 1015, CTC.

**1603WS:** 2037LTS Locomotive, 6424, 6014, 6818, 6112, 6017, eight 1013s, three 1018s, 6029, 1053, CTC.

**1587S:** 2037-500LT Locomotive, 6462-500, 6464-510, 6436-500, 6464-515, 6427-500, eight 1013s, five 1018s, 6029, 1043-500, CTC.

**1601W:** 2337 Diesel, 6800, 6464-425, 6801, 6810, 6017, eight 1013s, three 1018s, 6029, 1053, CTC.

**1600:** 216 Diesel, 6572, 2432, 2436, eight 1013s, three 1018s, 6029, 1015, CTC.

**1605W:** 208 Twin Diesel, 6800, 6464-425, 6801, 6477, 6802, 6017, eight 1013s, three 1018s, 6029, 1053, CTC.

**1607WS:** 2037LTS Locomotive, 6465, 6818, 6464-425, 6112, 6660, 6119, eight 1013s, five 1018s, 6029, 1044, CTC.

**1608W:** 209 Twin Diesel, two 2432s, 2434, 2436, eight 1013s, five 1018s, 6029, 1053, CTC.

**2501W:** 2348 Diesel, 6464-525, 6802, 6560, 6119, twelve 31s, three 32s, 48, 39-5.

**2502W:** 400 Diesel, 2559, 2550, twelve 31s, three 32s, 48, 39-5.

**2503WS:** 665 Locomotive & Tender, 3361, 6434, 6801, 6536, 6357, twelve 31s, three 32s, 48, 39-20.

**2505W:** 2329 Locomotive, 6805, 6519, 6800, 6464-500, 6357, twelve 31s, three 32s, 48, 39-5.

**2513W:** 2329 Locomotive, 6556, 6425, 6414, 6434, 3359, 6427-60, twelve 31s, three 32s, 48, 39-20.

**2509WS:** 665LTS Locomotive, 6414, 3650, 6464-475, 6805, 6357, twelve 31s, three 32s, 48, 39-5.

**2507W:** 2242 Double-Unit Diesel, 3444, 6464-425, 6424, 6468, 6357, twelve 31s, three 32s, 48, 39-5.

**2515WS:** 646LTS Locomotive, 3662, 6424, 3444, 6800, 6427, twelve 31s, three 32s, 48, 39-20.

**2511W:** 2352 Locomotive, 3562, 3424, 3361, 6560, 6119, twelve 31s, three 32s, 48, 39-10.

**2518W:** 2352 Locomotive, 2533, 2534, 2531, twelve 31s, three 32s, 48, 39-5.

**2517W:** 2379 Diesel, 6519, 6805, 6434, 6800, 6657, twelve 31s, three 32s, 48, 39-5.

**2519W:** 2331 Diesel, 6434, 3530, 6801, 6414, 6464-275, 6557, twelve 31s, three 32s, 48, 39-5.

**2525WS:** 746LTS Locomotive, 345, 342, 6519, 6518, 6560, 6419, twelve 31s, five 32s, 48, 39-5.

**2521WS:** 746LTS Locomotive, 6805, 3361, 6430, 6424, 3356, 6557, twelve 31s, three 32s, 48, 39-15.

**2523W:** 2383 Twin Diesel, 264, 6434, 6800, 3662, 6517, twelve 31s, three 32s, 48, 39-20.

**2526W:** 2383 Twin Diesel, 2530, two 2532s, 2531, twelve 31s, seven 32s, 48, 39-5.

### OTHER 1958 SETS

**Sears 79N09657:** 2037LTS Locomotive, boxcar (6014?), hopper (6476?), 6818, 6112, 6800, 1013, eight 1013s, five 1018s, 6029, 1053.

**Sears 79N09656:** 210AA Diesel, 6801, 6014, 6112, flatcar (6802?), hopper (6476?), 6017, 1015, eight 1013s, three 1018s, 6029, CTC. Similar to Lionel Set 1599.

**Sears 79N09655:** 249LT Locomotive, 6014, 6112, hopper (6476?) 6151, 6017, eight 1013s, two 1018s, 1015, 1018. Similar to Lionel Set 1590.

**Sears 79N09658:** 2337 Wabash Diesel, 6800, crane (6560?), 6464-425, operating lumber car (3361?), flat with autos (6424?), 6818, flat with autos (6424?), 6818, 6119, eight 1013s, seven 1018s, 90-watt transformer.

**Wards 48T3001M:** 249LT Pennsylvania Locomotive, 6112, flat with autos (6424?), Boxcar (6014?), flat with van (6810?), caboose, twelve 1013s, four 1018s, 1015.

**Wards 48T3002M:** 205AA Missouri Pacific Diesel, flat with boat (6801?), box (6014?), flat with autos (6424?), gondola (6112?), two-dome oil car, caboose, eight 1013s, three 1018s, 1015.

**Wards 48T3003M:** 2037LTS Locomotive, 6424, 6014, 6818, 6112, caboose, eight 1013s, three 1018s, 1053.

### 1959
### LIONEL CATALOGUE SETS

**1609:** 246LT Locomotive, 6162-25, 6476, 6057, eight 1013s, 1018, 1008-50, 1016, CTC.

**1611:** 614 Diesel, 6825, 6162-50, 6465, 6027, eight 1013s, 1018, 1008-50, 1016, CTC.

**1612:** 1862LT Locomotive, 1866, 1865, eight 1013s, two 1018s, 1015, CTC.

**1800:** 1862LT Locomotive, 1877, 1866, 1865.

**1613S:** 247LT Locomotive, 6826, 6819, 6821, 6017, eight 1013s, 1018, 1008-50, 1015, CTC.

**1617S:** 2018LT Locomotive, 6816, 6536, 6812, 6670, 6119, eight 1013s, three 1018s, 6029, 1015, CTC.

**1615:** 217 Double-Unit Diesel, 6800, 6464, 6812, 6825, 6017-100, eight 1013s, three 1018s, 6029, 1015, CTC.

**1619W:** 218 Twin Diesel, 6819, 6802, 6801, 6519, 6017, eight 1013s, three 1018s, 6029, 1053, CTC.

**1626W:** 208 Twin Diesel, 3428, two 2412s, 2416, eight 1013s, five 1018s, 6029, 1053, CTC.

**1625WS:** 2037LTS Locomotive, 6636, 3512, 6470, 6650, 6017, eight 1013s, five 1018s, 6029, 1053, CTC.

**1621WS:** 2037LTS Locomotive, 6825, 6519, 6062, 6464-475, 6017, eight 1013s, three 1018s, 6029, 1053, CTC.

**1623W:** 2349 Diesel, 3512, 3435, 6424, 6062, 6017, eight 1013s, three 1018s, 6029, 1053, CTC.

**2527:** 44 Missile Launcher, 3419, 6844, 6823, 6814, 943, twelve 31s, 32, 48, 39-25.

**2528WS:** 1872LT Locomotive, 1877, 1876, 1875W, twelve 31s, 32, 48, 39-25.

**2529W:** 2329 Locomotive, 3512, 6819, 6812, 6560, 6119, twleve 31s, three 32s, 48, 39-25.

**2531WS:** 637LTS Locomotive, 3435, 6817, 6636, 6825, 6119, twelve 36s, three 32s, 48, 39-25.

**2533W:** 2358 Locomotive, 6650, 6414, 3444, 6470, 6357, twelve 31s, three 32s, 48, 39-25.

**2539WS:** 665LTS Locomotive, 3361, 464, 6464-825, 3512, 6812, 6357, twelve 31s, three 32s, 48, 39-35.

**2535WS:** 665LTS Locomotive, 3434, 6823, 3672, 6812, 6357, twelve 31s, three 32s, 48, 39-35.

**2537W:** 2242 Double-Unit Diesel, 3435, 3650, 6464-275, 6819, 6427, twelve 31s, three 32s, 48, 39-25.

**2543WS:** 736LTS Locomotive, 264, 3435, 6823, 6434, 6812, 6557, twelve 31s, three 32s, 48, 39-25.

**2541W:** 2383 Twin Diesel, 3356, 3512, 6519, 6816, 6427, twelve 31s, three 32s, 48, 39-25.

**2544W:** 2383 Twin Diesel, 2530, 2563, 2562, 2561, twelve 31s, five 32s, 48, 39-25.

**2545WS:** 746LTS Locomotive, 175, 6175, 6470, 3419, 6650, 3540, 6517, twelve 31s, three 32s, 48, 39-25.

## 1960

### LIONEL CATALOGUE SETS

**1609:** 246LT Locomotive, 6476, 6162-25, 6057, eight 1013s, 1018, 1008-50, 1016, CTC.

**1627S:** 244LT Locomotive, 6062, 6825, 6017, eight 1013s, 1018, 1008-50, 1015, CTC.

**1612:** 1862LT Locomotive, 1866, 1865, eight 1013s, two 1018s, 1015, CTC.

**1629:** 225 Diesel, 6650, 6470, 6819, 6219, eight 1013s, 1018, 1008-50, 1015, CTC.

**1631WS:** 243LTS Locomotive, 6519, 6812, 6465, 6017, eight 1013s, three 1018s, 1008-50, 1053, CTC.

**1637W:** 218 Twin Diesel, 6475, 6175, 6464-475, 6801, 6017-185, eight 1013s three 1018s, 6029, 1053, CTC.

**1633:** 224 Double-Unit Diesel, 6544, 6830, 6820, 6017-200, eight 1013s, three 1018s, 6029, 1015, CTC.

**1639WS:** 2037LTS Locomotive, 6816, 6817, 6812, 6530, 6560, 6119, eight 1013s, three 1018, 6029, 1053, CTC.

**1635WS:** 2037LTS Locomotive, 6361, 6826, 6636, 6821, 6017, eight 1013s, three 1018s, 6029, 1053, CTC.

**1640W:** 218 Twin Diesel, 3428, two 2412s, 2416, eight 1013s, three 1018s, 6029, 1053, 1640-100, CTC.

**1800:** 1862LT Locomotive, 1877, 1866, 1865.

**1805:** 45 Missile Launcher, 3429, 3820, 6640, 6824.

**2528WS:** 1872LT Locomotive, 1877, 1876, 1875W, twelve 31s, 32, 48, 39-25.

**2527:** 44 Missile Launcher, 3419, 6844, 6823, 6814, 943, twelve 31s, 32, 48, 39-25.

**2547WS:** 637LTS Locomotive, 3330, 6475, 6361, 6357, twelve 31s, 32, 48, 39-25.

**2549W:** 2349 Diesel, 3540, 6470, 6819, 6650, 3535, eighteen 31s, two 32s, five 34s, 48, 120, 39-25.

**2551W:** 2358 Locomotive, 6828, 3512, 6827, 6736, 6812, 6427, 110, twenty-four 31s, thirteen 32s, 48, 39-25.

**2553WS:** 736LTS Locomotive, 3830, 3435, 3419, 3672, 6357, eighteen 31s, seven 32s, two 33s, six 34s, 48, 120, 142-125, 260, 39-35.

**2544W:** 2383 Twin Diesel, 2530, 2563, 2562, 2561, twelve 31s, five 32s, 48, 39-25.

## 1961

### LIONEL CATALOGUE SETS

**1641:** 246-244T Locomotive, 3362, 6162, 6057, eight 1013s, 1018, 1008-50, 1010, CTC.

**1642:** 244-1130T Locomotive, 3376, 6405, 6119, eight 1013s, 1018, 1008-50, 1025, CTC.

**1643:** 230 Diesel, 3509, 6050, 6175, 6058, eight 1013s, 1018, 1008-50, 1025, CTC.

**1644:** 1862LT Locomotive, 3370, 1866, 1865, twelve 1013s, four 1018s, 1020, 1025, CTC.

**1645:** 229 Diesel, 3410, 6465, 6825, 6059, eight 1013s, three 1018s, 1008-50, 1073, 147, CTC.

**1646:** 233LTS Locomotive, 6162, 6343, 6476, 6017, eight 1013s, three 1018s, 1008-50, 1073, 147, CTC.

**1647:** 45 Missile Launcher, 3665, 3519, 6830, 6448, 6814, eight 1013s, three 1018s, 6019, 1073, CTC.

**1648:** 2037LTS Locomotive, 6062, 6465, 6519, 6476, 6017, eight 1013s, three 1018s, 1008-50, 1063, CTC.

**1649:** 218P Diesel, 218C, 6343, 6445, 6475, 6405, 6017, eight 1013s, three 1018s, 1008-50, 1063, CTC.

**1650:** 2037LTS Locomotive, 6544, 6470, 3330, 3419, 6017, eight 1013s, three 1018s, 6029, 1063, CTC.

**1651:** 218 Twin Diesel, 2414, two 2412s, 2416, eight 1013s, three 1018s, 6029, 1063, CTC.

**1810:** 231 Diesel, 3665, 3519, 3820, 6017.

**1809:** 244-1130T Locomotive, 3370, 3376, 1877, 6017.

**2570:** 616 Diesel, 6822, 6828, 6812, 6736, 6130, twelve 31s, two 32s, 39-25.

**2528WS:** 1872LT Locomotive, 1877, 1876, 1875W, twelve 31s, 32, 48, 39-25.

**2571:** 637LTS Locomotive, 3419, 6445, 6361, 6119, twelve 31s, two 32s, 39-25.

**2572:** 2359 Diesel, 6544, 3830, 6448, 3519, 3535, twelve 31s, four 32s, 39-25.

**2573:** 736LTS Locomotive, 3545, 6416, 6475, 6440, 6357, twelve 31s, four 32s, 39-25.

**2574:** 2383 Twin Diesel, 3665, 3419, 448, 3830, 6437, twelve 31s, three 32s, 34, 109, 39-25, 943.

**2575:** 2360 Locomotive, 6530, 6828, 6464, 6827, 6736, 6560, 6437, twelve 31s, six 32s, 39-35.

**2576:** 2383 Twin Diesel, 2563, two 2562s, 2561, twelve 31s, six 32s, 39-25.

### OTHER 1961 SETS

**Quaker Oats Set X-600:** 246(A) Locomotive & Tender, 6076, 6042, 6047, 6406. John Divi Collection.

## 1962

### LIONEL CATALOGUE SETS

**11201:** 242LT Locomotive, 6042-75, 6502, 6047, eight 1013s, two 1018s, 1010, CTC.

**11212:** 633 Diesel, 3349, 6825, 6057, eight 1013s, 1018, 1008-50, 1010, CTC.

**11232:** 232 Diesel, 3410, 6062, 6413, 6057-50, eight 1013s, 1018, 1008-50, 1025, CTC.

**11222:** 236-1050T Locomotive, 3357, 6343, 6119, eight 1013s, 1018, 1008-50, 1025, CTC.

**11252:** 211 Twin Diesel, 3509, 6448, 3349, 6463, 6057, eight 1013s, three 1018s, 1008-50, 1025, CTC.

**11242:** 233LTS Locomotive, 6465, 6476, 6162, 6017, eight 1013s, three 1018s, 1008-50, 1073, 147, CTC.

**11278:** 2037LTS Locomotive, 6473, 6162, 6050-110, 6825, 6017, eight 1013s, three 1018s, 1008-50, 1073, 147, CTC.

**11268:** 2365 Diesel, 3619, 3470, 3349, 6501, 6017, eight 1013s, three 1018s, 6029, 1073, CTC.

**11288:** 229P Diesel, 229C, 3413, 6512, 6413, 6463, 6059, eight 1013s, three 1018s, 1008-50, 1073, 147, CTC.

**11298:** 2037LTS Locomotive, 3419, 6544, 6448, 3330, 6017, eight 1013s, three 1018s, 6029, 1063, CTC.

**11308:** 218 Twin Diesel, 2414, two 2412s, 2416, eight 1013s, three 1018s, 6029, 1063, CTC.

**12502:** 1862LT Locomotive, 3376, 1877, 1866, 1865.

**12512:** 45 Missile Launcher, 3413, 3619, 3470, 3349, 6017.

**13008:** 637LTS Locomotive, 3349, 6448, 6501, 6119, twelve 31s, 32, 34, 39-25.

**13018:** 616 Diesel, 6500, 6650, 3519, 6448, 6017-235, twelve 31s, 32, 34, 39-25.

**13036:** 1872LT Locomotive, 6445, 3370, 1876, 1875W, twelve 31s, 32, 34, 39-25.

**13028:** 2359 Diesel, 3665, 3349, 3820, 3470, 6017-100, twelve 31s, 32, 34, 943, 39-25.

**13058:** 2383 Twin Diesel, 3619, 3413, 6512, 470, 6437, twelve 31s, three 32s, 34, 39-25.

**13048:** 736LTS Locomotive, 6822, 6414, 3362, 6440, 6437, twelve 31s, three 32s, 34, 39-25.

**13088:** 2383 Twin Diesel, 2523, two 2522s, 2521, twelve 31s, five 32s, 34, 39-25.

**13068:** 2360 Locomotive, 6464-735, 6828, 6416, 6827, 6530, 6475, 6437, twelve 31s, five 32s, 34, 39-35.

**13078:** 2360 Locomotive, 2523, two 2522s, 2521, twelve 31s, five 32s, 34, 39-35.

## 1963

### LIONEL CATALOGUE SETS

**11311:** 1062 Locomotive, 6409-25, 6076-100, 6167, eight 1013s, 1026, CTC.

**11321:** 221P Diesel, 3309, 6076-75, 6042-75, 6167-50, eight 1013s, two 1018s, 1026, CTC.

**11341:** 634 Diesel, 3410, 6407, 6014-325, 6463, 6059-50, eight 1013s, 1018, 6139, 1010, CTC.

**11331:** 242-1060T Locomotive, 6473, 6476-25, 6142, 6059-50, eight 1013s, 1018, 6139, 1010, CTC.

**11351:** 237-1060T Locomotive, 6050-100, 6465-150, 6408, 6162, 6119-100, eight 1013s, 1018, 6139, 1025, CTC.

**11361:** 211P-150 211T Twin Diesel, 3665-100, 3413-150, 6470, 6413, 6257-100, eight 1013s, three 1018s, 6139, 1025, CTC.

**11375:** 238LTS Locomotive, 6822-50, 6465-150, 6414-150, 6476-75, 6162, 6257-100, eight 1013s, three 1018s, 6139, 1073, 147, CTC.

**11385:** 223P-50 Diesel, 218C, 3619-100, 3470-100, 3349-100, 3830-75, 6407, 6257-100, eight 1013s, three 1018s, 6139, 1073, 147, CTC.

**11395:** 2037LTS Locomotive, 6484, 6469-50, 6536, 6440-50, 6560-50, 6119-100, eight 1013s, three 1018s, 6029, 1073, 147, CTC.

**11405:** 218 Twin Diesel, 2414, two 2412s, 2416, eight 1013s, three 1018s, 6029, 1073, 147, CTC.

**13108:** 617 Diesel, 3665, 3419, 6448, 3830, 3470, 6119-100, twelve 31s, 32, 34, 39-25.

**13098:** 637LTS Locomotive, 6469, 6464-900, 6414, 6446, 6447, twelve 31s, 32, 34, 39-25.

**13128:** 2383 Twin Diesel, 3619, 3413, 6512, 448, 6437, twelve 31s, three 32s, 34, 39-25.

**13118:** 736LTS Locomotive, 6446-60, 6827, 3362, 6315-60, 6560, 6429, twelve 31s, 32, 34, 39-25.

**13148:** 2383 Twin Diesel, two 2523s, 2522, 2521, twelve 31s, five 32s, 34, 39-25.

**13138:** 2360 Locomotive, 6464-735, 6828, 6416, 6827, 6315-60, 6436-110, 6437, twelve 31s, five 32s, 34, 39-25.

## 1964

### LIONEL CATALOGUE SETS

**11420:** 1061LT Locomotive, 6042-250, 6167-25, eight 1013s, 1026, CTC.

**11430:** 1062LT Locomotive, 6176, 6142, 6167-125, eight 1013s, 1018, 6149, 1026, CTC.

**11440:** 221P Diesel, 3309, 6176-50, 6142-125, 6167-100, eight 1013s, 1018, 6149, 1026, CTC.

**11450:** 242-1060T Locomotive, 6473, 6142-75, 6176-50, 6059-50, eight 1013s, 1018, 6149, 1010, CTC.

**11460:** 238LTS Locomotive, 6014-325, 6465-150, 6142-100, 6176-75, 6119-110, eight 1013s, 1018, 6149, 1073, 147, CTC.

**11480:** 213 Twin Diesel, 6473, 6176-50, 6142-150, 6014-325, 6257-100, twelve 1013s, three 1018s, 1020, 6149, 1025, CTC.

**11490:** 212 Twin Diesel, 2404, 2405, 2406, eight 1013s, three 1018s, 6149, 1073, 147, CTC.

**11500:** 2029LTS Locomotive, 6465-150, 6402-50, 6176-75, 6014-325, 6257-100, eight 1013s, three 1018s, 6149, 1073, 147, CTC.

**11510:** 2029-1060T Locomotive, 6465-150, 6402-50, 6176-75, 6014-325, 6257-100, eight 1013s, three 1018s, 6149, 1025, CTC.

**12700:** 736LTS Locomotive, 6464-750, 6162-100, 6414-75, 6476-125, 6437, eight TOCs, five TOSs, UCS.

**12740:** 2383 Twin Diesel, 3662, 6822, 6361, 6464-525, 6436-110, 6315-60, 6437, eight TOCs, five TOSs, UCS.

**12780:** 2383 Twin Diesel, two 2523s, 2523, 2521, eight TOCs, five TOSs, UCS.

**13150:** 773LTS Locomotive, 3434, 6361, 3662, 6415, 3356, 6436-110, 6437, 112, sixteen 31s, nineteen 32s, four 34s, two 39-25s, ZW.

### OTHER 1964 SETS

**Sears 3-9820:** 240 Locomotive, unnumbered gray flatcar with green tank, 64709, unnumbered Rescue Caboose without stretchers, 1249 Marx transformers, 10 plastic soldiers. Lewis Striebeck Collection.

## 1965

### LIONEL CATALOGUE SETS

**11520:** 242-1062T Locomotive, 6176, 3364, 6142, 6059, eight 1013s, 1018, 6149, 1010, CTC.

**11530:** 634 Diesel, 6014, 6142, 6402, 6130, eight 1013s, 1018, 6149, 1010, CTC.

**11550:** 239LTS Locomotive, 6473, 6465, 6176, 6119, eight 1013s, 1018, 6149, 1073, 147, CTC.

**11560:** 211 Twin Diesel, 6473, 6176, 6142, 6465, 6059, twelve 1013s, three 1018s, 1020, 6149, 1025, CTC.

**11500:** 2029LTS Locomotive, 6465, 6402, 6176, 6014, 6059, eight 1013s, three 1018s, 6149, 1073, 147, CTC.

**11490:** 212 Twin Diesel, 2404, 2405, 2406, eight 1013s, three 1018s, 6149, 1073, 147, CTC.

**11540:** 239-242T Locomotive, 6473, 6465, 6176, 6119, eight 1013s, 1018, 6149, 1025, CTC.

**12730:** 2383 Twin Diesel, 6464-735, 6162, 6414, 6476, 6437, eight TOCs, five TOSs, UCS, LW.

**12800:** 2346 Diesel, 6428, 6436, 6464-485, 6415, 6017, eight TOCs, five TOSs, UCS.

**12710:** 736LTS Locomotive, 6464-735, 6162, 6414, 6476, 6437, eight TOCs, five TOSs, UCS, LW.

**12820:** 2322 Diesel, 3662, 6822, 6361, 6464-735, 6436, 6315, 6437, eight TOCs, five TOSs, UCS, LW.

**12780:** 2383 Twin Diesel, two 2523s, 2522, 2521, eight TOCs, five TOSs, UCS.

**13150:** 773LTS Locomotive, 3434, 6361, 3662, 6415, 3356, 6436, 6437, 112, sixteen 31s, nineteen 32s, four 34s, two 39-25s, ZW.

## 1966

### LIONEL CATALOGUE SETS

**12840:** 665LTS Locomotive, 6464-375, 6464-450, 6431, 6415, 6437, eight TOCs, five TOSs, UCS, LW.

**11520:** 242-1062T Locomotive, 6176, 3364, 6142, 6059, eight 1013s, 1018, 6149, 1010, CTC.

**11530:** 634 Diesel, 6014, 6142, 6402, 6130, eight 1013s, 1018, 6149, 1010, CTC.

**11560:** 211 Twin Diesel, 6473, 6176, 6142, 6465, 6059, twelve 1013s, three 1018s, 1020, 6149, 1025, CTC.

**11550:** 239LTS Locomotive, 6473, 6465, 6176, 6119, eight 1013s, 1018, 6149, 1073, 147, CTC.

**11540:** 239-242T Locomotive, 6473, 6465, 6176, 6119, eight 1013s, 1018, 6149, 1025, 147, CTC.

**11500:** 2029LTS Locomotive, 6465, 6402, 6176, 6014, 6059, eight 1013s, three 1018s, 6149, 1073, 147, CTC.

**11590:** 212 Diesel, 2408, 2409, 2410, eight 1013s, three 1018s, 6149, 1073, 147, CTC.

**12800:** 2346 Diesel, 6428, 6436, 6464-475, 6415, 6017, eight TOCs, five TOSs, UCS.

**12710:** 736LTS Locomotive, 6464, 6162, 6414, 6476, 6437, eight TOCs, five TOSs, UCS, LW.

**12730:** 2383 Twin Diesel, 6464, 6162, 6414, 6476, 6437, eight TOCs, five TOSs, UCS, LW.

**12850:** 2322 Diesel, 3662, 6822, 6361, 6464, 6436, 6315, 6437, ten TOCs, fourteen TOSs, UCS, T022, LW, CTC.

**12780:** 2383 Twin Diesel, two 2523s, 2522, 2521, eight TOCs, five TOSs, UCS.

**13150:** 773LTS Locomotive, 3434, 6361, 3662, 6415, 3356, 6436, 6437, 112, sixteen 31s, nineteen 32s, four 34s, two 39-25s, 36-1, ZW 275.

## 1967

No Catalogue was issued for 1967. We believe that Lionel offered the 1966 sets.

## 1968

### LIONEL CATALOGUE SETS

**11600:** 2029LTS Locomotive, 6014, 6476, 6315, 6560, 6130, 1122, 1020, 1044, 6149, 260, twelve 1013s, six 1018s, CTC.

## 1969

### LIONEL CATALOGUE SETS

**11710:** 1061 Locomotive & Tender, 6402, 6142, 6059, eight 1013s, two 1018s, 1025, CTC.

**11720:** 2024 Diesel, 6142, 6402, 6176, 6057, eight 1013s, three 1018s, 6149, 1025, CTC.

**11730:** 645 Locomotive, 6402, 6014, 6142, 6176, 6167, eight 1013s, five 1018s, 6149, 1025, CTC.

**11740:** 2041 Twin Diesel, 6315, 6142, 6014, 6476, 6057, eight 1013s, seven 1018s, 6149, 1025, CTC.

**11750:** 2029LTS Locomotive, 6014, 6476, 6473, 6315, 6130, eight 1013s, seven 1018s, 6149, 1025, CTC.

**11760:** 2029LTS Locomotive, 6014, 6315, 6476, 3376, 6119, eight 1013s, seven 1018s, 6149, 1044, CTC.

# Chapter XIII
# UNCATALOGUED SETS

## POSTWAR PRODUCTION, 1946-1969

This is our first listing of a category which is growing in importance to the collector of Lionel Postwar - uncatalogued sets. These sets were numerous; they were sometimes depicted in the yearly Advance Catalogues but not in the Consumer Catalogues. Moreover, these sets included all those which were made by Lionel for a particular store or chain - Montgomery Ward, Sears, etc. The manufacture of special sets for specific department stores was a long tradition with Lionel, going back at least to 1911 and continuing even today in the Fundimensions era.

We expect this initial listing to grow considerably as time goes by. Much information is still to be learned even in the sets we list here, but the picture becomes more clear with each report from readers. Curiously, the Lionel uncatalogued sets we list seem to gravitate either towards the very low end or the very high end of the price scale. Some of these sets can only be considered as cheap loss-leaders. On the other hand, a few of the sets rival even the great Norfolk and Western and Virginian sets of the early and middle fifties. Arguably, the Sears set with the rare 2347 diesel locomotive might have been the greatest set ever made by Lionel!

We do not know the numbers of several of the sets we list. Therefore, we have listed these sets by the numbers of the locomotives contained in them. This strategy has the added advantage of listing by a familiar component, since very few collectors know set numbers that well.

If you have an uncatalogued set to report to us, be sure to let us know the set number, the date and all the contents - even the lubricant, wires and instruction leaflets. Photographs of the set box are an immense help. We also know very little about the value of these sets; establishing the value is much more than just adding up the values of the parts. Intact sets usually command a substantial premium over the individual pieces as long as the contents are in their original set box.

### A WORD ON OUTFIT CODING
#### By I. D. Smith

By the early sixties, Lionel had acquired many subsidiary firms in an attempt to diversify. This necessitated a change in Lionel's numbering system for its train sets. The 1962 Advance Catalogue explains that five-numbered sets are coded as follows: the first digit (1) explains that the item is a train set. The second, third and fourth digits are the set numbers themselves. The fifth digit indicates a packaging code, as follows: 1, 2 or 3 meant a display pack; 4 meant a display box with component packing; 5 or 6 meant conventional non-display packaging; and 7 or 8 meant a conventional box with component packing. This coding may help a collector to determine whether a set box is original or not.

**215 SANTA FE** Alco AA Units Set 19444, 1965, 027 gauge: contents included 215P and 215T Santa Fe Alco units, 6176 gray Lehigh Valley hopper with black lettering, 6465 Lionel Lines orange tank car, 6142 green gondola with white Lionel lettering and two white canisters, 6130 Santa Fe work caboose, 1025 transformer, 12 curved and three straight track, one 6149 uncoupler, one 90-degree crossover, five billboards, an accessory catalogue, a service station directory, guarantee, and envelope 1103-40 with wire, controller and lockon. Ambrose Collection.

**220 SANTA FE** Alco AA Units Set X568NA, 1960, 027 gauge: contents included 220P and 220T Santa Fe Alco units, 6476 red Lehigh Valley hopper with white lettering, 6044 blue Airex boxcar, 6045 gray two-dome tank car, 3386 Bronx Zoo giraffe car with telltale and spring cam, 6047 red SP caboose, 902 elevated trestle set, 1015 transformer, eight curved and four straight track, 1008 cam-trol track, wire, lockon, five billboards, accessory catalogue, service station directory and guarantee. Ambrose Collection.

**221 RIO GRANDE** Alco A Unit Set 19152, Diesel Freight Set: contents included 221 Rio Grande Alco A unit, unlettered red flatcar (mold 6511-2, Timken trucks, dummy couplers, three light gray plastic pipes, no brakewheel); 6042 blue gondola (dummy couplers and two red canisters); 6045 LIONEL LINES orange tank car (dummy couplers); and 6167 red unlettered caboose (one operating and one dummy coupler). Frangillo Collection.

**221 U. S. MARINE CORPS** Alco A Unit Set 19334, 1963-64, made for J. C. Penney: contents included 221 U. S. Marine Corps Alco A Unit (two-position E-unit, light, no weight, Magnetraction; and four unlettered freight cars, all in olive drab: hopper car, gondola car, turbo missile launcher and rescue unit work caboose. The caboose has a white cross, "RESCUE UNIT" and "LIONEL" on its frame in white (see 6824 entry). Also included: 1010 transformer, eight curved and three straight tracks, one 6149 uncoupler. Reportedly, only 400 of these sets were made; it was only available by mail order. Ambrose Collection.

**222 RIO GRANDE** Alco A Unit Set 11011, 1962, shown in Advance Catalogue, "The Constellation": contents included 222 Rio Grande Alco A unit, 3510 satellite launching car, 6076 hopper car, 6120 work caboose, eight curved and two straight tracks, 1026 25-watt transformer, CTC lockon, oil, wires and instruction sheet. The satellite and hopper cars are pictured with Timken trucks, but the caboose is pictured with arch bar trucks. I. D. Smith observation.

**227 CANADIAN NATIONAL** Alco A Unit Set X616, Diesel Freight Set: set box has large "LIONEL" in red on top cover, picture of steam and diesel engines below logo and broad red stripe running along bottom of cover; white rectangle within red band reads "No. X-616/DIESEL FREIGHT". Contents included 227 Canadian National Alco A unit (green with yellow lettering and stripes); unlettered tuscan General-style flatcar, mold 1877-3, with gray-bumpered yellow auto held by two rubber bands (auto is like those premium cars listed for 6414); 6042 blue gondola (white "LIONEL" lettering and number, two red canisters); unlettered red SP-type caboose with one coupler, no lights. All rolling stock has Timken trucks and dummy couplers. Also included 1026 25-watt transformer; eight curved and two straight tracks (027); lockon and wires packed in envelope marked "Part No. 1103-12", lubricant and instruction leaflets Nos. 1125-10 and 1123. Cordone Collection.

**241 LIONEL LINES** 2-4-2 steam locomotive, Set 19563, circa 1963; contents include 241 2-4-2 locomotive (smoke, "LIONEL LINES", short tender with one Timken and one arch bar truck, disc coupler); 6076 black Lehigh Valley gondola; 6050 red Swift short boxcar; 6142 blue "LIONEL" gondola; unlettered gray General-style flatcar with unknown trailer load; unlettered brown General-style flatcar with three plastic pipes; red 6167 "LIONEL LINES" caboose (galvanized base, tab fasteners, white lettering, recessed stack plug); 1020 90-degree crossover; 110 trestle set; 45-watt transformer; 16 curved and 11 straight 027 tracks, uncoupler track, instructions, wire, lockon, smoke tube and guarantee. Bratspis Collection.

**242 LIONEL LINES** 2-4-2 steam locomotive, Set Number unknown; contents included 242 Lionel Lines steam locomotive and tender, 638-2361 Van Camp boxcar, unlettered 3309 turbo missile launching car, unlettered 1887

General-style gray flatcar and unlettered SP-type caboose. Further details requested. Dunn Collection.

**243 LIONEL LINES** 2-4-2 steam locomotive Set X-573NA, "Channel Master Promotion No. 9745", 1959-60: special promotional set made for Channel Master Corporation. Contents included 243 Lionel Lines steam locomotive (plastic boiler shell, white heat-stamped number on cab, two-position E-unit, no whistle, motor and boiler like 249, smoke unit like 746 liquid unit but different lever system, curved E-unit slot, no rubber traction tires, tender like 242 but not numbered, lettered "LIONEL LINES"); 6162(B) New York Central blue gondola with three white canisters; 3376(A) Bronx Zoo giraffe car with telltale and spring cam; 3512(A) Hook and Ladder firefighting flatcar; 6812(B) Track Maintenance Car; 6017(G) Lionel Lines SP-type caboose; also included 128 Animated Newsstand with 364C controller; 1008 Cam-Trol track, 1015 45-watt transformer, 1020 90-degree crossover, 12 curved and eight straight 027 tracks; and billboards 82, 79, 77 and G. I. D. Smith Collection.

**635 UNION PACIFIC** NW-2 Switcher Set 19440, 1965, 027: contents included 635 Union Pacific NW-2 switcher; 6076 black Lehigh Valley hopper with white lettering; 6473 Horse Transport Car; 6465 Lionel Lines two-dome orange tank car; 3362/64 green log dump car; 6059 Minneapolis & St. Louis red SP-type caboose. Also included 1025 transformer, eight curved and three straight 027 tracks, one 6149 uncoupler, five billboards, accessory catalogue, service station directory, guarantee and 1103-40 envelope with wire, controller and lockon. Ambrose Collection.

**1060 LIONEL LINES** Steam Locomotive Set 11001, 1962, shown in Advance Catalogue, "The Trailblazer": contents included 1060 Lionel Lines steam locomotive with 1130T tender; 6402 flatcar with cable reels; 6042 gondola with canisters, 6067 Lionel Lines SP-type caboose. Engine's tender and cable reel car pictured with Timken trucks; gondola and caboose pictured with arch bar trucks. Set also included 1026 25-watt transformer, CTC lockon, oil, wires and instruction sheet. I. D. Smith observation.

**1882 GENERAL** 4-4-0 Steam Locomotive The following two sets may be identical; reader comments requested.
(A) Set number unknown, "GENERAL" set, 1959: contents included 1882 General engine and tender; 1885 unlighted passenger car; 1887 General-style flatcar, 1866 mail-baggage car. Also included 12 curved and four straight 027 tracks; 1020 90-degree crossover; 45-watt transformer; instruction sheet dated 10-59. Many Bachmann Plasticville accessories were also included: windmill in light gray, nine dark brown corral fence pieces, hand water pump, round pail, two black standing cows, one brown reclining cow, one tan hog, two black, two white and five brown horses (brown horses

probably for flatcar), and dark brown log cabin. LaFayette Collection.
(B) Set number unknown, made for Sears, circa 1960: contents included 1882 General engine and tender; 1887 flatcar with horses; 1885 blue passenger car; 1866 mail-baggage car. Track is 027; transformer make is "ALLSTATE" identical to Marx production of the period, but Marx trademark not on transformer. Sears also sold "ALLSTATE" train sets made by Marx which used this transformer during this time. The best inference is that Sears cut its costs by using Marx transformers for its inexpensive sets rather than Lionel ones. Not true of all Sears Lionel sets, however: see 2347 entry below. Feldman Collection.

**2029 LIONEL LINES** 2-6-4 Steam Locomotive Set 11620, 1966, 027: contents included 2029 Lionel Lines steam engine with 234T tender; 6176 hopper car; 6012 gondola car; 6402 flatcar with empty reels; and 6130 work caboose. Further details requested. Ambrose Collection.

**2347 CHESAPEAKE & OHIO** GP-7 Road Switcher Set 9836, Sears "ALLSTATE TRAIN SET", circa 1964 (9836 is Sears catalogue number). This set is one of the most spectacular train sets made by Lionel in the Postwar period. It came packed in a large white cardboard carton marked "ALLSTATE"and included the following components: 2347 Chesapeake and Ohio GP-7 Road Switcher; 3662-1 Automatic Refrigerated Milk Car with platform; 6342 New York Central Culvert Gondola Car; 6315 three-dome tank car; 6464-725 New Haven boxcar; 6414 Auto Loader Car with four gray-bumpered premium red automobiles; 6437 Pennsylvania N5C lighted caboose. Also included 346 manually-operated culvert unloader; five 310 billboards; three 76 street lamps; one pair of 022 remote switches; two UCS remote track sections; LW 125-watt transformer; 321 trestle bridge, an unknown quantity of O Gauge track, lockon, wires and instructions. Beavin Collection. — — — **2000**

**2349 NORTHERN PACIFIC** GP-9 Road Switcher Sears uncatalogued set, number unknown, circa 1965: contents included 2349 Northern Pacific GP-9; 6175 flatcar with rocket; 3419 helicopter launching car; 6476 hopper car and 6017-100 dark blue Boston and Maine SP-type caboose. Came in Lionel box with track and unknown transformer. Further details requested. Beavin Collection.

**6110 LIONEL LINES** 2-4-2 Scout steam locomotive Set 1461S, circa 1948-49: contents included 6110 die-cast Scout locomotive and tender (passive air-driven smoke unit, tender box marked 0001T but no number on tender bottom); 6002 New York Central black gondola; X6004 Baby Ruth boxcar (blue lettering, orange Type I body); 6007 red SP-type caboose, Die 3. All rolling stock had peculiar combination of Scout plastic trucks with magnetic couplers. I. D. Smith Collection.

# Chapter XIV
# CATALOGUES

## THE LIONEL CATALOGUES

Joshua Lionel Cowen was certainly a man of many talents. Ron Hollander's biography, **All Aboard!**, documents admirably the abilities Cowen possessed as inventor, administrator and manager. However, whatever talents Cowen may have had paled before his greatest talent: his ability to market and sell a product. His salesmanship took many forms, all of which worked. The greatest of all his sales tools was the annual consumer catalogue.

These catalogues did much more than illustrate and list the products of the Lionel Corporation. The best of these catalogues also created a world of magic and power for children. In the early postwar years, at least, the idol of young people was still the railroad engineer - though not so much as in the great prewar years. To be the engineer of a great Lionel railroad was a childhood treat beyond description. Youngsters would agonize over the choices they had to make; when their parents were spending a fair sum of money, or when the children themselves were saving money from paper routes, these decisions could not be taken lightly. The choices were all there - in the Lionel catalogues.

As sales tools, the catalogues did not just offer pictures of the locomotives, rolling stock and accessories. The artists' drawings of the trains showed them in action. It was easy for the imagination to visualize a whole world in miniature - and that's exactly what the catalogues were designed to do. The text of the descriptions freely indulged in exaggeration, but somehow all the hype seemed believable. It wasn't just the trains which were sold through the catalogues - it was a whole philosophy which implicitly stated that if Lionel was in the home, a child's future was secure. That was a message with very feeble grounding in reality, but it was what America wanted to believe in the early and middle postwar years. The message resulted in the largest toy company in the world.

Every collector of postwar Lionel has a favorite catalogue year, perhaps as much because of personal association as the year's production. Many prefer the first catalogues of 1946 and 1947 for their beautiful pictures of die-cast equipment, before plastic took over for good. In addition, the classic picture of father and son ("Which Lionel do you want, Son?") coming together over Lionel trains has an irresistible appeal to many. This editor's favorite is the great 1957 catalogue, the last "good year" for Lionel, when Super 0 track was introduced, the Canadian Pacific passenger set emerged and the great Norfolk and Western and Virginian sets were made. After that came the military and space sets, cheapened production and oblivion. The truth is that nobody can make a definite pronouncement about the "best" Lionel catalogue. The choice is simply too subjective and personal!

Despite that disagreement, collectors are in accord that the Lionel catalogues are extremely helpful to research, even if they are not always completely accurate. No other toy company documented its production as thoroughly as did Lionel through its catalogues. For the social historian, to look at the sales pitches is to look back into history; of such small stuff is an age categorized. For the Lionel researcher, dates can be established, varieties sorted out and features delineated.

Through other forms of paper, Lionel also made sure that its quality was maintained. Great quantities of operating instructions were printed, many of which included expertly-drawn diagrams and schematics. The serviceman's repair manual was as complete as Lionel could make it, frequently drawing from the experiences of repairmen from around the country. Much of this material has been researched and reprinted for today's collectors, and the operating and repair instructions are just as timely today as they were when they were first issued. Lionel did not achieve its reputation for superb engineering on a lark! Each set had a booklet of instructions for operating the trains, including all the basics needed by anyone to set up and run the outfits. The instructions were simply and skillfully written so that anyone could read and understand them - no easy feat for us, even with our heightened sense of readability. Each operating accessory had complete diagrams and instructions for its correct use. Nothing was left to chance in Lionel Land!

The promotional literature written by Lionel is tremendously interesting; it shows that Lionel was not above the "hard sell" in promoting its products. This is, of course, understandable, given the highly competitive nature of the toy industry, then as well as now. Store owners were shown how to promote Lionel's advantages over all others and, above all, how to demonstrate Lionel's attention to quality construction and operation. The company's ads extolled the virtue of "togetherness" between father and son; that word was an important "buzzword" during the fifties which meant harmony and understanding. Lionel played off family sensitivities like a virtuoso, even if such claims as "Control of a Lionel today...control of his life tomorrow" had little, if any, basis in truth.

The little billboards Lionel produced in the early to late fifties are a fascinating parenthetical study of their own. Two years ago, Will Sykes, then thirteen years old, wrote us a letter asking why we didn't say anything about these little billboards. That letter began an extensive effort to study these paper products. Since then, I.D. Smith has completed a major study of the Lionel 310 billboards; this edition features his first revision of the original listing which appeared in our last edition. The billboards offer a fascinating insight into the sales pitches used during what has been called the "golden years" of advertising.

The world, it is said, runs on paper. The world of Lionel Land was no different from the real one, it would seem. The best research into the varieties of toy trains has always combined shrewd observation of the artifacts with careful reading of the documents contemporary to them. We have learned that there is tremendous interest in Lionel's paper, and we are glad to see it. We appreciate your assistance in updating and expanding these chapters.

# POSTWAR PAPER 1945-1969
## I. D. Smith, Jr., P.E.

In mid-1982 we published our first listing of Lionel Postwar Paper. That listing filled less than four pages. But what interest it generated! Never could we have anticipated the response, the flood of "unknown paper". There obviously is another type train buff out there - a "Lionel Train Paper Collector".

This postwar paper chapter has been separated into three sections for simplicity. They are catalogues, instruction books, pamphlets, record and miscellaneous paper, No. 310 Billboards and Service Station Bulletins.

This listing is an update of the past year's responses from our many readers. Please look in your boxes. See if you can find paper that we have not listed! We would appreciate your comments and additions to this listing.

## CATALOGUES, INSTRUCTION BOOKS
## PAMPHLETS, RECORD AND MISCELLANEOUS PAPER
### INTRODUCTION

Most Lionel paper is printed on white paper. Sometimes, to initial appearance a booklet or catalogue will appear to be printed on blue or black paper with white ink. Actually the ink coverage is approaching 90 to 95 percent and the white lettering is produced by the absence of ink. A single ink color (such as red) can also produce very different visual effects depending on its density. Run as very small dots with white space between the dots, the red appears pink. Run as a solid it produces a very strong red. The "blue" paper usually turns out to be blue ink with the uncovered areas appearing as white ink but actually is simply unpainted paper. A magnifying glass will usually show this.

### MAGAZINES

**MODEL BUILDER** (1937-April 1949). Published by the Lionel Corporation, 1945, six issues; 1946-48, eight issues per year; 1949, four issues. Early issues in the 1930s are scarce. Late issues considered very common. A complete set demands a premium price.

**ALL ABOARD AT LIONEL** 1947 to ?.

This publication was the Lionel Company's major communication with its people. Current data indicates it was first published in early 1947. From a letter from the editor, dated February 17, 1954, it appears that its circulation was limited to management and employees at the Irvington, New Jersey plant. But on that date, it was announced that Approved Service Stations would now be included in its circulation from February, 1954.

This publication covered a wide variety of subjects about the employees (marriages, births, retirement, their hobbies, promotions, deaths, job descriptions and their everyday activities). After reading one of these, you will soon realize that these were real people making toy trains, with many varied interests besides trains.

**Gd VG Exc Mt**

### 1945

**ADVANCE CATALOGUE** Confirmation and description requested. **NRS**

**CATALOGUE** 8-1/2" x 11", four-page folder, "The Lionel Line for Christmas 1945".
(A) Original. **NRS**
(B) Lester Gordon reproduction, red or red-orange, black ink on white-coated stock, reproduction logo on top of page 1: "Original printed black and red ink. Reproduced April 1, 1969 by LESTER GORDON". Smith Collection. .25 .50 .75 1
(C) Greenberg reproduction on uncoated paper, cover states "1974 Reproduction" with Columbia, Maryland address, page 2 with same address. .25 .50 .75 1
(D) Greenberg Reproduction on coated stock, cover states "1974 Reproduction" with Columbia, Maryland, address, but page 2 has Sykesville, Maryland, address. .25 .50 .75 1

**CANDID CAMERA SHOTS LIONEL TRAINS** in action 5-7/8" x 8-3/4", 20 pages, black and white with red caption backgrounds, no printing on inside covers. Note that 226 locomotive on trestle on cover is pulling an American Flyer gondola! Page 3 bottom "Entire Contents Copyright 1945..." Weber Collection. .50 1 2 3

**PLANS & BLUE PRINTS FOR LIONEL MODEL RAILROADERS** 5-7/8" wide x 8-13/16" high, 20 pages. Front cover shows block signal and what appears to be a 700E. Front cover is printed in yellow, black and blue ink, on white paper. Unpaginated center fold, interior printed in black ink, pages 8 and 9 show four different layouts and 12 different track plans. Salamone Collection. 1 2 3 5

**PLANS & BLUE PRINTS FOR LIONEL MODEL RAILROADERS** size unknown, 16 pages, yellow, black and blue cover with white border showing 5344 passing a light signal. Contains track plans, photographs and tips with many of the photos coming from "LIONEL RAILROAD PLANNING BOOK" 1944... "Copyright 1945...". Inside back cover advertises the new knuckle coupler truck and predicts: "More sensational improvements coming in 1946." Weber Collection. 1 2 3 5

### 1946

**ADVANCE CATALOGUE** "World's Finest Lionel Trains for 1946", 10-1/2" x 8-5/16", 24 pages, self-covered, red and black, includes "Price Sheet May 1, 1946" with brown ink on yellow paper. 20 30 40 60

**CATALOGUE**
(A) 8-3/8" x 11-1/4", 16 pages plus four page cover, full cover, cover illustration shows trains and boy holding gray work caboose. 3 5 10 15
(B) Reproduction of (A) by Greenberg, with "1946" on cover; and "1975 Reproduction" with Columbia, Maryland, address on inside cover. .50 1 2 3
(C) 8-1/4" x 11-1/4", 16 pages, full color, some similar to (A). Page 1 "Which LIONEL do you want, Son?" with father with arm around son. Son is wearing plaid shirt. Smith Collection. 2 5 10 20
(D) Reproduction of (C) by Fundimensions on heavier stock than original, inside cover states "Reproduced by Lionel of Fundimensions...1975" at lower left corner. .50 .75 1.00 2

**1946 PRICE SHEET - LIONEL TRAINS** 7-1/4" wide x 8-3/8" high, one sheet printed both sides, plain white paper, black ink. Information keyed to Catalogue (C) above. Smith Collection. .25 .50 .75 2

**INSTRUCTIONS FOR ASSEMBLING AND OPERATING LIONEL TRAINS** 5-1/2" x 8-1/2", 40 pages plus covers, black and white pages.
(A) Dark and light blue cover. .50 1 2 3
(B) Green and orange cover. .50 1 2 3
(C) Orange and black cover, Greenberg reproduction, page 1 (inside) states "1975 Reproduction" with Columbia, Maryland, address. .25 .50 .75 1
(D) Same as (C), but numbered "No. 497" on back cover. Ocilka Collection. **NRS**

**INSTRUCTIONS FOR ASSEMBLING AND OPERATING ELECTRONIC CONTROL LIONEL TRAINS** 12 pages, black and white. .50 1 2 4

**SCENIC EFFECTS FOR MODEL RAILROADS - LIONEL TRAINS** (24 pages) including covers 6" wide x 9" high. Front cover printed in black and red ink on paper. Interior pages printed in red and black ink on white paper. Information on table building, mountain building, right of way scenery and cutaway view of new Atomic motor with double worm-gear drive. Piker and Salamone Collections. 1 2 3 5

**SCENIC EFFECTS FOR MODEL RAILROADS - LIONEL TRAINS** pink, orange, black and white cover, artist's drawing, 22 pages, contains construction tips, plans and photos, copyright 1946. Weber Collection. 1 2 3 5

### 1947

**ADVANCE CATALOGUE** "The Lionel Line for 1947", 14" x 11", 22 pages including tan, red and black cover, red, black and white interior. Zydlo Collection. 5 10 25 40
(A) The Lionel Line for 1947, Advance Catalogue, 18 pages, red background, black border, two edges, tan printing, black ink on white interior pages. Salamone Collection. 5 10 25 40

**CATALOGUE** 11-1/4" x 7-5/8", 32 pages, full color, cover shows 6200 passing crossing shanty.
(A) Lower prices for 11 sets from pages 8-16. Example: Page 10: $45, $55 and $67.50. Bowers Collection. 3 10 15 20
(B) Higher prices for 11 sets from pages 8-16. Example: Page 10: $47.50, $57.50 and $70.00. Bowers Collection. 3 10 15 20

**INSTRUCTIONS FOR ASSEMBLING AND OPERATING LIONEL TRAINS** 5-1/2" x 8-1/2", 40 pages plus covers, black and white pages, red and yellow wraparound cover, number "No. 497" on back of cover. Schreiner and Ocilka Collections. .50 1 2 3

**INSTRUCTIONS FOR ASSEMBLING AND OPERATING LIONEL TRAINS** bright red cover with yellow lettering, 40 pages, copyrighted inside front cover 1947. Additional sheet that came with this book, an artist's drawing of "an ideal Lionel Model Layout", designed by Robert M. Sherman, 1947. Weber Collection. **NRS**

**FUN WITH LIONEL MODEL RAILROADING** 32 pages, red-black and white. Comes in two sizes.
(A) 8-1/2" x 5-3/8" plus. Smith, Zydlo and Salamone Collections. 2 3 4 5
(B) 10-3/4" x 8-1/4". Zydlo Collection. 2 3 4 5

**LIONEL RAILROAD GUIDE** wall poster, 16-1/2" wide x 10-1/2" high, printed on one side, in yellow, black and red ink on white paper, shows 0-6-0 switcher numbered 8976 and five other locomotives. Advertising copy reads "LIONEL RR GUIDE". For another variety, see next entry. Salamone Collection. 2 4 6 10

**LIONEL RAILROAD GUIDE** wall poster, 20-3/4" wide x 15-3/4" high, printed (one side only) in yellow, black and red ink on white paper. Shows 0-4-0 switcher numbered 1662 and five other locomotives. Advertising copy reads "LIONEL R.R. GUIDE". For another variety, see previous entry. Salamone Collection. 2 4 6 10

## 1948

**ADVANCE CATALOGUE**
(A) "LIONEL FOR 1948", 14" x 11", 20 pages including cover. Cover has picture of 6200 in black and white plus red circle. Interior black, red and white. Advance catalogue does not show F-3s. Zydlo Collection. 5 10 25 40
(B) "LIONEL FOR 1948", 14" wide x 11" high, 16 pages plus covers, front cover printed in black and red on white paper shows Pennsylvania steam turbine, black and red ink on white interior paper. Salamone Collection. 5 10 25 40

**CATALOGUE** 11-1/8" x 8", 36 pages, cover illustration shows PRR turbine passing streamline passenger train, with overpass in the background. 3 10 15 20

**INSTRUCTIONS** 5-1/2" x 8-1/2", 40 black and white interior pages, coated, plus yellow wraparound cover, with blue ink on front outside cover, black ink on inside front and rear covers, and no printing on rear outside cover, "Form No. 703" on inside front cover. Smith Collection. .50 .75 2 3

**PROMOTIONAL POSTER** 18" x 19-1/8", one side, two-color printing, features three horizontal photos of Lionel trains. .50 1 2 5

**PAPER CITY** 38" x 25", one side, color printing, six cut and assemble buildings: cottage, service station, suburban or country house, church and garage. .50 1 2 5

**1948 MAKE THESE REALISTIC MODELS FOR YOUR LIONEL RAILROAD** 23-1/4" wide x 25" high, coated paper, printed one side in red, green and blue ink. Models include grocery store, cottage, service station, country house, church and garage. "Copyright 1948 by The Lionel Corporation". Smith Collection. 1 2 3 7

**1948 3D Poster** 18" wide x 19" high, printed in red and blue ink on coated stock with red ink printed from 5/16" to 7/8" to the right of the blue ink, three images, top image captioned "Away They go! Magnificent LIONEL TRAINS - So Real, So True to Life" and showing 726 set, 671 set and Santa Fe set; middle caption: "Here they are..."; lower caption: "Swift as an arrow! - The Brand New LIONEL Santa Fe Diesel". Included is a pair of glasses with left red lens and right blue (card stock 3D viewer by "American Colortype Co.") came as insert in 1948, 36 page catalogue. Schreiner and Smith Collections. 1 2 5 9

## 1949

**ADVANCE CATALOGUE** "LIONEL ADVANCE CATALOGUE FOR 1949", 17" x 8-1/4", 24 pages. Gray and white cover with silhouette of Hudson in yellow, blue, red and black. Interior pages blue, yellow and black and white. Shows Lionel construction sets on rear covers. Salamone and Zydlo Collections. 5 10 25 40

**CATALOGUE**
(A) 11-1/4" x 8", 38 pages, cover illustration shows family viewing Lionel layout with Santa Fe twin diesels in foreground, top locomotive on page 11 is 622. 5 10 18 30
(B) Same as (A), but top locomotive on page 11 is 6220. 5 10 18 30

**INSTRUCTIONS** 5-1/2" x 8-1/2", black and white, printing on coated stock, 56 pages, No. 926-49.
(A) Green and black wraparound cover. .50 .75 1 2
(B) Two-tone blue cover. Dixon, Ocilka and Smith Collections. .50 .75 1 2

**LIONEL 3D POSTER WITH GLASSES** sheet of three pictures circa 1949 (see description under 1948). Weber Collection. 1 2 5 9

**TRACK LAYOUTS** 11" x 8-1/2", 16 pages, printed in green and black on coated white stock. Cover is photo of a section of the N.Y. Lionel showroom layout. Copyright 1949. Contains tips, drawings and photos of Lionel accessories. Weber Collection. .50 .75 1 2

**LIONEL TRAIN LAYOUT PLANNING BOOK FOR POP** A small booklet 5" x 7-1/8", containing artist's drawings of layouts and building tips, 14 pages, circa 1949. The cover is a drawing by Peter Stevens of "Pop" watching a train under the Christmas tree. Weber Collection. 2 3 5 7

**LIONEL TRAIN LAYOUT PLANNING BOOK FOR POP** (1949, no date on cover) 5-1/16" wide x 7-1/16" high, 16 pages, front cover shows pipe-smoking Pop. Printed in multiple colors on white paper, black and red printing on interior white paper. Shows 15 different train layouts. Salamone and Weisblum Collections. 2 3 5 7

## 1950

**ADVANCE CATALOGUE** Gold cover, black and white inside pages. 5 10 18 25

**CATALOGUE**
(A) "Golden Anniversary Year", 11-1/4" x 8", 44 pages full color, page 30 not numbered. 5 10 18 25
(B) Same as (A), but page 30 numbered. 5 10 18 25
(C) "Sorry! ...We are substituting this complete catalogue in 2 colors", 11" x 8", 40 pages, red and black on white-coated stock, 2343 shown on cover. 3 8 15 20

**RECORD** "Lionel Train Sound Effects", 5-1/2" in diameter, clear vinyl with cardboad insert, steam locomotive with train on one side, twin diesels with train on other, blue lettering. — — 20 —

**WHISTLES & BELLS - LIONEL TRAINS** 5-3/4" x 5-13/16", came in yellow and brown four-page folder, jacket copy reads, "Whistles and Bells and Puffing Lionel Trains". Weisblum Collection. — — 25 —

**INSTRUCTIONS**
(A) 5-1/2" x 8-1/2", 64 black and white pages, dark blue and light yellow cover, "256 Pages - Hundreds of Pictures Just Published 25 cents", "No. 926-50" on inside front cover. Dixon and Smith Collections. .50 .75 1 2
(B) 5-1/2" x 8-1/2", 64 black and white pages plus ivory and blue cover, No. 926-50, Ocilka Collection. .50 .75 1 2

**ART PRINTS OF 19TH CENTURY LOCOMOTIVES PRESENTED BY LIONEL** As part of Lionel's 50th Anniversary Celebration (1950), Lionel published four handsome color prints of historical locomotives. "The Best Friend of Charleston", "Civil War Period 1860 - 1875", "The Famous 999 - 1893", and "The Big Mogul - 1900". It is not currently known how these were distributed. However, they are not difficult to locate. Weber and Ulmer Collections. 2 3 5 10

**THE MAGIC OF LIONEL MAGNETRACTION** 5" wide x 7" high, 16 pages including covers, front cover printed in red and black ink on white paper, interior pages printed in black and red on white paper. Salamone and Magner Collections. 1 2 3 4

**RAILROADING IS FUN** poster, 17-1/4" wide x 23" high, printed in green and black ink on both sides. 2 3 5 9

## 1951

**ADVANCE CATALOGUE**
(A) "1951 Lionel Trains Advance Catalog", 11" x 8", 24 pages, red, black and white cover, black, white, yellow and red interior. Salamone and Zydlo Collections. 5 10 25 40

(B) "1951 Lionel Trains", advance catalogue, red and blue front cover with 1951 in very large script made from engine smoke, cover train set is headed by a 679, 11" x 8" format. Tompkins Collection.　　**15　25　35　50**

**CATALOGUE** 11-1/8" x 7-3/4", 36 pages, full color, cover illustration shows family in column at left and five trains to the right.

**3　8　15　20**

**INSTRUCTIONS** 5-1/2" x 8-1/2", 64 pages, black and white-coated, usually dark and light green wraparound cover, "No. 26-51".

(A) Rear cover reads, "25 Cents For This Complete Book On Model Railroading" at top and "Just Published" in lower right side of page. Smith Collection.　　**.50　.75　1　2**

(B) Rear cover has same type on page top cited in (A), but with red "X" overprint over 25 Cents and new red type "35 Cents New Edition Bigger 384 Pages" at top and "New Edition Of 384 Pages 35 Cents" in red towards bottom and at very bottom in red "Old 25 Cents Edition Out Of Print". Smith Collection.　　**.50　.75　1　2**

(C) New rear cover with booklet "Romance of Model Railroading" at top with light gray background and dark green lettering, front cover background also light gray. Smith Collection.　　**.50　.75　1　2**

(D) Same rear cover image but now in light gray with dark blue lettering, front cover is dark blue rather than usual dark green with very light blue background. Smith Collection.　　**.50　.75　1　2**

**QUESTIONS:** What is the order of the four items? Clearly (A) preceeds (B), but the relationship of (C) and (D) to each other, and to (A) and (B), is unknown.

**ROMANCE OF MODEL RAILROADING WTH LIONEL TRAINS** 9" wide x 6" high, 32 pages including covers, front cover shows pipe-smoking engineer and two boys and a railroad yard in right corner, printed in black ink and the interior pages are printed in black and orange ink on white paper. Salamone and Zydlo Collections.　　**2　3　5　9**

**LIONEL RAILROADING IS FUN** poster, 17-1/4" wide x 23-3/4" high, printed on both sides in blue and black ink on white paper. Shows track plans and accessories inside. Salamone and Smith Collections.

**2　3　5　9**

### 1952

**ADVANCE CATALOGUE** 11-1/8" x 8", 40 pages, red, black and yellow two-tone pages, red and black cover.　　**5　10　18　25**

**CATALOGUE** 11-1/8" x 7-3/4", 36 pages, cover illustration shows boy overlooking "LIONEL" arch bridge; Santa Fe switcher with train is crossing bridge and six locomotives are lined up beneath it.　　**3　7　13　25**

**INSTRUCTIONS**

(A) 8-1/2" wide x 5-1/2" high, 64 black and white pages plus yellow and blue wraparound cover, No. 926-52. Ocilka Collection.

**.50　.75　1　2**

(B) 8-1/2" wide x 5-1/2" high, 64 black and white interior coated pages plus yellow and dark blue wraparound covers, "Form 926-52". Dixon and Smith Collections.　　**.50　.75　2　3**

(C) 8-1/2" wide x 5-1/2" high, 64 pages, black and white and green on gray-brown cover, No. 926-51.　　**.50　.75　1　2**

**1952 CONSUMER CATALOGUE** 9-1/2" wide x 11" high, color cover, inside pages are either red and black or blue and black, printed on pulp paper, cover language, "1952 Lionel Trains" with Real Puffing Smoke, Built in Remote Control Whistle, and Sensational new Magnetraction in all Diesel Locomotives, Bryan Collection. This catalogue was printed for dealer distribution and contained a block on the rear cover for dealer name and address.　　**5　10　20　25**

**LIONEL TRAIN CATALOGUE** 11-1/4" wide x 7-5/8" high, 36 pages including covers and interior pages printed in full color on coated paper; this catalogue shows retail prices; was probably a Lionel authorized reprinting in conjunction with a distributor. The retail store name appeared on the front cover; sample observed marked, "Playworld Toy Shop, Utica, N.Y." Salamone and Smith Collections.　　**2　3　4　6**

**LIONEL ACCESSORIES** 9" wide x 7" high, 16 pages, black and red cover and interior pages, coated stock, cover language, "Give You True Railroading Realism and Operating Excitement."　Bryan Collection.

**.50　.75　1　2**

**PAPER CITY** 42" x 22", full color printing, includes two oil trucks, two passenger automobiles, service station, packing plant, pump station and other items. Available as part of coupon offer reported in December 1952 issue of **The Whistle Stop**, page 27. C. Lang and Schreiner Collections.

**1　2　3　5**

**1952 OFFICIAL BOOK OF RULES FOR MODEL RAILROADING** 4-3/16" wide x 6-1/8" high, blue cover, 16 pages, inside pages have blue ink with red and green ink on signals. Available as part of coupon offer depicted in advertisement in December 1952 issue of **The Whistle Stop**, page 27. C. Lang, Bryan and Schreiner Collections.　　**.50　1　2　4**

**1952 RAILROADING IS FUN** Fold out poster, 17-1/4" x 22-3/4", printed in black and white on both sides with orange background. Ocilka and Salamone Collections.　　**1　2　3　5**

**DETAILED LAYOUT DIAGRAMS**, booklet, 8-1/2" x 11". Magner Collection. Further information needed.　　**NRS**

### 1953

**ADVANCE CATALOGUE** 11-1/4" x 7-5/8", 44 pages, color cover with Santa Fe 2343 diesels, black and white inside pages with red and orange backgrounds and headings.　　**5　10　18　25**

**CATALOGUE**

(A) 11-1/4" x 7-5/8", 40 pages, coated stock, full color; cover illustration shows four trains against pale blue background, red "LIONEL", centerfold has "High Powered Triple Diesel Freights", page 8 lists "No. 2046 Lionel Steam Loco" and "No. 2055 Steam Loco", page 14 shows "Lionel New No. 685 Steam Loco".　　**3　6　12　17**

(B) Same as (A), but page 8 "No. 2046 Lionel Steam Loco and Tender" and "No. 2055 Lionel Steam Loco and Tender", page 14 same as (A).

**3　6　12　17**

(C) Same as (B), but page 14 has "Lionel New No. 685 Steam Loco and Tender".　　**3　7　13　18**

(D) Same as (A), but page 14 has "Lionel New No. 685 Steam Loco and Tender", page 8 same as (A).　　**3　6　12　17**

(E) 8" x 5-5/8", 32 pages, coated stock, two-tone inside pages, color cover like (A), centerfold has three sets in a layout different than the others (may be imprinted with store name on front).　　**2　3　6　12**

**DISTRIBUTOR'S ADVERTISING PROMOTIONS CATALOGUE.**

(A) Usually imprinted with store advertising, 8-1/2" x 11", 16 pages, pulp paper, color covers, red, black, and blue interior pages, "New Lionel Trains for 1953" on cover.　　**.50　1　2　3**

(B) Same as (A), no "New Lionel Trains for 1953" known as UNEEDA Catalogue. Ocilka Collection.　　**NRS**

(C) Same as (E), four-page cover added to (E). Covers are white heavy stock and shows "UNEEDA TRAIN TOWN" store front, 736 steam engine, "Trains Are Our Business, Not a Sideline." Smith Collection.　　**NRS**

**HOW TO OPERATE LIONEL TRAINS AND ACCESSORIES** 8-1/2" x 5-3/8", 64 black and white pages plus wraparound cover No. 926-53.

(A) Black and yellow wraparound cover. Weisblum Collection.

**.25　.50　1　2**

(B) Orange and black wraparound cover. Ocilka Collection.

**.25　.50　1　2**

**LIONEL ACCESSORIES** "Gives you true Railroading Realism and Operating Excitement", 9" wide x 6" high, 16 numbered pages, coated stock, red and black print on white paper. Bryan, Smith and Salamone Collections.　　**2　3　5　9**

**1953 ADVERTISING FLYER** 7" x 10", printed in black or full color, four sets on front, accessories on back with prices. Schreiner Collection.

**.25　.50　1　1.50**

**LIONEL TRACK LAYOUT PRINTING KIT** 9-1/2" x 12-1/2", red and black printing. "A Few of the Many LIONEL Track Layouts to Make", one piece of 9-1/2" x 12-1/2", plastic dies, 0 and 0-27 crossovers, switches, straight and curve tracks, yellow plastic ring, die with big L, Copyright 1953. Koff and Smith Collections.　　**NRS**

### 1954

**ADVANCE CATALOGUE** 11-1/4" x 7-5/8", 44 pages, color covers, red and black interior, coated stock.　　**5　10　15　20**

**NEW LIONEL BOXCARS** Supplement to Advance Catalogue, 10-1/2" x 7-1/4", one-side, black and white on coated stock, illustrates 6464-125, 6464-100, 6464-150, 6464-175 and lists others.　　**1　2　3　5**

## CATALOGUE

(A) 11-1/4" x 7-5/8", 44 pages, full color, coated stock, yellow cover with four locomotive fronts.   **3  6  9  18**

(B) 8-1/8" x 5-3/4", 32 pages, color covers like (A), red and black interior printing, coated stock.   **2  4  8  12**

**DISTRIBUTOR'S ADVERTISING PROMOTIONS CATALOGUE** 8-3/8" x 11", 16 pages, stock, color covers, front cover shows 2321 LACKAWANNA, black, red and yellow interior pages, cover illustration shows two boys watching 2321 FM traverse girder bridge.   **.50  1  2  3**

**ACCESSORIES CATALOGUE** 9" x 6", 20 pages, coated stock, green and black printing, four-page blue center section, pages not numbered. Smith Collection.   **1  2  3  4**

**ALL ABOARD AT LIONEL** 8-5/8" x 11-1/2", 20 pages, coated stock, pink cover, black and white inside pages.   **1  2  3  4**

**HOW TO OPERATE LIONEL TRAINS AND ACCESSORIES** 5-1/2" x 8-1/2", 64 black and white pages, plus black and light green wraparound cover, No. 926-54. Dixon, Ocilka and Smith Collections.   **.25  .50  1  2**

**1954 LET'S PLAN THE FINEST LIONEL LAYOUT IN TOWN** 16 pages including covers. 10-7/8" wide x 8-1/4" high, front cover shows dad and son with Lackawanna Train Master, Seaboard NW-Z and 736 steamer; front cover and interior pages printed in black and red ink on white paper. Salamone Collection.   **2  3  5  9**

**STORE DISPLAY CATALOGUE,** 12" x 9", white-coated stock, black and red ink, 12 pages. Contains "1954 PRICE SHEET ON LIONEL TRAINS" with retail prices and the statement that "LIONEL PRODUCTS ARE PRICE FIXED AND SOLD UNDER FAIR TRADE ACT". Then it showed three different dealer assortments: $5,000, $2,000 and $1,000. It also showed store merchandisers and displays. The largest store display, D-132, was 8' x 8' and operated three trains on two different levels. Net cost was $273. Diggle Collection.   **NRS**

### 1955

**ADVANCE CATALOGUE**

(A) 11-1/4" x 7-3/4", 20 black and white pages, lightweight coated stock.   **5  10  15  20**

(B) 11-1/4" x 7-3/4", 20 pages including covers, orange and black ink on white stock featuring magnetraction. Salamone Collection.   **5  10  25  40**

**A SPECIAL DEALER'S CATALOGUE** showing set compositions and components, cars, track, etc. White with black and white halftones of 1955 sets on gloss paper, 27 pages printed on one side only, no cover, sheets stapled together on left-hand side, shows 27 sets (rare). Zydlo and Diggle Collections.   **NRS**

**CATALOGUE** 11-1/4" x 7-5/8", 44 pages, full color, coated stock, cover illustration in white with five trains and six happy faces.   **3  6  9  12**

**ELLIOTT ROWLAND CATALOGUE** Usually imprinted with store advertising.

(A) 8-3/8" x 11-1/8", yellow covers with "Lionel Trains by (Store Name)", pages 5 and 14 are yellow, pulp paper; cover illustration shows father leaning against easy chair while grandfather operates the trains and children look on.   **.50  1  2  3**

(B) Same as (A), but color cover with blue background.   **.50  1  2  3**

(C) 8-3/8" x 11-1/8", color covers, pulp paper, cover illustration shows family looking at Lionel layout through store window.   **.50  1  2  3**

**HOW TO OPERATE LIONEL TRAINS AND ACCESSORIES** Includes Service Station listing, 8-1/2" x 5-1/2", 64 pages in black and white, plus brown and white wraparound cover, Form 926-55.   **.25  .50  1  2**

**ACCESSORY CATALOGUE** 11-1/4" x 7-3/4", front cover printed in black and orange ink on white stock, inside pages printed in black ink on white stock, 20 pages including covers. This is the same as Advance Catalogue (B), except for title and ink. Salamone Collection.   **2  5  12  20**

**TEMPLATES FOR LIONEL "027" LAYOUTS** Form 1061 Rev 11-55 upper left corner. Peel-off track templates (reusable if used on surface such as porcelain, linoleum, etc.) 8-1/2" x 11", one-page depiction of track, switches and crossovers one-eighth actual size. Algozzini Collection.   **.50  1  2  3**

### 1956

**ADVANCE CATALOGUE** 11" x 8", 48 pages, black and white, red cover with "Order Now!"   **5  10  15  20**

**CATALOGUE** 11-1/4" x 7-5/8", 40 pages, full color, coated stock, cover illustration shows PRR and NH Electric, Lionel Lines steam locomotive, 3530, 3360 and 3927.

(A) "Remember: Lionel Train Sets Start as Low as $19.95...." in white block on back cover.   **3  5  7  10**

(B) No lettering in white block on back cover.   **3  5  7  10**

**ACCESSORY CATALOGUE** 11" x 8", 24 pages, red and black on pulp paper.   **1  2  3  4**

**HOW TO CLEAN AND LUBRICATE...** 5" x 4", 12 pages, black and white, coated stock.   **.10  .25  .35  .50**

**HOW TO OPERATE LIONEL TRAINS AND ACCESSORIES**

(A) Includes Service Station listings, 8-1/2" x 5-1/4", 64 pages, black and white, red and blue wraparound cover, form 925-56. Graham Collection.   **.25  .50  1  2**

(B) Pale yellow and dark blue cover, drawing of dad and son playing trains, 64 pages copyrighted inside front cover of 1950, came with advertising sheet, "Send for Billboards" (25 cents) one side and send for "Romance of Model Railroading Book" on other side, copyrighted 1956, contains individual items only. Weber Collection.   **NRS**

**1956 ELLIOTT ROWLAND CATALOGUE** 24 pages including covers, 8-1/4" wide x 11" high, front covers, in full color, shows mom, dad and two children looking in a store window at a Lionel layout, catalogue shows retail prices. Rowland was authorized by Lionel to print and distribute these inexpensive catalogues depicting the Lionel line. Salamone Collection.   **2  3  4  6**

### 1957

**ADVANCE CATALOGUE** 11" x 8-1/4", 54 pages, red and black covers, black and white-coated stock.   **5  10  15  20**

**AND NOW H0 - BY LIONEL** 10-3/4" x 7-5/8", "For the Discriminating Hobbyist...", supplement to Advance Catalogue, four-page color folder, may have been distributed separately and/or in consumer catalogue in addition to Advance Catalogue.   **.25  .50  1  2**

**COLLECTOR TRADING CARDS**   **.10  .25  .35  .50**
Boston And Maine
Virginian
Seaboard
Canadian Pacific
Rock Island
Southern
New Haven
Northern
Santa Fe
Western Pacific
Alaskan
M-K-T
Norfolk & Western
Rio Grande
Baltimore and Ohio
Pennsylvania
Great Northern
General
Milwaukee
Wabash
Union Pacific
Burlington

**SALES SHEET: VITAL SMALL PARTS FOR LIONEL TRAINS, SUPER "O" TRACK FOR LIONEL TRAINS** 19-3/4" x 14", black and white. Graham Collection.   **.50  1  2  3**

**CATALOGUE** 11-1/4" x 7-1/2", 52 pages, full color, coated stock, cover has "New Super '0' Track".   **1  2  3  7**

**ACCESSORY CATALOGUE** With Service Station Directory for 1957-58, 10" x 7-1/2", 32 pages, red and black covers, black and white pulp paper.   **.25  .50  1  2**

**HOW TO OPERATE LIONEL TRAINS AND ACCESSORIES** 8-1/2" x 5-1/2", 64 black and white pages plus red and black wraparound cover, pulp paper. .25 .50 1 2

**BANNER: H0 BY LIONEL THE LEADER IN MODEL RAILROADING** 21-3/16" x 6-1/2", yellow paper printed with black and red ink. Graham Collection. .50 1 2 3

**POSTER: LIONEL TRAINS AND ACCESSORIES COME IN AND GET YOUR NEW FREE CATALOGUE** 28" x 12", full color, six engines with 2379 and 746 in center. Graham Collection. 1 2 3 5

**BANNER: COME IN AND GET YOUR BIG NEW LIONEL CATALOGUE** 10-/4" x 4-1/4", red and black ink on white paper. Graham Collection. .25 .50 .75 1

**TRACK LAYOUT BOOK FOR SUPER 0**, details needed. Magner Collection. NRS

**DEALER PROMOTION BOOKLET** "TAKE THE THROTTLE AND MAKE YOUR SALES ROLL". Features Steve Allen, Ed Sullivan and the 2373 Canadian Pacific F-3, 12" x 18", 10 pages. Magner Collection. 3 7 10 20

### 1958

**ADVANCE CATALOGUE** 10-7/8" x 8-1/4", 64 pages, red and black cover, NH and M & StL trains passing missile launching site, black and white, H0 scale section has burgundy marker with gold-stamped "H0". 5 10 15 20

**CATALOGUE** 11-1/4" x 7-5/8", 56 pages, cover like Advance Catalogue but in full color on coated stock. 2 4 6 8

**ACCESSORY CATALOGUE** With Service Station Directory, 11-1/8" x 8", 32 pages, red and black cover, black and white, pulp paper. Title "Lionel 1958 Accessory Catalogue" contains individual items only. Cover picture is similar to regular catalogue, inside front cover copyrighted 1958. Weber Collection. .50 1 2 3

**ADVANCE H0 CATALOGUE** 10-7/8" x 8-1/8", 8 pages, black and white, cover has red background and illustration of H0 display, rear cover shows dealer displays "For Your H0 Department". .50 1 2 3

**H0 CATALOGUE**
(A) 8-1/8" x 10-7/8", six-page fold-out, full color, coated stock. .50 1 2 3
(B) 8-1/4" x 11-1/4", 8 pages, full color, coated stock. .50 1 2 3
(C) 8" x 11", six-page fold-out, full color, coated stock, copyright 1958 by The Lionel Corporation. Published in **Railroad Model Craftsman** magazine, October 1958, as unnumbered pages 35 through 40. 1 2 3 4

**LIONEL RAILROAD MAP:** 52" x 37", published by Rand-McNally. Magner Collection. 3 7 10 20

### 1959

**ADVANCE CATALOGUE** 8-1/2" x 10-7/8", 44 pages, full color, black and white, fold-out pages, coated stock, cover lettered "Lionel 1959", illustration shows 1872 General and 44 missile launcher. 3 7 12 18

**CATALOGUE** 11" x 8-1/2", 56 pages, full color, coated stock, cover illustration shows 736, 1872 General and 44 U.S. Army. 3 5 9 12

**ACCESSORY CATALOGUE** 11" high x 8" wide, red and black front cover with 1872 and 44 locomotives, black ink only on pulp interior pages, 36 pages. Schreiner Collection. .75 1.50 2 3

**H0 CATALOGUE** 8-1/8" x 11", eight pages, full color, coated stock, copyright 1958 by The Lionel Corporation, published in **Railroad Model Craftsman** magazine, October 1959, as unnumbered pages 35 through 42. 1 2 3 4

**CARDBOARD GAME SHEET,** "The Great Locomotive Race", 10-7/8" x 11-7/8", included in catalogued set 2527, a Super 0 set with a 44 Missile Launcher locomotive. Spins of a cardboard wheel move cardboard engines around the sheet. Was this sheet produced in conjunction with the Walt Disney movie **The Great Locomotive Chase**, which was made in 1959? Reader comments invited. Ambrose and Algozzini Collections. NRS

### 1960

**ADVANCE CATALOGUE** 8-1/2" x 11", 60 pages, color cover, black and white, red and white back cover with promotional slogan, coated stock, cover illustration shows father and son viewing twin railroad layout. 3 5 7 12

**CATALOGUE** 11" x 8-3/8", 56 pages, full color, coated stock, cover illustration shows family viewing close-up section of twin railroad layout. 3 5 9 12

**ACCESSORY CATALOGUE** With Service Station listing, 8-5/8" x 11", 40 pages, color cover, black and white pulp paper. 1 2 3 4

**HOW TO OPERATE LIONEL TRAINS AND ACCESSORIES**
(A) 8-1/2" x 5-3/8", 64 black and white pages on coated stock, heavy paper wraparound cover in black and white with red background, Form 926-60. 1 2 3 4

(B) Cover shows black and white photo of N & W Y6b, left and rear side with orange-red right half with black and white lettering, 62 pages, copyrighted 1960 inside rear cover. Smith and Weber Collections. 1 2 3 4

**CATALOGUE POSTER** 10-1/4" x 4-1/4", one-side, coated stock, apparently intended for store window.
(A) "Come in and get your Big New Lionel Catalog", red and black letters on white background. 1 2 4 6
(B) Same as (A), but black and white letters on red background. 1 2 4 6

**GET SET FOR ACTION....** Promotional flier, 22-1/4" x 27-1/2" folded to 11-1/8" x 7-1/8", two sides, red and black on heavy white stock. 1 2 4 6

**PLEDGE POSTER** 9-1/4" x 11-3/4", black and white, green border, "We pledge to all Lionel Customers....", small tear-off section at bottom reads, "Mr. Dealer: Display this message prominently". .50 1 2 3

**PROMOTIONAL POSTER** 22" x 8-1/2", one side, coated stock, black and white, "Lionel Trains and Accessories" in red letters. 1 2 4 6

**CONTEST POSTER** 22" x 8-1/2", one-side, coated stock, black and white on red background, "Hey Kids! Big Lionel Contest..." 1 2 4 6

**CONTEST INSTRUCTIONS** 11" x 8-3/8", four-page folder, color cover similar to catalogue cover, black and white interior, coated stock. .50 1 2 3

**UNION PACIFIC RAILROAD, A BRIEF HISTORY** 5-3/16" wide x 8-7/8" high, printed April 1946, 16th printing, March 1960, 16 pages, coated stock. Railroad buffs will find in this brief history of the Union Pacific Railroad a wealth of information. Lionel is indebted to the Union Pacific Railroad for providing this material. Smith Collection. .50 .75 1 2

**LIONEL TRACK LAYOUTS FOR "027", SUPER "O" AND H0 GAUGES, START BUILDING YOURS TODAY!** 8-3/8" x 11", 4 pages, not numbered.
(A) Price 10 cents on front, page 2 has "1-115" on lower right, heavy white paper black and gray. "Address inquiries to: Lionel Service, Dept 74-E, Hoffman Place, Hillside, NJ 07205" on back page. Smith Collection. .25 .50 .75 1

(B) Similiar to (A), but no price, no number, coated paper stock. On bottom last 3 pages concerning inquires, "simply write to: Engineer Bill c/o The Lionel Corp., 15 East 26th St., New York, 10 NY." Smith Collection. .25 .50 .75 1

**H0 CATALOGUE** 8-1/2" x 10-7/8", 12 pages, full color, coated stock, cover reads, "Operating Cars - 1960's Most Exciting H0 News". 1 2 3 4

**HOW TO OPERATE LIONEL H0 TRAINS** 8-1/2" x 5-1/2", 24 pages plus red and black covers. .50 1 2 3

### 1961

**ADVANCE CATALOGUE** 8-1/2" x 11", 76 pages, John Bruce Medaris on cover, color cover, black and white-coated stock. 3 5 7 10

**SALES TIPS** 8-1/2" x 11", four-page folder, John Bruce Medaris on cover, black and white coated stock, sales tips for dealers. .50 1 2 3

**CATALOGUE**
(A) 8-1/2" x 11", 56 pages, layout and science sets on cover, red and black covers, inside black and white pulp paper, "Honorary Stockholder" on rear cover. .50 1 2 3
(B) 8-1/2" x 11", 72 pages, cover same as (A), but catalogue differs, full color coated stock, H0 raceways on rear cover. 1 2 4 6

**JOIN WITH LIONEL** Dealer flier, 25-7/8" x 22", order form for custom ad mats (used for store windows and advertisements), one-side, black and white. .50 1 2 3

**LIONEL-PORTER SCIENCECRAFT CATALOGUE**
(A) 8-1/2" x 11", 8 pages, red and black, coated stock, "The Lionel Corporation, Hagerstown, Maryland". .50 1 2 3
(B) 8-1/2" x 11", 8 pages, red and black ink on white-coated stock, "The Lionel Corporation, Hagerstown, Maryland". This catalogue was initially dated as 1961 based on associated materials. However, a price sheet supplied by I. D. Smith states, "Net billing prices to you are guaranteed against voluntary . . . decline during 1962". This could indicate a 1961-62 catalogue since schools would be one of the principal purchasers of this equipment and school years span the calendar year. Further comments requested. Smith Collection. .50 1 2 3
**VITAL SMALL PARTS FOR LIONEL TRAINS** sales sheet, 8-1/2" x 11", folded, unfolds to 17" x 11", printed one side, black ink on heavy paper, Lockons, Sayer 0 track parts, 0 and 0-27 track pens and adapter pens, contractors, controllers actuators, No. 2524, 11-61, Printed in U.S. of America, lower left. Smith Collection. .50 1 2 3

## 1962
**CATALOGUE** 8-1/2" x 11", 100 pages, cover lettered "Lionel 1962". 1 2 4 6
**ADVANCE CATALOGUE** "Lionel Trains and Accessories - The Leader in Model RR 1962", 64 pages, four-color cover, black and white inside, includes displays and HO, 8-1/2" x 11" vertical. Zydlo Collection. **NRS**
**ACCESSORY CATALOGUE** 8-3/8" x 10-7/8", 62 pages, full color cover, first 2 and last 2 pages are coated stock, rest is black and white pulp. Ocilka Collection. **NRS**
**ACCESSORY CATALOGUE** 8-3/8" x 10-7/8", 40 pages, red and black cover, black and white, pulp paper. 1 2 3 4
**LIONEL-SPEAR-TRIANG ADVANCE CATALOGUE** 8-3/8" x 11", 56 pages, color-coated stock, top cover illustration shows science lab, bottom illustration shows phonographs, rear cover features "Scalextric" racing. 1 2 4 6
**LIONEL-SPEAR CATALOGUE** 8-3/8" x 11", 56 pages, color-coated stock, cover lettered "Lionel-Spear '62". 1 2 3 4
**LIONEL PHONOGRAPH AND TAPE RECORDER PARTS AND SERVICE GUIDE**, 8-1/2" x 11", further details needed. Magner Collection. **NRS**

## 1963
**CATALOGUE** 8-3/8" x 10-7/8", 56 pages, color cover, red and black interior coated stock 1 2 4 6
**ADVANCE CATALOGUE** "Lionel 1963", 8-1/2" x 11", 80 pages, yellow, black and white cover, interior black and white, includes trains, Lionel-Porter and racing sets, etc. Smith and Zydlo Collections. **NRS**
**ACCESSORY CATALOGUE** With Service Station listing, 8-3/8" x 10-7/8", 40 pages, blue and black cover, interior black and white pulp paper. .50 1 2 3
**SCIENCE CATALOGUE** 8-3/8" x 10-7/8", 32 pages, red and black two-tone pulp paper, cover lettered "Lionel 1963 Science Catalogue". 1 2 3 4

## 1964
**CATALOGUE** 8-3/8" x 10-7/8", 24 pages, black and blue.
(A) Pulp paper, page 13 lists 6402 flatcar at $2.50. 1 2 4 5
(B) Same as (A), but 6402 is incorrectly listed at $3.95. 1 2 4 5
(C) Same as (A), but coated stock. 1 2 5 7
(D) Same as (B), but coated stock. 1 2 5 7
**LIONEL RACEWAYS CATALOGUE** 8-1/2" x 11", 12 pages, green and black-coated stock, cover lettered "Lionel Raceways and Accessories for 1964". .50 1 2 3
**HELIOS 21** Remote Control Space Craft, 8-1/2" x 11", four-page folder, red and black with black and white photos, cover lettered "Hey! Hey Helios 21 is Here", Advance for dealers. .50 1 2 3
**PROJECT X CATALOGUE** 22-7/8" x 11", tri-fold, red and black with silver, Lyter-N-Air remote control space ships, Advance for dealers. .50 1 2 3
**LIONEL "U-DRIVE" BOAT** 8-1/2" x 11", 2 pages. This versatile boat can be used in a backyard, local pond or small lake. Stekoll Collection. .50 1 2 3

**LIONEL COMBINES SIGHT WITH SOUND** Phono-Vision, 8-1/2" x 11", 4 pages, two-color printing, front cover shows boy and girl with record player with slide projector lens on right side and image shown on inside of record player case, believed to be 1964. (Verification of date requested.) Stekoll Collection. .50 1 2 3

## 1965
**CATALOGUE** 8-1/2" x 10-7/8", 40 pages, multi-color printing and backgrounds.
(A) Pulp paper. 1 2 4 5
(B) Coated stock. 1 2 5 7
(C) Same as (A), 6119 and 6401 (errata). 1 2 4 5
(D) Same as (B), 6119 and 6401 (errata). 1 2 5 7
**HOW TO OPERATE LIONEL TRAINS** 8-1/2" x 11", 32 pages, black and white plus yellow wraparound cover, uncoated paper. .50 1 2 3
**LIONEL-PORTER SCIENCE SETS CATALOGUE** 8-3/8" x 10-7/8", 8 pages, two-tone brown and black, coated stock, eight items illustrated on cover. .25 .50 .75 1
**LIONEL-SPEAR CATALOGUE** 8-1/2" x 11-1/8", four-page folder, two-tone brown and black-coated stock, cover lettered "Lionel-Spear 1964". .25 .50 .75 1
**PHONO-VISION CATALOGUE** 8-1/2" x 11", 4-page folder, two-tone yellow and black coated stock, cover lettered "Lionel Combines Sight with Sound! Phono-Vision". .25 .50 .75 1
**HOW TO SELL LIONEL TRAINS AND ACCESSORIES:** Dealer promotion booklet, 5-3/4" x 8-1/2", 40 pages including covers. Front cover is orange with white border and black sans-serif lettering; rear cover is white with Lionel logo at bottom. Pages are tabbed for easy use. General contents give specific selling points for Lionel features such as magnetraction, smoke, etc. Algozzini Collection. 3 5 8 10

## 1966
**CATALOGUE** 10-7/8" x 8-3/8", 40 pages, full color coated stock, cover illustration shows father and son watching trains rush by.
(A) Set illustrations on pages 8 and 10. .50 1 2 3
(B) No illustrations as in (A). .50 1 2 3
**WELCOME TO THE WONDERFUL WORLD OF LIONEL** Trains, race-ways, phonographs, science sets, 8-1/2" x 21-3/4" folded to 3-1/2" x 8-1/2", black and white with orange and blue trim, No. 1-117. Dixon Collection. **NRS**
**LIONEL TRAIN & ACCESSORY** Operating and Wiring Manual for 0-27 and Super 0, $1.00, 36 page illustrated booklet No. 4080, $1.25 to cover cost of postage and handing charge. Shown on page 17 of 1966 Catalogue. **NRS**

## 1967
**CATALOGUE NOT ISSUED**

## 1968
**TRAINS AND ACCESSORIES CATALOGUE** 8-1/2" x 11", 8 pages, folds out to 34" x 11", full color coated stock. 1 2 3 5
**HAGERSTOWN SET** 11" x 8-1/2", two-sided, blue on white-coated stock, shows 11600 set on one side with "Lionel '68", track and accessories on the other with "The Lionel Toy Corporation - Hagerstown, Maryland 21740".
(A) Original. .50 1 2 3
(B) Reproduction by Greenberg Publishing Co. — — — .50
**LIONEL TRACK LAYOUTS** and **No. 4080 LIONEL TRAIN & ACCESSORY** Manual again shown as available for a cost in the 1968 Train and Accessory Catalogue. **NRS**

## 1969
**CATALOGUE**
(A) 11" x 8-1/2", 8 pages, full color coated stock. 1 2 3 5
(B) 11-1/8" x 8-1/2", 8 pages, similiar to (A), but printed on brown and white-coated stock, pages not numbered. 1 2 3 5
**No. 4080 LIONEL TRAIN & ACCESSORY** Manual again shown as available for a fee on page 7 of Catalogue (A) and unnumbered page 7 of Catalogue (B). **NRS**

### DATE UNKNOWN
Help us date this material.
**THE LIONEL PARTS STORY** 8-1/2" x 11", 4 pages, heavy paper, black ink. 3 pictures on each page, shows "The Permanent Staff", Lennie Dean, Parts

Supervisior, Emma Alvino, Lorraine Ciasullo, John Farley, Alex Charron, and Al Visicaro. See 1966 and 1968 LIONEL TRACK LAYOUTS. Printed black, white and gray.

(A) White-coated stock, no page numbers or identifying numbers, address, Engineer Bill, c/o The Lionel Corp., 15 East 25th St., New York 10, N.Y. **NRS**

(B) White uncoated heavy paper stock. Price $.10 lower right corner, front. Inside (page 2) lower right "1-115". Pages are not numbered. "Address inquiries to: Lionel Service, Dept. 74-E, Hoffman Place, Hillside, N.J. 07205". **NRS**

**RECORD**, date unknown, appears to be from mid-fifties; probably 33-1/3 RPM 10" disc molded from translucent vinyl with designs on both sides. "LIONEL TRAINS SOUND EFFECTS" in bold block letters around rim of both sides. One side portrays a steam train alongside a lake; the other side shows a Santa Fe diesel passing through farm country. Presumably, the steam and diesel pictures indicated the type of sounds on each side. Kirby Collection.

|  | Gd | Exc | Mt |
|---|---|---|---|

### SERVICE STATION LISTINGS

**1948-49** 7-1/2" wide x 8-3/4" high, white, folds out to 8-3/4" high x 22-1/2" wide, coated stock. Smith Collection. .25 .50 1

**1950-51** (August 1 above 1950 and July 31 above 1951, front cover), 5-3/8" wide x 8-1/2" high, white, 12 pages, numbered pages except front and rear, coated stock, Form 927-51-TT. Smith Collection. .25 .50 1

**1952-52** 5-3/8" wide x 8-1/2" high, white, 12 pages, numbered pages (except front and rear), coated stock, Form 927-51-TT. Smith Collection. .25 .50 1

**1952-53** 5-3/8" wide x 8-1/2" high, 12 pages, white-coated stock, numbered, "Form 927-51-TT. Smith Collection. .25 .50 1

**1952-53** 8-1/2" wide x 5-1/2" high, 12 pages, white-coated stock, pages numbered, Form 927-52-TT, except inside front cover pages not numbered. Smith Collection. .25 .50 1

**1953-54** 8-3/8" wide x 5-1/2" high, 12 pages, white-coated stock, numbered pages, except inside front cover and rear not numbered, Form 927-53-TT. Smith Collection. .25 .50 1

**1954-55** 8-3/8" wide x 5-1/2" high, 12 pages, white-coated stock, numbered pages, except inside front cover and rear not numbered, Form 927-Revised 4-19-54-TT. Smith Collection. .25 .50 1

**1954-55** 8-3/8" wide x 5-1/2" high, 12 pages, white-coated stock, numbered pages, except inside front cover and rear not numbered, Form 927-Revised 8-30-54-TT. Smith Collection. .25 .50 1

**1955-56** 8-1/2" wide x 5-1/2" high, 12 pages, white-coated stock, numbered pages, except inside front cover and rear not numbered, Form 927-Revised-2-28-55-TT. Smith Collection. .25 .50 1

**1956-57** 8-1/2" wide x 5-1/2" high, 12 pages, white-coated stock, numbered pages, except inside front cover and rear not numbered, Form 927-Revised 7-30-56-TT. Smith Collection. .25 .50 1

**1962-63** 8-1/2" wide x 5-1/2" high, pages white-coated, four pages, pages not numbered, no form number. Smith Collection. .25 .50 1

**1963-64** 8-1/2" wide x 5-1/2" high, pages white-coated, four pages, pages not numbered, no form number. Smith Collection. .25 .50 1

**1964-65** Same as 1963-64. Smith Collection. .25 .50 1

**1965-66** LIONEL APPROVED SERVICE STATIONS, 8-9/16" wide x 11" high, four pages, not numbered, (926-65 lower right page 1), white paper, black ink. .25 .50 1

**1966-67** LIONEL RACEWAY APPROVED STATIONS, 8-9/16" wide x 11" high, four pages, uncoated, black ink on yellow paper, not numbered, Form No. 5100-166. Smith Collection. .25 .50 1

**1966-67** LIONEL PHONOGRAPH APPROVED STATIONS, 8-9/16" wide x 11" high, four pages, not numbered, no form number, green paper, black ink. Smith Collection. .25 .50 1

**1966-67** LIONEL TRAIN APPROVED STATIONS, 8-9/16" wide x 11" high, four pages, not numbered, no form number, white paper. .25 .50 1

**1968-69** LIONEL TRAIN APPROVED STATIONS, 8-9/16" wide x 11" high, four pages, not numbered, white paper, Form No. 926-68 rear lower left corner. Smith Collection. .25 .50 1

**1969-70** LIONEL TRAIN APPROVED STATIONS, 8-1/2" wide x 13-7/8" high, four pages, not numbered, white paper. Smith Collection. .25 .50 1

# Chapter XV
# FACTORY ERRORS

## FACTORY ERRORS AND PROTOTYPES, POSTWAR PRODUCTION: 1946-1969

The following is our first separate list of factory errors and prototypes. Previously, these items were included in the main listings, but they now have been separated for two distinct reasons. The most obvious reason is that the number of such items reported to us has climbed so drastically that such a separate list has become feasible. The second reason is, that for a long time, certain collectors have specialized in the acquisition and research of these mistakes and pre-production samples. When one considers the immense production of the Lionel factory during the postwar period, it is amazing that more odd pieces have not emerged. The sorting out of postwar factory errors is child's play when compared to the awesome variations faced by collectors of prewar Ives and American Flyer. Ives, for example, all but hand-made its pieces. Where does the collector draw the line between a variation and a factory error?

As a tentative answer, consider that variations are produced in much greater quantities (as a rule) than are factory errors. A variation may occur because of a slight difference in the color of a paint batch or a change in a component subcontracted by the factory. This is not the case with a factory error. These pieces involve mistakes within the production itself - a missing stripe here, a forgotten decal there. The sample on the mass production line both before and after the error is usually made according to specifications. Human error plays a considerable role, despite the best of intentions and the most stringent quality control. A worker may be distracted for an instant, and the flatcar he is rubber-stamping may not get its "LIONEL" stamp on one or both sides. It must be remembered that assembly line jobs are by their very nature rather repetitive and even boring - and that produces mistakes.

Stories have spread throughout the train collecting world that during the last years of the Lionel Corporation's production, some factory errors were deliberately made. While it is not our purpose to resolve such a matter, the mere presence of such stories points out that the collection of factory errors is the riskiest specialty of all for even the most experienced train collector. Some factory errors are indeed highly prized and very rare - thus, quite valuable. However, factory errors can and have been faked by the unscrupulous within the hobby. We strongly urge that you exercise the greatest of caution and fiscal prudence when you consider the purchase of a factory error. Many features are easily switched, repainted or substituted.

Prototypes are quite another matter. Frequently, the factory would produce a small number of a particular item to test reaction to it or to study the feasibility of its mass production. These prototypes would differ from normal production in some way; perhaps the company would decide that a different color was more appropriate for a car, for example. Some factory prototypes were produced as salesman's samples to demonstrate a new year's line. From time to time, the decision would be made not to produce the item as a mass production piece; these prototypes are the rarest of all train collectibles. Over the years, many of these prototypes escaped the factory and emerged in the train collecting world, where they are now sought after and highly prized.

The factory errors and prototypes below are listed by number of the item, rather than in categories of rolling stock. We do not think this list is anywhere near complete, and we ask our readers to supply other examples of factory errors. We are reasonably sure that the items below did come from the factory and were not produced as fakes. If we are wrong - let us know! We also need to know values for most of the items presented.

### STEAM LOCOMOTIVES

**726 LIONEL LINES** 2-8-4 Berkshire steam locomotive.
(A) Decal 726 on cab, red motor plate instead of black. Reportedly, 12 of these engines were produced as pre-production samples for use by salesmen at toy shows. Klaassen Collection.  — — — **1000**

**2037-500 LIONEL LINES** 2-6-4 steam engine, "Girls' train" variant.
(A) No numbers or letters on either engine or tender. Algozzini Collection.  **NRS**

**2037-500** 2-6-4 "Girl's set" locomotive.
(C) Same as listing for (A), but no lettering or numbering; probable factory error. Algozzini Collection.  **NRS**

### DIESELS

**59 MINUTEMAN SWITCHER**
(A) Lettering only on one side. Algozzini Collection.  **NRS**
(B) Lettering is present, but star emblem is missing. Algozzini Collection.  **NRS**

**232 NEW HAVEN** Alco A Unit.
(A) On one side, black in the "H" of the "NH" logo carries upward to form a narrow stripe on the bottom of the white "N". Halverson Collection.  **NRS**

**611 JERSEY CENTRAL** NW-2 Switcher.
(A) No lettering or numbering on either side. Algozzini Collection.  **NRS**

**613 UNION PACIFIC** NW-2 Switcher.
(A) No lettering or numbering on either side. Algozzini Collection.  **NRS**

**645 UNION PACIFIC** NW-2 Switcher.
(A) Lettered only on one side. Algozzini Collection.  **NRS**

**1062 LIONEL LINES** steam locomotive.
(A) No lettering or numbering on either engine or tender. Algozzini Collection.  **NRS**

**2028 PENNSYLVANIA** GP-7 Road Switcher.
(A) Double-stamped on one side. Algozzini Collection.  **NRS**

**2322 VIRGINIAN** Fairbanks-Morse Trainmaster.
(A) No number or decal on either side. Algozzini Collection.  **NRS**

**2339 WABASH** GP-9 Road Switcher.
(A) No lettering or decals on either side. Algozzini Collection.  **NRS**

**2346 BOSTON AND MAINE** GP-9 Road Switcher.
(A) White unpainted plastic GP-9 fan shroud. Arpino Collection.  **NRS**

**2348 MINNEAPOLIS AND ST. LOUIS** GP-9 Road Switcher.
(A) Factory painted 2329 rectifier metal chassis. Rohlfing Collection.  **NRS**
(B) No lettering or decals on either side. Algozzini Collection.  **NRS**

**2359 BOSTON AND MAINE** GP-9 Road Switcher.
(A) Black unpainted plastic GP-9 fan shroud. Algozzini Collection.  **NRS**

**2041 ROCK ISLAND** Alco AA units, 1969, no lettering. Degano Collection.  **NRS**

**2355 WESTERN PACIFIC** F-3 AA units, 1953, no lettering on one side. Kraemer observation. **NRS**

**2379 RIO GRANDE** F-3 AB units, 1957-58, no silver stripe on B unit. Kraemer observation. **NRS**

**55 TIE-JECTOR** Same as listed, but no lettering, probable factory error. Catalano observation. **100 130 165 210**

**58 GREAT NORTHERN** Rotary Snowplow: Unpainted green cab sides, no logo, Pauli Collection. **NRS**

**59 MINUTEMAN** Switcher.
(B) Same as (A), but factory error: "U.S. AIR FORCE" on both sides, but one blank cab side and number "59" and only small part of insignia on other. Further examples of factory errors requested. Algozzini Collection. **NRS**

**520 BOX CAB ELECTRIC:** Same as (A), except re-stamped on one side to form double letter image, probable factory error. Blotner Collection. **NRS**

**635 UNION PACIFIC** NW-2 Switcher.
(A) Factory error: no lettering on one side. Kraemer observation. **NRS**
(B) Factory error: no number on front. Kraemer observation. **NRS**

**645 UNION PACIFIC** NW-2 Switcher.
(A) Heat-stamped lettering on only one side. This version was reported in our 1977 edition but subsequently dropped because questions of its collectibility arose. A subsequent report by J. Breslin indicates a second example which was obtained from Rosewood Hobbies. The questions are, therefore: Is this a collectible variation? Are there other examples in collector hands? Is this a legitimate factory error? Reader comments invited. **NRS**

## ACCESSORIES

**394 ROTARY BEACON.**
(A) Red base, aluminum tower and tower top, no evidence of switching part. Herdt Collection. **NRS**

## BOXCARS

**3454 AUTOMATIC MERCHANDISE CAR.**
(A) Same as (B) in main listing, but heat-stamped only on one side. Sattler Collection. **— — 200 —**

**3494 STATE OF MAINE** Operating Boxcar.
(A) Printed on only one side. **NRS**

**3656 STOCKYARD CORRAL.**
(A) Nameplate present, but no chains or holes for chains; appears to be a hybrid of older and newer type. Cummings Collection. **NRS**

**6445 FORT KNOX GOLD RESERVE** Mint Car.
(A) Gold-painted clear plastic, no lettering. Possible special production for Junior Achievement program. Algozzini Collection. **NRS**

**6464-50 MINNEAPOLIS AND ST. LOUIS** Boxcar.
(A) Type 1 light green mold, 1953-type doors, green-painted body, gold lettering, black plastic doors painted green, has "BUILT 5-53" on left side of door, unlike production pieces which have no built dates. Klaassen Collection. **NRS**

**6464-150 MISSOURI PACIFIC** Boxcar.
(A) No white lettering on top or on bottom of sides, blue stripes on one side of car. Klaassen Collection. **NRS**

**6464-375 CENTRAL OF GEORGIA** Boxcar.
(A) Entire car is maroon plastic Type IV body, unpainted pink-tinged doors. Algozzini Collection. **NRS**
(B) Regular 1956-type, but without decals. Algozzini Collection. **NRS**

**6464-425 NEW HAVEN** Boxcar.
(A) Lettered only on one side. Kraemer and Algozzini Collections. **NRS**

**6464-510 NEW YORK CENTRAL PACEMAKER** Boxcar.
(A) Same as Entry 216A, but door is the same as that found on 6464-515, Entry 217 - Navy blue-painted light greenish-blue. Strong evidence that this particular piece is a factory error where the doors were reversed with a 6464-515; see entry listed below. Budniak Collection. **NRS**

**6464-515 KATY** Boxcar.
(A) Same as Entry 217, but door is painted as described in Entry 216A

under 6464-510; possible door switch at factory, see 6464-510 above. Budniak Collection. **NRS**

## PROTOTYPE BOXCARS
See photograph on page 90.
These cars, from the collection of Elliott Smith, are now in the collection of Bill Eddins.

**6464(A) PARKER KALON** Type IIB* unpainted gray plastic body, 1956-type unpainted black plastic door, decal lettering, "6464(B)" does not appear on car. **— — 400 —**

**6464(B) 0000 HOTPOINT** Type III white plastic body painted yellow and black, 1956-type red plastic door painted yellow, black decal lettering, different designs on each side, "6464(B)" does not appear on car. **NRS**

**6464(C) 0000 HOTPOINT** Type IIB gray plastic body painted red and white, 1956-type yellow plastic door painted red, black decal lettering, different designs on each side, "6464(C)" does not appear on the car. **— — 1500 —**

**6464(D) PARKER KALON** Type IIB black plastic body painted white, 1956-type unpainted orange plastic door, decal lettering, "GENUINE PK SELF TAPPING SCREWS," "6464(A)" does not appear on the car, reportedly shown at 1964 Toy Fair, Parker Kalon was a Lionel subsidiary. **NRS**

**6464(E) CLEMCO AERO PRODUCTS INC** Type IV gray plastic body painted red, 1956-type gray plastic door painted red, paper label loosely fastened on car, "6464(E)" does not appear on the car, reportedly shown at 1964 Toy Fair, Clemco was a Lionel subsidiary. **NRS**

**6464(F) HATHAWAY DENVER** Type IV gray plastic body painted red, then blue, 1956-type gray plastic door painted red then blue, paper label loosely fastened on car, "6464(F)" does not appear on the car, reportedly shown at 1964 Toy Fair, Hathaway Denver was a Lionel subsidiary. **NRS**

**6464(G) M. STEINTHAL & Co** Type IV opaque plastic body painted red, then white, 1956-type opaque plastic door painted white, paper label loosely fastened on car, "6464(G)" does not appear on the car, reportedly shown at 1964 Toy Fair, M. Steinthal was a Lionel subsidiary. **NRS**

**6464(H) NO LETTERING** Type IIB bright blue unpainted plastic body, 1953-type black unpainted plastic door. **NRS**

**6464(I) 0000 M & SL** Type I clear plastic body painted green, 1953-type black plastic door painted green, yellow decal lettering. Louis Knapp Collection. **NRS**

**6464(J) 0000 (XP476) D & R G W COOKIE BOX** Type HB blue plastic body painted shiny gloss white, 1956-type blue plastic door painted shiny gloss white, black and red decal lettering, body screws and two tabs painted white. **NRS**

**6464(K) 6464-0000 (XP572)** TIDEWATER SOUTHERN Type IIB blue plastic body painted brown, 1956 blue plastic door painted brown, yellow decal lettering. **NRS**

**6464(L) 0000000 (XP540)** NORFOLK SOUTHERN Type IIB blue plastic body painted light brown, 1956-type blue plastic door painted light brown, white decal lettering. **NRS**

**6464(M) 0000000 (XP 521)** WABASH Type IIB gray plastic body painted tuscan, 1956-type gray plastic door painted tuscan, white decal lettering. **NRS**

**6464(N) 0000000 (XP527)** DULUTH, SOUTH SHORE AND ATLANTIC Type IIB gray plastic painted red and black, 1956-type blue plastic door painted red, white decal lettering, marked "XP476" on underframe. **NRS**

**6464(O) 0000000 (XP571)** LOUISVILLE & NASHVILLE Type IIB gray plastic body painted red, 1956-type yellow plastic door painted red, white decal, underframe marked "XP570". **NRS**

**6464(P) 0000000 (XP709)** LOUISVILLE & NASHVILLE Type III gray plastic body painted blue, 1953-type red plastic door painted blue, yellow decal lettering. **NRS**

**6464(Q) 0000 BURLINGTON** Type III blue plastic body painted red, 1956-type gray plastic door painted red, white decals. **NRS**

**6464(R) 0000 GREAT NORTHERN** Type IV gray plastic body painted green, 1956-type gray plastic door painted green, white and red decal lettering. **NRS**

**6464(S) 0000 (XP670)NYC** Type I black plastic body painted chocolate brown with double automobile doors, gray plastic doors painted chocolate brown, white decals. **NRS**

**6464(T) 0000 (XP534)** NYC **(NYMX)** Type I reefer, white plastic body painted yellow with black stripe, red plastic roof painted aluminum, red plastic door with yellow paint and black stripe, white and black decal. **NRS**

## CABOOSES

**6517 LIONEL LINES** Bay Window Caboose, same as (B), but missing all bay markings and radio wave on side. **NRS**

## CRANES AND SEARCHLIGHTS

**2460 LIONEL LINES** Crane Car.
(A) Cast aluminum unpainted boom, possible factory prototype. Krempel Collection. **NRS**

**2562 REGAL PASS** Passenger Car.
(A) "REGAL PASS" off-centered to right on one side only. Algozzini Collection. **NRS**
(B) "SANTA FE" off-centered to right on one side only. Algozzini Collection. **NRS**

**3620 LIONEL LINES** Searchlight Car.
(A) One bar-end metal truck and one plastic Timken truck, heavy lettering, orange generator. Timken truck is roller truck; fastenings of trucks to frame are identical rivet types. Schwartzel Collection. — — **50** —

**6560 BUCYRUS ERIE** Crane Car.
(A) Entry (D) in main listing is a probable limited test run; 6460 screw-attached trucks on plastic frame. Also applies to black cab version with stack. Ambrose comment. **NRS**
(B) Black cab and stack, 1954-type couplers, screws fasten trucks to frame, no lettering or numbering on cab or frame. Algozzini Collection. **NRS**

## FLAT CARS

**3545 TELEVISION CAR.**
(A) Heat-stamped lettering on one side only. Algozzini Collection. **NRS**
**6111 LIONEL** Flatcar with pipes, cream.
(A) Lettered only on one side. Halverson Collection. **NRS**

**6816 FLAT WITH ALLIS-CHALMERS BULLDOZER.**
(A) Same as listing (A), but dark orange bulldozer with "HD 16 DIESEL" missing on both sides. Algozzini Collection.
(B) Same as listing (A), but "HD 16 DIESEL" missing on one side of bulldozer. Algozzini Collection.

## GONDOLAS

**6162-60 NYC** Gondola.
(A) Lettered only on one side. Algozzini Collection **NRS**
**6342 NYC** Culvert Gondola.
(A) Timken trucks, 6462-2 frame, lettered only on one side. Kraemer and Algozzini Collections. **NRS**
**6462 NYC** Gondola.
(A) Pink-painted body, no lettering. Algozzini Collection. **NRS**
(B) Maroon body, two brakewheels, no lines under NYC, lettering on one side only. Algozzini Collection. **NRS**

## HOPPERS AND DUMP CARS

**6346-56 ALCOA** Covered Hopper.
(A) Dark red deep heat-stamped lettering and numbering instead of blue; may be one of a kind. Halverson Collection. — — **1000** —
**6436 LEHIGH VALLEY** Hopper Car.
(A) Rust-painted 1963-type body, no lettering on either side. Algozzini Collection. **NRS**
(B) Pink-painted 1957-type body, no lettering on either side. Algozzini Collection. **NRS**
**6536 MINNEAPOLIS AND St. LOUIS** Covered Hopper.
(A) No lettering on one side. Kraemer Collection. **NRS**

## PASSENGER CARS

**2422 CHATHAM** Passenger Car.
(A) Heat-stamped lettering on one side only. Algozzini Collection. **NRS**

## TANK AND VAT CARS

**6465 SUNOCO** Tank Car.
(A) Same as (I) in main listings, but Sunoco herald is double-stamped. Halverson Collection. **NRS**

## LIONEL BILLBOARDS
### By I. D. Smith
With major contributions from Don Corrigan's research

### Introduction

This list is organized from the Lionel Catalogues starting in 1950. I first used numbers instead of letters for each change as it appeared. There were many repeats in the years following the initial listing.

My second step was to take my collection, fill in a better description where not clear from the catalogues and verify dates where shown on uncut billboard poster set(s).

Thirdly, I used slides of Alan T. Weaver's collection following the same steps. Mr. Weaver's slides show a number of billboard posters designated "Outdoor Adv." and "Indoor Adv." where "Standard" showed in the early 1950s. These have NOT been included as they appear NOT to be Lionel. If "Standard" shows on a billboard, it is noted by "STD". Otherwise, it was not shown.

For each year(s) I have listed the page number of the catalogues where the No. 310 Billboard is listed, the number of plastic frames and the number of billboards or posters noted in the catalogue as a set for that year. Following this, if there were possible billboards shown in the catalogue, I have listed those pages on which they appear. Obvious advertisements on particular sets or train features printed inside the green billboard frame picture are not included.

However, since this article was first published, I have been made aware of several significant new facts. First there was Mr. Don Corrigan's research article which was published in **The Train Collector's Quarterly**, Spring 1980, and a number of update notes. Don Corrigan was aided in his research by J. E. Felber, Jim Gates, William Mekalian, George Shewmaker, Don Simonini and Joe Snuggs.

Secondly, there was the announcement which appeared in **The New York Times** in October, 1949, which clearly established the 1949 Billboard Connection as furnished by Mr. William Mekalian and published in **The Train Collector's Quarterly**, Summer 1980.

Mr. Corrigan and Mr. Mekalian have given their permission to use their data in the major revision of this article. Where practical, I will note Mr. Corrigan's direct comments and quotes with a single reference to reduce repetitious printing. Due to the 1949 billboards, this entire section will be re-numbered.

See **Greenberg's Price Guide To Lionel Trains: 1901-1942** for Standard Gauge billboards.

### Lionel Billboards

**No. 310 BILLBOARD 1949-68** unpainted green plastic frame with cardboard advertisements.

Beginning in 1949, Lionel offered a billboard assortment, the No. 310. The assortment consisted of an uncut sheet of eight different billboards. In 1950, the billboard assortment usually consisted of five green unpainted plastic frames with an uncut sheet of different billboards. In 1950, ten different billboards were offered. Later this was reduced to eight, six and in the later years to three different billboards.

The billboards made through 1956 include the words "Standard" in white letters with black background. Thereafter "Standard" was dropped from the sign. Many different billboard advertisements were offered. It appears that there were partial annual changes in the billboards as shown each year in the Lionel catalogues starting in the 1950s. In later years changes in billboards show up on other catalogue pages. The dating of these billboards has been based on the Lionel catalogues and uncut dated billboard sheets. In my correspondence with Mr. Corrigan, he states that "A complete billboard collection consists of 15 sheets containing 104 boards, 73 of which are different. This includes two almost duplicate sheets, one for 1951-52 and one for 1953." It may be that our readers have reliable source information that will contradict or supplement these billboard dates. Readers' comments are welcomed as this is our second listing of these signs. (It is very important to note the date that appears on uncut billboard sheets which will aid in establishing and verifying other billboard set dates as well as those that were never made.)

In describing these signs, I have noted the exact words and spelling including upper and lower case letters as appear on the sign. Additional descriptive words have been added to aid in the description.

As additional information, it is noted that in the August 1, 1959, numerical parts list, part No. 310-3 frame was listed. However, in the 1968 listing part No. 310-2 billboard had been added; this part was also shown in the 1970 MPC Lionel parts listing. It has not been determined if the number 310-2 covered an uncut sheet of the specified number of various individual billboards.

Mr. Corrigan also provides us with the following comments from his research efforts:. "Item numbers 9, 21, 38, 40, 68, 86, 87 and 90 were never produced, at least for the consumer market. These generally were pre-production mock-ups, used for their Lionel catalogues and the showroom and dealer layouts; some probably were never made. The number produced may never be known, given the transient nature of these layouts. I have never seen one in the flesh, but have several photos in which boards like these appear.

"Item 80 was produced in H0, and it was made to be used with the 6100 Race Set. Item 89 was never produced. As for the Lionel Porter and Spear Phonograph boards, I am certain they were never made."

This listing does not include any of the small size H0 or Raceway Game Lionel Billboards. Many of those were reduced sizes of the No. 310 billboards.

### 1949
#### "The 1949 Billboard Connection"

The following appeared in the N.Y. Times on October 24, 1949, and was sent by William Mekalian (as published in the **TCA Quarterly**).

## ADVERTISING NEWS AND NOTES

Toy Railroads Get Billboards. "Lionel Corporation", manufacturer of model railroads and equipment, will distribute with its Christmas catalogue 2,400,000 miniature outdoor billboards in 300,000 sets of eight designs, it was announced over the week-end. The toy-size poster panels have been produced by Lionel in cooperation with Standard Outdoor Advertising, Inc. and seven leading national advertisers. They are designed to strengthen home interest in advertising as part of the nation's identity, it was said. Their use in model railroad settings also is expected to satisfy model railroaders' desire for another touch of authenticity. Costs of the project were met by the advertisers, Standard and Lionel.

Although not catalogued, the billboards were available through a special catalogue offer, the ads for which appeared in various magazines. The 1949 catalogue offer included the billboards, the consumer catalogue, a sound effects record and a train layout planning book for "Pop". The billboard ads included Ford, Lionel Construction Sets, Kleenex, Nash, Baby Ruth, Wrigley's Spearmint, Kellogg's and Heinz Soup, identical to one in the 1951 sheet.*

The following billboards have been observed:

**1** LIONEL Construction Kits (shows boy with wrecker truck built from kit), Std.

**2** FORD (in reverse) (shows man, boy and dog looking through window with FORD on window), Std.

**3** FRESH Kellogg's CORN FLAKES (shows box of Corn Flakes on right, bowl with bananas on left), Std.

**4** He'll only chase a Nash (shows black dog on right, two girls on left), Std.

**5** Your nose knows, your best buy in tissues! (shows box of Kleenex Tissues on right. Girl pointing to her nose on left), Std.

**6** Compare...and you'll know they're better; Heinz Soups (bowl of tomato soup with can of Heinz Tomato Soup), Std.

**7** Enjoy Chewing Wrigleys SPEARMINT GUM (with light green background) (man with hat placing piece of gum to his mouth), Std.

**8** Slice and Serve, Baby Ruth (candy bar shown partly in wrapper with slices falling into dish), Another CURTISS Candy, Std.

**Sources:** Hudzik and Weaver Collections, uncut sheet, 1 through 8. Corrigan and Bohn Collections, 1 through 8.

### 1950

This was the first year the billboards were catalogued. Ads included those for Ford, Wrigley's, Silver Springs, Nash, Plymouth, Baby Ruth, DuPont Anti-Freeze and Northern Tissue. They came in a sheet of eight, two wide by four deep.*

**1950** Page 41, (five frames, billboards).

**9** LIONEL MAGNE-TRACTION GIVES YOU MORE SPEED, MORE PULL, MORE CLIMB, MORE CONTROL (1950 red and silver Santa Fe with part of second diesel unit, blond-haired boy).

**10** AMERICA'S BIG THREE; GRAND CANYON, NIAGARA FALLS, SILVER SPRINGS, (American flag design in red, white and blue), Std.

**8** See 1949 description.

**11** Get a DUPONT ANTI-FREEZE, ZEREX, ZERONE $3.50-1.25, Std.

**7** See 1949 description.

**12** Wow! FORD V-8 (bear with tree), Std.

**13** GREAT CARS SINCE 1902 NEW Nash...RAMBLER (ad shows old car and current model), Std.

**14** YOUR PLYMOUTH DEALER INVITES YOU TO DRIVE THE NEW PLYMOUTH 1950 (blue car, red background), Std.

**15** Snowy-Soft with "FLUFF" NORTHERN TISSUE (ad shows dog and boy on red sled), Std.

**Sources:** Sykes Collection, 10, 8, 11, 7, 12, 13, 14. Smith Collection, 10, 8. Weaver Collection, uncut billboard sheets dated 1950; 10, 7, 12, 13, and 8, 11, 14, 15. Bohn and Corrigan Collections, uncut billboard sheet, 10, 8, 11, 7, 12, 13, 14, 15.

### 1951

Lionel expanded the sheet to ten billboards this year. Plymouth, Wrigley's, Hallicrafters, Heinz Soups, Frigidaire, Baby Ruth, Atlantic Gas, Silver Springs, General Tires and DuPont Anti-Freeze were illustrated. The DuPont prices changed this year.*

**1951,** Page 31 (five frames, show 10 billboards).

**8** See 1950 catalogue.

**10** See 1950 catalogue.

**16** Same as 1950 catalogue, but price now $3.75 and $1.50, Std.

**17** Level best on the roughest roads, NEW PLYMOUTH (green Plymouth; man, woman and dog in car), Std.

**6** See 1949 description.

**18** Made for once-a-week shopping. The new FRIGIDAIRE, SEE YOUR FRIGIDAIRE DEALER (open refrigerator in center of yellow background), Std.

**19** Safe Traveling, THE GENERAL TIRE, SEE YOUR GENERAL TIRE DEALER (shows tire on right, squaw and papoose on left), Std.

**20** I'm a television cameraman... and in my home we have Hallicrafters. (shows TV on right, man on left), Std.

**21** WOW! ITS A "LIONEL" (shows blond-haired boy on floor with steam engine, dog, part of passenger car, automatic gateman).

**22** Enjoy Wrigley's Spearmint Gum daily-chewing aids teeth, breath, digestion (shows pack of gum lower right of billboard), Std.

**23** Keeps your car on the go-ATLANTIC (shows waterway with city in background, red and white Atlantic sign), Std. This billboard does not appear in the 1951 catalogue but Weaver Collection ties this billboard to 1951.

**Sources:** Smith Collection, 16, 17, 6, 18, 19, 20, 22, 23. Weaver Collection, 7, 6, 22, 20, 18, 16, 17, 23, 19. Bohn, Weaver and Corrigan Collections, uncut billboard sheet dated 1951, 17, 6, 22, 20, 10, 8, 16, 18, 19, 23.

### 1952

Ten billboards were again offered this year. The sheet at first was printed as being for 1951, but it was later changed to 1952. Products included were Plymouth, Wrigley's, Sunsweet Prunes, Heinz Beans, Frigidaire, Baby Ruth, DuPont Anti-Freeze, Sunoco High-Test, Silver Springs and General Tires.*

**1952** Page 33 (five frames, 10 billboards).

**24** HEINZ OVEN-BAKED BEANS (shows blond-haired boy holding a plate of beans on left and can on right), Std.

**25** You mean you haven't seen FLORIDA'S SILVER SPRINGS! (shows baby's face on left), Std.

**26** WRIGLEY'S SPEARMINT for real chewing enjoyment (shows pack of gum), Std.

**27** SUNSWEET good to feel-good! (lady in two-piece white sunsuit on beach. Box of Sunsweet Prunes on right), Std.

**28** HIGH-TEST at regular gas price BLUE SUNOCO ANTI-KNOCK PERFORMANCE! (shows man on left winking, red arrow Sunoco sign), Std.

**8** See 1950 catalogue.

**29** Shelves roll out . . . All the way! CYCLA-MATIC FRIGIDAIRE Automatic Defrosting! SEE YOUR FRIGIDAIRE DEALER (shows refrigerator on left and closer view of roll-out shelves on right), Std.

**30** Straight to the Point...TOP QUALITY, SEE YOUR GENERAL TIRE DEALER, THE GENERAL TIRE (shows tire on right, dog on left) Std.

**31** VOTE FOR VALUE Plymouth (shows red X by word Plymouth, Plymouth car on right side of billboard), Std.

**16** See 1951 catalogue.

**Sources:** Smith Collection, 24, 28, 30; Bohn, Corrigan and Weaver uncut billboard sheets dated 1952, 24, 26, 27, 31, and 8, 16, 25, 28, 29, 30. Corrigan and Bratspis uncut billboard sheets dated 1951; Weaver Collection, 26, 29, 24, 27, 31, 30, 28, 25.

### 1953

The sheet was reduced to eight billboards again, the start of a continued reduction throughout the remaining years. Plymouth, Wrigley's, Coca Cola, Frigidaire, DuPont Anti-Freeze, Sunoco, Silver Springs and Heinz Beans were made. For some reason, a second sheet was produced, the difference being instead of Heinz Beans, Heinz Ketchup was now illustrated.*

**1953,** Page 33, (five frames, eight billboards) (also page 21).

**33** Travel refreshed. DRINK Coca-Cola IN BOTTLES (shows train

* Comment by Don Corrigan

* Comment by Don Corrigan

engineer drinking a bottle of Coca-Cola, portion of steam locomotive to right) Std.

**33** NO SHIFTING! NEW PLYMOUTH HY-DRIVE (shows new Plymouth blue convertible), Std.

**16** See 1951 catalogue.

**34** WRIGLEY'S SPEARMINT CHEWING GUM (shows earth in background with infinite packs of gum coming from earth. Planet Saturn also shows in background), Std.

**35** Save at Sunoco, Tires and Batteries (shows Kelly tire on left, Sunoco battery center, SUNOCO yellow sign with red arrow pointing to the left) Std.

**24** See 1952 catalogue.

**36** Relax now! at FLORIDA'S SILVER SPRINGS (shows lady in two-piece red swim suit on beach), Std.

**37** Cycle-matic FRIGIDAIRE Food Freezer-Refrigerator YEARS AHEAD (shows open refrigerator on left), Std.

**24** See 1952 catalogue. This billboard does not show in 1953 catalogue, but Weaver Collection ties this billboard to 1953.

**38** (See page 21) LIONEL "0" GAUGE plus LIONEL MAGNE-TRACTION, MORE PULL, MORE SPEED, MORE POWER.

**39** RED MAGIC, HEINZ Ketchup (shows bottle of Heinz Tomato Ketchup, a hamburger with pickles on a plate), Std. This billboard does not show in 1953 catalogue, but Weaver and Corrigan Collections tie this billboard to 1953.

**Sources:** Smith Collection, 32, 33, 34, 36, 37, 39. Corrigan Collection, uncut billboard sheets, 33, 34, 32, 24 and 37, 16, 35, 36 also 33, 34, 32, 39 and 37, 16, 35, 36. Bohn and Weaver Collections, uncut billboard sheets, 37, 38, 34, 39 and 32, 33 34, 24; Weaver Collection, 36, 37, 34, 32, 39, 33, 35, 36.

### 1954

A sheet of eight billboards was offered this year, products advertised being Lipton Tea, Wrigley's, New Departure Safety Brakes, Campbell's Soups, Sunoco, Fram Filters, Breck Shampoos and DuPont Anti-Freeze. Again changed were the DuPont prices. Zerex was priced at $2.95 and Zerone at $1.50.*

**1954** Distributor's Advertising Promotions Catalogue, page 14, shows eight billboards. Those shown are the same as shown in the 1952 catalogue which are 16, 24, 25, 26, 27, 28, 30, 31.

**1954** Accessories Catalogue page 8, lists set of five frames and eight billboards.

**1954** Page 40 (five frames, eight billboards).

**40** Only LIONEL has MAGNE-TRACTION, MORE SPEED-MORE POWER-MORE CLIMB (shows boy on left), Std.
Note: Description of eight firms represented on page 40 indicates this was NOT a billboard.

**41** Change now for LONG Mileage (shows service station man on right holding in his hand on left side of billboard a can of Sunoco Dynalube Motor Oil), Std.

**42** GET a DUPONT ANTI-FREEZE ZEREX-ZERONE $2.95/$1.50., Std.

**43** BRECK Beautiful Hair THREE BRECK SHAMPOOS (shows woman and hair trademark in center and bottles of shampoo on left side), Std.

**44** NEW DEPARTURE, Safety Brake, STEER WITH YOUR HANDS STOP WITH YOUR FEET (shows brake on right, boy riding red bike on left), Std.

**45** It's Still Clean, FRAM-OIL-AIR-FUEL-WATER FILTERS, FOR NEAREST DEALER CALL WESTERN UNION OPERATOR 25 (shows service man looking at clean oil on oil dip stick, filter on right, yellow background), Std.

**46** Campbell's SOUPS MMM, GOOD! (shows can of Campbell's Tomato Soup on right, Campbell's Chef on left, yellow background), Std.

**47** WRIGLEY'S SPEARMINT GUM, (ad is full-size face of gum package). (Set of six uncut billboards from Smith Collection dated 1955 shows this billboard to have man driving car. On bottom "Chew—freshen your taste" on billboard), Std. Weaver Collection of uncut billboards shows same as Smith Collection except dated 1954.

**48** Coolest drink under the sun LIPTON ICED TEA (shows tall glass of iced tea on left, man sitting on grass holding glass of iced tea and leaning against push lawn mower. Box of Lipton Tea pictured in lower right corner) Std.

**Sources:** Smith Collection, 46, 47, 48, 45, 41, 42; Weaver, Bohn and Corrigan Collections, uncut billboard sheets dated 1954, 43, 44, 45, 46, 47, 48, 42, 41; Weaver Collection 48, 46.

### 1955

The sheet was reduced to six this year. Ads for Wrigley's, Snow Crop Peas, Log Cabin Syrup, Kool-Aid, Fram Filters and DuPont Anti-Freeze were made. The DuPont was changed for a last time, prices for Zerex and Zerone now at $3.25 and $1.60 respectively.*

**1955** Page 38 (five frames, eight billboards) (shown or listed, see page 19 for pictures).

**40** See 1954 catalogue.

**49** SNOW CROP PEAS (shows package of frozen peas with peas spilling out left end. Bear on right), Std.

**50** LOG CABIN SYRUP (shows bottle and famous "Log Cabin Tin" of Syrup).

**51** Makes the Cakes! LOG CABIN SYRUP (shows picture of sausage, forks, pitcher of syrup, pancakes with butter. Bottle and tin of syrup lower right) Std.

**52** FRAM FILTERS (shows red filter on right) CLEAN OIL MONTHLY CHANGE OIL AND FILTER NOW, FOR NEAREST DEALER CALL WESTERN UNION OPERATOR 25, Std.

**53** KOOLAID (shows package of Kool-Aid with glass on package).

**54** DUPONT ANTI-FREEZE ZEREX-ZERONE (does NOT show prices in catalogue. However, set of the same uncut billboards from Corrigan, Smith and Weaver Collections shows $3.25/$1.60), Std.

**47** See 1954 catalogue.

**55** Kool-Aid, .05 package makes two quarts (shows package of Kool-Aid lower left. Pitcher of Kool-Aid with happy face being drawn by finger) Std.

**Sources:** Smith and Weaver Collections uncut billboard sheet dated 1955; 49, 51, 52, 54, 47, 55; Weaver Collection, 51, 49, 53, 52, 54.

### 1956

Lionel did not produce a new sheet for this year, the catalogue showing the 1955 billboards. It is assumed the 1955 sheet was offered both years.*

**1956** Page 34 (five frames, six posters) (also see page 13 and 23).

**40** See 1954 catalogue.

**47** See 1955 and 1954 catalogues.

**55** See 1955 catalogue.

**54** See 1955 catalogue.

**52** See 1955 catalogue.

**50** See 1955 catalogue.

**49** See 1955 catalogue.

### 1957

The design of the billboards was altered this year, the most noticable difference being the elimination of the "Standard" logo. Ads included Airex, Nabisco Shredded Wheat, Wrigley's, the Navy and Lionel Trains. For this year only, the five rows of squares along the bottom of the billboards were pale yellow instead of white.*

**1957** Page 48 (five frames, five posters) (also see page 4, 5, 8, 15, 24, 32).

**56** NAVY, Graduates choose your field (shows young man with diploma on left and five Navy insignia over NAVY).

**57** WRIGLEY'S SPEARMINT CHEWING GUM, pure, wholesome, inexpensive (shows man with hat reaching way out with right arm showing pack of gum).

**58** NABISCO, the original SHREDDED WHEAT (shows boy holding box of Shredded Wheat).

**59** AIREX-REELS-RODS-LINE-LURES.

**60** LIONEL TRAINS (red letters) with MAGNE-TRACTION (shows lion with engineer's cap on left on page 48).

**Sources:** Smith Collection 60; Weaver Collections, 56, 57, 58, 60; Corrigan Collection uncut sheet; Bohn Collections, 56, 57, 58, 59, 60.

### 1958

Five billboards were again offered, with ads for the Navy, Airex, Juicy Fruit, Purolator and Chevrolet being made.*

---

* Comment by Don Corrigan

**1958** Page 39 (five frames, five posters) (see page 21, 37, 38, 40).

**61** Train and gain new nuclear NAVY (shows nuclear sub, two white hat sailors, officer and missile).

**62** CHEVROLET OK USED CARS AND TRUCKS (shows CHEVROLET emblem and red "OK" in yellow background in green circle).

**63** "Change-um oil filter...car run heap better". Purolator (shows new American Indian driving car).

**64** WRIGLEY'S JUICY FRUIT CHEWING GUM DIF-FERENT, DELICIOUS (shows pack of Juicy Fruit gum in yellow wrapper. Leaf with picture of a woman's face superimposed on leaf).

**65** AIREX-REELS-RODS-LINES-LURES (shows man in stream fishing near

rocks about to net hooked fish).

**Sources:** Weaver Collection, 61, 64, 63, 65; Smith Collection, 65; Bohn Collection, 61, 62, 63, 64, 65; Corrigan Collection, uncut billboard sheet, 61, 62, 63, 64, 65.

### 1959

This is another year in which no new ads were produced, as far as we know.*

**1959** Advance Catalogue, page 25 (five frames, five posters) (see page 31).

**61** See 1958 catalogue.

**64** See 1958 catalogue.

**60** See 1957 catalogue.

**66** AIREX-REELS-RODS-LINES-LURES (shows reel on left, man in water reaching out with net to catch hooked fish jumping out of water).

**67** TWICE AS POPULAR, CHEVROLET OK USED CARS AND TRUCKS (shows three children's faces and "OK" symbol in yellow circle at lower right and left with Chevrolet emblem).

**56** See 1957 catalogue.

**57** See 1957 catalogue.

**Sources:** Weaver Collection, 66, 67.

**1959** Page 35 (five frames, five posters) (see page 34).

**68** JOIN THE NAVY (white letters blue background).

**69** (Description needed).

**70** (Description needed).

**71** (Description needed).

**72** (Description needed).

### 1960

Five billboards were produced. Products shown were Underwood, the Navy, Cities Service, Airex and a bulls-eye Target range.*

**1960** Advance Catalogue page 32 (five frames, five posters) (see page 42, 45).

**73** GOOD TRAINING FOR GETTING AHEAD, Underwood PORTABLE TYPEWRITERS (shows portable typewriter on right side, boy with first prize cup on left).

**74** SPACE AGE TRAINING NAVY (shows Planet Earth in background with

navy jet in center and red rocket).

**64** See 1958 catalogue.

**60** See 1957 catalogue.

**60** (Description needed.

Page 42.

**63** See 1959 catalogue.

**61** See 1959 catalogue.

**64** See 1958 catalogue.

**67** See 1959 advanced catalogue.

**65** See 1958 catalogue.

**1960** Accessory Catalogue (page 13 shows name as 1960 Advance Catalogue).

**1960** Page 39 (five frames and billboards) (see page 29, 13, 30).

**68** See 1959 catalogue.

**76** EAGER BEAVER SERVICE all the way (shows gasoline pump on left and Cities Service emblem on right. Beaver reading road map center left).

**73** See 1960 advance catalogue.

**74** See 1960 advance catalogue.

### 1961

This was the last year five different billboards were offered. Ads for the Navy, Cities Service, Swift's Premium Franks and the Lionel Science Series were made along with a Target Range billboard.*

**1961** Page 58 (five frames, five posters) (see page 23, 29, 30, 32, 39).

**77** BIG GALLON, BIG Mileage Performance (shows a gas pump as the "I" in BIG. Cities Service emblem upper right).

**78** Hot Diggety! Swift Premium FRANKS. (shows a frank on fork, cheese on frank).

**79** NAVY Diploma—Stay in school (shows American flag on staff in center).

**80** FINISH LINE (shows black and white checkered flag with two cars racing).

**81** SEE THE NEW LIONEL SCIENCE SERIES (ad shows atom model at bottom center).

**75** See 1960 Catalogue.

**Sources:** Weaver Collection, 77, 78, 74, 81, 75; Bohn, Corrigan and Smith uncut billboard sheet (no date) 77, 78, 79, 81, 75.

**1961** Advance Catalogue (see page 53, billboards shown are the same as shown in the 1960 Accessory Catalogue and the 1960 Advance Catalogue).

### 1962

Only three billboards were printed and how anyone can spread these among five frames is a mystery to me. Pictured were ads for Cities Service, the Navy and Van Camp's Pork and Beans.*

**1962** Page 50 (five frames, five posters) Billboards pictured are the same as shown in the 1961 Advance Catalogue. (items 10, 13, 22, 24, 25).

**82** AMERICA'S FIRST, FINEST, FAVORITE (shows can of Van Camp's Pork and Beans on left. Ladle of beans on right).

**83** Get close to America by car! BIG GALLON, Quality alone makes it BIG! (shows City Service emblem on right, part of car center bottom. Big Gallon in red).

**79** See 1961 catalogue.

**84** (Description needed).

**85** (Description needed).

**Sources:** Weaver Collection 82, 83; Bohn and Corrigan Collection, uncut billboard sheet (no date), 82, 83, 79.

**1962** Trains and Accessories Catalogue 63 pages, (page 41 billboards shown are the same as shown in the 1961 catalogue).

### 1963

On page 33 of the Lionel consumer catalogue of this year appeared an illustration of the 1961 billboards, with the first two changed to promote Lionel Porter and Spear Phonographs. No one I know has ever seen examples of these, and I believe they do not exist.*

**1963** Page 33 (five frames, five posters) (see page 18, 19).

**86** LIONEL PORTER (shows Microcraft Student Microscope).

**87** LIONEL Spear (shows Mickey Mouse phonograph).

**79** See 1961 catalogue.

**81** See 1961 catalogue.

**80** See 1961 catalogue.

**1963** Accessory Catalogue, 40 pages (page 13) (five frames, five posters).

**88** Serve with Pride, GO NAVY.

**89** MODEL RACING LIONEL (shows two race cars).

**90** LIONEL PORTER (shows young man performing chemical tests).

**81** See 1961 catalogue.

**80** See 1961 catalogue.

**1963** Advance Catalogue (Lionel 1963 on cover, cover yellow, black and white, 80 unnumbered pages) (page 10, billboards shown are the same as 1963 accessory catalogue).

### 1964-65

The catalogues for these years shows the 1961 sheet continously.*

**1964** Page 14 (five frames, five posters) Billboards shown are the same as shown in the 1961 catalogue and the 1962 Trains and Accessory Catalogue.

**1965** Page 15 (set of billboards with five frames). Billboards shown are as shown in 1964 catalogue.

---

* Comment by Don Corrigan

* Comment by Don Corrigan

Lionel produced a five-billboard sheet during these years. The border was radically changed from the forest green of previous years to a purple. Two ads for U.S. Savings Bonds (identical), two ads for Education (also identical) and an ad for Dodge.*

Correspondence with Mr. Corrigan notes the following: "Blister Pack No. B310 is the above described 1966-68 billboard set." He also notes the blister pack may have different color arrow design. Reader comments requested.

Blister Pack B310, Billboard set of five plastic frames. Top frame shows poster "Buy U.S. Savings Bonds" (shows package of savings bonds, Series E, color light purple) Lionel with red and blue arrow design on pack like 1966 catalogue. Weaver Collection.

**91** Billboard: "Education is for the birds (the birds who want to get ahead). To get a good job get a good education." Light purple. Weaver Collection.

**92** Billboard: Horse cartoon-horse with collar—speaking "Get a Dodge". Light purple. Weaver Collection.

**93** Billboard: "Buy U.S. Savings Bonds", shows package of savings bonds, Series E, color light purple.

**1966** Page 15 (Set of billboards with five frames). Billboards shown are as shown in 1964 catalogue.

**Source** Corrigan Collection uncut sheet.

**1967** Catalogue not issued.

**1968** (Inside of back page) (Set of billboards with five frames). Billboards shown are as shown in 1964 catalogue.

(LAST YEAR LISTED)

The following billboard has been observed but has yet to be dated.

**A** Curtis Baby Ruth (red letters on large Baby Ruth candy bar—background white. No green billboard outline, may be printing error).
**Source** Weaver Collection.

## POSTSCRIPT

This listing would not be complete without presenting the following additional comments on billboards from Mr. Corrigan's research.

## H0 BILLBOARDS

### By Don Corrigan

As far as I can determine, Lionel made only two sheets of H0 billboards. (There are possibly others, but I could not locate them.) The first sheet was produced in 1960 and the illustrations were identical (see note) to the 0 Gauge sheet for that year. The second sheet was made the next year and was identical to the 1961 0 Gauge sheet with the following exceptions: instead of a Target Range board, Lionel substituted a "Finish Line" board to be used with the H0 Raceway sets. Also, the Lionel Science Series board was printed without the white molecular diagram which appeared below the word "Series" on the 0 Gauge version.

Except as noted above, the illustrations on these sheets are identical to the 0 Gauge boards, but the H0 sheets did not have

---

* Comment by Don Corrigan

the green borders, just the illustrations on a die-cut white card. The uncut sheets are 9-1/2" long and 2-11/16" wide.

In addition to the regular Lionel production billboards, a crop of decidedly different billboards have appeared. The size and format of these boards are identical to the Lionel boards, but these cannot be placed among the others. In fact, most were not made by Lionel at all.

### Silver Springs*

During the 1950s, Lionel made up lists of Lionel train set owners which it then gave to Florida's Silver Springs Amusement Park. Silver Springs printed up their own billboards, then sent them out in groups of three or more to the people on Lionel's list. The exact number, variety and years these boards were made is unknown, since the management of Silver Springs does not have any records of them. Because of all this, the final counts of these boards will probably never be known.

The Silver Springs billboards came in at least two styles, the difference being the color of the border. All of them had the logo "Outdoor Adv." instead of "Standard" in the bottom border. Group A has the traditional green border that Lionel used on their boards. While the "Tommy Bartlett" board is unique, the "Relay Now!" board is exactly like the one in Lionel's 1953 sheet, the difference being the "Outdoor Adv." logo. A third board has an ad for the Glass-Bottom Boat Ride. (NOTE: With the duplication of Lionel's "Relax Now!", the possibility exists of Silver Springs duplicating the other two billboards made by Lionel.)

Group B is quite different from any other because the border is sky blue rather than green. This is the only group that I have seen with this color.

### Mystery Boards*

Two billboards I have seen are absolute mysteries to me. The ads are for Narragansett Beer and Fisher's Golden Roll Creamery Butter. The 'Gansett board is different in that the ad is printed on a separate sheet of paper, which is glued to the cardboard billboard. I have come up with three possible explanations: It is either 1) a pre-production mock-up, 2) a special run printed by or for the 'Gansett Brewery to distribute for themselves, or 3) a home-made board. I tend to rule out the third alternative, since the ad is the perfect size, layout and format for the billboard.

The Fisher's Butter billboard is unusual in that it has the "Outdoor Adv." logo rather than the "Standard". This is the only non-Silver Springs board I have seen like this.

All of these non-Lionel billboards are, needless to say, very hard to come by.

---

* All by Don Corrigan.

# Chapter XVII
# ORIGINAL OR REPRODUCTION, AND PERIPHERALS

### By Len Carparelli
### with appreciation to Ed Kraemer

Several articles have been written on the age-old collecting question, "Is it original?" Although most experienced collectors can recognize an original, there are many who can not. It is to this aim that this article is being written.

All collectable items (Lionel trains among them) are and have been reproduced. The reason for a reproduction in any collecting field is so that a fellow collector could have a particular item in his collection which is rare, and in most instances, hard to find or very expensive.

Almost all of the post WW II (1946-1968) diesel and electric engine bodies (sometimes called cabs or shells) are being reproduced so a collector can enjoy operating his trains without fear of damaging a valuable original. The original has many times the value of a reproduction, and of course, always will have.

The main reason for this article is to determine whether the item in question is a genuine original, or a reproduction. This will insure that none of these reproductions will be sold as originals. The following paragraphs will explain and compare the differences between the original LIONEL painting processes and the reproduction painting processes.

Lionel used two types of lettering and line (striping) process. The first is HEAT-STAMPING. This is done by applying heat to a line or word area through a colored heat ribbon. The heat, when applied to the cab, causes the plastic or paint to soften and raise around the now indented words or lines. This can easily be felt by running a finger lightly across the lines or words and feeling the indentation.

The RUBBER-STAMPING process is self-explanatory, similar to rubber-stamps used in offices, businesses and schools for clerical work. Line and work PAINT DENSITY in this process is THIN. Almost always a smeared or blurry outline or shadow around the edges of letters is present. Rubber-stamping is never clear, crisp or distinct. This process was used by Lionel mostly on rounded noses of cabs and CANNOT be felt by running a finger across.

SILK-SCREENING is the method used on 99½ of all better reproductions. This is done by forcing paint through a silk screen, depositing the paint (which is only in the lines or words) directly onto the surface of the cab. Hardly any height can be felt. Silk-screening is a very CLEAR printing process. The distinct difference between silk-screening and rubber-stamping is that there is no shadow or outline with silk-screening as there is with rubber-stamping. There is definitely no indentation of words or lines as there is with heat-stamping.

Below is a list of reproductions that are currently available. Painting processes and other discrepancies are shown for comparison by a collector. The list will compare a Lionel item to a reproduction item.

### F3-TYPE CABS

(O)-Original
(R)-Reproduction

**2240/2367 WABASH:**
(O) Blue plastic cab; heat-stamped words.
(R) Spray painted blue cab; silk-screened words.

**2242 NEW HAVEN:** Checkerboard
(O) Heat-stamped, nose and sides.
(R) Decal nose; silk-screened sides.

**2343/53/83 SANTA FE:**
(O) Heat-stamped words; rubber-stamped top & side stripes.
(R) Silk-screened sides; decal top

**2344/54 NEW YORK CENTRAL:**
(O) Rubber-stamped lines; heat-stamped words (early 2333 has rubber-stamped words-also true for Santa Fe).
(R) Decal nose; silk-screened sides

**2345/55 WESTERN PACIFIC:**
(O) Heat-stamped words.
(R) Silk-screened words.

**2356 SOUTHERN:**
(O) Rubber-stamped.
(R) Silk-screened.

**2363 ILLINOIS CENTRAL:**
(O) Rubber-stamped lines & words; orange plastic cab on B UNIT ONLY.
(R) Silk-screened lines & words; painted orange A & B.

**2368 BALTIMORE & OHIO:**
(O) Blue plastic cab; rubber-stamped lines & nose; heat-stamped words.
(R) Painted blue cab; silk-screened lines & words; decal nose.

**2373 CANADIAN PACIFIC:**
(O) Heat-stamped on top & sides.
(R) Silk-screened.

**2378 MILWAUKEE ROAD:**
(O) Grey plastic cab; heat-stamped lines & words.
(R) Painted grey cab; silk-screened sides.

**2379 RIO GRANDE:**
(O) Heat-stamped words & lines; decal nose.
(R) Silk-screened sides; decal nose.

**2245 TEXAS SPECIAL:**
(O) Glossy red paint; silk-screen sides & nose. Decal on side is slightly yellowed.
(R) Semi-gloss red paint; decal nose; side decal clear.

### FM TRAINMASTER CABS:

**2341 JERSEY CENTRAL:**
(O) Heat-stamped. Different spacing between "Jersey" and "Central" on each side.
(R) Silk-screened; same spacing both sides.

**2331 VIRGINIAN:** Black and gold or blue and yellow.
(O) Rubber-stamped words & end criss-cross.
(R) Silk-screened words & end cross-cross. Words are slightly higher.

**2321 LACKAWANNA: gray or red top.**
(O) Lines & words rubber-stamped.
(R) Lines & words silk-screened.

### GP-7 OR 9 TYPE CABS:

**2349 NORTHERN PACIFIC:**
(O) Heat-stamped in gold leaf.
(R) Silk-screened.

**2348 MINN & ST. LOUIS:**
(O) Heat-stamped.
(R) Silk-screened.

**2338 MILWAUKEE ROAD:** Orange cab variation.
(O) Orange plastic cab; words & herald rubber-stamped.
(R) Painted orange cab; words & herald silk-screened.

**2328 BURLINGTON:**
(O) Words & herald rubber-stamped.
(R) Silk-screened.

**2028 PENNSYLVANIA:**
(O) Brown plastic cab; rubber-stamped.
(R) Painted brown; silk-screened.

**0000 ALASKA:**
(O) Approx. four prototypes hand-painted & water decals.
(R) Sprayed & silk-screened.

**2365/2347 CHESAPEAKE & OHIO:**
(O) Heat-stamped.
(R) Silk-screened.

### EP-5 TYPE (ELECTRIC) CABS

**2350 NEW HAVEN (All variations]:**
(O) Black plastic cab; heat-stamped words.
(R) Painted black; silk-screened.

**2351 MILWAUKEE ROAD:**
(O) Yellow plastic cab; heat-stamped words.
(R) Painted yellow; silk-screened.

**2352 PENNSYLVANIA:**
(O) Heat-stamped in gold leaf.
(R) Silk-screened, dull gold.

**2358 GREAT NORTHERN:**
(O) Heat-stamped.
(R) Silk-screened.

### GG-1 TYPE CABS:

**2340/2360 PENNSYLVANIA: Five-stripe.**
(O) 5 stripes rubber-stamped; words heat-stamped.
(R) Silk-screened.

**2360 PENNSYLVANIA: Solid stripe.**
(O) Heat-stamped words; some have decal words.
(R) Silk-screened words.

### MISCELLANEOUS:

**6427 VIRGINIAN: Caboose.**
(O) Heat-stamped.
(R) Silk-screened.

**2625 MADISON: Cars.**
(O) Heat-stamped words.
(R) Silk-screened words; rivets around words occasionally sanded off.

**2329 VIRGINIAN: Rectifier.**
(O) Heat-stamped.
(R) Silk-screened.

I hope this information will be of value to my fellow collectors. Additional help in verification will gladly be given. Remember, reproductions do have a place in the hobby and can be very enjoyable, provided they are not sold as originals. The reproduction is not the villian; it is the PERSON who FAILS to identify it as such. Collecting trains is a great hobby, but let's be aware of exactly what we are buying and selling!

## POSTWAR PERIPHERALS: 1946-1969

In an attempt to make our Guide as complete as possible, we are beginning the listing of peripherals with this edition. Peripherals are defined as items not readily fitting into the paper category which are designed primarily for display use, mostly by dealers, but sometimes by collectors (as the recent Fundimensions Lionel wall mirror would indicate). These items include banners, clocks, signs, display cases, pens and other advertising and display paraphernalia. There is a small but recognizable collector's market for items which fit this category.

We only have one entry for Postwar peripherals in this edition, but as time goes by we expect to see this listing grow considerably. If you have a peripheral item to report to us, be as specific as you can and try to estimate the value of your item - which might be extremely difficult. One of the difficulties with this category is that the Lionel Corporation seldom (if ever) manufactured its own peripherals, but subcontracted these items to other firms. Therefore, also try to identify the subcontractor if it is possible.

**BANNER:** No number, approximately 3 feet x 6 feet, dark blue with dark red border and white lettering: "HEADQUARTERS/ FOR/LIONEL TRAINS". Banner fastens to rod or wire with white upper hanging strip. Identification in upper right portion of hanging strip is as follows: black monkey figure in orange circle, black lettering "(obliterated) BUNTING" and orange lettering "DYED WITH OUR EVERLASTING DYES" to right of monkey emblem. To right of this lettering is a black shield containing "DETTRAS/FLAG" in black and "PRODUCT" in orange. May have been commissioned by Lionel for department stores in early to mid fifties; this banner is meant to hang from a high ceiling typical in such stores. E. Mancinelli Collection. **NRS**

# INDEX
## by Dr. W. Jeffery Miller

# Appendix

## INFORMATION SOURCES

Seeking advice is especially important because of the danger posed by fakes and frauds. Recently, the Train Collectors Association, the largest train collecting organization in the United States, published the details of a chemical dyeing process which can alter a common plastic locomotive cab or freight car's color into an apparently real and "rare" but spurious color. While it is not the purpose of this book to be judgmental about this matter, we urge our readers to exercise extreme caution in purchasing Lionel Postwar equipment purported to be a "factory error" because of a difference in color. The Factory Errors chapter, new with this edition, contains entries which are known to be genuine factory errors. Readers should consult expert opinion before contemplating any such purchase.

The Lionel collector and operator has several additional sources for toy train information. First there is the companion **Greenberg's Price Guide for Lionel Trains** manufactured before World War II. It presents a comprehensive listing of Lionel 0 and 0-27 from their beginnings in 1915 through 1942, of Standard, from its beginning in 1906 through 1940 when production ceased, and of Lionel 2-7/8 Gauge from 1901-1906.

Also we will publish, in late 1985, Greenberg's Guide to Fundimensions Trains: 1970-1985, providing in depth coverage of this production.

Tom McComas has written and published several handsome books on prewar and postwar Lionel trains. **Lionel: A Collector's Guide:** Volume IV, Fundimensions; V, Archives; and VI Art and Advertising. All are well written, handsomely illustrated and informative.

There are several other volumes of interest to the Lionel enthusiast. Between 1946 and 1966 Lionel issued hundreds of pages of service and instruction sheets for its dealers. These have been skillfully edited and organized into **Greenberg's Repair and Operating Manual for Lionel Trains.** This manual is the ultimate operator's guide. It helps him solve most operating problems; problems often due to design limitations. This book also describes the development of Lionel trains. In addition we offer **Plasticville: An Illustrated Price Guide** which provides a comprehensive photographic record with current prices. These books are available directly from Greenberg Publishing Company or from your local book or hobby store.

## REPORTING POSTWAR VARIATIONS

The first edition of Greenberg's Price Guide to Postwar and Fundimensions Lionel trains was published in 1977 as a response to collector demand for a comprehensive and reliable price guide to the toy train market. In the last seven years the Guide went through four editions and is now in its fifth edition. The book has rapidly developed; hundreds of new variations have been added and hundreds of entries have been changed. The Guide is the standard descriptive and price reference for the Lionel trains.

The main reason for the Guide's success has been the response and interest of you, the collector and enthusiast. Over the years, collectors from all over the United States and Canada have written with comments, suggestions and advice. These contacts have enabled the Guide to become accurate and thorough, although it still needs reader input.

In a little over the year between the fourth and the fifth editions, enough data was amassed to provide over 500 new entries, new variations and corrections to previous entries, as well as several new articles of research on various aspects of Lionel Postwar production. The sheer volume of contact has been a tribute to your interest, generosity and sincerity.

However, the incoming volume of mail and information, desirable as it is, has created a serious problem: the need to better respond to and organize new data. One approach will be to use computer-based compilation to increase the accuracy of our recording methods. Another approach is explained in this article.

The decision-making process concerning the listing of new items is surprisingly complex - and sometimes quite agonizing. Sometimes a variation is difficult to establish, and upon follow-up letters asking for specific information, reveal that the item is not in fact a new variation. At other times, a really odd item may strain one's credibility - yet the variation is genuine. In general, there are three major criteria used by the editors before listing a variation:

(1)**CREDIBILITY:** Obviously, we are not referring to the trustworthiness of the enthusiast! That is something we assume all along. Rather, we are trying to answer the classic question of the skeptic: "How do you know this variation came from the factory?" Two examples will show what is meant. One very experienced and knowledgeable collector reported a No. 50 gang car with light gray bumpers instead of blue ones, and three blue men instead of two blue and one gray, as a rare variation. The problem here is that bumpers and men are easily replaced, so there is no way to tell whether it is a true factory variant or a post-factory alteration. In this case, our listing might read: "Same as (A), but three blue men and gray bumpers. Confirmation requested. NRS" (No reported sales). Perhaps someone else will be able to furnish data to show that this gang car is really a factory variant. For example, a reader may be the original owner of a similar piece with the same characteristics. Another example is a 9134 Fundimensions Virginian covered hopper with a silver cover instead of the normal blue cover. This 9134 came straight out of its factory sealed box, so it was clearly factory production. We have assumed that it is a factory error. The car body had been spray-painted with its cover on. We would like to know how many cars the factory similarly processed. It is most likely only a curiosity, not a rarity, and it is listed as such. Besides, the covers for such hoppers are easily interchanged.

(2)**CORROBORATION:** Many times the type of proof sent along with the report is crucial. Photographic evidence is very helpful. Of greater importance is independent verification by other collectors.

(3)**COMPLETENESS:** Several possibly good variations have fallen victim to incomplete reports. It's not enough to say that one has a 6560 crane car with no smokestack on the cab. There are several different 6560 cranes - which one is being reported? However, if the correspondent says that his crane is "the same as (B), but has no stack," he has given us the proper basis for comparison. Many major variations turn on a minor item - and so does the value. For example, the common variety of the Fundimensions 9737 Central Vermont boxcar and a scarce variation appear identical from the outside. Both are painted tuscan brown. However, the common one is painted over brown plastic, while the scarce one has an orange plastic body. The correspondent would have to look inside the boxcar to see the difference! The common one is worth only $6, the scarce one $35. The more complete your description's, the better.

If you wish to report a new entry, variation or correction to us, please use the reporting sheet enclosed with this book. We appreciate very much your cooperation, enthusiasm and good will in helping us document Lionel train production. As has been our custom, we will acknowledge all varieties noted in the Guide as coming from your collection and/or observation. Every letter to us will be answered. Varied sections of the book will help you with types of couplers, trucks, frames, etc.